The Apple II® Circuit Description

by Winston Gayler

Howard W. Sams & Co., Inc.
4300 WEST 62ND ST. INDIANAPOLIS, INDIANA 46268 USA

International Standard Book Number: 0-672-21959-X
Library of Congress Catalog Card Number: 82-61966

Edited by: *Welborn Associates*
Illustrated by: *D. B. Clemons*

Printed in the United States of America.

Preface

This book is a detailed circuit description of the Apple II® computer. Specifically, it covers the main logic board including all revisions from the earliest through the latest (Rev. 0 through RFI Rev. D). Also covered are the current two-piece keyboard and the older single-piece keyboard.

The intended audience includes engineers, technicians, students, and hobbyists. An attempt has been made to appeal to most skill levels and backgrounds. This is done by dividing each chapter into two sections: Overview and Detailed Circuit Analysis. You may choose to read one, the other, or both.

The book consists of eight chapters. Chapter 1 discusses nomenclature and symbols used throughout the text and figures. This chapter also contains a glossary of terms. Chapter 2 presents a description of the Apple II computer at the block diagram level.

The detailed descriptions start in Chapter 3. Chapters 3 and 4 cover the system clocks and part of the video circuitry. Chapter 5 explains the memory system and Chapter 6 examines the 6502 microprocessor and the system bus. Chapters 5 and 6 contain overview sections dedicated to the 4116 RAM and the 6502 microprocessor. As a result, the reader need not have prior knowledge of these devices.

The keyboard and other on-board I/O are discussed in Chapter 7. The video display (graphics and text) is the subject of Chapter 8. Much of the Apple's circuitry serves to generate a video signal. Due to the importance of this topic, Appendix A is included to provide an introduction to video techniques.

Appendix B is a gathering of all known circuit revisions of the Apple II mother board and keyboard. While the body of the book describes the latest Apple II revision, Appendix B describes differences between this latest Apple and all earlier revisions. Appendix C contains a set of mother board and keyboard schematics. These schematics cover all revisions. The book concludes with a list of references.

WINSTON D. GAYLER

EDITOR'S NOTE: In order to present the illustrations as large as possible many have been placed on the foldout pages at the back of the book. These illustrations are indicated with an asterisk(*) immediately following the figure number in the text, e.g., Fig. 3-4* indicates that Fig. 3-4 is located at the back of the book.

Acknowledgments

I wish to thank fellow Apple enthusiast Dr. James Alinsky for his many suggestions and general inspiration during the research and writing of this book. I am very appreciative for his review, from the reader's viewpoint, of the complete manuscript.

Thanks also go to the numerous employees of Apple Computer, Inc., who assisted by providing documentation and answering questions. I appreciate the assistance of Apple's engineering department in coordinating much of this activity.

Finally, I wish to acknowledge Stephen Wozniak who designed the Apple II, making it all possible.

Contents

CHAPTER 7

CHAPTER 8

APPENDIX A

APPENDIX B

APPENDIX C

APPENDIX D

CHAPTER 1

Introduction

Have you ever wanted to know the detailed circuit operation of your Apple II®† computer? Perhaps you were designing a peripheral or making a modification. Maybe you were repairing an Apple. You may have just been curious about how it works.

This book started as an exercise in understanding the Apple II hardware. The initial goal was to evaluate or design circuit modifications. It soon became apparent that the information obtained would be useful to others. Thus, the plans for a book developed.

The result is a detailed circuit description and analysis of the main circuit board and keyboard of the Apple II. In this introductory chapter, we present the organization of the book and explain some of the terms and symbols used.

THE AUDIENCE

This book is intended for engineers, technicians, students, and serious hobbyists. The engineer and hobbyist can use the descriptions and timing diagrams as a preparatory step to designing peripherals or modifications. The service technician can use the timing diagrams and schematics as aids to troubleshooting. The waveform drawings are particularly handy for troubleshooting with an oscilloscope. The student can use the Apple II for examples of practical circuit design. In many cases the reasons behind the design are presented here. All readers can use the descriptions to better understand how the Apple II works.

CHAPTER ORGANIZATION

Chapter 2 is a block diagram description of the Apple II mother board. There we introduce the names such as "address multiplexer" and "video address generator" given to various functional circuit blocks. Chapter 2 contains the discussion of the power supply, a simplified circuit description.

Chapters 3 through 8 comprise the body of the book. Each of these chapters takes a functional part of the circuit and examines it in detail. These chapters are

---

†Apple and Apple II are registered trademarks of Apple Computer, Inc.

each divided into two sections: Overview and Detailed Circuit Analysis. The Overview presents the circuit concepts and often contains block diagrams and simplified timing diagrams. If the material is new to you, you may want to read only the Overviews and save the Detailed Circuit Analyses until you need specific details. On the other hand, you may already be familiar with Apple II hardware. In that case, you may want to jump directly into the Detailed Circuit Analyses and skip the Overviews.

Chapter 3 presents the master oscillator, clock generator, and horizontal portion of the video address generator. Clocks are always important in a digital circuit, and they are especially important in the Apple II due to their interplay with the video circuitry.

Chapter 4 completes the video address generator by presenting its vertical portion. The chapter also covers video sync, blanking, and color burst.

The random access memory in the Apple II is shared by the microprocessor and the video generator. Chapter 5 covers this shared access scheme. The chapter also contains an introduction to the type 4116 dynamic RAM (random access memory).

Chapter 6 starts with an introduction to 6502 microprocessor hardware. The chapter then describes all the 6502 cycle types that are used in the Apple. Included are read cycles, write cycles, RAM cycles, ROM cycles, I/O cycles, keyboard cycles, interrupts, and DMA (direct memory access).

Chapter 7 describes the Apple II on-board I/O devices, such as cassette I/O, game I/O, and speaker. This chapter also contains the circuit description for the current *two-piece* keyboard.

The video generator is described in Chapter 8. There you will learn how text, LORES, and HIRES are generated by the hardware under software control.

Appendix A is an introduction to video signal techniques. If you are not familiar with video signals, such as sync, blanking, and color burst, then you may want to read Appendix A. Doing so may increase your appreciation of Chapters 3, 4, and 8.

Appendix B covers the topic of Apple II circuit revisions. The most recent circuit available (RFI mother board, Rev. D) is covered in the body of the book. Circuit variations dating back to the earliest Apple II (Rev. 0) are then covered in Appendix B. The appendix also contains modified waveform drawings for signals that differ in earlier revisions. The circuit description for the old *single-piece* keyboard is contained in Appendix B.

Appendix C contains schematic diagrams for all revisions of the Apple II.

A list of references follows the appendices—it is arranged by chapter.

TRADEMARKS, PATENTS, AND COPYRIGHTS

The names Apple, Apple II, Apple II Plus, and Applesoft are registered trademarks of Apple Computer, Inc. BASIC is a registered trademark of the trustees of Dartmouth College.

Portions of the Apple II circuitry are protected by U.S. patents 4,130,862; 4,136,359; and 4,278,972.

The Apple II schematics are copyrighted by Apple Computer, Inc. These schematics have been redrawn and printed with the permission of Apple Computer.

WHAT YOU SHOULD KNOW

As a reader of this book, you should be familiar with TTL (transistor-transistor logic), such as gates, flip-flops, shift registers, and multiplexers. While reading, you may want to have a copy of a TTL data book, such as Reference 1.2. You need not be familiar with the 4116 RAM or the 6502 microprocessor. Special sections in Chapters 5 and 6 will cover these devices. However, you should have a basic knowledge of microprocessor and microcomputer architecture. And of course you should be familiar with the binary and hexadecimal number systems.

Concerning your Apple II background, you should be familiar with the *Apple II Reference Manual* (Reference 1.1).

REVISIONS

There have been several circuit revisions to the Apple II since its introduction in 1977. The revisions are discussed in detail in Appendix B. Here in Chapter 1 we simply summarize the changes and establish a revision nomenclature for use throughout the book.

There are two categories of the Apple II mother board: *Non-RFI* (the early mother boards) and *RFI* (recent mother boards that have been designed to reduce radio-frequency interference).

Non-RFI mother boards have the part number 820-0001-XX where XX is the revision. The first non-RFI mother board was Revision 0; we will call it simply *Rev. 0*. It had only four HIRES colors. Revision 0 also lacked color killer and power-on reset circuits.

Revision 1 came next and added two more HIRES colors (for the current total of six). Revision 1 also added color killer and power-on reset circuits and made other small changes. Revisions 2, 3, and 4 had the same circuit as Rev. 1. In this book, we include them with Rev. 1.

The next significant change occurred at revision 7—the memory jumper blocks were removed and the character generator IC was changed.

The next significant change occurred with the switch to the RFI mother board. This board has the part number 820-0044-XX where XX is the revision. All revisions of this board to date (through Rev. D) have the same functional circuit. We refer to it simply as *RFI*.

The part numbers are found either along the left edge of the mother board or under the 6502 IC. See Appendix B for more details. In summary, the mapping from mother board part numbers to our nomenclature is shown in Table 1-1.

Table 1-1. Mapping From Mother Board Part Numbers

	Part No.	Revision
Non-RFI	820-0001-00	Rev. 0
	820-0001-01 820-0001-02 820-0001-03 820-0001-04	Rev. 1
	820-0001-07 & up	Rev. 7
RFI	820-0044-01 820-0044-C 820-0044-D	RFI

IC AND SIGNAL NOMENCLATURE

The ICs on the mother board are designated by their location on an X-Y grid. The grid coordinates consist of the letters A through K along the left edge of the board and the numbers 1 through 14 along the front edge of the board (Fig. 1-1*). Within an IC, the individual gates or sections are designated by the pin number of the gate output. For example, a reference in the text to "flip-flop B10-9" refers to a flip-flop in the IC located at coordinates B10. The specific flip-flop is the one whose Q output is on pin 9.

Signals use a similar nomenclature. For example, signal "C11-4" is the signal at pin 4 of IC C11. Some signals have already been given names on the Apple schematics—"LD194" is an example. When a signal name has a bar over it (such as $\overline{CAS}$), it means that the signal is active low. All signal names are printed using uppercase letters.

WAVEFORMS

When we say a digital signal is *low,* we mean it is about 0 volts. When a digital signal is *high,* we mean it is about 4 or 5 volts. The exact voltage level varies with logic family, load, and power supply voltage. For typical 74LSXX logic, a low *output* is less than 0.5 volt and a high *output* is greater than 2.7 volts. The same logic family will accept an *input* of less than 0.8 volt as a low, and greater than 2.0 volts as a high. Input levels between 0.8 and 2.0 volts result in an indeterminate state.

When we say a digital IC's output signal is *high impedance,* we mean that the IC neither drives nor appreciably loads the signal line. The high-impedance state is the third state of *three-state* logic: low, high, and high impedance. We sometimes refer to the high-impedance state as the *off* state. The off state of a three-state IC allows other ICs to turn *on* and drive a common signal line.

Digital waveforms are not drawn to vertical scale. Instead, the three possible states are depicted as shown at the top of Fig. 1-2. The rest of this figure shows the symbols used for transitions between states.

RESEARCH

The research for this book consisted of two major steps: paper analysis and laboratory verification. In the first step, the schematics were analyzed to ascertain the circuit operation and the timing waveforms. In the second step, the waveform drawings were taken into the laboratory and verified using equipment, such as the frequency counter, oscilloscope, logic analyzer, and light pen recorder.

The two research steps were first performed on a Revision 3 non-RFI Apple II. Later, Rev. 0, Rev. 7, and RFI Apples were obtained so that waveforms unique to these revisions could be verified. Operation and waveforms for both the single-piece and two-piece keyboards were also confirmed. Thus, the complete set of Apple II waveforms presented in this book have been laboratory verified.

GLOSSARY OF TERMS

ac—Alternating current.
access time—The time from accessing a memory IC (with an address or clock) until the data becomes stable at the output.
active high—A high level represents a logic 1.
active low—A low level represents a logic 1.
AN—Annunciator.
architecture—Block diagram.
ASCII—American Standard Code for Information Interchange. A common 7- or 8-bit code used by computers and peripherals.

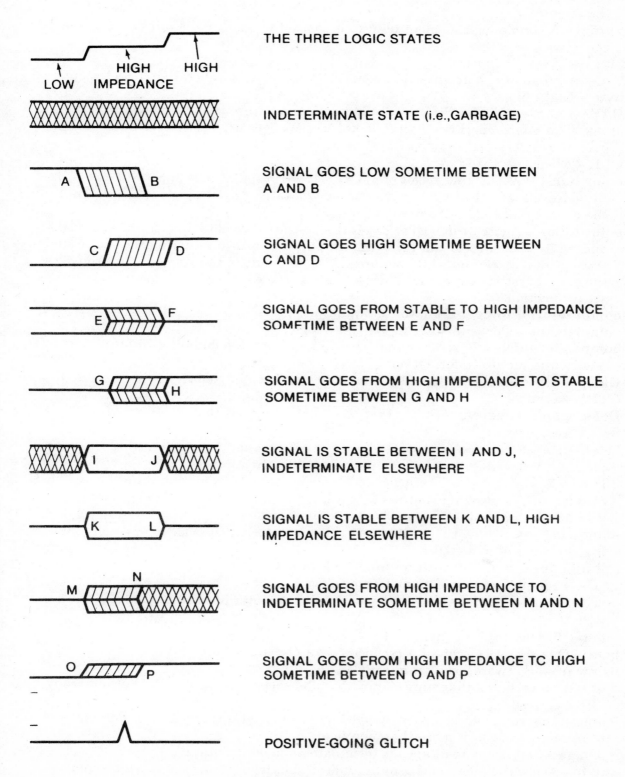

THE THREE LOGIC STATES

LOW   HIGH IMPEDANCE   HIGH

INDETERMINATE STATE (i.e.,GARBAGE)

SIGNAL GOES LOW SOMETIME BETWEEN
A AND B

SIGNAL GOES HIGH SOMETIME BETWEEN
C AND D

SIGNAL GOES FROM STABLE TO HIGH IMPEDANCE
SOMETIME BETWEEN E AND F

SIGNAL GOES FROM HIGH IMPEDANCE TO STABLE
SOMETIME BETWEEN G AND H

SIGNAL IS STABLE BETWEEN I AND J,
INDETERMINATE ELSEWHERE

SIGNAL IS STABLE BETWEEN K AND L, HIGH
IMPEDANCE ELSEWHERE

SIGNAL GOES FROM HIGH IMPEDANCE TO
INDETERMINATE SOMETIME BETWEEN M AND N

SIGNAL GOES FROM HIGH IMPEDANCE TC HIGH
SOMETIME BETWEEN O AND P

POSITIVE-GOING GLITCH

Fig. 1-2. Digital waveform symbols.

blanking—The part of a video signal that turns off the scanning electron beam during retrace.

bow tie—A PC board foil pattern in the shape of a bow tie. Meant to be cut to break the circuit.

buffer—A simple logic element used to increase the quantity of gates that a signal can drive.

burst—(See color burst).

bus—A group of signal lines that connect in common to several circuit elements.

byte—Eight bits.

CAS—Column Address Strobe. (Strobes column address into 4116 RAM.)

clock—An often repetitive digital signal whose edges are used to advance the outputs of counters and flip-flops.

CLR—Clear.

color burst—About nine cycles of a 3.579545 MHz signal that appear in a composite video waveform just following the horizontal sync pulse; used to synchronize the color circuitry in a tv receiver.

color killer—A circuit in a color tv set that defeats the color circuitry when a black and white transmission is received. Its purpose is to eliminate color noise and tinting from black and white pictures. Also, a circuit in the Apple II that removes the color burst in text mode. This is to allow the color killer in the associated tv set to function.

combinatorial logic—Logic consisting of just gates.

complement—Opposite state in two-state logic.

composite video—A video signal containing sync and blanking information in addition to picture information.

CRT—Cathode ray tube; usually a monitor or terminal containing a crt.

CTRL—Control.

DeMorgan's Theorem—States that $\overline{A \cdot B} = \overline{A} + \overline{B}$, and that $\overline{A + B} = \overline{A} \cdot \overline{B}$.

dc—Direct current.

DMA—Direct memory access; the ability of peripherals to directly access the main memory of a system without going through the microprocessor.

don't care—A signal whose logic state will not affect circuit operation.

dynamic—Depending on continuous clocking or sequencing for proper operation.

EPROM—Erasable programmable read-only memory.

equalizing interval—The portion of a video waveform just prior to and just following the vertical sync pulse.

falling edge—Signal transition from high to low.

FCC—Federal Communications Commission.

ferrite bead—A toroid or cylinder of magnetic material that is threaded with a wire to make an inductor.

fetch—To read from memory.

field—One complete scan of a crt face by an electron beam.

firmware—Software executing in ROM.

flag—A bit or signal that stores a binary state, such as on or off, ready or not-ready, set or cleared.

frame—One complete picture displayed on the face of a crt by a scanning electron beam; may consist of more than one field.

garbage—Data that is in an indeterminate or unstable state.

glitch—A usually short and usually undesirable level change in a logic signal.

high—A digital signal voltage of about 4 volts.

high-order—Bits representing the larger place values of a binary number.

HIRES—High resolution.

hold time—The time after a clock edge during which the input data to a flip-flop or other clocked IC must remain stable.

hue—Color tint (red, blue, etc.).

Hz—Hertz (cycles per second).

IC—Integrated circuit.

INH—Inhibit

inte lace—The process by which the lines of two or more fields are interleaved on the face of a crt to create a video frame.

I/O—Input/output.

IRQ—Interrupt request.

K or k—Kilo. (× 1000 when dealing with ohms, hertz, etc., × 1024 when dealing with memory locations, etc.)

KBD—Keyboard

LORES—Low resolution.

low—A digital signal voltage of about 0.

low-order—Bits representing the smaller place values of a binary number.

LSB—Least significant bit (the lowest order bit).

luminance—The brightness or black and white portion of a color video signal.

M—Mega (× 1,000,000).

mask—To cause to ignore.

mother board—The main logic board into which peripheral boards plug.

mS—Millisecond (0.001 second).

MSB—Most significant bit (the highest order bit).

negative true—A low level represents a logic 1.

NMI—Non-maskable interrupt.

non-interlaced—The video technique where each frame consists of one field; that is, the field and frame are identical (see interlaced).

non-maskable—Incapable of being ignored.

nS—Nanosecond (10^{-9} second).

off—High-impedance state of three-state logic.

on—Low-impedance state (either 0 or 1) of three-state logic.

op code—Operation code; the first byte of an instruction.

open collector—A logic output with two states: low (about 0 volt) and high impedance.

overscan—The loss of picture information caused by the electron beam scanning beyond the edges of a crt.

PC—Printed circuit.

PDL—Paddle.

period—Reciprocal of frequency.

pixel—Picture element.

positive true—A high signal represents a logic 1.

PROM—Programmable read-only memory.

RAM—Random access memory.

RAS—Row address strobe (strobes row address into 4116 RAM).

RDY—Ready.

refresh—The process by which the data contents of a dynamic RAM are maintained at their correct values by continuously clocking the IC.

REPT—Repeat.

RES—Reset.

retrace—The return of the scanning electron beam to the left of a crt after displaying a line. Also the beam's return to the top after displaying a field.

RF—Radio frequency.

RFI—Radio-frequency interference.

rising edge—Signal transition from low to high.

ROM—Read-only memory.

R/W—Read/write.

saturation—1. The intensity of color in a video signal (red is more saturated than pink).

2. The state of a linear device (such as an operational amplifier) that is operating outside its linear range.

serration—One of several narrow pulses within the vertical sync pulse. Serrations serve to maintain horizontal synchronization during the vertical sync pulse.

setup time—The time prior to a clock edge during which the data input to a flip-flop or other clocked IC must be stable.

Soft 5—A pull-up to a high TTL level.

Soft Switch—A register that can be set or reset under software control. The register then acts as a switch to control a hardware function.

solder pad—A PC board foil pattern to which wire jumpers are soldered.

STB—Strobe.

subcarrier—A carrier that modulates a main carrier. The subcarrier itself is modulated by information to be transmitted (such as the color information in a video signal).

SW—Switch.

sync—Synchronization.

transceiver—A bidirectional buffer.

TTL—Transistor-transistor logic.

UART—Universal Asynchronous Receiver/Transmitter.

V—Volts.

V$_{be}$—The voltage between the base and emitter of a transister; about 0.6 volt for a forward-biased silicon transistor.

wait state—An extra clock cycle inserted into the normal memory cycle of a microprocessor; used to accommodate peripherals with long access times.

$—Indicates a hexadecimal number, for example: $C0FF.

μS—Microsecond (10^{-6} second).

ϕ—Phase.

+—Logical OR.

●—Logical AND.

——Logical NOT ($\overline{A}$ = NOT A).

CHAPTER 2

The Apple II®
Block Diagram

In this chapter we describe the Apple II at the block diagram level. The material will probably not be new to most readers. It may be useful, however, to read the chapter for review. And of course if you read this material, we can then be assured of speaking the same language in later chapters.

We will discuss each of the blocks in the diagram and follow the signal paths for several major computer functions through the Apple. The Apple II block diagram is shown in Fig. 2-1.*

BASIC ARCHITECTURE AND BUSES

At first glance the Apple II's basic architecture appears to be standard for a single board microcomputer. There are several significantly uncommon features, however, and we will point them out as we go.

Microprocessor

At the heart of the Apple II is the 6502 microprocessor (A in Fig. 2-1*). The 6502 is an 8-bit processor. This means that it operates on data in chunks of eight bits, or one byte. The 6502 can directly address 64K bytes of memory. Thus, it outputs a 16-bit address.

Input/output (I/O) operations in the 6502 are memory mapped. This means that I/O or peripheral devices share the same 64K address space with the memory. There is no separate I/O address space as provided in some microprocessors, such as the 8080. In addition to the 8 data lines and 16 address lines, there are various clock and control lines connected to the 6502. These will be described shortly.

Buses

There are three major buses in the Apple II: the 16-bit address bus, the 8-bit data bus, and the control bus. These buses run throughout the computer and appear at the eight peripheral I/O connectors.

Address Bus—The 16 address lines from the 6502 are buffered by a three-state driver (B in Fig. 2-1*) which then drives the address bus. This driver can be turned

17

off (switched to the high impedance state) by signal $\overline{\text{DMA}}$ from the control bus. The function of $\overline{\text{DMA}}$ will be described shortly.

Data Bus—On write cycles, the eight data lines from the 6502 are buffered by transceiver C which then drives the data bus. On read cycles, signal R/W (read/write) reverses the drive direction of transceiver C. This allows data from the data bus to pass to the 6502.

Control Bus—The major control bus signals are the interrupt, ready, reset, read/write, $\overline{\text{DMA}}$, and clock lines. There are two interrupt lines that allow peripherals to signal the 6502 that they need its immediate attention. The first of these lines is $\overline{\text{IRQ}}$ (interrupt request). It can be selectively ignored (masked) by the 6502. The second interrupt line is $\overline{\text{NMI}}$ (non-maskable interrupt). It cannot be ignored; the 6502 always responds to $\overline{\text{NMI}}$.

The ready line allows "slow" peripherals to momentarily stop the 6502 while they fetch their data and put it on the bus. The reset line allows any device connected to it to reset (initialize) all other devices connected to the reset line.

We have already mentioned the read/write line. Its function is to control the direction of data transfers on the data bus. Data is *read from memory* or I/O devices into the 6502. Data is *written to memory* or I/O devices from the 6502.

Direct memory access (DMA) refers to the ability of peripheral devices to exchange data directly with the system's memory without the need of first sending data through the microprocessor. During a DMA cycle, the $\overline{\text{DMA}}$ line turns off bus driver B so that the DMA device can put its own address on the bus. Also during DMA cycles, transceiver C does not drive the data bus. This frees that bus for data transfers between the DMA device and the system memory.

Clocks—The system clocks are the key to controlling the timing of data and address transfers on the buses. The clocks are also used throughout the Apple for such functions as video generation. The clocks have their origin in crystal oscillator D. Its output of about 14 MHz is used by clock generator T to produce the system clocks. One of these clocks (at about 1 MHz) is supplied to the 6502. The 6502 uses this 1 MHz clock to time its accesses to the buses. Memory and I/O devices use the same clock to synchronize their bus accesses with the 6502.

A read or a write operation can take place in one period of the 1 MHz clock. While the 6502 is running a program, it is executing individual instructions of that program. Each instruction executes in an integer number of clock cycles. On each clock cycle, the 6502 either writes to the bus, reads from the bus, or performs an internal operation. Each instruction consists of a mixture of these cycle types. The shortest instruction is two clock cycles and the longest is seven.

The 6502, the buses, and such topics as interrupts and DMA will be discussed in Chapter 6. The clock generator will be discussed in Chapter 3.

MEMORY

Two types of memory are provided on the Apple II mother board: ROM (read-only memory) and RAM (random access memory). The mother board can contain up to 12K bytes of ROM and up to 48K bytes of RAM.

ROM

Up to six 2K byte ROMs (E) can be installed on the mother board. Address decoder F decodes the high-order address bits to provide individual chip select lines for the six ROMs. The low-order address bits connect directly to the ROMs. On ROM read cycles, the ROM's data output is placed directly on the data bus. Fig. 2-2* shows the main address and data paths through the Apple for a ROM read cycle. ROM cycles will be discussed in detail in Chapter 6.

RAM

Up to 48K bytes of RAM (G) can be installed on the mother board. Individual RAM locations are selected for read/write operations by addresses on the address bus. The address passes through address multiplexer H on its way to the RAM. The data input (DI) of the RAM connects directly to the data bus. This is the source of data for RAM write cycles. Fig. 2-3* shows the main address and data paths through the Apple for RAM write cycles.

On RAM read cycles, the data output (DO) of the RAM is stored in latch I. The read data then passes through data multiplexer J to the data bus. Fig. 2-4* shows the main address and data paths through the Apple for RAM read cycles. The RAM cycles will be discussed in detail in Chapters 5 and 6.

INPUT/OUTPUT

On-Board I/O

A computer may have a large memory and a fast processor, but it is of no use unless the computer can communicate with humans or other machines. That communication is the purpose of the computer's I/O (input/output) facilities. In the Apple II, some of the most frequently used I/O devices are located on the mother board. These on-board I/O devices include the speaker, cassette I/O, game I/O, and keyboard (K). Although the use of on-board I/O by the Apple is not unique, it is a distinguishing feature of the Apple II.

Write to I/O — Individual address select lines for the on-board I/O are provided by address decoder F. The 6502 processor writes to on-board I/O devices using these address lines; it does not use the data bus. For example, the 6502 may address one location to turn an I/O function *on*. The 6502 may then address another location to turn that same function *off*. It is the act of addressing specific locations that performs the functions. The data bus is not used.

Read from I/O — When the 6502 reads from an on-board I/O device, the data bus *is* used. Most on-board I/O devices provide just one bit, bit 7. This single data bit (D7) connects directly to the data bus as shown in Fig. 2-1*. The keyboard is an exception since it provides seven data bits. Fig. 2-5* shows the address and data paths for a keyboard read cycle. When the 6502 reads the keyboard, the keyboard data passes through multiplexer J. Keyboard cycles are described in Chapter 6.

Soft Switches — The soft switches are output locations that let the Apple configure its own hardware. The soft switches are set under software control to configure the video circuitry for various display modes. Their names of TEXT MODE, MIX MODE, PAGE 2, and HIRES MODE suggest this application.

On-board I/O is discussed in detail in Chapter 7. The soft switches are also discussed in Chapters 5 and 8.

Peripheral I/O

There is a need for flexibility and expansion beyond the on-board I/O. To meet this need, the Apple II mother board is provided with eight 50-pin peripheral connectors (L in Fig. 2-1*). The address, data, and control buses appear at each connector. Each connector is also provided with individual select lines from address decoder F. The select lines reduce the amount of address decoding circuitry needed on each peripheral card. This feature of the Apple II will be discussed in detail in Chapter 6.

VIDEO

The video output of the Apple contains text and graphics information for display on a monitor, or tv set. Video signals require high-frequency components that are too fast to be generated directly by the 6502 microprocessor. (If you are not familiar with video signals, you may wish to review Appendix A at this time.) As a result of the high frequencies, dedicated hardware is provided to generate the Apple's video output. Of course, software-control gives the 6502 command over this hardware to generate specific text and graphics patterns.

The patterns that are to be displayed on the screen are generated by the 6502 and stored as data in the RAM in the Apple. The video circuitry then reads the data from the RAM, converts it to a video format, and sends it to the video output for display on a monitor. The accesses to RAM by the 6502 and the video circuitry are time-shared as described here. During the first half of a 6502 cycle, the video circuitry reads from RAM. During the second half of the cycle, the 6502 reads from RAM or writes to RAM.

In the sections that follow, we will examine the blocks in Fig. 2-1* that comprise the video circuitry.

Video Address Generator

Using the system clock as a reference, video address generator M creates a 15-bit *video address*. The video address consists of six horizontal bits and nine vertical bits. The address is continuously running through an incrementing sequence that repeats about 60 times a second. During each pass through the sequence, the vertical address has 262 different values. For each value of vertical address, the horizontal address increments through 65 counts.

Together, the horizontal and vertical addresses can select a location anywhere on the screen. Each screen location has a height of one scan line, and a width of about one microsecond. The video address also includes locations that do not appear on the screen since they occur during horizontal or vertical blanking.

Each location on the screen corresponds to a unique video address. As we will see shortly, the scanning electron beam in the crt is synchronized to the video address. One function of the video address is to "tell" other hardware sections the current screen location of the beam. The other hardware sections then fetch the appropriate character or graphics symbol for display at that location.

Fig. 2-1* shows a feedback path from the video address generator to the clock generator. This feedback signal delays the system clock by about 140 nS every horizontal scan line. The purpose of this unique arrangement is to simplify the generation of color graphics—it will be described in Chapter 3.

Memory Mapper

The video address is not a bit-for-bit equal of the memory address used to store the corresponding screen data. As a result, the video address must be converted to a memory address in order to fetch the correct screen data from memory. Memory mapper N performs this function. Screen locations go into the mapper, and the corresponding memory location comes out.

The memory mapper will map to different memory address blocks under control of the soft switches. In HIRES mode, for example, the video address maps to a different memory range than it would in text mode.

Fig. 2-6 shows the path through the Apple for a video cycle. The video address goes into the memory mapper and the memory address comes out. During video cycles, address multiplexer H connects the output of the mapper to the address input of the RAM. Data out of the RAM is then stored in latch I. The latched data then appears as an input to video generator P.

Video Generator

The video generator configures the latched data into video data that it sends to mixer Q. In the mixer, the video data is combined with the sync and color burst signals to become the composite video output.

The conversion process in the video generator is controlled by the soft switches. In LORES mode, for example, the video generator acts on the data in a manner different from the way it would act on the same data in text mode.

Sync Generator

Sync generator R uses the video address to generate the sync, color burst, and blanking signals. SYNC and COLOR BURST are mixed with the video in mixer Q. The sync component of the composite video output allows the scanning electron beam in the display crt to synchronize with the video address. The color burst component allows the color circuitry in the display device to synchronize with the internal color reference clock of the Apple. BLANKING connects to the video generator where it forces the video signal to go black during the horizontal and vertical blanking intervals.

POWER SUPPLY

The Apple II is equipped with a *switching power supply* that provides +5 V, +12 V, −5 V and −12 V to the mother board, keyboard, and peripheral I/O connectors. Switching power supplies are noted for their higher efficiency and lower bulk than more conventional designs. The power supply design of the Apple eliminates the need for a heavy line transformer. The ac line input is rectified, then converted to a high-frequency ac. This high-frequency ac is then coupled to the secondary of the supply via a small transformer.

Basic Operation

Fig. 2-7 is a simplified diagram of the power supply. Bridge rectifier CR1 rectifies the ac line input to provide a dc potential that is filtered by C1. This dc potential causes a current to flow through a primary winding of transformer TR1 when Q3 is on. Transistor Q3 switches on and off at a high frequency. On each cycle, energy is stored in TR1 while Q3 is on. When Q3 turns off, this energy is coupled to the secondary windings and causes current to flow in the output load.

Circuitry is provided to control the conduction of Q3 via its base. This control circuitry derives its operating potential from a second primary winding of TR1.

At the secondary, rectifier diodes and filter capacitors are used to obtain the four dc output potentials.

Regulation—Transistor Q4 is wired as a comparator that senses the voltage on the +5 V output. Resistor R15 and zener diode CR19 derive a reference voltage from

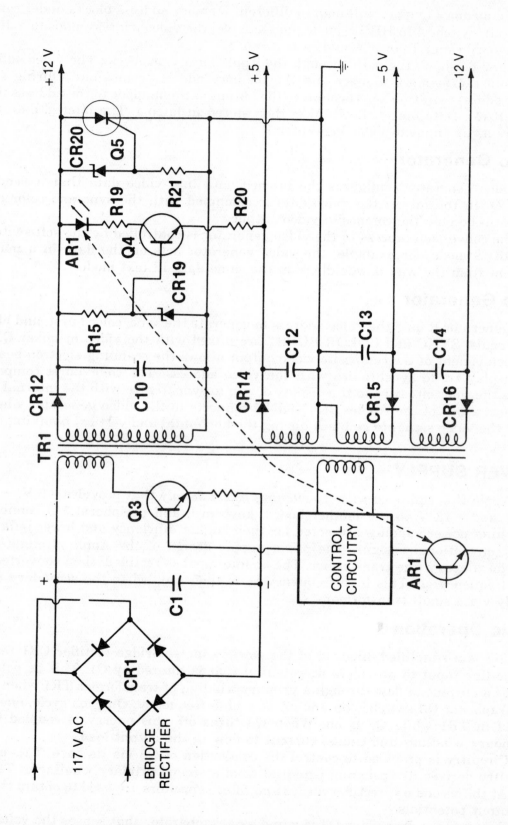

Fig. 2-7. Power supply—simplified diagram.

the +12 V output. This reference is applied to the base of Q4. The emitter of Q4 is connected through R20 to the +5 V output. When Q4 conducts, current flows through the LED (light emitting diode) that is part of optical coupler AR1. The amount of light emitted is a function of the voltage on the +5 V output. If the +5 V output decreases, for example, Q4 conducts more heavily and the LED emits more light. This light is coupled to the phototransistor portion of AR1. Increasing light causes the phototransistor to conduct more heavily. Via the control circuitry, this feedback causes Q3 to deliver more energy to TR1. This will in turn increase the voltage on the +5 V output. The other three voltages will track the regulation of the +5 V output.

Overvoltage —In the event of a fault that causes an overvoltage, the increased potential on the +12 V output will cause zener diode CR20 to conduct. This makes the gate of silicon controlled rectifier Q5 go positive—Q5 conducts, shorting the +12 V output to ground. This action will shut down the whole supply.

The complete power supply schematic is shown in Fig. C-23*. **CAUTION:** This schematic is reprinted directly from the *Apple II Reference Manual*. It has not been verified for accuracy with respect to any product shipped by Apple Computer. You are also cautioned against attempting to repair or modify your power supply. Much of the circuitry is not isolated from the ac line input and thus contains hazardous voltages. If you wish to read additional material on the power supply, obtain a copy of U.S. Patent No. 4,130,862.

SUMMARY

In this chapter we have presented a brief overview of the Apple II computer. At the heart of the Apple II is a basic single-board microcomputer consisting of microprocessor, buses, bus drivers, bus transceivers, ROM, and RAM. This basic architecture is enhanced by the inclusion of on-board I/O for many of the frequently used I/O functions. Expandability is provided by eight peripheral I/O connectors. The use of these connectors is simplified by an address decoding scheme that provides individual select lines for each connector.

A large part of the Apple II hardware consists of the built-in video text and graphics capability. Since the video screen memory resides in the address space of the microprocessor, the microprocessor can quickly output data to the screen with a simple memory write operation. Access to the screen memory is time-shared by the microprocessor and the video circuitry. This is an efficient arrangement that does not slow the processor.

In the chapters that follow, we will examine in detail the elements that make up the Apple II block diagram. We start in the next chapter with the clock generator.

CHAPTER 3

Clock Generator and Horizontal Timing

We begin our discussion of the Apple II with signals that are essential for the operation of the computer, the clocks. While it might not be very exciting, a knowledge of the clocks will provide a basis for the explanation of many of the functions of the Apple. In this chapter we will derive the clocks and horizontal timing and make some interesting discoveries about the processing speed of the 6502.

Schematic reference: Figs. C-2* and C-3*.

OVERVIEW

Clocks

The Apple II circuit design is based on clocked logic. There are thus many flip-flops, counters, and shift registers. These circuit elements all perform their tasks upon receiving a signal transition (or edge) at their clock inputs. For example, a 74LS161 counter will count and update its output pins upon receiving a rising edge at its clock input. The counter then sits idle until the next clock edge is received. Clearly the faster the clock, the higher the throughput. If the clock is too fast, however, the circuitry may not have time to respond between clock edges. The 74LS161, for example, may not respond to clock frequencies higher than 25 MHz.

Other devices in the Apple also use clocks. The 6502 microprocessor advances through a program one step at a time as it receives its clock input. The 6502 used in the Apple II is limited to a clock frequency of 1 MHz.

The type 4116 dynamic RAMs are also clocked devices. They load their address inputs upon receiving a clock edge. The RAMs in the Apple II are accessed at a 2 MHz rate.

The composite video output of the Apple contains an accurate 3.579545 MHz color reference signal. This signal is derived in the clock generator.

As you can see, there is a requirement in the Apple II for several clocks of different frequencies. By deriving the various clocks from a common high frequency master oscillator, all sections of the Apple are made to operate synchronously with each other. Synchronous operation is a highly desirable trait in a digital system.

The master oscillator is selected to be an integer multiple of the individual clock frequency that is the most critical. In the Apple, the color reference is the most critical frequency, and the multiplication factor is 4. Thus, the master oscillator frequency is 4 × 3.579545 MHz = 14.31818 MHz. The Apple makes use of counters and shift registers to divide the master oscillator frequency into the various lower frequencies required.

Clock Generator Block Diagram

Fig. 3-1 is a block diagram of the clock generator. The ICs that comprise each block are noted in the figure. The master oscillator frequency is divided by 2 to generate a complementary pair of 7.2 MHz clocks, 7M and $\overline{7M}$. Signal 7M is divided by 2 to create COLOR REF. Signals 7M, $\overline{7M}$, COLOR REF, and 14M are used in the video generator.

Signal 14M is divided by 7 to generate $\overline{RAS}$, AX, $\overline{CAS}$, and Q3 (all at 2 MHz). Row address strobe ($\overline{RAS}$), AX, and $\overline{CAS}$ are used by the RAM and memory address multiplexer. Clock Q3 is a general purpose clock made available to the peripheral I/O connectors. Clock Q3 is divided by 2 to create a complementary pair of 1-MHz clocks, $\phi 0$ and $\phi 1$. These two clocks are used by the 6502 and all other devices that read from or write to the system data bus.

Combinatorial logic then derives the LD194 and $\overline{LDPS}$ clocks from the other

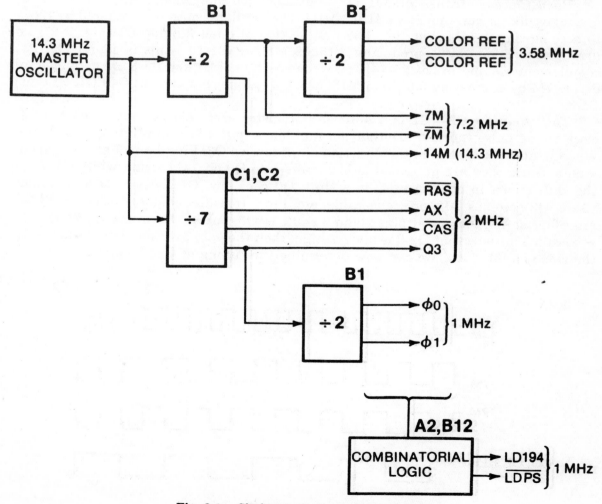

Fig. 3-1. Clock generator block diagram.

clocks previously described. LD194 is used in the video generator and $\overline{\text{LDPS}}$ is used in the video address generator.

Video Address Generator

The video address generator (Fig. C-3*) consists of a string of counters. These counters increment every microsecond to generate a new video address. The video address represents the instantaneous screen location of the scanning electron beam in the monitor connected to the Apple. The video address is used to fetch the video data that is to be displayed at each screen location. The video address is comprised of horizontal and vertical parts. The six bits of the horizontal part (H0 through H5) select one of 40 visible screen locations along a scan line. Later chapters will cover the use of the video address. In this chapter, however, we must examine the horizontal video address in detail. This is due to a feedback path from the video address generator to the clock generator. This feedback path plays a key role in the operation of the clock generator.

DETAILED CIRCUIT ANALYSIS

Clock Generator

Basic Clocks — Transistors Q1, Q2, and associated components (Fig. C-2*) form a crystal oscillator running at 14.31818 MHz. The oscillator output is buffered by B2-8 to become signal 14M, Fig. 3-2. The first section of quad flip-flop B1 (Fig. C-2*) is arranged to divide by 2, producing 7.15909 MHz at B1-15—this is signal 7M. Its complement $\overline{7M}$ appears at B1-14. The second section of B1 and B2-3 are arranged to divide 7M by 2, creating 3.579545 MHz at B1-2 and its complement COLOR REF at B1-3.

Shift Register C2 — C2 is a 4-bit shift register arranged so that on each 14M clock rising pulse (pin 10) it either parallel loads (pin 9 low) or shifts (pin 9 high). When it shifts, it does so in the direction of Q0 toward Q3. Pins 2 and 3 are the serial inputs. Since they are grounded, a low shifts into Q0 on 14M rising while C2 is in the shift mode. In other words, on a shift, Q0 goes low, Q1 becomes Q0's previous value, Q2 becomes Q1's previous value, etc. Pin 9 (parallel enable) is tied to Q3, so after four shifts, the low at pins 2 and 3 shifts to Q3, putting C2 in the load mode. If we assume for now that D2-6 is always high, then the only external signal into C2 is the steady 14M clock. We can now determine the timing of C2's outputs.

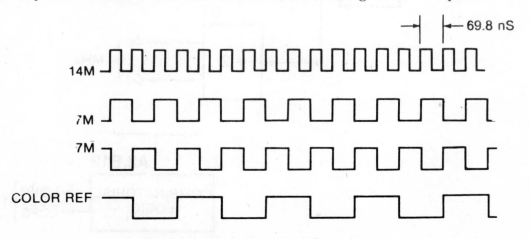

Fig. 3-2. Basic clock signals.

More Clocks—Referring to Fig. 3-3, let's start at the point where the low has just shifted into Q3 (point A). Shift register C2 is a synchronous load device, so after the next clock pulse the outputs will take on the values of the parallel inputs that existed before the clock pulse. Signal Q0 ($\overline{RAS}$) will remain low since PO (AX) was low. Signal Q1 (AX) will go high since P1 is assumed to be high for now. Signal Q2 ($\overline{CAS}$) will remain low since P2 (AX) was low. And finally, Q3 will stay low since P3 ($\overline{RAS}$) was low.

We are now at point B and still in the load mode. This time P0 and P2 (AX) are high, so on the next clock pulse, Q0 ($\overline{RAS}$) and Q2 ($\overline{CAS}$) will both go high. On the third load, Q3 goes high since P3 ($\overline{RAS}$) was high. We now stay in shift mode for four clock cycles before the low shifts into Q3 to put us back into the load mode. You can see the low's shifting along at points E, F, G, and H. The cycle begins again at point H which is the equivalent of point A. Since this cycle takes seven clock periods, $\overline{RAS}$, AX, $\overline{CAS}$, and Q3 all have a frequency of 14.31818 MHz ÷ 7 = 2.045454 MHz.

Microprocessor Clock—The circuit next divides by 2 to get the microprocessor's clock frequency of about 1 MHz. The third flip-flop in B1 (Fig. C-2) performs this function, aided by data selector C1-9. The 1 MHz signal that we are looking for will be at B1-10. The fourth B1 flip-flop delays B1-10 by one 14M clock pulse to generate $\phi 0$ at B1-7. Let's start with pins 10 and 7 of B1 low; this is in line with point A of Fig. 3-3. With both AX and $\phi 0$ low, select inputs S0 and S1 of C1 are low, and input pin 10 is gated to output pin 9. Thus, the low at B1-10 appears at B1-12. Both B1-10 and B1-7 remain low after the next clock edge, and we move to point B in Fig. 3-3.

At point B, AX is high, causing C1-9 (Fig. C-2*) to select input pin 11. Pin C1-11 connects to C2-11 and is high at this time. On the next clock pulse, B1-10 goes high and we move to point C (Fig. 3-3). The select inputs of C1 do not change, so on the next clock pulse, B1-10 stays high and B1-7 goes high to follow B1-10. We are now at point D. With B1-7 high, C1-9 selects input pin 13 which is high. Nothing changes on the following clocks until AX falls. Now C1-9 selects input pin 12 which is high. Still there is no change until Q3 falls at point H causing C1-9 to select input pin 10. Still no change until AX rises at point I. This selects C1-9 input pin 13 which is now low. On the next clock pulse, B1-10 falls and we move to point J. The select inputs of C1 do not change but B1-7 follows B1-10 to go low at point K. With B1-7 low, C1-9 selects input pin 11 which is low, so there is no change at point M. Signal AX is low at point N causing C1-9 to select input pin 10. Pin 10 is low, so there is no change at point O. The cycle begins again at point P which is the equivalent of point A.

Since this cycle takes 14 clock periods, signal $\phi 0$ has a frequency of 14.31818 ÷ 14 or about 1 MHz. Phase 1 at B1-6 is the complement of $\phi 0$. Phase $\phi 0$ and $\phi 1$ are the clocks for the 6502 microprocessor.

$\overline{LDPS}$ Clock—The signal $\overline{LDPS}$ is obtained by the combinatorial logic of gates B13-10 and A2-3 (Fig. C-2*). When AX is low *and* $\overline{CAS}$ is low *and* $\phi 0$ is high, then $\overline{LDPS}$ is low; see Fig. 3-3. Even though the waveforms in Figs. 3-2 and 3-3 are all derived from 14M, we have not combined them on one drawing yet since we do not know their relative phase. This will come later after we develop some of the video timing.

Horizontal Timing

In Fig. C-3* (Video Address Generator), D11, D12, D13, and D14 are a string of 4-bit binary counters chained together to provide the video address. The counters clock on the $\overline{LDPS}$ signal when it is rising. On each clock pulse, each counter will either

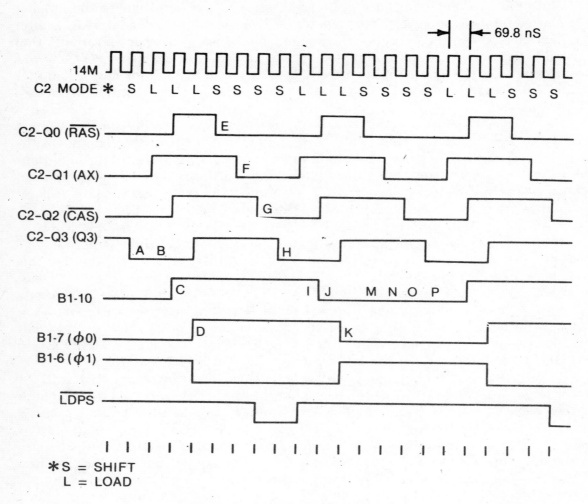

Fig. 3-3. Simplified system timing.

count (advance in binary sequence) or parallel load from its P inputs. The 74LS161 counts when pin 9 is high and loads when pin 9 is low.

The first seven counter bits (H0, H1, H2, H3, H4, H5, and $\overline{HPE}$) have the potential for 128 counts. Only 65 counts are used here. Let's start with all seven bits low, point A in Fig. 3-4*. Since $\overline{HPE}$ is low, D13 and D14 are in the load mode. On the next clock pulse ($\overline{LDPS}$ rising), the six low order bits load in zeros (so remain low), and $\overline{HPE}$ loads in a 1 (so goes high). We are now at point B and in the count mode. Counter D14 now counts up to 15 at which time its carry output (pin 15) goes high (point C in Fig. 3-4*). This enables D13 so that on the next clock D13 counts (H4 goes high). Counter D14 simply counts from 15 back to 0 and we are at point D. The enable input of D13 is removed (D14-15 low), so D13 does not count again until D14 reaches a count of 15 at E. Counter D13 counts at point F and again at points G and H. At point H, $\overline{HPE}$ is low again and the cycle restarts.

The decimal values of the bits H0 through H5 are shown in Fig. 3-4*. Note that there are two counts in the cycle with the value 0, and that there are 65 counts total per cycle. Counters D13 and D14 thus divide $\overline{LDPS}$ by 65. Each cycle (65 counts) through the waveforms of Fig. 3-4* corresponds to one horizontal line of the Apple video output. Each of the 65 counts corresponds to the width on the screen of one character in text mode (or one pixel in LORES mode). We know that the Apple displays only 40 characters per line. It so happens that the other 25 counts occur during horizontal blanking. There will be much more on this in later chapters. First let's examine how $\overline{HPE}$ feeds back to the clock generator to affect shift register C2.

Note: The remainder of the waveforms in Fig. 3-4* will be discussed in Chapter 4.

The Extended Cycle

Fig. 3-5 is similar to Fig. 3-3, but some new signals have been added. Bit $\overline{HPE}$ will go low on an $\overline{LDPS}$ rising edge, let's say at point A. Bit $\overline{HPE}$ is inverted by B2-6 (Fig. C-2*) to put a high at D2-1. This meets one of the conditions necessary for D2-6 to go low. The others are AX low *and* $\overline{CAS}$ low *and* $\phi0$ high *and* COLOR REF low (note that D2-2 is the complement of COLOR REF via B1). These conditions are the same as $\overline{LDPS}$ low *and* COLOR REF low. At this point we do not know the phase of COLOR REF relative to the other signals in Fig. 3-5. There are four possibilities shown as CR1, CR2, CR3, and CR4. The correct COLOR REF phase will turn out to

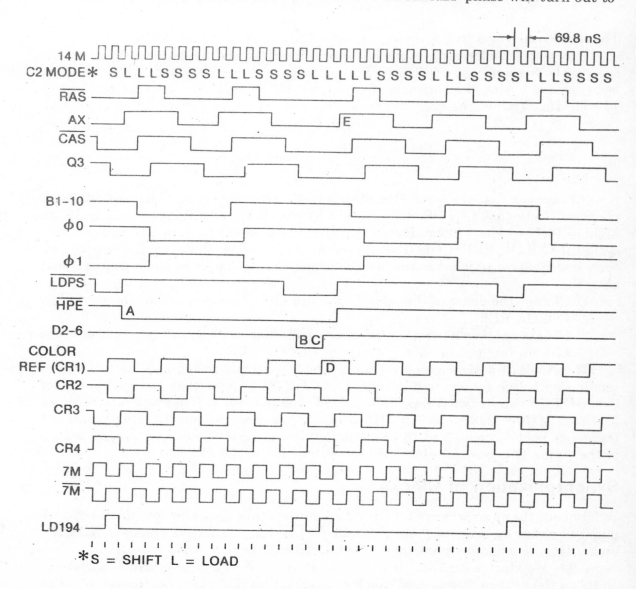

Fig. 3-5. System timing with extended cycles.

be CR1. Assume for now that our Apple powers up with COLOR REF shown as CR1; we will worry about the other three cases later.

Everything proceeds as previously described until point B when $\overline{\text{LDPS}}$ and COLOR REF are both low. Pulse D2-6 goes low, so that on the next clock cycle a low loads into AX instead of the usual high. We are now at point C and another low loads into AX. At point D, COLOR REF and D2-6 go high so that on the next clock pulse AX goes high (point E). The timing continues from this point as previously described in Fig. 3-3. The result of the low at $\overline{\text{HPE}}$ is to extend $\overline{\text{RAS}}$, AX, $\overline{\text{CAS}}$, Q3, $\phi 0$, $\phi 1$, and $\overline{\text{LDPS}}$ for two 14M clock cycles. The normal cycle is $14 \div 14.31818$ MHz $= 978$ nS (nanoseconds). The extended cycle is $16 \div 14.31818$ MHz $= 1117$ nS. In other words, most 6502 cycles are 978 nS long, but every 65th cycle is 1117 nS long. The average processor speed is then

$$14.31818 \text{ MHz} \times \frac{65}{(64 \times 14) + 16} = 1.020484 \text{ MHz}.$$

The horizontal video frequency is 1.020484 MHz $\div 65 = 15.700$ kHz.

Why the extended cycle every horizontal line? For the Apple to work with color tv sets, the frequency of COLOR REF must be very close to 3.579545 MHz. This has been achieved. Also, the horizontal frequency must be near (but need not be exactly) 15.734 kHz. Without the extended cycles, the circuit would divide 14M by (14×65). Since

$$\frac{14.31818 \text{ MHz}}{14 \times 65} \doteq 15.734 \text{ kHz}$$

it would appear that the second requirement is easily met. It is, but there is a complication. Note that COLOR REF divided by this horizontal frequency is 3.579545 MHz $\div 15.734$ kHz $= 227.5$. Every horizontal line would contain 227 and *one-half* cycles of COLOR REF. COLOR REF would thus change phase by 180 degrees on each line relative to what it was on the previous line. There are two ways to deal with this:

1. Change the phase of the color data every line to compensate for the change in COLOR REF.
2. Choose another horizontal frequency such that one horizontal line would contain an integer number of cycles of COLOR REF.

The Apple II design uses Number 2. The 227.5 ratio is increased to 228 by extending each line by one-half period of COLOR REF. Note that one-half period of COLOR REF equals two full periods of 14M. The horizontal frequency now becomes 3.579545 MHz $\div 228 = 15.700$ kHz, a number derived previously. This horizontal frequency is close enough to 15.734 kHz for most tv sets. The extended cycle design of the Apple II is a major claim of U.S. Patent No. 4,136,359.

Synchronization of Clocks

What about the cases where COLOR REF and the other clocks do not start in correct phase at power up (Fig. 3-5)? We will take each of the alternative phases (CR2, CR3, and CR4) and examine what they do while $\overline{\text{HPE}}$ is low.

CR2– We start with CR2 in Fig. 3-6. At point A, D2-6 goes low. Register C2 shifts on the next clock pulse, so this low has no effect. D2-6 goes high again at point B. Since the cycle was not extended, CR2 will have an extra one-half period left over

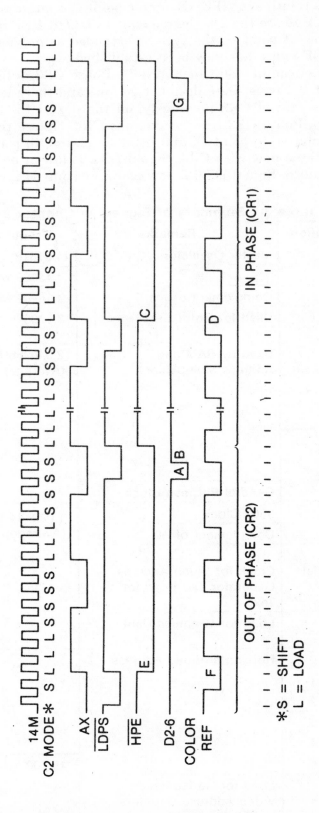

Fig. 3-6. Clock synchronization—CR2.

at the end of the line. The next time $\overline{\text{HPE}}$ is low (point C), COLOR REF will have shifted 180 degrees relative to $\overline{\text{HPE}}$. (Examine point C relative to point D, and point E relative to point F to see the 180 degree shift.) COLOR REF now has phase CR1. When D2-6 goes low at point G, the cycle is extended as previously described. The correct COLOR REF phase has now been established.

CR3—Next we examine CR3 in Fig. 3-7*. Phase CR3 is high (point A) when $\overline{\text{LDPS}}$ is low (point B). Thus, D2-6 does not go low, and there is no extended cycle. However, as in the case of CR2 previously, on the next $\overline{\text{HPE}}$ low, CR3 will have shifted 180 degrees. Phase CR3 has now become CR4. (To see the 180 degree shift, examine point C relative to point D, and point E relative to point F.)

CR4—We continue now with CR4. Signal D2-6 is low at point G and C2 shifts on the next clock pulse. Signal D2-6 is low again at point H and on the next clock

Table 3-1 Summary of Signals in Chapter 3

Signal	Description	Remarks	Frequency	Period
14M	14 MHz	Master Oscillator	14.31818 MHz	69.8 nS
7M	7 MHz		7.15909 MHz	140 nS
$\overline{7M}$	7 MHz	Complement of 7M	7.15909 MHz	140 nS
COLOR REF	Color Reference	Used for Color Burst	3.579545 MHz	279 nS
$\overline{\text{RAS}}$	Row Address Strobe	Used by RAM and Address Multiplexer	2.040968 MHz (Average)	489 nS or 628 nS
AX	Address Multiplex			
$\overline{\text{CAS}}$	Column Address Strobe			
Q3		General Purpose Clock		
ϕ0	Phase ϕ	6502 Clock	1.020484 MHz (Average)	978 nS or 1117 nS
ϕ1	Phase 1	Complement of ϕ0		
$\overline{\text{LDPS}}$	Load Parallel to Serial	Clock for Video Address Generator and Load for Text		
LD194	Load (74LS)194	Load for Graphics Data		
H0	Horizontal 0	Horizontal Video Address		
H1	Horizontal 1			
H2	Horizontal 2			
H3	Horizontal 3			
H4	Horizontal 4			
H5	Horizontal 5		15.700 kHz	63.7 μS
$\overline{\text{HPE}}$	Horizontal Parallel Enable	Load for Horizontal Video Address Counters		

pulse a low loads into AX. At point I, COLOR REF is high, so on the next clock pulse, AX loads a high (point J) and the timing continues as usual. The cycle has been extended by only one 14M period. The result of this extension is to convert COLOR REF from phase CR4 to phase CR1. (By examining point K relative to point M, and point N relative to point 0, you can see that the phase established immediately following the extension is indeed phase CR1.) Once phase CR1 has been established, there will be an extended cycle (point P) everytime $\overline{HPE}$ is low.

No matter which of the four phases COLOR REF takes at power up, it will quickly assume CR1. Phases CR2, CR3, and CR4 exist only momentarily at power up. It may avoid confusion to note that the *absolute* phase of COLOR REF does not really change after power up. The absolute phases of the other clocks *do* change as a result of extended cycles. References previously to a change in COLOR REF's phase mean a change *relative* to the other clocks.

SUMMARY

Now that the correct phase for COLOR REF has been established, 7M and $\overline{7M}$ can be transferred from Fig. 3-2 to Fig. 3-5. We can also add LD194 which is $\overline{7M}$ high *and* $\phi 0$ high *and* AX low *and* $\overline{CAS}$ low—LD194 is used later in the video generator. Table 3-1 is a summary of the signals presented so far.

In the next chapter we will complete the description of the video address generator. We will then examine the portion of the video generator that creates the video sync, video blanking, and color burst signals.

CHAPTER 4

Video Timing

This chapter continues the analysis of the video address generator that was started in Chapter 3. First we will finish the investigation of the D11, D12, D13, and D14 counter chain in order to develop the vertical timing. Then we will combine the horizontal and vertical timing to create the video sync, the video blanking, and the color burst signals.

Schematic reference: Figs. C-3*, C-16*, and C-20*.

OVERVIEW

Vertical Timing

Just as we needed a horizontal video address counter to define the horizontal position of the video data at any instant in time, we need a vertical address counter to define the vertical position of the video data. The horizontal and vertical address counters are not independent. The crt beam must trace a complete horizontal line before the vertical counter can advance to the next line (see Appendix A for an explanation of video techniques). The vertical counter advances once each time the horizontal counter runs through a complete count of 65. Each count of the vertical counter corresponds to a different horizontal line on the screen.

The Apple II video output consists of 262 lines. Of these lines, 70 are not visible on the screen since they occur during vertical blanking. The remaining 192 are used as follows:

1. TEXT Mode: TEXT mode characters are made of a 5 by 7 dot matrix in a 7 by 8 dot cell. The eight vertical dots per cell times 24 lines of text per screen = 192.

2. LORES: LORES pixels are 4 dots high by 7 dots wide. The 4 vertical dots per pixel times 48 pixels per screen vertically = 192.

3. HIRES: In HIRES, there are simply 192 dots vertically.

A counter with 262 possible states needs nine bits (eight bits would be too few since $2^8 = 256$). This 9-bit counter consists of two 4-bit counters (D11 and D12 (Fig. C-3*)) and the last stage of D13. The 9 bits are named VA, VB, VC, V0, V1, V2, V3, V4, and V5 in sequence from least to most significant. Their timing is shown in Fig. 4-1*.

In TEXT mode, the bits V0, V1, V2, V3, and V4 define one of 24 lines of text and the bits VA, VB, and VC define 1 of 8 vertical dots within the character cell. In HIRES mode, all 8 bits VA through V4 define 1 of 192 vertical dots. The ninth bit (V5) was needed to count beyond 256 to 262, but is not used elsewhere since 8 bits are sufficient to define 192 lines. Since only 8 of 9 bits are decoded, there are 6 addresses that repeat during each vertical scan. These addresses occur during vertical blanking and are not seen.

Video Sync

The Apple must provide sync signals in the video output for the external display. A horizontal sync pulse is provided between each horizontal line, and a vertical sync pulse is provided between each vertical scan. See Appendix A if you are not familiar with these concepts. The sync pulses are derived from the video address by combinatorial logic. The ICs involved are parts of A12, A14, B11, B14, C11, and C13 (Fig. C-20*). The sync output appears at C13-8. It is mixed with the video data and the color burst at transistor Q3. Transistor Q3 then provides the composite video output. The sync timing is shown in Figs. 4-1* and 4-2*.

Blanking

Blanking turns off the beam in the video display so it will be invisible during retrace. A blanking pulse is wider than the associated sync pulse which it straddles. The blanking signal is derived in gate C14-6 from signals already generated for SYNC. Its timing is shown in Figs. 4-1* and 4-2*. In standard tv, blanking has a unique voltage level in the composite signal. This level is slightly darker than black, but well above sync level. In the Apple II, blanking has the same level as black. In fact, the blanking signal is used in A9 (Fig. C-16*) to simply turn the video on and off. Off or low at A9-5 corresponds to black. More on this in the detailed analysis.

Color Burst

The color burst is a burst of 3.579545 MHz that appears in the composite video just following the horizontal sync pulse. A color display device uses the burst as a reference. COLOR BURST is obtained by gating $\overline{\text{COLOR REF}}$ with A14-1, B13-1, and B12-12 (Fig. C-20*). Its timing is shown in Figs. 4-2* and 4-3. Adjusting capacitor C3 (Fig. C-20*) trims the hue of the color display by delaying COLOR BURST a variable amount.

European TV

Signal V5, bow ties 12 and 16, and solder pads 13, 14 (Fig. C-20*), and 15 (Fig. C-3*) are used to configure the Apple II for use with European tv sets. The resulting operation is not covered in this book. See page 10 of the *Apple II Reference Manual* for more information.

DETAILED CIRCUIT ANALYSIS

VA

Signal VA is the vertical least significant bit (LSB) and toggles every horizontal line (Fig. 3-4*). Assume VA starts out low at point I. Counter D13 is in count mode and at a count of 7, so on $\overline{\text{LDPS}}$ rising, VA goes high (count 8). At J, $\overline{\text{HPE}}$ is low, loading VA into itself (D13-11 connected to D13-6 in Fig. C-3*). Signal VA stays high until

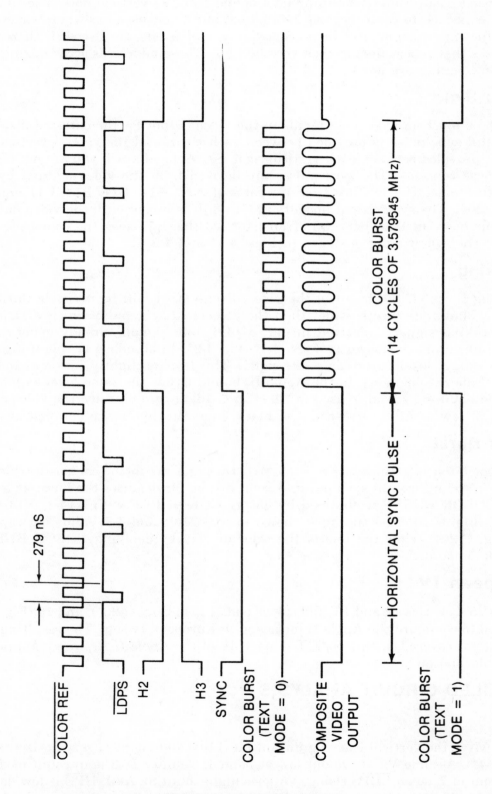

Fig. 4-3. Color burst signals.

the next time D13 is enabled (D14-15 high) *and* at a count of 15 (point K). On $\overline{\text{LDPS}}$ rising, D13 counts to 0 and VA goes low. Now $\overline{\text{HPE}}$ is low (point H), so VA loads into itself to stay low. This cycle repeats giving VA a period equal to two horizontal lines.

Before we leave Fig. 3-4*, let us examine the enable and load inputs of D12 and D11. Signal D13-15 goes high (point L) when D13 is enabled *and* at a count of 15. This enables D12. When D12 is enabled *and* at a count of 15 (D12-15 high), D11 is enabled (point M). When D11 is enabled *and* at a count of 15 (point N), C11-8 will go low (point P) to load D12 and D11. Note that D12 and D11 count (or load) on the clock *after* they are enabled, point Q.

The signals at points M, N, and P are drawn dotted to indicate that they are not active on every horizontal line. That is. on most lines these signals follow the solid trace. When the counters enable these signals, they follow the dotted trace. These signals are shown in Fig. 3-4* so that you may see their full width and timing relative to other signals. The signals will be shown again in later figures without ambiguity. These later figures have reduced time scales, however, and the signals will appear as mere "blips" with no width.

VB Through V5

Counters D12 and D11 are wired as an 8-bit counter. The counters load 125 decimal following a full count of 255 decimal. They count once per VA period (Fig. 3-4* point Q). This makes VB the next significant bit and V5 the most significant bit (MSB). Signals VA through V5 are the vertical video address bits and are shown in Fig. 4-1*. Let D12 and D11 start off with all bits high, point A. This makes C11-8 low when the counters are enabled, loading 125 decimal into the counters (point B). The two counters now count up to 255 decimal at point C where the cycle repeats. The vertical cycle consists of $255 - 125 + 1 = 131$ counts of D12 and D11. Each of these counts consists of 2 states of the LSB (VA). Therefore, the video output of the Apple consists of $2 \times 131 = 262$ counts or lines per vertical cycle. We will find that 70 lines occur during vertical blanking, resulting in 192 lines visible on the screen.

The vertical frequency of the Apple is

$$\frac{15,700 \text{ Lines/Sec}}{262 \text{ Lines/Field}} = 59.92 \text{ fields/sec, or } 59.92 \text{ Hz}$$

Combinatorial Logic

The next step in our investigation requires picking a few intermediate points in the circuit for plotting in the figures. Analyzing gates B14-10, A12-4, and B14-13 we see that B14-13 = $\overline{\text{VC} + \text{V0} + \text{V1}}$. B14-13 will be low when any of VC, V0, or V1 are high. Examine B14-13 in Fig. 4-1* and you will see that this is so.

At this point we introduce Fig. 4-2* which combines portions of the horizontal and vertical timing in one figure. The left portion of the figure shows the last two visible lines at the bottom of the screen. This portion also shows the start of vertical blanking. The center portion shows the area near the vertical sync pulse. Finally, the right portion shows the end of vertical blanking and the first visible line at the top of the screen. These three separate portions are marked in Fig. 4-1* for reference.

The signals at the top of Fig. 4-2* (H2 through B14-13) have been derived previously. Continuing now with signal B14-1 by examining gates C11-10, B14-4, A14-4, A14-10, and B14-1 (Fig. C-20*) and using DeMorgan's theorem, we get B14-1 = V2 ●

(H3 + H4 + H5). B14-1 is plotted in both Figs. 4-1* and 4-2*. Next, gates C13-C and B11-8 give us C13-C = B14-1 • B14-13 • V3 • V4. C13-C is plotted in both Figs. 4-1* and 4-2*. Note that signal C13-C appears internally to IC C13 only (see Fig. C-20*).

Blanking

Signal HBL (Horizontal Blanking) is derived in gate C13-6 (Fig. C-20*). HBL = $(\overline{H3} + \overline{H4})$ • $\overline{H5}$, and is shown in Fig. 4-2*. BLANKING = HBL + (V3 • V4) and is shown in Figs. 4-1* and 4-2*. When BLANKING is high, the screen is blanked. In Fig. 4-1*, you can count the 192 visible lines between the top and bottom of the screen (points D to E). There are 70 lines in the vertical blanking interval (point E to point F). Note that vertical blanking extends quite far to either side of vertical sync. This is so no text or graphics will be lost at the top or bottom of the screen.

Selected portions of BLANKING are shown extended in Fig. 4-2*. The segment between points A and B is a horizontal blanking interval. (This segment is reduced to a thin line in Fig. 4-1*.) The interval between points B and C (Fig. 4-2*) is the unblanked or visible portion of the line; in this case the next to last line at the bottom of the screen. Note that this interval aligns with the video information in the COMPOSITE VIDEO OUTPUT for line 190. The screen is blanked again from points C to D and the segment from points D to E is the visible portion of line 191. Vertical blanking starts at point E. Horizontal blanking extends to either side of the horizontal sync pulses at points F and G. This is so no text or graphics are lost at the left or right sides of the screen. Vertical blanking ends at point H, and line 0 is at the top of the screen.

Let us deviate here to examine how BLANKING gets through A10, A9, and B10-5 to meet with SYNC and COLOR BURST at Q3 (Figs. C-16* and C-20*). Register A10 is a 4 bit shift register wired never to shift. It is used as a register with an *enable* (pins 9 and 10). It counts on 14M rising when LD194 is high (every 978 nS or one character width). Thus, BLANKING is delayed by one character going through A10 (in on pin 5, out on pin 13). Pin 13 of A10 is the strobe input for A9, a data selector. The data inputs of A9 contain the video from three sources: TEXT, LORES, and HIRES. The select inputs of A9 simply select the source. More on this in later chapters. For now, it is the blanking signal at the strobe input that turns output A9-5 on and off. When BLANKING is high, the strobe is off, and A9-5 is low corresponding to black. When BLANKING is low, the strobe is on, and the selected video passes to A9-5.

The video is delayed one 14M clock (70 nS) by B10-5 before reaching Q3. The point of all this is that BLANKING is delayed by the time it reaches Q3. The amount of the delay is 978 nS + 70 nS = 1.048 μS. This delay cannot be seen in Fig. 4-2* due to the compressed time scale of the figure.

Sync

Signal C13-D = $\overline{H2}$ • H3 • HBL. It is shown in Fig. 4-2*. SYNC = $\overline{C13\text{-}C + C13\text{-}D}$ and is plotted in Figs. 4-1* and 4-2*. In Fig. 4-1*, each thin line is a horizontal sync pulse. The vertical sync pulse is four horizontal lines long and has three serrations. SYNC is shown expanded in Fig. 4-2* where you can see how the horizontal sync pulses at points F and G appear in the COMPOSITE VIDEO OUTPUT at points I and J. The vertical sync pulse starts at point K and extends to point L. One of the serrations is at point M.

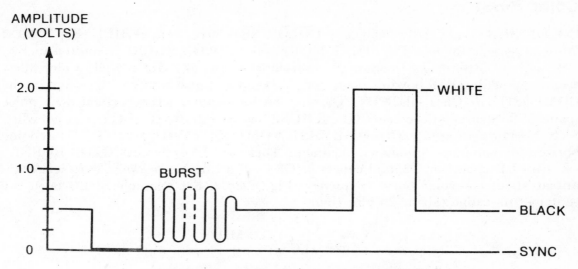

APPLE II COMPOSITE VIDEO OUTPUT MEASURED OPEN
CIRCUIT WITH R11 AT MAXIMUM.

SYNC LEVEL	0 V
BLACK LEVEL	.5 V
WHITE LEVEL	2.0 V
BURST	.7 V PEAK–PEAK CENTERED ABOUT .45 V

Fig. 4-4. Video levels.

Table 4-1. Summary of Signals in Chapter 4

Signal	Description	Frequency	Period	Remarks
VA	Vertical	7.85 kHz	127 μS	LSB
VB	Video	*		
VC	Address	*		
V0		*		
V1		*		
V2		*		
V3		*		
V4		59.92 Hz	16.7 mS	
V5		59.92 Hz	16.7 mS	MSB
BLANKING	C14-6	*		Combined Horizontal & Vertical Blanking
HBL	Horizontal Blanking	15.700 kHz	63.7 μS	Horizontal Blanking Only
SYNC	Synchronization	*		Combined Horizontal & Vertical Sync
COLOR BURST	B12-12	3.579545 MHz	279 nS	14 Cycles Every Horizontal Line
COMPOSITE VIDEO OUTPUT		H = 15.700 kHz V = 59.92 Hz	63.7 μS 16.7 mS	
VIDEO DATA				Video Without Sync or Burst

Complex waveforms, see Figs. 4-1 and 4-2*.

Color Burst

COLOR BURST = (TEXT MODE + $\overline{\text{COLOR REF}}$) • H2 • H3 • HBL (Fig. C-20*). We will assume for now that TEXT MODE = 0. COLOR BURST is plotted in Fig. 4-2* without attempting to show the individual cycles of COLOR REF. Color burst occurs immediately following each horizontal sync pulse and can be seen in the COMPOSITE VIDEO OUTPUT. There is no burst during the vertical sync pulse (point N for example) because COLOR BURST is essentially shorted out at Q3 when SYNC is low. In Fig. 4-3, COLOR BURST, COMPOSITE VIDEO OUTPUT, and one horizontal sync pulse are shown expanded. There are 14 cycles in COLOR BURST.

Coil L1, capacitor C2, and capacitor C3 form a tunable network parallel resonant at about the color burst frequency (Fig. C-20*). For example, if C3 is in the center of its range (about 25 pF), then

$$f = \frac{1}{2\pi\sqrt{LC}} = 3.6 \text{ MHz}$$

As C3 is tuned, COLOR BURST will experience a variable delay passing through R5 and the LC network. This is so the color hue of the Apple may be adjusted. The LC network also filters COLOR BURST to make it look more like a sine wave (see Fig. 4-3).

In TEXT mode, A14-2 is high, holding A14-1 low. This prevents COLOR REF from reaching COLOR BURST. Without a color burst present, the receiving tv activates its color killer and displays only black and white. *With* a color burst present, most tv sets would display text characters with an annoying color tint or fringe. To see this effect, observe the four lines of text in a LORES or HIRES *mixed mode* display.

Transistor Q6 and resistor R27 in Fig. C-20* are remnants from previous revisions. They perform no function since gate A14-1 is present.

Composite Video

The three signals VIDEO DATA, SYNC, and COLOR BURST are combined in Q3 (Fig. C-20*) to 'produce the COMPOSITE VIDEO OUTPUT. Transistor Q3 is an emitter follower with summing inputs. The values of the three input resistors R6, R7, and R8 are selected to give the required relative levels of sync, black, white, and burst in the output. Resistor R11 is a level adjust and R10 protects Q3 from shorts at the output.

To see the effect of the input resistor values, let's take white level as an example. For white, VIDEO DATA is high so we have about 3.5 V going into R7. During the visible portion of a line, SYNC is high and COLOR BURST is low, so we have about 3.5 V going into R8 and R6 grounded (through L1). Some easy math gives 2.6 V at the base of Q3. Subtracting V_{be} we get 2.0 V at the emitter of Q3. This will be the white level output voltage into an open circuit with R11 adjusted all the way up. Into a 75-ohm load, the output drops about 30% due mostly to the drop across R10. Fig. 4-4 is a sketch (to vertical scale) of the measured output of an Apple II.

SUMMARY

Table 4-1 is a summary of the signals introduced in this chapter.

In the next chapter we will discuss the memory system and explain how it is accessed by both the 6502 and the video circuitry. Also covered will be memory refresh and the mapping from screen locations to memory locations.

CHAPTER 5

The Memory System

One of the more clever design features of the Apple II is the efficient memory system. Memory access is shared by the 6502 microprocessor and the video display. This allows the video access to automatically refresh the memory; separate refresh circuitry is not needed.

First we review the 4116 dynamic RAM. You may wish to skip that discussion if you are already familiar with this IC. Then we introduce the memory circuitry and explain the reasons behind the design. Finally we analyze the circuit and signal waveforms in detail.

Schematic Reference: Figs. C-5*, C-6*, C-7*, and C-13*.

THE 4116

Memory Cell

The 4116 is a dynamic random access memory (RAM). It is organized 1 bit wide by 16K bits deep. Each of the 16K memory cells consists of a small capacitor and a transistor. The state (0 or 1) of the cell is stored as the presence or absence of charge on the capacitor. When the cell is accessed, the transistor turns on to connect the capacitor to the internal circuit. On a write cycle, the circuit charges or discharges the capacitor as appropriate for the state to be stored. On a read cycle, the circuit senses the presence or absence of charge as a 1 or a 0.

Refresh

The cell capacitor is so small that its charge is greatly reduced by the circuit that reads it. To compensate, the circuit restores the capacitor to its original charge at the end of the read cycle. Thus, cells that are read frequently are kept "refreshed." The charge on nonaccessed cells, however, will quickly leak away. To prevent this, cells that are not read with sufficient frequency must receive refresh cycles. A refresh cycle is nothing more than a dummy read cycle. There must be continuous read or refresh activity if the 4116 is to retain the correct data. This is why it is labeled "dynamic."

Multiplexed Address

The 16K cell locations inside the 4116 are selected by a 14 bit address ($2^{14} = 16$K). In order to conserve package size, these 14 bits are multiplexed onto 7 pins. Multiplexing means that the 14 bits are divided into two groups of seven each. Each time the memory is accessed, the first group of seven bits is placed on the address pins and strobed, then the second group of seven bits is placed on the address pins and strobed. After the second strobe, all 14 bits will be in the RAM, and a unique location will be selected.

The cells are arranged logically into 128 rows by 128 columns ($128 \times 128 = 16,384$). The first seven address bits are named the *row address* since they select the row. The second set of seven bits is the *column address* and selects the column. The two strobes or clocks are named the $\overline{RAS}$ (*row address strobe*) and the $\overline{CAS}$ (*column address strobe*). The strobes are active low, and the address is clocked into the 4116 on the falling edge of the strobe.

When a cell is read, all cells in the selected row are refreshed. This means the complete IC can be refreshed by reading a cell in each row. Stated another way, to refresh all cells, perform 128 read cycles using all 128 different row addresses—the column address is a "don't-care." You can also omit the $\overline{CAS}$. This turns what was a read cycle into a refresh-only cycle.

Again, if the RAM is read often enough, the normal read cycles will keep it refreshed, and refresh-only cycles will not be needed. By often, we mean all 128 rows every 2 milliseconds.

If any 7 of the 14 address bits constantly sequence through all 128 states in less than 2 milliseconds, you should assign these 7 bits to the row address. This will give you free refreshes. Apart from this consideration, the 14 bits may be arbitrarily assigned to the rows and columns.

Read Cycle

Fig. 5-1A shows a typical 4116 read cycle. We start at point A, the time you place the row address on the address pins. After waiting the needed setup time, take $\overline{RAS}$ low to strobe the row address, point B. After a *hold time*, you may multiplex (change) the address to the column address, point C. After a *setup time*, take $\overline{CAS}$ low to strobe the column address, point D. After a hold time, you may change the address (it has become a don't-care), point E. Write ($\overline{WR}$) is active low and stays high during a read cycle. Data in (DI) is a don't-care on a read cycle. After the *access time* from $\overline{RAS}$ or $\overline{CAS}$ (whichever comes later), DO (data out) will change from high impedance to the value stored in the addressed cell, point F. Data out will remain valid until $\overline{CAS}$ goes high, point G. At that time, DO returns to high impedance. The $\overline{RAS}$ may return high either before or after $\overline{CAS}$, points H or I.

The setup, hold, and access times mentioned previously vary depending on the specified speed of the RAM. There are also minimum $\overline{RAS}$ and $\overline{CAS}$ low times and minimum times allowed between cycles. A common specification for data access time from $\overline{RAS}$ is 200 nanoseconds. All of the parameters may be found in a 4116 data sheet.

Write Cycle

Two different write cycles are possible with the 4116, *early-write* and *read-modify-write*. The Apple II uses an early-write cycle, shown in Fig. 5-1B. The sequence for address, $\overline{RAS}$, and $\overline{CAS}$ is the same in the write cycle as it was in the read cycle. In

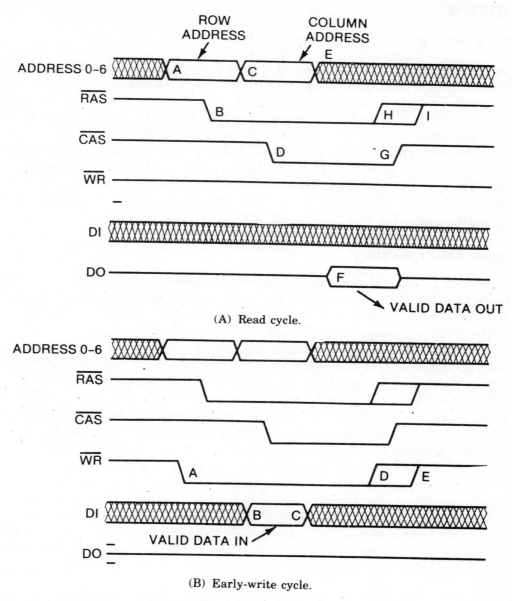

(A) Read cycle.

(B) Early-write cycle.

Fig. 5-1.   4116 RAM cycles.

the early-write cycle, however, you take $\overline{WR}$ low (point A) prior to taking $\overline{CAS}$ low. You also set up valid data on DI (point B) prior to taking $\overline{CAS}$ low. On $\overline{CAS}$ falling, the data is clocked into the RAM. The DI must remain valid until point C to allow a hold time after $\overline{CAS}$ falls. Data out remains high impedance during an early-write cycle. At the end of the cycle, $\overline{WR}$ may return high either before or after $\overline{CAS}$, points D or E. Other cycle types are available with the 4116, but only the two shown in Fig. 5-1 are used in the Apple II.

Data stored in the RAM is not inverted. If you write a 1 (high), you read a 1 (high).

So far we have been discussing a single IC—a RAM one bit wide. In a typical application, the 4116 is used in groups of 8 ICs to give an 8-bit-wide byte. In this example, the eight ICs would give you 16K bytes of memory. Deeper memories (more addresses) are obtained by using additional groups of eight ICs.

OVERVIEW

Memory Array

The memory array of the Apple is eight ICs wide by three ICs deep (Fig. C-7*). This organization provides a memory space 8 bits wide by 48K deep. You may plug the RAMs into the mother board in groups of eight, giving you a 16K, 32K, or 48K byte capacity. Each group of eight ICs has a separate $\overline{CAS}$ line. Only one $\overline{CAS}$ line is activated at a time, selecting a unique 16K range.

The $\overline{RAS}$, $\overline{WR}$, and address lines of all RAMs are tied in common. The DI pins for each bit from all three groups are tied in common and connected directly to the data bus. The DO pins for each bit from all three groups are tied in common and connected to registers B5 and B8. From there the data finds its way back to the data bus via multiplexers B6 and B7 (Fig. C-13*).

Address Multiplexing

Fig. 5-2A is a simplified diagram of the RAM address multiplexing scheme. We mentioned that the RAM is shared by the 6502 and the video display. Multiplexer A provides this sharing function. It selects bits coming from either:

1. The 6502 via the address bus, or
2. The video address.

The selection is under control of $\phi0$, one of the 6502 clocks. The 14 low order address bits (AD0–AD13) are divided into two groups of 7 bits each. Multiplexer B selects one or the other of these groups under control of signal AX (address multiplex). Similarly, 14 bits of the video address are divided into two groups for selection by multiplexer C. This selection is also under control of AX. Multiplexers B and C reduce 14 bit addresses to 7-bit row and column addresses for the 4116s.

Do not confuse "rows and columns" as used in this section with rows and columns on the video screen or rows and columns of ICs on the mother board.

Fig. 5-2B shows the timing associated with the address multiplexing. The signals shown were derived in Chapter 3 and presented in Fig. 3-3. One period of $\phi0$ (points A to C) corresponds to one 6502 cycle. We will learn more about the 6502 in Chapter 6, but for now we can say that the 6502 reads and writes memory while $\phi0$ is high (points B to C). The video circuitry reads the memory while $\phi0$ is low (points A to B).

Let's follow the sequence. At point A, $\phi0$ is low causing multiplexer A to select the video address. Signal AX is high causing multiplexer C to select the video row address. The $\overline{RAS}$ strobes the video row address at point D. At point E, AX goes low and multiplexer C selects the video column address. The $\overline{CAS}$ strobes the video address at point F. The video data is available from the RAM at about point G. Signals $\overline{RAS}$, AX, and $\overline{CAS}$ return high before point B. At point B, $\phi0$ goes high causing multiplexer A to select the 6502 address bus. Signal AX is high causing multiplexer B to select the 6502 row address. Signal $\overline{RAS}$ strobes the 6502 row address into RAM at point H. Signal AX goes low at point I causing multiplexer B to select the 6502 column address. Signal $\overline{CAS}$ strobes the 6502 column address into RAM at point J. Data is available from the RAM at about point K. This sequence repeats every $\phi0$ period, interleaving the video and 6502 accesses.

The multiplexers of Fig. 5-2A are implemented by ICs C1, E11, E12, and E13 (Figs. C-5* and C-6*).

In the previous discussion, we said that the 6502 puts the address on the bus.

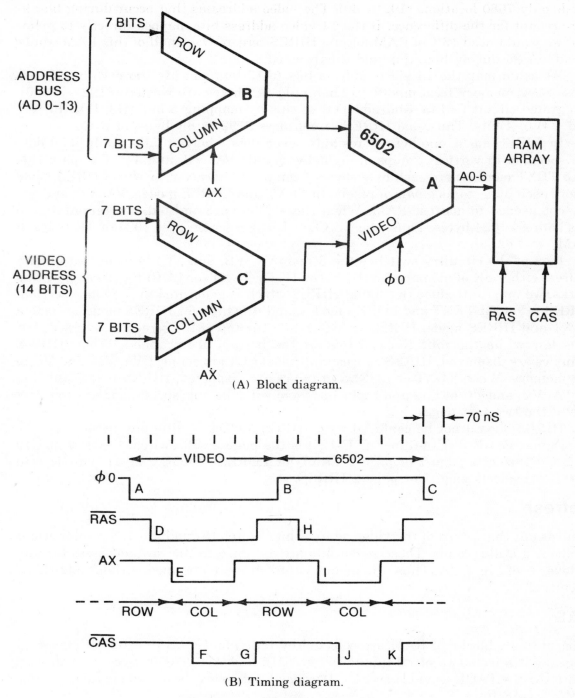

(A) Block diagram.

(B) Timing diagram.

Fig. 5-2. RAM address multiplex.

This is not always true. If a peripheral device has DMA capability, then it may put the address on the bus. The address multiplexing scheme, however, will be the same. We will cover DMA in Chapter 6.

Video Memory Mapping

The video address consists of the 14 bits H0, H1, H2, H3, H4, H5, VA, VB, VC, V0, V1, V2, V3, and V4. Fourteen bits can address 16384 locations. The **HIRES** screen needs only 7680 locations (192 × 40). The video addresses that occur during blanking account for the difference. If the 14 video address bits mapped directly to memory, we would need 16K of RAM for one HIRES screen. Over half of this RAM would be addressed during blanking and thus wasted.

We could map the 14 video address bits to 13 bits and use those 13 bits to address 8192 memory locations (2^{13}). Then only 512 bytes are wasted (8192 − 7680). Integrated circuit E14 (a 4-bit adder) does this by mapping 5 bits (H3, H4, H5, V3, and V4) to 4 bits. Thus, one HIRES screen uses 8192 or 8K bytes of RAM.

In HIRES mode, one byte stores only seven dots—horizontally. Additional dots are specified in vertical groups of eight by signals VA, VB, and VC. Compare this with TEXT mode where each byte stores a complete character, or with LORES mode where each byte stores a pair of pixels. In TEXT and LORES modes, VA, VB, and VC are not needed to address RAM. When these 3 bits are omitted, the remaining 10 bits address 1024 bytes. Thus, one TEXT or LORES screen uses 1024 or 1K bytes of RAM.

Part of the circuitry switches the 3 bits (VA, VB, and VC) in or out so we can address either 8K of memory for HIRES or 1K for TEXT (or LORES). To see how this works, we must introduce the signal HIRES which is generated in the video section. HIRES is low for TEXT and LORES modes, and it is high for HIRES mode. In mixed TEXT and HIRES mode, HIRES is high while the top of the screen is scanned, but goes low while the four lines of text at the bottom are scanned. When HIRES graphics are displayed, HIRES causes multiplexer C12 to connect VA, VB, and VC to the memory. When TEXT or LORES graphics are displayed, HIRES is low, turning off VA, VB, and VC at C12 and replacing them with the appropriate address to select one of the two text pages.

HIRES should not be confused with HIRES MODE, a different signal.

Signal PAGE 2 (F14-6 in Fig. C-12*) is the page 2 soft switch. PAGE 2 at C12 (Fig. C-6*) selects page 1 or page 2 TEXT (or LORES). PAGE 2 at J1 (via H1-8 in Fig. C-5*) selects page 1 or page 2 HIRES.

Refresh

It turns out that seven of the video address bits switch through all 128 combinations in about 2 milliseconds. These seven bits are assigned to the row addresses at multiplexer C of Fig. 5-2A. Thus, the memory refreshes are obtained without additional circuitry.

$\overline{\text{CAS}}$

Separate 16K blocks of RAM are selected by individual $\overline{\text{CAS}}$ lines. Multiplexer J1 (Fig. C-5*) selects two of its inputs to be AD15 and AD14 (6502 access) or ground and HIRES • PAGE 2 (video access). Decoder F2 decodes these two signals into one of three $\overline{\text{CAS}}$ lines.

Data Path

Input—The RAM data inputs simply connect to the data bus.

Output—The RAM data outputs are latched in registers B5 and B8 where they remain stable for a complete memory cycle. The video circuitry uses the latched data directly. However, for the 6502 to read the data, it must be put on the data bus. Multiplexers B6 and B7 do this, selecting either the latched RAM data or the keyboard output.

DETAILED CIRCUIT ANALYSIS

Memory Array and Data Path

We start our detailed analysis with the 24 IC memory array (Table 5-1).

Table 5-1. Physical and Logical IC Assignments

Address Range	Data Bits							
	0	1	2	3	4	5	6	7
32K – 48K	E3	E4	E5	E6	E7	E8	E9	E10
16K – 32K	D3	D4	D5	D6	D7	D8	D9	D10
0 – 16K	C3	C4	C5	C6	C7	C8	C9	C10

Right

Front   Top View

The $\overline{RAS}$, $\overline{WR}$, and address lines of all 24 ICs are tied in common. These inputs are largely capacitive and this can lead to reflections and ringing in a large array. Resistors RA02, RA03 (Fig. C-6*), R31, and R32 (Fig. C-5*) form terminations to alleviate this problem. The six low order memory address lines are driven by multiplexers E11, E12, and E13. The high order memory address line is driven by multiplexer C1-7.

$\overline{RAS}$—The $\overline{RAS}$ line for the array is the same line that was discussed in Chapter 3 and shown in Fig. 3-5. The $\overline{WR}$ line for the array is derived from the R/W (read/write) line on the system bus. This line is in turn driven by either the 6502 or by a peripheral with DMA capability.

$\overline{CAS}$—The $\overline{CAS}$ pins for each IC in a row of RAMs are tied in common. The $\overline{CAS}$ for each row is kept separate, however, since this is how the Apple selects unique 16K ranges. The driving device is one-of-four decoder F2 (Fig. C-5*). The decoder will take only one $\overline{CAS}$ low at a time, selecting one of three rows of RAMs. When the range 48K–64K is addressed, F2 will not activate any $\overline{CAS}$.

Data—The DI pin for each bit in the array is tied in common (Fig. C-7*). These eight lines then connect directly to the system data bus, D0 – D7. They are driven by either the 6502 or by a peripheral with DMA capability. The DO for each bit in the array is also tied in common. These eight lines are latched in registers B5 and B8 on $\overline{RAS}$ rising at the end of each read cycle. On video cycles, the latched data (signals DL0 – DL7) is used directly by the video generator. On 6502 or DMA cycles, the latched data is put on the data bus so that the 6502 or DMA device can read it. Multiplexers B6 and B7 (Fig. C-13*) perform this function under control of leads $\overline{RAM\ SEL}$ and $\overline{KBD}$. On a memory read in the range 0 to 48K, F2 (Fig. C-5*) will take low one of its output pins 10, 11, or 12. These lines pass to gate D2-8. Any input low at D2-8 will cause A2-5 to be high. Read/write is high (this is a read cycle) so $\overline{RAM\ SEL}$ goes low. The $\overline{RAM\ SEL}$ turns on B6 and B7 via their enable inputs. Then B6 and B7 drive the data bus. This is not a keyboard cycle, so $\overline{KBD}$ will be high at the B6 and B7 select inputs. This causes them to select the latched data to put on the data bus. The other function of B6 and B7 is to select the keyboard output when $\overline{KBD}$ is low. When neither the RAM nor the keyboard is selected, the B6 and B7 outputs remain high impedance.

Read Cycle—Fig. 5-3 shows the timing of memory read cycles. Note how video and 6502 cycles are interleaved. Signal $\overline{LDPS}$ rising at point A advances the video address at point B. With $\phi 0$ low and AX high, the row bits of the video address are

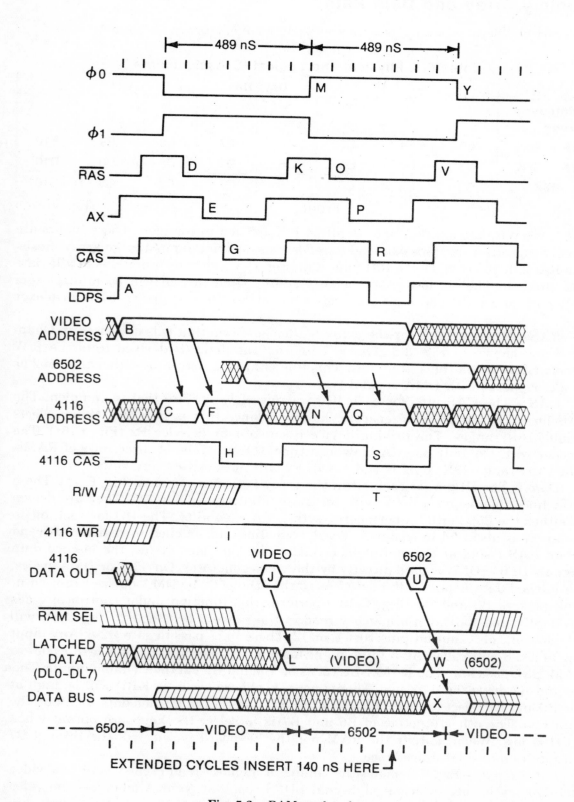

Fig. 5-3. RAM read cycle.

sent to the RAM at point C. They are strobed when $\overline{RAS}$ goes low at point D. AX goes low at point E to send the video column address bits to the RAM at point F. Meanwhile, the two high order address bits at decoder F2 prepare it to select one of the three 4116 $\overline{CAS}$ lines when $\overline{CAS}$ (F2-1) goes low at point G. When this happens, the selected 4116 $\overline{CAS}$ goes low (point H) to strobe the column address bits. When $\phi1$ is high, 4116 $\overline{WR}$ is high via gate C14-11 (Fig. C-7*). Thus, 4116 $\overline{WR}$ is high at point I (Fig. 5-3) to start a 4116 read cycle when $\overline{CAS}$ goes low. After the 4116 access time from $\overline{CAS}$, the 4116 outputs go low impedance and contain the addressed data, point J. On $\overline{RAS}$ rising (point K), the 4116 data is latched into registers B5 and B8, point L. The latched data is now available for the video generator.

Now comes the 6502 read cycle. Thus, $\phi0$ goes high at point M and AX is already high to send the 6502 row address bits to the 4116s at point N. They are strobed when $\overline{RAS}$ goes low at point O. Now AX goes low at point P to send the 6502 column address bits to the 4116s at point Q. Meanwhile, address bits AD14 and AD15 (Fig. C-5*) prepare decoder F2 to select one of the three 4116 $\overline{CAS}$ lines when $\overline{CAS}$ (F2-1) goes low at point R (Fig. 5-3). When this happens, the selected 4116 $\overline{CAS}$ goes low (point S) to strobe the 6502 column address. Note that the 4116 $\overline{CAS}$ shown in Fig. 5-3 represents all three 4116 $\overline{CAS}$ lines. Thus, the strobes at points H and S will not occur on the same 4116 $\overline{CAS}$ line unless the two cycles shown address the same 16K range.

We are discussing a 6502 read cycle, so R/W and 4116 $\overline{WR}$ are both high at point T. Thus, a 4116 read cycle starts when $\overline{CAS}$ falls. After the access time, the 4116 data outputs go low impedance and contain the addressed data, point U. On $\overline{RAS}$ rising (point V), the 4116 data is latched (point W). The $\overline{RAM\ SEL}$ is low at this point, so multiplexers B6 and B7 drive the latched data onto the data bus (point X). The 6502 reads the data from the bus on $\phi0$ falling, point Y. This concludes the cycle.

Recall from the clock discussion in Chapter 3 that every 65th $\phi0$ period is extended by 140 nS. We have drawn Fig. 5-3 to represent a RAM read cycle without this extension. At the bottom of the figure we have indicated the location for the extension. All the waveforms from Fig. 5-3 are redrawn in Fig. 5-4 with the 140 nS extension added. Even though the timing is altered, the extended cycle of Fig. 5-4 functions just like the normal cycle of Fig. 5-3.

Write Cycle—Fig. 5-5 shows a RAM write cycle. It is interleaved between two video cycles just like the 6502 read cycle of Fig. 5-3. The video cycles are the same as described previously. (Note that video cycles always *read* from RAM.) On a write cycle, the address is strobed into RAM the same as on a read cycle. The address is divided into row and column bits at points A and B (Fig. 5-5) and these are strobed at points C and D. Since this is a write cycle, the 6502 takes R/W low at about point E. When $\phi1$ falls at point F, 4116 $\overline{WR}$ goes low (point G). Since $\overline{WR}$ goes low before $\overline{CAS}$, the 4116 will enter an early-write cycle when $\overline{CAS}$ falls at point D. Meanwhile, the 6502 has output the data to be written at about point H. This data is driven onto the data bus and becomes stable at point I. The data bus is connected directly to the RAM inputs, so when $\overline{CAS}$ falls at point D, the data at point I is written into the RAM. Note that in a 4116 early-write cycle, the 4116 data out pin remains high impedance, point J.

Write cycles can be extended 140 nS just like read cycles. At the bottom of Fig. 5-5 we indicate where the extra 140 nS go.

Chapter 6 will discuss RAM read and write cycles again from the viewpoint of the 6502.

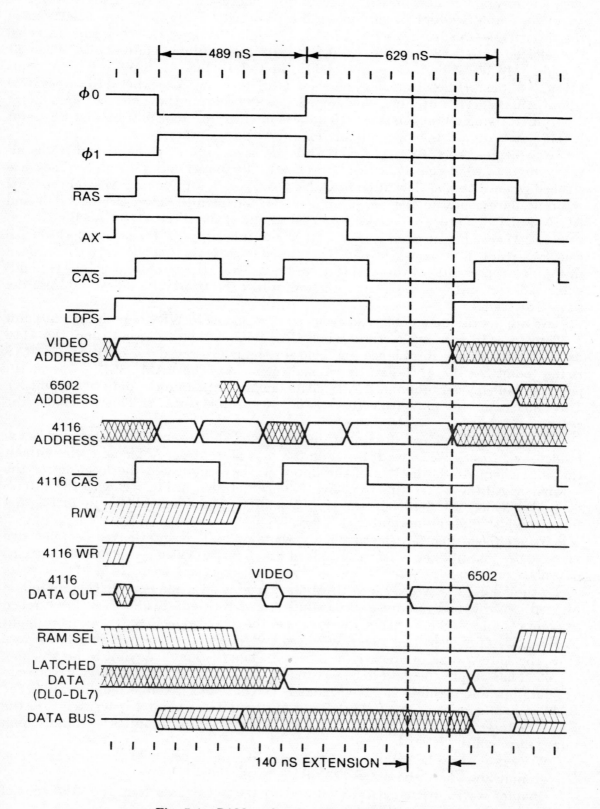

Fig. 5-4. RAM read cycle with extended φ0 clock.

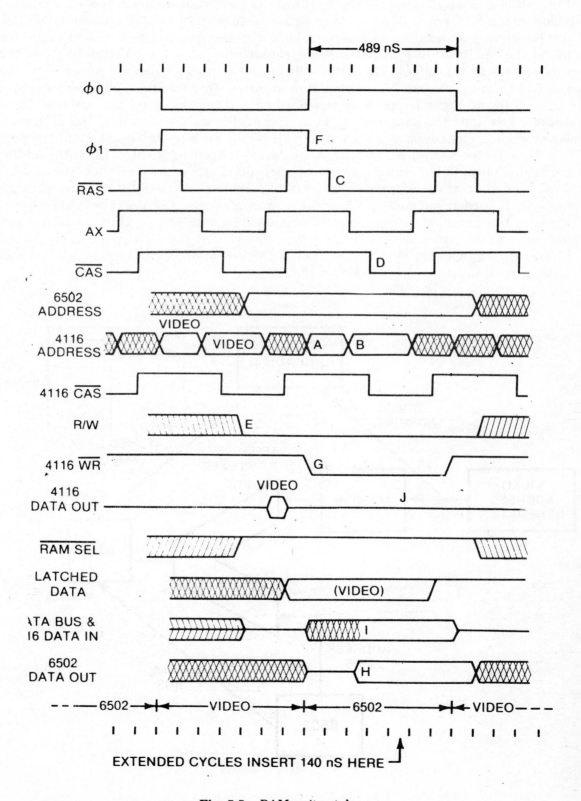

Fig. 5-5. RAM write cycle.

Address Multiplexing and Mapping

Fig. 5-6 is a block diagram of the hardware process that occurs when we write to a video screen location. Say we want to write the pixel that is "2 down and 3 over" (we are being very general here). We have looked in the *Apple II Reference Manual* and found the "address" of that pixel. What we have found is the location in RAM that corresponds to that pixel. The address from the *Apple II Reference Manual* is what the 6502 should put on the address bus to access that location. Now let's examine Fig. 5-6 to see what happens in the hardware. The 6502 puts the address on the address bus, puts the data (on, off, blue, green, etc.) on the data bus, and performs a RAM write cycle. On such a cycle, the address multiplexer selects the address bus.

How do we see on the crt what we have written to RAM? The video address generator outputs the video address of each pixel in sequence. When the pixel "2 down and 3 over" is addressed, this address is mapped to a RAM address by the mapper. It is then selected by the address multiplexer and sent to the RAM where it accesses the same location previously written. The data held in that location is read and sent to the video generator to create the desired pixel characteristics (on, off, blue, etc.). You can see that the mapper is the key to determining which RAM locations correspond to which screen locations.

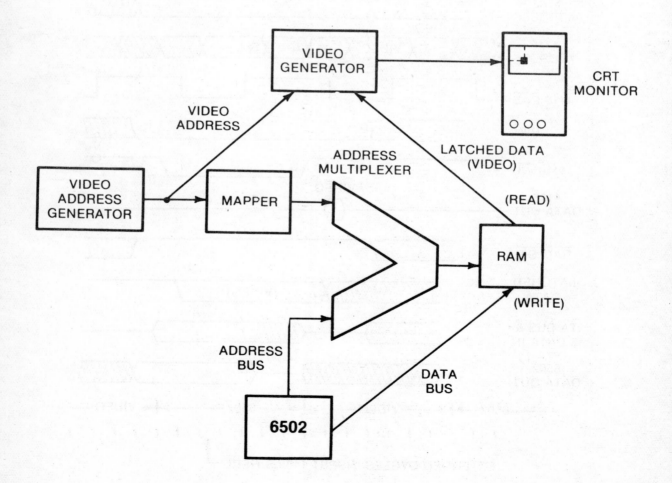

Fig. 5-6. Block diagram displaying a picture element.

Fig. 5-7* is an aid to analyzing the mapping circuitry. The video address bits (H0 to V4) appear on the left They map through ICs C1, C12, and E14 to the RAM. The RAM address is shown as 14 row and column bits. The 6502 address bits are shown in the center of the figure. The 14 low order bits map to the RAM as shown. The two high order bits are decoded by ICs J1 and F2 to select one of three $\overline{\text{CAS}}$ lines. On video cycles, C1, J1, and F2 decode signals HIRES and PAGE 2 to select the correct $\overline{\text{CAS}}$ line. The four columns on the right of the figure represent four possible configurations of the mapper.

We now follow the diagram in detail, referring to Fig. 5-7* when needed.

6502 Access—E11, E12, E13, and C1 are four-to-one multiplexers (Figs. C-5* and C-6*). They multiplex 28 lines to 7 lines for the RAM addresses. At the beginning of a 6502 memory access, $\phi 0$ and AX are high (Fig. 5-3 point N). This causes the multiplexers to select inputs AD0, AD1, AD2, AD3, AD7, AD8, and AD12 as the 4116 row address—they are mapped as shown in Fig. 5-7*. For the column address, AX goes low causing the multiplexers to select inputs AD4, AD5, AD6, AD9, AD10, AD11, and AD13—they are mapped as shown in Fig. 5-7*. Meanwhile, $\phi 0$ is also high at J1-1 (Fig. C-5*). Thus, J1 selects AD14 to output on pin 9 and AD15 to output on pin 12. Addresses AD14 and AD15 then appear on the select inputs of F2. When $\overline{\text{CAS}}$ (F2-1) goes low, F2 is enabled and outputs a $\overline{\text{CAS}}$ on one of its three output pins (4, 5, or 6). The selected $\overline{\text{CAS}}$ then selects a unique 16K memory range. Consequently F2 output pins 10, 11, and 12 are gated in D2-8 to create $\overline{\text{RAM SEL}}$ as previously described. If the address is above 48K, then both AD14 and AD15 are high, and none of the *used* outputs of F2 are activated. This is correct since we do not want $\overline{\text{RAM SEL}}$ or any of the 4116 $\overline{\text{CAS}}$ lines activated when we are not accessing RAM.

Page 1 Text—When the Apple is displaying Page 1 Text, HIRES and PAGE 2 are both low. Since this is a video access, $\phi 0$ will also be low. $\phi 0$ low at J1-1 causes it to select ground (pin 14) to output on pin 12. Recall that on a 6502 access, AD15 is connected to pin 12. Thus, a ground maps to AD15 as shown in Fig. 5-7*. The IC J1 also selects HIRES • PAGE 2 (gate H1-8) to output on pin 9. Recall that on a 6502 access, AD14 is connected to pin 9. Thus, H1-8 maps to AD14 and is 0 as shown in Fig. 5-7* for Page 1 Text.

HIRES is low at C12-1 (Fig. C-5*) causing it to select HBL (pin 14) to output on pin 12. Also, C12 selects ground (pin 11) to output on pin 9. During the first part of the video cycle, AX is high (Fig. 5-3 point C). Thus, $\phi 0$ low and AX high at C1 pins 2 and 14 (Fig. C-5*) cause it to select HBL (via C12-12) to be 4116 row address 6. As shown in Fig. 5-7*, row address 6 maps to AD12. During the visible portion of a line, HBL is low, so a 0 is shown in Fig. 5-7* for AD12 during Page 1 Text When AX goes low (Fig. 5-3 point F), C1 (Fig. C-5*) selects ground (via C12-9) to be 4116 column address 6. As shown in Fig. 5-7*, column address 6 maps to AD13.

HIRES low at C12-1 will cause it to select PAGE 2 (low at this time) to output on pin 7. Furthermore $\phi 0$ and AX low at E11 pins 14 and 2 (Fig. C-6*) cause it to select PAGE 2 (low) to output as 4116 column address 3. Fig. 5-7* shows that column address 3 maps to AD11. Also, C12 selects the high at C11-2 ($\overline{\text{PAGE 2}}$ in Fig. C-5*) to output on pin 4. Data selector E11 then selects this high to output as 4116 column address 0. Fig. 5-7* shows that column address 0 maps to AD10. Note that for Page 1 Text (Fig. 5-7*), AD10 is 1 and all *higher* bits are 0. This address is 1024 decimal which we know to be the start of Page 1 Text. The 10 LSBs give a range of 1K which we also know to be correct.

But what about those 10 LSBs; where do they come from? They are derived from the video address. Signals H0, H1, H2, V0, V1, and V2 connect directly to multiplexers E11, E12, and E13 and map as shown in Fig. 5-7*. The five lines H3, H4, H5, V3, and V4 are reduced to four lines ($\sum 0$, $\sum 1$, $\sum 2$, and $\sum 3$) at the output of 4-bit adder E14 (Fig. C-6*). These four lines then connect to the multiplexers and map as shown in Fig. 5-7*. Their waveforms are shown in Fig. 5-8* along with signals previously derived. The address bit to which each signal maps is shown in parentheses next to the signal name. Ignore the numbers in brackets for now; they apply to HIRES mode only.

Let's examine how the $\sum$ signals are derived. A 74LS283 adder performs a binary addition of two 4-bit inputs and a single carry-in bit:

$$
\begin{array}{cccc}
 & & & C_{in} \\
A3 & A2 & A1 & A0 \\
+\quad B3 & B2 & B1 & B0 \\
\hline
C_{out}\quad \sum 3 & \sum 2 & \sum 1 & \sum 0
\end{array}
$$

In the Apple this addition becomes:

$$
\begin{array}{cccc}
 & & & V3 \\
\overline{H5} & V3 & H4 & H3 \\
+\quad V4 & \overline{H5} & V4 & 1 \\
\hline
\sum 3 & \sum 2 & \sum 1 & \sum 0
\end{array}
$$

The carry-out is not used. Note that the symbol "+" used in this section represents *binary addition* and not logical OR.

Let's derive the signals for point A in Fig. 5-8*:

$$
\begin{aligned}
\sum 0 &= V3 + H3 + 1 \\
&= 0 + 1 + 1 \\
&= 0, \text{ carry } 1
\end{aligned}
$$

We plot a low for $\sum 0$ at point A then continue:

$$
\begin{aligned}
\sum 1 &= H4 + V4 + \text{carry from } \sum 0 \\
&= 1 + 0 + 1 \\
&= 0, \text{ carry } 1
\end{aligned}
$$

$$
\begin{aligned}
\sum 2 &= V3 + \overline{H5} + \text{carry from } \sum 1 \\
&= 0 + 1 + 1 \\
&= 0, \text{ carry } 1
\end{aligned}
$$

$$
\begin{aligned}
\sum 3 &= \overline{H5} + V4 + \text{carry from } \sum 2 \\
&= 1 + 0 + 1 \\
&= 0, \text{ carry } 1
\end{aligned}
$$

We end up plotting a low for all four $\sum$ signals at point A. This method can be used to determine the values of the $\sum$ signals at all points in Fig. 5-8*. Note how the waveforms change as a function of V3 and V4 (points B, C, D, and E).

We know from Chapters 3 and 4 that point A occurs at the upper left of the screen. We know this based on the value of the video address at point A. Let's find the memory location which maps to this video address. Examining point A of Fig. 5-8*, we see that AD3 through AD9 are low. We have not shown H0, H1, and H2 in Fig. 5-8*, but let's assume they are low. They map to AD0, AD1, and AD2 (see Fig. 5-7*). We are still discussing Page 1 Text mode, so AD10 is high. This gives us a decimal address of 1024. If you check Figure 1 (page 16) of the *Apple II Reference Manual*, you will find that the character at the upper left indeed has an address of 1024. This method of adding up the address bits can be used to determine the address of every point in Fig. 5-8*. We have done this for several points.

Point F is at the upper right of the screen. There are 40 bytes or characters between points A and F. (In Fig. 5-8*, the addresses increment by eight since the three LSBs are not shown.) Note that the addresses between F and G (shown in parentheses) are outside the range used for Page 1 Text. This does not matter since they occur during blanking. The second horizontal scan line starts at G and addresses location 1024 again. In fact, the first eight scan lines all start by accessing location 1024.

Recall that a text character is displayed in a 7 by 8 dot cell. The eight vertical dots account for the eight separate accesses of the same location. (Chapter 8 will illustrate the video display in more detail.) Point H starts the ninth scan line and the second text line. Find its address (1152) in Figure 1 of the *Apple II Reference Manual*. Points I and J (1064 and 1104) occur one-third and two-thirds of the way down the screen. Point K is at the lower right of the screen and vertical blanking extends from points K to L. The next field starts at point L, which is at the upper left of the screen.

Page 2 Text—Page 2 Text differs from Page 1 Text only as described here. PAGE 2 is high at C12-5, so C12-7 is high (Fig. C-6). This maps to AD11. C12-2 and C12-4 are low, and this maps to AD10. We have shown AD11 = 1 and AD10 = 0 in the Page 2 Text column of Fig. 5-7*. This makes Page 2 Text range from 2K to 3K decimal.

Page 1 HIRES—Page 1 HIRES is similar to Page 1 Text; it differs as follows. HIRES is high at C12-1 causing it to select C11-2 to output on C12-9 (Fig. C-5*). PAGE 2 is low, so C12-9 is high. Signals $\phi 0$ and AX low at C1 pins 2 and 14 cause it to select C12-9 to output on C1-7. This high maps to AD13 as shown in Fig. 5-7*. HIRES high at C12-1 causes it to select VC to output on C12-12. Signals $\phi 0$ low and AX high at C1 cause it to select VC (via C12-12) to output on C1-7. Thus, VC maps to AD12. HIRES high at C12-1 causes it to select VB and VA to output on C12 pins 7 and 4. Thus, VB and VA map to AD11 and AD10.

Note from Fig. 5-7* that for Page 1 HIRES, AD13 = 1, AD14 = 0, and AD15 = 0. This address is 8192 decimal which we know to be the start of Page 1 HIRES. The 13 LSBs give a range of 8K which we also know to be correct. These 13 LSBs are all shown in Fig. 5-8* where we have used brackets to indicate the address bits to which VA, VB, and VC map.

Recall that point A in Fig. 5-8* is at the upper left of the screen. Let's find the memory location that maps to this point. At point A, AD3 through AD12 are all low. Signals H0, H1, and H2 (not shown) are also low and map to AD0, AD1, and AD2. From Fig. 5-7*, we see that AD13 = 1, AD14 = 0, and AD15 = 0 for Page 1 HIRES. This gives us a decimal address of 8192. If you check Figure 3 (page 21) of the *Apple II Reference Manual*, you will find that the byte at the upper left indeed has an address of 8192. This method of adding up the address bits has been used to find the decimal addresses of several points in Fig. 5-8*. They are listed along the bottom of the figure.

Point F is at the upper right of the screen and there are 40 bytes between points A and F. Each byte generates seven dots horizontally. The addresses increment by eight since the three LSBs are not shown. The addresses between F and G occur during blanking. The second horizontal scan line begins at G and accesses location 9216. Recall that in TEXT mode, each location was accessed eight times. In HIRES mode, each location is accessed once. Point H starts the ninth scan line. Find its address (8320) in Figure 3 of the *Apple II Reference Manual*. Point K is at the lower right of the screen and vertical blanking extends from points K to L. The next field starts at point L which is at the upper left of the screen.

Page 2 HIRES — Page 2 HIRES differs from Page 1 HIRES only as described here. The signals PAGE 2 and HIRES are both high at H1-9 and H1-10 (Fig. C-5*). Thus, J1-11 and J1-9 are high, and this high maps to AD14 on Fig. 5-7*. PAGE 2 is high at C11-1 causing C12-10 and C12-9 to be low. When $\phi 0$ and AX are low at C1-2 and C1-14, C12-9 is selected to output on C1-7. Thus, a low maps to AD13. We have shown AD14 = 1 and AD13 = 0 in the Page 2 HIRES column of Fig. 5-7*. This makes Page 2 HIRES range from 16K to 24K.

Refresh

Remember that memory refreshes can be obtained without additional circuitry only if two requirements are met: The 4116 row addresses switch through all 128 combinations in 2 milliseconds or less.

Let's see if we will get free refreshes. From Fig. 5-7* we find the seven signals that map to the row address as shown in Table 5-2.

Table 5-2. Refresh Address Mapping

RAM Address Bit	Signal
Row 2	H0
Row 5	H1
Row 1	H2
Row 4	$\sum 0$
Row 6	HBL (TEXT Mode) or VC (HIRES Mode)
Row 0	V0
Row 3	V1

The signals are listed in order of increasing period. By examining their waveforms (found in Figs. 3-4, 4-2, and 5-8)*, you can see that each signal in the list has a period at least twice that of the preceding signal. Thus, in one period of V1, the seven bits switch through all 128 combinations. From Fig. 4-1*, we can find that V1 has a period of 2038 microseconds. This is close enough to 2 milliseconds to meet the requirement. We have now proven that the video accesses indeed refresh the memory.

SUMMARY

Table 5-3 lists a summary of the signals presented in this chapter.

Table 5-3. A Summary of Signals Presented in Chapter 5

Signal	Description
AD0 – AD15	System Address Bus
AX	Address Multiplex (high for row, low for column)
$\overline{\text{CAS}}$	4116 Column Address Strobe
DI	4116 Data In
DO	4116 Data Out
D0 – D7	System Data Bus
DL0 – DL7	Latched Data
HIRES	Goes high for HIRES display
$\overline{\text{KBD}}$	Keyboard (low for keyboard access)
PAGE 2	Goes high for Page 2 Text or Graphics
$\overline{\text{PAGE 2}}$	Complement of PAGE 2
$\phi 0$	6502 Phase 0 Clock
RA0 – RA6	RAM Address
$\overline{\text{RAM SEL}}$	RAM Select (low for keyboard or RAM read)
$\overline{\text{RAS}}$	4116 Row Address Strobe
R/W	Read/Write on system bus
$\Sigma 0 - \Sigma 3$	Mapping of H3, H4, H5, V3, and V4
$\overline{\text{WR}}$	4116 Write

6

The 6502 and System Bus

The Apple II provides a complete microcomputer system bus with the added bonus of decoded address select lines. This efficient design technique reduces the address circuitry needed on peripheral cards. In this chapter we cover the 50 pin system bus and the 6502 microprocessor. As usual, we start with an overview before digging into the details.

Schematic Reference: Figs. C-5*, C-7*, C-9*, C-10*, C-11*, C-12* and C-13*.

OVERVIEW

The 6502

The 6502 is a single-voltage, 8-bit, NMOS (n channel metal oxide semiconductor) microprocessor with a 64K byte address range. The device used in the Apple II is specified for a clock frequency of 1 MHz. This results in a 1 microsecond clock period or *clock cycle*. Each read or write of a single memory location requires one of these clock cycles. In addition to memory operations, some clock cycles are used for processing that occurs inside the 6502. The clock cycles are strung together to generate *instructions*, a term that should be familiar to assembly language programmers. An instruction is the smallest part of the microprocessor's time that can be specified by a programmer. Normally, an instruction ranges in duration from 2 to 7 clock cycles. In the hardware realm we have an opportunity to adjust the duration of an instruction by inserting *wait-states* or altering the clock's period. We can also interrupt the microprocessor between instructions. More on these features later.

The signals in and out of the 6502 can be divided into three groups: address, data, and control. Fig. 6-1 shows the 6502 pin assignments.

Address—The address bus (A0–A15) is a group of 16 lines that presents a binary address to the system memory and peripherals. The 16 lines allow the 6502 to access (read or write) 65,536 unique locations. The address bus is *undirectional* with addresses coming *out* of the microprocessor.

Data—The data bus (D0–D7) is a group of eight lines over which data is transferred between the 6502 and the addressed memory or peripheral location. On a write cycle, data is transferred from the 6502 to the addressed location. On a read

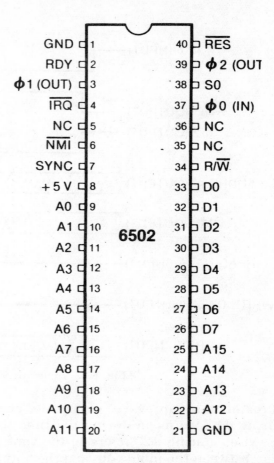

Fig. 6-1. 6502 Microprocessor.

cycle, data is transferred from the addressed location to the 6502. Thus, the data bus is *bidirectional*.

Control—The control group consists of the following signals:

Inputs

$\phi0$—Clock In
RDY—Ready
$\overline{\text{NMI}}$—Non-maskable Interrupt
$\overline{\text{IRQ}}$—Interrupt Request
$\overline{\text{RES}}$—Reset
SO—Set Overflow

Outputs

$\phi1$—Clock Out
$\phi2$—Clock Out
R/W—Read/Write
SYNC

Clocks—The timing of all 6502 data transfers is controlled by the clocks of the microprocessor. $\phi0$ is a clock input on which you normally place a square wave. For a 6502 specified at 1 MHz, this would be a 1 MHz square wave (Fig. 6-2). From this input, the 6502 generates two clock outputs: $\phi1$ and $\phi2$. These clock outputs are

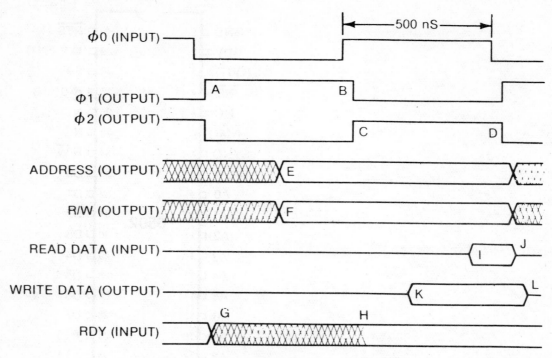

Fig. 6-2. Standard 6502 read/write timing.

approximate square waves of opposite phase. When we speak of an event occurring "during $\phi1$," we mean during the time that $\phi1$ is high (points A to B in Fig. 6-2). Likewise, "during $\phi2$" refers to the time between points C and D. Note the slight delay between the input ($\phi0$) and the outputs ($\phi1$ and $\phi2$). The 6502 $\phi2$ output is not used in the Apple II—$\phi0$ is used in its place. We will still refer to events occurring "during $\phi2$."

Read/Write—Signal R/W controls the direction of the data bus. R/W is high for a read cycle and low for a write cycle. The R/W and the address bus stabilize during $\phi1$ (points E and F in Fig. 6-2). The data transfer takes place during $\phi2$. We will examine the exact sequences later.

Ready—Signal RDY is used to delay a 6502 read cycle momentarily so that slow memory or peripherals can have time to place their data on the data bus. Signal RDY is *high* to indicate that the memory is ready. Signal RDY is *low* to delay the 6502. The RDY signal must change only during $\phi1$ or during the first 100 nS of $\phi2$ (points G and H). See References 6.2, 6.9, 6.12, and 6.15 for timing details. The RDY signal is sampled during $\phi2$, and if high, the cycle will complete. If RDY is low, the cycle will be extended to the next $\phi2$ when RDY is again sampled. In this manner, the RDY line can insert an integer number of clock cycles or *wait-states*. The RDY line is ignored during write cycles. No circuitry on the mother board uses the RDY line, but it is available at the peripheral connectors. It is usually driven by open collector devices.

Interrupts ($\overline{IRQ}$ and $\overline{NMI}$)—Signals $\overline{IRQ}$ and $\overline{NMI}$ are inputs to the 6502. When activated (low), they request the 6502 to interrupt the current program and jump to another routine. After executing the new routine, the processor usually returns to the interrupted program. An application of interrupts would be a real time clock. For example, the clock could interrupt the processor every second to run a routine. This routine could do something like update a clock display on the screen.

The $\overline{IRQ}$ line is *maskable*. This means that the 6502 can be programmed to ignore the $\overline{IRQ}$ line by using the SEI instruction (Set Interrupt Disable Status). The SEI instruction sets the interrupt disable flag which is one bit in the internal status register of the 6502. The bit may be cleared by using the CLI instruction (Clear Interrupt Disable Bit). A situation that might call for disabling interrupts would be a time-critical process. For example, if you used a "software UART" routine to drive your printer, you would not want an interrupt to divert the 6502 in mid-character.

The $\overline{IRQ}$ input is *level-sensitive*. This means that whenever $\overline{IRQ}$ is low (and interrupts are enabled), the 6502 will be interrupted. Because of this, the 6502 automatically sets the disable interrupt flag when it recognizes an interrupt. It is up to the user to restore interrupts using the CLI or RTI (Return from Interrupt) instruction. However, this should not be done until the interrupting device has released the $\overline{IRQ}$ line. Otherwise the interrupt from that device would be recognized again.

As the name says, the $\overline{NMI}$ line is *non-maskable*; it cannot be disabled by the processor. An application for a non-maskable interrupt would be to run a *trap* routine. For example, the hardware may detect an error condition and activate the $\overline{NMI}$ line. The 6502 would always recognize $\overline{NMI}$ and run the trap routine. This routine could then read various registers and send the results to the printer for diagnostic purposes.

Note that the presence of both maskable and non-maskable interrupts in the 6502 provides a method of prioritizing interrupts. When $\overline{NMI}$ is recognized, the interrupt disable flag is set and the 6502 ignores $\overline{IRQ}$. When $\overline{IRQ}$ is recognized, the interrupt disable flag is also set. However, this has no effect on $\overline{NMI}$. If $\overline{NMI}$ is activated while the processor is servicing an interrupt from $\overline{IRQ}$, the first interrupt routine will be interrupted and the 6502 will service the request from $\overline{NMI}$. Afterwards, it will return to the first interrupt routine and then finally to the main program. Thus a non-maskable interrupt request can interrupt a maskable interrupt routine, but not vice versa. This gives non-maskable interrupts priority over the maskable type.

The $\overline{NMI}$ input is *edge-sensitive*. This means that it is recognized once for each negative transition. It must return high then low to be recognized again.

Interrupts $\overline{IRQ}$ and $\overline{NMI}$ are sampled during $\phi2$. If either signal is low, the 6502 will finish the current instruction, then start the appropriate interrupt routine. An interrupt request will not be recognized if RDY is low. Interrupts $\overline{IRQ}$ and $\overline{NMI}$ are normally driven with open collector devices. Interrupts $\overline{IRQ}$ and $\overline{NMI}$ are not used on the mother board, but they are available at the peripheral I/O connectors.

Note that applications for non-maskable interrupts in the Apple II are limited. This is due to the software timing loops used in the floppy disk operating system. You can probably imagine the chaos that could occur if a non-maskable interrupt altered a critical timing loop while the disk was spinning.

Reset—The $\overline{RES}$ input is used to start the 6502 from a powered-down condition, or to set the program counter to a known location at any time. Simply stated, whenever $\overline{RES}$ is taken low, then returned high, the 6502 will start executing code from a known location, usually in ROM. In the Apple II, this location is in the monitor ROM. There are three sources of reset in the Apple as follows:

1. A power-up reset circuit (555 timer A13)
2. The keyboard reset button
3. The peripheral connectors

Sync—The 6502 SYNC output goes high during clock cycles that are op code fetch cycles—SYNC is not used in the Apple II.

Set Overflow—The 6502 SO (set overflow) input is used to set the overflow flag—SO is not used in the Apple II and is tied low.

6502 Read and Write Cycles

Before leaving Fig. 6-2, let's discuss the sequence of read and write cycles. We will assume that RDY is high.

On a read cycle, the address and R/W become stable no later than points E and F. The R/W signal will be high for a read cycle. The devices on the bus must now decode the address and the device that is selected must put its data on the bus no later then point I. The data must be held until point J. The data is strobed into the 6502 on φ2 falling at point D. This concludes the read cycle.

On a write cycle, the address and R/W have the same timing that they do on a read cycle. The R/W signal will be low, however, for a write cycle. The 6502 puts the write data on the bus no later than point K and holds it until point L. The accessed device must strobe in the data sometime between these two points. This concludes the write cycle. Additional 6502 cycle types will be described later in this chapter.

In this overview we have made only a brief exploration of the 6502. We must move ahead, however, to topics related more specifically to the Apple II. The references for this chapter contain more information on the 6502.

Address Decoding

We learned in Chapter 5 that addresses in the range 0 to 48K are decoded to access the RAM. Now we will discuss the remaining 16K of address space. The top 12K of this space is assigned to six 24-pin sockets. These sockets are arranged to accept type 9316B 2K-byte by 8-bit ROMs that are similar to (but not completely pin compatible with) 2716 EPROMs. The sockets are usually referenced by their address range rather than by their X-Y location on the mother board. In this book, we too will refer to the ROMs by their address. See Fig. C-10* for the physical locations of the ROM sockets. Fig. 6-3 shows the pin assignments for a 9316B ROM.

The F8 socket usually contains one of the monitor ROMs (original or autostart). In the original Apple II, F0, E8, and E0 contain the Integer BASIC ROMs. Sockets D8 and D0 are available for optional firmware such as the Programmer's Aid No. 1.

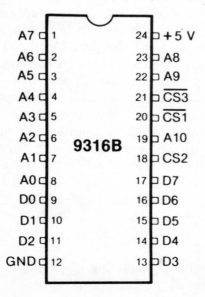

Fig. 6-3. 9316B ROM.

In the Apple II Plus, sockets F0, E8, E0, D8, and D0 contain the Applesoft floating point BASIC ROMs. These ROM variations are just optional ways of arranging the firmware. All the hardware really needs is a ROM in the F8 socket so that the 6502 will have a program to execute on power-up.

Let's look at the circuitry involved with the address decoding. One-of-eight decoder F12 divides the top 16K of address space into eight 2K blocks. The top six blocks ($D000–$FFFF) are assigned to the six ROM sockets. The next block down ($C800–CFFF) is assigned to the peripheral connectors (pin 20, $\overline{\text{I/O STB}}$). The final block ($C000–$C7FF) is further decoded by H12. Decoder H12 divides this 2K block into eight blocks of 256 bytes each. The top seven of these blocks are assigned to peripheral connectors 1 through 7 (pin 1, $\overline{\text{I/OSEL}}$). The remaining 256 byte block is further decoded by H2 and F13. Decoder H2 divides the upper half of the block ($C080–$C0FF) into eight blocks of 16 bytes each. These eight blocks are assigned to the peripheral connectors (pin 41, $\overline{\text{DEV SEL}}$). There now remain 128 bytes of address space ($C000–$C07F) unaccounted for. Decoder F13 and associated ICs decode this block for the on-board I/O. Address decoding will be covered in detail later in this chapter. Decoding of the 128 on-board I-O locations will be covered in Chapter 7.

You will note from the previous discussion that a peripheral connector has both 16-byte and 256-byte address blocks decoded for it. This decoding scheme uses only two ICs on the mother board and eliminates several potential ICs on each peripheral card. The ICs eliminated are ones that would be needed if the peripheral card had to decode its address range directly from the 16-bit address bus. This reduction of ICs is the efficient design which we mentioned in the introduction.

The bus signal $\overline{\text{INH}}$ (inhibit) is used by a peripheral to inhibit the on-board ROM. A typical application of this signal is the Apple ROM card. It uses $\overline{\text{INH}}$ to switch out the on-board ROM so that it can substitute its own ROM into the same memory space.

Direct Memory Access

Direct memory access (DMA) is a process whereby a peripheral gains direct access to the system memory, bypassing the microprocessor. A common reason for using DMA is speed; for example, when transferring data between memory and a hard disk. Without DMA, the processor must transfer data a byte at a time using a software routine. This routine would take many clock cycles per byte as it fetches op codes, computes addresses, etc. A peripheral with DMA capability can transfer one byte per clock cycle.

While a peripheral is using DMA, the processor cannot access memory. A method used to avoid conflict is to place the processor in a stopped or *hold* state. When an Apple II peripheral wishes to perform DMA, it takes the $\overline{\text{DMA}}$ line low. This stops the 6502 and forces the address bus and R/W to a high impedance. When the 6502 stops, its ϕ1 output is high and this forces the data bus to a high impedance. With R/W, address, and data buses at high impedance, the peripheral can put its own address and data on the buses. It can also control R/W. The peripheral now has access not only to memory, but also to the peripheral connectors and the on-board I/O. In other words, a peripheral with DMA capability can access any location that the 6502 can.

Daisy Chains

The $\overline{\text{DMA}}$ line is connected in common to all peripheral I/O connectors. What if more than one peripheral pulls low on $\overline{\text{DMA}}$ at the same time? An obvious conflict would occur. A DMA daisy chain is provided that can prevent a bus conflict if used with the proper circuitry. The daisy chain forms a series circuit running through the peripheral connectors. Circuitry is provided on each peripheral (with DMA capability) to break the daisy chain when DMA is requested. The nature of the chain is such that higher priority is given to peripherals in lower slot numbers. Should two or more peripherals simultaneously request DMA, only the highest priority peripheral will seize the bus. The exact operation will be described later in this chapter.

There is also a daisy chain for interrupts that can be used for the same purpose as the DMA daisy chain. Use of the interrupt daisy chain is optional, however, since a software polling routine could be used to detect and prioritize simultaneous interrupt requests.

Keyboard

The keyboard plugs into mother board location A7. When a key is pressed, a 7-bit code representing that key appears at A7 along with a strobe signal. The strobe is used to set a latch. When the 6502 addresses the keyboard, the seven data bits plus the latched strobe are driven onto the data bus. The 6502 then reads the data. If the program finds the strobe bit set, it uses the other seven bits to determine the key pressed. The program also resets the latch to wait for the next character. Fig. 6-4 shows the keyboard connector pin assignments at A7.

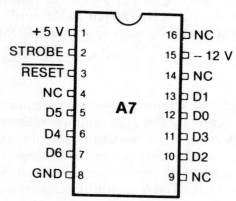

Fig. 6-4. Keyboard connector.

DETAILED CIRCUIT ANALYSIS

6502 Read from RAM

Fig. 6-5 depicts a cycle in which the 6502 reads from RAM. Note that we have shown the length of a half cycle as it actually is in the Apple—489 nS. This means the Apple's 6502 runs about 2% faster than the recommended 1 MHz maximum rate of a standard-speed part.

To start the cycle, the 6502 outputs the address during $\phi 1$. The address becomes stable by point A. The $\overline{\text{DMA}}$ is high due to pull-up resistor RA01-3 (Fig. C-9*). Thus, C11-12 is low to enable address bus drivers H3, H4, and H5. The address arrives on the system bus at point B (Fig. 6-5). Since this is a read cycle, 6502 R/W stabilizes high at point C. H5-5 is enabled, so BUS R/W goes high at point D. Since we are addressing RAM in the space 0–48K, one of the inputs of D2 (pins 9, 10, or 12 of Fig.

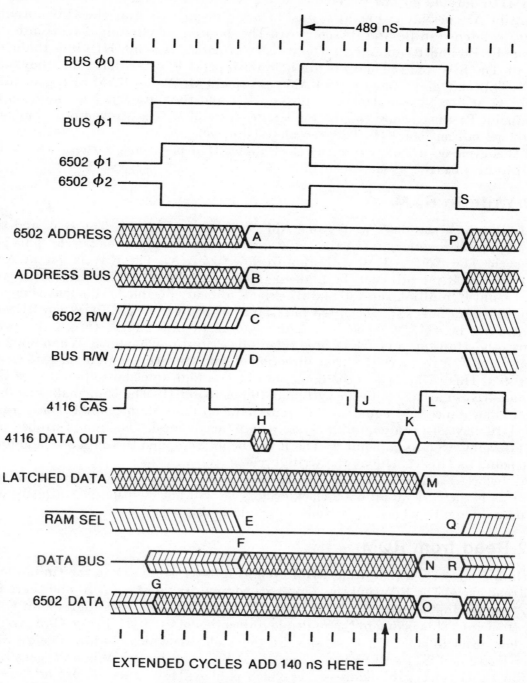

Fig. 6-5. 6502 read from RAM.

C-5*) will go low when the address stabilizes. Thus $\overline{\text{RAM SEL}}$ goes low by point E (Fig. 6-5). The low on $\overline{\text{RAM SEL}}$ will enable multiplexers B6 and B7 (Fig. C-13)*, and they drive garbage onto the data bus at point F (Fig. 6-5). Signal 6502 ϕ1 is high, so starting at point G, data transceiver H10 (Fig. C-9*) drives the data bus into the 6502. Meanwhile, a video RAM read cycle is occurring during ϕ1 as described in Chapter 5. The 4116s output the video data at point H (Fig. 6-5).

Next the address bus is multiplexed into row and column bits (also described in Chapter 5). The row and column addresses are strobed into the RAMs at points I and

J. The 4116 outputs go low impedance with valid data at point K and the data is held until $\overline{CAS}$ goes high at point L. Just before it disappears from the 4116 outputs, the data is latched in B5 and B8 (point M). The data is immediately driven onto the data bus by B6 and B7 (point N). The data then passes through H10 into the 6502 (point 0). The R/W and the address are held until point P. After that time, they may change. This change propagates to $\overline{RAM\ SEL}$ (point Q). When $\overline{RAM\ SEL}$ goes high at point Q, it disables multiplexers B6 and B7, and the data bus goes high impedance (point R). Just before the data is lost from the bus, it is strobed into the 6502 on 6502 $\phi2$ falling (point S). This completes the cycle.

If this cycle occurs on one of the clock cycles that is extended, there will be an extra 140 nS inserted as shown in Fig. 6-5.

6502 Write to RAM

A cycle in which the 6502 writes to RAM is shown in Fig. 6-6. The R/W and the addresses stabilize during $\phi1$ at the same time they do during a read cycle. This is a write cycle, however, so R/W will stabilize low (point A). The R/W is low at A2-4 (Fig. C-5*), so $\overline{RAM\ SEL}$ will be high (point B of Fig. 6-6). When $\overline{RAM\ SEL}$ goes high at point B, multiplexers B6 and B7 (Fig, C-13*) are disabled. This leaves no one driving the data bus, so it goes high impedance at point C (Fig. 6-6). When BUS $\phi1$ falls at point D, 4116 $\overline{WR}$ goes low (point E) due to gate C14-11 (Fig. C-7*). This prepares the 4116s for an early-write cycle as described in Chapter 5. When 6502 $\phi1$ falls at point F, it reverses the drive direction of data transceiver H10 via gate C14-8 (Fig. C-9*). This reversal lets the 6502 data bus go high impedance (point G of Fig. 6-6), and drives garbage onto the system data bus (point H). The 6502 makes its data bus low impedance and equal to the write data no later than point I. Data transceiver H10 drives the data onto the system data bus, point J. The data is strobed into the 4116s on $\overline{CAS}$ falling, point K. The R/W, the address, and the data are held until about point L. This concludes the write cycle.

As before, there is a 1 in 65 chance that this cycle could be extended 140 nS. Since this is the case on all 6502 clock cycles, we will not mention it again. We will note on each figure where the extension would be inserted.

6502 Read from ROM

The timing for a 6502 read from ROM cycle (Fig. 6-7) is similar to the timing for a RAM read cycle. The R/W and the addresses become stable at point A, and there is a video read during $\phi1$ with output at point B. The $\overline{RAM\ SEL}$ goes high (point C) on BUS $\phi0$ rising. This is due to the multiplexing action of $\phi0$ at J1-1 (Fig. C-5*). While $\phi0$ is low (prior to point C), J1 selects the video address which is always below 32K. Either F2-12 or F2-11 will be low. Thus, $\overline{RAM\ SEL}$ will be low. When $\phi0$ goes high at point C, J1 selects the address bus which is above 48K since we are addressing ROM. None of F2-10, 11, or 12 are low and $\overline{RAM\ SEL}$ is high. The high on $\overline{RAM\ SEL}$ disables B6 and B7 (Fig. C-13*) so they release the data bus (point D of Fig. 6-7).

Right at this same time ($\phi0$ rising), $\phi1$ falls to partially enable decoder F12 via pins 4 and 5 (Fig. C-10*). Since we are addressing above 48K, both AD14 and AD15 are high. Thus, H1-6 is high to fully enable F12 via pin 6. Decoder F12 now decodes address lines AD11, AD12, and AD13 to select one of eight 2K blocks above 48K. Since we are addressing ROM, one of the six F12 outputs assigned to a ROM chip select will go low (point E of Fig. 6-7). The F12 outputs are assigned to chip select input pins 20 and 21. A third chip select pin on each ROM is tied in common to

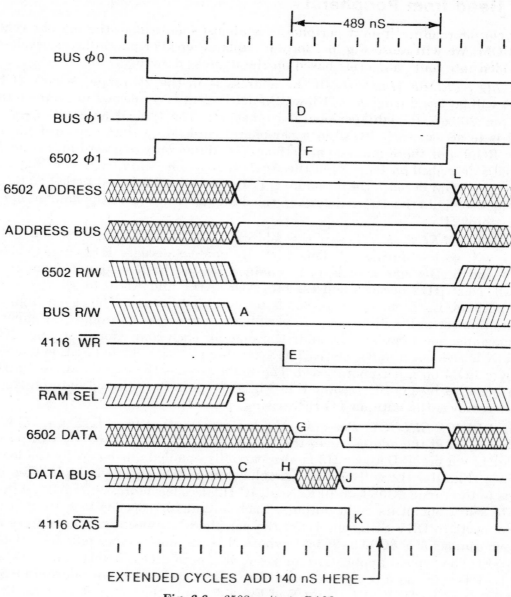

Fig. 6-6. 6502 write to RAM.

signal $\overline{INH}$. It is held high (ROMs enabled) by resistor RA01-7. Address lines AD0 through AD10 connect to the address inputs of the ROM. These 11 lines select one of the 2K locations in each ROM. After the IC's access delays from address and chip select, the ROM outputs will equal the data contained in the addressed location (point F of Fig. 6-7). This data is driven into the 6502 by H10 (point G). The ROM chip select goes high again on ϕ1 rising, point H. This disables the ROM which removes its data from the bus after a short delay, point I. Just before the data disappears from the 6502 data inputs (point J), it is strobed into the 6502 on 6502 ϕ2 falling (point K). This concludes the cycle.

Since the address for this cycle is above 48K, there is no active $\overline{CAS}$ at point L. It follows that the 4116 outputs remain high impedance at point M, and that the latched data at point N is garbage.

6502 Read from Peripheral

The cycle for reading from a peripheral is almost identical to the one for reading from ROM. We will reuse Fig. 6-7 for our explanation. Peripheral access cycles can be divided into four categories based on the address decoding:

1. I/O STROBE (Pin 20)—If the address is in the 2k range, $C800–$CFFF, F12-14 will go low during $\phi2$ ($\phi1$ low). Signal F12-14 is connected in common to $\overline{\text{I/O STB}}$ (pin 20) of all eight peripheral connectors. The typical application for this signal is to access a 2K ROM on a peripheral card. More than one card can have such a ROM, but there must be a method of enabling only one card at a time. This method is described on Page 84 of the *Apple II Reference Manual* under "Expansion ROM." The ROM decodes the 11 address LSBs and when accessed by $\overline{\text{I/O STB}}$ (point E of Fig. 6-7), puts the selected data on the data bus. It removes the data on $\overline{\text{I/O STB}}$ rising, point H.

2. I/O SELECT (Pin 1)—If the address is in the 2K range, $C000–$C7FF, F12-15 will go low during $\phi2$. This partially enables decoder H12 (Fig. C-11*) via pins 4 and 5. Decoder H12 is fully enabled by the high on pin 6 from resistor RA01-8. Next, H12 decodes address bits AD8, AD9, and AD10 to select one of its eight outputs. Each output corresponds to a 256 byte range. The seven high order outputs connect to $\overline{\text{I/O SEL}}$ (pin 1) of peripheral connectors 1 through 7. Connector 0 has no connection to pin 1. The address range for each connector is $CN00–$CNFF where N is the slot number (1–7). The typical application for $\overline{\text{I/O SEL}}$ is to access a 256 byte ROM on a peripheral card. The ROM decodes the eight address LSBs and when accessed by $\overline{\text{I/O SEL}}$ (point E of Fig. 6-7), puts the selected data on the data bus. It removes the data on $\overline{\text{I/O SEL}}$ rising, point·H.

3. DEVICE SELECT (Pin 41)—The low order output from H12 (pin 15) will go low during $\phi2$ if the address is in the range $C000–$C0FF. This low will partially enable H2 via pin 4. Decoder H2 is also partially enabled during $\phi2$ by the low ($\phi1$) on pin 5. Finally, H2 will be fully enabled when AD7 (H2-6) is high. This corresponds to the range $C080–$C0FF. Next, IC H2 decodes address bits AD4, AD5, and AD6 to select one of its eight outputs. Each output corresponds to a 16 byte range and connects to $\overline{\text{DEV SEL}}$ (pin 41) of the peripheral connectors. The address range for each connector is $C0N0–$C0NF where N is the slot number plus 8 (that is N = $8 to $F). The typical application for $\overline{\text{DEV SEL}}$ is to access assorted latches, registers, UARTs, etc., on a peripheral card. The card decodes the four address LSBs and when accessed by $\overline{\text{DEV SEL}}$ (point E of Fig. 6-7), puts the selected data on the data bus. It removes the data on $\overline{\text{DEV SEL}}$ rising, point H.

4. Full Address Decode—A peripheral card does not have to use the decoded address on pins 1, 20, and 41. The card can perform its own decoding of the address bus (AD0–AD15). An application would be a card that is addressed in a range not available on pins 1, 20, or 41. For example, the Apple ROM card responds to the range $D000–$FFFF; not available as a predecoded select line. Note that the address bus becomes stable (point O) before the decoded select lines (point E), an advantage of this decoding method. However, the peripheral should still wait until $\phi1$ is low to output to the data bus. This is to avoid a bus conflict since B6 and B7 drive the bus until point D.

A Caution for Designers—A few words about the read data hold time are in order. They apply to all four addressing methods discussed previously. The 6502 data sheet specifies that at the end of a read cycle, the data must remain stable on the 6502 data inputs for a 10 nS *hold time* after 6502 $\phi2$ falling. Referring to Fig.

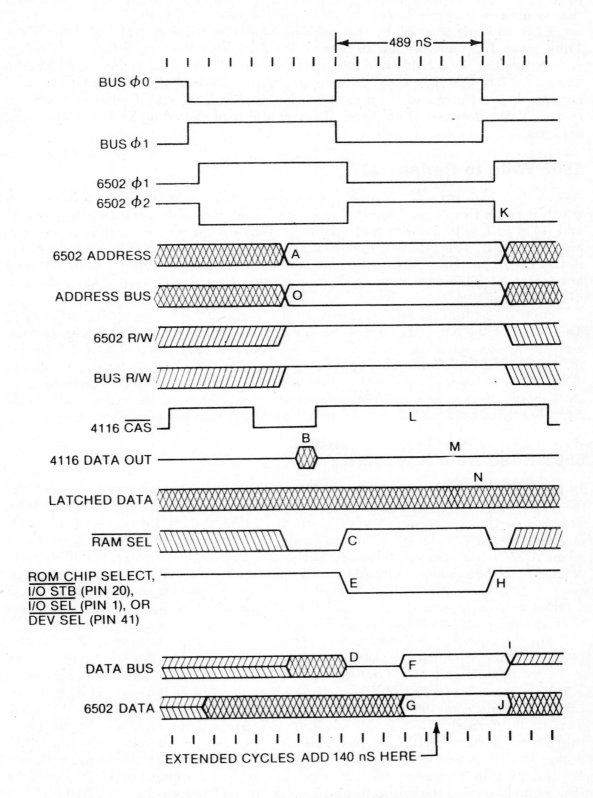

Fig. 6-7. 6502 read from ROM or peripheral.

6-7, we see that point J (6502 data no longer valid) must occur at least 10 nS after point K (6502 $\phi2$ falling). Recall that 6502 $\phi2$ is not used in the Apple II. The signal that is used in its place to enable data onto the bus is BUS $\phi0$.

BUS $\phi0$ leads 6502 $\phi2$ by the propagation delays through B11-3 and the 6502. Thus, when BUS $\phi0$ goes low to remove the data from the bus, it may remove the data *before* the 6502 hold time has been satisfied. This problem can be helped by using $\overline{\text{I/O STB}}$, $\overline{\text{I/O SEL}}$, $\overline{\text{DEV SEL}}$, or inverted $\phi1$ instead of $\phi0$ to enable the data onto the bus. Also, the use of a data bus buffer that is slow to disable will help. In summary, the designer of an Apple II peripheral card should make a careful timing analysis.

6502 Write to Peripheral

A cycle in which the 6502 writes to a peripheral (Fig. 6-8) is similar to a cycle in which it reads from a peripheral. On a write cycle, R/W will stabilize low (point A) and $\overline{\text{RAM SEL}}$ will stabilize high (point B). When $\overline{\text{RAM SEL}}$ goes high, it will disable B6 and B7 (Fig. C-13*), releasing the data bus at point C. On $\phi1$ falling, $\overline{\text{I/O}}$ $\overline{\text{STB}}$, $\overline{\text{I/O SEL}}$, or $\overline{\text{DEV SEL}}$ will go low (point D). Also on $\phi1$ falling, 4116 $\overline{\text{WR}}$ goes low (point E). This does nothing, however, since there is no 4116 $\overline{\text{CAS}}$ while this 4116 $\overline{\text{WR}}$ is active.

On 6502 $\phi1$ falling, data transceiver H10 (Fig. C-9*) reverses its drive direction. This releases the data bus toward the 6502 (point F of Fig. 6-8) and drives garbage onto the system data bus (point G). The peripheral card is selected by $\overline{\text{I/O STB}}$, $\overline{\text{I/O}}$ $\overline{\text{SEL}}$, $\overline{\text{DEV SEL}}$, or a full decoding of the address bus. It then waits for the write data of the 6502 to become valid and driven onto the data bus, point H. The peripheral card should strobe the data into its memory or registers on the rising edge of $\overline{\text{I/O}}$ $\overline{\text{STB}}$, $\overline{\text{I/O SEL}}$, $\overline{\text{DEV SEL}}$ (point I), or $\phi1$ (point J). This completes the write cycle.

6502 Read from Keyboard

In our discussion of the peripheral address decoding, we determined that H12-15 (Fig. C-11*) goes low during $\phi2$ when the address is in the range $C000–$C0FF. This low partially enables decoder F13 via pin 5 (Fig. C-12*). Decoder F13 is further enabled via pin 6 when $\phi0$ is high. Decoder F13 is finally fully enabled via pin 4 when AD7 is low. This corresponds to the 128 byte address range $C000–$C07F. Next, F13 decodes address bits AD4, AD5, and AD6 to select one of its eight outputs. Each output corresponds to a 16 byte range. The low order output (pin 15) is of interest to us here; it is the signal $\overline{\text{KBD}}$—$\overline{\text{KBD}}$ will go low during $\phi2$ if the address is in the range $C000–$C00F. When programming, we simply use $C000.

Fig. 6-9 shows a cycle during which the 6502 reads the keyboard. (It is similar to Fig. 6-7, a cycle during which the 6502 reads from ROM.) The 6502 puts out the keyboard address at point A and takes R/W high at point B. When R/W goes high, $\overline{\text{RAM SEL}}$ goes low (point C). When $\phi0$ goes high at point D, multiplexer J1 switches (Fig. C-5*). Since we are addressing above 48K, D2 pins 9, 10, and 12 all go high. This would normally take $\overline{\text{RAM SEL}}$ high. We are addressing the keyboard, however, so on $\phi0$ rising, $\overline{\text{KBD}}$ goes low (point E of Fig. 6-9). A low $\overline{\text{KBD}}$ signal at D2-13 makes D2-8 high and keeps $\overline{\text{RAM SEL}}$ low (point F). Thus, $\overline{\text{KBD}}$ low at multiplexers B6 and B7 (pin 1) causes them to select the keyboard connector A7 (Fig. C-13*). (Data bits 0–6 go to the connector; bit 7 is the latched keyboard strobe, B10-9.) With $\overline{\text{RAM SEL}}$ low at B6 and B7 pin 15, they drive the keyboard data and strobe onto the

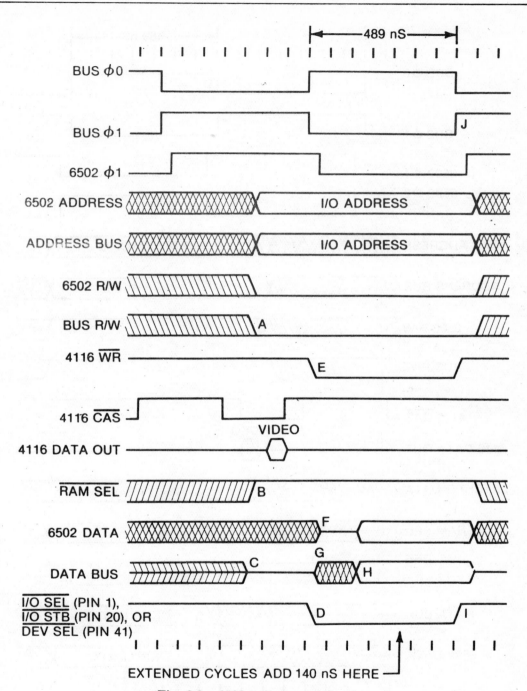

Fig. 6-8. 6502 write to peripheral.

data bus, point G. Data transceiver H10 drives the data into the 6502 which strobes it on 6502 ϕ2 falling, point H. This concludes the keyboard cycle.

When any character key is pressed on the keyboard, A7-2 goes high (Fig. C-13*). This sets flip-flop B10 and its pin 9 goes high. When a program scans or reads the keyboard, it checks data bit 7 (B10-9). A 1 (high) indicates that a key has been pressed and that data bits 0–6 contain the character. The program must then address location $C010. This takes $\overline{\text{CLR STB}}$ low and clears B10-9 via C11-4 and A12-1. If this is not done, B10-9 will still be high on the next scan, and the same character will be read again.

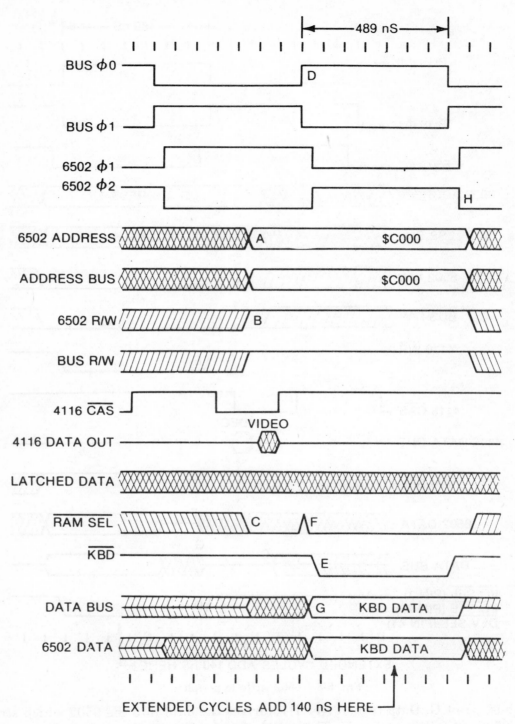

Fig. 6-9. 6502 read from keyboard.

USER 1

A signal named USER 1 is connected in common to pin 39 of all eight peripheral connectors (Fig. C-11*). USER 1 then connects to a jumper on the mother board. When this jumper is absent, USER 1 can be used as a signal line between two or more peripheral cards. Its application would be up to the designer of the peripherals.

When the jumper is installed, USER 1 connects to H12-6. This gives the peripherals control over the 2K address space $C000–$C7FF. This range consists of the on-board I/O and the memory blocks selected by $\overline{\text{I/O SEL}}$ and $\overline{\text{DEV SEL}}$. When USER 1 is high, this range is not affected. When USER 1 is low, the range $C000–$C7FF is inhibited.

The Ready Line

The RDY (Ready) line gives the peripheral cards the ability to momentarily delay the 6502 an integer number of clock cycles. An application would be the use of peripheral devices with long access times.

Fig. 6-10 depicts a read cycle that has been extended by one *wait state*. The basic cycle is similar to the read from peripheral shown in Fig. 6-7. The main difference occurs when the peripheral takes RDY low to indicate that it will not have data ready within the usual one cycle. This occurs during $\phi1$ after the peripheral recognizes its address, between points A and B in Fig. 6-10. During $\phi2$, the 6502 will sample RDY and see that it is low. As a result, the 6502 will not strobe in the data at the end of $\phi2$. Instead, it maintains R/W and the address for another clock cycle. Our peripheral is ready now, so during $\phi1$ of the second cycle (points C to D) it releases RDY. Resistor RA01-5 pulls RDY high (Fig. C-9*). The 6502 again samples RDY during $\phi2$ and, seeing that it is high, completes the read cycle.

The peripheral card can start decoding the address as early as point E (Fig. 6-10). However, it should not drive the data bus unless $\overline{\text{I/O STB}}$, $\overline{\text{I/O SEL}}$, $\overline{\text{DEV SEL}}$, or $\phi1$ is low. This is to avoid a bus conflict with multiplexers B6 and B7. Note that any number of wait states may be inserted to extend the cycle. With the appropriate circuitry, RDY can be used to single step the processor one clock cycle at a time.

DMA Daisy Chain

We introduced the concept of DMA in the overview. The DMA allows a peripheral card to gain direct access to the system bus and take over in place of the 6502. Only one card at a time can be allowed to do this. Fig. 6-11* shows the DMA daisy chain that allows access to the bus, one card at a time, on a priority basis. We have shown cards with DMA capability plugged into slots 0, 2, and 7. The card plugged into slot 1 does not have DMA capability. A line on this card simply connects DMA IN (pin 27) to DMA OUT (pin 24).

The daisy chain starts at slot 0 pin 27 and continues through the cards and the mother board to slot 7 pin 24. The DMA OUT from slot 7 (pin 24) goes nowhere and is a don't care. (The optional connection at solder pad "7," Fig. C-11*, is not associated with DMA.) The DMA IN at slot 0 also has no connection on the mother board. Although not shown in this example, slots 3 through 6 must contain cards so that the daisy chain will be continuous. You do not need eight cards to use DMA. If you have fewer cards, they must be arranged so that the chain is continuous. The chain need not start in slot 0 or end in slot 7. The cards with higher priority are placed toward slot 0.

Normally, the signal CHAIN on each card is high. A pull-up resistor is provided on each card so that DMA IN of the highest priority card will be high. As a result, the daisy chain is normally high all along its path.

For DMA operation, suppose the card in slot 2 needs to perform a DMA. The logic on the card checks DMA IN and finds it to be high. This "tells" the card it may proceed since no higher priority card needs DMA. The slot 2 card then takes CHAIN

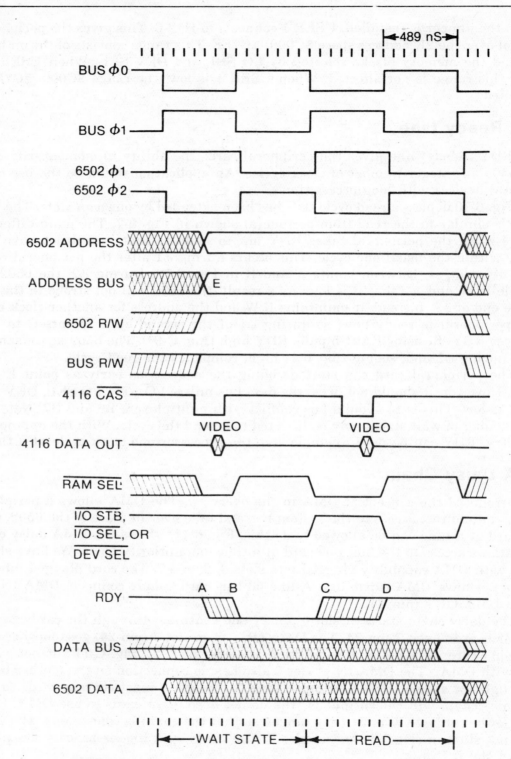

Fig. 6-10. 6502 read from peripheral extended by ready line.

low with the result that DMA OUT goes low. This low will propagate down the chain to lower priority cards, preventing them from starting DMA cycles. The slot 2 card also takes $\overline{DMA}$ low via an open collector gate. When $\overline{DMA}$ is low, it removes the 6502 from the bus—more on this later.

Now suppose a higher priority card (slot 0) needs to perform a DMA. Slot 0

DMA IN is high, so the card in slot 0 proceeds. It takes CHAIN and DMA OUT low. This low propagates to slot 2 where it prevents that card from performing a DMA.

The DMA operation must be *synchronous*. This means that peripheral cards must get their timing from the system clocks and start DMA cycles only during $\phi 1$. Otherwise, a peripheral could cut short a 6502 cycle and higher priority peripherals could cut short cycles of lower priority peripherals.

DMA Read from RAM

Fig. 6-12 shows a DMA read from RAM followed by a 6502 read from RAM. On $\phi 1$ rising (point A), the peripheral card checks DMA IN (point B). The DMA IN is high,

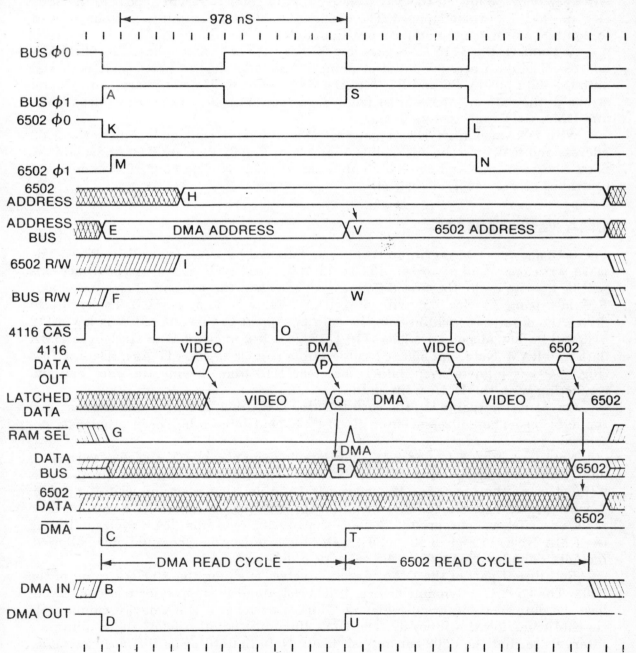

Fig. 6-12. DMA read from RAM.

so the card takes $\overline{DMA}$ low (point C) and DMA OUT low (point D). It also drives an address onto the bus (point E) and takes R/W high (point F). The $\overline{DMA}$ low at C11-13 takes C11-12 high to disable bus drivers H3, H4, and H5 (Fig. C-9). Thus, the 6502 address and R/W are removed from the bus so they will not conflict with the DMA address and R/W.

This is a RAM read cycle, so $\overline{RAM\,SEL}$ goes low as soon as the DMA address is decoded on the mother board (point G of Fig. 6-12). The 6502 address and R/W become valid at points H and I, but have nowhere to go yet. Note that the DMA cycle does not interfere with the video read from RAM at point J. The $\overline{DMA}$ low at B11-1 will keep 6502 $\phi 0$ low all the way from point K to point L. It will appear to the 6502 as if its clock input had stopped. The 6502 will hold its $\phi 1$ output high from point M to point N and will not enter $\phi 2$ until point N.

At point O, the 4116 $\overline{CAS}$ goes low for the memory bank selected by the DMA address. The data becomes valid at point P and is latched at point Q. It is driven onto the data bus by B6 and B7 (Fig. C-13*) at point R. The peripheral card should strobe in the data on $\phi 1$ rising at point S. Also on $\phi 1$ rising, the card returns $\overline{DMA}$ and DMA OUT high (points T and U).

With $\overline{DMA}$ now high, H3, H4, and H5 (Fig. C-9*) are enabled and drive the 6502 address and R/W onto the bus (points V and W of Fig. 6-12). Gate B11-3 now lets the 6502 clock continue and the 6502 enters $\phi 2$ at point N. The 6502 read from RAM continues as previously described.

DMA Write to RAM

Fig. 6-13 shows a DMA write to RAM cycle followed by a 6502 read from RAM. The DMA write operation is very similar to the DMA read cycle just described. Since this will be a write cycle, the first difference occurs when the peripheral card takes bus R/W low (point A). Bus R/W will cause $\overline{RAM\,SEL}$ to be high, point B. The card also drives the data to be written onto the data bus, point C. Since bus R/W is low, 4116 $\overline{WR}$ will go low at point D. The 4116 $\overline{CAS}$ goes low at point E to strobe the DMA data into RAM. Note that 6502 $\phi 1$ is high from point F to point G. As a result, C14-8 (Fig. C-9*) is high to keep data transceiver H10 from driving the data bus and conflicting with the DMA write data.

On $\phi 1$ rising (point H), the card releases $\overline{DMA}$, bus R/W, the address bus, and the data bus. The 6502 read from RAM cycle that follows has been previously described.

Note that Figs. 6-12 and 6-13 show simple examples of DMA cycles. Variations and refinements are possible. Also note that peripheral cards can have direct access to much more than memory. We showed DMA cycles that read and write the RAM. A card can also access ROM, on-board I/O, and other peripherals. It can perform reads or writes as appropriate. We have shown 6502 read from RAM cycles following the DMA cycles in Figs. 6-12 and 6-13. Of course, any cycle type could have followed, including another DMA from the same or a different card.

Recall that part of the DMA process involves stopping the $\phi 0$ clock input of the 6502. The 6502 is a dynamic device. If its clock input is stopped for too long, it will lose the data in its internal registers. Thus, a peripheral DMA device cannot hold the $\overline{DMA}$ line low continuously. The $\overline{DMA}$ line must be released at 10 μS minimum intervals so that the 6502 can refresh itself. Note that 10 μS is the *most restrictive* value obtained from the 6502 data sheets (References 6.9, 6.12, and 6.15 in Appendix D).

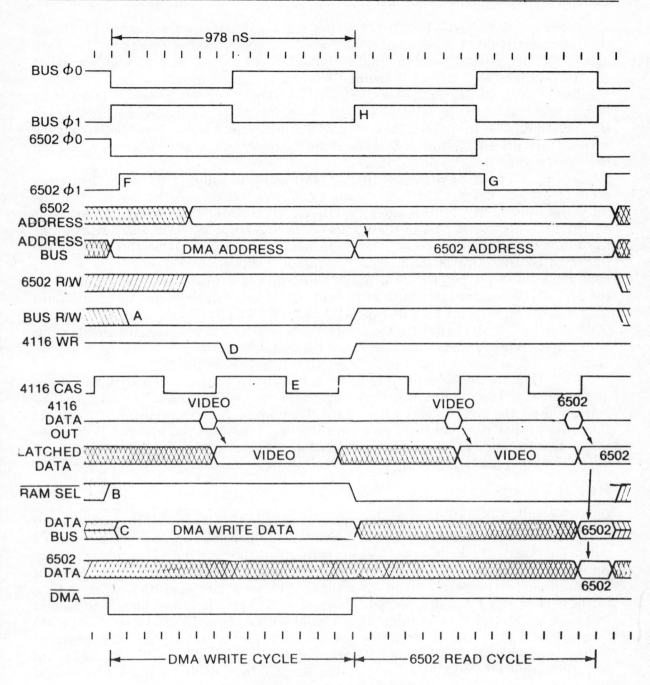

Fig. 6-13. DMA write to RAM.

Interrupts

Interrupt Daisy Chain — Interrupts of the 6502 microprocessor were discussed in the overview of this chapter. There we mentioned that an interrupt daisy chain was available that could be used to prioritize interrupt requests. This interrupt daisy chain operates just like the DMA daisy chain shown in Fig. 6-11*. Just substitute INT IN (pin 28) and INT OUT (pin 23) for DMA IN and DMA OUT. Also substitute $\overline{\text{IRQ}}$ or $\overline{\text{NMI}}$ for $\overline{\text{DMA}}$. (Note: The optional connection at solder pad "8," Fig. C-11*, is not associated with interrupts.)

Interrupt Sequence—Fig. 6-14* shows a typical interrupt sequence. Let's say that at about point A a peripheral card needs to interrupt the processor. The card checks INT IN (point B) and finding it high, proceeds to take $\overline{\text{IRQ}}$ or $\overline{\text{NMI}}$ low (point A). It also takes INT OUT low (point C).

Note that the interrupt request ($\overline{\text{IRQ}}$ or $\overline{\text{NMI}}$) may be *asynchronous*. This means it may occur at any time relative to the system clocks. It is sampled during $\phi2$, and if it is found to be low, the 6502 will start its interrupt routine on $\phi1$ following the current instruction. Note that the processor finishes the current instruction and not just the current clock cycle.

In Fig. 6-14, we have shown $\overline{\text{IRQ}}$ or $\overline{\text{NMI}}$ going low during $\phi1$ of the last clock cycle of an instruction. This means the next clock cycle *could* be the start of the interrupt routine. It *is*, if the interrupt request is on $\overline{\text{NMI}}$. If the interrupt request is on $\overline{\text{IRQ}}$, the 6502 first checks the status of the interrupt mask bit. In our example the mask bit is off (low, point D), so the next clock cycle will be the start of the interrupt routine. One of the first things the interrupt routine does is set the interrupt mask bit (high, point E). The 6502 then proceeds with the interrupt routine. At the end of the routine, commands are sent to the interrupting card to let it return $\overline{\text{IRQ}}$ or $\overline{\text{NMI}}$ high (point F). The card also returns INT OUT high, point G. Then the 6502 executes the RTI (Return from Interrupt) or CLI (Clear Interrupt Disable Bit) instruction, resetting the interrupt mask bit (point H). This concludes the sequence and the 6502 is now ready to receive another interrupt request.

Note that the sequence in Fig. 6-14 is merely an example and that variations are possible. For example, it may be desirable for the peripheral to release $\overline{\text{IRQ}}/\overline{\text{NMI}}$, and for the 6502 to execute a CLI instruction *early* in the routine. This would then allow other peripherals to interrupt the first interrupt routine. See References 6.3, 6.4, 6.11, and 6.17 for more information. Also note that use of the interrupt daisy chain is optional.

Reset

Fig. 6-15 shows the Apple II power-up reset sequence. At point A the power is off and V_{cc} (the +5 V supply) is at 0. At point B the power is on and V_{cc} is near +5 volts. This starts the logic and clocks operating, but they are not yet stable (point C). As power is applied, the $\overline{\text{RESET}}$ line starts to pull high via resistor RA01-6 (point D). As soon as the power is on, 555 timer A13 goes into operation (Fig. C-13*). Initially capacitor C4 is discharged. This low at A13 pins 2 and 6 cause it to trigger and take its output (pin 3) high. This provides base drive to Q5 through R14. Q5 turns on and pulls the $\overline{\text{RESET}}$ line low (point E in Fig. 6-15). Now C4 begins to charge through R26. After a time determined by the formula $T = 1.1\,RC$, A13 will turn its output off (low). This releases the $\overline{\text{RESET}}$ line (point F). $\overline{\text{RESET}}$ is low for about 240 mS.

The 6502 reset sequence actually starts on $\overline{\text{RESET}}$ rising at point F. The 6502 waits six clock cycles, then loads the program counter with the vector stored at $FFFC and $FFFD (point G). The processor then fetches the first op code (point H) and is off and running.

Note that the 240 mS power-up reset is available on the bus to reset circuitry on the peripherals. Also, a reset signal could originate on a peripheral. When the reset button on the keyboard is pressed, A7-3 (Fig. C-13*) goes low sending a reset to the 6502 and the peripherals. (There is a switch option on newer keyboards that can require both CONTROL and RESET to be pressed to take A7-3 low.) The power-up reset from A13 also clears (initializes) the keyboard strobe via A12-1.

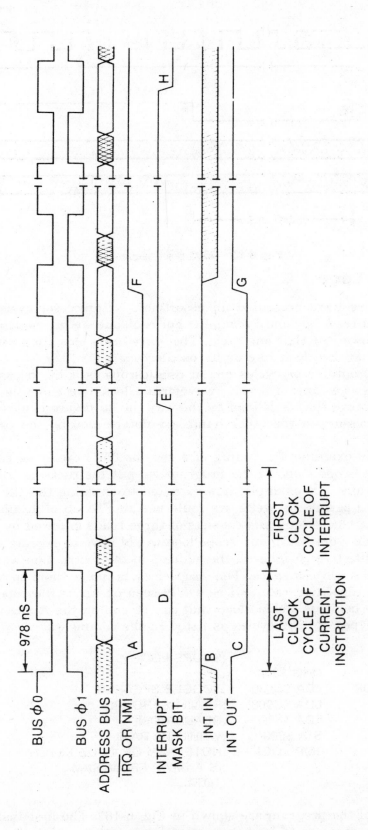

Fig. 6-14. 6502 interrupts.

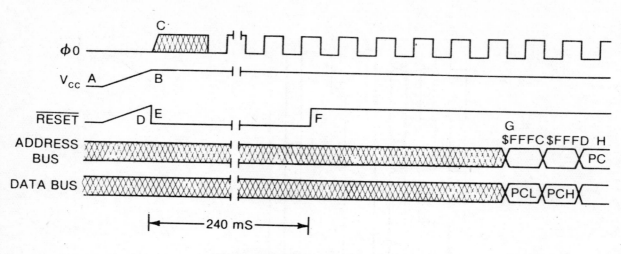

Fig. 6-15. 6502 reset sequence.

6502 'Scope Loop

In this chapter we have presented an assortment of processor cycles: RAM read, RAM write, ROM read, keyboard read, etc. For each one we have examined a timing diagram that shows just that one cycle. The waveforms look nice when printed on paper, but what do they look like on an oscilloscope?

Viewing microprocessor cycles on an oscilloscope is a bit tricky. It is not as simple as looking at a clock or a video waveform. Clocks, for example, are repetitive and follow a sequence that is defined by the way the hardware is wired. The signals from a microprocessor, on the other hand, are determined by the program that is running.

If we want to examine the timing of a specific 6502 cycle, we can use a short program called a 'scope loop. In the program we put instructions that contain the cycle types we want. For example, if we wanted to examine the timing of a RAM read followed by a peripheral write, we could use an STA-absolute instruction. This instruction is four clocks long and consists of three reads followed by a write. Since we specified a read from RAM, our 'scope loop would have to execute in RAM. Since we specified a write to a peripheral, the address in the instruction would have to be in the peripheral's address space. The 'scope loop is made short so the waveforms will have a high repetition rate and be easily seen on an oscilloscope.

The program below is a short loop that can be run on the Apple II. It allows us to view several types of 6502 cycles as listed in the comments.

```
                              ;SCOPE LOOP.                  CLOCK
                    ORG $800  ;                             CYCLES:
0800 AD30C0 LOOP    LDA $C030 ;TOGGLE SPEAKER                 4
0803 AD00C0         LDA $C000 ;READ KEYBOARD                  4
0806 AD00F8         LDA $F800 ;READ PROM                      4
0809 8D0009         STA $900  ;WRITE TO RAM                   4
0812 4C0008         JMP LOOP  ;NOTE: ANY OP CODE FETCH        3
                              ;IS A READ FROM RAM           _____
                              ;TOTAL =                        19
```

The results of the program are shown in Fig. 6-16*. The first instruction (LDA $C030) tells the processor to load its accumulator with the data found at location

$C030. Location $C030 is the address assigned to the on-board speaker. Whenever we access that location, the speaker toggles. We do not care that the speaker does not return any data; we are using the LDA instruction merely as a means to generate the address.

This instruction consists of four clock cycles. The first three cycles read the op code and its operand from consecutive RAM locations. These locations ($800, $801, and $802) are shown in Fig. 6-16* on the address bus. At location $800, the op code ($AD) is read from RAM as shown on the 4116 DATA OUT trace. This data is then latched, put on the data bus, and finally put on the 6502 data lines. At location $801, the operand low order byte ($30) is read. The high order byte ($C0) is read from location $802.

On the fourth cycle, the processor performs the operation specified by the op code. It first outputs $C030 on the address bus (point A). This is decoded on the mother board and found to be above 48K. Thus, there is no 4116 $\overline{CAS}$, and $\overline{RAM\ SEL}$ goes high during $\phi 2$ (point B). The address is further decoded by the string of decoders F12, H12, and F13 (see Figs. C-10*, 11*, and 12*). The specific address $C030 causes F13-12 to go low during $\phi 2$ (point C of Fig. 6-16*). The rising edge of F13-12 causes flip-flop J13-5 to toggle and create a sound in the speaker (point D). More on this in Chapter 7. Notice that the speaker does not respond with any data, so the data bus goes high impedance during $\phi 2$ (point E). The resulting garbage on the data inputs of the 6502 is strobed on $\phi 2$ falling at the end of the cycle. Remember that we do not care about this data anyway.

You will notice the video cycles (indicated by a "V") interleaved with the 6502 cycles throughout Fig. 6-16*.

If you were to actually enter the 'scope loop program (or any other program) into the Apple and view the processor signals on an oscilloscope, you would see the effect of the extended clock cycles. This is a messy display that could cause confusion. To eliminate the extended cycles, lift IC D2 pin 6 (Fig. C-2*). Everything except color displays should continue to operate properly, and you will get cleaner oscilloscope displays.

If you wish to view one complete period of the loop, you need to trigger the oscilloscope on a signal that occurs once each period. You could use F13-12 (Fig. C-12*) in our example.

Let's return to Fig. 6-16* and discuss the remaining instructions. The second instruction (LDA $C000) is similar to the first. Notice that the RAM locations for the op code and its operand start at $803 which follows the last address used by the previous op code. In the fourth cycle of this instruction we address the keyboard ($C000) which *does* respond with data (point F).

The third instruction (LDA $F800) is similar to the first two. Here we load the first byte from the monitor ROM ($4A) into the accumulator.

The fourth instruction (STA $900) tells the processor to store the contents of the accumulator at location $900. The first three clock cycles of this instruction fetch the op code ($8D) and its operand ($900) from RAM locations $809, $810, and $811. On the fourth cycle, the 6502 takes R/W low (point G). When R/W goes low, $\overline{RAM\ SEL}$ goes high. Since R/W is low, 4116 $\overline{WR}$ goes low during $\phi 2$ (point H). Later during $\phi 2$, the 6502 outputs the contents of its accumulator ($4A obtained in the previous instruction). The data is strobed into the RAM on 4116 $\overline{CAS}$ falling during $\phi 2$ (point I).

The fifth and last instruction is JMP $800. This tells the processor to jump to location $800 and execute the op code found there. Since $800 is the beginning of the program, the loop repeats.

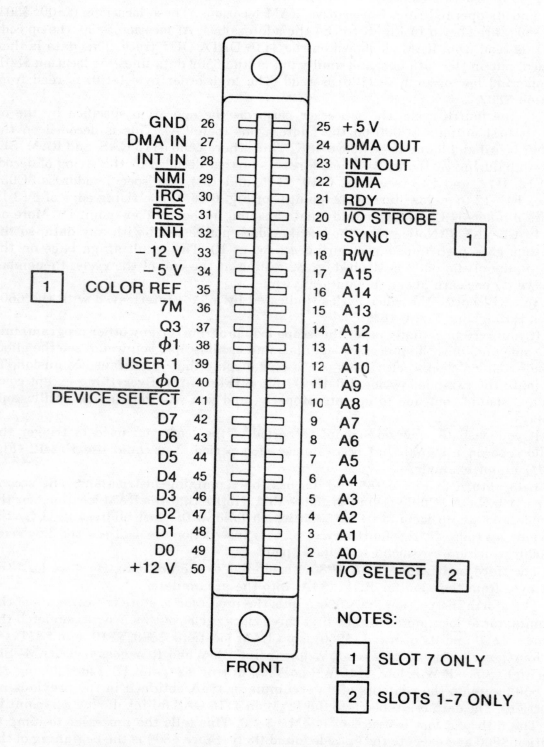

GND	26		25	+5 V	
DMA IN	27		24	DMA OUT	
INT IN	28		23	INT OUT	
NMI	29		22	DMA	
IRQ	30		21	RDY	
RES	31		20	I/O STROBE	
INH	32		19	SYNC	
−12 V	33		18	R/W	
−5 V	34		17	A15	
COLOR REF	35		16	A14	
7M	36		15	A13	
Q3	37		14	A12	
φ1	38		13	A11	
USER 1	39		12	A10	
φ0	40		11	A9	
DEVICE SELECT	41		10	A8	
D7	42		9	A7	
D6	43		8	A6	
D5	44		7	A5	
D4	45		6	A4	
D3	46		5	A3	
D2	47		4	A2	
D1	48		3	A1	
D0	49		2	A0	
+12 V	50		1	I/O SELECT	2

FRONT

NOTES:

1 SLOT 7 ONLY

2 SLOTS 1–7 ONLY

Fig. 6-17. Peripheral connector pinout. (Courtesy Apple Computer, Inc.)

Table 6-1 The Apple II Bus

Pin Number	Signal Name [1]	Mode [2]	Description
1	I/O SEL	I	INPUT/OUTPUT SELECT. Seven individually decoded lines for slots 1–7. I/O SEL at any one connector goes low during $\phi2$ when \$CN00–\$CNFF is accessed; N = slot number.
2–17	AD0–AD15	B	16-bit address bus. Address becomes valid during $\phi1$ and remains valid throughout $\phi2$.
18	R/W	B	READ/WRITE. Becomes valid during $\phi1$ and remains valid throughout $\phi2$. High for read; low for write.
19	SYNC	I	Video synchronization signal (C13-8). Connects to slot 7 only.
20	I/O STB	I	INPUT/OUTPUT STROBE. Common select line that goes low during $\phi2$ when \$C800–\$CFFF is accessed.
21	RDY	B	READY. Taken low during $\phi1$ to insert wait states. The 6502 recognizes low on RDY only during read cycles.
22	DMA	O	DIRECT MEMORY ACCESS. Taken low at the beginning of $\phi1$ to halt the processor and make the address, data, and R/W lines high impedance.
23	INT OUT	O	INTERRUPT OUT. Daisy chain to lower priority slots. Normally driven high if used; connects to pin 28 if not used.
24	DMA OUT	O	DIRECT MEMORY ACCESS OUT. Daisy chain to lower priority slots. Normally driven high if used; connects to pin 27 if not used.
25	+5 V		+ 5 volts
26	GND		Ground
27	DMA IN	I	DIRECT MEMORY ACCESS IN. Daisy chain input from higher priority slots. Normally high.
28	INT IN	I	INTERRUPT IN. Daisy chain input from higher priority slots. Normally high.
29	NMI	O	NON-MASKABLE INTERRUPT. Taken low to start a 6502 non-maskable interrupt.
30	IRQ	O	INTERRUPT REQUEST. Taken low to start a 6502 maskable interrupt. Recognized only if interrupt disable flag is not set.
31	RESET	B	As an output, taken low to reset the 6502 and other peripherals. As an input, goes low during resets from the keyboard, on power-up, and from other peripherals.

Table 6-1—cont. The Apple II Bus

Pin Number	Signal Name [1]	Mode [2]	Description
32	INH	O	INHIBIT. Taken low to inhibit the ROM address space ($D000–$FFFF).
33	–12 V		– 12 volts
34	–5 V		–5 volts
35	COLOR REF	I	COLOR REFERENCE. Connects to slot 7 only.
36	7M	I	7MHz. 7.15909 MHz clock.
37	Q3	I	2.040968 MHz (average) clock.
38	ϕ1	I	PHASE 1. 1.020484 MHz (average) system clock. Used on bus in place of 6502 ϕ1.
39	USER 1	O	Taken low to inhibit the I/O address space ($C000–$C7FF).
40	ϕ0	I	PHASE 0. 1.020484 MHz (average) system clock and compliment of ϕ1. Used on bus in place of 6502 ϕ2.
41	DEV SEL	I	DEVICE SELECT. Eight individually decoded select lines, one for each slot. DEV SEL at any one connector goes low during ϕ2 when $C0X0–$C0XF is accessed; X = N + 8, N = slot number.
42–49	D7–D0	B	Eight bit bidirectional data bus. Data becomes valid during ϕ2 and remains valid to the end of ϕ2.
50	+12 V		+ 12 volts

Notes: [1] Unless otherwise specified, all signals appear on all eight connectors.

[2] I: Input   With respect
O: Output   to peripheral
B: Bidirectional   card.

There are 19 clock cycles in the loop, giving a period of 19×978 nS = 18.58 μS. However, if an extended clock cycle falls during a period of the loop, then that period will be 18×978 nS + 1117 nS = 18.72 μS. Note the slight difference.

The extended clock cycles produce some subtle effects. We have just demonstrated the first effect. That is, if you are using a sequence of processor instructions to produce a short and precise delay, an extended cycle will increase your delay by 140 nS. A second effect was discussed in Chapter 3; extended cycles decrease the processor's speed from 1.023 MHz to 1.020 MHz. This slight difference would have an effect on the computation time of *very long* calculations.

A third effect arises since the processor clock is not a pure frequency—it has a 15.7 kHz component. To demonstrate this effect, consider our 'scope loop. It has an average period of $19 \div 1.020$ MHz = 18.63 μS. Each time through the loop the speaker is toggled. A complete period of speaker cone movement requires two passes through the loop. This period is 37.3 μS. The frequency is 26.8 kHz—too high to hear. Yet when you run the 'scope loop, you *do* hear a high pitched sound from the speaker. What you hear is the beat between 26.8 kHz and the 15.7 kHz clock component—this is 11.1 kHz, clearly audible.

SUMMARY

This chapter concludes with a summary of the Apple II bus. A brief review of each signal is given in Table 6-1. Fig. 6-17 shows the physical arrangement of the bus on the peripheral connectors.

In the next chapter we will examine the on-board I/O and the soft switches.

CHAPTER 7

On-Board I/O

A computer is of little use unless it communicates with the outside world via its I/O facilities. Minimum I/O usually consists of a keyboard for input and a crt display for output. Some computer architectures require plug-in peripheral boards to provide *any* I/O, including this minimum set. In the Apple II, many of the frequently used I/O devices are located on the mother board. This built-in I/O contributes to your ability to just plug in the Apple II and start computing.

In this chapter we cover the built-in or *on-board* I/O. This includes the cassette I/O, the game port, the speaker, and the keyboard.

Schematic Reference: Figs. C-12*, C-13*, and C-22*.

OVERVIEW

In Chapter 6 we mentioned that the address range $C000–$C07F was used for the on-board I/O. This range is decoded by ICs F13 and F14 (Fig. C-12*). There are nine inputs and 13 outputs listed as follows:

Inputs	Outputs
Keyboard	Clear Keyboard Strobe
Cassette Tape	Cassette Tape
Game Switches 0–2	Speaker
Game Paddles 0–3	Game Paddle Trigger
	Game Utility Strobe
	Game Annunciators 0–3
	TEXT Soft Switch
	Mixed Mode Soft Switch
	Page 2 Soft Switch
	HIRES Soft Switch

Keyboard

The built-in keyboard consists of two printed-circuit boards. On one board are mounted the 52 keys. On the second board are mounted five ICs and assorted discrete components. Keyboard encoder IC B6 scans the 47 character keys looking for one that is depressed. These 47 keys are arranged in a 9 by 10 matrix as shown in Fig. C-22*. Not every point in the matrix is occupied by a key. This matrix arrangement allows B6 to detect a key closure using only 19 instead of 47 pins. When B6 detects a depressed key, it generates the corresponding ASCII character at its output. If the SHIFT key, CTRL key, or both are also depressed, B6 generates the ASCII character for a shift, control, or shift-control function. The output of B6 is buffered by B5 and B4-3 then connects by a short flat cable to A7 on the mother board.

Timer IC B2 is connected to oscillate at about 15 Hz. It provides a repeat strobe to B3-3 when the REPT key is depressed. The RESET key connects directly via the flat cable to A7 on the mother board. Note that the SHIFT, CTRL, and REPT keys do not generate characters unless used with another key. The RESET key also does not generate characters since it connects directly to the 6502.

Cassette Tape

The Apple II can store and retrieve digital data using a standard audio cassette tape recorder. The hardware involved is fairly simple; all the intelligence is in the firmware. When you store a program, routines in the monitor ROM cause flip-flop J13-9 (Fig. C-12*) to generate square or rectangular waveforms. Thus, J13-8 then drives the CASSETTE DATA OUT jack. This jack is meant to be connected to the microphone input of the recorder.

The earphone output of the recorder connects to the CASSETTE DATA IN jack of the Apple. When you load a program, the signals from the tape pass through operational amplifier K13, then appear at an input of data selector H14. The 6502 can read the output of H14 under program control. The program (again in the monitor ROM) then processes the cassette signal to reproduce the data.

Speaker

Tones are produced in the speaker of the Apple by toggling flip-flop J13-5 under program control. Transistor Q4 amplifies the output of J13-5 to drive the speaker.

Game Connector

Several of the on-board inputs and outputs appear at connector J14 (Fig. 7-1). Although J14 is called the "game connector," it can have other applications.

Up to three switches can connect to the J14 pins named SW0, SW1, and SW2

Fig. 7-1.   Game connector.

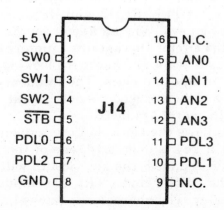

The 6502 can select and read the switches via H14 (Fig. C-12*). In the game application, the switches are usually momentary-operate push buttons.

Up to four variable resistors can connect to J14 at the pins named PDL0– PDL3. These external variable resistors control the timing of quad timer H13. The four outputs of H13 connect to H14 which selects one of them to be read by the 6502. By using a software timing routine, the 6502 can measure the pulse duration of the timer. This duration is in turn a function of the external resistance connected to PDL0– PDL3. In the game application, the external resistance is usually a paddle or joystick.

Signal $\overline{STB}$ on the game connector is a utility strobe. It is activated under program control and its application is determined by the user. Signal $\overline{STB}$ goes low for 489 nS whenever the address range $C040–$C04F is accessed.

The application of game connector signals AN0 (Annunciator 0) through AN3 is also up to the user. These four signals are *soft switches*. This means they act like switches that are under software control. The software can turn them on or off, and they will stay in that condition until accessed again. An application for one of the annunciator outputs is use as a serial output port driven by a software UART.

More Soft Switches

Four of F14's outputs are soft switches used by the video circuitry to configure the video memory mapping. We made use of one of these (PAGE 2) in Chapter 5. We will find uses for the others in Chapter 8. All four are listed in Table 7-1.

Table 7-1. F14 Soft Switches

IC Pin	Signal Name
F14-4	TEXT MODE
F14-5	MIX MODE
F14-6	PAGE 2
F14-7	HIRES MODE

DETAILED CIRCUIT ANALYSIS

Two-Piece Keyboard

Keyboard Encoder IC—At the heart of the keyboard is B6 (Fig. C-22*), a type AY-5-3600 scanning keyboard encoder IC. The 9 X outputs and 10 Y inputs of B6 are arranged in a matrix with the character keys at the cross points. (*Character keys* exclude SHIFT, CTRL, REPT, and RESET.) Only 47 of the possible 90 cross points are occupied by keys. When a key is depressed, it connects the X line to the Y line.

Integrated circuit B6 contains counters that count through an X sequence and a Y sequence as it scans the keyboard looking for a depressed key. These counters are driven from an internal clock. The frequency of the clock is about 90 kHz and is set by R1 and C5. The frequency is not critical, but it must be between 10 kHz and 100 kHz for B6 to operate properly.

Fig. 7-2 shows the clock and the sequence of pulses generated on the X outputs of B6. When a key is depressed, one of the X outputs connects to a Y input. When this Y input is scanned, the key closure will be detected. Keyboard encoder B6 then "looks" at the SHIFT and CTRL key inputs and encodes the key into the proper ASCII character. The character is latched and appears inverted at B6's output (B1

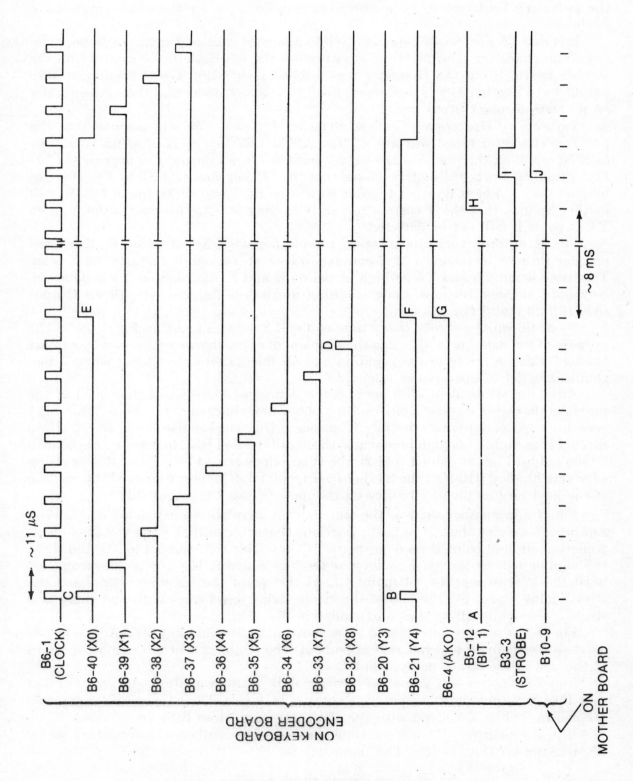

Fig. 7-2. X scan (two-piece keyboard).

through B7). (B6 is a mask programmed device. The mask determines the exact encoding of matrix cross points into output codes. The device used in the two-piece keyboard has been custom programmed for Apple Computer. This custom IC allows the two-piece keyboard to be a functional replacement for the older single-piece keyboard.)

Inverter B5 and NAND gate B4-3 buffer the character and invert it to positive-true. The character then finds its way through the flat cable to location A7 on the mother board. Since the character was latched inside B6, it will remain at B6's output until another key is depressed. Each time a key is closed, B6 outputs a pulse on its Data Strobe Output (pin 16).

Sequence of Operation—(Follow along on Fig. 7-2.) We will assume that the previous character typed was an "8." The ASCII LSB for "8" is 0, so B5-12 will be latched low from the previous character (point A). Now suppose you depress the "7" key. From the keyboard matrix we see that the "7" key connects X0 to Y4. Thus, as long as the "7" key is down, Y4 (point B) will be the same as X0 (point C). We will further assume that the Y scan is currently looking at Y3. This means the high on Y4 at point B will not be detected.

The X outputs continue to scan, completing with X8·at point D. Keyboard encoder B6 now increments its Y counter to look at Y4, and it restarts·the X scan. This time when X0 and Y4 go high at points E and F, the high on Y4 *is* detected. Keyboard encoder B6 now stops scanning and takes its Any Key Down Output (AKO) high (point G).

Next, B6 waits a *Strobe Delay* time of about 8 mS (set by C2 in Fig. C-22*). The purpose of the delay is to alleviate the problem of extra characters caused by contact bounce. (Bounce refers to the rapid on and off fluctuations that occur when a mechanical switch is operated or released.)

After the strobe delay, B6 encodes the depressed key. Recall that bit 1 of the previous character was low, point A. Bit 1 of our new character (7) is high. Thus, bit 1 goes high (point H) when the key is encoded. One clock pulse later, B6-16 (Data Strobe) goes high. This high propagates through B3-6 and B3-3 to take the keyboard's strobe output high at point I. The strobe is one clock period long. The strobe's rising edge sets flip-flop B10-9 on the mother board, point J. (Chapter 6 covered the reading of the keyboard as far as circuitry on the mother board is concerned.)

Fig. 7-3 is another view of the signals that were shown expanded in Fig. 7-2. Again let's assume that "8" was the previous character so that B1 is low at point A. Sometime around point B we depress the "7" key. This connects Y4 to X0, and these two signals will be the same as long as the key is down. The key is not recognized until the Y scan reaches Y4 (point C). At this point the scanning stops, and the strobe delay starts. At the end of the strobe delay, bit 1 goes high and there is a strobe pulse (point D) as shown expanded in Fig. 7-2.

Fig. 7-4 is a more compressed view showing a complete key stroke. The key is depressed at point A and released at point B. The strobe is sent to the mother board at the end of the strobe delay, point C.

Non-TTL Levels—If you observe the matrix with an oscilloscope, you will find that B6's X outputs and Y inputs are not at TTL levels. Their typical voltage levels are shown in Fig. 7-5 along with the clock waveform from B6-1.

Repeat Function—B2 is a 555 timer connected to oscillate at a frequency set by R8, R7, and C7 (Fig. C-22*). The frequency is

$$\frac{1.44}{(R8 + 2R7)C7} = 15 \text{ Hz}$$

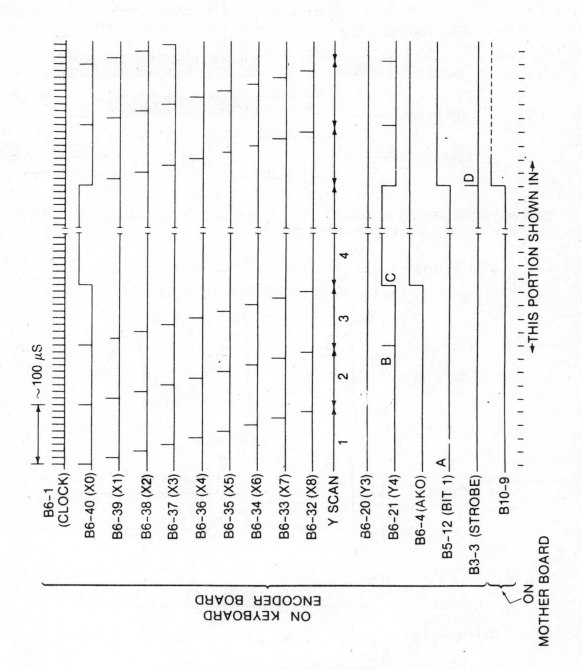

Fig. 7-3. Y scan (two-piece keyboard).

B2 is normally held reset by R10. When the REPT key is depressed, and another key is also pressed (AKO high), then the reset is removed. Timer B2 now oscillates and its output is coupled through C6 to gates B4-11, B4-8, and B3-3. The 15-Hz pulses at B3-1 create additional strobe pulses to the mother board.

Roll Over and Phantoms—The keyboard encoder IC is capable of *N-key roll over*. N-key roll over means that you can have any number of keys down simultaneously, and the encoder will correctly send the characters in the order keyed. This capability, however, can be used only if there is a diode at every cross point in the key matrix. The Apple II keyboard does not have these diodes. Without them, de-

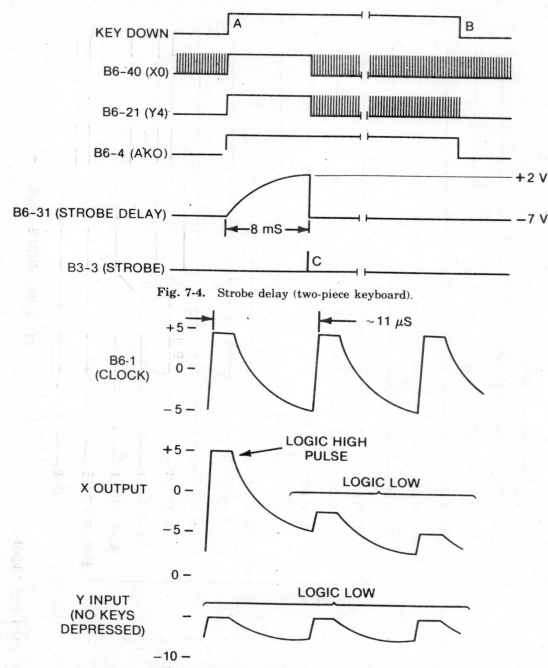

Fig. 7-4. Strobe delay (two-piece keyboard).

Fig. 7-5. Typical AY-5-3600 keyboard encoder waveforms (two-piece keyboard).

pressing three or more keys simultaneously may generate extraneous or *phantom* characters. As a result, the keyboard is described as having *2-key roll over*. No more than two keys may be depressed simultaneously if phantom characters are to be avoided.

It is the sneak paths that are possible in a matrix without diodes that generate the phantom characters. For example, simultaneously pressing the space, N, and B keys will connect X4 to Y4. This creates a phantom "A." Simultaneously pressing space, N, and M will connect X4 to Y6. No key is assigned to this matrix cross point. However, the AY-5-3600 will still output a character. In the original AY-5-3600 mask, all unused matrix cross points were programmed to be an ASCII *null*. A null typed inadvertently in a Pascal program can be undesirable. A later mask for the AY-5-3600 programs all unused cross points to be an ASCII *space*. These two versions of encoder IC are identified as 331-0931-A and 331-0931-B, respectively.

Quad-Mode Operation—B6 is a *quad-mode* encoder. This means each key can generate up to four different characters as a function of the SHIFT and CTRL keys (Table 7-2).

Table 7-2. Characters as a Function of Control and Shift

B6-28 (CTRL)	B6-29 (SHIFT)	Character Group
0	0	Unshift
0	1	Shift
1	0	Control
1	1	Shift-Control

The four characters for each key are shown in Fig. C-22*. Only the "P," "M," and "N" keys generate four different characters. The rest generate fewer.

Lowercase—There are two bow ties on the board with the ICs. They may be cut as a user option. The circuit is then restored by adding switch S2. In the normal position of S2, the circuit functions as previously described. When S2 is operated, output bits 9 and 8 are substituted for bits 5 and 6. Encoder B6 has been programmed with ASCII lowercase letters. This substitution of bits will make the lowercase letters available. Lowercase operation is as follows: with the shift key not depressed, pressing any letter key will output lowercase. With the shift key pressed, pressing any letter key will output uppercase. The three characters @,], and ˆ are not available directly from the keyboard when S2 is in its lowercase position.

Numeric Pad—As a user option, a nine-pin connector may be installed on the keyboard at J2. Then J2 can be extended to a numeric pad as shown in Fig. C-22*.

Accidental Reset—To prevent accidental resets, S1 may be moved to its "CTRL" position (pins 1 and 2 connected). In this position of S1, it is necessary to press both CTRL and RESET to reset the Apple.

Cassette Tape

In this section we will describe the hardware involved in writing and reading cassette tapes. We will also touch on some aspects of the cassette system that are actually determined by the firmware.

Data to be recorded on tape is formatted into *records*. Each record consists of several seconds of *header tone* followed by a *sync bit,* the actual data, and a *check sum*. Binary files and machine code are recorded as one record (Fig. 7-6A). BASIC

HEADER	SYNC	DATA	CHECK SUM

(A)   Binary files or machine code.

HEADER	SYNC	LENGTH	CHECK SUM	HEADER	SYNC	PROGRAM	CHECK SUM

(B) BASIC programs.

Fig. 7-6. Cassette tape formats.

programs are recorded as two records (Fig. 7-6B). The first record contains the BASIC program's length in the record's data field. The second record contains the BASIC program itself.

Fig. 7-7 shows individual bits or cycles of the tones that make up the format. The times shown are approximate, but they are within 2% of measured values. The header tone consists of half cycles of 650 microseconds each. This is a frequency of 770 Hz. The sync bit contains one-half cycle of 200 microseconds followed by one-half cycle of 250 microseconds. A 0 bit consists of two 250 microsecond half cycles. Data of all 0's would be a tone of 2000 Hz. A 1 bit consists of two half cycles of 500 microseconds each. Data of all 1's would be a 1000-Hz (1-kHz) tone. It takes 500 microseconds to transmit a 0 and 1000 microseconds to transmit a 1. The average transmission rate for random data is therefore 1333 bits per second.

Data is recorded low byte first. Within each byte the MSB is recorded first.

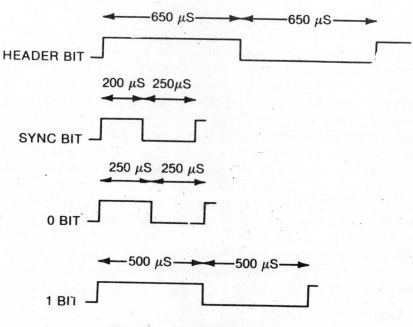

Fig. 7-7. Cassette bit timing.

Fig. 7-8 shows typical tape cassette waveforms near the time of the sync bit. When the cassette output ($C020–$C02F) is accessed, J13-11 goes low for 489 nS (point A). On J13-11's rising edge, J13-8 is clocked (point B). Since J13-8 connects to J13-12 (Fig. C-12*), this flip-flop will toggle when clocked. In Fig. 7-8 we have shown the last two and one-half cycles of the header tone. The sync bit comes next, followed by the first data byte. In this example, the first byte is $B0 or 10110000 (binary).

Note that on power-up, J13-8 can be either low or high. The processor can neither initialize nor read the state of J13-8. As a result, the J13-8 waveform could be inverted from what is shown in Fig. 7-8. No matter in which state J13-8 starts, it toggles every time J13-11 goes high. That is all that matters.

Resistors R18 and R19 attenuate J13-8 to about 0.8%, or 32 mV peak-peak open circuit. The attenuated signal appears at the CASSETTE DATA OUT jack of the Apple. It is connected to the microphone input of the recorder when data is stored. This concludes the discussion of the hardware used in the write direction. We now turn our attention to the read process.

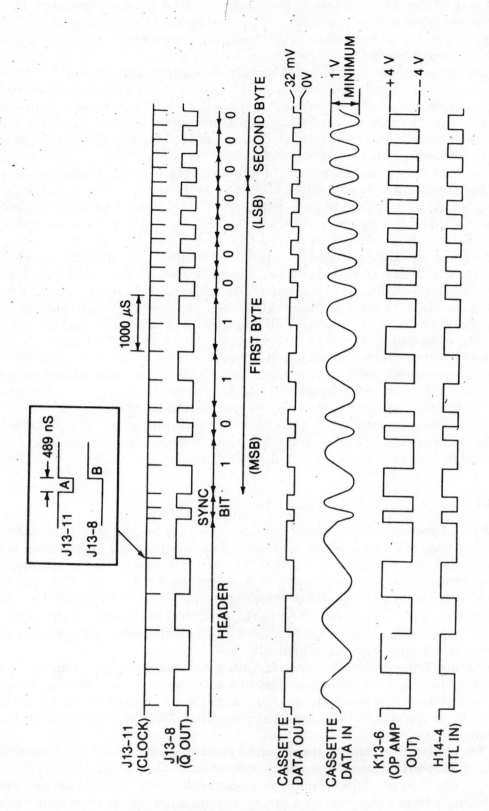

Fig. 7-8. Tape cassette waveforms.

On data retrieval, the earphone jack of the recorder connects to the CASSETTE DATA IN jack of the Apple. There may or may not be a polarity inversion in going through the recorder; it does not matter. The cassette input is ac coupled by C10 and attenuated to 50% by R17 and R30. The signal then connects to the inverting input of operational amplifier K13.

Operational amplifier K13 is wired to act as a comparator. Ground through R16 provides an average comparator threshold of 0 volt and R15 provides about 100 mV of hysteresis at the input of the comparator. This circuit arrangement is called a zero crossing detector. The minimum cassette input that produces good results is about 1 volt peak-peak. While reading tapes, the output of K13 swings from plus-saturated to minus-saturated, or about ± 4 volts.

Resistor R29 limits current out of the input of H14 when K13-6 is low. Resistor R29 and the input clamping diode of H14 effectively convert the signal to a TTL level at H14-4. Note that the signal is inverted by K13. Except for an inversion, the TTL signal at J13-8 has been recreated at H14-4. To see this, compare the waveforms for J13-8 and H14-4 as shown in Fig. 7-8.

At this point we must discuss how the cassette signal gets through data selector H14 (Fig. C-12*). If the address is in the range $C060–$C06F, then F13-9 will go low during φ2. This enables H14 via pin 7. Data selector H14 selects one of its eight inputs as a function of address lines AD0, AD1, and AD2. When the address is $C060 or $C068 (AD0, AD1, and AD2 all equal 0), H14 is enabled and selects input pin 4 to output on pin 5. Pin H14-5 connects to data bus bit 7. Thus, at either of these addresses, the cassette input is put on data bus bit 7. Bit 7 is used since it is easily tested by various 6502 instructions. Since AD3 is not decoded by this part of the circuit, there are two addresses eight locations apart that can access the cassette input. In such cases, we usually use the lower address ($C060).

Routines in the monitor scan bit 7 at location $C060 every 12.8 microseconds looking for a transition. By measuring the time between transitions, the routines can distinguish between header, sync, 0, and 1 bits.

Speaker

Decoder F13-12 goes low during φ2 whenever the range $C030–$C03F is addressed. On the rising edge of F13-12, J13-5 is clocked. This flip-flop will toggle since pin 6 is tied to pin 2. It takes two accesses to $C030 to generate one period of speaker oscillation. The square or rectangular wave at J13-5 is coupled through C11 and R24 to the base of Q4. Diode CR1 provides a discharge path for C11. Transistor Q4 is a Darlington pair that amplifies the signal to drive the speaker through R25. Capacitor C12 provides some integration and also absorbs some of the energy stored in the speaker winding when Q4 turns off.

To generate tones from the speaker, you must calculate the number of clock cycles needed between each toggle. The clock cycles are then obtained using a software loop. Using this method, you can generate tones from below to above the audible range. If you want absolute pitch, remember that the average clock cycle is 980 nS long.

Fig. 7-9 shows the voltage (to ground) measured at the internal speaker for 1002-Hz and 10.4-kHz tones. Note the overshoot at each transition.

You can get a much fuller sound by disconnecting the small internal speaker and connecting a larger external speaker. Be careful with the speaker leads; one side is connected directly to +5 volts.

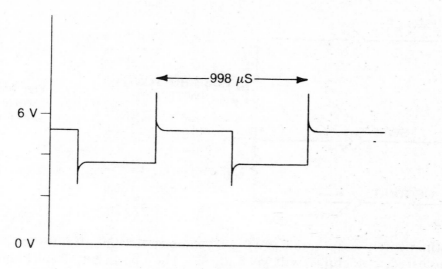

(A) 1002-Hz tone.

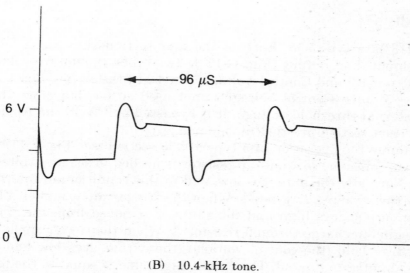

(B) 10.4-kHz tone.

Fig. 7-9. Speaker output.

Game Switches

The three game switches (SW0–SW2) connect to inputs of data selector H14 (Fig. C-12*). The operation of H14 was described in the section on the cassette input. Here we list the addresses that will select the game switches (Table 7-3).

Table 7-3. Addresses and Game Switches

Location	Game Switch
$C061 and $C069	SW0
$C062 and $C06A	SW1
$C063 and $C06B	SW2

A game switch is typically wired as shown in Fig. 7-10. With the switch normal, the 560-ohm resistor pulls SW0 low. When $C061 is accessed, data bit 7 will go low

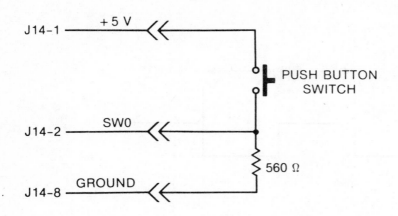

Fig. 7-10. Game switch—SW0 is shown as typical.

(0). When the switch is operated, SW0 will connect to +5 volts (high). Now when $C061 is accessed, data bit 7 will go high (1). The operation of SW1 and SW2 is identical to that of SW0.

Game Paddles

Quad timer H13 is a type 558. Each of the four sections has an isolated trigger input, timing input, and output (Fig. C-12*). Two other inputs are common to all sections: $\overline{\text{Reset}}$ (pin 13) and Control Voltage (pin 4). In the Apple, $\overline{\text{Reset}}$ is not used and is tied to +5 volts. Control Voltage is not used either, but since this pin can influence an internal threshold voltage, it is bypassed by C9. In the Apple, the trigger inputs for each section are tied in common.

Let us examine the operation of a typical 558 section (see Fig. 7-11A). The output stage is open collector, so a pull-up resistor is needed to see any voltage changes at the output. Normally the output is low, and in this condition an internal transistor shunts the timing input to ground. When the trigger input makes a high-to-low transition, the output goes high and the shunt is removed from the timing input. Capacitor C begins to charge through resistor R. When the timing input reaches an internally set threshold (the control voltage), the output goes low and the timing input is again shunted to ground. The output high time is equal to the product RC.

Once the timer has triggered, the trigger input has no effect until the output is low again. This characteristic of the trigger input will be used later in this section to explain a well-known paddle phenomena. First, however, we will see how the 558 is used in the Apple.

Apple's paddle scheme functions by replacing R in Fig. 7-11A with a variable resistor and measuring the timer's pulse width using the 6502. Here are the circuit details. The trigger inputs of all four sections connect in common to F13-7 (Fig. C-12*). This line goes low during $\phi2$ in the address range $C070–$C07F. The 6502 uses address $C070 to trigger all four timers. The output of each timer connects to an input of H14. This IC can select one of these inputs in the same manner that it selects an input from the game switches or the cassette (described in previous sections). The 6502 reads the timer outputs by addressing the locations shown in Table 7-4.

The timing capacitors for each section (C5, C6, C7, and C8) have values of 0.022 microfarad. The timing resistors for each section consist of 100 ohms (Ω) on the mother board (R20, R21, R22, and R23) plus the resistance of the paddles. Fig. 7-12

Table 7-4. Addresses and Game Paddles

Location	Paddle
$C064 and $C06C	0
$C065 and $C06D	1
$C066 and $C06E	2
$C067 and $C06F	3

shows the usual wiring of a game paddle. Apple recommends a 150 kΩ value. The longest pulse width is

$$(150 \text{ k}\Omega + 100 \text{ }\Omega) \times 0.022 \text{ }\mu\text{F} = 3.30 \text{ mS}$$

The shortest pulse is

$$100 \text{ }\Omega \times 0.022 \text{ }\mu\text{F} = 2.2 \text{ }\mu\text{S}$$

The purpose of the 100 Ω resistor is to provide some protection for H13 from external shorts and from the condition when the external resistance goes to 0.

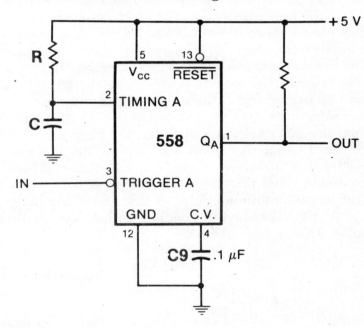

(A) Typical wiring diagram.

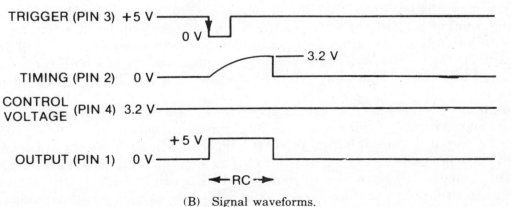

(B) Signal waveforms.

Fig. 7-11. 558 timer.

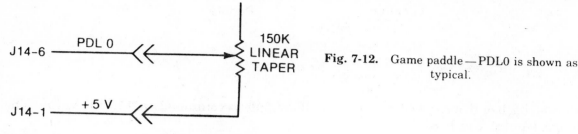

Fig. 7-12. Game paddle — PDL0 is shown as typical.

That's it for the hardware, now how does the firmware determine the position of the paddle? There is a monitor routine at $FB1E that triggers H13, then enters a loop to count until the output of H13 returns low. Fig. 7-13 shows the flowchart. You enter the routine with the paddle number (0–3) in the X register. The routine first triggers H13 (F13-7 goes low). Next the Y register, used for the counter, is initialized to 0. The routine now delays about 4 μS, then reads the timer output for the specified paddle (F13-9 goes low). If the paddle output is low on the first read, this indicates a very short pulse (low resistance). You exit the routine with Y = 0.

If the first read is not low, the routine increments the counter (Y register) and then checks for counter overflow. By overflow we mean that the Y register overflows (counts) from 255 to 0. If there is no overflow, the routine reads the paddle again. The time around the loop is 11 clock cycles, or 10.8 μS. When the timer output goes low, you exit the routine with the paddle position value in the Y register. At the high resistance end of the paddle, the counter may overflow. In this case, the routine decrements the counter and you exit with Y = 255. Note that as the paddle moves from lowest to highest resistance, the paddle value changes from 0 to 255.

Recall that there is a minimun of 100 Ω designed into the circuit. The game paddle may also have some "end resistance." These two items together produce a minimum timer pulse of several microseconds. The 4 μS initial delay in the routine bridges this minimum pulse so that the minimum paddle value can be 0.

At the other end of paddle rotation, we found that 150 K gave us a 3.30 mS pulse. This is equivalent to

$$\frac{3.30 \text{ mS}}{10.8 \text{ } \mu\text{S}} = 305 \text{ counts}$$

Thus, we are assured of reaching the maximum paddle value of 255.

You may already know that if you read the value of one paddle too soon after reading another paddle, the value of the second paddle may be in error. Fig. 7-14 shows why this is so. We will take the case where PDL 0 is set for a value of 45 and PDL 1 is set for a value of 240. At point A, the program triggers both timers. After about 500 μS, timer 0 times out (point B), and the program displays a PDL 0 value of 45.

As fast as Integer BASIC can, it triggers the timers again (point C). Timer 0 outputs another pulse (point D), but we don't care since we are now reading timer 1. Timer 1's output is still high from the first trigger; it will not time out until point E. Timer 1 has ignored the trigger at point C. The monitor routine times from point C to point E (about 450 μS) and returns with a PDL 1 value of 40, clearly in error. To correct the situation, you must insert some delay between consecutive reads of different paddles. The total delay between consecutive triggers should be greater than 4 mS.

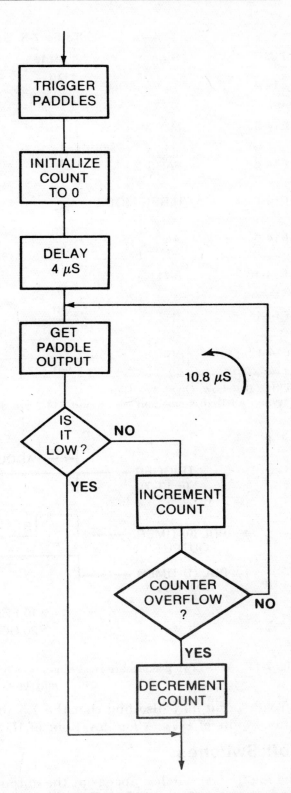

Fig. 7-13. Read game paddle flowchart.

If you examine the outputs of H13 with an oscilloscope, you may see some strange voltage levels. This is due to the lack of pull-up resistors on H13's open collector outputs. The only pull-up on these lines comes from the inputs of H14. The result is a high level of about 1.5 volts instead of the more typical TTL high level of

Table 7-5. Soft Switches

Pin	Signal	State*	Location	Function
F14-4	TEXT MODE	Off	$C050	Graphics or mixed
		On	$C051	All-Text**
F14-5	MIX MODE	Off	$C052	All-Text or graphics
		On	$C053	Mixed
F14-6	PAGE 2	Off	$C054	Select page 1
		On	$C055	Select page 2
F14-7	HIRES MODE	Off	$C056	Select LORES
		On	$C057	Select HIRES
F14-9	AN0	Off	$C058	
		On	$C059	
F14-10	AN1	Off	$C05A	
		On	$C05B	
F14-11	AN2	Off	$C05C	
		On	$C05D	
F14-12	AN3	Off	$C05E	
		On	$C05F	

*Off = 0 = Low, On = 1 = High
**When All-Text is selected, F14-5 and F14-7 are don't cares.

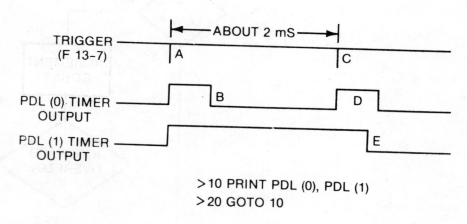

>10 PRINT PDL (0), PDL (1)
>20 GOTO 10

Fig. 7-14. When two paddles are read consecutively without inserting delay, the second paddle value may be in error.

3.5 volts. You may also find that the 1.5 volt high level varies as a function of the other inputs of H14. A *low* level out of H13 looks normal however (0 to 0.4 volt).

Soft Switches

The eight soft switches appear at the outputs of addressable latch F14 (Fig. C-12*). Whenever the range $C050–$C05F is accessed, F13-10 goes low during φ2. This enables F14. The three address bits AD1, AD2, and AD3 select one of the eight outputs of F14. When enabled, F14 latches the data on pin 13 into the selected output. Input F14-13 connects to address bit AD0, so even addresses will latch a 0 into the output. Likewise, odd addresses will latch a 1 into the selected output.

Table 7-6. On-Board I/O Locations

Location	Function	Remarks
$C000	Keyboard Data Input	*
$C010	Clear Keyboard Strobe	*
$C020	Toggle Cassette Output	*
$C030	Toggle Speaker	*
$C040	Game Utility Strobe	*
$C050-$C05F	Soft Switches	See Table 7-5
$C060 & $C068	Cassette Input	
$C061 & $C069	Game SW0	
$C062 & $C06A	Game SW1	
$C063 & $C06B	Game SW2	
$C064 & $C06C	Game PDL0	
$C065 & $C06D	Game PDL1	
$C066 & $C06E	Game PDL2	
$C067 & $C06F	Game PDL3	
$C070	Game Paddle Trigger	

*Any of 16 locations starting with the listed location will perform the same function.

Two output states times eight different outputs is equal to 16. Thus, all 16 locations in the range $C050–$C05F are separately decoded by F14. Table 7-5 shows each location and its function. For example, to select a mixed TEXT and LORES display from page 1, you would access locations $C050, $C053, $C054, and $C056. Use of the soft switches to control the display will be covered in detail in Chapter 8.

SUMMARY

Table 7-6 is a summary of the I/O address locations covered in this chapter.

In the next chapter, we will explore the video display modes of TEXT, LORES, HIRES, and mixed.

8

The Video Display

The Apple II's video display is one of its greatest assets. There are three basic modes: black and white text, 16-color low resolution graphics (LORES), and 6-color high resolution graphics (HIRES). Two additional modes allow text to be mixed with either LORES or HIRES graphics. All three basic modes can display either a primary page of memory (Page 1) or a secondary page of memory (Page 2). This chapter describes the video display circuitry and explains how colors are generated by the digital electronics.

OVERVIEW

We start our overview of this chapter with a review of Apple's video display characteristics. In text mode, the display is 40 characters wide by 24 characters high. Each of these 960 characters is stored as one byte in a 1024 byte block of memory. The range of this block is shown as follows:

Page 1 $400–$7FF
Page 2 $800–$BFF

The page to be displayed is selected by the PAGE 2 soft switch. (Table 7-5 lists the soft switch address locations.)

In LORES mode, the display contains 1920 *pixels* arranged 40 wide by 48 high. A pixel is a *picture element,* and is used here to describe one of the LORES color blocks. LORES uses the same Page 1 and Page 2 memory ranges as text mode. In LORES, each byte stores two vertically adjacent pixels. Of a byte, the four low order bits store the upper pixel, and the four high order bits store the lower pixel. The information stored in the four bits is the pixel's color. There are 16 colors possible.

In HIRES mode, the display is 192 pixels high. A HIRES pixel is a mere dot, much smaller than a LORES pixel. It is a little difficult to specify the number of HIRES pixels in the horizontal direction. The width of a pixel is such that 280 pixels can fit on one horizontal line. Thus, the HIRES horizontal resolution is usually defined as 280 pixels. However, there are actually 560 *positions* where pixels can be placed. Here is how we explain this concept. Divide the line into 280 equal parts called *cells*. The design of the Apple is such that you can position a pixel to be coincident with a cell. You can also position a pixel so that it overlaps two cells, one-half in one and one-half in another. Taken over the full width of the line, there are then 560 positions where you can locate a pixel.

We have not yet said anything about the color of the pixel. On a black and white monitor, there is no color and each pixel is either on (white) or off (black). In black and white HIRES we have 560 horizontal plotting positions.

Color HIRES is a different matter. Here the pixel's exact position will determine its color. If we step a single pixel across the screen, stopping at each of the 560 locations, the pixel's color will sequence through violet, blue, green, orange, violet, etc. Any one color can appear at only one out of four positions. Thus, the color HIRES horizontal resolution could be defined as 140 pixels.

There are two more limitations on color HIRES resolution. First, two adjacent pixels will not display in color, but will be a white dot. Of course you may want a white dot. Second, the pixels stored by any one byte must be selected from one and only one of the following two lists:

List 1	List 2
Violet	Blue
Green	Orange
White	White
Black	Black

Thus, for example, you cannot mix green and orange pixels in the same byte.

One memory byte stores the pixels for seven adjacent cells. The 280 cells per line result in 40 bytes per line, and the 192 lines per screen result in 7680 bytes per screen. In practice, an even 8K-byte memory block stores one HIRES screen:

Page 1	$2000–$3FFF
Page 2	$4000–$5FFF

There are two varieties of mixed mode: text mixed with LORES graphics and text mixed with HIRES graphics. In both cases, the lower one-sixth of the screen contains four lines of text characters.

Fig. 8-1 is a high level block diagram of the video display process. When you display text or graphics, you first configure the circuitry for the desired mode by setting the soft switches under 6502 software control. Next you again use the 6502 to write to the desired locations in the screen memory. Meanwhile the video address generator is always running, using the system clock to create the video address, blanking, sync, and color burst signals. The video address maps to a memory address, and then accesses the screen memory (RAM). The RAM's data is latched and made available to the video generator. The video generator is enabled and disabled by the blanking signal. The video generator also uses inputs from the soft switches to configure itself for the selected mode. Its function is to convert the latched data into a video output. This video output is combined with the sync and color burst signals in Q3 (Fig. 8-1). The output of Q3 is the Apple's composite video output which is used to drive a monitor or an rf modulator. The video generator is the subject of this chapter; the other blocks in Fig. 8-1 have been covered in preceding chapters as noted in the figure.

Fig. 8-2 is a block diagram of the video generator. The ICs that make up each

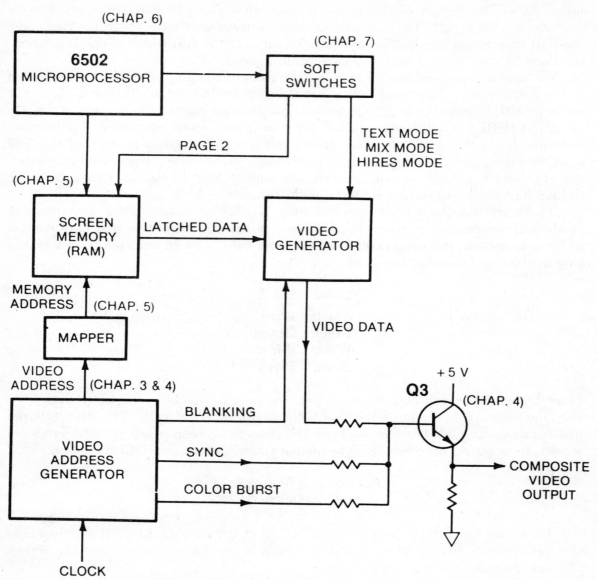

(CHAP. 6)

6502
MICROPROCESSOR

(CHAP. 7)

SOFT
SWITCHES

TEXT MODE
MIX MODE
HIRES MODE

PAGE 2

(CHAP. 5)

SCREEN
MEMORY
(RAM)

LATCHED DATA

VIDEO
GENERATOR

MEMORY
ADDRESS

(CHAP. 5)

MAPPER

VIDEO DATA

VIDEO
ADDRESS

(CHAP. 3 & 4)

+ 5 V

Q3   (CHAP. 4)

VIDEO
ADDRESS
GENERATOR

BLANKING

SYNC

COLOR BURST

COMPOSITE
VIDEO
OUTPUT

CLOCK

Fig. 8-1. Block diagram of video display process.

block are noted in the figure. The text generator consists of a character generator, a shift register, a timer (for flashing characters), and gates to produce flashing and inverse text. The text generator is always running. It processes the latched data at its input into text at its output. The text video becomes an input to data selector A9.

Shift registers B4 and B9 are configured by data selector A8. When HIRES MODE is low, each shift register takes four bits of latched data at its input and produces a LORES pixel at its output. The LORES video becomes another input to data selector A9.

When HIRES MODE is high, A8 configures B4 and B9 into one long shift register. This long shift register takes the latched data at its input and produces seven HIRES pixels at its output. The HIRES video becomes a third input to A9. Note that shift registers B4 and B9 are always running, producing either LORES or HIRES video.

The TEXT MODE, MIX MODE, and HIRES MODE soft switches cause data

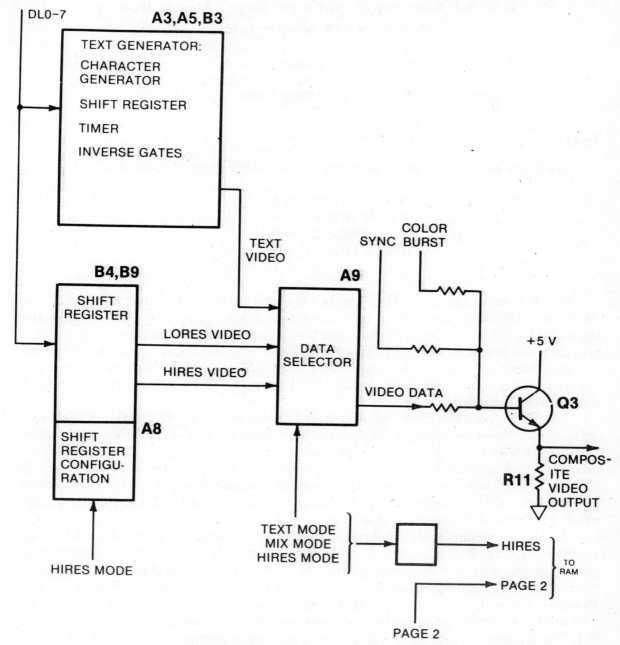

Fig. 8-2. Block diagram of video generator.

selector A9 to select either text video, LORES video, or HIRES video to output toward Q3. There, the video is mixed with SYNC and COLOR BURST to create the composite video output.

TEXT MODE, MIX MODE, and HIRES MODE are combined to generate the signal HIRES. HIRES and PAGE 2 map to memory as described in Chapter 5 and as summarized in Table 8-1.

The way in which data selectors A8 and A9 reconfigure the circuit under control of the soft switches is a key concept in understanding the video generator. Each configuration will be covered separately in the sections that follow.

Table 8-1. Summary of HIRES and Page 2 Map to Memory

PAGE 2	HIRES	Memory Space
0	0	Page 1 Text/LORES
0	1	Page 1 HIRES
1	0	Page 2 Text/LORES
1	1	Page 2 HIRES

Text

The following soft switch settings configure the video generator for All-Text:

$$\text{TEXT MODE} = 1$$
$$\text{MIX MODE} = X$$
$$\text{PAGE 2} = 0 \text{ or } 1$$
$$\text{HIRES MODE} = X$$
$$(X = \text{Don't care})$$

Fig. 8-3 shows the block diagram for this configuration. The first block, A5, is a 2K by 8-bit ROM that has been programmed to contain the same ASCII character set as contained in a type 2513 character generator. Thus A5 takes the six low order latched data bits and interprets them as a set of 64 characters. This character set includes numerals, uppercase letters, and most ASCII symbols. It does not include lowercase letters and some remaining ASCII symbols. The output of A5 is a 5 by 7 dot matrix character (Fig. 8-4).

The ROM, A5, generates the character one row at a time. Each row in the character is displayed by adjacent horizontal scan lines on the crt. It takes eight scan lines to display a complete character (including a vertical space above each character). Of course these 8 scan lines also display the other 39 characters in a line of text. As the crt beam scans down the screen, the signals VA, VB, and VC increment at each line. This is shown in Fig. 8-4. Signals VA, VB, and VC address the appropriate contents of A5 on each new row.

At any particular row, the dots on that row are output in parallel by A5. Shift register A3 (Fig. 8-3) converts the dots from parallel to serial. This means that it shifts out the dots one at a time as the crt beam scans across the screen. For each character, shift register A3 shifts seven times. It first shifts out a 0 (low), then the five dots that make the character, then finally another 0. The two 0s are stored in A5 and are used to create the horizontal space between characters. This is seen in Fig. 8-4. The figure also shows the video waveform that is generated for the third row of the character "A."

Referring again to Fig. 8-3, flashing timer B3 provides the rate for flashing characters and the cursor. Gates B11-11 and B13-4 decode the high order two bits (DL6 and DL7) of each character to determine its display mode (see Table 8-2).

Table 8-2. DL6 and DL7 Determine Display Mode

DL7	DL6	Mode
0	0	Inverse
0	1	Flashing
1	0	Normal
1	1	Normal

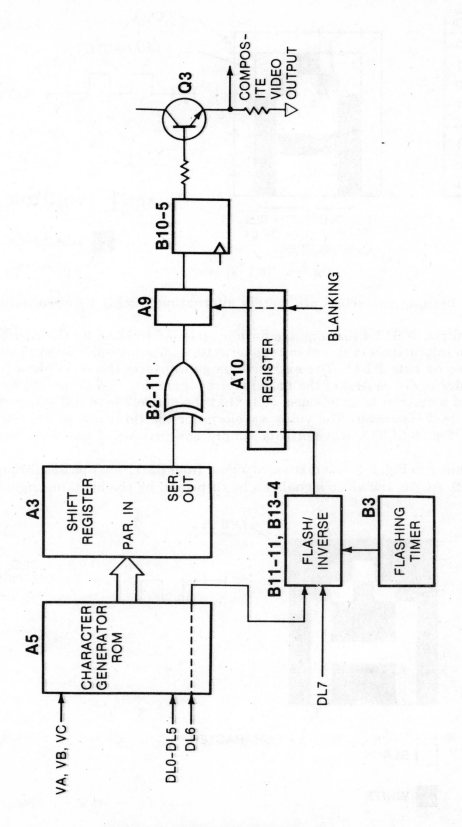

Fig. 8-3. Block diagram of text mode.

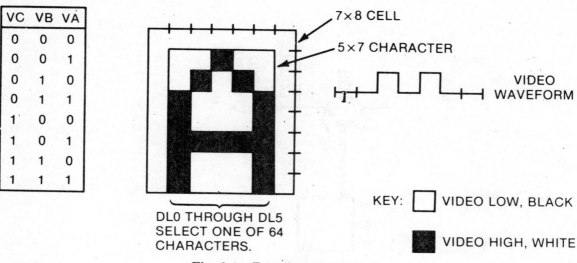

VC	VB	VA
0	0	0
0	0	1
0	1	0
0	1	1
1	0	0
1	0	1
1	1	0
1	1	1

7×8 CELL

5×7 CHARACTER

VIDEO WAVEFORM

DL0 THROUGH DL5
SELECT ONE OF 64
CHARACTERS.

KEY: ☐ VIDEO LOW, BLACK

■ VIDEO HIGH, WHITE

Fig. 8-4. Text character format.

Note that flashing characters are merely alternating quickly between normal and inverse.

The output of B13-4 contains the flash/inverse information for the current character. This information is stored in register A10, and is then presented to one input of exclusive OR gate B2-11. The exclusive OR gate inverts the serial data from the shift register under control of the flash/inverse signal. Fig. 8-5 shows the letter "A" as it would appear in inverse video. Note that the entire 7 by 8 cell is inverted, not just the 5 by 7 character. The video waveform for the third row in the cell is also shown in Fig. 8-5. The waveform is simply the inverse of the waveform from Fig. 8-4.

Returning to Fig. 8-3, the text video signal from B2-11 next passes through data selector A9. At A9, the video signal can be turned off by the blanking signal stored

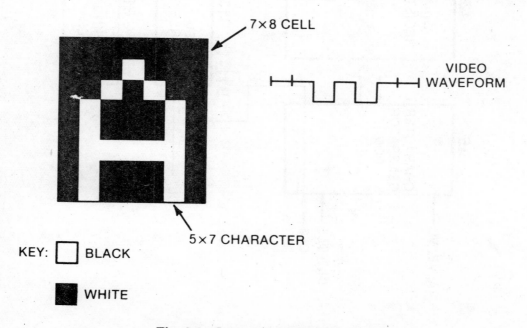

7×8 CELL

VIDEO WAVEFORM

5×7 CHARACTER

KEY: ☐ BLACK

■ WHITE

Fig. 8-5. Inverse text character.

in register A10. By this, we mean that during the blanking interval, the video signal is forced to 0 (low) to create a black portion of the screen. After A9, the video next passes through flip-flop B10-5 and then to Q3. At Q3, the video is mixed with SYNC and COLOR BURST to create the composite video output. (Blanking and the Q3 mixing process were described in Chapter 4.) This completes the path of the text characters through the video generator.

HIRES

The following soft switch settings configure the video generator for HIRES:

$$
\begin{array}{rl}
\text{TEXT MODE} &= 0 \\
\text{MIX MODE} &= 0 \\
\text{PAGE 2} &= 0 \text{ or } 1 \\
\text{HIRES MODE} &= 1
\end{array}
$$

Fig. 8-6 is the block diagram for HIRES mode. Data selector A8 configures 4-bit shift registers B4 and B9 into one long 8-bit shift register. Each byte to be displayed is loaded into the parallel input of this shift register. The contents are then shifted out one HIRES pixel at a time as the crt beam sweeps across the screen. If the byte contains green or violet pixels, the high order bit (DL7) will be 0, and data selector A9 will select the output of the shift register. If the byte contains blue or orange pixels, DL7 will be 1, and data selector A9 will select the output of flip-flop A11-9. The output of A11-9 is the shift register's output delayed by one 14M clock.

The output of data selector A9 passes through flip-flop B10-5 on its way to Q3. At Q3, it is mixed with SYNC and COLOR BURST to create the composite video output. Just as was the case in text mode, a blanking signal is applied to A9 to force the video to black during the blanking interval—DL7 and BLANKING are stored in register A10 on their way to A9. The key elements of Fig. 8-6 are the shift register

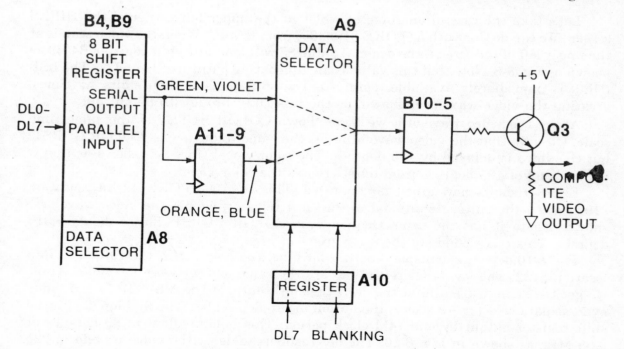

Fig. 8-6. Block diagram of HIRES generator.

and the ability of A9 to select the shift register's output either directly or delayed by A11-9. This selection is under control of DL7.

Now that we have the circuit arrangement in mind, let's see how it actually produces colors. Recall from color television theory that a video signal with a component at 3.58 MHz (the color burst frequency) will produce a color on the screen. The hue or tint of that color will be a function of the signal's phase relative to the phase of the color burst signal. (If you are not familiar with color video techniques, you should review Appendix A at this time.) Fig. 8-7 shows color hue as a function of phase angle relative to color burst.

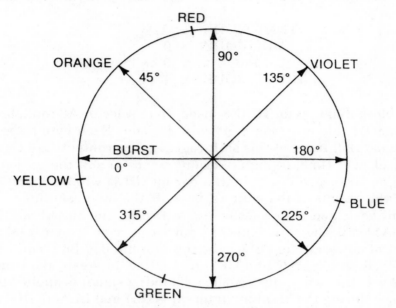

Fig. 8-7. Color hue as a function of phase angle relative to burst.

Let's take the case of one byte of violet in the upper left corner of the HIRES screen. We can do this with a "POKE 8192, 85" from BASIC. When the video scan is at the upper left of the screen, the decimal value 85 will load into shift register B4/B9 as shown in Fig. 8-8. Note that this value is an alternating pattern of 1s and 0s. The LSB (DL0) is immediately available (point A). The shift register then shifts six times, creating the video waveform shown, as the bits DL0 through DL6 shift out.

Above the video waveform we have shown COLOR BURST at the same time scale. Observe that the video waveform has the same frequency as COLOR BURST, but the video is delayed by 135 degrees. The color wheel (Fig. 8-7) shows us that a phase delay of 135 degrees from burst creates the color violet.

Fig. 8-9 shows how green is generated. This time we POKE 42 into location 8192. When the pattern shifts out of the shift register, we get the video waveform shown. Again it has the same frequency as COLOR BURST, but is delayed 315 degrees. This corresponds to the color green in Fig. 8-7.

Fig. 8-10 depicts the display method for blue. Here we POKE the value 213 into location 8192. The low order seven bits are the same as they were for violet. Thus, we get the same waveform at the shift register's output. The MSB (DL7) is 1, however, so data selector A9 selects the output of flip-flop A11-9. The flip-flop delays the shift register output by one 14M clock period. This is equivalent to 90 degrees at 3.58 MHz as shown in Fig. 8-10. The net result is to delay the video waveform 225 degrees relative to burst. This corresponds to the color blue in Fig. 8-7.

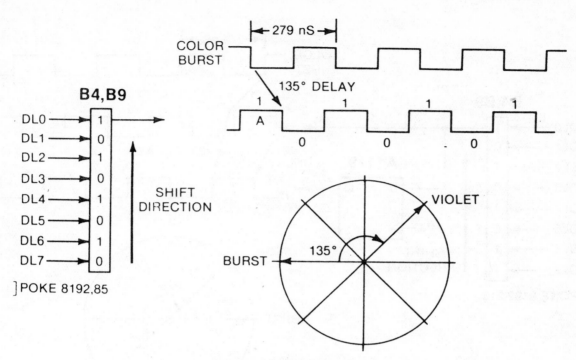

Fig. 8-8. HIRES violet.

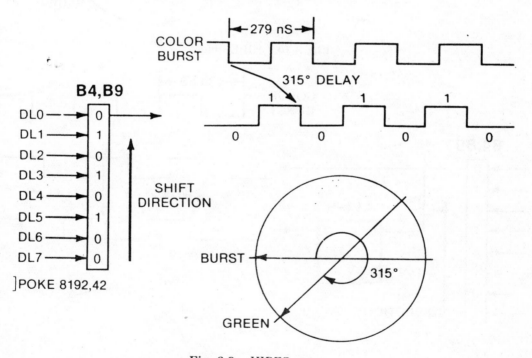

Fig. 8-9. HIRES green.

Finally, in Fig. 8-11, we show how orange is produced. We poke the value 170 into location 8192, and this generates the "green" waveform at the shift register's output. The MSB (DL7) is 1, so A9 selects the output from A11-9. A11-9 delays the "green" waveform by one 14M clock. The net result is a video waveform delayed 45 degrees from burst. This corresponds to the color orange in Fig. 8-7.

There now remain the two "colors" black and white. For black we simply store 0

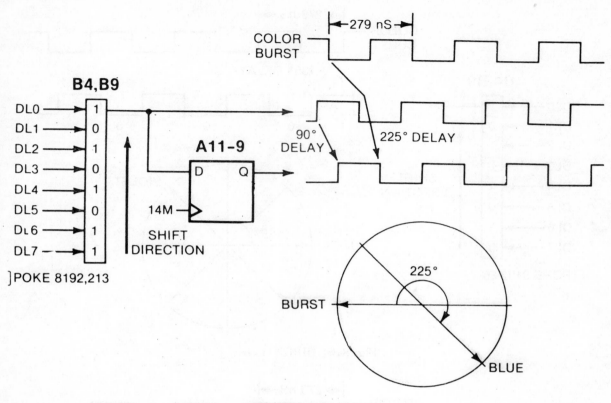

Fig. 8-10. HIRES blue.

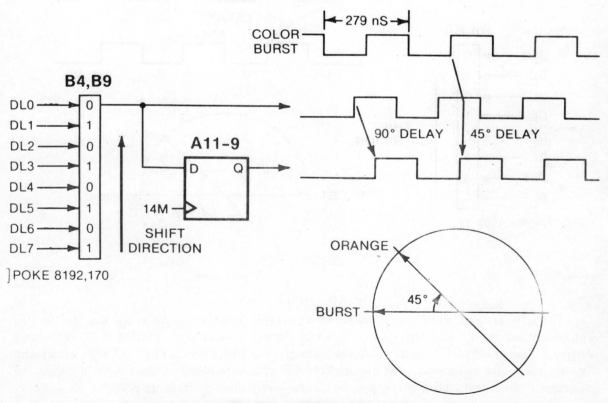

Fig. 8-11. HIRES orange.

or 128 in memory (Fig. 8-12). The seven 0s will shift out creating a continuous low signal. This corresponds to black. For white, we store 127 or 255 (Fig. 8-13). The seven 1s will shift out creating a continuous high signal. This signal has no component at 3.58 MHz, so there is no color. A high level corresponds to white, so that is what we get.

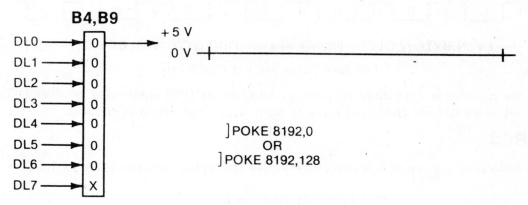

Fig. 8-12. HIRES black.

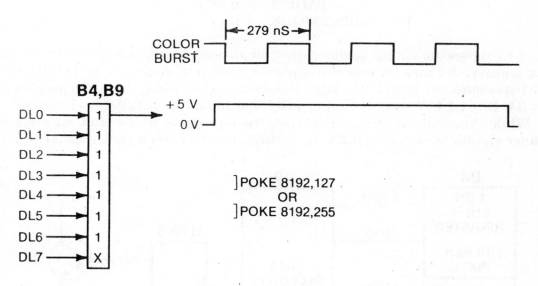

Fig. 8-13. HIRES white.

Before leaving our overview of the HIRES display, we must introduce the topic of even and odd bytes. The previous examples showing the six HIRES colors all used an even byte, location 8192. Fig. 8-14 shows what happens when we consider both even and odd bytes. At the top of the figure we have shown color burst. The second waveform is the video output for a violet line. It starts out just like the example in Fig. 8-8. The value 85 produces the alternating pattern 1010101.

The next segment of the line is stored in an odd location. If the line is to continue with the same color (same phase relative to burst), the odd segment must have the pattern 0101010. This is the value 42, the complement of 85. The same color is stored as *two different values,* depending on whether the byte is *even* or *odd.* This can be explained by noting that the time used to display one byte contains three and one-half cycles of 3.58 MHz. Thus, the relative phase of COLOR BURST changes by 180 degrees every byte. HIRES plotting routines take this into account.

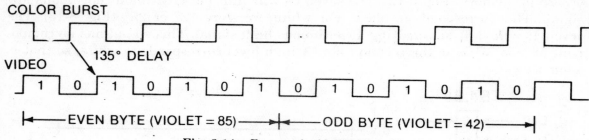

Fig. 8-14. Even and odd HIRES bytes.

We have now explained in concept how the HIRES colors are produced. There remain more details that will have to wait until later in this chapter.

LORES

The following soft switch settings configure the video generator for LORES.

$$\begin{aligned}
\text{TEXT MODE} &= 0 \\
\text{MIX MODE} &= 0 \\
\text{PAGE 2} &= 0 \text{ or } 1 \\
\text{HIRES MODE} &= 0
\end{aligned}$$

Fig. 8-15 shows the circuit configuration for this mode. Data selector A8 arranges shift registers B4 and B9 into two separate 4-bit shift registers. In LORES mode, each byte stores two pixels. Bits DL0–3 store the upper pixel; these bits parallel load into B4. Bits DL4–7 store the lower pixel and these bits parallel load into B9.

While the pixels are being displayed, the bits rotate in the shift registers in a manner similar to that of HIRES. In LORES, however, each shift register provides

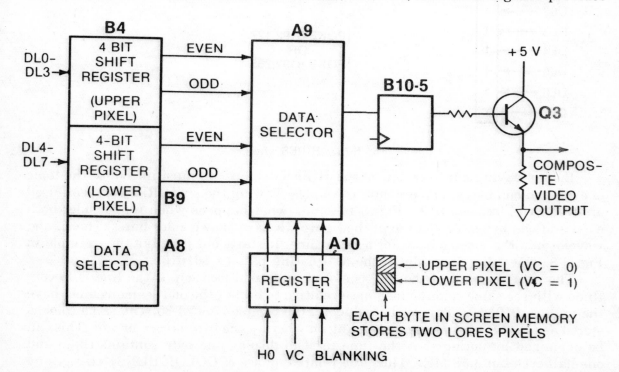

Fig. 8-15. Block diagram of LORES generator.

both an even and an odd output. Data selector A9 selects between even and odd outputs under control of signal H0. Signal H0 alternates between 0 and 1 as the crt beam scans over alternating even and odd bytes. You can refer to Fig. 3-4* to see the timing of H0. The purpose of this even/odd circuit configuration will be explained shortly.

Data selector A9 also selects between the upper and lower pixels under control of signal VC. Here you should refer to Fig. 4-1* to see the timing of VC. Signal VC alternates between 0 and 1 every four scan lines. The height of a LORES pixel is also four scan lines. When VC=0, A9 selects the upper pixel. When VC=1, A9 selects the lower pixel. This is depicted in Fig. 8-16 where we have shown signals VC and H0 coordinated with four LORES pixels.

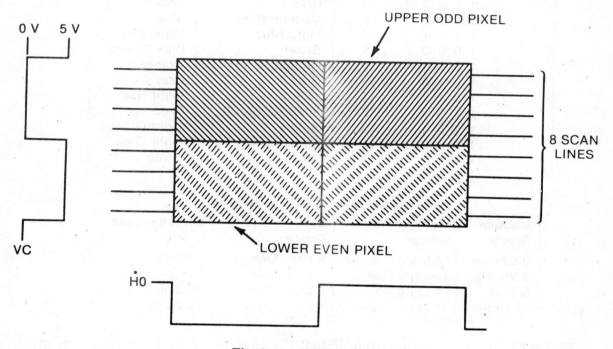

Fig. 8-16. LORES pixels.

The blanking signal at data selector A9 forces the video to black during the blanking interval. Signals H0, VC, and BLANKING are stored in register A10 before they go to A9. The video out of A9 passes through flip-flop B10-5 on its way to Q3. At Q3, the video is mixed with SYNC and COLOR BURST to create the composite video output.

Let's briefly review the LORES block diagram. The key elements are: (1) the shift registers with separate odd and even outputs, and (2) data selector A9 which selects upper and lower, even and odd inputs under control of VC and H0.

We now move from the block diagram to an explanation of LORES color generation. Each pixel is stored as four bits in memory. The pixel color is coded by these four bits as listed in Table 8-3. The table lists the color names used in Apple's documentation and alternative color names used in this book. The alternative names will aid our discussion, and you may assume that hereafter any LORES color mentioned in this book will use the alternative name.

In Table 8-4 the 16 colors are divided into four groups. We will examine one color from each of the first three groups and three colors from the miscellaneous group.

Table 8-3. LORES Colors

Bit Positions				Color Names	
Upper Pixel: 3 2 1 0 Lower Pixel: 7 6 5 4		Decimal		From *Apple II Reference Manual*	Alternative Names
0 0 0 0		0		Black	Black
0 0 0 1		1		Magenta	Dark Red
0 0 1 0		2		Dark Blue	Dark Blue
0 0 1 1		3		Purple	Violet
0 1 0 0		4		Dark Green	Dark Green
0 1 0 1		5		Gray 1	Gray 1
0 1 1 0		6		Medium Blue	Blue
0 1 1 1		7		Light Blue	Light Blue
1 0 0 0		8		Brown	Dark Orange
1 0 0 1		9		Orange	Orange
1 0 1 0		10		Gray 2	Gray 2
1 0 1 1		11		Pink	Light Red
1 1 0 0		12		Light Green	Green
1 1 0 1		13		Yellow	Light Orange
1 1 1 0		14		Aquamarine	Light Green
1 1 1 1		15		White	White

Table 8-4. LORES Groups

Medium Group	Light Group	Dark Group	Miscellaneous Group
9 Orange	13 Light Orange	8 Dark Orange	0 Black
3 Violet	11 Light Red	1 Dark Red	5 Gray 1
6 Blue	7 Light Blue	2 Dark Blue	10 Gray 2
12 Green	14 Light Green	4 Dark Green	15 White

Fig. 8-17 shows the generation of LORES blue. We start by poking a 6 into memory location 1024 (the upper left pixel on the screen). When the video address scans this pixel, the low order four bits load into shift register B4. Bit DL0 (a 0) is immediately available at the video output, point A. The shift register now shifts 13 times. On each shift, the serial output is loaded into the other end of the register. Thus, the same four bits *recirculate* through the shift register, generating the waveform shown.

COLOR BURST is drawn above the video waveform at the same time scale. Both signals have the same frequency, 3.58 MHz. We have drawn tic marks at the center of the positive portion of each signal so that we can measure their relative phase. As shown, the video signal is delayed 225 degrees relative to COLOR BURST. From Fig. 8-7 we see that 225 degrees corresponds to blue. You may also wish to note that the video signal for LORES blue is the same as that for HIRES blue, Fig. 8-10.

Fig. 8-18 shows the generation of LORES *light* blue. This time we POKE a 7 into location 1024. Again, when the upper left pixel is scanned, four bits load into the shift register then rotate to create a video waveform at the serial output. This waveform has the same frequency as burst and is delayed 180 degrees. From Fig. 8-7 we see that 180 degrees also corresponds to blue.

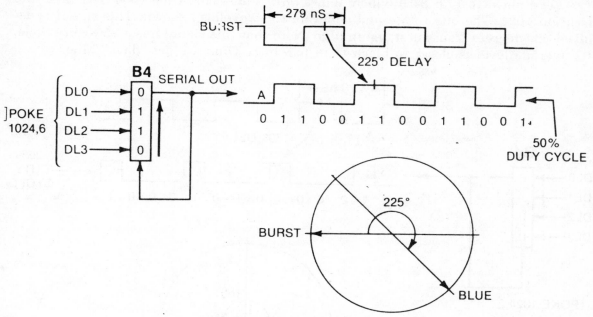

Fig. 8-17. LORES blue.

The color waveform in Fig. 8-18 differs from those presented up to now; it does not have a 50% duty cycle. This waveform is high for three out of four counts, so it has a duty cycle of 75%. Stated another way, its average value is 75% of the way from black (low video level) to white (high video level). This means the color display of this signal will be brighter than the display of the 50% duty cycle signal of Fig. 8-17. Thus, Fig. 8-17 shows "medium" blue and Fig. 8-18 shows "light" blue.

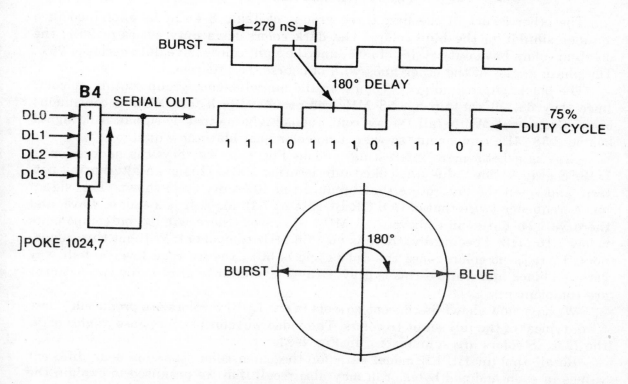

Fig. 8-18. LORES light blue.

Let's move to Fig. 8-19 which shows *dark* blue. This time we POKE a 2 into location 1024. The bits rotate and generate the waveform shown. This signal is delayed 180 degrees from burst, again blue. Note that this signal has a 25% duty cycle. Its average level is closer to black than to white. Thus, we get "dark" blue.

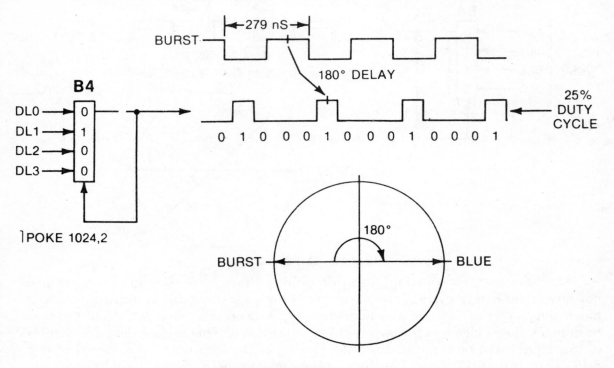

Fig. 8-19.   LORES dark blue.

The other colors in the first three groups of Table 8-4 can be explained in a manner similar to the blue colors. The dark colors have duty cycles of 25%, the medium colors have duty cycles of 50%, and the light colors have duty cycles of 75%. The phase angles of the other hues will, of course, be different.

The black, white, and gray "colors" in the miscellaneous group contain no color since they do not contain a 3.58 MHz component. Black (all 0s) is a continuous low—a dc signal. White (all 1s) is a continuous high; another dc signal. A dc signal has no 3.58 MHz component, so we get no color, just black or white.

Gray is a little more interesting, and in Fig. 8-20 we show the generation of LORES gray 1. The value 5 is poked into location 1024. This is an alternating pattern, and when the bits rotate they produce the 50% duty cycle shown. This signal has a frequency twice that of COLOR BURST or 7.16 MHz. It is a square wave, and there will be harmonics above 7.16 MHz. However, there will be no components below 7.16 MHz. Specifically, there is no 3.58 MHz component. Without this component, there is no color. Since the duty cycle is 50%, the average level is half way between black and white—this is gray. Gray 2 is similar to gray 1; the two patterns are complements.

We have now shown in concept how six of the LORES colors are produced. These 6 are typical of the full set of 16 colors. The video waveforms and phase angles of *all* the LORES colors are summarized in Fig. 8-21.

Recall that in HIRES mode, data for the same color was stored as different values in even and odd bytes. You may also recall that we promised to explain the separate even and odd shift register outputs in the LORES block diagram, Fig. 8-15.

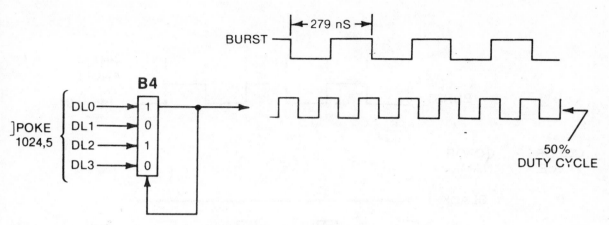

Fig. 8-20. LORES gray 1.

The Apple's method for handling the even/odd problem in LORES differs from the method used in HIRES. In HIRES, it is left to the software to sort out even and odd bytes. In LORES, the problem is solved in hardware. Fig. 8-22 shows the scheme, using blue as an example. First, data from an even byte is loaded into shift register B4. The data is decimal 6 which has the binary pattern 0110. The pattern rotates and generates the video waveform shown, starting at point A and ending at point B. This is the same waveform that was shown for the even byte blue of Fig. 8-17.

The next adjacent pixel is stored in an odd byte. Its display starts at point C. To continue the video signal at the same phase angle, the pattern starting at point C must be 1001. Here is how it works. We store the same decimal value (6) in the odd byte. When the pixel is scanned, the 6 loads into B4. Since this is an odd byte, signal H0 causes data selector A9 to select the "odd" tap of shift register B4. When B4 is loaded, the 1 at the odd tap is immediately available at the video signal, point C. The bits then rotate from this starting point, giving us a 1001 pattern.

In summary, A9 selects even and odd outputs of B4, allowing one data value to represent the same LORES color for both even and odd bytes. Since this is handled in the hardware, the programmer need not worry about it.

Our overview of LORES graphics has used shift register B4 as an example. The operation of shift register B9 is the same as that of B4. B9, however, operates on the high order four bits of data, and displays the lower pixel.

Mixed HIRES and Text

The following soft switch settings configure the video generator for mixed HIRES and text:

$$
\begin{aligned}
\text{TEXT MODE} &= 0 \\
\text{MIX MODE} &= 1 \\
\text{PAGE 2} &= 0 \text{ or } 1 \\
\text{HIRES MODE} &= 1
\end{aligned}
$$

Note that both the text and HIRES will come from the same page (determined by the PAGE 2 soft switch). Fig. 8-23 shows the block diagram for this configuration. Both the text generator and the 8-bit shift register operate on the latched data as previously described. While the crt scan is in the top portion of the screen, data selector A9 selects the HIRES from the 8-bit shift register. When the scan gets five-sixths of

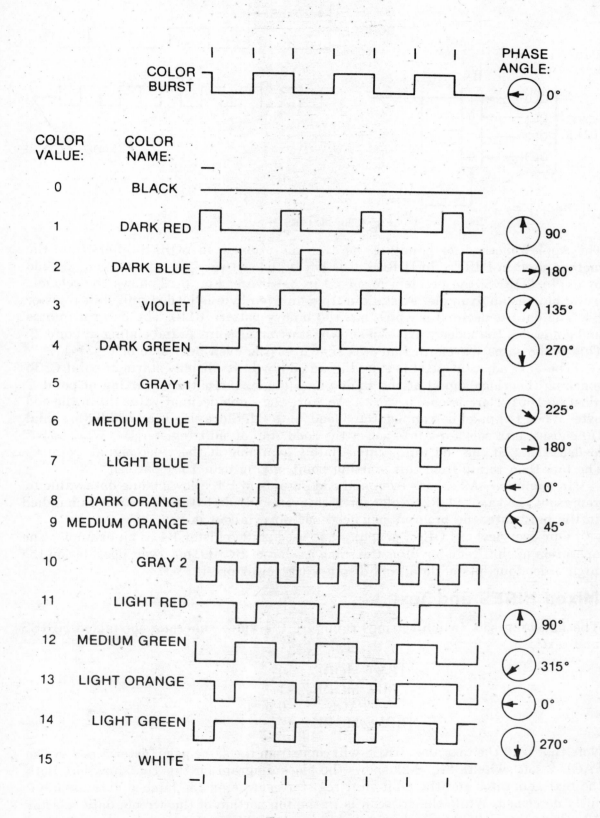

Fig. 8-21. LORES colors.

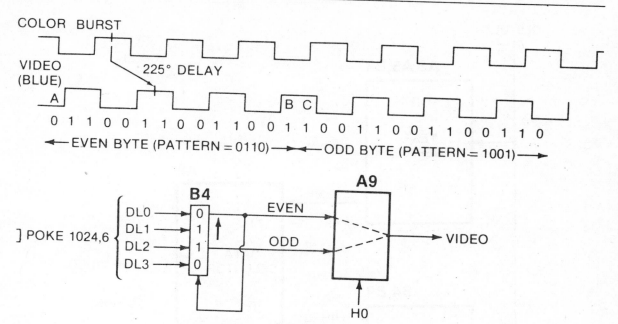

Fig. 8-22. Even and odd LORES bytes.

the way down the screen, video address lines V2 and V4 both go high. This causes A9 to select the text generator output. As a result, the bottom one-sixth of the screen contains four lines of text.

Mixed LORES and Text

The following soft switch settings configure the video generator for mixed LORES and text:

$$
\begin{aligned}
\text{TEXT MODE} &= 0 \\
\text{MIX MODE} &= 1 \\
\text{PAGE 2} &= 0 \text{ or } 1 \\
\text{HIRES MODE} &= 0
\end{aligned}
$$

Both the text and LORES will come from the same page. Fig. 8-24 shows the block diagram for this configuration. Both the text generator and the two shift registers operate on the latched data. While the crt scan is in the top portio. of the screen, data selector A9 selects LORES pixels from the shift registers. When the scan gets five-sixths of the way down the screen, video address lines V2 and V4 both go high. This causes A9 to select the text generator output. As a result, the bottom one-sixth of the screen contains four lines of text.

This concludes the overview of the Apple II video display. The block diagrams and signal waveforms in this section were drawn to illustrate only the concepts. As a result, some of the drawings may. not correspond exactly to the actual circuit implementation or to waveforms actually observed on an oscilloscope. These details will be provided in the circuit analysis that follows.

DL0–DL7

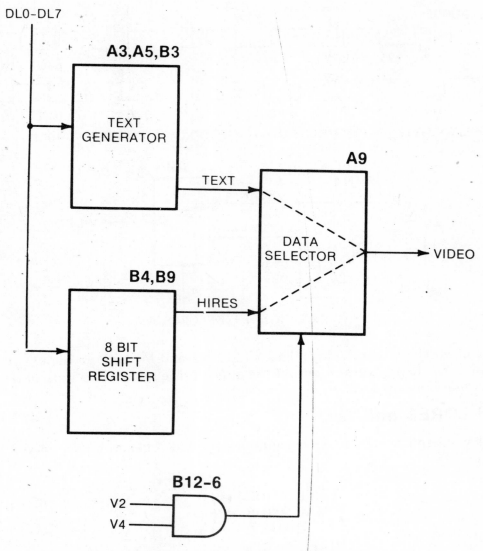

Fig. 8-23. Block diagram of mixed HIRES and text.

DETAILED CIRCUIT ANALYSIS

Text Mode

Our detailed analysis of text mode starts with character generator A5 and shift register A3 (Fig. C-16*). We then follow the signal through data selector A9 and flip-flop B10-5.

Character Generator—IC A5 is a type 2316B ROM that stores all the row and column dots for a set of 64 dot matrix characters. Inputs A3 through A8 are the character address. They receive latched data bits DL0 through DL5. These are the six bits of each byte in text memory of the Apple that store the character. Inputs A0, A1, and A2 of IC A5 are the row address. They receive the video address lines VA, VB, and VC. As the crt beam moves down the screen, these address lines select one of the eight rows that make up each character.

Input A9 of IC A5 connects to DL6. Character generator A5 is programmed so

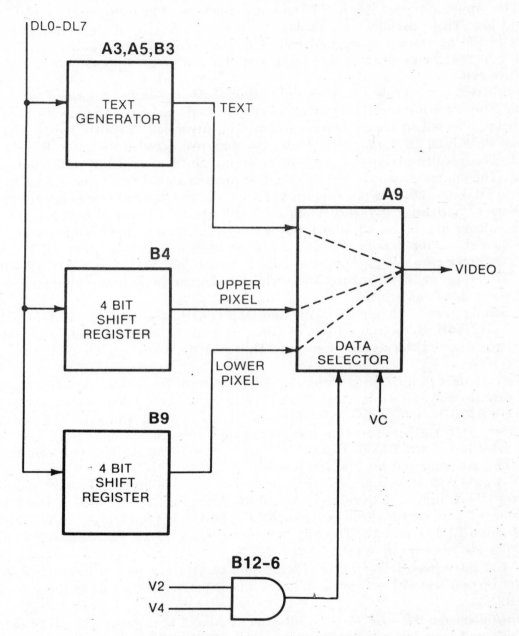

Fig. 8-24. Block diagram of mixed LORES and text.

that output O8 exactly follows address input A9. The effective result is to connect DL6 to B11-12.

Input A10 of IC A5 connects to DL7. A5 is programmed such that input A10 is a don't care.

As we have just described, the connection of DL6 and DL7 to A5 has no effect with the ROM supplied by Apple Computer. The purpose of the connections is so that you can provide your own ROM or EPROM containing additional characters. The additional characters would be accessed via DL6 and DL7. Additional flexibility is provided by bow ties 9, 10, and 11. These may be cut and connections made to A5 inputs A9 and A10 from external sources, such as the game I/O or a simple switch. The external source could then select a character set via A5 inputs A9 and A10. Specific implementation of user character sets is not covered in this book.

The Apple supplied A5 ROM is programmed so that outputs O1 and O7 are always low. This provides a blank dot on the left and right of each character. The result is the horizontal space between characters. In a user supplied ROM, these blank dots may be programmed to form part of a character. An example would be a graphics symbol.

Shift register A3 takes the parallel output of A5 and shifts it out one bit (dot) at a time. The resulting serial bit stream passes through exclusive OR gate B2-11 where it can be inverted to create inverse video. The inversion is controlled by the two latched data bits, DL6 and DL7. These two bits are decoded by gates B11-11 and B13-4. The resulting signal is applied to input pin 6 of register A10 where it is stored. The signal exits A10 on pin 12. The inverse signal has to be stored in A10 because DL6 and DL7 do not remain valid for the full character display time.

Normal and Inverse Text—When DL7 is high, B13-4 and A10-12 will be low. The resulting low at B2-12 allows the serial bit stream to pass noninverted. This gives us a character in *normal* video (white on black). Note that when DL7 is high, DL6 is a don't care. When DL6 and DL7 are both low, B13-4 and A10-12 will be high. This high at B2-12 inverts the serial bit stream, giving us a character in *inverse* video (black on white).

Flashing Text—When DL7 is low and DL6 is high, the signal at B11-11, B13-4, and A10-12 will follow the output of timer B3. B2-11 now alternately inverts or passes noninverted the serial bit stream. This gives us a *flashing* character at about 2 Hz.

Text Mode Circuit Configuration—Before moving on to the detail timing, we must explain how data selectors A8 and A9 configure the video generator for text. The TEXT MODE soft switch will be set, so B13-12 is high. NOR gate B13-13 is low, and after three $\overline{\text{RAS}}$ pulses, this low propagates through flip-flops B5-2 and B8 to make B8-2 low. Thus B11-6 (HIRES) is low, assuring that we will fetch characters from the text page and not the HIRES page.

NOR gate A12-10 is high, A12-13 is low, and A11-6 is high. (A11-5 is used as an inverter.) This high at data selector A8 causes it to select its "1" inputs. Pin B5-2 is low, and this low passes through A8 to A8-7. The low is then stored in A10 on 14M rising while LD194 is high. The low next appears at A9-10. Recall that A12-13 is low. This low appears at A9-9.

If you have been following this discussion carefully, you will notice that A9 is now set up to select either input pin 3 or 4. These pins both connect to the video text from B2-11.

Shift Register A3—As we ease into the details of text generation, let's explore the clock and load inputs of shift register A3. These three inputs are driven from signals previously discussed and shown again at the top of Fig. 8-25A. Pins 6 and 7 are connected internally to a NOR gate that provides the IC's internal clock. The device is clocked on the falling edge as shown in the fourth line of Fig. 8-25A. On each clock, the IC either shifts (if pin 15 is high) or loads parallel data (if pin 15 is low). Signal $\overline{\text{LDPS}}$ controls the mode (shift or load) of A3.

Text Mode Timing Diagram—Fig. 8-26* shows the display timing of two text characters. Signals 14M and $\overline{\text{A3 CLOCK}}$ are shown at the top. The mode of A3 is shown next to each falling edge of $\overline{\text{A3 CLOCK}}$ (S = shift, L = load). (Remember that $\overline{\text{A3 CLOCK}}$ is an internal IC signal and cannot be viewed on an oscilloscope.) Also shown in the figure are LD194, the video address, and the latched data—all previously discussed.

The first character that we have shown is the left-most character on a line,

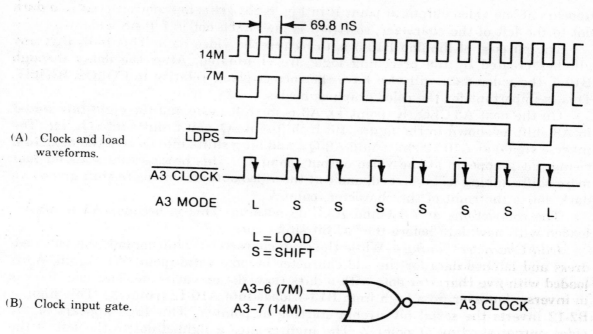

(A) Clock and load waveforms.

L = LOAD
S = SHIFT

(B) Clock input gate.

Fig. 8-25. Clock and load inputs—shift register A3.

character 0. The second is the right-most character on a line, character 39. The 0 is an even character and 39 is an odd character. To add even more variety, we have made character 0 be in normal video and character 39 be in inverse video. We have drawn the timing as if these were the only two characters on a line. This is so the timing relationship between adjacent characters can be shown. There are, of course, really 40 characters per line.

Note that Fig. 8-26* shows one horizontal scan line or one row through the characters. The uppercase letters in the figure are references to the text (our normal practice in this book). The lowercase letters represent the data values of the waveform at various points. The seven signals A3-Q_A through A3-Q_G are shown as aids to understanding the timing. They are not available externally to IC A3.

Even Character Timing—At point A, the video address for character 0 becomes valid. Since we are at the left edge of the display, the video address is decoded to remove blanking at point B. After the video address maps to memory, the character appears as latched data at point C. During the time that the video address and the latched data are both valid (point D), VA, VB, VC, and DL0 through DL5 all address character generator A5 (Fig. C-16). Character generator A5 responds with seven horizontal dots on its outputs O1 through O7. On A3 CLOCK falling (point E in Fig. 8-26*), these seven bits load into shift register A3 (points F through M). The values of these seven bits are represented in Fig. 8-26* as b through h (corresponding to their 74166 signal names).

Also while the latched data is valid, DL6 and DL7 are decoded by B11-11 and B13-4 to become the inverse signal. It is loaded into A3 at point N. It is also loaded into register A10 on 14M rising pulse while LD194 is high, point O. The signal at A10-12 is low, so the output of A3 passes to B2-11 noninverted, point P. BLANKING (C14-6 in Fig. C-20*) is now low, so on 14M rising pulse while LD194 is high, A10-13 goes low (point Q in Fig. 8-26*). This enables data selector A9 (Fig. C-16*) via its pin 7. We already know that A9 is set to select input pin 3 or 4. Thus when enabled, A9 sends the text to B10-2. This flip-flop is clocked every 14M rising pulse, so the text appears at the video output at point R in Fig. 8-26*. This first dot is actually a dark dot to the left of the character, so B10-5 is low. Each dot is 140 nS wide.

The purpose of flip-flop B10-5 is to *reclock* the video data. This is so that any glitches created by the preceding logic are eliminated. After the delay through B10-5, the video data will also have the correct phase relative to COLOR BURST. This is important for the color graphics modes.

On the next $\overline{\text{A3 CLOCK}}$ (point T), A3 is in shift mode and the eight bits stored in A3 shift as shown in the figure. Bit b shifts into Q_C, bit c shifts into Q_D, etc. The inverse signal at A10-12 shifts into A3-Q_A, and bit g shifts into Q_H. On the next 14M rising, bit g appears at the video output (point U). This process continues for four more shifts, giving us bits f, e, d, and c at the video output. One more shift gives us a dark dot to the right of the character, point V.

The connections at A3-1 and A3-2 do nothing. This is because A3 is always loaded with new data before the "a" bit shifts out.

Odd Character Timing — While the even character is shifting out, the video address and latched data for the odd character become valid (point W). Again, A3 is loaded with five character dots with a dark (low) dot on each side. This character is in inverse, however, so a high from B13-4 loads into A10-12 (point X). This high at B2-12 inverts the serial bit stream starting at point Y. This high appears at the video output starting at point Z. The high creates a lighted dot to the left of the inverse character. On the next five shifts of A3, the bits g through c appear inverted at the video output. One more shift creates a lighted dot to the right of the character, point AA.

Since this is the right-most character on the line (character 39), BLANKING goes high when the video address changes (point BB). On the next 14M rising pulse while LD194 is high, A10-13 goes high (point CC). This disables A9, and horizontal blanking starts after one more 14M clock pulse (point DD). This concludes our detailed analysis of text mode.

HIRES Mode

Our analysis of HIRES mode starts with the configuration of the video generator by the soft switches. Then we follow in detail the timing of the signals through the circuitry.

HIRES Mode Circuit Configuration — For HIRES graphics, the TEXT MODE and MIX MODE soft switches are low. This results in a high at B13-13 (Fig. C-16*). After three $\overline{\text{RAS}}$ pulses, this high propagates through flip-flops B5-2 and B8. This makes B11-5 high. Since the HIRES MODE soft switch is high at B11-4, B11-6 (HIRES) is high. This arranges the memory system to map video addresses to the HIRES page.

HIRES MODE high at A12-12 results in a high at A11-6. (Recall that A11-5 is used as an inverter.) This high at data selector A8 pin 1 causes it to select its "1" inputs. Thus $\overline{\text{7M}}$ at A8-10 passes through to A8-9 and pin 10 of shift register B4 and B9. Pins 9 and 11 of B4 and B9 connect to LD194 and 14M. Pin 11 is the clock input and pins 9 and 10 control the shift modes of B4 and B9 as shown in Table 8-5. B4 and B9 load on 14M rising while $\overline{\text{7M}}$ *and* LD194 are high. B4 and B9 shift left on 14M rising pulse while $\overline{\text{7M}}$ is high *and* LD194 is low. A left shift is a shift in the direction of D3 toward D0. The clock edges on which the loads and shifts occur are shown in Fig. 8-27. This figure also shows the clock edges on which A10 loads.

Returning to A8, pin 1 is high, so data input on pin 3 is output on pin 4. Thus,

Table 8-5. S1 and S0 Control Shift Modes

S1 (Pin 10)	S0 (Pin 9)	Mode
0	0	Do Nothing
0	1	Shift Right
1	0	Shift Left
1	1	Load

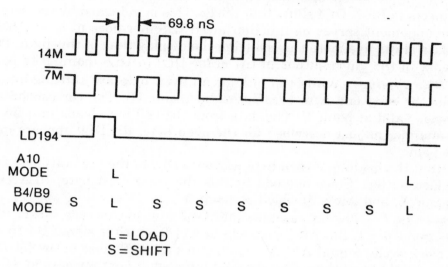

Fig. 8-27. Clock and shift inputs—ICs A10, B4, and B9.

bits that shift out of B9-15 shift into B4-7. This is how B4 and B9 become one long 8-bit shift register.

The signal at B5-2 is high as previously described. This high at A8-6 passes to A8-7, is latched in A10, then appears at A9-10. The signal at A12-13 is low (again as previously described), and this low appears at A9-9. Signal DL7 at A8-13 passes to A8-12, is latched in A10, then appears at A9-11. These three select inputs of A9 (pins 9, 10, and 11) cause it to select either input pin 1 or pin 2 under control cf DL7. When DL7 is low, A9-2 is selected. This comes from B4-15, the direct output of the shift register. When DL7 is high, A9-1 is selected. This comes from A11-9, the shift register's output delayed by one 14M clock cycle.

HIRES Mode Timing Diagram—Fig. 8-28* shows the detail timing of HIRES data. The timing for 14M, the video address, and the latched data have been derived previously. The clock edges on which A10, B4, and B9 shift and load are also shown. This information has been duplicated from Fig. 8-27.

The two bytes shown are the left-most display byte (an even byte), and the right-most display byte (an odd byte). The waveforms represent one horizontal scan line. We have shown the timing as if only two bytes were displayed on a line. In practice, 40 bytes are displayed.

Even Byte Timing—The video address for the even byte becomes valid at point A. Since this is the left-most byte, BLANKING goes low at the same time (point B). The video address maps to the HIRES screen memory, and the memory returns the byte to be displayed as latched data, point C. While the latched data is still valid, it is loaded into B4 and B9, points D through K. The numbers (0 through 7) shown in the waveforms correspond to the bit's origin. For example, at point K, bit DL0 loads into B4 and appears at B4-15.

At the same time that B4 and B9 are loaded, DL7 loads into A10-14 and BLANKING loads into A10-13 (point M). Data selector A9 is enabled by the low on A10-13. Assume for now that DL7=0. This causes A9 to select input pin 2. Thus, bit DL0 from B4-15 appears immediately at A9-5, point N. On the next 14M rising pulse, bit DL0 appears at B10-5, the video output (point P). The bit is 140 nS wide when displayed.

On the next 14M rising pulse, B4 and B9 shift. This moves bit DL1 to B4-15, point Q. The other seven bits also shift as shown by the arrows. Note that since B9-15 connects to B9-7, DL4 shifts into B9-12. This is indicated by the arrow to point R. This arrangement serves no function in HIRES, nor does it do any harm.

The data shifts five more times during the display time of this byte. The latched data appears in the video output in the order DL0 to DL6 (point P to point T).

Odd Byte Timing—While the bits for an even byte are shifting out, the video address for the next odd byte becomes valid (point U). The corresponding latched data becomes valid at point V. The data from the odd byte loads into B4 and B9 in the same manner as just described for the even byte. Bit DL0 appears in the video output at point W.

Note that the loading of each byte prevents DL7 of the previous byte from reaching the video output. Since our odd byte is the right-most byte, BLANKING goes high at point X, and A9 is disabled at point Y.

Effects of DL7—Now let's assume that DL7 = 1. In this case, A9-11 is high, and A9 selects input pin 1. Pin A9-1 connects to A11-9 which is signal B4-15 delayed by one 14M clock cycle. Signal A11-9 is shown in Fig. 8-28* just below B4-15. The one clock delay should be evident. The delayed bit stream next appears at A9-5, then at B10-5 after another delay of one 14M clock cycle.

Compare the B10-5 waveforms in Fig. 8-28* for the cases where DL7 = 0 and DL7 = 1. You should see that under control of DL7, we can shift any pixel by 70 nS. This is a distance equal to half of the pixel's width. Thus, there are twice as many horizontal plotting locations on a line as there are pixel cells. This gives us 560 horizontal plotting locations for black and white HIRES, as mentioned in the overview.

We have now shown exactly how each bit of a typical HIRES byte appears in the video output. We will now use this new information to demonstrate the generation of HIRES colors.

HIRES Color Generation—Fig. 8-29 shows the video output for two adjacent HIRES bytes. The first four signals in Fig. 8-29 are simply duplicated from Fig. 8-28*. We have shown the even byte shifting out while the video address is odd, as is the case. COLOR REF is then added to the figure in the proper phase relationship.

Next we show COLOR BURST, but recall that COLOR BURST is active only for a short time following the sync pulse. The *phase* established by COLOR BURST is important, so we have shown that phase continuing into the visible portion of the display as a dotted line. COLOR BURST is delayed about 35 nS by the LC network (L1, C2, and C3 in Fig. C-20*), so we also show this delayed COLOR BURST at Q3.

The next signal in the figure (line A) shows the video output for two bytes, both with the value 85. Bits DL0, DL2, DL4, and DL6 are set when the data equals 85. Since DL7 is not set, the timing will correspond to the signal labeled "DL7 = 0." When the phase angle of the video is compared with that of burst, you can see that the value 85 in an *even* byte is violet while the same value in an *odd* byte is green. The next signal (line B) shows the same two bytes with a value of 213. Bits DL0, DL2, DL4, DL6, and DL7 are set when the data is 213. The timing of this signal will

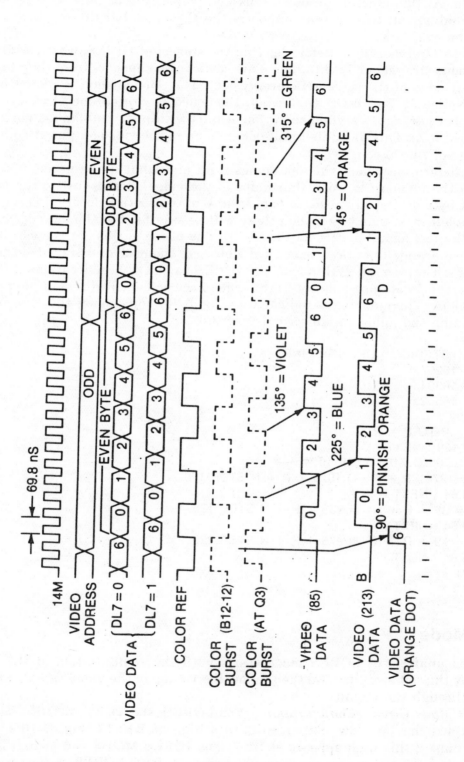

Fig. 8-29. HIRES colors.

correspond to the signal labeled "DL7 = 1." The phase angle results in blue for an even byte and orange for an odd byte.

At points C and D, two adjacent bits are both high. This results in a white dot on the screen. At this juncture in our discussion, you should be able to see how the circuit, as analyzed in this section, supports the theory of HIRES graphics as explained in the overview.

Mysterious Orange Line—Before leaving the subject of HIRES, we must discuss the "Mysterious Orange (or Pink) Line." This vertical line appears from time to time along the left edge of the screen (Reference 8.2). The phenomenon is rooted in the hardware. Notice in Fig. 8-28* that when the video is shifted one clock cycle by A11-9, 70 nS of garbage is shifted such that it falls within the unblanked portion of the screen (point Z). This unwanted half-dot ends up in the video output at point AA (the left edge of the screen)

Can we determine where this dot comes from and what its value is? It comes from bit 6 of the memory location that maps to the video address just to the left of the left-most byte displayed on the screen. If bit 6 of this critical location is set, *and* if bit 7 of the left-most byte is set, then there will be a half-dot at the left edge of the screen (see the last signal plotted in Fig. 8-29). The phase of this dot is such that it will be pinkish-orange in color. The critical addresses themselves can be determined from Fig. 5-8*. They are all within the 16K HIRES page. Of these locations, 128 are legitimate screen locations along the right edge of the screen. The remaining 64 are unused locations. The mapping is indicated in Fig. 8-30. You can see the Mysterious Line by running the following 20 second program.

```
>10 REM MYSTERIOUS ORANGE LINE
 20 POKE -16297,0
 30 POKE -16304,0
 40 POKE -16302,0
100 P = 8192
110 FOR I = P TO P + P
120 POKE I,128 : NEXT I
130 FOR N = 0 TO 7168 STEP 1024
140 FOR I =127 + P + N TO 1023 + P + N STEP 128
150 POKE I,64 : NEXT I
160 FOR I = 39 + P + N TO 935 + P + N STEP 128
170 POKE I,64 : NEXT I
180 FOR I = 79 + P + N TO 975 + P + N STEP 128
190 POKE I,64 : NEXT I
200 NEXT N
999 END
```

LORES Mode

Our detailed analysis of LORES mode starts with the configuration of the video generator by the soft switches. We then follow the timing of the video signals as they propagate through the circuit.

LORES Mode Circuit Configuration—For LORES, the TEXT MODE and MIX MODE soft switches are low. This results in a high at B13-13 (Fig. C-16*). After three $\overline{RAS}$ pulses, this high appears at B8-2. The HIRES MODE soft switch is low, so HIRES is low. This arranges the memory mapper to fetch LORES characters from the text page.

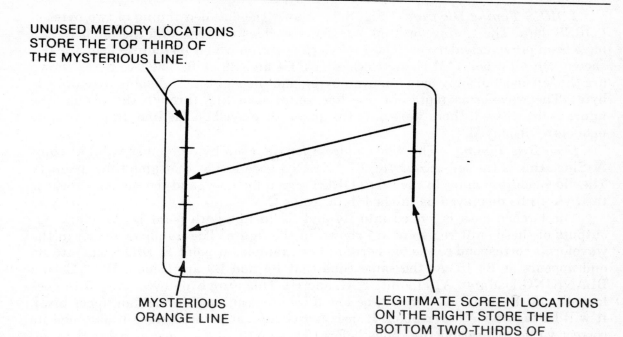

UNUSED MEMORY LOCATIONS
STORE THE TOP THIRD OF
THE MYSTERIOUS LINE.

MYSTERIOUS
ORANGE LINE

LEGITIMATE SCREEN LOCATIONS
ON THE RIGHT STORE THE
BOTTOM TWO-THIRDS OF
THE MYSTERIOUS LINE.

Fig. 8-30. Mysterious orange line.

The high from B8-2 makes A12-10 low. Since HIRES MODE is also low, A12-13 is high. Flip-flop A11-6 inverts this, and we get a low at data selector A8's input pin 1. This causes A8 to select its "0" inputs. Thus, the high pull-up at A8-11 appears at A8-9 which connects to B4-10 and B9-10. Since this line is a continuous high, B4 and B9 are limited to two modes: load and shift left. Signal LD194 connects to their pin 9, so B4 and B9 will load when LD194 is high, and shift when LD194 is low. Of course they only shift or load on 14M's rising edge. A left shift is a shift in the direction from Q3 toward Q0.

Bits shifting out of B4-15 will pass through A8 (A8-2 to A8-4) and back into B4 and pin 7. Bits shifting out of B9-15 will immediately shift back in on pin 7. Thus, the four bits loaded into each shift register rotate on each shift as described in the overview.

Signal VC passes through A8 (A8-5 to A8-7) and is stored in A10. It then appears at pin 10 of data selector A9. Signal H0 follows a similar path through A8 (A8-14 to A8-12) and is also stored in A10. It then appears at A9-11. Nor gate A12-13 is high as previously described, and this high appears at A9-9. These three most recently mentioned inputs to A9 are its *select* inputs. They cause A9 to select outputs from the shift registers as shown in Table 8-6.

Table 8-6. Signals VC and HO Influence the Output of A9

VC	HO	Selected Source	Description
0	0	B4-15	Upper Pixel, Even Byte
0	1	B4-13	Upper Pixel, Odd Byte
1	0	B9-15	Lower Pixel, Even Byte
1	1	B9-13	Lower Pixel, Odd Byte

LORES Timing Diagram—Fig. 8-31* shows the detailed timing of two bytes of LORES data. The timing for 14M, LD194, the video address, and the latched data have been previously derived. The 14M clock edges on which B4 and B9 load are also shown. On all other 14M rising clock edges, B4 and B9 shift. The two bytes shown are the left-most display byte (an even byte), and the right-most display byte (an odd byte). The waveforms represent one horizontal scan line through the pixels. The figure is drawn as if there were only two pixels displayed on the line. In practice, 40 pixels are displayed.

Even Byte Timing—The video address for the even byte becomes valid at point A. Since this is the left-most byte, BLANKING goes low at the same time, point B. The video address maps to the text/LORES screen memory, and the memory returns the byte to be displayed as latched data, point C.

The latched data is loaded into B4 and B9 in line with point D. All eight "Q" outputs of these shift registers are shown in the figure. The numbers shown in the waveforms correspond to the bit's origin. For example, at point E, DL0 loads into B4 and appears at B4-15. At the same time that B4 and B9 are loaded, H0, VC, and BLANKING load into A10 (points F, G, and H). This is an even byte, so A10-14 goes low at point F. Signal A10-15 will be low if we are scanning through an upper pixel. It will be high for a lower pixel. It does not change at point G since it assumed its correct value several microseconds before. Thus, A10-13 goes low at point H to enable A9.

We will assume in this example that VC is low (upper pixel). H0 (latched at A10-14) is also low, so A9 selects B4-15. Thus, bit DL0 appears at A9-5 (point I). On the next 13 rising edges of 14M the shift registers recirculate their contents as shown in the figure. Data selector A9 continues to select the bits at B4-15, and they appear at A9-5 as shown. After one 14M pulse delay, the bits at A9-5 appear at B10-5 (the video output). Each bit is 70 nS wide.

Odd Byte Timing—While the bits for an even byte shift out, the video address and latched data for the next adjacent odd byte become valid (points J and K). In line with point M, the odd data is loaded into B4 and B9. At the same time, H0 is loaded into A10. Signal A10-14 goes high (point N) since this is an odd byte.

For the next 13 clock pulses, the bits recirculate in the shift registers just as they did for the even byte. Signal A10-14 is high for the odd byte, however, so A9 selects B4-13 to output on A9-5. For example, bit DL2 at point P appears at point Q. After a one clock pulse delay, A9-5 appears at the video output, B10-5.

When the video address changes at point R, BLANKING goes high (point S) since we are at the right edge of the screen. At point T, A10 loads again, and A10-13 goes high to disable A9.

Note that the output bit sequence remains in order at the boundary between even and odd bytes (point Q). This is a result of H0's control over data selector A9. In this example, we assumed that VC is low. If VC is high, the video output contains bits 4, 5, 6, and 7 in that order.

LORES Color Generation—We have shown above bit for bit how the LORES data appears in the video output. In Fig. 8-32, we demonstrate by two examples how these bit positions create colors. The first four waveforms in the figure have been duplicated in the correct relative phase from Figs. 8-29 and 8-31*. We have shown two bytes. Remember that even bytes shift out while the video address is odd and vice versa.

The fifth signal in Fig. 8-32 is the video output that results if both bytes equal 2. Note that the DL1 bit is high. The phase delay from burst is 180 degrees (blue), and

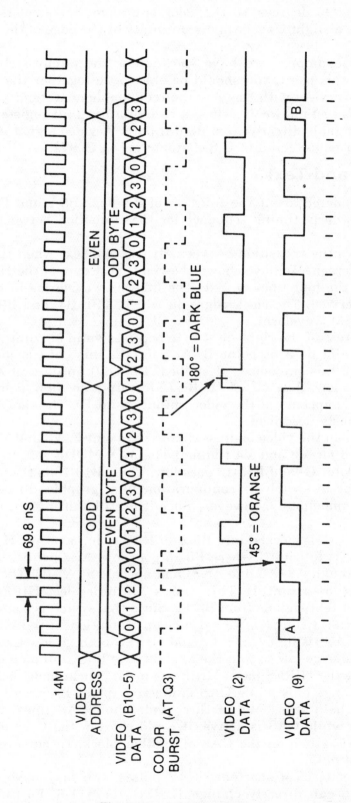

Fig. 8-32. LORES colors.

the duty cycle is 25% (dark). Thus, the color is *dark blue*. The last signal in the figure shows both bytes equal to 9. Note that bits DL0 and DL3 are high. The phase delay from burst is 45 degrees, so the color is orange. Some colors (orange is an example) will have a slight waveform discontinuity at the edge of the pixel, points A and B.

By these two examples, we have shown how the circuit actually produces LORES colors. At this point, you should be able to tie together the LORES theory presented in the overview with the actual circuit implementation.

In the previous section, we described a recirculating shift register that can generate color video signals directly from digital data. A video signal generator using this technique is a major claim of U.S. Patent No. 4,278,972.

Mixed HIRES and Text

You may have wondered about the function of flip-flops B5-2 and B8 (Fig. C-16*). They provide an orderly timing sequence for the transition between graphics and text displays.

Fig. 8-33 shows the transition between HIRES and text when these two modes are mixed on the screen. We have shown the right-most byte of the HIRES scan line that is just above the four lines of text. The first six waveforms in the figure have been previously derived. The clock edges on which A10, B4, and B9 load are indicated under the 14M waveform.

The video address of the right-most byte becomes valid at point A. The memory system provides valid data at point B. At point C, this data is loaded into shift registers B4 and B9 as previously described. Bit DL0 appears at B4-15. We will assume that DL7 is low, thus A9 selects B4-15 to output on A9-5 (point D). After one clock delay, bit DL0 appears at the video output (point E). The remaining bits then shift out as previously described.

Meanwhile, when the video address changes at point F, V2 and V4 both go high. (Refer to Chapter 4 for V2 and V4 timing.) The MIX MODE soft switch is high, so B12-6 goes high (point G) and B13-13 goes low. Thus, B13-13 is the signal that tells the video generator to switch its configuration from graphics to text. The circuit can't reconfigure immediately, however, since it is still shifting out the last HIRES byte.

The low at B13-13 is clocked into B5-2 on $\overline{RAS}$ rising at point H. The next $\overline{RAS}$ rising edge brings us to point I where B8-15 goes low. Meanwhile, the low at B5-2 has propagated through A8 (A8-6 to A8-7) and appears at A10-3. The next time A10 loads, A10-15 goes low (point J). This causes A9 to deselect HIRES signals from B4-15, and to select text signals from B2-11. Since this switch is coincident with the beginning of blanking (point K), we get a clean transition in the video output.

On the next $\overline{RAS}$ rising edge, B8-2 and HIRES both go low (points M and N). HIRES must of course go low so that the next 32 scan lines will map to the text page of memory and not the HIRES page. HIRES is made synchronous with $\overline{RAS}$ so that it (HIRES) will change only while $\overline{CAS}$ is inactive (point P). Recall that HIRES is decoded by F2 to help select one of three individual $\overline{CAS}$ lines. If HIRES were allowed to change while $\overline{CAS}$ is active, it could shorten the $\overline{CAS}$ for one memory block and produce a glitch on the $\overline{CAS}$ of another block. Either event would most likely cause loss of data.

While on the subject of shortened $\overline{CAS}$ pulses, you may have noted that the HIRES soft switch can directly change HIRES via B11-6. Fortunately the soft switches change state on $\phi 0$ rising, which occurs while $\overline{CAS}$ is inactive.

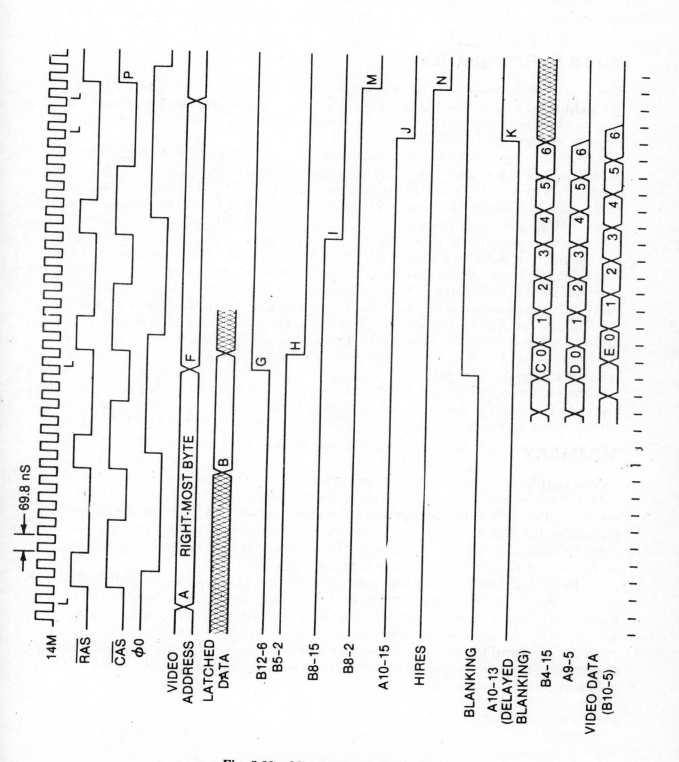

Fig. 8-33. Mixed HIRES and text.

Following the four lines of text, the video generator has to reconfigure itself to display graphics. This transition occurs during vertical blanking with HIRES being synchronized to $\overline{RAS}$ in a manner similar to that shown in Fig. 8-33.

In summary, flip-flops B5-2·and B8 delay the transition from graphics to text until blanking. The flip-flops also synchronize HIRES to $\overline{RAS}$ so that there will be no shortened $\overline{CAS}$ pulses. This concludes our discussion of mixed HIRES and text.

Mixed LORES and Text

The transition between LORES and text is depicted in Fig. 8-34*. The figure shows the right-most byte of the LORES scan line that is just above the four lines of text. Most of the waveforms in the figure have been previously presented, so we will concentrate on new information.

When the video address changes at point A, V2 and V4 both go high. The MIX MODE soft switch is high, so B12-6 goes high (point B) and B13-13 goes low. This low is clocked into B5-2 on $\overline{RAS}$ rising at point C. On the next $\overline{RAS}$ rising edge, B8-15 goes low (point D). Signal VC also goes low at point A, so when A10 next loads, A10-15 goes low (point E). In a similar manner, H0 goes low at point A, so A10-14 goes low at point F.

On the next $\overline{RAS}$ rising edge, B8·2 goes low (point G). This causes A12-13 to go low, point H. Since A12-13 connects to one of A9's select inputs (Fig. C-16*), A9 deselects the LORES graphics coming from the shift registers. This is a satisfactory point for the transition since we are now into blanking (which started at point I).

The low at A12-13 makes A11-6 go high, point J. This high appears at A8-1 causing A8 to reconfigure the circuit. The low at B5-2 passes through A8 (A8-6 to A8-7) and A10 (A10-3 to A10-15), then finally appears at A9-10. This causes A9 to select text signals from B2-11.

The circuit is now in text mode so the four lines of text can be displayed. During vertical blanking, the circuit switches back to LORES mode in a manner the reverse of that shown in Fig. 8-34.* This concludes the discussion of mixed LORES and text.

SUMMARY

In this chapter we have explained both the concepts and circuit details of the video modes of the Apple II. The Apple video generator consists of shift registers and data selectors. The data selectors configure the shift registers into circuit arrangements that differ for each mode. In each arrangement, the shift registers convert parallel graphics data into a serial bit stream. This serial data then becomes the video component of the composite video output of the Apple II.

This chapter also marks the conclusion of *The Apple II Circuit Description*. If you are designing peripherals or modifications for the Apple II, this book should have given you a major start. If your goal is repair of the mother board, the waveform drawings and large schematics should be a valuable maintenance aid. For students of digital design, a very popular and practical product has been described. And finally, if you were simply curious about the operation of Apple's hardware, that curiosity should now be satisfied.

Video Techniques

The Apple II has a composite video output that may be connected to a video monitor or to the antenna terminals of a television receiver via an rf (radio frequency) modulator. In order to understand the Apple video circuitry, it is first necessary to understand some basics about television. In this appendix we provide a brief introduction to video, using actual parameter values from the applicable U.S. standards. We also compare the video of the Apple II with these standards.

The signal we are discussing is called *composite video*. Such a signal is found at the video output of the Apple, at the video input of a video monitor, at the video input of an rf modulator, or inside a tv receiver at the *output* of the tuner. This signal has information content from near dc to several megahertz. It has an amplitude of about 1 volt. For our purposes, there is no audio in this signal.

The composite video signal should not be confused with an *rf* signal. An rf signal as used in television is a carrier in the range from 54 MHz to 900 MHz that has been modulated by a composite video signal. An rf signal would be found at the *output* of an rf modulator or at the antenna terminals of a tv set. Such an rf signal usually ranges from 300 to 2000 microvolts.

THE BASIC VIDEO DISPLAY

A video display is created by sweeping an electron beam across the face of a crt (cathode ray tube) as in Fig. A-1. Of course in practice, there are many more lines than shown. The solid lines are visible and form the image. The dashed lines are not visible. The dashed lines show the path of the beam as it retraces back to the left at the end of each line and as it retraces to the top after each field. A *field* is one complete journey of the beam from top to bottom including retrace back to the top. The rapid motion of the beam (about 60 fields/sec) makes the screen appear to the eye to be lighted at all points simultaneously.

The video display of Fig. A-1 is *noninterlaced*. This term will have more meaning shortly when we show an interlaced video display. Noninterlaced video has many applications, but it is not the broadcast standard used for transmitting television signals over the air.

The image you see on the screen is formed by modulating the intensity of the

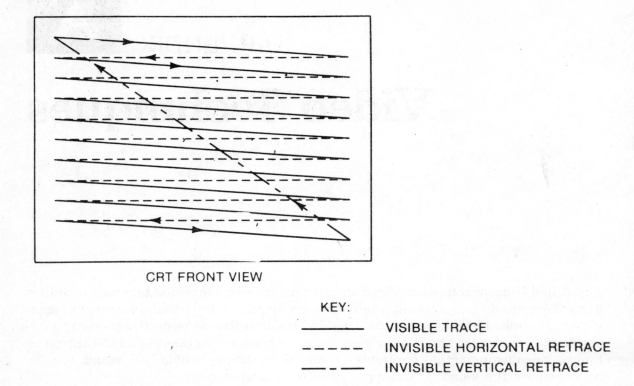

CRT FRONT VIEW

KEY:

———————— VISIBLE TRACE

– – – – – INVISIBLE HORIZONTAL RETRACE

——–·—— INVISIBLE VERTICAL RETRACE

Fig. A-1. Basic video display (noninterlaced).

beam. The beam is *blanked* during retrace, causing the retrace lines to be invisible. Blanking is accomplished by applying a modulation that corresponds to a level slightly darker than the blackest picture elements. The horizontal and vertical retrace times are shorter than the display times. This is so the beam can spend most of its time displaying picture material.

A video system must provide a synchronization means so that the beam in the crt will sweep in step with the beam in the transmitting device (often a tv camera tube). Both beams must return to the left simultaneously at the end of each horizontal line. Both beams must also return to the top simultaneously after each field. To accomplish this, the video signal contains a *horizontal sync* (synchronization) pulse between lines and a *vertical sync* pulse between fields. A composite video signal consists of the picture modulation for the beam, the blanking signals and the sync signals.

In Fig. A-2A we show the composite video signal for two complete horizontal lines. *White* picture level is in the positive direction and *black* is in the negative direction. Blanking level is slightly more negative than black, and sync pulses are more negative still. In Fig. A-2B we see the signal in the area of a vertical sync pulse. Horizontal sync pulses continue throughout vertical blanking and vertical retrace. This is to maintain the horizontal oscillator of the receiver on frequency during this interval. Since there are no horizontal sync pulses during the vertical sync pulse, the vertical sync pulse is interrupted at the horizontal rate by *serrations*. The serrations thus provide horizontal timing information during the vertical sync pulse. Note that the horizontal and vertical blanking intervals extend beyond each edge of their respective sync pulses.

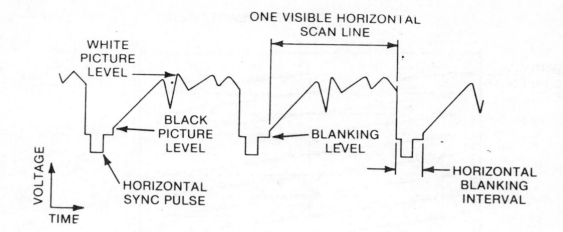

(A)   Typical horizontal scan lines.

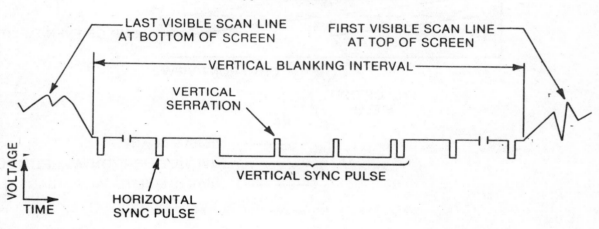

(B)   Vertical blanking interval.

Fig. A-2.   Composite video waveforms (noninterlaced).

BROADCAST STANDARDS

Broadcast television uses a technique called *2:1 interlace*. For a fixed bandwidth and line quantity, interlacing reduces visible flicker. In 2:1 interlace, each complete picture or *frame* is divided into two fields with the lines of one field interlaced between the lines of the other field, Fig. A-3. The figure shows fewer lines than actually exist in practice. In the U.S. there are 262.5 lines per field and 525 lines per frame. Each frame consists of two interlaced fields, one named *even* and one named *odd*. For black and white tv, the frame rate is 30 Hz and the field rate is 60 Hz. The horizontal line rate for black and white television is 525 lines/frame × 30 frames/sec = 15,750 lines/sec, or 15.750 kHz.

The horizontal sync and blanking signals are the same for both interlaced and noninterlaced tv, so Fig. A-2A still applies. However, the vertical signals differ (see Fig. A-4). Note that after each field, the vertical sync pulse alternately advances and delays one-half horizontal line. This is how the interlaced scans are generated. Note also the addition of the *equalizing interval*. This allows the sync separator in the tv

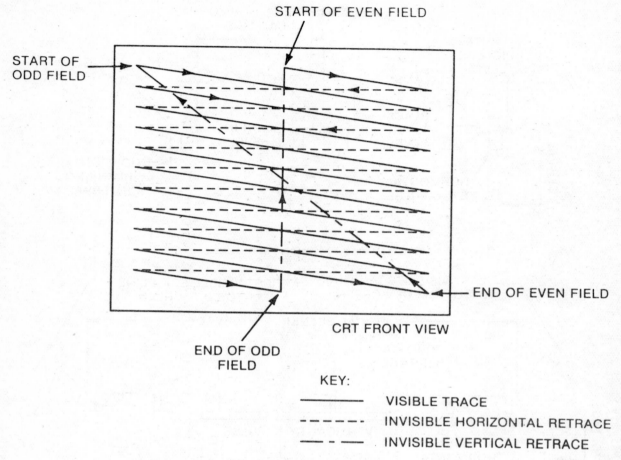

Fig. A-3. Video display (2:1 interlace).

set to trigger the vertical retrace at the same time (relative to the vertical sync pulse) on both odd and even fields.

We do not need to explore further the interlaced signal to understand the Apple's video; the Apple II's output is noninterlaced. Our object is to simply introduce the topic and point out that the Apple II does not output a broadcast standard 2:1 interlaced signal.

COLOR

The color tv process starts by dividing the image into three primary colors: red, blue, and green. This is often done with a tv camera that contains three camera tubes, one for each color. The three signals for the three colors are then combined in the proper proportions to create a brightness, or *luminance*, signal. The luminance is the same signal described previously for black and white tv. It is the signal that modulates the beam of a black and white crt to produce a picture. One purpose of including the luminance signal in the color broadcast signal is compatibility. This compatibility allows a black and white set to display a signal that is broadcast in color.

What about color tv sets? For the benefit of color sets, the red, blue, and green signals are used to modulate a 3.579545 MHz *subcarrier* that is added to the composite video. A color receiver demodulates the subcarrier and uses the resulting information along with the luminance to create a color image. A color crt displays the

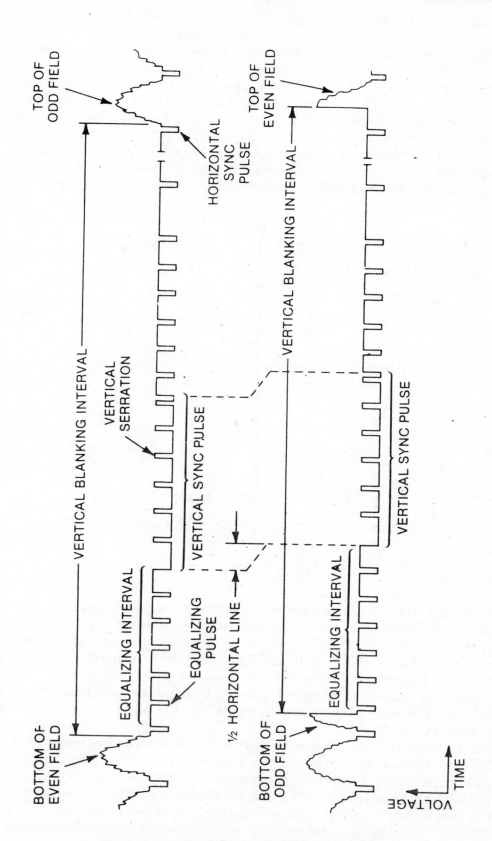

Fig. A-4. Vertical blanking interval (2:1 interlace).

image as many small dots or rectangles of the primary colors. Your eye blends the small dots together to create a continuous color image.

In Fig. A-5 we introduce the color circle as an aid to understanding how the subcarrier can contain the color information. Note that all colors can be represented by points around the circle. After modulation at the transmitting end, the phase of the 3.579545 MHz component determines the *hue* and its amplitude determines the intensity or *saturation*. In Fig. A-5, 0 degrees is the phase of a *burst* of subcarrier that is transmitted after each horizontal sync pulse. There are typically 9 cycles of the subcarrier in the burst. A color tv set uses this color burst to synchronize its internal 3.579545 MHz oscillator. It is with respect to this internal oscillator that the color set interprets the phase of the subcarrier to determine the hue.

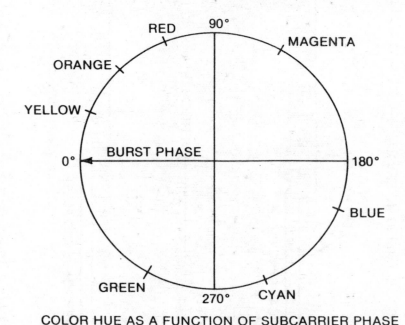

COLOR HUE AS A FUNCTION OF SUBCARRIER PHASE

Fig. A-5. Color circle.

In summary, the two important parts of the color signal are the color burst (which sets a reference) and the subcarrier (whose phase relative to the burst determines the hue). Recall that the luminance signal is still present and its importance is in determining the brightness. For example, a subcarrier at "red" phase added to a high luminance level will be light-red or pink.

Fig. A-6 shows a color burst signal followed by a video signal that creates a blue horizontal line. The line is blue since its phase lags the burst phase by 180 degrees (refer to the color circle).

When the standards for color television were formed, the frequency of the color subcarrier was selected to be toward the high end of the video band. This would reduce interference with the luminance signal. The color subcarrier also had to be below the 4.5 MHz sound subcarrier used in broadcast tv. The exact frequency was selected to reduce interference, such as beat patterns between the video, color, and sound signals. This was accomplished by adjusting some of the frequencies to be exact multiples of other frequencies contained in the composite video.

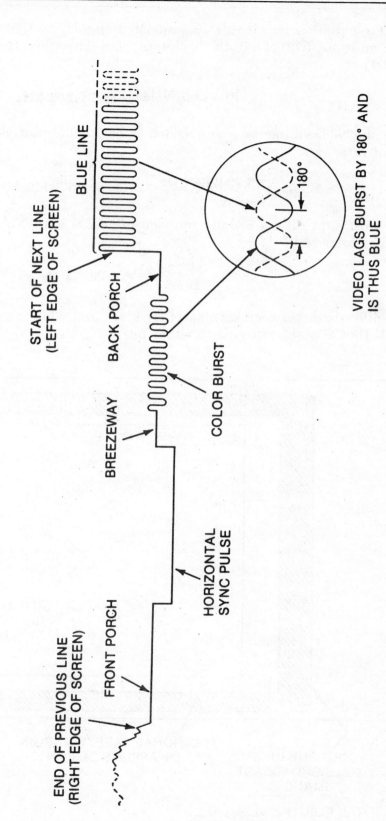

Fig. A-6. Color burst.

First the horizontal rate was adjusted slightly so that the sound would be an even multiple (572) of half the horizontal rate. Therefore, the horizontal line rate for color tv is

$$2 \times \frac{4.5 \text{ MHz}}{572} = 15.734266 \text{ kHz}$$

Next the color subcarrier was selected to be an odd multiple (455) of half the horizontal rate, or

$$\frac{15.734266 \text{ kHz}}{2} \times 455 = 3.579545 \text{ MHz}$$

The horizontal rate is usually rounded to 15.734 kHz. Note that the vertical field rate for color tv is

$$\frac{15.734 \text{ kHz}}{262.5 \text{ lines}} = 59.94 \text{ Hz}$$

The differences between scan rates for black and white and color broadcasts are so small that a tv set can sync to either one.

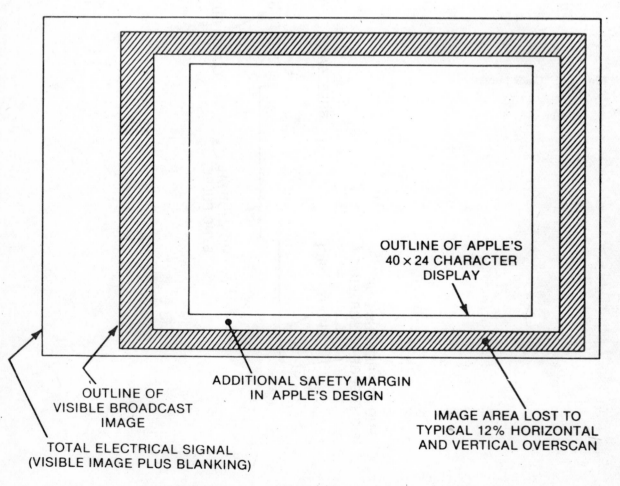

Fig. A-7.   The video area of the Apple compared with the standard broadcast image.

Table A-1 Apple's Video Parameters

Parameter	Broadcast Standard	Apple II		
		Rev. 0	**Rev. 1**	**Rev. 7 and RFI**
Interlacing	2:1		No	
Lines per Field	262.5		262	
Line Rate	15.734 kHz (Color) or 15.750 kHz (B&W)		15.700 kHz	
Field Rate	59.94 Hz (Color) or 60 Hz (B&W)		59.92 Hz	
Color Subcarrier	3.579545 MHz		3.579545 MHz	
Burst Length	9 Cycles[1] (2.24 μS min)		14 Cycles (3.9 μS)	
Front Porch	1.27 μS min		7.9 μS	
Hor Sync Pulse	4.45–5.08 μS	7.8 μS		3.9 μS
Breezeway	381–735 nS		70 nS	
Color Backporch	1.27 μS min	5.0 μS		8.9 μS
B & W Backporch	4.25 μS min	8.9 μS		12.8 μS
Sync to Blanking End	9.2 μS min		16.7 μS	
Sync to Burst End	7.78–7.94 μS	11.7 μS		7.8 μS
Hor Blanking	10.5 μS min		24.6 μS	
Sync to Burst Start	5.3 μS[1]	7.9 μS		4.0 μS
Vert Serration	4.5 μS	None		8.9 μS[2]
Vert Blanking	1.14 mS min		4.48 mS	
Vertical Sync Pulse	190 μS (3H)[3]	1.02 mS (16H)		255 μS (4H)
Intended Output Load Impedance	75 Ω		75 Ω	
Peak-Peak Level into 75 Ω	1.0 V		0–1.4 V (Adjustable)	
Black Level	+7.5 Units[4]		0 Units	
White Level	+100 Units		+110 Units	
Sync Level	–40 Units		–30 Units	
P–P Burst Level	20 Units		25 Units	

Notes: [1] Recommendation.

[2] Rev. 7 vertical serration is a double pulse, see Fig. B-2*.

[3] H = 1 horizontal line.

[4] Level relative to blanking. 140 Units = peak-peak signal amplitude.

OVERSCAN

The sweep circuits in a standard tv set are designed to *overscan* the face of the picture tube. As a result, parts of the picture as broadcast are lost around the edges. This is done so that even with component aging or line voltage fluctuations that tend to shrink the picture, the screen will still be full. A 12% horizontal overscan is typical. This means that the picture area available for Apple's output is limited if we are to avoid losing part of the display due to overscan. Fig. A-7 shows (to scale) Apple's video area relative to that of a standard broadcast image.

SUMMARY

The parameters of the Apple II video output are listed in Table A-1 next to the applicable broadcast standard. Even though it does not meet the standards in all ways, the Apple II works well with most tv sets and monitors. However, there have been cases of partial incompatibility with some color sets, projection tv sets, video cassette recorders, and broadcast switching equipment. Table A-1 contains information for those researching such problems. Note that later revisions of the Apple II conform more closely to broadcast standards.

Apple's Revisions

Like many electronic products that are manufactured for several years, the Apple II has undergone revision from time to time. Some revisions are product enhancements, such as adding more graphics colors. Some changes, like adjusting the cassette input gain, improve performance or reliability. Other revisions reduce cost by taking advantage of changing technology. An example is elimination of the ability to use the old 4K RAMs. One revision expands the market by providing optional compatibility with European television. Finally, some changes are mandated by government regulation. Here we speak of the redesign required for compliance with FCC rules on radio frequency interference.

The list of revisions may seem long, but the Apple II has actually sustained little functional change since its initial release in 1977. This can be credited to the foresight and innovation of the original design.

In this appendix we describe mother board and keyboard circuit changes that have occurred since the Apple II's initial design. We also note which changes occurred at which revision level and how to determine the revision of a particular Apple.

The circuit description in the body of this book covers the current Revision D RFI mother board and the two-piece keyboard. When earlier revisions require different descriptions, those descriptions are provided in this appendix.

OVERVIEW OF REVISIONS

Mother Board

The Apple II mother board has been manufactured in two basic varieties: *Non-RFI* and *RFI*. The non-RFI board was produced until 1981 when Apple switched to the RFI board. Radio frequency interference (RFI) refers to the electromagnetic noise given off by high-speed circuits such as computers. This noise often interferes with radio and tv sets. The FCC can restrict the sale of computers that exceed certain RFI limits. For this reason, Apple redesigned the mother board to reduce RFI. This redesigned board is referred to as the "RFI Mother Board." Earlier boards are referred to as "Non-RFI Mother Boards."

The RFI redesign involved such things as interchanging the location of + 5 volt and ground buses, isolating some circuit grounds, and adding ferrite beads. There were few functional changes. (Note that the Apple II RFI redesign involved more than the mother board. Part of the change involved shielding the plastic case and using shielded cable to the peripherals.)

Within the two major categories of RFI and non-RFI, there are additional revisions. We will list these in later sections.

Non-RFI—The non-RFI mother boards are designated by the nine digit part number 820-0001-XX. The "XX" is an incrementing revision number that starts with 00. The part number is found near the F1 location (left edge of board) on later revisions, and under the 6502 microprocessor IC on earlier revisions. (In this latter case, it is necessary to remove the 6502 to see the part number.) On the first or "Rev. 0" board, there may be no part number at all.

It is possible to determine the revision of a non-RFI mother board by examining certain features on the board. This is handy if the part number is not visible. A Rev. 0 board does not have an Auxiliary Video Pin. This pin is a single vertical pin located between the four-pin Auxiliary Video Connector and the video level adjust potentiometer (see Fig. B-1).

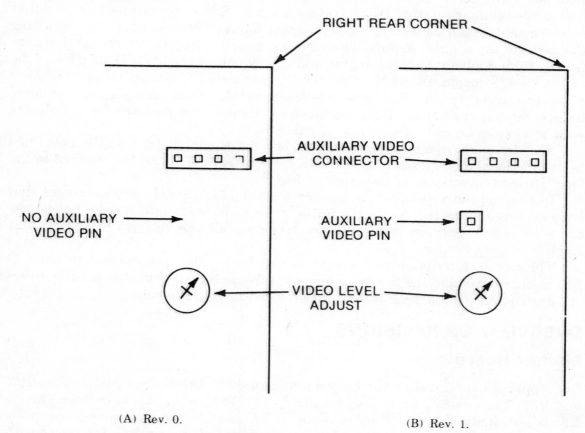

(A) Rev. 0.   (B) Rev. 1.

Fig. B-1. Identification of early non-RFI mother boards.

Non-RFI revisions 0 through 6 all have Memory Select Jumpers at locations D1, E1, and F1. Revision 7 does not have these jumpers.

There are no significant circuit differences between the revision 1 through 6 mother boards. Also, we have not found any distinguishing visible features (other than the part number) that can be used to differentiate these revisions. *In this book, we refer to the revision 1 through 6 non-RFI mother boards as simply "Rev. 1." Similarly, revision 7 and higher non-RFI boards are referred to as "Rev. 7."*

RFI—The RFI mother boards are identified by the part number 820-0044-XX. The "XX" is the revision and to date (July 1982) the latest revision is "D." There have been previous revisions of "01" and "C." The part number is found near the F1 location (left edge of board). The differences between RFI revisions involve locations and quantities of ferrite beads and other changes intended to further suppress RFI emissions. To date there have been no functional circuit changes between RFI revisions. *We refer to all RFI mother boards (through revision D) as simply "RFI."*

Keyboard

Single-piece—The early Apple II computers contain a single-piece keyboard; the keys and electronic components are mounted on a common PC board. This keyboard uses the National Semiconductor MM5740-AAE encoder IC which is no longer manufactured. The single-piece keyboard is described in this appendix.

Two-piece—At about the time that Apple introduced the Rev. 7 non-RFI mother board, they also introduced a two-piece keyboard. In this design, the keys are mounted on one PC board, and the electronic components are mounted on another. The two boards then plug together. There have been revisions of the board containing the keys. These revisions allow for key-switches from different manufacturers. These different boards, however, are all plug-compatible with the electronics board. The two-piece keyboard uses the General Instrument AY-5-3600 encoder IC and is described in Chapter 7.

Apple II Plus

The Apple II Plus is not a revision in the same sense as the mother board circuit revisions listed in this appendix. The difference between the Apple II and the Apple II Plus is the choice of firmware plugged into the mother board. Integer BASIC is on the Apple II mother board, and Applesoft BASIC is on the Apple II Plus mother board. In this book we have made no distinction between the Apple II and the Apple II Plus.

DETAILED CIRCUIT ANALYSIS

In this section we work backwards in time, describing circuit differences between revisions of the Apple. Remember that the RFI mother boards (part numbers 820-0044-01, -C, and -D) are described in the body of the book. It is with respect to the RFI board that we describe circuit variations.

Revision 7 Non-RFI Mother Board

The revision 7 non-RFI mother boards are identified by part numbers 820-0001-07 and up.

Color Killer—Early Rev. 7 boards do not have IC A14 (Fig. C-19*). These boards use transistor Q6 as a color killer. When TEXT MODE is high, base current through R27 drives Q6 into saturation. This shunts COLOR BURST to ground. This use of Q6 is not fully effective and some tv sets still display tinted text characters. In later Rev. 7 boards, A14-1 and A14-4 are added to force COLOR BURST to a low when TEXT MODE is high. For these boards, the last waveform of Fig. 4-3 is always low. Note that A14 is inserted into the circuit differently on Rev. 7 boards than it is on RFI boards. Also note the use of COLOR REF versus $\overline{\text{COLOR REF}}$.

Soft 5—Rev. 7 and earlier boards use high outputs of gates A2-8 and A2-11 instead of R28 to pull up unused logic inputs (Fig. C-2*).

Data Transceiver—Rev. 7 and earlier boards use two 8T28 quad transceivers on the data bus (H10 and H11 in Fig. C-8) instead of a single 8304 octal transceiver.

H2 Inverter—Rev. 7 boards use Q7 and associated resistors (Fig. C-19*) instead of A14-13 (Fig. C-20*) to invert signal H2. Q7 is located near IC B13.

Vertical Sync—Rev. 7 boards do not use A14-4 and A14-10 in the vertical sync circuit (Fig. C-19*). This results in a slightly different vertical sync pulse waveform as shown in Fig. B-2*. The waveforms that differ between Rev. 7 and RFI boards are B14-1, C13-C, SYNC, and the COMPOSITE VIDEO OUTPUT. For Rev. 7, Fig. B-2* replaces the vertical sync portion of Fig. 4-2*.

Auxiliary Video Pin—The Auxiliary Video Pin on some Rev. 7 boards is mounted in a four-pin connector as shown in Fig. C-19*. Two pins in this connector connect to unused solder pads 3 and 4 nearby. The fourth pin connects to signal AN2 and solder pad 2.

Video Filter—Rev. 7 and earlier boards do not have the high frequency filter consisting of L7 and C16 in the composite video output (Fig. C-19* and C-20*).

Miscellaneous—On Rev. 7 boards, the Clear input for text mode shift register A3 connects to SOFT 5 via bow tie 5.

Revision 1 Non-RFI Mother Board

The revision 1 non-RFI mother boards are identified by part numbers 820-0001-01 through -06.

Color Killer—Rev. 1 boards use Q6 as their only color killer. The operation of Q6 was described previously under Rev. 7.

Text Points—Rev. 1 and Rev. 0 boards do not have test points 3 and 4 or solder pad 1 (Figs. C-2*, C-12*, and C-16*).

Memory Jumper Blocks—Rev. 1 and Rev. 0 boards have 16-pin Memory Jumper Blocks at locations D1, E1, and F1 (Fig. C-4*). These blocks allow 16K-bit *or* 4K-bit RAMs to be used. The jumper blocks in Fig. C-4* are drawn in the configuration for use of *all* 16K RAMs. In this configuration, the memory system operates as described in Chapter 5. The following ICs and gates are part of the 4K/16K memory arrangement of Rev. 1 and Rev. 0 boards: H1-11, H1-3, C14-3, and E2. The IC E2 may be removed if you are using all 16K RAMs in a Rev. 1 or Rev. 0 Apple.

RAM Address 6 Termination—R31 and R32 which terminate signal line RA6 are not present on Rev. 1 or Rev. 0 boards.

Solder Pads 7 and 8—Solder pads 7 and 8 (Fig. C-11*) are not present on Rev. 1 or Rev. 0 boards. These pads are used to connect signals to peripheral I/O slot 7 for use by European color video generators.

Cassette Input—The gain of the cassette input circuit is different on Rev. 0 and some Rev. 1 boards (Fig. C-12*).

Test Connector—Rev. 1 and Rev. 0 boards do not have a multipin test connector near IC B2 (Fig. C-3*).

Character Generator—On Rev. 1 and Rev. 0 boards, IC A5 is a 2513 character generator (Fig. C-15*). A 2513 is really a ROM containing the same set of 64 ASCII characters that have been programmed into the 2316B ROM of the Rev. 7 and RFI boards. The 2513 cannot be directly replaced by a user-supplied EPROM, however, due to its supply voltages and pinouts.

The 2513 supplies only five outputs; the five horizontal dots of a character. As a result, the B and H inputs of shift register A3 are tied to ground. Bow ties 9, 10, and

11 are not present on Rev. 1 or Rev. 0 boards. Apart from these differences, the text mode operation of Rev. 1 and Rev. 0 boards is the same as described in Chapter 7.

Video Sync—Rev. 1 mother boards do not have IC A14 (compare Figs. C-18* and C-20*.) The result is a horizontal sync pulse twice as wide on Rev. 1 as on Rev. 7 and RFI boards. Fig. B-3 shows as typical the horizontal sync pulse that follows the vertical sync pulse. When dealing with a Rev. 1 board, use Fig. B-3 to replace the appropriate parts of Fig. 4-2*.

Fig. B-4 *shows the wider sync pulse and COLOR BURST in detail. When dealing with Rev. 1, Fig. B-4 replaces Fig. 4-3. In summary, the video signals that differ between Rev. 1 and RFI boards are B14-1, C13-C, C13-D, SYNC, COLOR BURST, and the COMPOSITE VIDEO OUTPUT.

Miscellaneous—The following items also differ between Rev. 1 and RFI boards: SOFT 5, Data Transceiver, and Video Filter. These items were described previously under Rev. 7.

Revision 0 Non-RFI Mother Board

The revision 0 non-RFI mother boards are identified as shown in Fig. B-1.

Power-On Reset—The Rev. 0 mother board does not have a power-on reset circuit. This function is provided by type 555 timer A13 on Rev. 1 and later boards (Fig. C-13*). This means that Rev. 0 users may have to press the reset key to initialize the 6502. This is not necessary, however, if a peripheral is installed that drives a reset pulse onto the reset line at power up. The Apple II floppy disk controller card is such an example.

Without power-on reset, the keyboard strobe flip-flop (B10-9) may be set when power is applied to a Rev. 0 board. As a result, the first keyboard command may contain an extra leading character. Note: If an autostart monitor ROM is installed in a Rev. 0 board, reset routines in the ROM will reset the keyboard strobe.

Color Killer—Rev. 0 boards use neither IC A14 nor transistor Q6 for a color killer. Without a color killer, COLOR BURST is not suppressed in text mode. This results in text characters with a color tint or fringe when using a color tv set.

Four HIRES Colors—The Rev. 0 mother board displays only four HIRES colors: black, white, violet, and green. By comparing Figs. C-14* and C-15*, you can see that some components are absent from Rev. 0. The key component not present is flip-flop A11-9. Recall from the HIRES discussion in Chapter 8 that A11-9 provides a delayed version of the HIRES serial bit stream from B4-15. Data selector A9 then selects either the delayed or nondelayed bit stream under control of DL7. When the delayed bit stream is selected, blue and orange are provided.

On Rev. 0 boards, there is no delayed bit stream, so there are no blue and orange colors. Data bit DL7 is ignored in HIRES mode on a Rev. 0 mother board.

Also on Rev. 0 boards, DL7 does not connect to A9 (this connection is via A8 and A10 on Rev. 1 and later boards). The data and select inputs of A9 are also arranged differently on Rev. 0 boards, with A12-10, A12-13, and A11-5 absent. Apart from the two missing HIRES colors, the graphics and text operation of Rev. 0 is the same as that of the RFI mother board described in Chapter 8.

24K Memory Size Problem—There is a problem on the Rev. 0 mother board that affects Apples with 20K or 24K bytes of RAM. The problem causes BASIC to "think" that there is more RAM in the computer than there is. This problem is corrected on the Rev. 1 board by gate C14-3 (Fig. C-4*). See page 72 of the *Apple II Reference Manual* for more details.

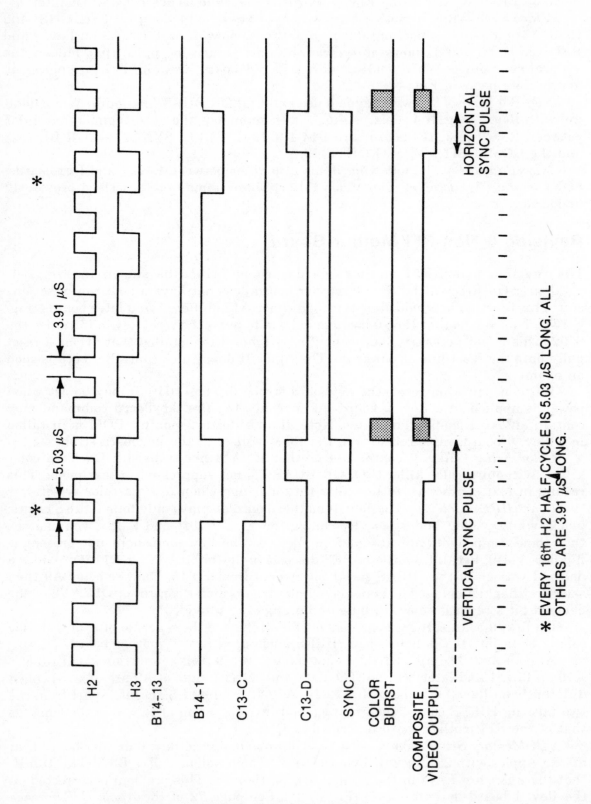

Fig. B-3. Vertical and horizontal sync—Rev. 1.

European TV Standards—Bow ties 12 and 16, and solder pads 13, 14, and 15 on Rev. 1 and later boards can be rearranged to convert the vertical frequency to 50 Hz for use with European tv sets. These pads and bow ties are not present on Rev. 0 boards. The circuit differences may be seen in Figs. C-3*, C-17*, and C-18*. The operation of the video address generator on a Rev. 0 board is the same as described in Chapters 3 and 4 for RFI boards.

Auxiliary Video Pin—Rev. 0 boards do not have an Auxiliary Video Pin (compare Figs. C-17* and C-18*).

Slot 7—Signals SYNC and COLOR REF do not connect to peripheral I/O slot 7 on Rev. 0 boards (Fig. C-11*).

Video Sync—Rev. 0 boards do not have ICs A14 and B14 (compare Figs. C-17* and C-20*). Since there is no A14, the Rev. 0 horizontal sync pulse is twice as long as the RFI horizontal sync pulse (see Figs. B-4 and B-6*). When dealing with the Rev. 0 mother board, substitute Fig. B-4 for Fig. 4-3.

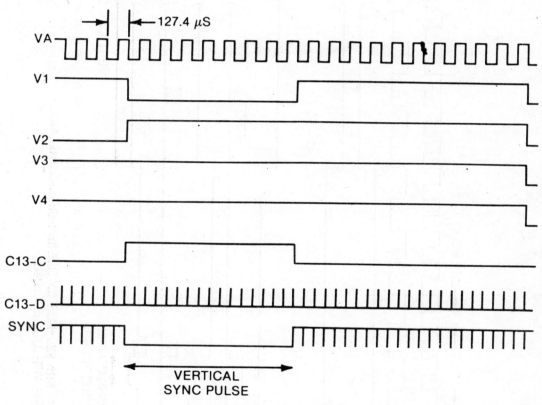

Fig. B-5.   Vertical sync—Rev. 0.

Since there is no B14, the Rev. 0 vertical sync pulse has no serrations and is four times as long as the RFI vertical sync pulse (compare Figs. B-5 and 4-1*). Note that to the scale of the figures, the Rev. 0 and RFI vertical sync pulses both start at the same time relative to the video address. When dealing with the Rev. 0 mother board, substitute Figs. B-5 and B-6 for the appropriate sections of Figs. 4-1* and 4-2*.

Miscellaneous—The following items also differ between Rev. 0 and RFI boards (they were described previously under Rev. 1):

Test Points
Memory Jumper Blocks

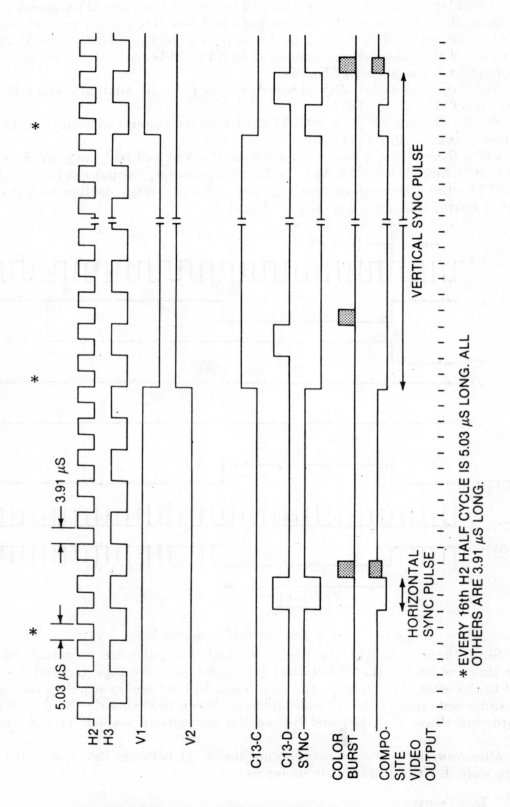

Fig. B-6. Vertical and horizontal sync—Rev. 0.

RA6 Terminator
Solder Pads 7 and 8
Cassette Input
Test Connector
Character Generator

The following additional items of difference between Rev. 0 and RFI boards were described previously under Rev. 7:

SOFT 5
Data Transceiver
Video Filter

Table B-1 lists a summary of the major differences between mother board revisions.

Table B.1 Summary of Major Mother Board Revisions

	Rev. 0	Rev. 1	Rev. 7	RFI
Color Killer	No	Q6	Q6 or A14-4	A14-1
Horizontal Sync Pulse	7.8 μS	7.8 μS	3.9 μS	3.9 μS
Vertical Sync Pulse	1.02 mS	255 μS	255 μS	255 μS
Vertical Serrations	No	Yes	Yes	Yes
H2 Inverter	None	None	Q7	A14-13
Auxiliary Video Pin	No	Yes	Yes	Yes
Optional 50 Hz Video	No	Yes	Yes	Yes
SYNC and COLOR REF on Slot 7	No	Yes	Yes	Yes
Solder Pads 7 and 8	No	No	Yes	Yes
HIRES Colors	4	6	6	6
Power-on Reset	No	Yes	Yes	Yes
Character Generator	2513	2513	2316B	2316B
Memory Jumper Blocks	Yes	Yes	No	No
Data Bus Transceiver	8T28	8T28	8T28	8304
SOFT 5	A2-8 & A2-11	A2-8 & A2-11	A2-8 & A2-11	R28

Single-Piece Keyboard

The single-piece keyboards used in early Apple II computers are identified by their physical arrangement. In the single-piece keyboard, the key switches and the ICs are all mounted on a common PC board. The functions performed on the single-piece keyboard are similar to those described in Chapter 7 for the two-piece keyboard. A different keyboard encoder IC is used, however, and there are other circuit differences. In this section, we provide a circuit description for the single-piece keyboard (Fig. C-21*).

(Note that *very early* single-piece keyboards use different reference designators than those shown in Fig. C-21*. These early keyboards use essentially the same parts and circuit, however. The early keyboards have a different PC layout that allows the ICs to be seen when the lid of the Apple is removed. This is how the early keyboards may be identified.)

Keyboard Encoder IC—The single-piece keyboard uses a type MM5740-AAE keyboard encoder IC, U5. The IC's 9 X outputs and 10 Y inputs are arranged in a matrix with the character keys at the cross points. Only 47 of the possible 90 cross points are occupied by keys. When a key is depressed, it connects the X line to the Y line.

Keyboard encoder U5 contains counters that count through an X sequence and a Y sequence as it scans the keyboard looking for a depressed key. These counters are driven from an external clock supplied to pin 3. An oscillator is formed by U4-6, U4-8, U4-11, C6, R6, and R7 that provides this clock. Its frequency (about 50 kHz) is not critical, but it must be between 10 kHz and 200 kHz for U5 to operate properly.

Fig. B-7 shows the clock and the sequence of pulses generated on U5's X outputs. When a key is depressed, one of the X outputs connects to a Y input. When this Y input is scanned, the key closure will be detected. Keyboard encoder U5 then looks at the SHIFT and CTRL key inputs and encodes the key into the proper ASCII character. The character is latched and appears inverted at U5's output (B1 through B9). The Apple II uses only the lower seven bits.

Gates U2 and U1-8 buffer the character and invert it to positive-true. The character then finds its way through the flat cable to location A7 on the mother board. Since the character was latched inside U5, it will remain at U5's output until another key is depressed.

Each time a key is closed, U5 outputs a pulse on its Data Strobe Output (pin 13). Pin 13 connects to pin 14 (Data Strobe Control), an arrangement that sets the pulse length at one clock period.

Sequence of Operation—Follow along on Fig. B-7 as we describe the timing. We will assume that the previous character was a "B." The ASCII LSB for "B" is 0, so U2-8 will be latched low from the previous character (point A). Now suppose you depress the "A" key. From the keyboard matrix we see that the "A" key connects X9 to Y4. Thus, as long as the "A" key is down, Y4 (point B) will be the same as X9 (point C). We will further assume that the Y scan is currently looking at Y4. This means the pulse on Y4 at point B will be detected by U5. Since the ASCII LSB for "A" is 1, U2-8 will go high (point D).

On the second clock falling pulse after detection (point E), U5 will generate a strobe pulse (point F). The pulse is one clock period long. The strobe is buffered by U1-6 and U1-3, then finds its way via the flat cable to location A7 on the mother board. There it sets flip-flop B10-9, point G. Chapter 6 covered the reading of the keyboard as far as circuitry on the mother board is concerned.

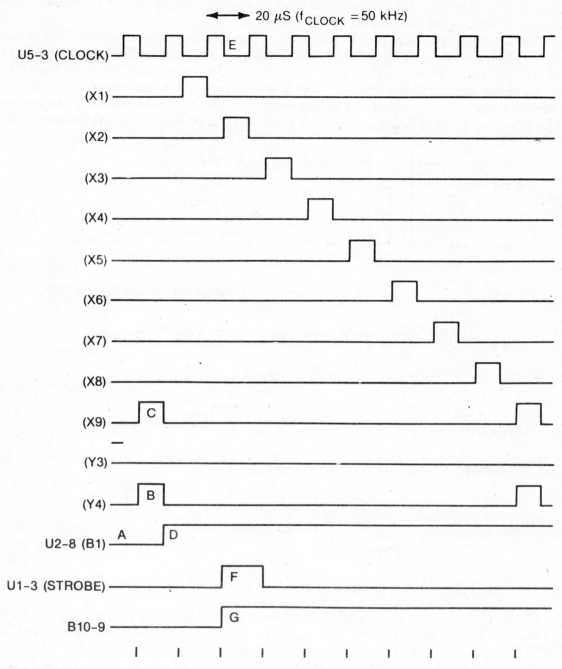

Fig. B-7. X scan—single-piece keyboard.

Fig. B-8* is another view of the signals shown expanded in Fig. B-7. In Fig. B-8* we can see one complete scan of the Y inputs. Again let's assume that "B" was the previous character so that B1 is low at point A. Sometime around point B we depress the "A" key. This connects Y4 to X9, and these two signals will be the same as long as the key is down. The key is not recognized until the Y scan reaches Y4 (point C). At this point, B1 goes high and there is a strobe pulse as was shown expanded in Fig. B-7.

The length of time it takes to detect a key closure is a function of where in the scan the key is depressed. The time ranges from 1 to 90 clock periods.

Non-TTL Levels—U5's X outputs and Y inputs are not at TTL levels. Their typical voltage levels are shown in Fig. B-9.

Contact Bounce—In most mechanical keyboards there is a possibility of contact bounce when a key is depressed and again when it is released. The bounce (rapid on and off fluctuations) can cause extra characters to be generated. Keyboard encoder U5 alleviates this problem by ignoring key closures for 8 mS after a key is first closed and again for 8 mS after a key is opened. This is accomplished by connecting C4 to U5's Key Bounce Mask pin. Fig. B-10 shows the timing and waveforms on C4.

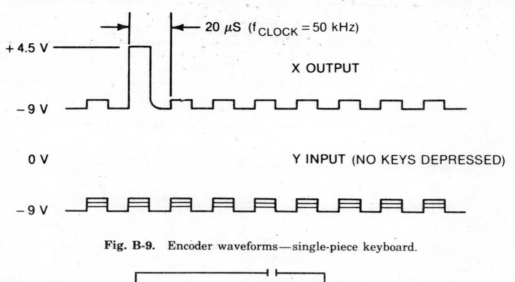

Fig. B-9. Encoder waveforms—single-piece keyboard.

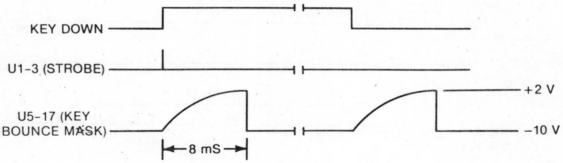

Fig. B-10. Key bounce mask—single-piece keyboard.

Repeat Function—U3 is a type 555 timer connected to oscillate at about 10 Hz as set by R3, R4, and C2 (Fig. C-21). U3 is normally held reset by R2. When the REPT key is depressed, the reset is removed and the resulting 10 Hz signal is applied to U5's Repeat input (pin 16). During each positive half cycle of the Repeat input, U5 will output a data strobe if a character key is also depressed.

Roll Over—The MM5740-AAE encoder IC is capable of *N-key roll over*. N-key roll over means that you can have any number of keys down simultaneously, and the encoder will correctly send the characters in the order keyed. This capability, however, can be used only if there is a diode at every cross point in the key matrix. The Apple II keyboard does not have these diodes. Without them, depressing three or more keys simultaneously may generate extraneous or *phantom* characters. As a result, the Apple II keyboard is described as having *2-key roll over*. No more than two keys may be depressed simultaneously if phantom characters are to be avoided.

The sneak paths that are possible in a matrix without diodes can be used in the single-piece keyboard to generate characters not normally available from the keyboard as shown in Table B-2.

Table B-2. Generate Special Characters

Character	Hold down these keys simultaneously
_ (Underscore)	SHIFT, U, I, Y
[(Left Bracket)	SHIFT, U, I, J
\ (Backslash)	SHIFT, U, I, H

With the proper editing, you can insert these characters into programs directly from the keyboard.

Quad-Mode Operation — U5 is a quad-mode encoder. This means each key can generate up to four different characters as a function of the SHIFT and CTRL keys (see Table B-3).

Table B-3. CHARACTERS as a Function of Control and Shift

U5-19 (CTRL)	U5-21 (SHIFT)	Character Group
0	0	Unshift
0	1	Shift
1	0	Control
1	1	Shift-Control

The four characters for each key are shown in Fig. C-21*. Only the "P," "M," and "N" keys can generate four different characters. The rest generate one or two.

Initialization — C7 and R8 form a delay circuit that initializes U5 on power up by taking SHIFT high for about 5 mS. Diode CR1 provides a rapid discharge path for C7.

Apple II Schematics

This appendix contains schematics for the Apple II mother board, keyboard, and power supply. Mother board schematics are provided for circuits dating from the earliest Apple II to the most recent revision available for publication. The paragraphs that follow contain information intended to help you use the schematics.

REVISIONS
Mother Boards

As described in Appendix B, the earliest Apple II mother board is known as Rev. 0. A short time after the Apple's introduction, several circuit changes resulted in the Rev. 1 mother board. Rev. 1 includes a color killer and two more HIRES colors. There were no more significant circuit changes until the introduction of the Rev. 7 mother board. Rev. 7 deletes the Memory Jumper Blocks and changes the character generator ROM. The next significant change involved modification of the mother board and packaging to reduce RFI. Some minor circuit changes were made at the same time. The major revisions of the mother board are denoted in this book as Rev. 0, Rev. 1, Rev. 7, and RFI.

Appendix B contains additional information on the differences between revisions. It also describes how you can examine the mother board to determine the revision of a particular Apple II. Note that the circuit description in the body of this book corresponds to the RFI schematics. Material in Appendix B describes the differences in operation of Revisions 0, 1, and 7 relative to the operation of the RFI mother board.

A notation on each schematic indicates the revision to which the schematic applies. Most schematics apply to two or more revisions. Minor circuit differences between the revisions are indicated by notes or insets on the drawing. When there are major differences between revisions, separate schematics are used for each revision. As you trace a signal from schematic to schematic, be sure to use the drawing that corresponds to the revision of interest.

Keyboards

The original Apple II keyboard was constructed on a single printed circuit board and is thus referred to as the "single-piece keyboard." Apple later introduced a "two-piece keyboard." The two-piece keyboard contains one printed circuit board on which the keys are mounted. A second printed circuit board containing the ICs then plugs onto the first printed circuit board. This appendix contains schematics for both the single- and two-piece keyboards.

SYMBOLS

Fig. C-1 shows some of the symbols used on the schematics. When a signal enters or exits a schematic, the signal name is shown beside an arrow symbol (Examples a through d). The direction of the arrow indicates the direction of signal flow. A double-headed arrow indicates bidirectional signal flow, such as on a data bus (Example c). If the signal is part of the system bus, a number inside the arrow symbol gives the peripheral I/O connector pin on which the signal appears (Examples c and d). A "To" or "From" notation beside a signal name indicates the other schematics on which the signal appears. The designations "Part 1" and "Part 2" refer to the two separate drawings used to show some schematics. For example, the video generator schematic is divided into two parts.

Logic functions that are active on a low level are shown by a small circle or

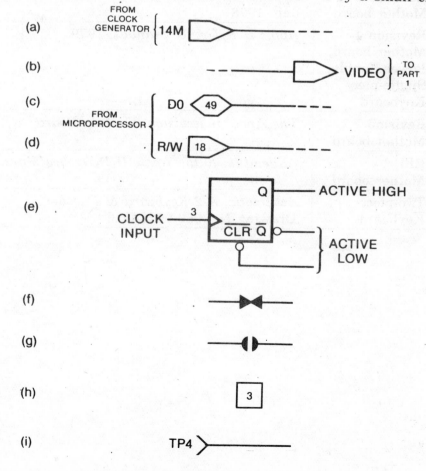

Fig. C-1. Schematic symbols.

"bubble." For example, see the $\overline{Q}$ output and $\overline{CLR}$ input in Example e. The symbol at pin 3 is a clock input.

The symbols in Examples f and g represent the shapes of printed circuit board traces that are meant to be altered in order to modify the circuit. The *bow tie* in Example f would be cut between the arrows to open the circuit. The semicircles in Example g would be bridged with solder to close the circuit.

A number in a square (Example h) refers to a note shown elsewhere on the drawing. The symbol in Example i represents a test point or other labeled solder point on the circuit board.

When an IC is powered from +5 volts and ground, and these voltages connect to the usual opposite corner pins of the IC, then the power pins are not shown on the schematic. If the +5 volts connects to an unusual pin or if the IC requires multiple voltages, then the power pins *are* shown. In general, bypass capacitors, ferrite beads, and isolated grounds are not depicted in the drawings.

The Apple II schematics are shown in Figs. C-2* through C-23*.

ACKNOWLEDGMENTS

The schematics in this appendix have been used with the permission of Apple Computer, Inc. They have been redrawn from the following Apple Computer documents:

Revision 0 Mother board	*Apple II Reference Manual* ("Red Book"), Jan. 1978
Revision 1 Mother board, Power Supply, Single-piece Keyboard	*Apple II Reference Manual*, 1979
Revision 7 Mother board	*The Apple II Revision 07 Main Board*
RFI Mother board	*Addendum to the Apple II Reference Manual*
Two-piece Keyboard	*Schematic, A-2 Keyboard & Encoder*, Drawing No. 050-0021-D

APPENDIX **D**

References

Chapter 1

1.1 Espinosa, Christopher. *Apple II Reference Manual*, Apple Computer, Inc., 1979.
1.2 *The TTL Data Book for Design Engineers*, 2nd ed., Texas Instruments, 1976.

Chapter 2

2.1 United States Patent No. 4,130,862, "DC Power Supply," Inventor: Frederick R. Holt, Assignee: Apple Computer, Inc., 19 Dec., 1978.
2.2 Wozniak, Stephen. "System Description—The Apple II," *Byte*, May 1977.

Chapter 3

3.1 United States Patent No. 4,136,359, "Microcomputer for use with Video Display," Inventor: Stephen G. Wozniak, Assignee: Apple Computer, Inc., 23 Jan., 1979.
3.2 Wozniak, Stephen. "The Impossible Dream: Computing *e* to 116,000 Places with a Personal Computer, "*Byte*, June 1981.

Chapter 5

5.1 *Memory Data Book and Designers Guide*, Mostek, 1979.

Chapter 6

6.1 "Apple II Product Specifications, Hobby/Prototyping Board," Apple Computer, Inc.
6.2 "Applications Information AN2—SY6500 Microprocessor Family," Microprocessor Products, Synertek, Jan. 1980.
6.3 DeJong, Marvin L. *Programming & Interfacing the 6502, with Experiments*, Howard W. Sams & Co., Inc., 1980.
6.4 Fischer, Dan and Caffrey, Morgan P. "Go Ahead and Interrupt your Apple," Parts 1 and 2, *Softalk*, Mar. and Apr. 1982.
6.5 Holland, John M. *Advanced 6502 Interfacing*, Howard W. Sams & Co., Inc., 1982.

6.6 *MCS 6500 Microcomputer Family Hardware Manual*, Commodore Business Machines, Inc. (MOS Technology), Jan. 1976.

6.7 *MCS 6500 Microcomputer Family Programming Manual*. Commodore Business Machines, Inc. (MOS Technology), Jan. 1976.

6.8 *R6500 Microcomputer System Hardware Manual*, Rockwell International, Aug. 1978.

6.9 "R6500 Microcomputer System Data Sheet," Rockwell International, Nov. 1981.

6.10 *R6500 Microcomputer System Programming Manual*, Rockwell International, Feb. 1979.

6.11 Scanlon, Leo J. *6502 Software Design*, Howard W. Sams & Co., Inc., 1980.

6.12 "6500 Microprocessors" (Data Sheet), Commodore Semiconductor Group, Feb. 1981.

6.13 *SY6500/MCS6500 Microcomputer Family Hardware Manual*, Synertek, Aug. 1976.

6.14 *SY6500/MCS6500 Microcomputer Family Programming Manual*, Synertek, Aug. 1976.

6.15 SY6500 Data Sheet, "8-Bit Microprocessor Family," Synertek, Apr. 1980.

6.16 Titus, Jonathan S., Larsen, David G., and Titus, Christopher A. *Apple Interfacing*, Howard W. Sams & Co., Inc., 1981.

6.17 White, George M. "Using Interrupts on the Apple II System," *Byte*, May 1981.

Chapter 7

7.1 *Apple II Monitors Peeled*, Apple Computer, Inc., 1981.

7.2 "AY-5-3600 Keyboard Encoder Operation," Bulletin 1402, General Instrument Corp.

7.3 *Data Catalog*, Standard Microsystems Corp., 1981 (KR3600 Keyboard Encoder).

7.4 Lancaster, Don. *TV Typewriter Cookbook*, Howard W. Sams & Co., Inc., 1976.

7.5 *Microelectronics Product Catalog*, General Instrument Corp., 1980 (AY-5-3600 Data Sheet).

7.6 "The Apple II Cassette Interface," *Apple Orchard*, Spring 1981.

Chapter 8

8.1 Bishop, Bob. "Apple II HIRES Graphics: Resolving the Resolution Myth," *Apple Orchard*, Fall 1980.

8.2 Rowe, Pete. "The Mysterious Orange Vertical Line," *Apple Orchard*, Fall 1980.

8.3 United States Patent No. 4,278,972, "Digitally Controlled Color Signal Generation Means for use with Display," Inventor: Stephen G. Wozniak, Assignee: Apple Computer, Inc., 14 July, 1981.

Appendix A

A.1 Bierman, Howard and Bierman, Marvin. *Color Television Principles and Servicing*, Hayden Book Co., Inc., 1973.

A.2 "EIA Television Systems Bulletin No. 4, EIA Recommended Practice for Horizontal Sync, Horizontal Blanking and Burst Timing in Television Broadcasting," EIA, Mar. 1976.

A.3 "EIA Standard RS-170, Electrical Performance Standards—Monochrome Television Studio Facilities," EIA, Nov. 1957.

A.4 "EIA Standard RS-189-A, Encoded Color Bar Signal," EIA, July 1976.

A.5 "EIA Standard RS-330, Electrical Performance Standards for Closed Circuit Television Camera 525/60 Interlaced 2:1," EIA, Nov. 1966.

A.6 Grob, Bernard, *Basic Television Principles and Servicing*, McGraw-Hill, 1975.

A.7 "Industrial Electronics Bulletin No. 1, Closed Circuit Television—Definitions," Electronics Industries Association, Sept. 1962.

A.8 "19-Inch Color TV's," *Consumer Reports*, Jan. 1981.

A.9 Schure, Alexander. *Basic Television*, Vol. 6, Hayden Book Co., Inc., 1975.

Appendix B

B.1 "Addendum to the Apple II Reference Manual," Apple Part No. 031-0004-B, Apple Computer, Inc. (Reduced RFI Mother Board).

B.2 *Apple II Reference Manual* (Red Book), Apple Computer, Inc., Jan. 1978.

B.3 "Application Note AN-80, MOS Keyboard Encoding," National Semiconductor Corp., April 1973.

B.4 "Data Sheet, MM5740 90-Key Keyboard Encoder," National Semiconductor Corp., 1977.

B.5 "The Apple II Revision 07 Main Board," Apple Part No. 031-0072-00, Apple Computer, Inc.

B.6 "2513 Data Sheet—High Speed 64 × 7 × 5 Character Generator," Signetics.

Index

SAMS APPLE® BOOKS

Many thanks for your interest in this Sams Book about Apple II® microcomputing. Here are a few more Apple-oriented Sams products we think you'll like:

POLISHING YOUR APPLE®
Clearly written, highly practical, concise assembly of all procedures needed for writing, disk-filing, and printing programs with an Apple II. Positively ends your searches through endless manuals to find the routine you need! By Herbert M. Honig. Approximately 64 pages, 5½ x 8½, comb. ISBN 0-672-22026-1. © 1982.
Ask for No. 22026 . . . . **$4.95 Tentative**

THE APPLE II® CIRCUIT DESCRIPTION
Provides you with a detailed circuit description of the Revision 1 Apple II motherboard, including the keyboard and power supply. Compares Revision 1 with other revisions, and includes timing diagrams for major signals. By Winston D. Gayler. Approximately 240 pages, 8½ x 11, comb. ISBN 0-672-21959-X. © 1983.
Ask for No. 21959 . . . . **$22.95 Tentative**

INTERMEDIATE LEVEL APPLE II® HANDBOOK
Hands-on aid for exploring the entire internal firmware of your Apple II and finding out what you can accomplish with its 6502 microprocessor through machine- and assembly-language programming. By David L. Heiserman. Approximately 364 pages, 6 x 9, comb. ISBN 0-672-21889-5. © 1983.
Ask for No. 21889 . . . . **$9.95 Tentative**

APPLE® FORTRAN
Only fully detailed Apple FORTRAN manual on the market! Ideal for Apple programmers of all skill levels who want to try FORTRAN in a business or scientific program. Many ready-to-run programs provided. By Brian D. Blackwood and George H. Blackwood. 240 pages, 6 x 9, comb. ISBN 0-672-21911-5. © 1982.
Ask for No. 21911 . . . . **$14.95**

APPLE II® ASSEMBLY LANGUAGE
Shows you how to use the 3-character, 56-word vocabulary of Apple's 6502 to create powerful, fast-acting programs! For beginners or those with little or no assembly language programming experience. By Marvin L. De Jong. 336 pages, 5½ x 8½, soft. ISBN 0-672-21894-1. © 1982.
Ask for No. 21894 . . . . **$15.95**

ENHANCING YOUR APPLE II® — Vol. 1
Shows you how to mix text, LORES, and HIRES anywhere on the screen, how to open up whole new worlds of 3-D graphics and special effects with a one-wire modification, and more. Tested goodies from a trusted Sams author! By Don Lancaster. 232 pages, 8½ x 11, soft. ISBN 0-672-21846-1. © 1982.
Ask for No. 21846 . . . . **$15.95**

CIRCUIT DESIGN PROGRAMS FOR THE APPLE II®
Programs quickly display "what happens if" and "what's needed when" as they apply to periodic waveform, rms and average values, design of matching pads, attenuators, and heat sinks, solution of simultaneous equations, and more. By Howard M. Berlin. 136 pages, 8½ x 11, comb. ISBN 0-672-21863-1. © 1982.
Ask for No. 21863 . . . . **$15.95**

APPLE® INTERFACING
Brings you real, tested interfacing circuits that work, plus the necessary BASIC software to connect your Apple to the outside world. Lets you control other devices and communicate with other computers, modems, serial printers, and more! By Jonathan A. Titus, David G. Larsen, and Christopher A. Titus. 208 pages, 5½ x 8½, soft. ISBN 0-672-21862-3. © 1981.
Ask for No. 21862 . . . . **$10.95**

INTIMATE INSTRUCTIONS IN INTEGER BASIC

Explains flowcharting, loops, functions, graphics, variables, and more as they relate to Integer BASIC. Used with *Applesoft Language* (No. 21811), it gives you everything you need to program BASIC with your Apple II or Apple II Plus. By Brian D. Blackwood and George H. Blackwood. 160 pages, 5½ x 8½, soft. ISBN 0-672-21812-7. © 1981.
Ask for No. 21812 . . . . **$8.95**

APPLESOFT® LANGUAGE

Only complete text available on Applesoft BASIC! Self-teaching format simplifies learning and lets you use what you learn FAST. Ideal for businessmen, hobbyists, and professionals! Many programs included. By Brian D. Blackwood and George H. Blackwood. 256 pages, 5½ x 8½, soft. ISBN 0-672-21811-9. © 1981.
Ask for No. 21811 . . . . **$10.95**

MOSTLY BASIC: APPLICATIONS FOR YOUR APPLE II®, BOOK 1

Twenty-eight debugged, fun-and-serious BASIC programs you can use immediately on your Apple II. Includes a telephone dialer, digital stopwatch, utilities, games, and more. By Howard Berenbon. 160 pages, 8½ x 11, comb. ISBN 0-672-21789-9. © 1980.
Ask for No. 21789 . . . . **$12.95**

MOSTLY BASIC: APPLICATIONS FOR YOUR APPLE II®, BOOK 2

A second gold mine of fascinating BASIC programs for your Apple II, featuring 3 dungeons, 11 household programs, 6 on money or investment, 2 to test your ESP level, and more — 32 in all! By Howard Berenbon. 224 pages, 8½ x 11, comb. ISBN 0-672-21864-X. © 1981.
Ask for No. 21864 . . . . **$12.95**

You can usually find these Sams products at better computer stores, bookstores, and electronic distributors nationwide.

If you can't find what you need, call Sams at 800-428-3696 toll-free or 317-298-5566, and charge it to your MasterCard or Visa account. Prices subject to change without notice.

For a free catalog of all Sams Books available, write P.O. Box 7092, Indianapolis IN 46206.

SAMS BRINGS YOU MIND TOOLS™ FOR FINANCIAL PLANNING IN BUSINESS

Special, ready-to-use software that temporarily interlocks with the spreadsheet in your regular version of Multiplan® or VisiCalc® so you can immediately perform 17 common financial planning calculations without wasting time manually setting up the sheet. All you do is enter the data — the proper formulas and column headings are there automatically!

Mind Tools allow you to instantly calculate present, net present, and future values, yields, internal and financial management rates of return, and basic statistics.

Also lets you do break-even analyses, depreciation schedules, and amortization tables, as well as compute variable- and graduated-rate mortgages, wraparound mortgages, and more!

Allows you to use your regular spreadsheet as you always have, at any time. Ideal for any businessman with financial planning responsibilities, as well as for business students and instructors.

Supplied with complete documentation, including 136-page text and 68-page quick-reference guide, all in a binder with the proper disk to match the brand of spreadsheet program you own.

Currently available for use with Multiplan or VisiCalc on the Apple II as follows:

EXECUTIVE PLANNING WITH MULTIPLAN

Apple II Version, ISBN 0-672-22058-X.
Ask for No. 22058 . . . . **$59.95**

EXECUTIVE PLANNING WITH VISICALC

Apple II Version, ISBN 0-672-22059-8.
Ask for No. 22059 . . . . **$59.95**

TO THE READER

Sams Computer books cover Fundamentals — Programming — Interfacing — Technology written to meet the needs of computer engineers, professionals, scientists, technicians, students, educators, business owners, personal computerists and home hobbyists.

Our Tradition is to meet your needs and in so doing we invite you to tell us what your needs and interests are by completing the following:

1. I need books on the following topics:

_____

_____

_____

_____

_____

_____

_____

_____

_____

2. I have the following Sams titles:

_____

_____

_____

_____

_____

_____

_____

3. My occupation is:

_____ Scientist, Engineer	_____ D P Professional
_____ Personal computerist	_____ Business owner
_____ Technician, Serviceman	_____ Computer store owner
_____ Educator	_____ Home hobbyist
_____ Student	Other _____
	_____

Name (print)_____

Address_____

City _____ State _____ Zip _____

Mail to: **Howard W. Sams & Co., Inc.**
　　　　Marketing Dept. #CBS1/80
　　　　4300 W. 62nd St., P.O. Box 7092
　　　　Indianapolis, Indiana 46206

21959

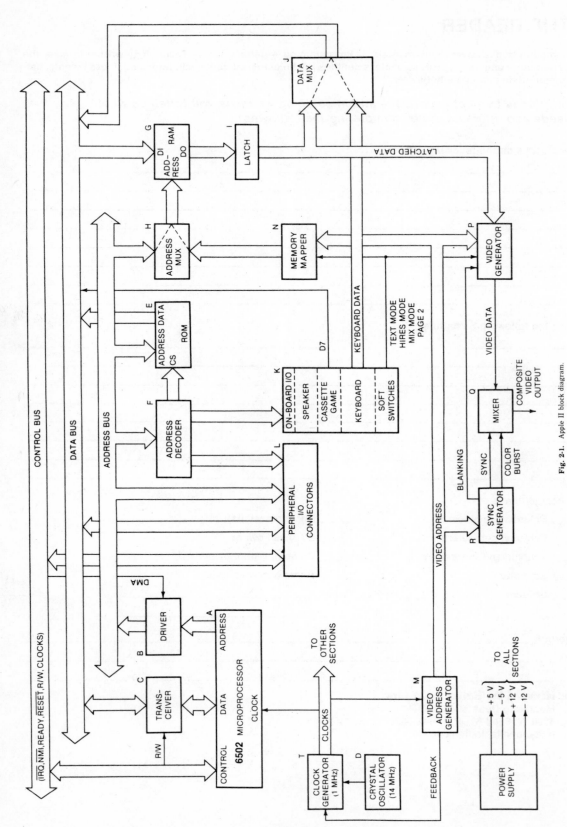

Fig. 2-1. Apple II block diagram.

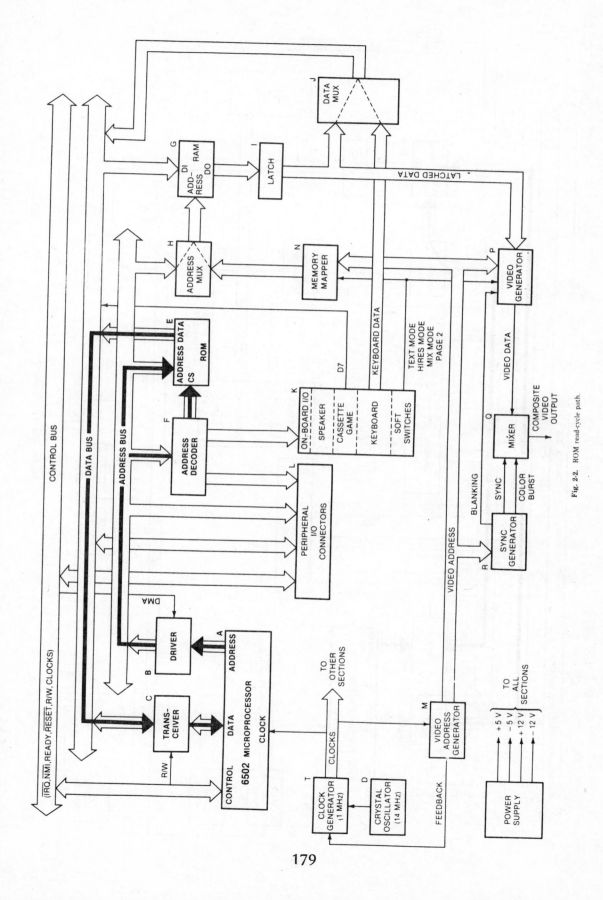

Fig. 2-2. ROM read-cycle path.

179

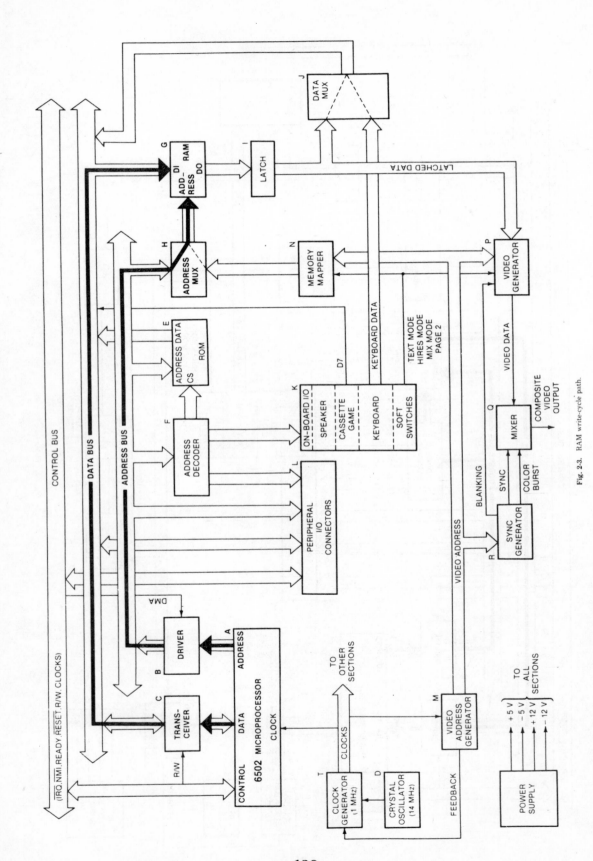

Fig. 2-3. RAM write-cycle path.

180

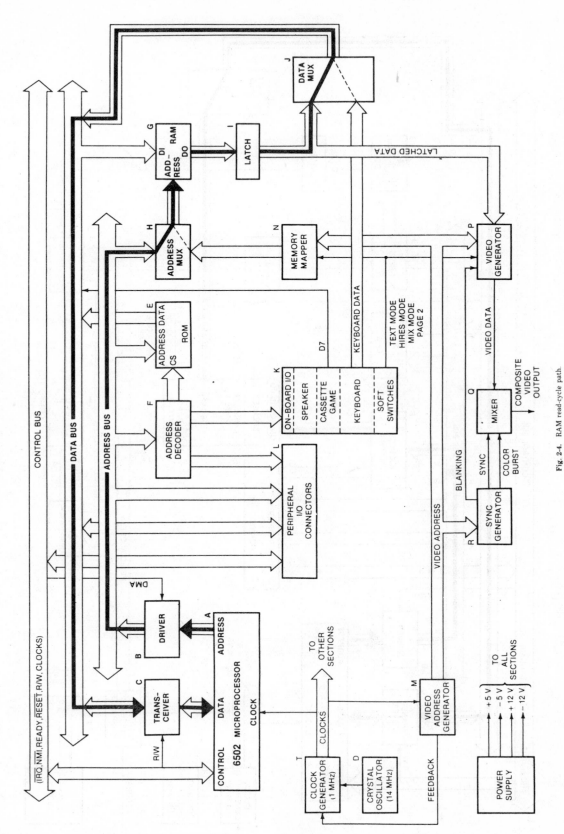

Fig. 2-4. RAM read-cycle path.

181

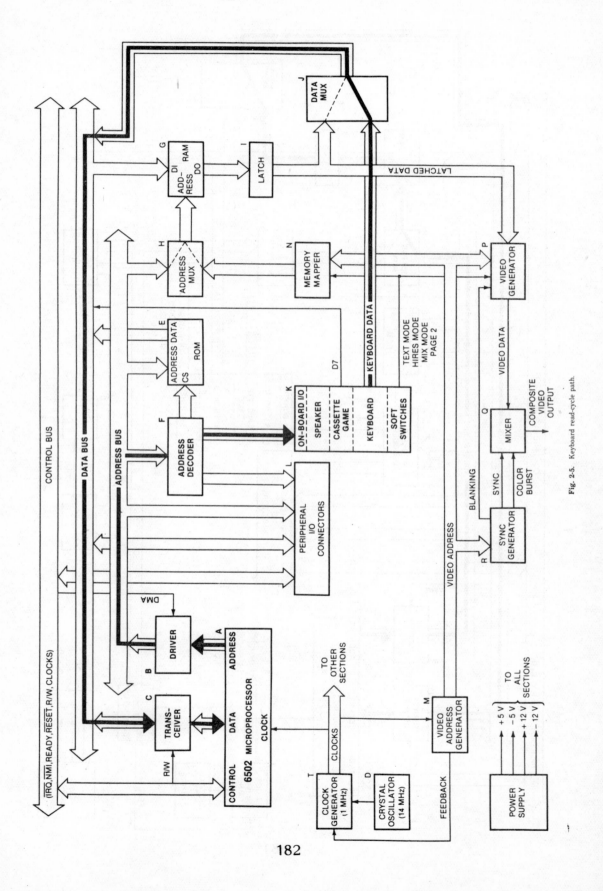

Fig. 2-5. Keyboard read-cycle path.

182

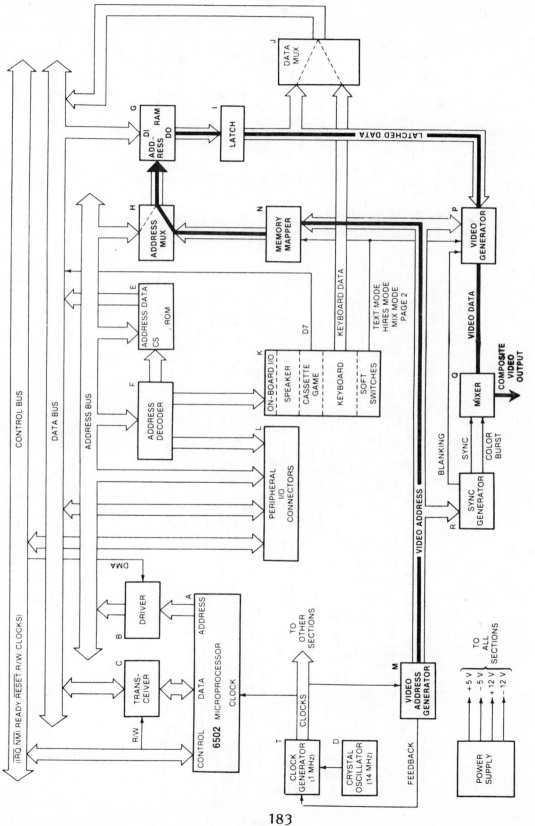

Fig. 2-6. Video-cycle path.

183

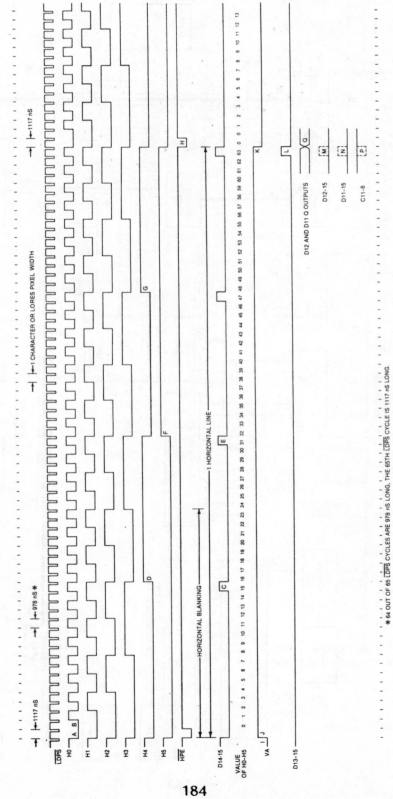

Fig. 3-4. Horizontal timing.

184

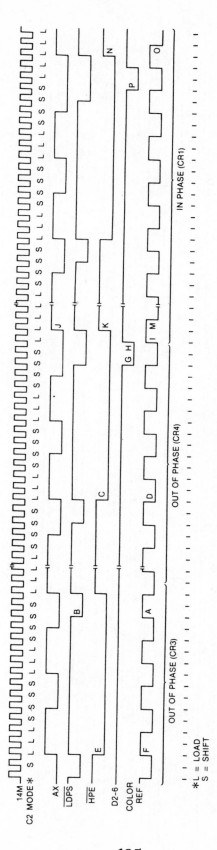

Fig. 3-7. Clock synchronization—CR3 and CR4.

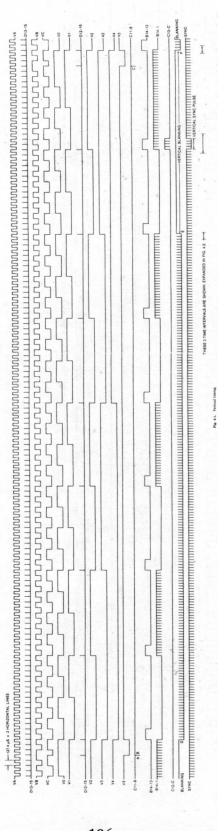

Fig. 4-1. Vertical timing

186

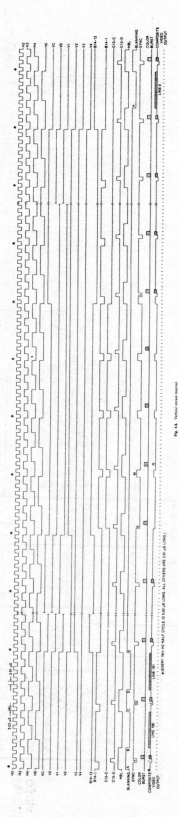

Fig. 4-2. Vertical retrace interval.

187

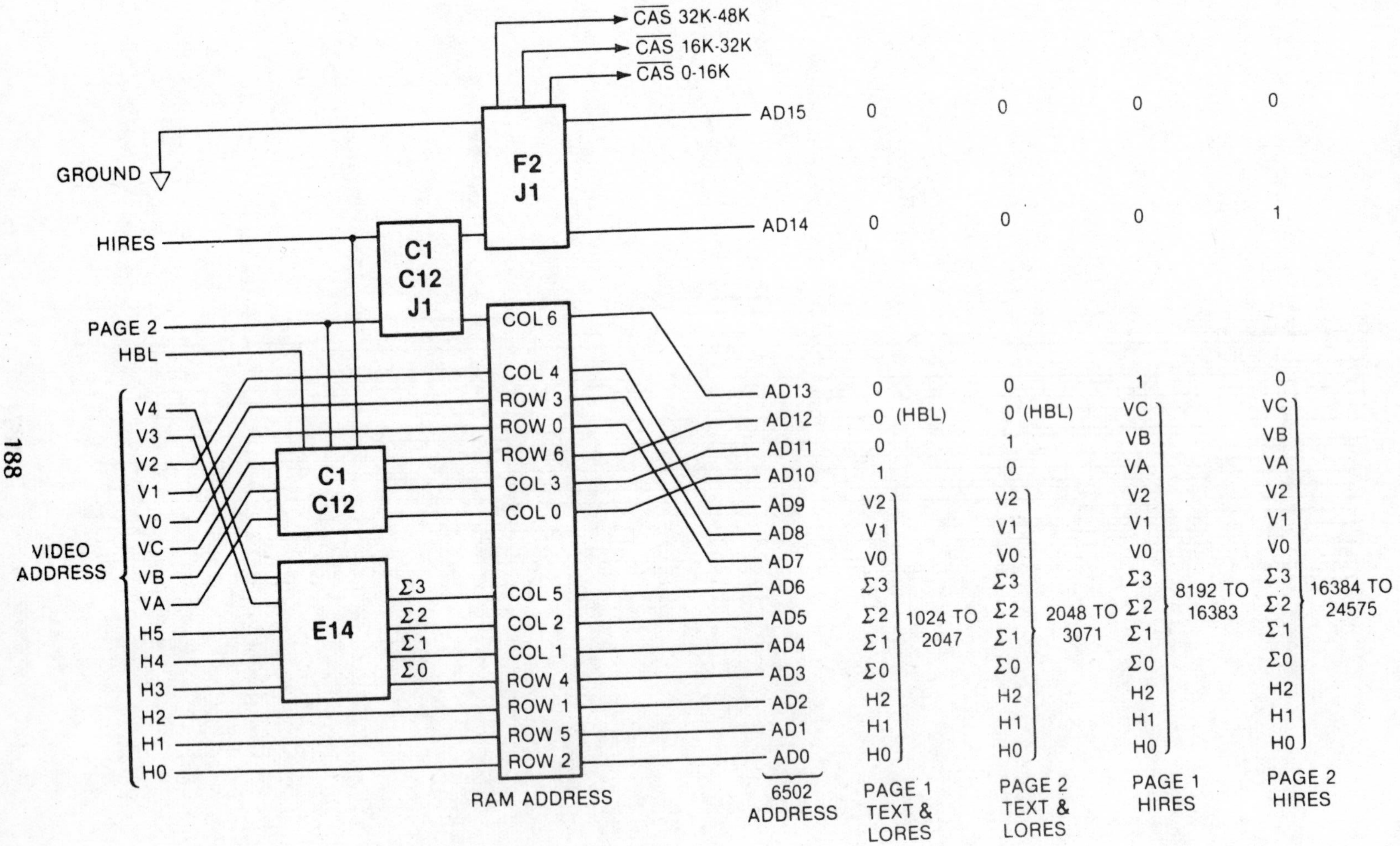

Video address mapping table (6502 address bits vs. display mode)

6502 ADDRESS	PAGE 1 TEXT & LORES 1024 TO 2047	PAGE 2 TEXT & LORES 2048 TO 3071	PAGE 1 HIRES 8192 TO 16383	PAGE 2 HIRES 16384 TO 24575
AD15	0	0	0	0
AD14	0	0	0	1
AD13	0	0	1	0
AD12	0 (HBL)	0 (HBL)	VC	VC
AD11	0	1	VB	VB
AD10	1	0	VA	VA
AD9	V2	V2	V2	V2
AD8	V1	V1	V1	V1
AD7	V0	V0	V0	V0
AD6	Σ3	Σ3	Σ3	Σ3
AD5	Σ2	Σ2	Σ2	Σ2
AD4	Σ1	Σ1	Σ1	Σ1
AD3	Σ0	Σ0	Σ0	Σ0
AD2	H2	H2	H2	H2
AD1	H1	H1	H1	H1
AD0	H0	H0	H0	H0

Block diagram labels

Inputs: GROUND, HIRES, PAGE 2, HBL, AD15, AD14

Logic blocks: F2 J1 → $\overline{CAS}$ 32K-48K, $\overline{CAS}$ 16K-32K, $\overline{CAS}$ 0-16K; C1 C12 J1; C1 C12 (Σ3, Σ2, Σ1, Σ0); E14 (Σ3, Σ2, Σ1, Σ0)

RAM ADDRESS: COL 6, COL 4, ROW 3, ROW 0, ROW 6, COL 3, COL 0, COL 5, COL 2, COL 1, ROW 4, ROW 1, ROW 5, ROW 2

VIDEO ADDRESS: V4, V3, V2, V1, V0, VC, VB, VA, H5, H4, H3, H2, H1, H0

Fig. 5-7. Video mapping.

188

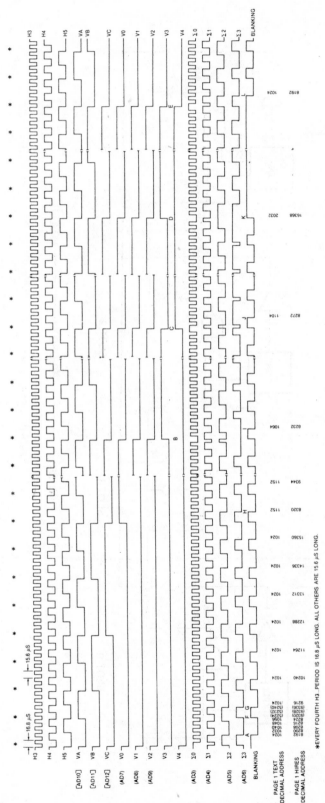

Fig. 5-8. Video address signals.

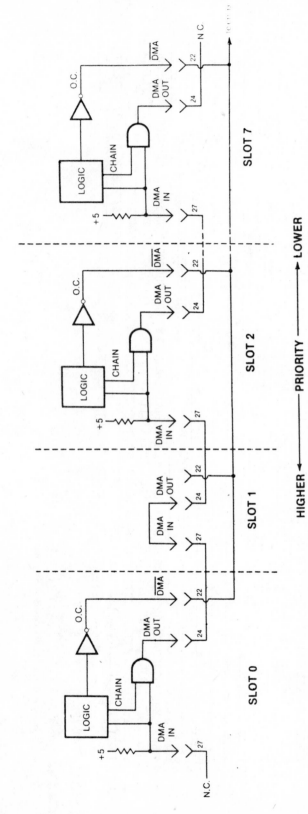

Fig. 6-11. DMA daisy chain.

190

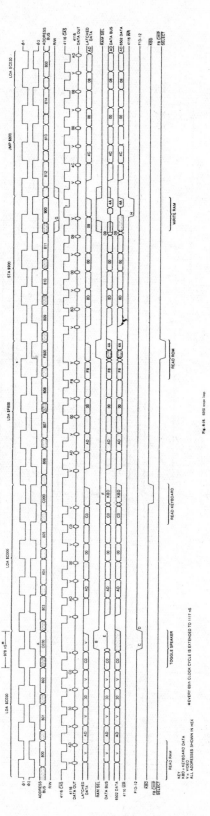

Fig. 6-18. 6502 scope loop.

191

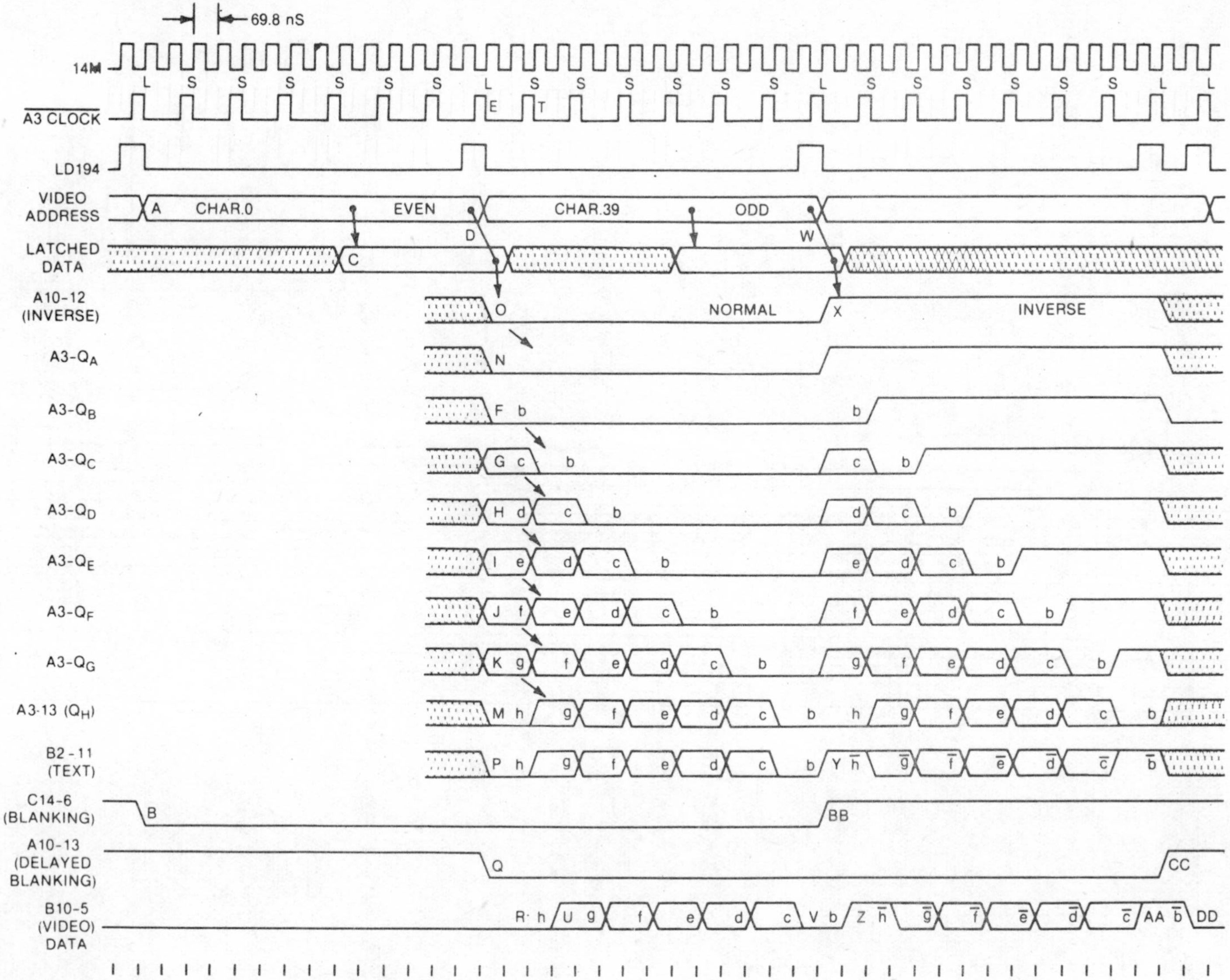

Fig. 8-26. Text mode timing diagram.

192

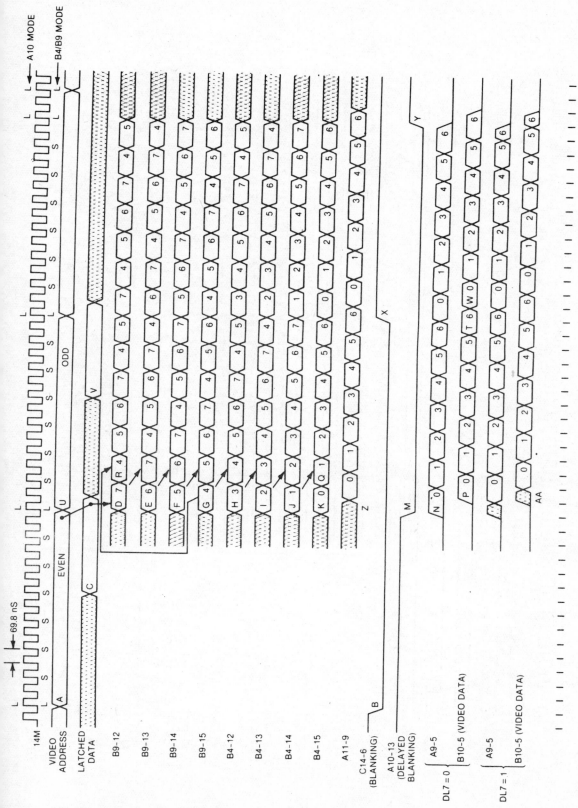

Fig. 8-28. HIRES-mode timing diagram.

193

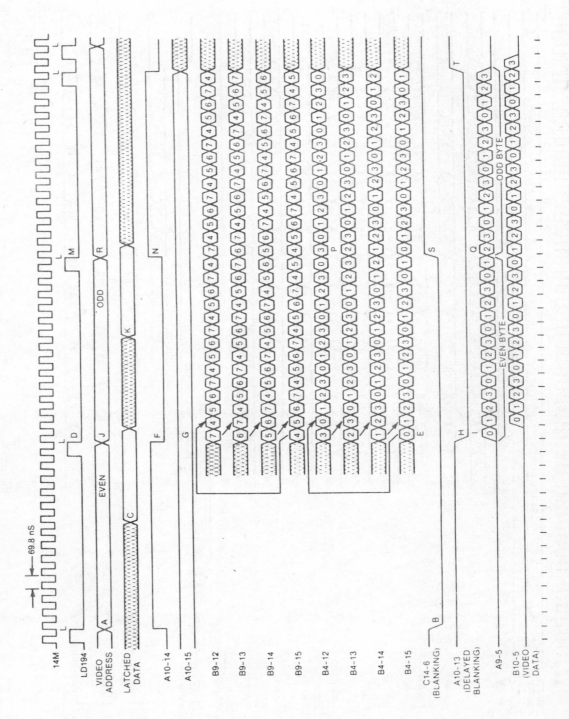

Fig. 8-31. LORES-mode timing diagram.

194

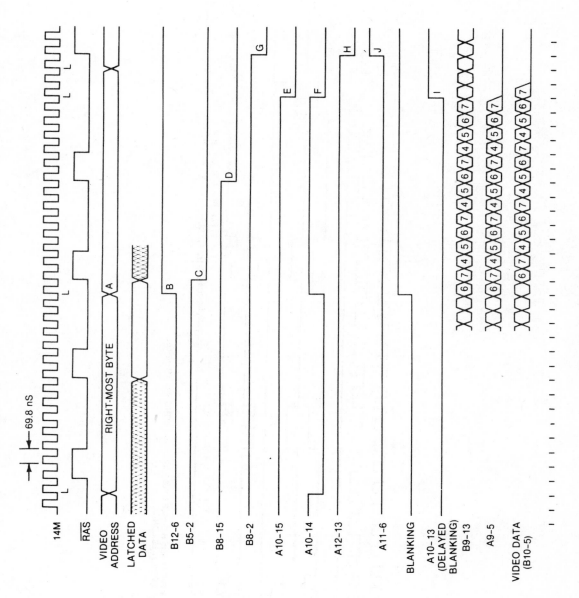

Fig. 8-34. Mixed LORES and text.

195

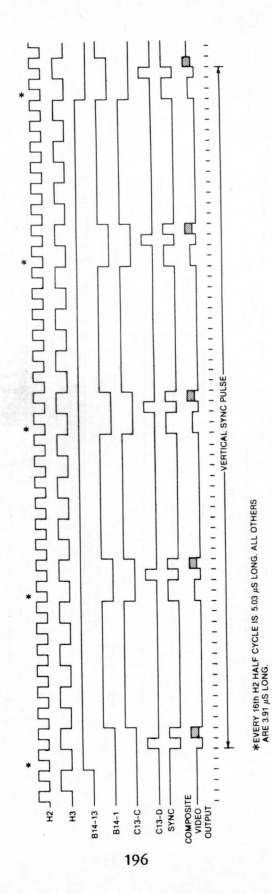

Fig. B-2. Vertical sync — Rev. 7.

*EVERY 16th H2 HALF CYCLE IS 5.03 μS LONG. ALL OTHERS
ARE 3.91 μS LONG.

VERTICAL SYNC PULSE

H2
H3
B14-13
B14-1
C13-C
C13-D
SYNC
COMPOSITE
VIDEO
OUTPUT

196

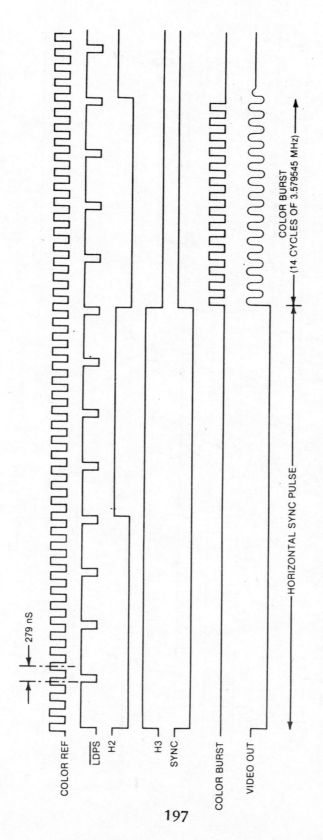

COLOR REF

279 nS

$\overline{\text{LDPS}}$

H2

H3

SYNC

COLOR BURST

VIDEO OUT

HORIZONTAL SYNC PULSE

COLOR BURST
(14 CYCLES OF 3.579545 MHz)

Fig. B-4. Color burst—Rev. 0 and 1.

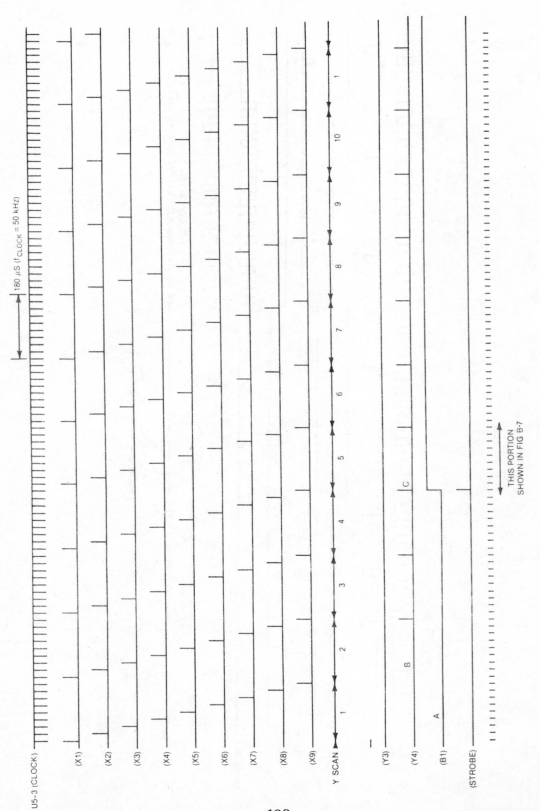

Fig. B-8. Y scan—single-piece keyboard.

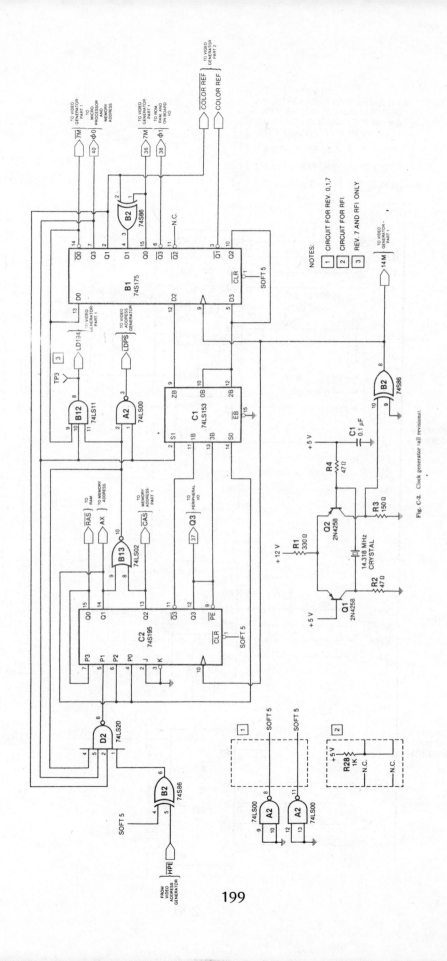

Fig. C-2. Clock generator (all revisions).

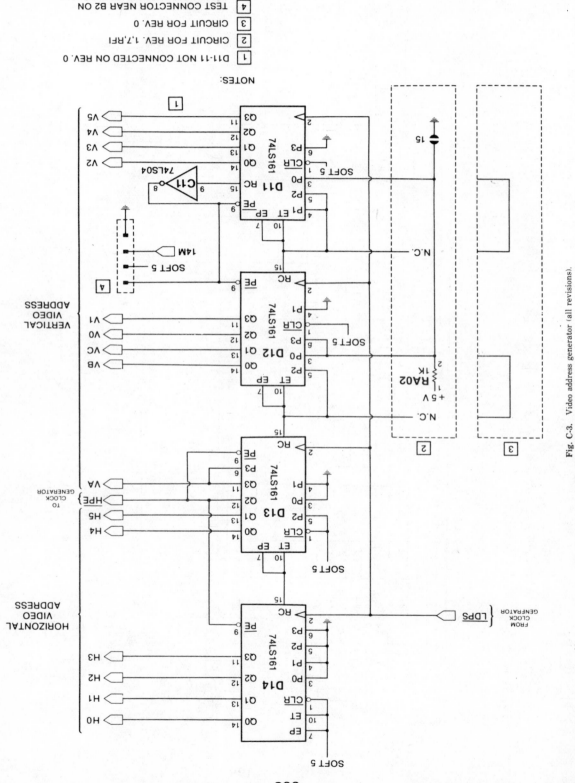

Fig. C-3. Video address generator (all revisions).

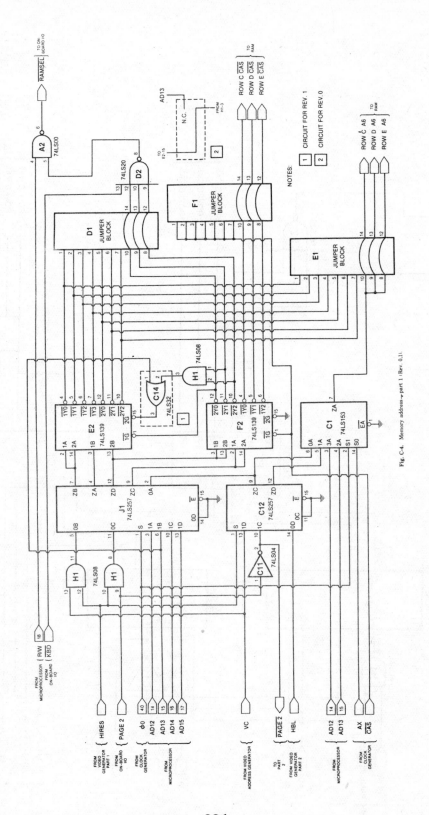

Fig. C-4. Memory address—part 1 Rev. 0,1).

201

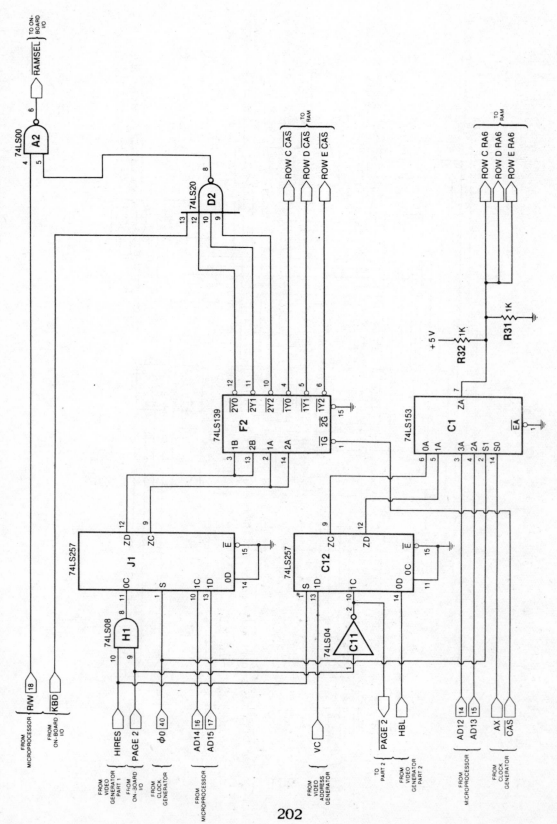

Fig. C-5. Memory address—part 1 (Rev. 7, RFI).

202

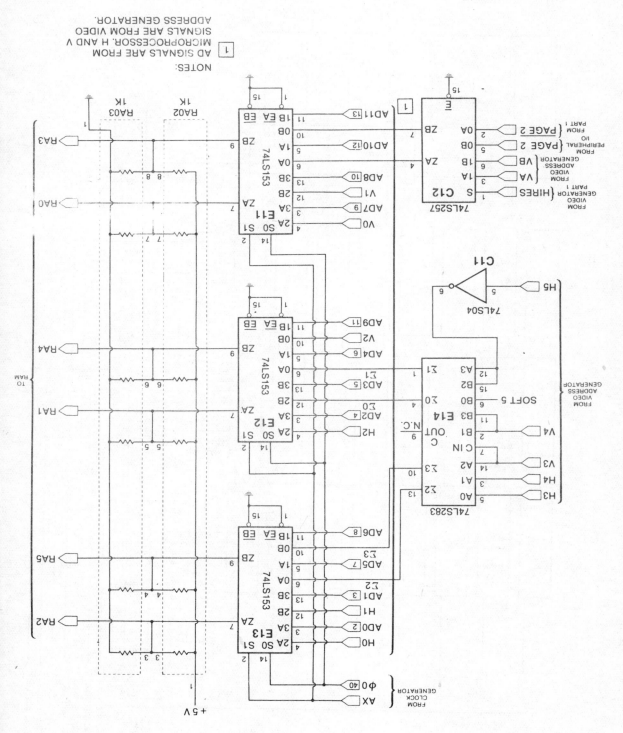

Fig. C-6. Memory address—part 2 (all revisions).

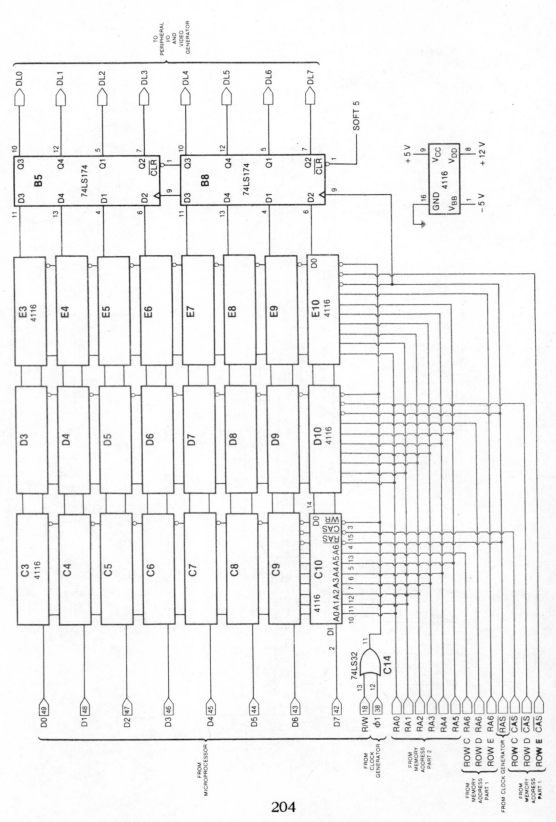

Fig. C-7. RAM (all revisions).

204

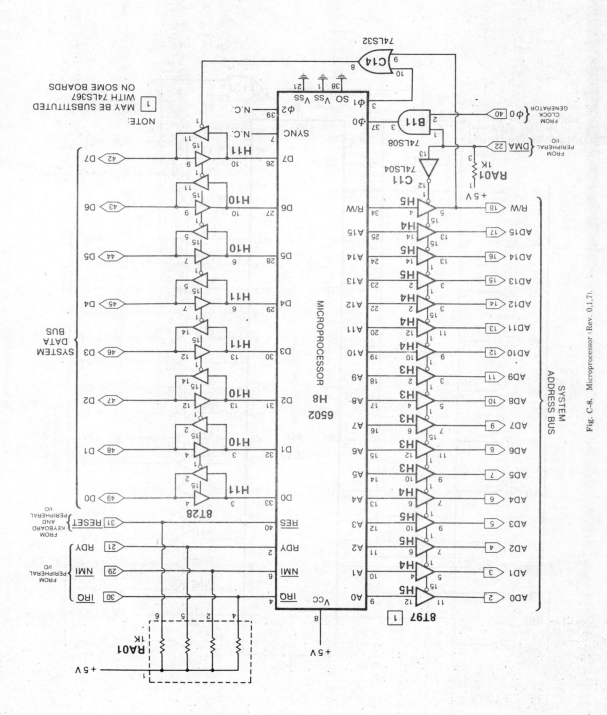

Fig. C-8. Microprocessor (Rev. 0,1,7).

205

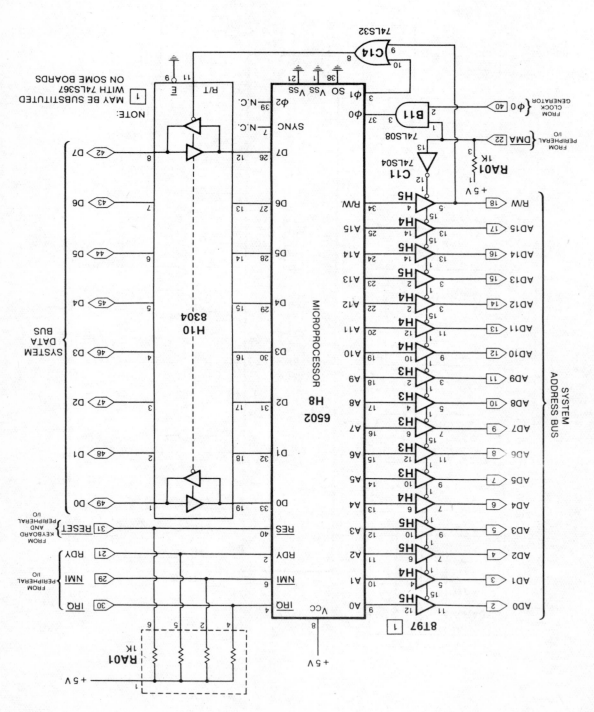

Fig. C-9. Microprocessor (RFI).

206

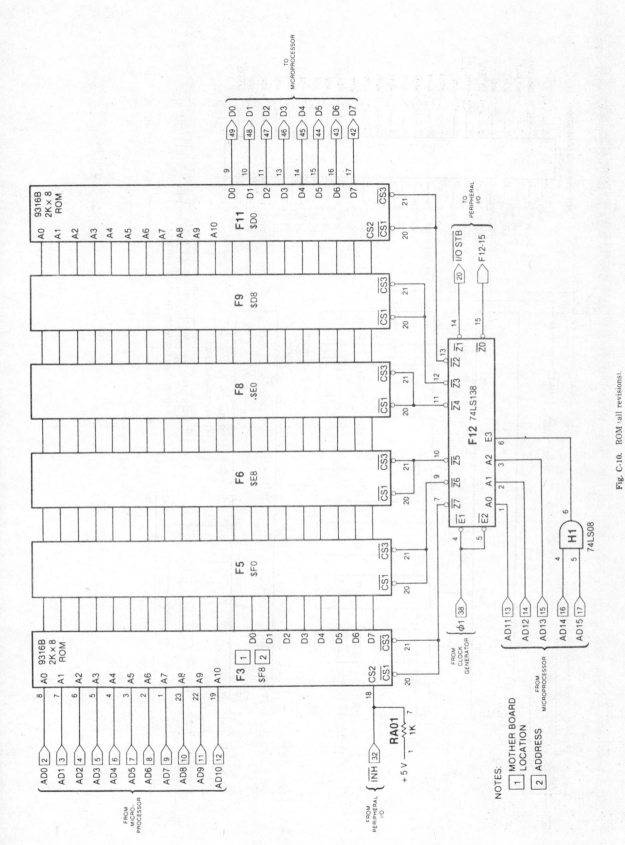

Fig. C-10. ROM (all revisions).

207

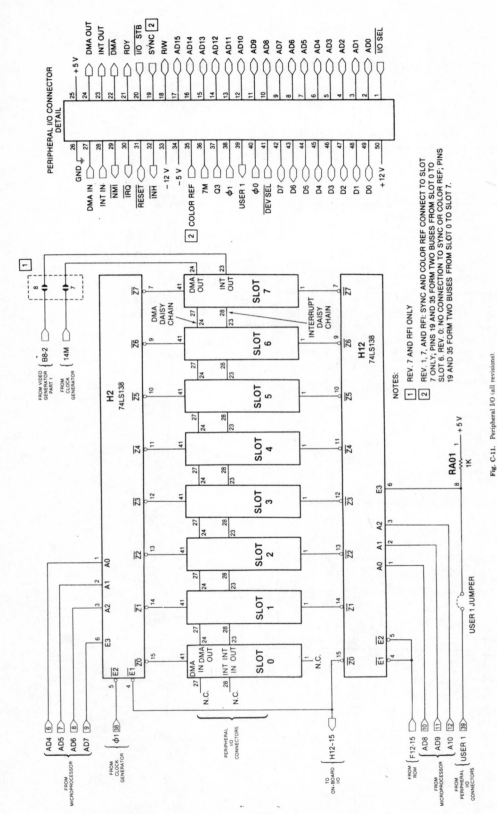

Fig. C-11. Peripheral I/O (all revisions).

208

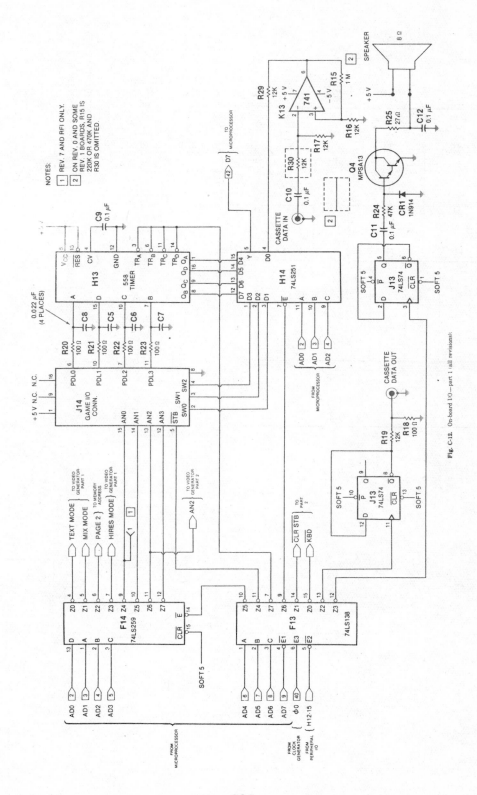

Fig. C-12. On-board I/O—part 1 (all revisions).

209

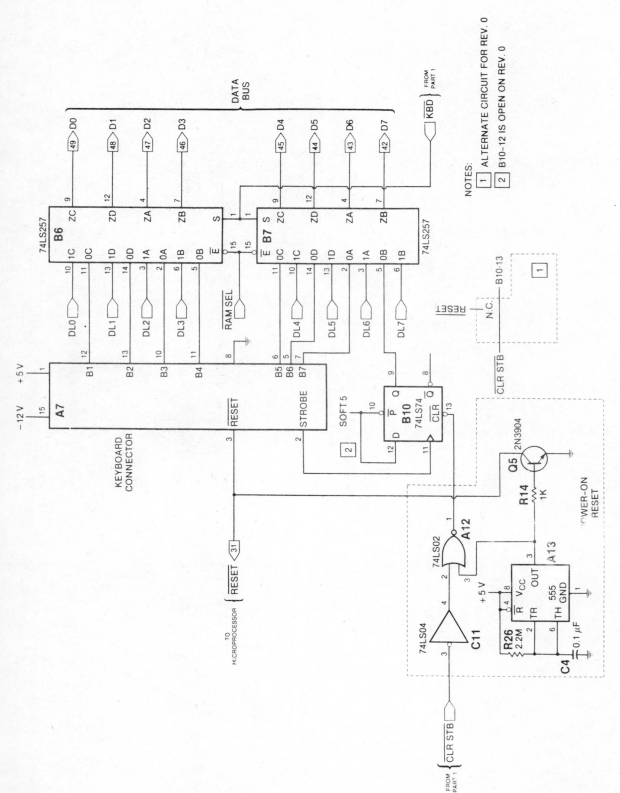

Fig. C-13. On-board I/O—part 2 (all revisions).

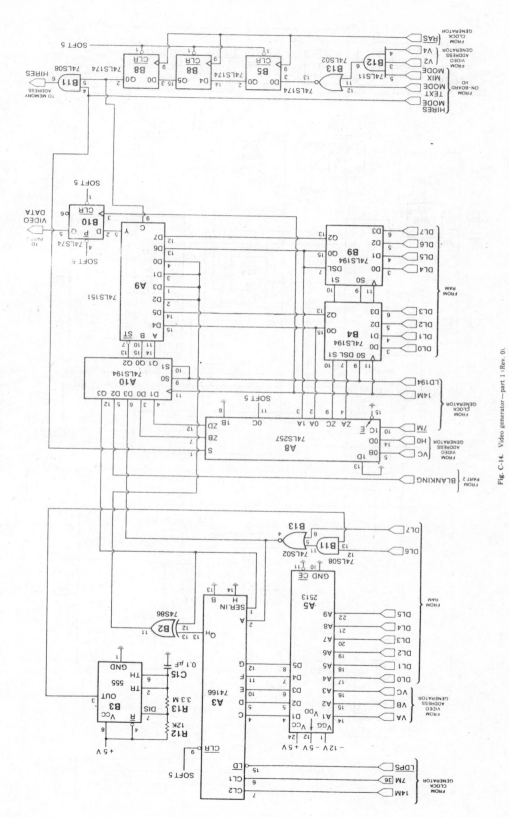

Fig. C-14. Video generator—part 1 (Rev. 0).

211

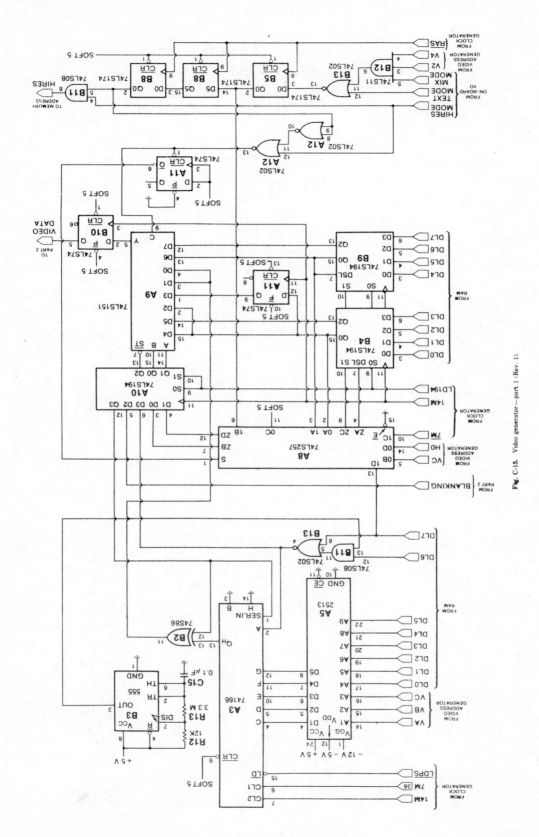

Fig. C-15. Video generator—part 1 (Rev. 1).

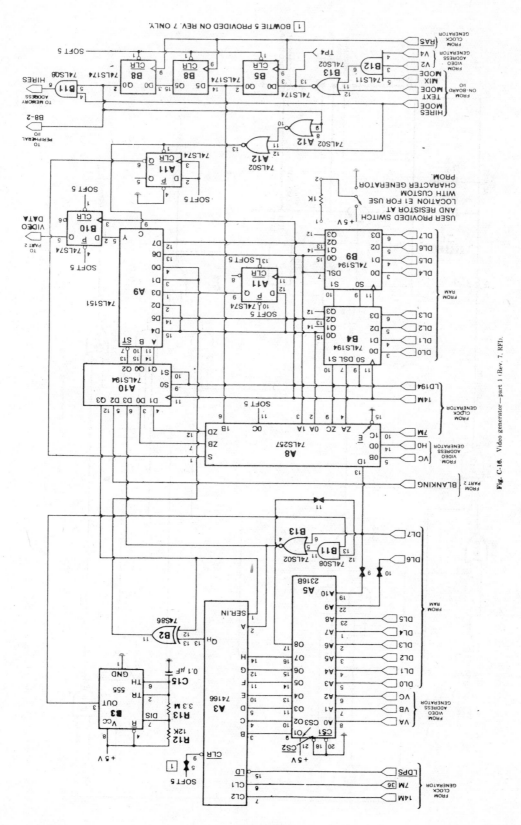

Fig. C-16. Video generator—part 1 (Rev. 7, RFI).

213

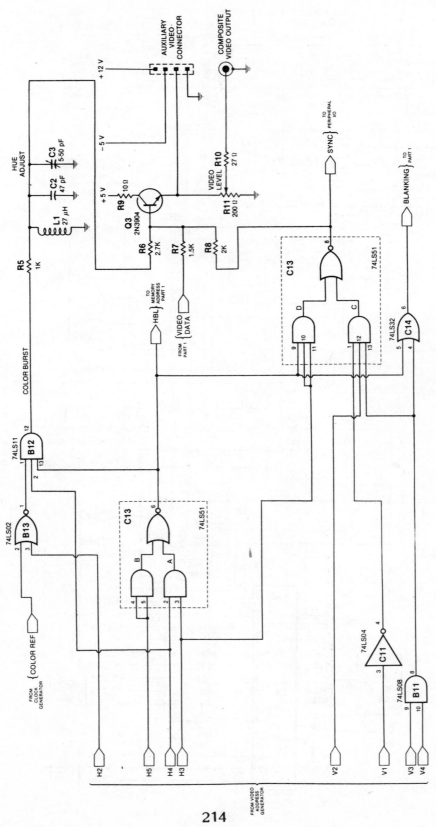

Fig. C-17. Video generator—part 2 (Rev. 0).

214

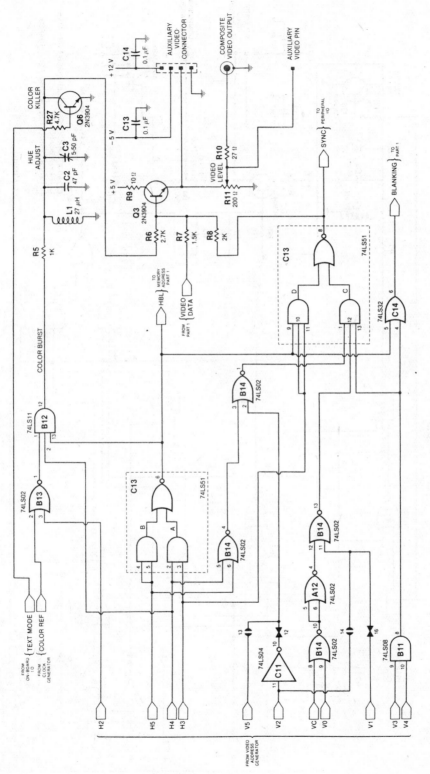

Fig. C-18. Video generator—part 2 (Rev. 1).

215

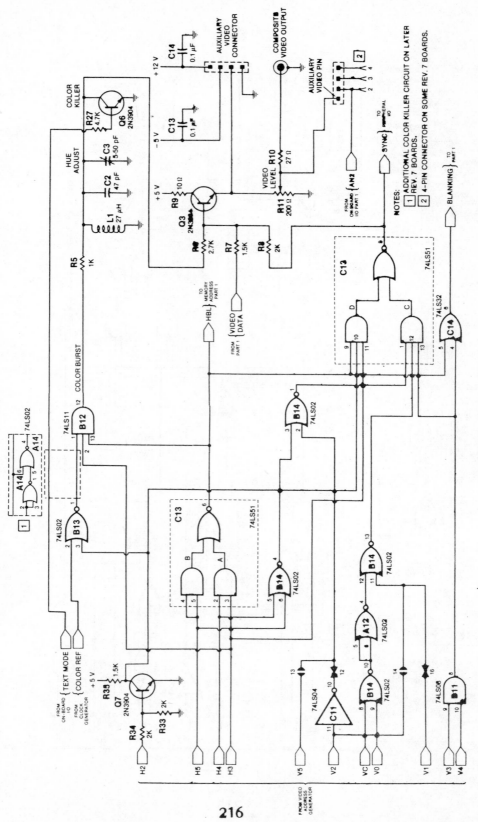

Fig C-10. Video generator—part 2 (Rev. 7).

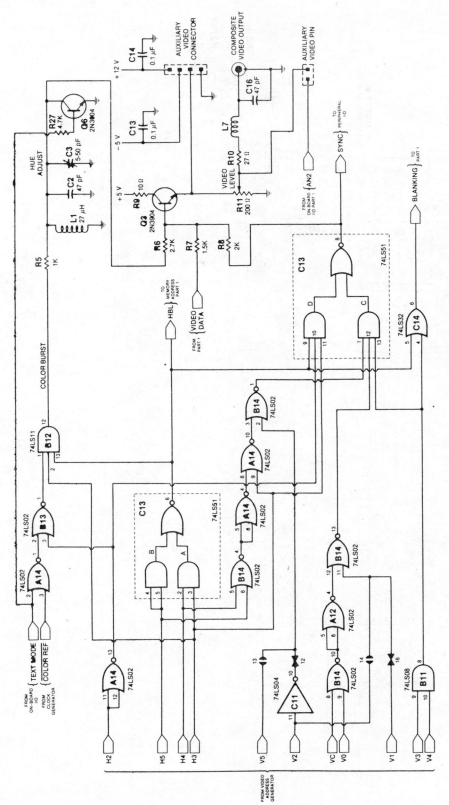

Fig. C-20. Video generator—part 2 (RFI).

217

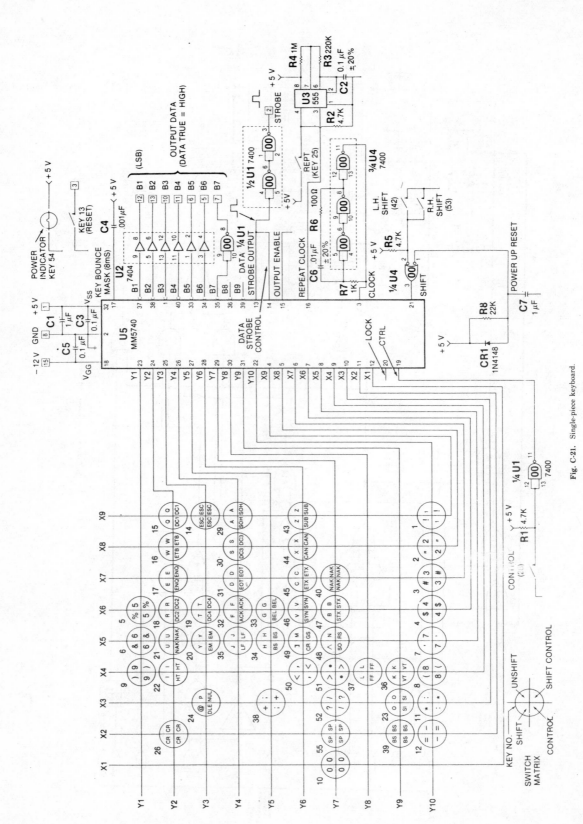

Fig. C-21. Single-piece keyboard.

218

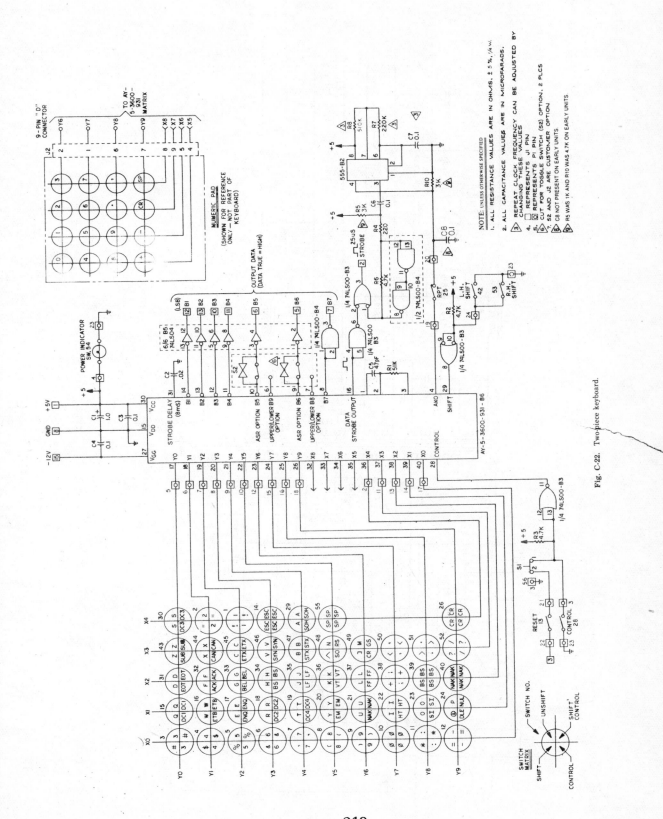

Fig. C-22. Two-piece keyboard.

219

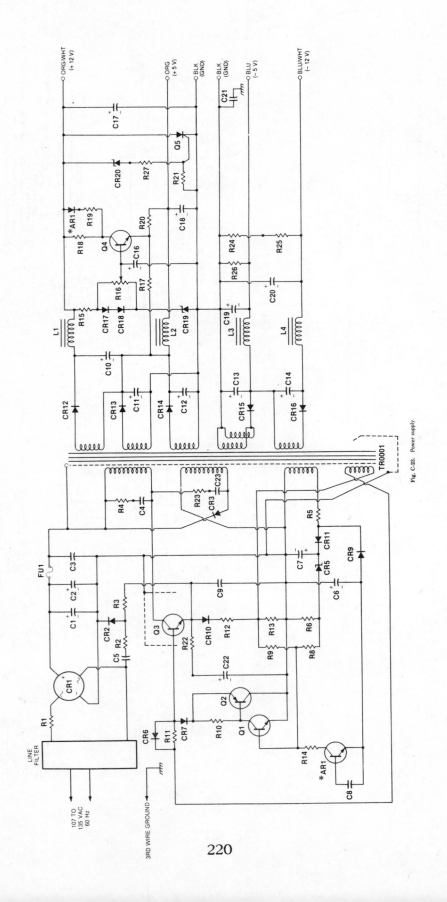

Fig. C-23. Power supply.

220

National College
of Ireland
Library

Project Silk

Client-side Web Development
for Modern Browsers

Bob Brumfield
Geoff Cox
Nelly Delgado
Michael Puleio
Karl Shifflett
Don Smith
Dwayne Taylor

ISBN: 978-1-62114-010-8

Contents

Foreword

I was in New York when I first got the call from Don Smith asking about Project Silk. The idea and vision that Don described to me over the phone that day were ambitious. At the time, very little had been published about large application architecture with jQuery. Don explained how he and the team planned to tackle the task, developing a working sample application alongside documentation that thoroughly described the approach and the architecture decisions. The result of that vision is the book that you hold in your hands today, and I can confidently say that the Project Silk team did an incredible job.

The most impressive and meaningful aspect of this book is the care taken to integrate and work with the open source community to develop this material. Karl, Don, and their team went above and beyond to talk with members of the jQuery community. They spent time researching the latest approaches recommended by the open source community. They held team trainings and brought in industry experts to learn the latest techniques. After the initial project had been completed, they solicited a number of community reviews to get feedback from several developers. This feedback was integrated into the guidance, which then underwent additional community reviews and releases.

The results of these efforts are clear. The approach and examples outlined in these pages are focused on helping you create an application in the best way possible. It is this intentional effort that makes the open source process sustainable. I couldn't be more proud to have been a part of it all and I highly commend Karl and Don for their leadership. The method by which this guidance was produced will stand as an example of how to properly tackle a project like this one.

The result of their work could not have been published at a better time. JavaScript, jQuery, HTML5, and CSS3 are gaining tremendous importance as unifying standards for producing cross-platform applications. This fact is only reinforced by the release of the Microsoft Windows 8 Developer Preview in September 2011. With many developers now choosing to use these technologies to produce software, high-quality guidance such as Project Silk is needed.

With this renewed emphasis on the use of these technologies, comprehensive guidance is required to leverage their full potential. The methods described here for how to successfully integrate standard web technologies into the Microsoft ASP.NET stack will help ensure that developers who depend on the Microsoft technology stack will be using the latest techniques when developing applications. Not only will developers be using the latest techniques to build maintainable applications, they will be participating as good citizens of the web by practicing the standards-based development that is exemplified in this book. This makes the web a better place for everyone, and it is exciting to see the leadership role Microsoft is taking in this effort.

From a technical perspective, the most exciting thing about the approach and guidance documented in Project Silk is the use of the jQuery UI Widget Pattern. In my personal opinion, the Widget Pattern is incredibly underutilized when building web applications. The Widget Pattern is a technique used to build user interface (UI) widgets in a maintainable and extensible way. Most jQuery UI Widgets in jQuery UI 1.8 are based upon this pattern, yet it is rarely seen outside of the jQuery UI project. With such an important project leveraging this pattern, I hope to see it used more and more.

It is my hope that as a developer, you will benefit greatly from reading the Project Silk guidance. Having been a small part of the process, I can testify to the care and research that went into producing Project Silk for your benefit. The developers behind this book and the application that accompanies it truly care about the web and about making your job easier. It is now your turn to adopt these patterns and principles to make better software. The completion and release of Project Silk is not the end, but the beginning, as it is now in your hands. Please join the Silk team in spending the time to adopt and leverage these patterns as we practice our craft together.

In closing, Microsoft has proven to be an incredible resource to the jQuery Community and it is exciting to see efforts like this. Project Silk represents that commitment in several ways. The way this guidance was produced is an example for similar projects that will follow it. The quality that it achieves sets a new standard in how to build and architect large, maintainable web applications with jQuery and ASP.NET.

I hope that this book serves you well and teaches you new and exciting ways to work with these technologies.

Mike Hostetler
CEO, appendTo—The Company Dedicated to jQuery

Foreword

We're in an incredibly exciting time where the Internet is dramatically changing the way we live our lives. From communication and shopping, to gaming and organizing groups, the Internet has become a vital part of our lives—as important as the basic utilities we take for granted daily. If we look at the evolution of the web, it's evident that the effort of developers to continuously push the capabilities and boundaries of web technologies has uniformly transformed the way users experience the web. No longer are we bound to simplistic pages with generic text and hyperlink navigation.

Technologies and frameworks like HTML5, CSS3, JavaScript, and jQuery have allowed us to dramatically alter the way information is presented to consumers by providing rich, immersive user interfaces that are engaging and, most importantly, responsive. They are impacting every aspect of development on every platform, from traditional browsers to the smallest mobile devices. If you consider, for example, that these technologies allow most anyone with a cell phone to shop online or map a route, you realize how important they are and the impact that the applications built with them have on our daily lives. The web is ubiquitous, and the developers who are leveraging these technologies are having a direct and positive impact on the lives of millions.

The obvious question that any developer should be asking is, "How do I leverage these technologies today so I can build the next great web experience?" One of Microsoft's greatest strengths is its commitment to ensuring that developers have the knowledge, tools, and infrastructure to be successful. This guide exemplifies that commitment by providing the information developers need to build and manage responsive websites using the latest web languages, tools, and best practices.

Creating guidance is not at all trivial, and all the time, research, and coding that went into this effort are truly a testament to the Microsoft patterns & practices team and their genuine desire to provide the absolute best and most timely information to developers. Vetted by professional web developers, both internal and external to Microsoft, including jQuery team members, this guidance will help you understand the real-world implications of designing a dynamic and responsive website. It's certainly possible to scour the Internet to compile a massive list of blog posts and articles that may (or may not) articulate how to approach web development, but the guidance offered in this book can realistically serve as a priority resource for developers wanting to acquire a firm understanding of how to use the best web development technologies and apply them professionally.

I'm so proud to have been a part of this incredible project and appreciate the impact it will have on the way developers build great experiences. It takes more than just sprinkling some JavaScript or HTML5 on a site to make it worthwhile. It takes thought, time, experience, and a firm understanding of how to use the technologies. This book will help you tackle these key points and make you a better developer.

Rey Bango
Senior Technical Evangelist
Microsoft Corporation
jQuery Team member

The Team Who Brought You This Guide

Authors	Bob Brumfield, Geoff Cox, Nelly Delgado, Michael Puleio, Karl Shifflett, Don Smith, and Dwayne Taylor
Reviewers	Mark M. Baker, Christopher Bennage, Larry Brader, Bob Brumfield, Colin Campbell, Geoff Cox, Nelly Delgado, Julian Dominguez, Dan Dole, Barry Dorrans, Norman Headlam, Israel Hilerio, Alex Homer, Simon Ince, Poornimma Kaliappan, Stuart Leeks, Roberta Leibovitz, Katie Neimer, Michael Puleio, Steve Sanderson, Chris Sells, Karl Shifflett, Adam Sontag, Don Smith, Aaron Sun, Jonathan Wall, Dave Ward, Bill Wilder, Rob Zelt
Editors	Nancy Michell and Roberta Leibovitz
Graphic Artist	Katie Niemer

Project Silk Development Team

The Microsoft patterns & practices team involves both experts and the broader community in its projects. Thanks to the individuals who contributed to Project Silk.

Project Silk Team	Christopher Bennage, Larry Brader, Bob Brumfield, Nelly Delgado, Alex Homer, Michael Puleio, Karl Shifflett, and Don Smith (Microsoft Corporation); Geoff Cox (Southworks SRL); Ara Pehlivanian; Aaron Sun (Content Master Ltd); Poornimma Kaliappan, Hailin Wei, Hongran Zhou (VanceInfo); Dwayne Taylor (RDA Corporation); Roberta Leibovitz and Colin Campbell (Modeled Computation LLC)
Editing / Production	Nancy Michell (Content Master Ltd); Roberta Leibovitz and Katie Niemer (Modeled Computation LLC); John Hubbard (Eson); Ted Neveln (Ballard Indexing Services); Tom Draper and Patrick Lanfear (Twist Creative LLC); Richard Burte (ChannelCatalyst.com, Inc.)
External Advisors	Scott González, Mike Hostetler, Jonathan Sharp, and Andrew Wirick of appendTo, LLC; Adam Sontag of the jQuery UI Project; Mark M. Baker of BNA Software; Norman Headlam; Michael Kenyon of IHS, Inc.; Chris Love of Tellago; Dave Ward of Encosia; Bill Wilder; Rob Zelt of Digital Commute LLC

Microsoft Corporation   Rachel Appel, Rey Bango, John Bristowe, Doris Chen, Dan Dole, Barry Dorrans,
Advisors   Damian Edwards, Phil Haack, Simon Ince, Tim Laverty, Stuart Leeks, Steve Sanderson, Giorgio Sardo, Justin Saint Clair, Brandon Satrom, Chris Sells, Amanda Silver, and Brad Wilson

Readme

Project Silk provides guidance for building cross-browser web applications with a focus on client-side interactivity. These applications take advantage of the latest web standards, including HTML5, CSS3 and ECMAScript 5, along with modern web technologies such as jQuery, Windows® Internet Explorer® 9, and ASP.NET MVC 3.

To illustrate this guidance, the project includes the Mileage Stats Reference Implementation (Mileage Stats) that enables its users to track various metrics about their vehicles and fill ups. Much of the effort in building Mileage Stats was applied to the usability and interactivity of the experience. Animations were included to enhance the enjoyment of the site and Ajax is used to keep the interface responsive and immersive. A great deal of care was also taken to ensure that the client-side JavaScript facilitates modularity and maintainability. To accomplish these design goals, the JavaScript code was structured into *widgets* that benefit from the jQuery UI Widget Factory.

This guidance is intended for existing web developers who are interested in taking advantage of the latest web standards and technologies.

Installation Overview

To install and run the reference implementation, you must perform the following steps:

1. Install system requirements.

2. Download and install Project Silk.

3. Run script to install NuGet packages.

4. Download external JavaScript libraries.

5. Install test libraries (optional).

6. Run Mileage Stats.

Step 1: Install System Requirements

Mileage Stats was designed to run on the Microsoft Windows 7 or Windows Server 2008 operating system. It has been smoke tested on Windows Vista and Windows XP. Before you can use Mileage Stats, the following must be installed:

- Microsoft® Visual Studio® 2010 Professional, Premium, or Ultimate edition
- Microsoft Visual Studio 2010 SP1
- ASP.NET MVC 3
- Microsoft SQL Server Compact 4.0
- ADO.NET Entity Framework 4.1 - Update 1
    - To install the Entity Framework, download it from the Microsoft Download Center rather than using NuGet.
    - For information about the Entity Framework 4.1 release, see EF 4.1 Released.
    - For information about the Entity Framework 4.1 - Update 1 release, see EF 4.1 Update 1 Released.
- NuGet version 1.4 or later
- Internet Explorer 9 or another modern web browser. Firefox 3.x is not supported. Use Firefox 4.0.1 or higher.
- Optional:
    - Web Standards Update for Microsoft Visual Studio 2010 SP1

Mileage Stats requires several external libraries that cannot be included in the download. These fall into two categories: NuGet packages and JavaScript libraries, which are explained below.

Step 2: Download and Install Project Silk

Project Silk includes written guidance and the source code for both Mileage Stats and the Widget QuickStart. To download and install, follow these steps:

1. Download **Project Silk** from the Microsoft Download Center.

2. To extract the download, run the .exe file. This will extract the source code and documentation into the folder of your choice.

3. Install external dependencies from NuGet and download the required external JavaScript libraries, as explained in the steps below.

Step 3: Run Script to Install NuGet Packages

Before building Mileage Stats, you will need to install the required NuGet packages. There are two scripts in the Solution Items folder, which are used to install and remove the NuGet packages.

TO INSTALL THE NUGET PACKAGES:

1. Open MileageStats.sln located in {silk}\MileageStats.

2. In Visual Studio, from the **Tools** menu, point to **Library Package Manager**, and select **Package Manager Console**.

3. Run the install script with the following command:

```
.\InstallRequiredNuGetPackages.ps1
```

You can remove the packages with the RemoveRequiredNuGetPackages.ps1 packages.

Step 4: Download External JavaScript Libraries

Mileage Stats requires several external JavaScript libraries. These libraries were chosen because they fit the needs of the project, not as a general recommendation or implied endorsement of these libraries. Every project is different and may have different needs.

JQPLOT

jqPlot is a jQuery plugin to easily create charts with JavaScript. To learn more about jq-Plot, see http://www.jqplot.com/.

TO OBTAIN THE FILES NEEDED TO RUN MILEAGE STATS:

1. Go to https://bitbucket.org/cleonello/jqplot/downloads/ and download the file jquery.jqplot.1.0.0a_r701.zip.

2. Unzip the downloaded file to a folder of your choice, for example c:\temp\.

3. Copy the following .js files from the \dist\ folder in the above folder into the {silk}\MileageStats\MileageStats.Web\Scripts folder:
   - excanvas.min.js
   - jquery.jqplot.min.js

4. Copy jquery.jqplot.min.css from the \dist\ folder in the above folder into the {silk}\MileageStats\MileageStats.Web\Content folder.

5. Copy the following .js files from the \dist\plugins folder in the above folder into the {silk}\MileageStats\MileageStats.Web\Scripts folder:
   - jqplot.cursor.min.js
   - jqplot.dateAxisRenderer.min.js
   - jqplot.canvasAxisTickRenderer.min.js
   - jqplot.canvasTextRenderer.min.js

Step 5: Install Test Libraries (Optional)

The test libraries are only required when you deploy the web site to a server running Microsoft Internet Information Services (IIS). Otherwise, if you are running Mileage Stats from Visual Studio, these files are optional.

JQUERY.SIMULATE.JS (OPTIONAL)

jquery.simulate is a JavaScript API that allows you to simulate user interaction to help with QUnit tests.

TO OBTAIN THE FILES NEEDED TO RUN MILEAGE STATS:

1. Go to http://code.google.com/p/jqueryjs/source/browse/trunk/plugins/simulate?r=6063&spec=svn6063 and download the files jquery.simulate.js.

2. Copy the saved file into the {silk}\MileageStats\MileageStats.Web\Scripts\tests folder.

   Note: *You can also download the file from the jQuery UI tests folder at:* **https://github.com/jquery/jquery-ui/tree/008def00bd565d0984c47cdd97d65e1c7bd73e04/tests.**

QUNIT (OPTIONAL)

QUnit is a JavaScript unit testing framework. To learn more about QUnit, see **http://docs.jquery.com/Qunit.**

TO OBTAIN THE FILES NEEDED TO RUN THE UNIT TESTS IN MILEAGE STATS:

1. Go to **https://github.com/jquery/qunit** and download the files qunit.js and qunit.css from the QUnit folder.

2. Copy the saved file into the {silk}\MileageStats\MileageStats.Web\Scripts\tests folder.

3. Build and run Mileage Stats, and navigate to http://localhost:23495/scripts/tests/tests.htm.

4. Wait while the QUnit tests execute.

Step 6: Run Mileage Stats

Mileage Stats is an application that provides you with information about your cars' fuel consumption, operational efficiency, and service records, allowing you to track and visualize data about your cars.

TO RUN MILEAGE STATS

1. Open MileageStats.sln located in {silk}\MileageStats.

2. Press F6 to build the solution.

3. Select the MileageStats.Web project as the startup project. To do this, right-click the project, and then click **Set as StartUp project**.

4. Press Ctrl+F5 to run the application.

5. (optional) In Internet Explorer 9, you can pin the Mileage Stats icon to the Windows Taskbar.

6. Click the **Sign in or Register** button.

7. On the **Mock Authentication** page, use the default name provided and click **Sign In**.

8. On the Dashboard page, click the **Add Vehicle** button.

9. Enter the name of your car in the **Name** textbox.

10. (optional) Select the year. You have **1997, 2003, 2010, 2011** as options.

11. (optional) Select one of the car manufacturers from the drop-down box.

12. (optional) Select one of the models from the drop-down box.

13. (optional) Browse to a photo.

14. Click **Save**.

15. You should then see your car added to the Dashboard. You can add a fill up, add a reminder, view/edit details, add a new vehicle, or visually view your data by clicking **Charts**.

16. You can update your profile on the Profile page.

17. You can look at the other default car's information.

You can learn more about the design and implementation of Mileage Stats in the documentation included with Project Silk.

Running in Release Mode

By default, Mileage Stats will run in Debug mode with non-minified JavaScript files.

TO RUN IN RELEASE MODE WITH MINIFIED JAVASCRIPT FILES

1. Set Visual Studio to **Release** mode.

2. Update the web.config file:
   - Change <compilation debug="true" targetFramework="4.0"> to <compilation debug="false" targetFramework="4.0">
   - Comment out the unity configSource section and replace it with the commented out version.

3. Build the solution. At the end of the build, the minified file Scripts\MileageStats.min.js will be available.

4. Press Ctrl+F5. When you run the app, the new minified file will be used. To verify this, sign into the RI, press F12 (Internet Explorer developer tools), go to the **Scripts** tab, and look at the much shorter list of scripts that are now available.

About Mileage Stats

Mileage Stats is a multi-page interactive web application whose pages are rendered without requiring full-page reloads. This creates the illusion of a desktop application. By not requiring the browser to reload the full page, the user sees rich UI transitions between states (pages). In addition, the browser application runs very fast because of client-side data caching.

The Mileage Stats JavaScript is modularized using jQuery UI Widgets. The widgets allow the UI to be broken down into small, discrete, stateful objects; this provides a clean separation of responsibilities and concerns. See the Widget QuickStart for an example application that uses the jQuery UI widget factory.

Mileage Stats uses OpenID for authentication.

Mileage Stats home page

Mileage Stats uses Internet Explorer 9 Pinned Sites features. Below you can see the notification icon that indicates there are more than three outstanding maintenance tasks for the owner's three vehicles. Mileage Stats also displays dynamic jump lists for maintenance tasks.

Notification icon in Internet Explorer 9

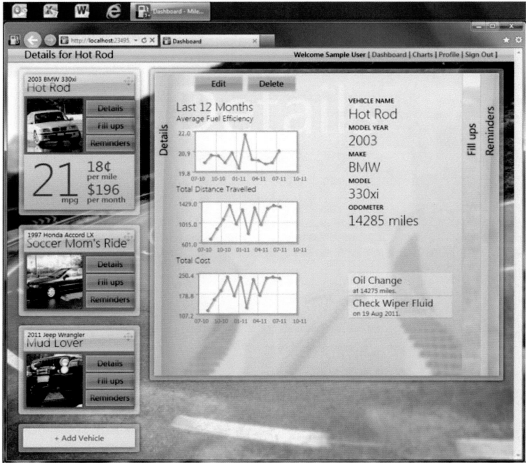

Mileage Stats contains a rich chart page that allows you to select three charts, vehicles, begin and end date, and data.

Charts in Mileage Stats

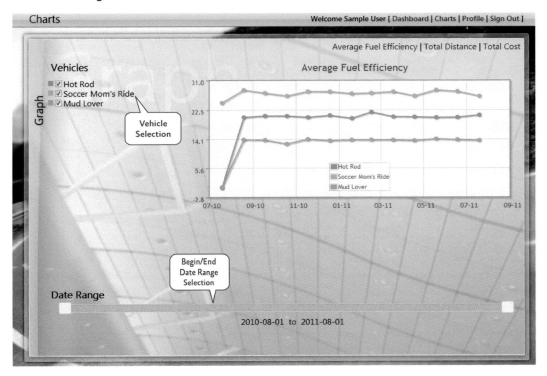

View a two minute video on Mileage Stats on Channel 9.

ABOUT THE BOOK

The chapters in this book cover a wide range of topics, including: planning and designing your web application, understanding and writing jQuery UI Widgets, writing server-side code that supports the client-side application, patterns and concepts used in JavaScript code, data and caching, and securing and testing your application. It also provides more information about Mileage Stats and the design decisions and challenges addressed by the team.

REQUIREMENT FOR JUMP LIST ITEMS TO APPEAR

In Internet Explorer, the Windows 7 taskbar jump list items can be disabled. If disabled, you will not see the jump list items display even though the website has been pinned to the taskbar. The **Store and display recently opened items in the Start menu and the taskbar** property setting needs to be checked for the jump list items to appear.

Taskbar and Start menu properties

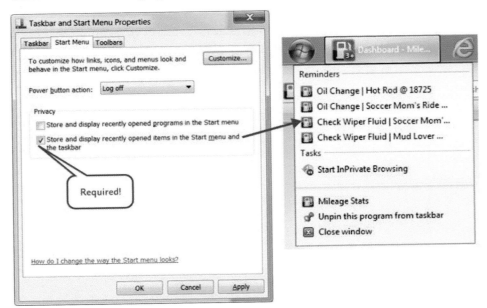

Known Issues

- After you upgrade to Visual Studio 2010 SP1, you may encounter an issue when deploying the web site to your Localhost on IIS. The SP1 update resets the IIS Application pool configuration so it is no longer the latest version. You will need to navigate to C:\Windows\Microsoft.NET\Framework64\v4.0.30319 on 64-bit computers and C:\Windows\Microsoft.NET\Framework\v4.0.30319 on 32-bit computers and run aspnet_regiis -i.

- In Internet Explorer 7, you will only see static charts in all scenarios (whether JavaScript is enabled or disabled). This is by design.

- When deploying a release-compiled version to IIS, there may be an extra Uri section definition in the web.config file added by installing one of the NuGet packages. Remove the following extra section definition from the web.config file:

```
<section name="uri" type="System.Configuration.UriSection, System,
Version=2.0.0.0, Culture=neutral, PublicKeyToken=b77a5c561934e089" />
```

The NuGet package that adds this extra Uri section is: Install-Package DotNetOpen-Auth -Project MileageStats.Web

- When upgrading from a community version of the Mileage Stats, you may encounter problems where a cached version of JavaScript is used. If so, clear the browser's cache. In some browsers this can be accomplished with Crtl+F5.

Community

Project Silk's community site is http://silk.codeplex.com. There, you can post questions, provide feedback, or connect with other users for sharing ideas. Community members can also help Microsoft plan and test future offerings. In addition, the community site has links to tutorial videos and MSDN content.

Resources and Further Reading

Download Project Silk from the Microsoft Download Center:
http://www.microsoft.com/download/en/details.aspx?id=27290

The online version of this document is on MSDN:
http://msdn.microsoft.com/en-us/library/hh404100.aspx

For information about the Entity Framework 4.1 release, see "EF 4.1 Released":
http://blogs.msdn.com/b/adonet/archive/2011/04/11/ef-4-1-released.aspx

For information about the Entity Framework 4.1 - Update 1 release, see "EF 4.1 Update 1 Released":
http://blogs.msdn.com/b/adonet/archive/2011/07/25/ef-4-1-update-1-released.aspx

Internet Explorer 9:
http://windows.microsoft.com/en-US/windows/downloads/internet-explorer

jqPlot:
http://www.jqplot.com/

ASP.NET MVC 3:
http://www.asp.net/mvc/mvc3

jQuery UI widget factory:
http://docs.jquery.com/UI/Developer_Guide

View a two minute video on Mileage Stats on Channel 9:
http://channel9.msdn.com/posts/Project-Silk-Mileage-Stats-Application

1 Introduction

Project Silk provides guidance for building maintainable cross-browser web applications that are characterized by an intentional design, rich interactivity, and a responsive user interface (UI), resulting in an immersive and engaging user experience (UX). Such applications take advantage of the latest web standards, including HTML5, CSS3, and ECMAScript version 5, and modern web technologies such as jQuery and ASP.NET MVC3.

An intentional design indicates that deliberate attention was paid to the modularity of the JavaScript code, and the usability of the application was an explicit focus. Under the direction of the team's web designer, UI and UX concerns received special attention, and this guidance aims to help you be successful addressing these concerns in your own applications. Modularity is important when building highly interactive web applications because they often require a significant amount of JavaScript code. This guidance aims to help you understand how to write maintainable JavaScript code that reaps the many benefits of a modular design.

Project Silk also illustrates how you can take advantage of the fast JavaScript engines of the modern, standards-based web browsers to achieve a user experience and execution speeds that rival desktop applications. Windows® Internet Explorer® 9 further enriches the user experience by taking advantage of integration with the operating system and hardware-accelerated graphics processing.

The concepts explained in the Project Silk written guidance are demonstrated via a real-world customer-facing web application called the Mileage Stats Reference Implementation (Mileage Stats). Mileage Stats allows users to track and compare their vehicles' fuel efficiency, usage, and operating costs, and to schedule vehicle maintenance reminders.

Prerequisites

This guidance is intended for web developers and assumes you have some hands-on experience with ASP.NET MVC, CSS, HTML, JavaScript, and jQuery. Mileage Stats relies heavily on a few important JavaScript and jQuery concepts that you need to understand. They include:

- **JavaScript**: Object literals, immediate functions, closures, object prototypes, scoping rules, use of the **this** keyword
- **jQuery**: Selectors, wrapped sets, chaining

If you are not familiar with these concepts or have not used them in your own projects, see the "Further Reading" section at the end of this chapter for more information on these topics.

Spectrum of Web Applications

There is a spectrum of web applications being built today that can be grouped into four application types. These types of web applications are categorized by their full-page reload behavior and the amount of client-side interactivity they provide. Each application type provides a richer experience than the one listed before it.

- **Static sites**. These consist of static HTML pages, CSS, and images. They are static in that as each page is navigated to, the browser performs a full-page reload and there is no interaction with portions of the page. In addition, the page does not change no matter who requests it or when.
- **Server rendered**. In this model, the server dynamically assembles the pages from one or more source files and can incorporate data from another source during the rendering. The client-side script in these applications might perform some data validation, simple hover effects, or Ajax calls. As each page is navigated to, the browser performs a full-page reload. ASP.NET applications that don't make heavy use of client-side JavaScript are examples of server-rendered web applications.
- **Hybrid design**. This model is similar to the server-rendered web application, except that it relies heavily on client-side JavaScript to deliver an engaging experience. This type of application has islands of interactivity within the site that do not require full-page reloads to change the UI as well as some pages that do require a full-page reload. Mileage Stats is an example of a hybrid design.
- **Single-page interface**. In this model, a full-page load happens only once. From that point on, all page changes and data loading is performed without a full-page reload. Hotmail, Office Live, and Twitter are examples of single-page-interface web applications.

Characteristics of Modern Web Applications

While there are many types of modern web applications, addressing many different needs, they all have some characteristics in common.

- **They are standards-focused.** To have the broadest reach across multiple platforms and devices, applications attempt to implement the current and evolving standards and adopt future standards once ratified.

- **They are interactive.** Modern web applications keep the user engaged by providing constant feedback on their actions. This feedback can come in the form of messages, animations to hide or show elements, mouse-over effects, drag and drop feedback, the automatic refreshing of screen data, animation of various elements, or the implementation of fade-in or fade-out effects. Interactive applications leverage the fast JavaScript engines in modern browsers to perform their client-side tasks.

- **They limit full-page reloads.** Modern web applications seek to limit the number of full-page reloads. Reloads are much slower than a localized Ajax call to update a portion of the UI. Full-page reloads also limit the ability to animate state or page changes. By not performing a full-page reload, users can be kept in context, providing a fluid experience as they navigate from one task to another.

- **They are asynchronous.** Modern web applications use Ajax to dynamically load data, page fragments, or other assets instead of performing a full-page reload to acquire data or HTML content. Because the loading of data is asynchronous, the UI is able to stay responsive and keep the user informed while the data request is being fulfilled. This asynchronous on-demand loading also reduces application response time because requests can be tuned to return only the data and other content that needs to change.

- **They manage data.** When applicable, modern web applications provide client-side data caching and prefetching to boost client-side performance. This enables the UI to immediately respond to user input gestures because it does not have to make a call to the server for data. Data caching also serves to minimize the impact on server resources, increasing application scalability because fewer calls to the server are required.

Considerations for Building Modern Web Applications

Building a rich modern web application can be rewarding and fun. For developers or web software firms that have typically delivered server-centric applications, possibly with small amounts of JavaScript, embarking on a modern web application project will involve a paradigm change that should not be minimized or overlooked.

In the next two sections we will examine the skill sets a project team will need and the technologies used when building a modern web application.

TEAM SKILLS

Developing modern web applications requires a broad range of skills. Depending on your application requirements, your team will need expertise provided by people in the following roles:

- **Designer roles**. These will be responsible for user experience, user interface, and graphics.
- **Client-side developer roles**. These will bring programming expertise in the areas of user interface, user interaction, and test.
- **Server-side developer roles**. These will have programming expertise in the areas of web pages, business objects and logic, databases, and test.

The composition of the web project team will vary from project to project based on the application's requirements and the team's resources. For example, on a large project, each of the roles above would probably be filled by a different person or possibly a team. On a small project, team members will likely fill multiple roles with augmentation from consultants as required to fill in the gaps.

On Project Silk, all of the above roles were filled by a lead developer, web designer, server-side developer, and two client-side developers. Project Silk also had a test team that consisted of a test manager, test program manager, and two software test engineers. The test team was responsible for testing browser compatibility, deployment testing, performance testing, stress testing, and security testing. To accomplish this, the test team set up a lab with servers running Windows Server® 2008, each with different configurations, and client computers configured with different operating systems and browsers. These systems were then used to perform daily automated and manual tests.

TECHNOLOGIES

This section will familiarize you with technologies and patterns used in building Mileage Stats. If any of these are new to you, please review the resources in the "Further Reading" section so you will get the most from the guidance and will be able to understand the Mileage Stats JavaScript, HTML5, CSS3, and C# code. This section does not intend to convey all of the important concepts you must know. Rather, you should consider it a list of indicators you may need to research further before building an application such as Mileage Stats.

Ajax

For over 10 years, the web has benefited from the ability to replace full-page reloads with Ajax calls. But given the advances in standards such as CSS3 and HTML5, browsers adherence to those standards, and the arrival of powerful, cross-browser JavaScript frameworks, we have all the tools necessary to build highly engaging client-side experiences.

Ajax facilitates a paradigm change in web development from the traditional full-page reload model of server-centric applications to rich, responsive client-centric applications. The client receives data and updates the UI using JavaScript. Bandwidth requirements are minimized because the server responds to requests by returning just the requested data instead of HTML pages (and all their elements) along with the data. The application runs faster because the data requests take less time to complete, and the UI is quickly updated without a full-page reload. Asynchronous calls are essential to keeping interactive and immersive applications responsive from the user's perspective.

JavaScript

JavaScript is a dynamic, functional, prototypal language that has a very close relationship with the document object model (DOM). For both JavaScript and the DOM, there are features you can use with confidence and others you should avoid. Over the past ten years, the web development community has learned a great deal about how to use these together to maximize success. See the "Further Reading" section for resources that explain the recommended ways of using JavaScript. Project Silk adheres to these practices, but we do not present a primer here.

As is true with all environments, you will be most successful using it as intended. If you aren't presently writing JavaScript code according to the patterns currently accepted in the JavaScript community, be sure your team has time to become familiar with them, because you may be surprised. For example, the Project Silk team members who had recently worked in the Microsoft .NET environment needed to ramp up on the following aspects of JavaScript:

- JavaScript uses object-oriented concepts, but classes and inheritance hierarchies are not the same as in other .NET languages such as Visual C# and Visual Basic.NET.

- Understanding closures and variable scoping is important. They are used intentionally and often by allowing variables defined within one scope to be used in another function.

- The object that the **this** keyword refers to changes based on where it is used. For example in a single method, **this** may refer to the object the method is defined on, and in a loop within that same method **this** may refer to the current item of the collection being iterated over. You should understand its rules.

- Objects without type definitions are very common and use an object literal syntax. The commas between properties and functions used in these object literals may cause syntax errors until you are familiar with them.

jQuery

jQuery is an open-source JavaScript library that addresses the challenges of working with the DOM across browsers. It has a straightforward API that can be divided into two calling conventions:

- **Functions** are called on the jQuery object itself. For example, the **extend** function merges the properties and methods of two different objects together. It looks like this: **$.extend(targetObject, objectToMerge)**.

- **Methods** are called on the **wrapped set**. A wrapped set is the result of a query that uses a **selector** to find elements in the DOM. To call a method on a wrapped set of elements, a selector is used to select elements in the DOM. For example, to add the **listing** CSS class to all **ul** elements directly inside a **div** element, **$('div ul').addClass('listing')** can be used.

jQuery also provides features to raise and handle events, make Ajax requests, and process the data returned from Ajax requests. To be successful developing with jQuery, you should:

- Know that the selector syntax uses and extends the CSS selector syntax. The better you're able to leverage this syntax, the cleaner your HTML can be.

- Understand what the wrapped set is, how it's different from an array of DOM elements, and which you're working with at any given time. For example, when using **$.each**, inside the callback, **this** is not wrapped.

- Understand that animations are asynchronous and are queued. Use a named queue or the **stop** method to gain more control over how the animations behave.

Modernizr

In the past, the client-side application would use **navigator.userAgent** to determine which browser was in use and choose its code paths accordingly. Today, the accepted practice is to explicitly detect each feature the application intends to use.

Modernizr is an open-source JavaScript library that detects the support for browser features (geolocation, canvas, SVG, border-radius, etc.) and exposes its findings in CSS and JavaScript. Once a script reference to Modernizr is included, Modernizr will add a CSS class to the **html** element for each feature it can detect. If the feature isn't supported, the CSS class will start with **no-**. For example, if a browser supports canvas and not webgl, its **html** element will look like this: **<html class="canvas no-webgl ...">**. Modernizr also exposes a **Modernizr** JavaScript object that has Boolean properties for each feature it can detect.

ASP.NET MVC Razor

Razor is the name of one of the view engines in ASP.NET MVC 3 (WebForms is the other). The razor view engine is used to render MVC views, which are comprised of HTML and server-side code.

The Razor syntax is clean and concise, and easy to learn, and Visual Studio includes IntelliSense® and syntax highlighting for Razor syntax.

For a more detailed overview of Razor, see "ASP.NET MVC 3 Overview, The Razor View Engine" in the "Further Reading" section.

Dependency Injection

Dependency injection is a variant of the Inversion of Control design pattern. Dependency injection containers reduce the dependency coupling between objects by providing a facility to instantiate instances of classes and manage their lifetimes based on the configuration of the container. During the creation of objects, the container injects into the object any dependencies the object requires. If those dependencies have not yet been created, the container creates and resolves their dependencies first.

Dependency injection provides several benefits:

- Reduced coupling; classes and components don't have to locate dependencies or manage their lifetimes.

- Improved testability; dependencies can be easily substituted with mocked implementations.

- Improved flexibility and maintainability; dependencies can be replaced easily.

ASP.NET MVC 3 provides better support for applying dependency injection and for integrating with dependency injection or inversion of control containers. For more information about dependency injection in ASP.NET MVC 3, see "ASP.NET MVC 3 Overview, Dependency Injection Improvements" in the "Further Reading" section. For an introduction to dependency injection and inversion of control, see "Loosen Up: Tame Your Software Dependencies for More Flexible Apps" in MSDN Magazine.

Exploring This Guidance

The purpose of this guidance is to show you how to plan, design, and build a rich, interactive web application your users will enjoy using. This guidance includes the following resources:

- **Mileage Stats Reference Implementation**. Comprehensive sample application demonstrating a real-world, interactive, cross-browser, consumer-facing, rich web application. The reference implementation is intentionally incomplete, but does illustrate the core concepts, design patterns, coding patterns, security requirements, web technologies, and unit testing necessary to be successful.
- **Widget QuickStart**. Small sample application that demonstrates how to use and develop jQuery UI Widgets.
- **Documentation**. This guidance provides an architectural overview of rich web applications and chapters that cover the design, concepts, patterns, security, testing, and implementation of Mileage Stats. This guidance also includes documentation that covers the Widget QuickStart and How-to topics on automated testing.

Exploring the Mileage Stats Reference Implementation

Mileage Stats is an ASP.NET MVC application that enables users to track and compare various metrics about their vehicles including fuel consumption, fuel costs, miles driven, and maintenance reminders. The application is a multi-page interactive web application where the pages are rendered without requiring a full-page reload. The lack of full-page reloads enables rich UI transitions between states (pages) and the application runs fast because of the client-side data caching and some data prefetching.

Much of the effort in building Mileage Stats was applied to the usability and rich interactivity of the experience. Animations were included to enhance the enjoyment of the site and Ajax is used to keep the interface responsive and immersive. A great deal of care was also taken to ensure that the client-side JavaScript was modularized for maintainability. To accomplish these design goals, the JavaScript code was structured using jQuery UI Widgets and JavaScript objects. Widgets allow you to break the UI into discrete stateful objects that provide a clean separation of responsibilities and concerns.

The Mileage Stats solution is partitioned into three layers: data, business, and web, spread across five Visual Studio projects pictured on the left side of the image below. Mileage Stats also includes four unit test projects for testing the C# projects, and a suite of JavaScript unit tests, pictured on the right side of the image below.

Mileage Stats project and unit tests

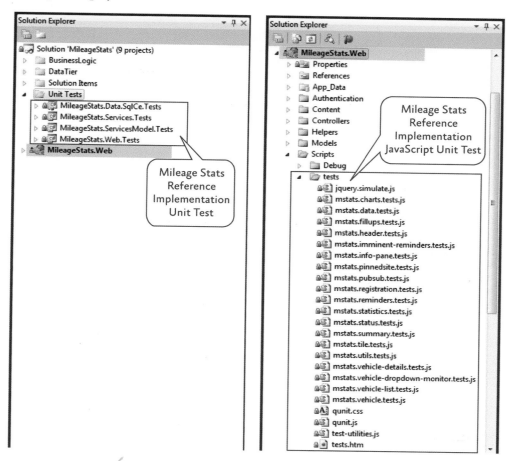

The design and implementation of the Mileage Stats solution is used for illustration throughout the guidance and will be covered in the remaining chapters. Now let's walk through Mileage Stats from a user's perspective.

Using Mileage Stats

Unauthenticated users accessing Mileage Stats will be redirected to the landing page to sign in. Mileage Stats uses third-party OpenID providers for user authentication. Mileage Stats supports deep linking, so that previously authenticated users returning to the website can go directly to any page.

For Internet Explorer 9 users, Mileage Stats provides a customized pinned sites experience that is accessed from the landing page. The image below shows the pinned site running in the pinned sites customized chrome of Internet Explorer 9. The menu, favorites bar, command bar, and status bar have been removed from view. The back and forward buttons are rendered with a custom color, and the site's favicon is displayed to the left of the back button, which navigates to the landing page.

Landing page

The first time a new user logs into Mileage Stats, the summary pane will display the "Complete your Registration" form pictured below. This form will continue to be displayed in the Summary pane until the user clicks the **Save** button. Further edits to the user's profile can be made by clicking the **Profile** link at the top right of the browser window.

Third-party authentication providers do not uniformly expose their user data to applications requesting authentication services. For example, a user may have an OpenID account, but Mileage Stats may not be able to request information such as the user's first and last name from the provider to populate the **Display Name** field. The UX designer did not want to force a new user to complete a form in order to use Mileage Stats. Instead, we implemented a non-intrusive form for collecting the new user's name, country, and postal code. New users can immediately use Mileage Stats and can complete the registration information at their leisure.

First time logging in

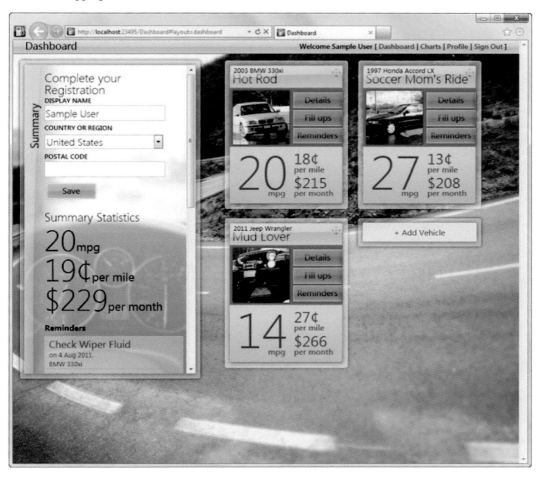

The dashboard provides a summary view of the user's vehicles. From here the user can add a new vehicle, drill down to more detail for a vehicle, and see maintenance reminders that are overdue or due soon. There is a navigation bar at the top of the browser window that provides top-level navigation to the Dashboard, Charts, or Profile pages and a link to sign out of the application.

Dashboard

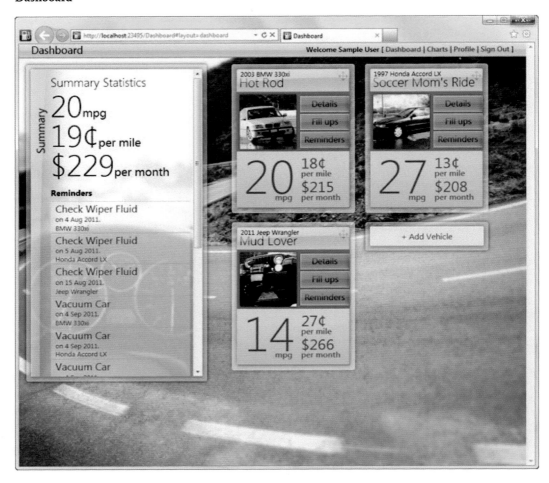

A high-value scenario for this guidance was to demonstrate fluid and rich UI transitions and animations. The image below shows the application transitioning from the Dashboard (two column vehicle listing) to the Details view (single column vehicle listing) in response to the user clicking the **Details** button in Hot Rod's vehicle tile. The image demonstrates the synchronization of opacity and position animations as the summary pane, vehicle tiles, and info pane animate into their respective positions.

Transitioning from the Dashboard to Details

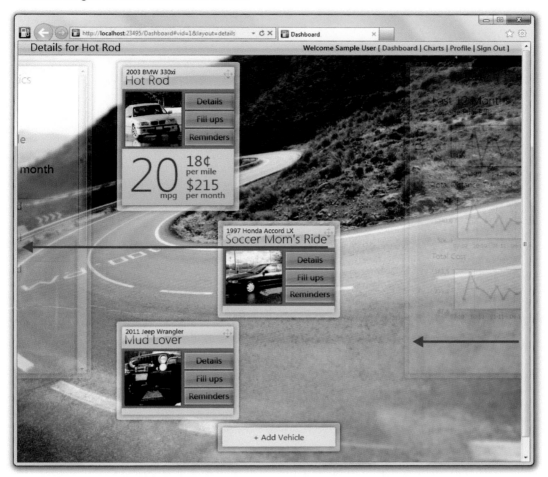

The Details view displays aggregated monthly trends for fuel efficiency, distance traveled, and fuel cost. Users are able to quickly see trends in their vehicle usage as well as overdue maintenance reminders. In addition to displaying maintenance reminders, the Details view allows users to edit or delete the vehicle, as well as navigate to the Fill ups and Reminders views.

Details

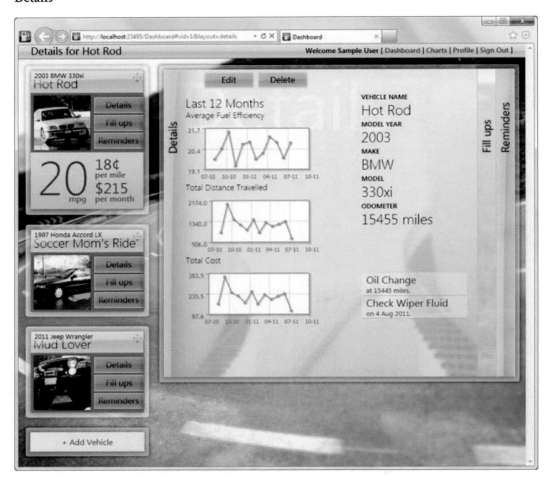

The Charts page provides three charts, which allow users to easily compare their vehicles' fuel efficiency, distance travelled, and cost. The displayed data can be filtered by vehicle and date range. The data displayed in these charts is prefetched and cached, providing a fast user experience.

Charts

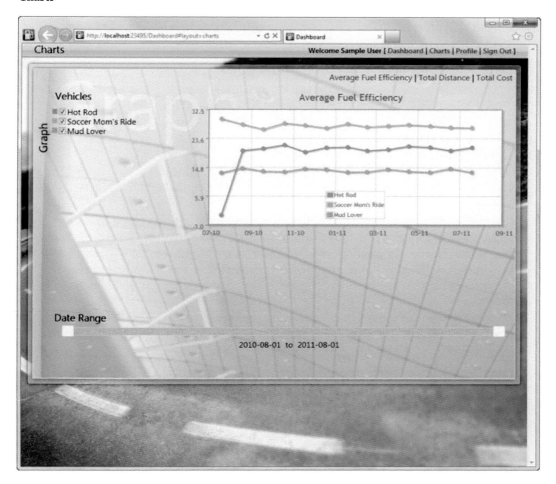

Exploring the QuickStart

The Widget QuickStart is a small, focused application that illustrates the way Mileage Stats uses the jQuery UI Widget Factory to create maintainable widgets that implement client-side behavior.

Exploring the Documentation

This guidance covers a wide range of topics, including: planning and designing your application, understanding and writing jQuery UI Widgets, writing server-side code that supports the client-side application, patterns and concepts used in JavaScript code, data and caching, and securing and testing your application.

The documentation includes the following:

- Chapter 2, "**Architecture**." This chapter explains the Mileage Stats client-side architecture by studying how its structure, modularity, communication, navigation, and data relate to one another.

- Chapter 3, "**jQuery UI Widgets**." An understanding of jQuery UI Widgets is important to comprehending this guidance and Mileage Stats because the application makes heavy use of widgets to modularize its JavaScript. This chapter provides instruction on widget fundamentals, lifetime, creation, events, properties and methods, and inheritance. It largely uses code examples from the Widget Quick-Start.

- Chapter 4, "**Design and Layout**." This chapter explains the importance of an iterative design process and the roles different team members fulfill. After a survey of user experience and UI design considerations, we will walk through the design and building of Mileage Stats and see how these considerations influenced the application.

- Chapter 5, "**Modularity**." Rich and interactive web applications can require a fair amount of JavaScript coding. Modularizing your JavaScript makes your code easier to maintain and evolve. In this chapter we will explain how the Mileage Stats JavaScript was modularized using jQuery UI Widgets and JavaScript objects.

- Chapter 6, "**Client Data Management and Caching**." This chapter covers how JavaScript objects in Mileage Stats request and send data. It also covers how the data manager façade performs the Ajax calls to the server and provides transparent data caching.

- Chapter 7, "**Manipulating Client-Side HTML**." This chapter discusses how an interactive application like Mileage Stats can manage client-side HTML changes without having to fully reload the page each time the user navigates or completes a task.

- Chapter 8, "**Communication**." This chapter explains how communication between widgets and JavaScript objects was implemented in Mileage Stats. Some topics include loosely coupled communication that uses the "publish and subscribe" metaphor, events, and inter-widget communication.

- Chapter 9, "**Navigation**." Rich web applications support client-side transitions, animations, and deep linking. Even when the site avoids the use of full-page re-freshes, users expect their browser back button to function as expected. This chapter explains the challenges client-side web developers face maintaining the browser history when using Ajax calls instead of full-page reloads. In addition, the Mileage Stats state-change management is fully explained.
- Chapter 10, "**Application Notifications**." Web applications that users consider responsive have one thing in common: they provide appropriate and timely feed-back to the user. In this chapter we show how to provide unobtrusive feedback to the user and how to implement notifications on the desktop with the Internet Explorer 9 Pinned Sites API.
- Chapter 11, "**Server-Side Implementation**." This chapter covers the Mileage Stats ASP.NET MVC application, the components it's dependent upon, and the services they provide to support the client-side JavaScript objects. The chapter takes you from the database, through the repositories, to the business objects that provide data validation and data shaping services to the controllers that consume their data and render it to the client.
- Chapter 12, "**Security**." Web security is critical to consumer confidence. Poor security can cause your customer's data, your own data, or your intellectual prop-erty to be compromised. This chapter covers some of the security features of the ASP.NET MVC platform and security features in Mileage Stats that provide coun-termeasures against the relevant threats for authentication, input validation, anti-forgery, and JavaScript Object Notation (JSON) hijacking.
- Chapter 13, "**Unit Testing Web Applications**." Unit tests are long-term investments that give the development team confidence when refactoring or evolving the application, and when updating external dependencies, such as when versions of external libraries are updated. This chapter is meant to help you get started unit testing JavaScript and ASP.NET MVC code.
- Chapter 14, "**Widget QuickStart**." This topic describes the Widget QuickStart and includes information on attaching widgets, widget initialization, and widget interac-tions.
- "**Project Silk Road Map**." This list helps you locate sections of the guidance by topic.
- "**Glossary**." This topic provides a summary of the terms, concepts, and technologies used in this guidance.

The following topics are included with the Project Silk download and on MSDN:
- "**Readme**." This file contains instructions on installing external dependencies from NuGet and downloading the required external JavaScript libraries to build and run Mileage Stats.
- "**How to: Check UIElement Properties Using Coded UI Test**." This How-to topic walks you through the creation of an automated test that checks that UIElement properties in Mileage Stats are displayed with the correct values. It uses Coded UI Test that is available in Visual Studio 2010 Premium or Ultimate Edition.

- **"How to: Create an Automated Negative Test Case Using Coded UI Test."** This How-to topic walks you through the creation of an automated negative test case that checks the error handling capability of Mileage Stats. It uses Coded UI Test that is available in Visual Studio 2010 Premium or Ultimate Edition.
- **"How to: Create a Web Client UI Test Using Coded UI Test."** This How-to topic walks you through the creation of an automated test that verifies that the correct controls are displayed with the correct values. It uses Coded UI Test that is available in Visual Studio 2010 Premium or Ultimate Edition.
- **"Bibliography."** This is a summary of the resources referred to in the guidance.

Community

Project Silk's community site is **http://silk.codeplex.com**. There, you can post questions, provide feedback, or connect with other users to share ideas. Community members can also help Microsoft plan and test future offerings. In addition, the community site has links to tutorial videos and MSDN content.

Further Reading

To download Project Silk source code and documentation, see "Project Silk: Client-Side Web Development for Modern Browsers" on MSDN at **http://msdn.microsoft.com/en-us/library/hh396380.aspx**.

If you have comments on this guide, visit the Project Silk community site at **http://silk.codeplex.com**.

View a two minute video on Mileage Stats on Channel 9: **http://channel9.msdn.com/posts/Project-Silk-Mileage-Stats-Application**.

Additional content is provided on MSDN:

"Readme" file online at **http://msdn.microsoft.com/en-us/library/hh404100.aspx**.

"How to: Check UIElement Properties Using Coded UI Test" online at **http://msdn.microsoft.com/en-us/library/hh404081.aspx**.

"How to: Create an Automated Negative Test Case Using Coded UI Test" online at **http://msdn.microsoft.com/en-us/library/hh404089.aspx**.

"How to: Create a Web Client UI Test Using Coded UI Test" online at **http://msdn.microsoft.com/en-us/library/hh404082.aspx**.

For information on the designer role, see Chapter 4, **"Design and Layout."**

For information on unit testing, see Chapter 13, **"Unit Testing Web Applications."**

Crockford, Douglas. *JavaScript: The Good Parts*. O'Reilly Media, 2008.

Stefanov, Stoyan. *JavaScript Patterns*. O'Reilly Media, 2010.

"ASP.NET MVC 3 Overview, The Razor View Engine" on ASP.NET:

http://www.asp.net/mvc/mvc3#BM_The_Razor_View_Engine

"ASP.NET MVC 3 Overview, Dependency Injection Improvements" on ASP.NET:
http://www.asp.net/mvc/mvc3#BM_Dependency_Injection_Improvements

"Loosen Up: Tame Your Software Dependencies for More Flexible Apps" in MSDN
Magazine:
http://msdn.microsoft.com/en-us/magazine/cc337885.aspx

"Entity Framework 4.1 Released" on the ADO.NET team blog:
http://blogs.msdn.com/b/adonet/archive/2011/04/11/ef-4-1-released.aspx

"Entity Framework 4.1 Update 1 Released" on the ADO.NET team blog:
http://blogs.msdn.com/b/adonet/archive/2011/07/25/ef-4-1-update-1-released.
aspx

jQuery Documentation Main Page:
http://docs.jquery.com/Main_Page

ASP.NET MVC 3:
http://www.asp.net/mvc/mvc3

NuGet version 1.4 or later:
http://nuget.org/

Internet Explorer 9:
http://windows.microsoft.com/en-US/windows/downloads/internet-explorer

Modernizr:
http://www.modernizr.com/

To access web resources more easily, see the online version of the bibliography on
MSDN: http://msdn.microsoft.com/en-us/library/hh404094.aspx.

2 Architecture

Introduction

The Mileage Stats Reference Implementation (Mileage Stats) is a cross-browser, ASP.NET Model-View-Controller (MVC) application that takes advantage of the features of modern browsers. The application offers two types of user experiences:

1. **A traditional website experience**. In this approach, a form post and page reload are executed each time a button or hyperlink is clicked.

2. **A rich website experience**. In this approach, the initial page is loaded once, and server requests are only made when new data is required or updated. In addition to other user-friendly features, the lack of a full-page reload enables the animation of client-side state changes.

The rich website approach provides a superior experience for the user, as the application feels more responsive and more like a desktop application. However, because some users do not have scripting enabled or available on their user agent (web browser or accessibility tool, such as a screen reader), which is necessary for the partial-page reloads, we must also support the traditional website experience.

In the traditional approach, the ASP.NET MVC controllers are responsible for acquiring data and for returning a built-up view that consists of HTML structure and data. In the case of the rich website experience, we perform asynchronous data requests and the controller returns only data. The client then renders the data in the user interface (UI) without reloading the whole page.

Supporting both these experiences introduces complexity that requires careful planning on both the client and server sides to ensure that the application is responsive, maintainable, has a clean separation of concerns, and is testable.

You should determine early in the design phase which experience the user should expect in each browser and browser version the application will support. If you choose to support older browsers, you may limit your technology choices and affect the run-time experience of the application. Shims and polyfills, such as those that provide HTML5 support, are available for adding support for some technologies in older browsers, but these come at the cost of additional dependencies (see "Further Reading" at the end of the chapter to learn more about shims and polyfill solutions). Making decisions early on about which technologies you will need to support allows you to establish realistic expectations for users and project stakeholders.

This chapter provides a high-level map of the Mileage Stats client-side architecture, and is divided into five areas of discussion: structure, modularity, communication, navigation, and data.

- **Structure** refers to client-side HTML structure and manipulation. It is represented below as the Template.
- **Modularity** refers to how a clean separation of JavaScript objects helps create a more maintainable application. It is represented below as the Widget.
- **Communication** defines how JavaScript objects communicate. It is represented below as Pub/Sub.
- **Navigation** explains how to manage user gestures and coordinate animations. It is represented below as Navigation and the Layout Manager.
- **Data** provides guidance for client-side data requests and data caching. It is represented below as the Data Manager.

Mileage Stats client architecture

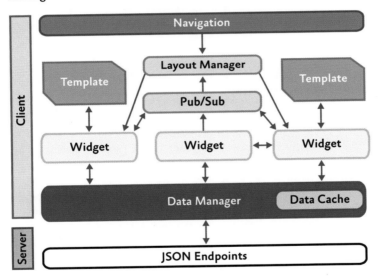

In this chapter you will learn:
- Options and strategies for getting the right HTML to the client.
- The advantages of modular code, and techniques for using jQuery UI widgets.
- How the Publish/Subscribe (pub/sub) pattern can be used for loosely coupled communication.

- How to solve browser history and back-button problems when the site doesn't perform full-page reloads.
- How a loosely coupled data layer can simplify caching for client-side data requests.
- How the Mileage Stats team solved a number of challenges related to structure, modularity, communication, navigation, and data.

The technologies and libraries discussed in this chapter are JavaScript, jQuery, jQuery UI Widgets, and jQuery Back Button & Query Library (jQuery BBQ).

Structure

Websites like Mileage Stats provide an engaging user experience when viewed using modern browsers with JavaScript enabled. The site can also be viewed without JavaScript enabled and will function when viewed in an older browser.

To provide an engaging, responsive, and interactive experience, the application needs to manage client-side structure changes without performing full-page reloads. This requires client-side loading, creation, and replacement of HTML fragments or pages.

To support both rich and traditional user experiences, the Project Silk team chose to have the web server generate the initial HTML; then, after using JavaScript to detect the browser capabilities, we enhanced the user experience in capable browsers by replacing the server-generated HTML structure with a client-side version. Elements replaced include portions of HTML, button actions, and CSS classes. Enhancement can mean adding animation, page transitions, or Ajax functionality to client-side elements. Client-side enhancement of server-generated HTML is called *progressive enhancement*. Progressive enhancement adds features to the client-side experience based on browser capabilities.

After the initial enhancement of the server-generated HTML, the client-side JavaScript responds to user gestures, requests data, and initiates UI changes without posting back to the server.

Client-side UI structure can be generated with JavaScript, loaded on demand from the server, or rendered by a plug-in or a library. Initially, the team tried on-demand loading of granular HTML fragments from the server. This approach was motivated by the team's desire to limit the creation of HTML to a single location. However, this approach failed to provide the desired result, so the team changed tactics and used jQuery templates instead. See Chapter 7, "**Manipulating Client-Side HTML**" for a full explanation of this choice.

jQuery Templates

jQuery templates are HTML markup with inline JavaScript expressions that are used to populate values in the markup. The jQuery Template plug-in applies data to the template and renders the output into the document object model (DOM). Mileage Stats uses jQuery UI widgets to coordinate the data retrieval, applying of the data to the template using the plug-in, and overwriting the DOM element.

jQuery template rendering in Mileage Stats

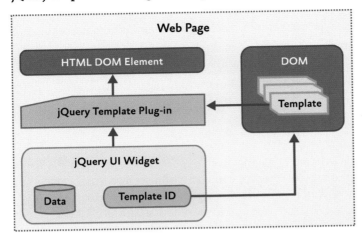

The data can be a single object or an array of objects. jQuery templates separate structure and data, making the application easier to code, test, and maintain.

If you use ASP.NET MVC or ASP.NET Web Forms, you can use the rendering engine to dynamically create or modify the jQuery template while it's being rendered. Mileage Stats uses this capability to inject URLs and **data-** (pronounced "data dash") attributes into the templates at render time.

Mileage Stats loads all jQuery templates as part of the initial page load. Preloading templates simplifies the client-side application and provides much faster client-side rendering than on-demand loading of templates.

For more information on the jQuery Template plug-in and authoring templates, see "**jQuery Templates**" in the "Further Reading" section. For more information on jQuery templates in Mileage Stats, see Chapter 7, "**Manipulating Client-Side HTML**."

Modularity

Modularized code simplifies the overall application, establishes clear boundaries of responsibility, provides separation of concerns, increases testability, eases maintenance, and enables reuse. The modularization of code in Mileage Stats is achieved by composing client-side JavaScript into jQuery UI widgets and JavaScript objects.

jQuery widgets are objects attached to page elements that supply services for managing lifetime, state, inheritance, theming, and communication with other widgets or JavaScript objects. Objects in Mileage Stats belong to one of the following functional categories:

- **UI**. Includes these jQuery UI widgets: vehicle, vehicle list, information pane, vehicle details, vehicle fill ups, vehicle reminders, registration, statistics, summary, status, header, and charts.

- **Behavior**. Includes the tile and layout manager widgets, and JavaScript objects for pinned sites and validation.

- **Infrastructure**. Includes JavaScript objects for data access, caching, and pub/sub messaging.

The jQuery widgets that compose the Mileage Stats Dashboard are pictured in the image below. The complexity of the application demonstrates the need for modularization. By breaking the implementation into discrete, loosely coupled objects, the client-side code is much easier to understand, author, maintain, test, and debug.

1. **Pinned sites.** JavaScript object that provides the pinned sites implementation for Windows® Internet Explorer® 9.

2. **Status widget**. Provides management and display of user notification messages.

3. **Summary widget**. Acts as a container, managing its child registration, statistics, and reminders widgets.

4. **Statistics widget**. Displays summary statistics for all vehicles.

5. **Reminders widget**. Lists overdue and upcoming maintenance reminders. Manages the action of clicking on a reminder.

6. **Layout manager widget**. Services navigation requests and coordinates UI layout changes.

7. **Vehicle list widget**. Displays the vehicle tiles in a one-column or two-column listing. Invokes the child widget animation when required and controls when child widgets are displayed in expanded or contracted view.

8. **Tile widget**. Provides drag-and-drop capability for the child vehicle widget.

9. **Vehicle widget**. Displays vehicle information in expanded or contracted view. Manages the actions of each button.

10. **Header widget**. Provides top-level navigation and user name display. Manages actions when a hyperlink in the header is clicked.

Modularization in Mileage Stats

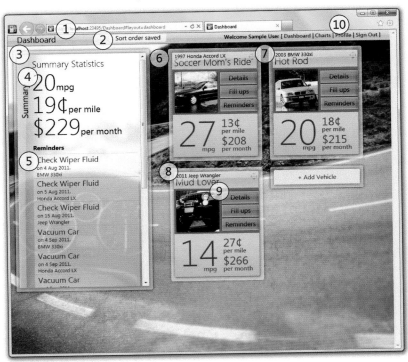

For more information on modularity in Mileage Stats, see Chapter 5, "Modularity." For more information on jQuery UI widgets see Chapter 3, "jQuery UI Widgets" and Chapter 5, "Modularity." For more information on pinned sites, see Chapter 10, "Application Notifications."

Communication

jQuery widgets and JavaScript objects help you modularize your code, but these objects are not isolated islands; rather they are small objects that work together to form the complete application. Well-defined communication between objects is critical not only from a functional view, but from an architectural view as well.

If not carefully planned, communication between objects can lead to tight coupling and undesirable dependencies. Mileage Stats objects either communicate *directly* with one another, or *loosely* by using a publish and subscribe pattern (pub/sub).

DIRECT COMMUNICATION

Direct widget communication is typically reserved for high-level widgets controlling lower-level widgets, such as when the layout manager tells a widget to hide or show itself.

Layout manager and pub/sub

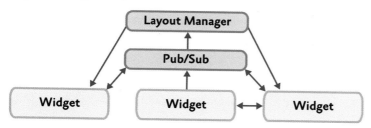

LOOSE COMMUNICATION

Pub/sub is a messaging pattern that enables loose communication between publishers and subscribers. When a message is published, zero or more subscribers will be notified. A pub/sub object manages communication, relieving the publishers and subscribers of needing direct knowledge of one another. Pub/sub messages are individually defined and can optionally contain a payload.

The pub/sub pattern provides clean separation between the object invoking the action and the object that handles the action. This separation allows the publisher and subscriber's internal implementations to evolve without affecting each other.

Mileage Stats has its own pub/sub implementation that provides for loose communication. For example, the **Status** widget subscribes to the **status** message. The **status** message has a payload that contains message, type, duration, and priority values. Publishers of the **status** message provide these values when publishing this message.

Mileage Stats widgets have publish and subscribe functions passed into their options object during construction to decouple them from the pub/sub implementation.

For more information about the pub/sub implementation in Mileage Stats, see Chapter 8, "Communication."

Navigation

Rich client-side web applications like Mileage Stats do not perform full-page reloads each time a button or hyperlink is clicked. Instead, client-side application code handles these events.

The jQuery BBQ plug-in is responsible for providing address bar URL changes. Changing the address bar URL performs two functions. First, it allows users to bookmark addresses so that they can return directly to a particular application state. This is known as deep linking. Second, it enables the browser history and back button to perform as the user expects.

The Mileage Stats layout manager is a widget that works in conjunction with the BBQ plug-in to service navigation requests. It subscribes to the BBQ plug-in **hashchange** event, and initiates layout changes based on address bar URL changes.

Navigation and layout manager

Along with hiding and showing UI elements, the layout manager is also responsible for initiating UI animations during navigation. The layout manager does not perform the animation, but sequentially calls methods on one or more lower-level widgets, resulting in an engaging UI transition.

As part of the layout manager's top-level widget responsibilities, it subscribes to several pub/sub messages and invokes lower-level widget data refresh methods when those messages are published. For more information about navigation and the layout manager, see Chapter 9, "Navigation."

Data

When designing your client-side data architecture, several key decisions will impact application performance, maintainability, and browser support. Will data requests flow through a central object or will objects make direct calls to the server? Will data be cached, and if so, how much? Will data be prefetched, and if so, how much? Answers to these questions will vary based on your application's specific requirements.

In Mileage Stats, all data requests are made via Ajax and are routed through the data manager. Having a single object handle data requests simplifies the client-side calling code, improves application testability, and facilitates cleaner application evolution when client-side libraries advance or change. The single data manager object also affords you the opportunity to implement client-side data caching in a central location. Data is cached in a JavaScript object, rather than using HTML5 local storage or similar APIs, in order to meet the cross-browser requirements of the application.

Mileage Stats prefetches chart data during the initial page load, enabling instant application response when the user navigates to the Charts page. Whenever data is returned from the server, it's cached. This can make the application more scalable because repeated requests to the server for the same data are no longer necessary, requiring less server processing per user.

Widgets and JavaScript objects request their data from the data manager. The data manager services the request, first checking if the request should be cached, and if so, checks the cache before making a call to the server. Upon successful completion of the request, the returned data will be added to the cache, and then passed to the calling widget. If an error occurs, the error will be returned to the calling widget.

Data request

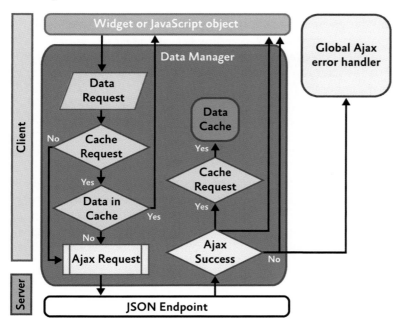

For in-depth coverage of data management and caching, see Chapter 6, "**Client Data Management and Caching.**"

Architectural Alternatives

The Project Silk team built Mileage Stats using jQuery UI Widgets as a way to provide modularity in JavaScript while keeping external dependencies on other libraries to a minimum. This is an effective way to separate different client-side concerns and facilitates testability and readability of the code base. This approach worked well for Mileage Stats, but it isn't the only option.

A common UI design pattern separates the application's user content (the model) from the details that dictate how that information is displayed (the view). This separation necessitates logic that connects these two concepts (the controller). The MVC pattern has been implemented as described here and has also been adapted to specialized uses such as data binding that have resulted in similar patterns such as the Model View View-Model (MVVM) pattern. There are popular JavaScript libraries such as **Backbone.js** and **Knockout.js** that, for all intents and purposes, implement the MVC and MVVM patterns, respectively. There are also more comprehensive JavaScript frameworks such as **Sprout-Core**, **YUI**, and the **Dojo Toolkit** that aim to address more aspects of the client-side application in a single framework rather than using various libraries, each with a specific purpose.

The use of these libraries does create more dependencies, but this usually has a positive impact on the overall design of the application by making it easier to control the separation of concerns that is so important to complex user interfaces. If your UI has a number of screens made up of multiple regions and includes complex interaction patterns, and having additional dependencies is acceptable to you, you should consider applying these patterns and using these libraries. A design the Project Silk team is interested in investigating in the future involves the use of jQuery UI Widgets that can be data bound within an MVVM implementation such as Knockout.js.

Summary

Building a rich web application that reduces the number of full-page loads, includes animations, and is responsible for updating the UI dynamically requires a thoughtful approach to managing structure, modularity, communication, navigation, and data. This chapter provided a high-level view of the Mileage Stats client-side application architecture. The following image shows the client-side objects and their implementation mapped to libraries or frameworks.

Mileage Stats client architecture technology map

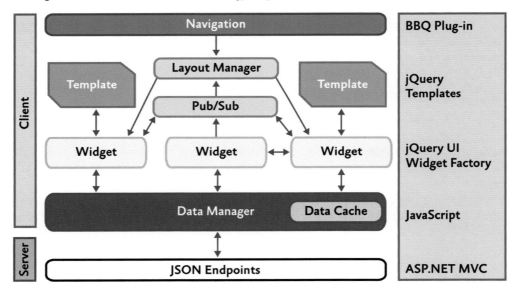

Further Reading

For more information on jQuery UI widgets see Chapter 3, "jQuery UI Widgets," and Chapter 5, "Modularity."

For more information on jQuery templates in Mileage Stats, see Chapter 7, "Manipulating Client-Side HTML."

For more information on pinned sites, see Chapter 10, "Application Notifications."

For more information on modularity in Mileage Stats, see Chapter 5, "Modularity."

For more information about the pub/sub implementation in Mileage Stats, see Chapter 8, "Communication."

For more information about navigation and the layout manager, see Chapter 9, "Navigation."

For more information about data management and caching, see Chapter 6, "Client Data Management and Caching."

For more information about the libraries and guidelines discussed in this chapter, see the following:

jQuery:
http://jquery.org

jQuery Templates:
http://api.jquery.com/category/plugins/templates/

Backbone.js:
http://documentcloud.github.com/backbone/

Knockout.js:
http://knockoutjs.com/

SproutCore:
http://www.sproutcore.com

YUI:
http://developer.yahoo.com/yui

Dojo Toolkit:
http://dojotoolkit.org

"jQuery BBQ: Back Button & Query Library" on Ben Alman's blog:
http://benalman.com/projects/jquery-bbq-plugin/

"Filling the HTML5 Gaps with Polyfills and Shims" from Rey Bango's MIX11 session:
http://channel9.msdn.com/Events/MIX/MIX11/HTM04

"Making HTML5 and CSS3 work with polyfills and shims" by Rey Bango on .net magazine:
http://www.netmagazine.com/features/making-html5-and-css3-work-polyfills-and-shims

To access web resources more easily, see the online version of the bibliography on MSDN: http://msdn.microsoft.com/en-us/library/hh404094.aspx

3

jQuery UI Widgets

Introduction

When building rich, client-side web applications, some of the visual elements on the page will naturally take on roles, responsibilities, and state. As more of these elements are added to the page, complexity will increase, so it's important for the design to support a maintainable code base. Maintainable solutions have at least three important characteristics: they have an intentional design, are modular, and they have unit tests. All of these characteristics should play to the strengths of the platform, language, and key parts of the environment.

The web browser is the platform, JavaScript is the language, and various JavaScript libraries represent key parts of the environment. Among other benefits, libraries such as jQuery and jQuery UI can simplify the code you write by:

- Decreasing the amount of code you need to write and maintain.
- Addressing typical challenges, such as browser compatibility issues.
- Providing consistency for Ajax interactions, animations, and events.
- Assisting in creating a maintainable code base through modularity.

A concept that is central to the visual parts of jQuery UI is the *widget*. According to the official jQuery UI project, jQuery UI "provides abstractions for low-level interaction and animation, advanced effects and high-level, themeable widgets, built on top of the jQuery JavaScript Library, that you can use to build highly interactive web applications." Widgets are objects attached to page elements that supply services for managing lifetime, state, inheritance, theming, and communication with other widgets or JavaScript objects.

One of the most valuable aspects of jQuery is that extensibility is built in and well defined. This extensibility is accomplished through the construction of jQuery plug-ins. Even though they have a number of extra features in addition to those in a typical jQuery plug-in, it's important to know that a widget *is* a jQuery plug-in. This may not be obvious because a widget is defined differently, but they are used the same way you use official jQuery methods and most custom plug-ins. Sometimes a plug-in is sufficient and other times a widget is more appropriate. When you need to apply behavior or state to *individual* elements and need to communicate between elements, widgets provide a number of capabilities you would otherwise have to write yourself. This chapter illustrates these capabilities. See the "Further Reading" section at the end of the chapter for more information about jQuery plug-ins and how to author them.

In this chapter you will learn:

- How to define and apply widgets.
- How to manage the lifetime of widgets.
- How to define default options that permit overrides and change notifications.
- How to use options for decoupling behavior and facilitating event subscriptions.
- How to use private methods to improve the readability of the code.
- How to define and use public methods, properties, and events.
- How to inherit from a base widget.

The technologies discussed in this chapter are jQuery Plug-ins and the jQuery UI Widget Factory. The code examples used here largely come from the Widget QuickStart included with Project Silk.

Widget Fundamentals

If you know how to use jQuery, you know how to use a widget. In practical terms, a jQuery UI widget is a specialized jQuery plug-in. Using plug-ins makes it easy to apply behavior to the elements they are attached to. However, plug-ins lack some built-in capabilities, such as a way to associate data with its elements, expose methods, merge options with defaults, and control the plug-in's lifetime. Widgets have these capabilities built in.

A plug-in can be made to have the same features as a widget, but you must add these capabilities yourself. However, before you can use a widget, it must be defined. Once it has been defined, it can be applied to elements. Widgets are defined using the widget factory. When the widget factory is invoked, it creates a *widget method* on the jQuery prototype, **$.fn**, the same place that plug-ins and other jQuery functions are located. The widget method represents the primary interface for applying the widget to elements and using the widget after it's applied. This important concept is covered in more depth in "The Widget Method" later in the chapter.

Unlike other chapters, this chapter uses the Widget QuickStart for the code examples rather than the Mileage Stats Reference Implementation (Mileage Stats). The focus of the Widget QuickStart is to enable the client-side behavior for tagged keywords. When a user hovers over a keyword, the browser will display a pop-up list of popular links for that keyword from the Delicious.com bookmarking service. The following figure illustrates the QuickStart and the corresponding widgets.

The tagger and infobox widgets displayed

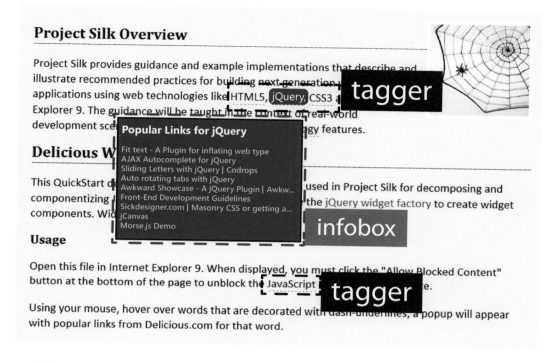

The page accomplishes this through the use of two widgets:

- **tagger** adds the hover behavior to the tagged keywords.
- **infoBox** retrieves the links and controls the box that displays them.

For more information about the QuickStart or to walk through the process of building it, see Chapter 14, "Widget QuickStart."

DEFINING A WIDGET

The dependencies for a widget can be fulfilled with script references to the **content delivery network (CDN) locations** for jQuery and jQuery UI. Widgets often reside in their own .js file and are wrapped in an immediate function, as you can see in the following code example. This wrapper creates a JavaScript closure, which prevents new variables from being globally scoped. A single solution should allow no more than one global object to be created, as per well-accepted JavaScript practices.

The jQuery argument at the end of the following code example becomes the **$** argument passed in, which allows you to use the common **$** symbol to represent the **jQuery** function. Because there is no second argument, the **undefined** argument becomes truly undefined. Therefore the **$** and **undefined** arguments reestablish their expected behavior inside the closure in case another script previously defined these variables as something else.

```
JavaScript
// Contained in jquery.qs.tagger.js
(function($, undefined) {
  $.widget('qs.tagger', {
    // definition of the widget goes here
  });
}(jQuery));
```

The call to **$.widget** invokes the widget factory, which makes the widget available for use. The first argument, **qs.tagger**, is the widget's namespace and name separated by a period (*namespace.name*). The name is used as the name of the widget method placed on the jQuery prototype. The second argument, called the *widget prototype*, is an object literal that defines the specifics of the widget. The widget prototype is the definition of the widget, and is used when the widget is applied to elements. The prototype is stored directly on the jQuery object under the namespace provided: **$.qs.tagger**.

USING A WIDGET

Once a widget has been defined, it's ready to be applied to DOM elements. To apply the widget to the matched elements, invoke the widget method just like you would other jQuery methods. The following code shows how to apply the **tagger** widget to all **span** elements with a **data-tag** attribute.

```
JavaScript
// Contained in startup.widget.js
$('span[data-tag]').tagger();
```

Because the widget method is used as the primary interface to the widget, it's not only called when initially applying the widget to the element, it's also used for calling methods and reading and writing options and properties on the widget. When widgets are applied to elements, an instance of the widget is created and stored inside each element. This is how the widget factory knows if a widget has already been attached to an element.

Managing Lifetime

There are three phases of a widget's lifetime that you can control: creation, initialization, and destruction.

CREATION

The first time the widget is applied to an element, the widget's **_create** function is invoked. Method names preceded with an underscore have private scope by convention, which means they only expect to be invoked from inside the widget. The following code shows the **_create** method in the **infobox** widget.

```
JavaScript
// Contained in jquery.qs.infobox.js
_create: function () {
    var that = this,
        name = this.name;
    that.infoboxElement = $('<div class="qs-infobox" />');
    that.infoboxElement.appendTo('body')
    .bind('mouseenter.' + name, function () {
        mouseOverBox = true;
    })
    .bind('mouseleave.' + name, function () {
        mouseOverBox = false;
        that.hideTagLinks();
    });
},
```

> **Note:** The **that** variable is defined to capture a reference to the widget so it can be accessed within the **mouseleave** event handler. Inside the event handler **this** refers to the element that raised the event, not the widget.
>
> An alternative to using **that** is to use the **jQuery.proxy** function. This function, according to the jQuery API documentation at http://api.jquery.com/jQuery.proxy/, "takes a function and returns a new one that will always have a particular context." When used with event handlers, the widget can be used as the context, and **event. target**, which is normally **this** inside the event handler, can be used to reference the object that raised the event.

The **_create** method is the most appropriate place to perform a number of common tasks:

- **Adding classes** to various elements the widget is attached to is the recommended way to apply styling, layout theming, and more to the widget.

- **Storing references** to commonly accessed elements can increase performance when a particular set of elements is used from a number of methods. Simply create object-level variables for them once, and all other methods can use them. This is an accepted jQuery performance best practice.

- **Creating elements** in the DOM is common for widgets that have requirements such as animations, effects, styling, accessibility, and cross-browser compatibility. As an example, consider the **div.qs-infobox** element created by the **infobox** widget.

- **Applying other widgets** is recommended during creation when your widget relies on other widgets. Even if your widgets don't require each other, consider using the standard jQuery UI widgets from inside yours to add useful behaviors and interactions.

INITIALIZATION

The **_init** method is called after **_create** when the widget is first applied to its elements. The **_init** method is also called every time thereafter when the widget is invoked with no arguments or with options. This method is the recommended place for setting up more complex initialization and is a good way to support reset functionality for the widget if this is required. It's common for widgets to not implement an **_init** method.

DESTRUCTION

The widget's **destroy** method is used to detach a widget from an element. The goal of the **destroy** method is to leave the element exactly like it was before the widget was attached. Therefore, it's not surprising that common tasks are to remove any CSS classes your widget added to the element, detach any elements your widget added to the DOM, and destroy any widgets your widget applied to other elements. Here is the **destroy** method for the **tagger** widget.

```JavaScript
// Contained in jquery.qs.tagger.js
destroy: function () {
    this.element.removeClass('qs-tagged');

    // if using jQuery UI 1.8.x
    $.Widget.prototype.destroy.call(this);
    // if using jQuery UI 1.9.x
    //this._destroy();
}
```

The last part calls the widget's base implementation of **destroy** and is a recommended practice when you provide your widget with a **destroy** method. The base **destroy** method will be called if you don't define one for your widget or if you explicitly call it, as in the code example above. The base implementation will remove the instance of the widget from the element and unbind all namespaced event bindings (this topic is discussed in more detail later in this chapter).

Defining Options

Options give widgets the ability to be extended with values and functions from the JavaScript code that creates and uses the widget. Options are automatically merged with the widget's default options during creation, and the widget factory supports change notifications when option values change.

Options and their default values are defined in the **options** property of the widget prototype, as shown below in the **infobox** widget.

```JavaScript
// Contained in jquery.qs.infobox.js
$.widget('qs.infobox', {
    options: {
```

```
        dataUrl: ''
        maxItems: 10,
    },
    ...
```

To override default options during the creation of the widget, pass them in as an object literal to the widget method, as shown in this startup code of the widget.

JavaScript
```
// Contained in startup.widget.js
var infobox = $('body').infobox({
    dataUrl: 'http://feeds.delicious.com/v2/json/popular/'
});
```

To read the options from inside the widget, use the **options** property directly, as shown in the last line of this code.

JavaScript
```
// Contained in jquery.qs.infobox.js
displayTagLinks: function (event, tagName) {
    var i,
        that = this,
        options = that.options,
        url = options.dataUrl + tagName + '?count=' + options.maxItems,
        ...
```

Reading the values directly from **options** is acceptable when reading values from inside the widget, but you should not use this approach when changing the value of options. Instead, use the **option** method (without an 's').

JavaScript
```
// Code illustration: not in QuickStart
var max = this.option('maxItems');
this.option('maxItems', max + 4);
```

The **option** method is called with one argument when reading an option's value, two arguments when setting a value, and a single object hash when setting more than one option. The **option** method should always be used to change the value of options so that change notifications will work as expected. Changing the option directly on the **options** property bypasses the notification mechanism.

WHEN OPTIONS CHANGE

The options on your widgets should be aware that their values can change and should be prepared when they do. To respond to changes, widgets use the **_setOption** method. This method is called by the widget factory just after the value has been set on the **options** property. The Widget QuickStart doesn't have a need for **_setOption**; but, as an example, if the number of links in the **infobox** widget were configurable by the user, the widget might need to adjust the size of the box when **maxItems** changes.

```javascript
JavaScript
// Code illustration: not in QuickStart
_setOption: function (name, value) {
    if(name === 'maxItems') {
        this._resizeBoxForMaxItemsOf(value);
    }
    $.Widget.prototype._setOption.apply(this, arguments);
},
```

In the code above, if **maxItems** is the name of the option being set, the **_resizeBox ForMaxItemsOf** method will be called. Rather than placing a lot of code in the **_set Option** method, you should place the logic in private methods. This allows you to call the logic from other places that might need it, such as **_create**. The last line calls the base widget's **_setOption** method. This will set the value of the option and will be useful for supporting a **disabled** state.

> **Note:** *All widgets support the notion of being disabled, whether they choose to implement it or not. The Boolean value is stored at* **this.options.disabled** *or* **$(selector).widget('option', 'disabled')** *if you're asking from the outside. In return for honoring this option (whatever that would mean for the user interface (UI) and behavior of your widget) the widget factory will default it to* **false** *and manage some CSS classes related to theming and accessibility.*

The **_setOption** method is not called for the options passed in during the creation of the widget.

FUNCTIONS AS OPTIONS

Defining functions as options is a powerful way to decouple the widget from functionality better located elsewhere.

> **Note:** *The widgets in Mileage Stats use this approach for publishing and subscribing to global events by using their* **publish** *and* **subscribe** *options and getting data from the* **dataManager** *using their* **sendRequest** *option. To learn more about the pub/sub engine, see Chapter 8, "Communication." For more details on the* **dataManager**, *see Chapter 6, "Client Data Management and Caching."*

For example, rather than forcing the **tagger** widget to know how to get a reference to the **infobox** widget and invoke the public methods on the **infobox** widget, the widgets can be kept free of any knowledge of each other by passing in the functions from the startup script, since the startup script already knows about both widgets. To set this up, the **tagger** widget defines **activated** and **deactivated** options.

```javascript
JavaScript
// Contained in jquery.qs.tagger.js
$.widget('qs.tagger', {
    options: {
        activated: $.noop,
        deactivated: $.noop
    },
```

Just like normal options, these can either define defaults or omit them. The use of **$.noop** as a default value saves you the effort of having to ensure that the value isn't **null** before calling the option. Calling **$.noop** has no effect and won't throw any exceptions. The startup script will provide these options when it applies the **tagger** widget to the **span** elements, as shown here.

JavaScript
```javascript
// Contained in jquery.qs.tagger.js
$('span[data-tag]').tagger({
    activate: function (event, data) {
        // call displayTagLinks() on infobox here
    },
    deactivate: function () {
        // call hideTagLinks() on infobox here
    }
});
```

In the code examples above, the options are defined inside the widget's implementation and passed in during creation. Later in this chapter you'll see how function-based options are used as callbacks for events.

The Widget Method

Well-designed objects have public interfaces that are intentional, intuitive, and focused. Widgets go one step further and provide a single method, referred to as the *widget method*, which is the entire public interface of the widget. The action the widget performs when you call this method depends on the number and type of arguments provided in the call. In addition to creating and initializing the widget, as shown earlier, the widget method is also used to do the following:

- Invoke public methods
- Read and write public properties
- Read and write options

PUBLIC METHODS

Public methods are defined on the widget prototype, as you can see here in the **infobox** widget. The public methods are **hideTagLinks** and **displayTagLinks**.

JavaScript
```javascript
// Contained in jquery.qs.infobox.js
$.widget('qs.infobox', {
    hideTagLinks: function() {
        ...
    },
    displayTagLinks: function(event, tagName) {
        ...
    }
```

Widgets must be created before their methods can be called. The following calls to the **infobox** widget assume the widget method has already been called once to apply the widget to the **body** element. To call **hideTagLinks** from outside the widget, use a jQuery selector to match the element and pass the name of the method to the widget method as its only argument.

JavaScript
```
// Code illustration: not in QuickStart
$('body').infobox('hideTagLinks');
```

When you need to pass any arguments into the call, such as **displayTagLinks**, simply add the arguments after the method name.

JavaScript
```
// Code illustration: not in QuickStart
$('body').infobox('displayTagLinks', event, tag.name);
```

The **option** method covered earlier (in the section "Defining Options") is an example of a public method. When one argument is passed to it, the method will return the value of that option. When two arguments are passed, it will set the option specified in the first argument to the value of the second argument. When calling the **option** method from outside the widget, pass the method name as the first argument, the name of the option as the second, and the value as the third argument, as shown here.

JavaScript
```
// Code illustration: not in QuickStart
$('body').infobox('option', 'maxItems', 10);
```

Public methods can also return values by placing the expression on the right-hand side of the assignment operator (=). Returning a value from methods on **infobox** is reasonable because **infobox** is only attached to a single element. But be aware that if you call a method on a wrapped set that contains more than one element, the method will only be called on and returned from the first element.

In the examples so far, each time the widget method is invoked it is being called on the instance returned by the jQuery function, **$(selector)**, which requires accessing the DOM. The next section recommends a couple of alternatives.

REUSING AN INSTANCE

Each time the jQuery function uses a selector to invoke the widget method, it must search the DOM. This has a negative impact on performance and is unnecessary because widget methods return a jQuery object, which includes the wrapped set of matched elements.

JavaScript
```
// Code illustration: not in QuickStart
var ib = $('body').infobox();  // queries the DOM
ib.infobox('displayTagLinks'); // does not query the DOM
```

Rather than use a selector with the jQuery method each time you need to call a method on a widget, create a variable when the widget is initially attached to the elements. The DOM will be accessed during this initialization, but it should be the only time you need to access it. In subsequent calls, such as the second line in the snippet above, you can call the widget method on the variable you created and it won't access the DOM.

Using the Pseudo Selector

In a situation where neither the selector nor the instance is available, there is still a way to obtain all instances of a particular widget. As long as you know the name of the widget, you can use a pseudo selector to get all instances that have been applied to elements.

```JavaScript
// Contained in an older, more tightly coupled version of startup.js
$('body').infobox();

// Contained in an older, more tightly coupled version of jquery.qs.tagger.js
var ibInstance = $(':qs-infobox');
ibInstance.infobox('displayTagLinks',    // method name
                   $(this).text(),       // tag
                   event.pageY + offsetY,  // top
                   event.pageX + offsetX); // left
```

A pseudo selector begins with a colon, followed by the widget's namespace and name separated by a hyphen. The pseudo selector in the example above is **:qs-infobox**. Pseudo selectors have the potential to increase coupling between widgets, so be aware of this if you intend to use them.

Private Members

Private methods and properties have private scope, which means you can only invoke these members from inside the widget. Using private members is a good idea because they improve the readability of the code.

METHODS

Private methods are methods that start with an underscore. They are expected to be accessed directly using the **this** keyword. Private methods are common and recommended.

Private methods are only private by convention and cannot be enforced. This means that if a widget isn't called according to the convention for calling public methods (described later), its private methods can still be accessed. The convention is easy and consistent, and the underscore makes it easy to distinguish between the public and private interface.

PROPERTIES

Methods are designated as private by using underscores. Unlike methods, properties on the widget prototype are private by default; they are not designated private by prepending an underscore. The reason properties don't need underscores is that they cannot be accessed through the widget method.

JavaScript
```
// Code illustration: not in QuickStart
$.widget('qs.infobox', {
    dataUrl: '',    // should only be accessed using this.dataUrl
    _maxItems: 10   // unnecessary; properties are already private
});
```

Because each element contains its own instance of the widget, the **dataUrl** property can be different for each element.

Clearly **dataUrl** is best exposed as an option, but if this was not a configurable option you would probably want to define it so that only one copy of the value is available to all instances of the widget. Let's call these static members.

Static Members

To define a variable that's available to all instances of the widget, but nowhere else, place them inside the self-executing function wrapper and above the call to the widget factory, as shown in the **tagger** widget.

JavaScript
```
// Contained in jquery.qs.tagger.js
(function ($) {

    var timer,
        hideAfter = 1000; // ms

    $.widget('qs.tagger', {
        ...
```

Because the **timer** variable is defined outside the widget prototype, only a single timer will be created and shared across all instances of the **tagger** widget. Functions that don't rely on the instance of the widget can also be defined here.

If you need access to static members from outside the widget, they can be added to the widget after the widget's definition. They are defined afterwards because they extend the widget, as you will see in a moment.

Let's make a fictitious change to the **infobox** widget to illustrate this by moving an isolated function to a more accessible location. Inside the **displayTagLinks** method in the **infobox** widget, a function variable called **displayResult** is defined.

JavaScript
```
// Contained in jquery.qs.infobox.js
var displayResult = function () {
    elem
    .html(html);
    .css({top: top, left: left});
    .show();
};
```

The variable, **displayResult**, is defined in **displayTagLinks** because this is the only method that uses it. In our fictitious change, let's say the **infobox** widget needs to make Ajax calls from other methods. That means the **displayResult** function will need to be moved so that it is available to all methods that need it. Defining it as a static member outside the scope of the widget is a way to make this happen.

JavaScript
```
// Code illustration: not in QuickStart
$.widget('qs.infobox', {
    ...
});
$.extend($.qs.infobox, {
    displayResult: function(elem, html, top, left) {
        elem
        .html(html);
        .css({top: top, left: left})
        .show();
    }
});
```

The **$.extend** method is used to merge the object passed as the second argument into the object passed as the first argument. Therefore, the **displayResult** method is merged into the prototype of the widget, **$.qs.infobox**. With **displayResult** defined here, the **infobox** widget can use it from anywhere, as shown in this code.

JavaScript
```
// Code illustration: not in QuickStart
// assume elem, html, top, and left variables were already defined
$.qs.infobox.displayResult(elem, html, top, left);
```

Events

Events are an effective way to communicate between widgets without forcing them to be tightly coupled. jQuery supports and extends the DOM event model and provides the ability to raise and handle custom events that are not defined in the DOM.

RAISING THE EVENT

A widget raises events by using the **_trigger** method. The first argument to **_trigger** is the name of the event you are raising. If the event you are raising originates from a DOM event, the DOM event can optionally be passed as the second argument. The third argument is any data to be passed to the event handler and is also optional. The following code sample shows one way the **tagger** widget might raise the **activated** event when the mouse enters the element.

JavaScript
```javascript
// Code illustration: not in QuickStart
_create: function () {
    var that = this,
        tag = that.infoboxElement.text();

    that.infoboxElement
        .bind('mouseenter', function (event) {
            that._trigger('activated', event, {name: tag});
        });
},
```

In this fictitious code example, **infobox** is raising an **activated** event by binding to the **mouseenter** event of an element. You can also use **bind**, as well as the **live** and **delegate** methods, to handle events triggered from widgets.

BINDING HANDLERS

Event handlers bind to widget events the same way as they bind to other events, although the name of the event is influenced by the widget's name.

JavaScript
```javascript
// Code illustration: not in QuickStart
$('span[data-tag]').bind('taggeractivated', function(event, data) {
    // handle the event
});
```

Notice how the name of the event being bound to has the name of the widget prepended. This is the default behavior for event names. If you prefer a different name so that your code is more readable, this behavior can be changed, as shown in the following section.

Event Naming

The **widgetEventPrefix** property defines what will be prepended to the names of the events the widget raises. By default, the value is the name of the widget and is set by the widget factory. If you want to use something other than the widget name, simply define this property and provide an alternative value.

JavaScript

```
// Contained in jquery.qs.tagger.js
$.widget('qs.tagger', {

    widgetEventPrefix: 'tag',

    ...
```

When **widgetEventPrefix** has a value, it will be used instead of the widget name. The code that uses this widget and binds to its **activated** event will use the event name **tagactivated**.

Options as Callbacks

When options are defined as functions and the option name corresponds to an event name (without the prefix), they are referred to as callbacks. The **_trigger** method on the base widget will automatically invoke the callback whose name matches the event being raised.

JavaScript

```
// Contained in jquery.qs.tagger.js
widgetEventPrefix: 'tag',

options: {
    activated: $.noop,
    deactivated: $.noop
},

_create: function () {
    var that = this,
        name = this.name(),
        tag = this.element.text();

    this.element
        .bind('mouseenter.' + name, function (event) {
            that._trigger('activated', event, {name: tag});
        });
},
```

The JavaScript that creates the **tagger** widget can now define the handler for the **activated** and **deactivated** events when it creates the widgets.

```JavaScript
$('span[data-tag]').tagger({
    activated: function (event, data) {
        infobox.infobox('displayTagLinks', event, data.name);
    },
    deactivated: function () {
        infobox.infobox('hideTagLinks');
    }
});
```

This allows the two widgets to interact without explicitly knowing about each other. Using this approach causes the script that invokes the widgets to act as connective tissue that describes a lot about the solution in a succinct, readable format.

Inheritance

Sometimes, when building a widget, another widget already has many properties and much of the functionality the new widget requires. The widget factory's inheritance support is designed for this case. For illustration purposes, consider the following widget.

```JavaScript
// Code illustration: not in QuickStart
(function ($) {
    $.widget('a.container', {
        ...
        resize: function() {
            // resize width and height
        },
        ...
    });
}(jQuery));
```

If this widget was built elsewhere and you wanted to change its resizing behavior to an animation, a reasonable approach would be to inherit from **a.container** and override its **resize** method. Inheritance is accomplished by passing three arguments into the widget factory. The first argument is the namespace and name of the widget, the second is the prototype of the widget you want to extend from, and the third argument is the object you want to extend it with.

```
JavaScript
// Code illustration: not in QuickStart
(function ($) {
    $.widget('an.animatedContainer', $.a.container, {
        ...
        resize: function() {
            // override with animations
        }
    });
}(jQuery));
```

The only difference between the signature above and the signature usually used for defining widgets is the addition of the second parameter.

Inheritance is a useful tool when you are using a widget that almost does what you want it to do. In version 1.9 of jQuery UI, widgets can inherit from themselves. This makes it easy to add functionality to a widget for your application without the need of changing the original implementation. The jQuery UI **bridge** method allows you to retain the name of the original widget to be used with your specialized widget.

Summary

Using jQuery UI widgets is a great way to add modularity to client-side web applications. Widgets are objects that attach to page elements and supply services for managing life-time, state, inheritance, theming, and communication with other widgets or JavaScript objects.

Options give widgets the ability to have state that is public, readable, writable, and callable. Options are automatically merged with the widget's default options during creation, and the widget factory supports change notifications when option values change. In addition, defining functions as options is a powerful way to decouple the widget from functionality better located elsewhere.

Widgets provide just a single method that represents the entire public interface of the widget. Widgets also allow for private methods that can only be invoked from within the widget.

jQuery supports and extends the DOM event model and provides the ability to raise and handle custom events that are not defined in the DOM. Widgets can trigger and handle these events and options can be used as callbacks.

Finally, widgets can inherit from other widgets, and in jQuery UI version 1.9, a widget can inherit from itself.

Further Reading

For more information about the QuickStart or to walk through the process of building it, see Chapter 14, "Widget QuickStart."

For more information about the pub/sub engine, see Chapter 8, "Communication."

For more information on the **dataManager**, see Chapter 6, "Client Data Management and Caching."

Widget Factory documentation on the jQuery UI wiki:
http://wiki.jqueryui.com/w/page/12138135/Widget-factory

jQuery Documentation for Plugins/Authoring:
http://docs.jquery.com/Plugins/Authoring

jQuery UI Developer Guidelines:
http://jqueryui.com/docs/Developer_Guide

jQuery UI source code:
https://github.com/jquery/jquery-ui

To access web resources more easily, see the online version of the bibliography on MSDN: http://msdn.microsoft.com/en-us/library/hh404094.aspx.

Resources

Microsoft Ajax Content Delivery Network (CDN) addresses:
http://www.asp.net/ajaxlibrary/cdn.ashx

4 Design and Layout

Introduction

The development of rich, responsive web applications requires an iterative design process to create applications that result in a user interface (UI) design that harmonizes beauty, simplicity, symmetry, and consistency. The combination of new web technologies and innovations in web browsers makes it possible for designers and developers to complement their UI with an engaging and intuitive user experience (UX).

The design process includes the collaboration of stakeholders and team members with different skills and perspectives. If your team invests in a design process, you are more likely to create an application that users enjoy, find useful, and continue to use. A goal of this chapter is to illustrate the importance of the design process, and UI and UX designer roles. If you are not able to have dedicated designers on your team, then think about the concepts discussed here as you plan and build your own site.

Many books have been written on UI and UX design. This chapter does not attempt to provide comprehensive UI and UX guidance, nor is it a primer on web technologies such as HTML5 or CSS3. Instead, this chapter explains the design process and considerations the team applied when building the Mileage Stats application.

In this chapter you will learn:

- The importance of the designer roles and the design process.
- UX and UI design artifacts and considerations.
- How the design of Mileage Stats evolved.

Technologies discussed in this chapter are HTML and CSS.

Design is a Worthwhile Investment

We cannot overstate the value of a high-quality design. Design may easily be the determining factor between a successful website and a website that does not get the expected traffic, repeat visitors, or recognition from its users. Design is beauty and function.

Design invokes the correct emotion. A successful design helps users feel confident that they are visiting a credible site. A high-quality design makes users feel valued and encourages them to explore the site.

Design communicates ideas that resonate with users and enriches the user experience. Design brings clarity to the presented information. But a successful design does more than that. It provides the user with an experience that naturally flows and is enjoyable. Effective design results in websites that are easier and faster to use. It helps users achieve a result and save time by making fewer mistakes and knowing what to do in case of an error.

Design improves the process and ensures the right result. Design is hard work. It takes time and effort, and there is a cost to working with one or more designers. However, investing in design early in the project will likely reduce the overall development costs and provide many other benefits as well. The design process helps to focus the project and set its priorities. It determines what the site will accomplish. The design artifacts facilitate communication with stakeholders. The iterative prototyping process allows the design to quickly and easily change and gives team members the freedom to be creative because they are not constrained by working code. Defining the user experience and user interface early clarifies scope. This facilitates the identification and prioritization of features and the technical requirements to deliver these features.

Web Project Designer Roles

Developing modern web applications requires a broad range of skills. Depending on your application requirements, your team will need expertise to fill the following roles: user experience designer, information architect, user interface designer, graphic designer, user interface and user interaction developer, production designer, integrator, producer, and server-side developers and testers. The UI designer and information architect are more focused on the audience and the consumption of the website than they are concerned about how the website is implemented. On the other hand, integrators are more concerned with how the design is implemented.

Designers don't necessarily care about how it gets done; they just assume that developers can do it. Developers may be frustrated at how difficult the design can be to implement. Designers may get frustrated that developers don't understand the importance of the design.

The composition of the web project team will vary from project to project based on the application's requirements and the team's resources. Depending on the size of the team, you may have a number of specialized people or one person filling multiple roles. A large project will typically include two or three designers, an information architect, a producer, and two integrators. A medium-sized project will probably have one designer and one integrator. A small team typically has a single integrator/designer who can do CSS, JavaScript, and visual design. The tradeoff is that this individual is probably not as strong in all areas because his or her skills are spread across many areas rather than having expertise in only one of these roles.

Teams that value the UX and UI roles receive a significant return on investment. This is illustrated by looking at websites that invested in UX; these sites exhibit a polished UI that is intuitive, responsive, and facilitates the easy completion of tasks. UX and UI designers positively impact the team by being the customer advocate, providing a user-centric perspective on what the site offers and how the site is used.

In this chapter, *designer* is an umbrella term that covers the above designer roles.

Focus on the User

When you are starting a project, the first thing you should focus on is the user. You should start by defining who the user is, what their characteristics are, and identify scenarios for each *persona*, which is a user in a particular context. A persona embodies work style, role, motivation, skills, and goals. If you have a complicated or large application, some features might target different personas. The process of identifying users and scenarios helps drive the design of both the experience and the branding of the application.

As your design evolves, continue to think about the user's characteristics and intentions. Think about creating the flow through the application that provides a path that is natural and makes sense to the user. Don't be afraid to reduce features or start over again.

Companies that research user behavior are able to evolve their applications to reduce failure rates and increase adoption. Many companies have dedicated user research teams for this purpose. They instrument their websites to track, for example, how long people take to navigate from page to page. This helps identify areas of confusion and difficulty. This is important because in a large company, even a very small percentage of people abandoning the order pipeline could cost millions of dollars.

Design Prototyping

Design prototyping begins after the application requirements, user scenarios, and user stories have been identified. Design prototyping provides structured time for stakeholders and team members to iterate on the application design. It is much cheaper to add and remove pages to the site earlier in the design, and it is cheaper to change paper diagrams than code. The iterative process of creating the following artifacts allows design decisions to be made at the right time with the right level of effort.

- **Mood board**. A mood board is a visual collage that can include words representing the concepts you want the application to convey, along with colors and images that would appeal to your users from a variety of sources. A mood board is created early in the project because you want everyone on the team to be on the same page about what you are building and to be inspired. The mood board allows you to set direction about the feel of the application and about your design principles, and allows you to eliminate unnecessary elements and ideas. It doesn't represent the end product, but helps you establish the personality of the product. If you are following a style guide or have an established experience, skip this step. If you are creating a new experience, this is a common first step. This is a low-cost, fast exercise that provides high value in establishing your brand.

- **Flow diagram**. Based on application requirements, the UX designer defines the pages in the site, actions available on those pages, and navigation between pages. These decisions need to consider the user stories identified in the requirements. The result of this work is a flow diagram, typically drawn on paper.

- **Wireframe**. The UX and UI designers collaborate to create wireframe models that depict rough placement of the text, data, and basic controls. These models are used to help organize the page's information. The wireframes can be hand drawn or created using an application such as **SketchFlow** or **Balsamiq**. Wireframes intentionally lack detail such as color, images, drop shadows, and finished controls.
- **Image-based Mockups**. UI and graphic designers work together to create images that show what the application will eventually look like. These mockups contain details such as typography, color, gradients, images, and transparency. Mockups should communicate all necessary details of the UI. Multiple mockups for a single page may be required to effectively convey details of the different states. Mockups can be created using a tool like Adobe PhotoShop or Illustrator.
- **Functional mockups**. The designers and UI developer build functioning HTML pages that include CSS and possibly JavaScript. These pages are autonomous and don't yet interact with the server, and use fake data when needed. It's during this phase that the team makes decisions about implementation details and balances browser capabilities with HTML, CSS, images, and JavaScript.

> **Note:** *Depending on the project scope and the team's resources or preferences, image-based mockups may be skipped. Note that it's cheaper to modify and iterate the design using a graphical image than HTML and CSS.*

User Experience Design Considerations

A UX design specifies the site's structure, the web pages it uses, what actions users can perform on each page, and the transitions that can occur once a user performs an action. A well-designed site has a short learning curve, makes the user feel successful, saves them time, is intuitive, and presents clear, useful information. The following sections discuss UX design considerations.

CONSISTENCY

User success is the primary motivation for consistency. User gestures, colors, metaphors, navigation, and similar concepts should be consistent across your application. Keep your navigation model consistent across your site and be sure that you don't change the way users do things on different pages. Make sure the user always knows the context they are in so they don't have to think about it.

The degree of consistency in your application is directly related to user success. When your users encounter inconsistency, it causes them to question their understanding. They are forced to determine whether this was an oversight in the application or whether they misunderstood how the application works. Regardless of the degree of the inconsistency or how much additional time it takes, the user has been taken out of the flow of what they were trying to accomplish.

An example of consistency in Mileage Stats is the use of vehicle tiles in both the dashboard and details layouts. Because the vehicle list animates the transitions between these layouts, the user sees the relationship, understands why some are collapsed, and never loses sight of the vehicle they selected. Animations should provide feedback or direct the user's attention but not be a distraction or be irritating to your users.

RESPONSIVENESS

Users appreciate a site that is responsive. The goal of a responsive website is to never leave the user wondering what is going on. Responsiveness means the site provides feedback when the user takes an action, and the site loads content quickly.

Feedback can be a visual cue such as a confirmation graphic that appears when the user clicks a **Submit** button or a progress bar displayed during a long-running task. Another example of immediate feedback is an error message that appears as soon as the user makes a mistake in a form rather than after the form has been submitted.

When loading content, you can improve a user's perception of responsiveness even if the actual load time is slow. Text, images, data, and scripts can be downloaded in the background. Mileage Stats demonstrates a responsive UI by prefetching chart data when the Dashboard loads, so that when the Charts page is accessed, the chart displays immediately. Data is also loaded asynchronously during UI transitions.

You can optimize page rendering times by putting script tags for JavaScript files at the bottom of the HTML page or by using a JavaScript loader so the JavaScript files are loaded in parallel to rendering the HTML page. Doing this allows the majority of the page content to be loaded and rendered first. When a script tag is found by the browser, all rendering stops until the script is downloaded and evaluated, so if the scripts are on the top, the user may see a white screen for a few moments.

FAMILIAR METAPHORS

People naturally associate new concepts with what they already know, so familiarity shortens the user's learning curve. The canonical metaphor is the shopping cart. People know what a shopping cart is, so you don't need to explain the virtual equivalent.

STREAMLINING THE EXPERIENCE

Streamlining is about optimizing the navigational flow through the site. Users should not have to spend time searching for information they care about most or reading about how to navigate the site.

One of the most important things in site design is global navigation. This is the top-level channel for how users get into your site and accomplish the tasks that are most important to them. Navigation should feel natural and familiar to users. If you want to innovate, innovate by building upon the familiar. Designers and developers should work together to create a prioritized list of the top-level actions based on your user scenarios.

Consider ways to improve the use of the site. Evaluate how easy it is for users to locate information or complete a task. Logically place features where users need them. An example of this is placing a reset password button next to the password field on a sign-in page. Additional examples of streamlining the experience are setting focus to the first field in an input form, and designing the UX so that the user does not have to use a mouse.

Think about how to get people to willingly do what you want them to do without feeling like they are being forced. For example, think about form registration. Don't ask the user for any more information than you will actually use. You can help the user progressively fill out the form by breaking the input process into multiple steps that build on each other based on the user's input. This will require less of the user's time, but you need to be clear about the number of steps it will take to complete the process. You can use a progress bar to communicate to the user where they are in the process. Save users as much time as you can by automatically filling in form fields whenever possible. For example, when given a zip code, fill in the city and state. Use a country field to control the display of address input fields, or a credit card type to change the security code prompt. Sites that take shipping and billing information should provide the option to use the same address for both.

Mileage Stats demonstrates a streamlined experience in a number of ways. It provides a simple site navigation experience, as shown below.

Navigation in Mileage Stats

[Dashboard | Charts | Profile | Sign Out]

It also has a Complete Registration form that is optional, asks for the minimum amount of information, and can easily be dismissed.

The Mileage Stats vehicle tiles on the Dashboard prominently display commonly used vehicle performance metrics. The vehicle tiles are easy to read and provide the user with the ability to drill down for more detail.

Example Mileage Stats vehicle tile

Design for desirability and usability. Think about how you progressively disclose information and options. You don't necessarily want everything to be at the same level of discoverability. You should think about what items you are putting above the fold, which means that they are immediately visible on the web page without scrolling.

ANTICIPATE USABILITY ISSUES

When possible, account for user actions that that can lead to frustration. For example, saving form data as the user completes a form prevents them from having to reenter data if they accidently press the backspace key and navigate to the previous page. Prompting the user to save unsaved form data when they close the browser is another technique for preventing unintended data loss. Another feature to help users be successful is to prevent data loss through the use of a trash can or by providing an undo action that is available after the user completes a destructive action. You can evaluate the impact of your design and reduce risk by gathering data through user research.

LIMIT THE CHOICES

UX designers encourage focused applications. These applications perform a limited number of tasks very well, rather than overwhelming the user with choices. Iterate on your design, reducing it down to its essence. Focus fiercely on the core scenarios and spend less effort on the edge cases that won't affect the majority of users. Elegance, usability, and desirability are easier to achieve with fewer concepts and less complexity. It is easier to limit the choices if you have a very clear understanding of who the user is.

User Interface Design Considerations

Users visiting your site get their first impressions from the visual elements and layout. You need to think about the visual aspects that will resonate with your users. Look at websites, applications, books, magazines, and anything that might help you gain inspiration for creating something new. Of course, you don't want to copy someone else's ideas. At the same time, however, you don't necessarily want to be different just for the sake of being different. Designing for the web is no different than designing clothing or anything else; you need to understand what the current trends are and what appeals to your user base.

One tool that you can use to convey ideas, personality, and emotion is a mood board, mentioned earlier. For more information about mood boards and to see an example, see the following resources:

- "Website Mood Boards: A Successful Precursor to Visual Prototyping" by Kevin Flahaut
  http://weblog.404creative.com/2007/02/14/website-mood-boards-a-successful-precursor-to-visual-prototyping/
- "Why Mood Boards Matter" by Mindy Wagner
  http://www.webdesignerdepot.com/2008/12/why-mood-boards-matter/

As we mentioned, a mood board should be created early in the design process. It helps get the whole team on the same page, facilitates important conversations between team members, and helps establish principles and direction for the project.

Focusing on the user can drive everything in the UI from the color palette to the design elements and typography. When you feel like your visual design is jelling, bounce your ideas off other designers, potential users, and customers to validate your ideas and help you focus.

Your UI design should be unified and provide a visual signal to your audience that all your elements belong together. The following sections provide some thoughts about the website's UI in terms of color, typography, symmetry, consistency, and simplicity.

Color

Color can be used effectively to communicate an idea or to focus a user's attention. Color discloses a mood, creates images, and highlights items. For example, the various shades of gray can create the illusion of depth or add drama. Be aware that many individuals perceive colors differently and so you should not rely solely on color to communicate information.

People tend to have a strong reaction to color. Color also has specific connotations in different cultures. Blue is one of the colors most commonly seen as neutral. When working on the branding and personality of the product, you should focus on your color palette early. There are many tools, such as **Kuler**, to help you select your color palette. The key to color is that it needs to evoke the correct emotion for your targeted users and/or your brand. Color contrast is also important. Make sure that there is enough contrast between your foreground and background colors.

For example, Mileage Stats uses red to indicate that a maintenance reminder is overdue.

Example overdue vehicle maintenance reminder

Typography

The font you choose greatly influences the emotion your website conveys. In general, you don't want to use more than three typefaces across your application. However, certain typefaces, especially similar typefaces, don't work well together. Certain fonts are designed specifically for headlines and some fonts can be used anywhere in your application. There are tools such as **Typekit** that you can use to choose a web font and font stack.

Font size, font weight, and the spacing between letters, words, and paragraphs are also important. You should avoid sizes that are too large or too small. It is often helpful to make the font size of a text field slightly larger than the surrounding text, but you need to take into consideration the size of the page and avoid forcing the user to scroll down if possible. Designers often set the font smaller than the 16 pixels that the browser uses as its default. You may want to adjust the line height as well.

Use a CSS reset file so that you can set the base font sizes explicitly and not depend on the default browser settings. A CSS reset file is also helpful in establishing default values for padding, margins, and borders to ensure consistency across browsers. These defaults are typically set to zero so other CSS rules can provide values on top of a known baseline. For an example of a CSS reset, see the reset.css file in Mileage Stat's Web\ Content folder.

Balance and Symmetry

Balance refers to the distribution of visual weight and whether it is symmetrical or asymmetrical. Symmetry can communicate stability and strength, which may be appropriate for a traditional audience. Asymmetry is a more informal balance that may be more appropriate for a modern audience or an entertaining website.

Studies have shown that there are certain proportions of a physical page layout that intrinsically feel better to users. You can use a grid system to help you set the width of the site navigation and the content of the page with the proper proportions. One example is the **960 Grid System**.

You should also think about using the **rule of thirds** in your layout. This is a rule of thumb for visual composition that states that an image should be imagined as divided into nine equal parts by two equally-spaced horizontal lines and two equally-spaced vertical lines. Important compositional elements should be placed along these lines or their intersections. The Mileage Stats landing page illustrates this idea by placing the title, description and login form on these intersections.

Mileage Stats landing page

CONSISTENCY

Page layout, branding, color, and typography should be consistent across the site. You can use master pages and CSS to help drive consistency. You should follow established conventions for UI elements so that users can quickly understand and use your site. You should think about your UI control choices and keep them consistent across your application. Don't confuse the use of radio buttons and check boxes. Don't interchangeably use links and buttons to do the same thing on different pages. Be aware that because of touch interfaces, people assume that everything is clickable.

SIMPLICITY

Lay out the page logically to help users accomplish the most important features or tasks. Don't put crucial elements in areas that usually contain ancillary information. Avoid technical jargon that users won't understand. Limit the number of animations, special effects, colors, gradients, fonts, and other design options.

Other Design Considerations

In addition to the considerations mentioned above, you should think about designing for accessibility, globalization, and localization. An accessible design is one that can be used by as many people as possible, with varying abilities. Globalization ensures that your application can be translated to another language and culture. Localization is the act of translating your application into another language.

Designing the Mileage Stats Reference Implementation

This section walks through the design process and decision points that influenced the design of the Mileage Stats application. Coverage includes UX and UI design prototyping, creating mockups, and integrating design assets with the application code.

IDENTIFYING USER STORIES

The team created a prioritized list of user stories identified from the application requirements and user scenarios. The user stories are a tool used by the designer to drive the creation of the flow diagrams and prototypes. Developers use the user stories to drive their weekly backlog task items and to validate the completed work. The user story below was used to describe the requirements for displaying the dashboard.

Mileage Stats User Story

The team wrote their acceptance criteria using the **given-when-then** template. This provides for clear and concise documentation that can be understood by all team members and can be used to generate both manual and automated test scripts. For more information, see the **"Introducing Behavior Driven Design"** in the "Further Reading" section below.

User Story: As an authenticated user, I want to see my dashboard so I can use the site.
Acceptance Criteria:
    Given an authenticated user
    when they navigate to the dashboard page
    then the user name
        and the word "Dashboard" are displayed.
    Given an authenticated user
    when they are redirected to the dashboard page
    then the user name
        and the word "Dashboard" are displayed.

USING FLOW DIAGRAMS TO PROTOTYPE THE UX

Based on the user stories, the UX design came to life on paper in the form of flow diagrams. The early diagrams were rough and only pictured main features of the application. These flow diagrams outlined the primary pages and how the pages would link to each other. The following figure illustrates an early application flow diagram.

Early UX flow diagram

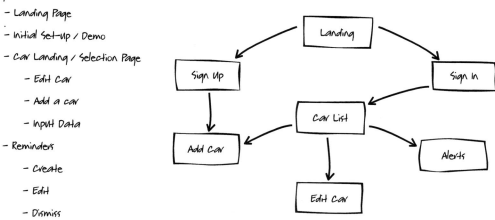

The flow diagram was then expanded to show data placement and the available actions for users, as pictured below. The flow diagram evolved through an iterative process with the team and stakeholders. As features were added or removed, the flow diagram was updated to reflect the current user stories, ensuring that no important functionality was left out.

Additional details for the flow diagram

Use Flows.   Desktop

① Registration

    - Click Register
    - Put Open ID / password or OAuth redirect
    - Start with new car

② New Car Entry   ✩ PowerPoint

    - Put nickname
    - Optional
        - Put year, make, model
        - Plate / VIN for reference?
        - Picture or Icon + color?
    - Done, go to homepage / cancel to exit
    - Readd recently removed cars.

③ Dashboard

    - If no cars one add car full size entry
    - else cars + small add another at the end.

④ View Cars   What stats here?

    - Car image, general stats
    - Graphs
    - Fill-up history
    - Trip history
    - Environmental message (+ donate to charity :P)
    - Reminder / Service History / + add / remove, etc.

⑤ Edit Car

    - Edit info
    - Add drivers (by Open ID/ OAuth email)

⑥ Settings

    - Units
    - Email reminders?

⑦ Export / Import

USING WIREFRAMES TO PROTOTYPE THE UI

Based on the flow diagrams, each section of the UI had multiple wireframes created for it. The wireframe was drawn on paper, with some pieces on sticky notes. The team tested each variation against user stories, moving the pieces around to decide what worked best. The following figure illustrates one of the wireframes.

Early wireframe

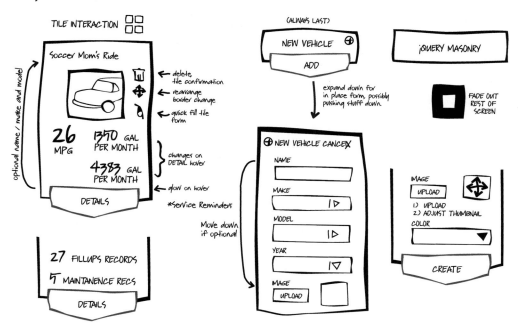

Wireframes can also be used to illustrate animations and interesting transition effects. In Mileage Stats the vehicle tiles animate into position when transitioning between the Dashboard and Details layouts. The vehicle tiles also expand and collapse based on the selected vehicle, and allow you to change the ordering of your vehicles. Using the wireframes allowed the team to easily iterate on the details of these animations. The following figure is a hand-drawn wireframe of a vehicle tile and its associated animations.

Early animation wireframe

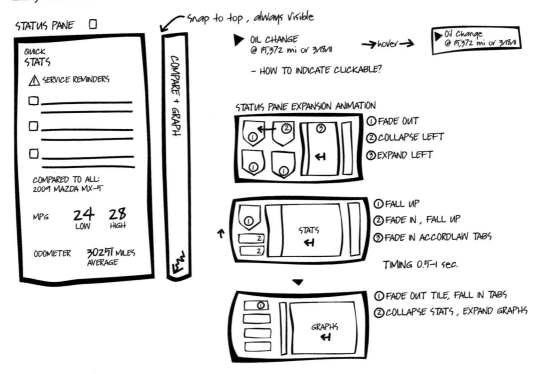

CREATING SITE MOCKUPS

Once everyone agreed on the wireframes, the designer began to create site mockups of the actual pages. As you would expect, there were several iterations before the final version. This section highlights a few things that we learned that led to changes in the design.

> **Note:** *You can conduct usability testing during the process of refining your design. During usability testing, users walk through the scenarios, using the interface, while you watch them. Let them do what they would normally do. Ask them to think out loud about what they are looking for, and what they expect to be available on any page. Be sure not to give them any clues or ask them leading questions. It's best if you can remain silent and just observe. After every walkthrough, refine the site based on the feedback.*

You can see how the Mileage Stats UI and UX evolved in the following images. The first image illustrates an early version of the Fill Up page. It gave the developers a good sense of what the end product would look like. The next image shows the final screenshot of the same page.

Early mockup of Fill Up page

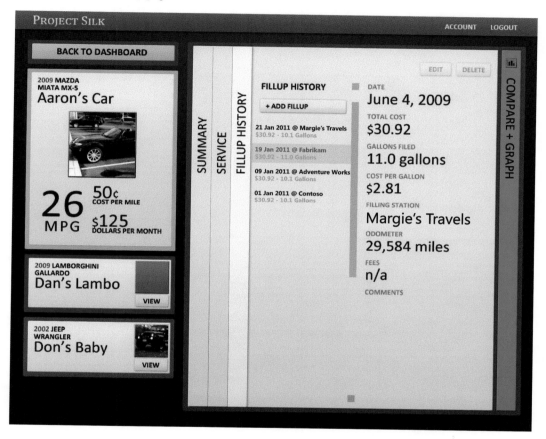

Final screenshot of Fill Up page

We wanted consistency in navigating between the pages. We also wanted users to realize that on some pages they are viewing information specific to a particular vehicle and on other pages they are viewing aggregate information about all vehicles. The links in the top, right corner in the final version of Mileage Stats provide a unified, consistent, and understandable way to navigate between the Dashboard, Profile, Sign In/Out, and Charts pages. The Dashboard and Chart pages show information pertaining to multiple vehicles, so it made sense to include those links with the more general Sign In/Out and Profile links. Adding the **Details**, **Fill ups**, and **Reminders** buttons on the vehicle tiles made it clear that those pages were only relevant to the individual vehicle.

User registration brought up several interesting questions: Should a user have to register in order to use the site? Will users be discouraged from using the site if they have to register? We decided that anyone should be able to use the site but it would be best if users signed in so that they could track their metrics, and this would allow us to build up an interesting database over time. We wanted to strike the right balance between encouraging the user to complete their registration and not annoying the user. The screenshot below shows user registration in Mileage Stats.

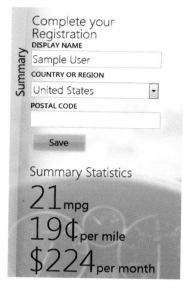

User registration in Mileage Stats

Once the team was satisfied with the Mileage Stats mockups, the developers began to code the site's infrastructure. They created static pages and basic forms that implemented the user actions. In the meantime, the designer started work on the final UI and graphics.

IMPLEMENTING THE DESIGN

A functional mockup can consist of a single HTML and CSS file, while the run-time rendering of the page is composed from multiple code fragments, files, and data sources that come from the client and/or server. This section explains some of the considerations for converting a mockup to HTML, organizing CSS styles, adopting new standards, and debugging.

Converting a Mockup to HTML

You can convert mockups to HTML by breaking down areas into component **div** block elements. Usually, the **div** blocks group together related elements, or they represent single text blocks, or single interactive elements. Once you decide how to lay out the **divs**, you can use different CSS styles to position and size them correctly. The following figure shows the boundaries of some of the elements that make up the vehicle tile and the classes applied to those elements. Not all elements are shown because it would have made the image too complicated, but this gives you the idea of how the tile is constructed.

Vehicle tile construction

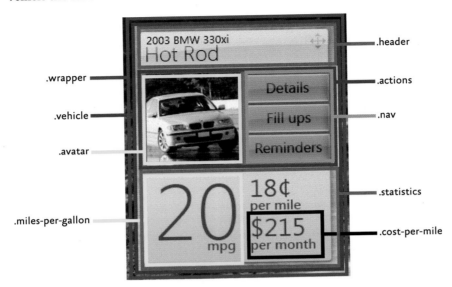

These tiles are meant to look exactly like the mockup, to the pixel, so absolute positioning is used. There are **div** groups for the header, navigation, and statistics in order to facilitate the animation that collapses the tiles. Depending on what vehicle a user selects, a tile can collapse into a more condensed version of itself, omitting some **divs** that represent information that is not relevant. For example, the currently selected vehicle is "Hot Rod" so the "Soccer Mom's Ride" vehicle tile is collapsed as shown below:

Collapsed and expanded vehicle tiles

For aesthetic reasons, there are extra layers of **divs** on the vehicle tile. For example, the semi-transparent outer border of the tile was created with CSS, so it required another nested **div** to hold the contents of the tile. In situations like this, it can be easier to use **parent > child** selectors and other relational selectors to style them rather than to create CSS classes for all the **divs**.

The following example shows portions of the template used when rendering the vehicle list.

CSHTML
```cshtml
<!-- Contained in _TemplateVehicleList.cshtml -->
<script id="mstats-vehicle-list-template" type="text/x-jquery-tmpl">
...
    <div class="wrapper">
        <div class="vehicle" data-vehicle-id="${VehicleId}">
            <div class="content">
                <div class="header">...</div>
                <div class="actions">...</div>
                <div class="statistics footer">...</div>
            </div>
        </div>
    </div>
</script>
```

The following CSS shows the rules applied to the **vehicle** and **content** classes. The CSS3 Color Module defines a color value that includes a parameter for the alpha channel. The form of this value is **rgba(red, green, blue, alpha)** where the red, green, and blue values are integers or percentages and the alpha value is between 0.0 (completely transparent) and 1.0 (completely opaque).

CSS3
```css
/* Contained in stylesheet.css */
.vehicle
{
    position: relative;
    width: 220px;

    overflow: hidden;
    padding: 9px;

    background-color: #bbb;
    background: rgba( 233, 233, 233, 0.6 );
    border: 1px solid #bababa;
    border: 1px solid rgba( 233, 233, 233, 0.8 );

    -webkit-border-radius: 5px;
    -moz-border-radius: 5px;
```

```
    -o-border-radius: 5px;
    border-radius: 5px;

    -webkit-box-shadow: 0px 0px 12px rgba( 0, 0, 0, 0.4 ),
                        inset 0px 0px 10px rgba( 233, 233, 233, 0.4 );
    -moz-box-shadow: 0px 0px 12px rgba( 0, 0, 0, 0.4 ),
                  inset 0px 0px 10px rgba( 233, 233, 233, 0.4 );
    -o-box-shadow: 0px 0px 12px rgba( 0, 0, 0, 0.4 ),
                inset 0px 0px 10px rgba( 233, 233, 233, 0.4 );
    box-shadow: 0px 0px 12px rgba( 0, 0, 0, 0.4 ),
            inset 0px 0px 10px rgba( 233, 233, 233, 0.4 );

    z-index: 0;
}

.vehicle .content
{
    width: 220px;

    -webkit-border-radius: 4px;
    -moz-border-radius: 4px;
    -o-border-radius: 4px;
    border-radius: 4px;

    -webkit-box-shadow: 0px 0px 10px rgba( 0, 0, 0, 0.5 );
    -moz-box-shadow: 0px 0px 10px rgba( 0, 0, 0, 0.5 );
    -o-box-shadow: 0px 0px 10px rgba( 0, 0, 0, 0.5 )
    box-shadow: 0px 0px 10px rgba( 0, 0, 0, 0.5 );
}
```

The above CSS code also illustrates other new CSS3 features such as **box-shadow** and **border-radius**.

Given some practice, the process of converting a mockup to HTML will become easier and more straightforward. It's a good idea to look at various websites and see how they construct their HTML and CSS structures. You can use the techniques in the "Debugging" section below to inspect other websites.

CSS Organization

You need to structure your CSS so that you know where things are and what you are changing. At the beginning, it is easiest to create a style for every element. When you start consolidating styles, it's a cost/benefit tradeoff. On the one hand, there is more to figure out. For example, you need to keep track of styles that you can override and styles that should cascade down. In the long run, if you group common styles together, it will be easier to maintain these centralized styles. It can be hard to know what common styles you need at the beginning of a project but easier to understand at the end. This is an exercise similar to refactoring code.

Good naming helps organization, and there aren't many restrictions to naming. In general, you should think about whether you know what CSS style is being applied to each element on the page and whether you can identify each element by looking at the HTML.

Here are some guidelines for assigning IDs to elements and naming CSS classes:

- Apply IDs only to elements unique to the page. Classes should be used for repeating elements.

- Use IDs and classes to apply style to elements using CSS. Do not use **data-** attributes to apply style to elements; **data-** attributes should only be used by developers.

- Use logical names in the domain. For example, Mileage Stats uses vehicle and chart. This is in contrast to naming the CSS rule based on its location on the page, for example, column2.

- Group logical elements together in the CSS file. For example, all navigation buttons should be together, and all elements in the header should be together. In Mileage Stats, there is only one place where there are tiles.

- Elements should be styled consistently across pages. Forms should all be styled the same.

In the Mileage Stats stylesheet.css file there are common elements for lists and forms and page-specific styles for elements such as vehicle tiles and panels.

Vendor-Prefixed Attributes

The standards that govern web technologies are always evolving, and CSS is not immune to this evolution. In order to maintain progress, new proposals should be implemented and tested soon and often by browser makers and the web-building community. Traditionally, the use of cutting-edge standards means more work in the future when the standard is approved. Vendor-prefixed attributes provide a way for the browser makers to implement early specifications so designers can use them right away. Browsers use the last attribute they understand. By placing the final attribute after the vendor-prefixed attributes, browsers will use the most appropriate one given their level of standards support. The following example shows this technique being applied to the **box-shadow** attribute.

CSS3
```
/* contained in stylesheet.css */
-webkit-box-shadow: 0px 0px 10px rgba( 0, 0, 0, 0.50 );
-moz-box-shadow: 0px 0px 10px rgba( 0, 0, 0, 0.50 );
-o-box-shadow: 0px 0px 10px rgba( 0, 0, 0, 0.50 );
box-shadow: 0px 0px 10px rgba( 0, 0, 0, 0.80 );
```

Debugging

You should understand how to debug styles using the browser tools for each of the common browsers. The **Internet Explorer 9 F12 developer tools** allow you to view the style stack of any DOM (document object model) element. It is very convenient to test style changes in the browser because you get instant feedback. Using the F12 tools you can also disable or enable specific styles for a selector, or add a style to an individual DOM element. This allows you to determine if the properties of one style override the properties of another. You can click on any of the styles and edit them in place. You can also check or uncheck the check box and it will enable or disable the value.

HTML styles shown in Internet Explorer 9 F12 developer tools

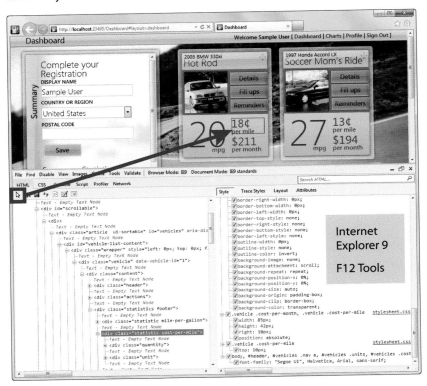

Summary

A UX design that empowers users to quickly accomplish tasks via a UI that resonates with them does not happen without a great deal of effort. Rely on a web designer to help you create a beautiful, useful website. Consider the designer to be the voice of the customer. Together with the designer, establish a design process for iteratively creating your UX and UI artifacts before you begin implementing any features of the application. As you create your design, remember the design considerations outlined in this chapter. Your customers will appreciate your responsive and easily understood site.

Useful Design Tools

Microsoft Expression® Web
http://www.microsoft.com/expression/

Balsamiq:
http://balsamiq.com/

SketchFlow:
http://www.microsoft.com/expression/products/Sketchflow_Overview.aspx

PhotoShop:
http://www.photoshop.com/

Typekit:
http://typekit.com/

Kuler:
http://www.adobe.com/products/kuler/

Image compression tools:

- OptiPNG:
  http://optipng.sourceforge.net/

- Pngcrush:
  http://pmt.sourceforge.net/pngcrush/

- jpegtran:
  http://sylvana.net/jpegcrop/jpegtran/

- CSS Compressor on CSSDrive.com:
  http://www.cssdrive.com/index.php/main/csscompressor/

- CSS Optimizer:
  http://www.cssoptimiser.com/

- Code Beautifer:
  http://www.codebeautifier.com/

- CSS Tidy:
  http://csstidy.sourceforge.net/

Further Reading

Krause, Jim. *Design Basics Index*. How, 2004.

Lidwell, William, Kritina Holden, Jill Butler. *Universal Principles of Design: 100 Ways to Enhance Usability, Influence Perception, Increase Appeal, Make Better Design Decisions, and Teach through Design*. Rockport Publishers, 2003.

Norman, Donald. *The Design of Everyday Things*. Doubleday Business, 1990.

Samara, Timothy. *Design Elements – A Graphic Style Manual. Understanding the rules and knowing when to break them*. Rockport Publishers, 2007.

Snyder, Carolyn. *Paper Prototyping: The Fast and Easy Way to Design and Refine User Interfaces*. Morgan Kaufmann, 2003.

Tidwell, Jenifer. *Designing Interfaces – Patterns for Effective Interaction Design*. Second edition. O'Reilly Media, 2011.

Weinman, Lynda and William Weinman. *<creative html design.2>: a hands-on web design tutorial*. Waite Group Press, 2001.

White, Alexander. *The Elements of Graphic Design: Space, Unity, Page Architecture, and Type*. Allworth Press, 2002. Web Form Design: Filling in the Blanks:
http://www.lukew.com/resources/web_form_design.asp

A Book Apart: *Brief books for people who make websites*:
http://www.abookapart.com/

A List apart: For People Who Make Websites:
http://www.alistapart.com/

Smashing Magazine:
http://www.smashingmagazine.com/

Six Revisions: Useful Information for Web Developers & Designers:
http://sixrevisions.com/

"10 Usability Tips Based on Research Studies" by Cameron Chapman on Six Revisions:
http://sixrevisions.com/usabilityaccessibility/10-usability-tips-based-on-research-studies/

Tuts+:
http://tutsplus.com/

52 weeks of UX: *A discourse on the process of designing for real people*:
http://52weeksofux.com/

UX Booth: User Experience & Usability Blog:
http://www.uxbooth.com/

Web Content Accessibility Guidelines (WCAG) 2.0:
http://www.w3.org/TR/2008/REC-WCAG20-20081211/

Marcotte, Ethan. *Responsive Web Design*. Available on A Book Apart:
http://www.abookapart.com/products/responsive-web-design

User Stories:
http://en.wikipedia.org/wiki/User_story

Behavior Driven Development:
http://en.wikipedia.org/wiki/Behavior_Driven_Development

Introducing Behavior Driven Design:
http://dannorth.net/introducing-bdd/

"Why Mood Boards Matter" by Mindy Wagner:
http://www.webdesignerdepot.com/2008/12/why-mood-boards-matter/

"Website Mood Boards: A Successful Precursor to Visual Prototyping" by Kevin Flahaut:
http://weblog.404creative.com/2007/02/14/website-mood-boards-a-successful-precursor-to-visual-prototyping/

"8 Definitive Web Font Stacks Article" by Aaron Boodman:
http://www.sitepoint.com/eight-definitive-font-stacks/

Windows Internet Explorer Developer Tools:
http://msdn.microsoft.com/en-us/ie/aa740478

Herding Code 108: Jin Yang and Nathan Bowers on Web Design:
http://herdingcode.com/?p=309

"Design Fundamentals for Developers" by Robby Ingebretsen on Channel 9:
http://channel9.msdn.com/Events/MIX/MIX09/02W

To access web resources more easily, see the online version of the bibliography on MSDN: http://msdn.microsoft.com/en-us/library/hh404094.aspx.

5   Modularity

Introduction

A modular application is divided into functional units named modules that can be integrated into a larger application. Each module provides a portion of the application's overall functionality and represents a set of related concerns. Within a browser-based application, a module can add or remove user interface (UI) elements, add or enhance functionality (or behavior) already available in the UI, or enhance the user experience (UX). Modules can be built independently of one another but still communicate with each other in a loosely coupled fashion. Modular applications can make it easier for you to develop, test, deploy, and extend your application. Modular designs also have well-understood benefits that help you unit test your applications and make them easier to maintain over time.

Achieving a modular design in a complex JavaScript application requires specific techniques that are not immediately obvious if your previous experience is with object-oriented languages such as C# or Microsoft® Visual Basic®. While environments such as the Microsoft .NET Framework allow you to use classes, interfaces, and assemblies to organize application functionality, there are fewer options for creating explicit boundaries in JavaScript. Without a modular approach, JavaScript source files tend to be large and hard to maintain, and often the entire application is found in a single source file with numerous unstructured global variables. You can easily end up with an application that is prone to defects and difficult to troubleshoot and maintain. An application with the feature set of Mileage Stats is much more straightforward to develop and test when its design is modular.

In this chapter you will learn:

- The benefits of modularity for hybrid-designed web applications.
- The factors that influence a modular design, such as the module's boundaries.
- Types of modules to consider for your application, along with their functional roles and categories.
- When to use a JavaScript object, a jQuery plug-in, or a jQuery UI Widget.

The technologies and libraries discussed in this chapter are JavaScript, jQuery, and jQuery UI.

Benefits of Modularity for Hybrid-Design Web Applications

There are a number of benefits of modular application design that apply specifically to hybrid-design web applications. These benefits can be seen through the whole application lifecycle, which includes design, development, testing, troubleshooting, and maintenance.

Modular design provides the following benefits:

- The ability to leverage frameworks
- Better support for an immersive UI
- Support for team-oriented development
- Explicit control over application initialization
- The ability to externally configure modules
- Decoupled module interactions
- Easier troubleshooting and debugging
- Easier code base maintenance
- Easier testing

LEVERAGING FRAMEWORKS

There are a number of approaches to creating modular applications. When writing applications with JavaScript, the simplest way to partition your code into modules is to use JavaScript objects. However, for a truly flexible system, using only JavaScript objects to create modules, as opposed to other options presented in this chapter, will result in a code base that is larger than needed.

Another option is to use a framework that allows for modular designs. The Project Silk team chose the jQuery library because it supports modular designs through *plug-ins* and *widgets* and because it helps avoid cross-browser compatibility issues.

- **jQuery plug-ins** allow developers to create libraries that extend the functionality of jQuery. There are jQuery plug-ins for everything from simplifying Ajax calls to implementing drag and drop.
- **jQuery UI Widgets** are high-level building blocks that are provided by the jQuery UI library. Widgets are a way to create modules within an application that already takes advantage of the jQuery library, and to help impose modular design on client-side code. For more information on widgets, see Chapter 3, "jQuery UI Widgets."

> **Note:** *This chapter uses the term* **module** *to refer to a JavaScript object, a jQuery plug-in, or a jQuery UI Widget, which contain cohesive sets of functionalities.*

Of course, there are other high-quality libraries besides jQuery to choose from, such as **Prototype** and **Script.aculo.us**. Finding a framework to act as a starting point for a modular application is important. If the framework allows you to avoid having to implement low-level DOM manipulation yourself and offers cross-browser support (as jQuery does), so much the better. For other examples of JavaScript libraries and frameworks, see "Architectural Alternatives" in Chapter 2, "Architecture."

SUPPORT FOR AN IMMERSIVE UI

Immersive experiences use modern UI design approaches to keep the user in context while inside the defined boundaries of the immersive experience. *In context* means that users are never confused about where they are in the application. Breadcrumbs are one way to help the user, but they do not match the intuitiveness of an immersive UI. The user expects either instant responsiveness or some indication of progress from an immersive web application. The experience must be fluid. This requirement places a number of non-trivial responsibilities on the client-side code. Some of these responsibilities have to do with Ajax data retrieval and caching, updating UI content, state management, and animating layout transitions.

It is difficult to implement the complex behavior required for an immersive UI without a design that is partitioned into modules with clear boundaries and responsibilities. Dividing functionality into widgets that are associated with specific HTML elements ensures that only a local region needs to be refreshed in the display. This can improve performance.

SUPPORT FOR TEAM-ORIENTED DEVELOPMENT

Most complex web applications will be written by a team rather than by a single person. Dividing the application into modules allows pieces of the application to be developed in parallel by different teams or individuals. For example, after this approach was decided upon for Mileage Stats, the fill ups and reminders modules were simultaneously developed by separate members of the development team.

EXPLICIT CONTROL OVER APPLICATION INITIALIZATION

One of the challenging parts of a complex application is initializing and cleaning up various parts of the application at the appropriate times. A modular design can help to orchestrate these tasks. Fortunately, widgets contain several hooks for controlling what happens during initialization and cleanup. See "Initializing Modules" later in this chapter for an example of how Mileage Stats uses these hooks.

ABILITY TO EXTERNALLY CONFIGURE MODULES

Modern applications often defer the configuration of components until the application is deployed. If you design your application in a modular way, you can implement ways to externally configure your modules. Without external configuration you must use hard-coded component dependencies, which result in brittle code that is hard to test and maintain.

DECOUPLED MODULE INTERACTIONS

A modular design allows you to formalize the interactions between the components of your system. For example, in Mileage Stats the interface of each widget allows the widget to work with other parts of the UI without unnecessary coupling. The interface of a widget is made up of three things: the options it accepts, the public methods it exposes, and the events it raises. To see an example of how modules in Mileage Stats collectively respond to user actions in a loosely coupled way, see "Communicating Between Modules" later in this chapter.

TROUBLESHOOTING AND DEBUGGING

Modular applications are easier to troubleshoot and debug. When a problem occurs, it is usually easy to isolate the source of the issue to either a single module or to the communication between modules. Once a faulty module is located, troubleshooting should be straightforward. For communication issues between modules, unit tests should indicate which side of the communication is causing the problem, allowing for a quick resolution.

CODE BASE MAINTENANCE

A modular design allows your code base to be more maintainable by making it easier to understand. Adding new features and evolving the application over time is easier than it is in a monolithic application. Since each module has a well-defined set of responsibilities, decisions about where a new feature belongs should be straightforward. If the new feature is an addition to the responsibilities that a module owns, then the feature should be added to the module. If the new feature is outside the areas of responsibility for existing modules, there may be a need for a new module. Changes to the code tend to be more localized in applications that were originally designed with a clear and well-motivated modular structure. This makes adding new features less costly.

For example, in the future the Project Silk team may want to add an additional chart to the Mileage Stats application. This chart would show the user's average fuel efficiency for each vehicle compared to the average fuel efficiency of other vehicles of the same make and model. This feature is a type of chart, so extending the charts module to show the new type of data is a good option. However, if the team decides that the responsibilities are too different from those of the existing chart module due to the types of data or how the data should be displayed and partitioned, they could create a new module to handle the retrieval and display of this information. Adding the new module to the application would simply require initializing it at the appropriate time in the mileagestats.js file, and modifying the layout manager to handle any new user interactions and navigation required for the new feature.

TESTING

Modular applications can be tested module by module. In addition, it is possible to create test frameworks that isolate modules from their application context. This technique, which is sometimes called *sandboxing*, allows components of the application to be tested before the entire application is complete. It also makes testing more robust by preventing software defects in one module from blocking or affecting the testing of other modules.

Factors That Influence a Modular Design

Numerous factors come into play when defining the roles and responsibilities of modules within an application. For interactive modules, some questions to consider are:
- What are the design goals and constraints for the application?
- How is the module defined visually?
- What will the module do?

Using the UI elements to determine the responsibilities of a module requires answers to a few questions:

- What UI element or elements define a visual boundary for the module?

- Does the module need to create, insert, remove, or replace elements in the UI?

- Will the module contain other modules? If so, will it be responsible for managing the lifecycle of the child modules?

In addition to defining the visual boundaries of a module, it is important to define what the module does. Several questions to consider are:

- What behaviors or interactions should the module add to the UI elements?

- What animations or screen transitions is the module responsible for?

- What data responsibilities does the module have?

- How does the module interact with other modules and the rest of the application?

To determine the boundaries of the modules in your application, a few techniques can be used. If you applied an approach for defining the UI and UX of your application, such as the one described in Chapter 4, "Design and Layout," you should already have the assets you need to begin defining application modules. After applying UX considerations you should have flow diagrams that illustrate user navigation and transitions throughout the application. After applying UI considerations you should have wireframes and various mockups that show the dimensions and relationship between UI elements. These assets can be used to influence the boundaries of modules. You can identify the modules in your application by evaluating the following three aspects:

- **Layout**. Wireframes and mockups are used to guide the design of UI modules that are made up of groups of related elements.

- **Animations**. Flow diagrams and navigation transitions are used to identify animations that are independent of the UI elements that the animation affects. Animations can influence the need for behavioral modules.

- **Data Refreshes**. UX considerations identify how user actions that update the data in portions of the UI will affect the design of modules. The boundaries of these updates can indicate the possible boundaries of additional UI modules as well as infrastructure modules to accommodate the refreshing of data.

The Mileage Stats team used the assets from the design phase to initially define module boundaries. As a result, the team found that most of these modules remained unchanged throughout the building and refactoring of the application. The remainder of this section illustrates how applying these techniques influenced Mileage Stats.

Page Layout

The UI layout gave the developers a good indication of how to begin defining widgets, most of which would be associated with visual elements. In Mileage Stats, a user can view statistics for each vehicle at three levels of granularity. A top priority was that users never see any page refreshes while switching from the dashboard to the details and charts layouts. In other words, these levels define the boundaries of an immersive experience. The following figure illustrates the three main layouts.

The three main screen layouts in Mileage Stats

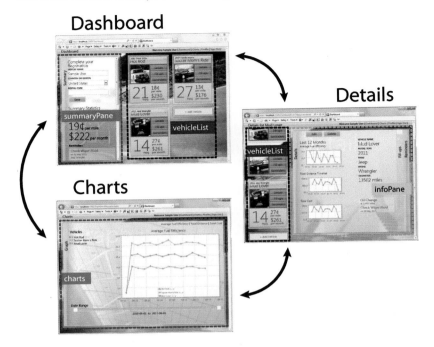

The dashboard contains a **summaryPane** region and the **vehicleList** region. The details layout contains **vehicleList** and **infoPane** regions, and the charts layout uses a single region.

The Dashboard Layout

The following figure shows the Mileage Stats dashboard.

The Mileage Stats Dashboard

The information presented to the user includes:

- Site navigation links
- A registration form
- A list of vehicles that the user has entered in the system
- Statistics aggregated across all the vehicles
- A list of reminders that are overdue or nearly due
- Status messages about actions the user has taken

After partitioning the screen based on its layout, the team arrived at the following module boundaries.

Dashboard regions

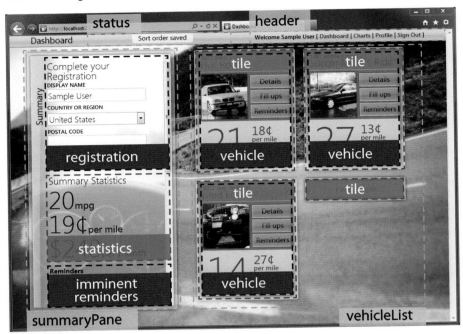

As you can see, the main components of the dashboard are the **summaryPane** region and the **vehicleList** region. The summary pane, like the vehicle list, is a parent widget with three child widgets. After registration is completed, the **registration** widget is no longer shown. The **status** and **header** regions appear in all layouts.

The Details Layout

The details layout, shown in the following figure, is another main screen that provides one of the three levels of granularity. The details layout is divided into the **vehicleList** region (which is shared with the dashboard layout) and the **infoPane** region. As you can see, the **tile** widget is applied to each child in the vehicle list while the **vehicle** widget is applied only to vehicle tiles. Only the **tile** widget is applied to the **Add Vehicle** button at the bottom of the vehicle list. The responsibilities of these widgets are described in the "Animations" section that follows.

Details regions

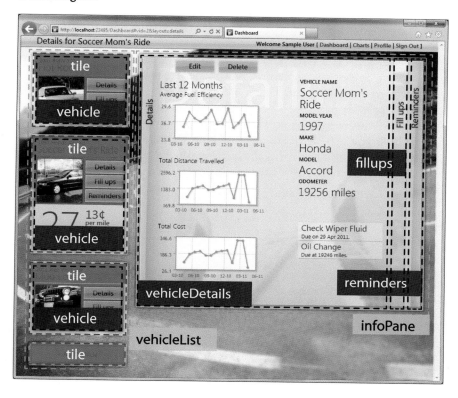

> **Note:** *Because the* **vehicleList** *region is used in both the dashboard and details layouts, users never lose sight of the selected vehicle, which keeps them in context.*

There are no full-page refreshes when users navigate to the different layouts, so each region of the page must know how to respond to **show**, **hide**, and **animate** directives. These requirements are good indications that the regions should be widgets. Also, some module must be responsible for telling each of these widgets to show, hide, or animate. This is the role of the **layoutManager**. This module has no UI, but it controls the operation of other widgets. For more information about the **layoutManager**, see Chapter 9, "Navigation."

ANIMATIONS
Animations are another factor that can influence the need for a module. Animation modules can be implemented as widgets, which permit them to focus on the details of the animation. This separates the animation code from the code that manages the state of the UI elements, such as data refreshes.

In Mileage Stats, the region that shows the list of vehicles appears in both the dashboard and details layouts. Transitions between the dashboard and details layouts are animated: the summary pane and the vehicle list regions enter and exit at the left side of the screen, and the info pane and chart regions enter and exit at the right. This animation influenced the decision to create the tile and vehicle widgets.

The vehicle list widget contains two types of elements: vehicle tiles and a tile that holds the **Add Vehicle** button. When a user transitions to and from the dashboard and details layouts, the animation uses a two-step process to move the vehicle tiles so that they are displayed in either one or two columns. At the same time, the vehicle tiles that were not selected shrink to a smaller size. These are two distinct cases, which indicate that there should be a widget for each type of animation.

Mileage Stats uses the **tile** widget to animate the position of all boxes horizontally and vertically, because both the vehicle boxes and the **Add Vehicle** box need that behavior. The **vehicle** widget expands and collapses the vehicle boxes, because only they need that behavior. The following figure illustrates the transition from the dashboard layout to the details layout.

Transitioning from the dashboard to details

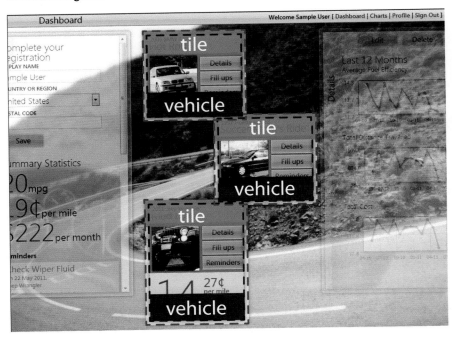

Modularizing these animations into widgets results in pieces of code that have clear boundaries and responsibilities.

> **Note:** *It would also be possible to separate the animation logic into its own widget that the **vehicleList** widget could then apply to itself. This would be particularly useful if you needed to apply the animation elsewhere or needed the ability to easily change the animation applied to the **vehicleList** widget.*

REFRESHING DATA

When all data updates happen through Ajax calls, the various parts of the UI must know how and when to request updates from the server and how to apply any necessary changes to the UI. Depending on the user's action, only parts of the UI, rather than all of the data on the page, may need to be updated. The boundaries that delineate the data to be refreshed and the data that remains the same can influence the boundaries of modules.

The statistics and imminent reminders regions of the summary widget are themselves widgets. They both must be able to request updates from the server and apply them. The following figure illustrates the summary widget, with two of the widgets it is responsible for.

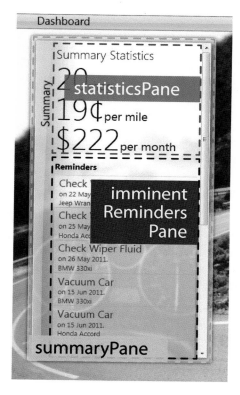

The summary widget

The statistics and imminent reminders regions each know how to request their own relevant data and update their content when changes in the vehicle, fill ups, or reminder data are detected. Many of the other widgets in Mileage Stats are also responsible for retrieving and applying updated content. However, the code that actually makes the requests and adds caching functionality is implemented in a separate module as a JavaScript object. To learn more about data abstraction in Mileage Stats, see Chapter 6, "Client Data Management and Caching."

Functional Roles and Categories for Modules

The role of a given module generally falls into one of three categories, each with a specific focus:

- **UI modules** are responsible for adding, removing, and modifying UI elements within the boundaries of the module.
- **Behavioral modules** are responsible for applying behavior to the elements within the module. Animation is an example of a behavior.
- **Infrastructure modules** are responsible for application-wide requirements that are not specific to the UI, such as data access and communication.

UI MODULES

UI modules, such as the **statistics** and **imminentReminders** widgets in Mileage Stats, are responsible for the visual representation of an element. UI modules can be commonly used controls such as date and time pickers, combo boxes, or tab controls. They can also be application specific, which is true of the Mileage Stats widgets.

Some of the Mileage Stats widgets rely on HTML and CSS for their appearance, and may correspond to elements with child elements. Alternatively, a widget may be applied to an element that has no child elements. In this case, the widget is responsible for adding the elements that make up the UI. This situation commonly occurs when the initial response from the server doesn't contain all of the necessary elements. When this happens, the widget may have to request the elements from the server or apply a data template. An example of this type of widget is the **infoPane** widget.

A widget can also act as a container for other widgets. An example of a container in Mileage Stats is the **summary** widget, which contains the **registration**, **statistics**, and **imminentReminders** widgets. Containers can have knowledge of their children because they are often responsible for creating those children, attaching children to the correct elements, and responding to events from their children.

> **Note:** *You should avoid creating children in container widgets that have knowledge of their parent because the resulting bidirectional dependencies make it more difficult to create a layered application. Bidirectional module dependencies also make the application harder to test.*

BEHAVIORAL MODULES

Behavior widgets and JavaScript objects add functionality to an existing element. The jQuery UI library calls these pieces of functionality *interactions*. Commonly used behavioral widgets include the **draggable**, **droppable**, **resizable**, **selectable**, and **sortable** widgets. In Mileage Stats, the behavior widgets include **tile** and **layoutManager**. There is also a JavaScript object for managing the process of pinning the site to the operating system's taskbar.

INFRASTRUCTURE MODULES

Infrastructure modules provide commonly needed functionality that isn't related to the visual aspects of the application. They don't interact with the UI. Typically, their functionality includes data access, communication, logging, or caching. The infrastructure modules in Mileage Stats are JavaScript objects. They include **dataManager, dataStore**, and **pubsub**.

JavaScript Module Implementations

Applications such as Mileage Stats that use JavaScript and jQuery can implement modules in any of the following ways:

- **JavaScript objects**. JavaScript objects are a good choice for implementing modules that are not associated with visual elements on the page. JavaScript objects are the most lightweight type of module.

- **jQuery plug-ins**. You should consider jQuery plug-ins when you need to extend the functionality of the jQuery framework. Plug-ins can encapsulate notions of UI and behavior.

- **jQuery UI Widgets**. When modules are associated with specific HTML elements, consider using jQuery UI Widgets. The jQuery UI framework provides helpful, built-in, functionality that makes widgets behave like user controls. These capabilities include creation, initialization, a property notification system, an event model, and teardown. Associating widgets with UI elements is an easy way to organize the code that supports your UI. For example, you can use a widget to populate a visual element with a new form dynamically in response to a UI event.

The following table shows the suitability of these three types of JavaScript modules for the functional roles or categories described in the previous section. These are not definitive rules, just suggestions on how to choose the appropriate module. The following sections describe the implementation of these JavaScript modules in more detail.

	JavaScript objects	jQuery plug-ins	jQuery UI widgets
UI modules	No	OK	Ideal
Behavioral modules	OK	Ideal	OK
Infrastructure modules	Ideal	OK	No

> **Note:** *Behavioral modules span a wide array of scenarios, which may or may not need to operate directly on DOM elements. Any of the three implementations may be appropriate. Use the guidance throughout this section to help you decide which module to use.*

For consistency, Mileage Stats uses widgets for everything that is associated with an HTML element or adds behavior to HTML elements, and uses JavaScript objects for everything else.

USING JAVASCRIPT OBJECTS AS MODULES

JavaScript objects are the most basic implementation of a module. They can be easy to write for simple modules, but they do not automatically provide the features available to plug-ins and widgets. Implementing a module as a JavaScript object is most appropriate when its functionality is not directly related to the HTML elements in the page. These modules only require logic that can be fulfilled by the language and don't need to extend existing libraries, such as jQuery, that abstract DOM manipulation. When a module extends the functionality of a library, for example to operate on DOM elements, it is more appropriate to use the library's extensibility points.

The following table lists the JavaScript objects that are used in Mileage Stats.

File	Purpose	Functional Category
mstats.pinnedsite.js	Provides the pinned sites implementation for Windows® Internet Explorer® 9	Behavioral
mstats.data.js	Data manager that retrieves and stores data; lets callers know when data is available	Infrastructure
mstats.pubsub.js	Manages subscriptions and publication of events	Infrastructure
mstats.events	Sets the event, which can be any button a user clicks, such as Details, or Add Vehicle	Infrastructure
mstats.vehicle-drop-down-monitor	Displays the Edit form	Infrastructure

USING JQUERY PLUG-INS AS MODULES

One of the characteristics of a good framework, such as jQuery, is a robust extensibility mechanism. Creating a plug-in is *the* recommended way to extend jQuery. In fact, a plug-in that follows the recommendations included in the "jQuery Plug-in Authoring Guidelines" is indistinguishable from the methods in the core library. Many features in jQuery began as external plug-ins that were later added to the library.

Note: *For more information on authoring plug-ins, see the "jQuery Plug-in Authoring Guidelines" in the "Further Reading" section at the end of the chapter.*

Because plug-ins behave just as other jQuery functions do, they can be invoked on elements by using jQuery selectors. Inside the plug-in, the **this** keyword is a reference to the set of DOM elements selected when the plug-in is applied. As an added advantage, the **each** function on **this** reassigns the **this** keyword to each DOM element of the selected elements.

The following code shows a plug-in named **doubleSizeMe** that doubles the size of an element.

JavaScript
```javascript
// Code example not in Mileage Stats
(function($){
    $.fn.doubleSizeMe = function() {
        return this.each(function() {
            var $this = $(this),
                width = $this.width(),
                height = $this.height();

            $this.width(width * 2);
            $this.height(height * 2);
        });
    };
})(jQuery);
```

This example code adds the **doubleSizeMe** method to the jQuery prototype so that it is available when you operate on a wrapped set. For example, to invoke the function on all elements with a class of **icon**, you would use the following call.

JavaScript
```javascript
$('.icon').doubleSizeMe();
```

> **Note:** *The example uses the jQuery functions for height and width, which provide cross-browser compatibility.*

There is much more functionality that you can add to your plug-ins. However, in some cases, plug-ins may not provide all the functionality you need. If you are writing a module that stores state internally, exposes methods you expect others to call, hides private methods, inherits from another object, or requires per-instance configuration, then a widget may be a better option.

USING WIDGETS AS MODULES

A jQuery UI Widget provides you with a number of capabilities that are useful when creating modules. These include features for object construction and destruction, storing state, merging options, and exposing public methods. To learn more about how to build widgets, see Chapter 3, "jQuery UI Widgets" and Chapter 14, "Widget QuickStart."

Mileage Stats uses UI widgets, which you can see on the web page, and behavioral widgets whose effects, such as animations, are visible. The UI widgets are responsible for visual elements and help to implement the application's presentation layer. Behavior widgets add functionality and help to implement the behavior layer of the application. The following table lists the main widgets that are used in Mileage Stats.

File	Purpose	Functional Category
mstats.status.js	Manages and displays user notification messages	UI
mstats.summary.js	Container that manages registration, statistics, and reminders widgets	UI
mstats.registration.js	Contained in summary widget; manages user registration	UI
mstats.statistics.js	Contained in summary widget; displays summary of vehicle statistics	UI
mstats.reminders.js	Contained in summary widget; lists overdue and upcoming maintenance reminders; manages click action when user selects a reminder	UI
mstats.layout-manager.js	Manages navigation requests and coordinates UI layout changes	Behavioral
mstats.vehicle-list.js	Displays vehicle tiles in one or two columns; invokes animation of child widgets; controls their contraction and expansion	UI
mstats.vehicle-list.js	Manages vehicle tiles, which are children of vehicle list widget	UI
mstats.vehicle.js	Displays vehicle information; manages actions of Details, Fill ups and Reminder buttons	UI
mstats.vehicle-details.js	Gathers and displays vehicle details	UI
mstats.charts.js	Creates charts displayed when user clicks Charts button	UI
mstats.info-pane.js	Controls display of fill ups, reminders, and vehicle details widgets, which are created in the same file	UI
mstats.tile.js	Moves vehicle tiles vertically and horizontally	UI

EXTERNALLY CONFIGURING MODULES

In Mileage Stats, some widgets are configured externally to reduce the coupling between them. For example, when the **layoutManager** widget is constructed in mileagestats.js, its **subscribe** option is populated with the **mstats.pubsub.subscribe** method. The rest of the options are references to the modules the layout manager is responsible for coordinating.

JavaScript
```javascript
// Contained in mileagestats.js
$('body').layoutManager({
    subscribe: mstats.pubsub.subscribe,
    pinnedSite: mstats.pinnedSite,
    charts: charts,
    header: header,
    infoPane: infoPane,
    summaryPane: summaryPane,
    vehicleList: vehicleList
});
```

Injecting dependencies through options allows the code that creates the widget to supply data, functions, and other modules during creation. This prevents the widget from needing to know how to resolve the dependencies itself, without sacrificing functionality. See "Defining Options" in Chapter 3, "jQuery UI Widgets" for more information about configuring modules.

INITIALIZING MODULES

The **_create** method of a widget contains initialization code, and the **destroy** method is used to clean up what the widget created. For example, in Mileage Stats, the vehicle list widget initializes the **vehicle**, **tile**, and **sortable** widgets when it is created. These widgets must be cleaned up in the **destroy** method.

JavaScript
```javascript
// Contained in mstats.vehicle-list.js
_create: function () {

    dataUrl = this.element.data('list-url');

    this._widgetizeVehicleTiles();
    this._bindEventHandlers();
    this._makeSortable();
    ...
},
destroy: function () {
    this.element
        .sortable('destroy')
        .find(':mstats-tile').tile('destroy')
```

```
        .find(':mstats-vehicle').vehicle('destroy');

    $.Widget.prototype.destroy.call(this);
}
```

The **_create** method uses private methods to initialize the other widgets. The **_widgetizeVehicleTiles** method initializes the **vehicle** and **tile** widgets and **_make Sortable** initializes the **sortable** widget. The **destroy** method cleans up these widgets by calling their **destroy** methods, and then calls the base widget's **destroy** method on the last line.

COMMUNICATING BETWEEN MODULES

In order to coordinate the responses to user actions, modules must be able to communicate with each other. Method calls and events are an effective way to accomplish this. As an example, the following sequence diagram shows some of the public methods that are called when a reminder is fulfilled in Mileage Stats.

Sequence diagram for fulfilling a reminder

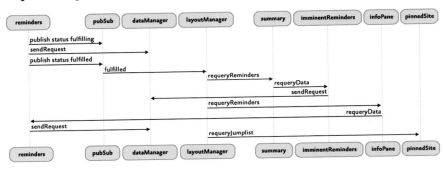

When the **Fulfill** button on the reminders pane is selected, it publishes its status, makes the Ajax call to save the reminder, and publishes an **mstats.events.vehicle.reminders.fulfilled** event. At this point, the **reminders** widget has not yet updated its UI with an updated list of reminders. The layout manager then instructs the summary, info pane, and pinned site modules to retrieve updated reminder data, and they coordinate the interactions with their child widgets. As a result, the reminders widget that initiated the action doesn't update its data until it is told to do so by the info pane.

These interactions illustrate the flexibility of a modular design. For more information on enabling communication between widgets, see Chapter 8, "Communication."

TESTING MODULES

Even without sandboxing, modular applications are easier to test using techniques such as unit testing. The modules can be tested by invoking each function of the interface that is exposed to other modules. For example, in Mileage Stats the **header** widget controls the header text it displays through its **title** option. The following test ensures that the header text changes each time the value of the option changes.

JavaScript
```javascript
// Contained in mstats.header.tests.js
test('when title option is changed, then it displays new title', function() {
    expect(1);
    var header = $('#header').header();
    header.header('option', 'title', 'test title');


    equal($('[data-title]').text(), 'test title', 'header text set properly');
});
```

When this test runs, it ensures that the **_setOption** method on the header widget, the code under test, updates the text for the header.

JavaScript
```javascript
// Contained in mstats.header.js
_setOption: function (key, value) {
    switch (key) {
        case 'title':
            this.element.find('[data-title]').text(value);
            break;
        ...
    }
    $.Widget.prototype._setOption.apply(this, arguments);
}
```

In order for the tests to run in isolation, each test file must contain a copy of the HTML markup that mirrors the markup to which the code under test will be applied. You can find this markup at the top of the test files.

JavaScript
```javascript
// Contained in mstats.header.tests.js
module('Header Widget Tests', {
    setup: function () {
        $('#qunit-fixture').append('<div class="header" id="header">' +
            '<div><div><h1 data-title>Dashboard</h1>' +
                ...
            '</div>'
        );
    }
});
```

For more information about unit testing, see Chapter 13, "Unit Testing Web Applications."

Summary

There are several possibilities for imposing a modular structure on complex JavaScript applications. JavaScript objects are a good choice for implementing modules that are not associated with elements on the page. When the boundaries of the module are defined by visual elements of the UI, consider using jQuery UI widgets. You can use jQuery plug-ins to extend the functionality of the jQuery library.

Independent of the types of modules you use, you can expect the same sorts of benefits from modularity that you see in solutions created with object-oriented languages. A modular design makes your code base more maintainable, easier to test, easier to troubleshoot, and suitable for team development.

The boundaries of your modules can be influenced by considering page layouts, animations used during transitions, and the need to selectively refresh parts of the UI based on user actions. When defining these boundaries, consider the various layouts in the application and the regions in those layouts. Also, take animations into account, as well as content that must be updated with Ajax. The modules should each be easily identifiable as belonging to the presentation (UI) layer, the behaviors layer, or the infrastructure layer.

Further Reading

jQuery Plug-in Authoring Guidelines: http://docs.jquery.com/Plugins/Authoring

For more information about how to build widgets, see Chapter 3, "jQuery UI Widgets" and Chapter 14, "Widget QuickStart."

To learn more about data abstraction in Mileage Stats, see Chapter 6, "Client Data Management and Caching."

For more information on enabling communication between widgets, see Chapter 8, "Communication."

For more information about how the tile widget performs its animation, see Chapter 9, "Navigation."

For more information about unit testing, see Chapter 13, "Unit Testing Web Applications."

For other examples of JavaScript libraries and frameworks, see "Architectural Alternatives" in Chapter 2, "Architecture."

For examples of other libraries that support a modular design, see:

- Prototype:
  http://prototypejs.org
- Script.aculo.us:
  http://script.aculo.us

To access web resources more easily, see the online version of the bibliography on MSDN: http://msdn.microsoft.com/en-us/library/hh404094.aspx.

6 Client Data Management and Caching

Introduction

Web applications are intended to present data to the user. In rich, interactive, client-centric applications like Mileage Stats, users expect the application to respond quickly to mouse gestures, page transitions, and the saving of form data. Delays caused by data retrieval or saving data can negatively impact the user's experience and enjoyment of the site. Therefore, carefully managed data retrieval and caching is critical to today's web applications.

> **Note:** *The term data caching used in this documentation refers to the caching of client-side JavaScript objects within the DOM (document object model) rather than using the browser's built-in page caching mechanism.*

A sound client-side data management strategy is critical to the success of a web application and will address fundamental concerns such as:

- **Maintainability**. Writing clean maintainable JavaScript code requires skill, discipline, and planning. The Mileage Stats data implementation addresses maintainability by providing a simple object for centralized data access that other application objects use to execute data requests and to cache the results.

- **Performance**. Client-side caching and prefetching of data plays a key role in achieving application responsiveness from the user's perspective. Eliminating unnecessary data calls to the server enables the browser to process other tasks, such as animations or transitions, more quickly.. Mileage Stats addresses these performance concerns by caching data returned from the server, using prefetching to acquire data that a user is likely to view, and using Ajax to perform asynchronous data calls to the server.

- **Scalability**. Client-side objects should avoid making repeated requests to the server for the same data. Unnecessary calls to the server require additional server-side resources, which can negatively impact the scalability of your application. Mileage Stats uses client-side data caching to increase scalability.

- **Browser support**. Your choice of a data caching mechanism will influence which browsers your application can support. Rather than employing a browser-specific feature such as local storage, Mileage Stats caches data using a generic JavaScript object caching mechanism so that older browsers such as Windows® Internet Explorer® 7 are supported.

In this chapter you will learn:

- How Mileage Stats manages and centralizes application data requests.
- The benefits of a client-side data manager and how data requests are abstracted.
- How to improve application performance by caching and prefetching data.

The technologies and libraries discussed in this chapter are Ajax, JavaScript, jQuery, and jQuery UI Widgets.

Note: *Data validation on the client and server is covered in Chapter 11, "Server-Side Implementation."*

Client-Side Data Design

The Mileage Stats data solution centers on the data manager, which handles client-side data requests and manages the data cache. The diagram below shows the relationship of the client-side JavaScript objects to one another and to the server JSON (JavaScript Object Notation) endpoints.

Mileage Stats client-side data architecture

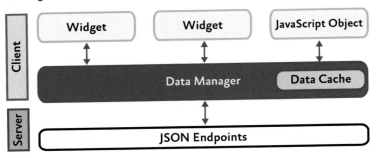

Mileage Stats objects use URLs when requesting data from the server. URLs were chosen because their use simplifies the data manager's design by providing a mechanism to decouple the server JSON endpoints from the data manager's implementation.

The URL contains the JSON endpoint and, optionally, a data record key value corresponding to the requested object. The URL typically aligns with the UI elements the object is responsible for. For example, the reminders widget uses "/Reminder/JsonList/1" to retrieve the reminders for the vehicle with the ID of 1.

When data is requested from the data manager, it returns the data to the caller and optionally caches it. The caching of data improves the performance of the application because repeated requests to the server for the same data are no longer necessary.

In addition to data caching, Mileage Stats also prefetches the chart data. The chart data is prefetched on the initial page load because there is a reasonable expectation that users will use the Charts page to compare their vehicles. The prefetching of this data enables an instant response when the user navigates to the Charts page.

In your applications, the amount of data you elect to prefetch should be based on the volatility of the data, the likelihood of the user accessing that data, and the relative cost to get that data when the user requests it. Of course, the number of concurrent users and the capabilities of your web and database servers also play a role in this decision.

Data Manager

All Ajax data requests are routed through the **dataManager** JavaScript object contained in the mstats-data.js file. The data manager is responsible for performing data requests and managing interactions with the data cache. The data manager has a simple public interface that exposes two methods: **sendRequest,** which processes Ajax calls to the server, and **resetData,** which removes a requested item from the data cache.

The next three sections examine the benefits of the data manager abstraction, look at how data requests are initiated by jQuery UI widgets, and show how those requests are executed by the data manager.

BENEFITS OF THE DATA MANAGER ABSTRACTION

Abstracting the data request implementation as a data manager object provides an injection point for data caching, which is a cross-cutting concern. Data requestors get the full benefit of data caching without taking on another dependency or implementing additional code. Isolating the data cache also makes it much easier to change the data cache implementation because only the data manager has a direct dependency on it.

The data manager improves application testability by allowing developers to unit test data requests and data caching in isolation. The data manager also facilitates changing the application over time. Evolution of an application is required not only after its release but during development as well. For example, the team added a feature to the data manager that would have required modifying all the Ajax request code. Had the data manager not been implemented, the change would have been riskier and potentially costlier.

The team discovered that when the website was deployed to a virtual directory as opposed to the root directory of the web server, the URLs in the JavaScript code had not taken the virtual directory into account. The fix for this problem only had to be applied to the data manager, which saved development and testing resources. This feature is discussed in the "Performing Ajax Requests" section below.

DATA REQUEST

Client-side data requests in Mileage Stats are initiated by jQuery UI widgets and Java Script objects, and performed by the data manger. The data manager **sendRequest** method has a signature similar to the signature of the jQuery **ajax** method. Widgets making requests set their calls up as if they are calling jQuery **ajax**, passing an **options** object that encapsulates the URL, a **success** callback, and optionally an **error** callback or other callbacks such as **beforeSend** or **complete**.

Data Request Options

When a widget is constructed, the options provided supply the methods needed to execute a data request or to remove an item from the data cache. Externally configuring widgets removes tight coupling and hard-coded values from the widget. Widgets can also pass their options, like **sendRequest**, to other widgets they create.

This technique of external configuration enables Mileage Stats widgets to have a common data request method injected during widget construction. In addition to run-time configuration, this technique also enables the ability to use a mock implementation for the data request methods at test time.

In the following code, the **summaryPane** widget is constructed, and its **sendRequest** and **invalidateData** options are set to corresponding data manager methods. The summary widget does not make any data requests; instead, these two methods will be passed into child widgets created by the summary widget.

```JavaScript
// Contained in mileagestats.js
summaryPane = $('#summary').summaryPane({
  sendRequest: mstats.dataManager.sendRequest,
  invalidateData: mstats.dataManager.resetData,
  publish: mstats.pubsub.publish,
  header: header
});
```

In the code snippet below, the summary widget constructs the child widget, **statisticsPane**, and passes the above **sendRequest** and **invalidateData** data manager methods as options. Setting these options replaces the default implementation defined in the statistics widget for making data requests. Now, when the statistics widget performs a data request, the method defined in the data manager will be executed.

```JavaScript
// Contained in mstats.summary.js
_setupStatisticsWidget: function () {
    var elem = this.element.find('#statistics');

    this.statisticsPane = elem.statisticsPane({
        sendRequest: this.options.sendRequest,
        dataUrl: elem.data('url'),
        invalidateData: this.options.invalidateData,
        templateId: '#fleet-statistics-template'
    });
},
```

The **dataUrl** option is the URL or endpoint for the data request. The **url** value is stored below in the **data-** attribute in the HTML. The **statisticsPane** widget is attached to and is queried by the **elem.data** method call seen above. Externally configuring data endpoints prevents you from having to hard-code knowledge about the server URL structure within the widget.

```
CSHTML
// Contained in \Views\Vehicle List.cshtml
<div id="statistics" class="statistics section"
    data-url="@URL.Action("JsonFleetStatistics","Vehicle")">
...
</div>
```

Performing a Data Request

The **sendRequest** method has the same method signature as the jQuery **ajax** method, which takes a **settings** object as the only argument. The **_getStatisticsData** method, below, passes the **sendRequest** method an object literal that encapsulates the **url**, **success**, and **error** callbacks. When the Ajax call completes, the appropriate callback will be invoked and its code will execute.

```JavaScript
// Contained in mstats.statistics.js
_getStatisticsData: function () {
    var that = this;
    that.options.sendRequest({
        url: this.options.dataUrl,
        success: function (data) {
            that._applyTemplate(data);
            that._showStatistics();
        },

        error: function () {
            that._hideStatistics();
            that._showErrorMessage();
        }
    });
},
```

The above pattern simplified the Mileage Stats data request code because it does not need to know about the data caching implementation or any other functionality that the data manager handles.

Now that you understand how widgets and JavaScript objects initiate a data request, let's examine how the data manager makes the Ajax request to the server and see how data caching is implemented.

PERFORMING AJAX REQUESTS

The data manager **sendRequest** method is used to request data from the server and in some places it is used to execute a command on the server, such as fulfilling a reminder. Because the jQuery **ajax** method signature is the same for requesting as well as posting data, the team chose to implement a single method for Ajax calls to the server. In addition to **success** and **error** callbacks, the **sendRequest** method has an option to cache the request or not. By default, requests are cached.

Mileage Stats has two use cases where data is not cached: data requests that only post data to the server, and the Pinned Sites requests. Results of the Pinned Sites requests are not cached because these requests are only initiated by events after data has changed. Because Pinned Sites only refreshes its data after a change, the data request needs to get fresh data from the server.

The diagram below illustrates the logical flow of a data request. The data manager services the request by first checking if the request should be cached and, if so, checks the cache before making a call to the server. Upon successful completion of the request, the resulting data will be returned to the user and added to the cache according to the option.

Data request

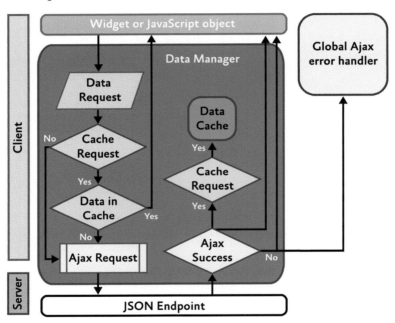

Now let's look at the code that implements the functionality of the above diagram. The **sendRequest** method, shown below, first modifies the URL to account for the virtual directory the website is deployed to by calling the **getRelativeEndpointUrl** function. Using the modified URL, it attempts to retrieve the requested data from the data cache. The options are then merged with the data manager's default options. If the caller wants the data cached, and data was found in the cache, it's immediately returned to the caller. If the data is not found, the jQuery **ajax** call is made. If successful, and the caller requested the data to be cached, it is added to the cache and the caller's **success** callback is invoked. If an error occurs and the caller implemented an **error** callback, it will be invoked. If a global Ajax error handler has been defined, it will be invoked after the **error** callback.

> **Note:** *The jQuery **ajax** method can be configured at the global level to define default options as well as default event handlers. Mileage Stats defines the global Ajax error handler shown above.*
>
> *For more information about how Mileage Stats implements the global Ajax error handler, see the "User Session Timeout Notification" section in Chapter 10, "Application Notifications."*

JavaScript
```javascript
// Contained in mstats.data.js
sendRequest: function (options) {
  // getRelativeEndpointUrl ensures the URL is relative to the website root.
  var that = mstats.dataManager,
          normalizedUrl = mstats.getRelativeEndpointUrl(options.url),
          cachedData = mstats.dataStore.get(normalizedUrl),
          callerOptions = $.extend({ cache: true },
                                    that.dataDefaults,
                                    options,
                                    { url: normalizedUrl });

  if (callerOptions.cache && cachedData) {
    options.success(cachedData);
    return;
  }

  callerOptions.success = function (data) {
    if (callerOptions.cache) {
      mstats.dataStore.set(normalizedUrl, data);
    }
    options.success(data);
  };

  $.ajax(callerOptions);
},
```

> **Note: getRelativeEndpointUrl** *is a utility method in the mstats.utils.js file that is used to modify the URL passed in the argument, inserting the virtual directory the website is installed under. This is necessary because the virtual directory is not known until run time.*

Data Cache

The Mileage Stats data manager uses an internal data cache for storing request results; the data cache is only accessed by the data manager. Making the data caching internal to the data manager allows the caching strategy to evolve independently without affecting other JavaScript objects that call the data manager.

The data cache is implemented using a JavaScript object named **dataStore** that is contained in the mstats-data.js file. Other data cache storage locations could include the DOM, a browser data storage API or a third-party library. The **dataStore** JavaScript object was implemented because Mileage Stats supports Internet Explorer 7, which does not support the HTML5 web storage specification.

Adding and Retrieving Cached Data

Note: *The Mileage Stats* **dataStore** *object is scoped to the page, not the browser window. Consequently, when the page is fully reloaded from the server, the cached data will no longer be cached since the data cache object will be recreated when the page loads.*

Mileage Stats integrates client-side data caching into the data manager's **sendRequest** method implementation that was described in the previous section.

Internally, the **dataStore** is implemented using name/value pairs. It exposes three methods: **get,** to retrieve data by a name; **set,** to cache data by a name; and **clear,** to remove data corresponding to a name.

```JavaScript
// Contained in mstats.data.js
mstats.dataStore = {

  _data: {},

  get: function (token) {
    return this._data[token];
  },

  set: function (token, payload) {
    this._data[token] = payload;
  },

  clear: function (token) {
    this._data[token] = undefined;
  },
};
```

Removing a Data Cache Item

In addition to the data manager retrieving and adding data to the cache, it also provides the **resetData** method for removing cached data by URL.

```JavaScript
// Contained in mstats.data.js
resetData: function (endpoint) {
  mstats.dataStore.clear(mstats.getRelativeEndpointUrl(endpoint));
}
```

Mileage Stats objects call the **resetData** method when client-side user actions make the cached data invalid. For example, when a maintenance reminder is fulfilled, the **requeryData** method shown below will be called by the layout manager widget. When designing your data architecture, it is important to consider which client-side actions should invalidate the cache data.

```JavaScript
// Contained in mstats.statistics.js
refreshData: function () {
  this._getStatisticsData();
},

requeryData: function () {
  this.options.invalidateData(this.options.dataUrl);
  this.refreshData();
},
```

The **requeryData** method first invokes the **invalidateData** method, passing the URL of the cache item to remove. The **invalidateData** method is an option on the statistics widget, which was passed the data manager's **resetData** method when the widget was created. Now that the data cache item has been removed, the next call to **refreshData** will result in the data manager not locating the cached data keyed by the URL, and then executing a request to the server for the data.

Summary

In this chapter, you have learned about the design, benefits, and implementation of a centralized client-side data manager that executes all Ajax requests and manages the caching of data. This approach simplifies testing, facilitates application or external library changes over time, and provides a consistent pattern for objects to follow to execute data requests.

You have also learned how Mileage Stats keeps its widgets free from external dependencies and the hard-coding of server URLs by constructing and configuring them externally. This approach of injecting external dependencies increases the flexibility and maintainability of the JavaScript code, and the absence of hard-coded server URLs prevents the creation of brittle JavaScript code.

Further Reading

For more information on jQuery UI widgets, see Chapter 3, "jQuery UI Widgets."

For more information on the global Ajax error handler, see Chapter 10, "Application Notifications."

For more information on data validation, see Chapter 11, "Server-Side Implementation."

HTML 5 Web Storage:
http://dev.w3.org/html5/webstorage/

jQuery:
http://jquery.com/

jQuery **ajax**() method:
http://api.jquery.com/jQuery.ajax/

jQuery **data**() method:
http://api.jquery.com/data/

jQuery **ajaxError**() method:
http://api.jquery.com/ajaxError/

Ajax Programming on Wikipedia:
http://en.wikipedia.org/wiki/Ajax_(programming)

To access web resources more easily, see the online version of the bibliography on MSDN: http://msdn.microsoft.com/en-us/library/hh404094.aspx.

7   Manipulating Client-Side HTML

Introduction

Both hybrid and single-page interface (SPI) web applications that do not perform full-page post backs in order to change the rendered user interface (UI) must use client-side techniques for manipulating the document object model (DOM). This DOM manipulation could include updating the content of the page, displaying new UI elements, or loading entire pages in response to user gestures and other events. The three client-side technologies you can use when implementing these techniques are HTML, cascading style sheets (CSS) and JavaScript.

This chapter discusses how you can clearly define the roles of HTML, CSS, and JavaScript on the client to ensure that developers and designers can work together without affecting each other's code. You will also see how to use JavaScript to manipulate HTML effectively in the browser.

In this chapter you will learn:

* The roles and responsibilities of HTML, CSS, and JavaScript within a client application.
* How to use jQuery to select and manipulate HTML elements.
* How to use jQuery to generate new HTML within the client.
* How to use jQuery Templates to generate new HTML within the client.
* How to choose the most appropriate option when manipulating HTML.

Technologies discussed in this chapter are HTML, CSS, and JavaScript.

The Roles and Responsibilities of Client-Side Languages

When building the client-side portion of a web application, you generally use three technologies that can be viewed as separate development languages: HTML, CSS, and JavaScript. You may not be accustomed to thinking of these technologies as development languages. However, considering them in this way can help to clarify the role that each one plays in your application, and can help you keep their responsibilities separate.

As with any development language, it is possible to use these languages in a way that makes the application harder to maintain and extend. This can be avoided by taking advantage of the strengths of each language, and by keeping their responsibilities clear and distinct.

STRUCTURE, APPEARANCE, AND BEHAVIOR

There are three areas of responsibility within client applications, and each client-side language is associated with one of those areas. The three areas are:

- **The structure of the UI**. HTML is used to define the logical structure of the UI. *Structure* refers to the hierarchy of objects that make up the UI, not the visual appearance or layout of the UI. Today, HTML is ideally used only for the logical, non-visual structure.

- **The appearance of the UI**. This is the responsibility of CSS, which applies styling to elements and manages visual layout (positioning and flow) for the UI. CSS allows designers and developers to change the layout, styling, and appearance of the UI elements without requiring changes to the structure defined by the HTML.

- **The behavior of the UI**. JavaScript is responsible for the behavior of the application. It is used to define or re-define how UI elements respond to user interactions and gestures, as well as other events not directly initiated by the user.

HTML also has an additional responsibility that might not be immediately obvious. It is frequently used to transport the data that the client requires from the server. For example, when the Mileage Stats Reference Implementation (Mileage Stats) renders a page, the information about the vehicles is stored as metadata in attributes within the HTML markup. Using metadata in this way is discussed in "Using Data- Attributes" later in this chapter.

It is surprisingly easy to blur the lines of responsibility among the client-side languages. For example, you might be tempted to use a CSS class to associate semantic or structural meaning to an HTML element. In fact, this approach was commonly used in the past to identify elements in order to attach some behavior.

An example of this approach would be to add an attribute such as **class="vehicleLink"** to relevant hyperlinks so that you can select these elements in your JavaScript code. However, using a CSS class in this way is problematic because it muddles the responsibilities of CSS as a language. In particular, if you use a CSS class to specify the style and the behavior of elements, your designer might unintentionally break your application by changing a class name or relocating a CSS class to another element when updating the layout and style of the page.

ADDING INTERACTIVE BEHAVIOR TO AN APPLICATION

When you have a simple web application, you can rely on the web server to handle changes to the HTML by posting back to the server so that it can update the page, or by loading a different page that contains the required HTML. However, this approach limits the level of interactivity in the application.

There are several ways that JavaScript code can add interactivity to a page through manipulation of the HTML structure and content without requiring a full-page reload.

Some typical approaches are:

* Using the existing page structure and simply hiding and showing elements as necessary. This is the simplest approach and is appropriate in some scenarios. For example, you might use JavaScript code to change the CSS properties that specify the visibility of elements within the page as it is loading, or in response to user actions.

* Using JavaScript to modify, add, or remove elements within the browser's DOM. The code can also add, remove, or update the attributes and style classes applied to elements. For small applications that do not require the appearance, structure, and behavior to change very much, this may be an acceptable solution. For example, you might want to add a new UI element to the page, enable or disable controls in the page, change the text displayed in elements, or show a different image.

* Using JavaScript to retrieve HTML fragments from the server and add them to the DOM. This is an ideal approach when the server-generated HTML fragments can be reused directly within the client. The HTML fragments may be generated dynamically on the server to include data relevant to the current state of the application, or may be static content, perhaps read directly from disk files.

* Using templates to generate HTML fragments dynamically on the client, and adding or replacing elements in the DOM with the generated HTML. This approach is ideal when there is a lot of content to be generated on the client. It can be used to combine HTML in the template with data provided by the server. This is the solution used in Mileage Stats.

Using a JavaScript Library to Manipulate the DOM

For a rich user experience, where your application can change the UI while avoiding full page reloads, it is obviously necessary to have a mechanism for manipulating the DOM. JavaScript is the primary way to do this. However, due to different DOM and JavaScript implementations within different browsers, using a JavaScript library to shield you from cross-browser compatibility issues is the only practical approach for anything more than very simple interactions.

There are several libraries that do this very well, but this chapter discusses only the jQuery library. Mileage Stats uses the jQuery library because it provides many powerful methods for selecting and changing elements in the DOM, modifying element attributes, wrapping existing elements, and creating new elements while remaining compatible with almost all modern browsers.

> **Note:** *For more information about jQuery, see "*jQuery Home Page*" in the "Further Reading" section of this chapter. For more information about browser support for jQuery, see "*jQuery Browser Compatibility*" in the "Further Reading" section of this chapter.*

jQuery uses an element selection syntax that is very similar to CSS, and extends it to provide additional ways to select elements within the HTML. This means that the same syntax you use in style sheets to select elements can be used to attach JavaScript behaviors to elements. Once the elements have been selected, the code can modify them, remove them, or insert new elements within them. Modifying these elements could be as simple as adding or removing a CSS style, or changing the contents of the element. The remainder of this chapter focuses on how you can select elements and modify them, and how you can add new HTML elements to the page rather than changing the behavior of existing elements.

Selecting and Manipulating Existing HTML Elements

Many scenarios for interactive web applications only require client-side languages such as CSS and JavaScript to modify existing elements. Modification usually involves adding, removing, or updating the attributes and style classes applied to elements. In some cases, CSS alone may be capable of performing the required changes, such as changing the style of hyperlink elements as the mouse pointer passes over them. In other cases, JavaScript code is required to manipulate the elements directly.

Before you can perform actions on elements, you must specify how the CSS or JavaScript will select them. You can select one or more elements, as described in the following section, and then use a range of techniques to manipulate the elements. These techniques are described in "Modifying Existing Elements," later in this chapter.

SELECTING ELEMENTS

There are several ways you can use selectors within an application to select elements you want to modify. Each approach has its own benefits and drawbacks:

- **Using data- attributes**. **data-** attributes (pronounced "data dash" attributes) provide a simple and efficient way to select elements based on the presence and value of attributes whose name starts with "**data-**". jQuery provides the **data** method for working with **data-** attributes, as you will see in the next section of this chapter. This is the preferred approach for most element selection scenarios.

- **Using the id attribute**. This works well when there is a single element in the DOM with the specified value for its **id** attribute. However, this approach often causes jQuery to search the entire DOM to find the element, which can have significant impact on the client-side performance of your application. In addition, using the **id** as a selector is not a valid approach when you must support multiple elements on the page that may have the same **id** attribute values.

- **Using element name selectors**. This is a useful technique when you want to apply an action to all elements of a specific type (for example, all of the **<tr>** elements in a table). However, it can cause problems because it is easy to select more elements than intended if the element occurs elsewhere in the page. It also means that changing the type of elements in the HTML in the future will require changes to the JavaScript code.

- **Using class name selectors**. This is a useful technique for selecting multiple elements across the element hierarchy, but (as described in the introduction to this chapter) it can cause confusion between class names used for applying CSS styles and class names used as selectors to apply JavaScript behavior. It can also lead to subtle bugs when the JavaScript adds and removes classes on elements; suddenly the class name you use to find an element is no longer there.

- **Using relative location**. You can select one or more elements by relative position within the DOM with respect to a known element. For example, you might select all of the elements that are the children of a target element. This can be an efficient way to locate elements because it is usually much faster than searching from the root element of the DOM. It can be combined with the previous selection methods. However, selectors that rely on this approach are fragile because they depend on the specific hierarchy of the HTML structure.

    > **Note:** *All of these selection methods run the risk of impacting client-side performance. It is important to ensure that you provide additional context with the selectors to prevent searching the entire DOM. See "Using Context" below for more information.*

For more information on jQuery selectors, see "jQuery Selectors" in the "Further Reading" section of this chapter.

It is important to note that your HTML structure becomes an unofficial contract between the server and the client. The JavaScript code will expect elements with specific **id**s to exist as well as expecting the presence of certain **data-** attributes. The more assumptions that the JavaScript makes about the HTML, the more fragile the application will become.

Writing unit tests to verify that the HTML provides the expected metadata can save significant effort if changes to the HTML structure are required at a later time. For more information on how the server can provide the correct initial HTML to the client, see "Providing HTML Structure" in Chapter 11, "Server-Side Implementation."

Using Context

One of the ways to achieve maximum performance when selecting elements is to specify a context to search within. This context allows searches based on a known and referenced element. There are two ways to provide this context. The jQuery method can take a second parameter, a known element, to scope the search through the DOM. Alternatively, the **find** method of an element can be used to obtain a collection of all or specific child elements. Both techniques are shown here.

```JavaScript
// Example: select the child element(s) with id="dashboard-link"
// Both of the following lines return the same elements.
var myLinkElements =$('#dashboard-link', someKnownElement);
var myLinkElementsByFind = someKnownElement.find('#dashboard-link');
```

Similar methods that you can use to select elements based on their relative position include **next**, **nextAll**, **prev**, **prevAll**, **siblings**, **closest**, and **parent**. You can use this approach to find a collection of elements, and then apply other selection techniques on the collection to maximize efficiency.

Using Data- Attributes

HTML5 provides **data-** attributes as a mechanism for applying metadata to elements. It turns out that this metadata is also useful when selecting elements. The browser does not use **data-** attributes when rendering the page. This means that they can be used to select elements independently of the element hierarchy and styling.

In addition, **data-** attributes can store other arbitrary metadata, such as the state of a UI element, because they are merely attributes on the element. For example, the attribute **data-action="reminders"** can represent the **action="reminders"** name/value pair.

In Mileage Stats, **data-** attributes are used to provide the client with useful information. The client will make Ajax requests to the server to load and save data, so the client must know the URLs corresponding to the endpoints for those data requests. Rather than hard-coding the URLs within the client-side script, the server can provide the URLs in the HTML by using **data-** attributes, and the code can extract this value when it needs to make a request to the server. This means that the code will continue to work if the URLs change, such as when changing the routing in a Model-View-Controller (MVC) application or when moving the application to a different virtual directory on the server.

The following code shows the CSHTML code that Mileage Stats uses to render the vehicle list on the dashboard. Both the **id** attribute and CSS class are set so that they can be used for styling the vehicle list with CSS. There are also two **data-** attributes that contain URL metadata for use within the JavaScript that controls the behavior of the vehicle list.

```
CSHTML
<!-- Contained in_VehicleList.cshtml -->
<div id="vehicles" class="article @compactClass"
    data-list-url="@Url.Action("JsonList","Vehicle")"
    data-sort-url="@Url.Action("UpdateSortOrder", "Vehicle")">
...
</div>
```

The server-side code shown above creates the following HTML in the page sent to the client.

```
HTML
<!-- result of _VehicleList.cshtml -->
<div id="vehicles" class="article"
    data-list-url="/Vehicle/JsonList"
    data-sort-url="/Vehicle/UpdateSortOrder">
...
</div>
```

> **Note:** *Only the first hyphen in the attribute name is significant. Everything in the attribute name after the first hyphen is treated as a simple string value. For example,* **data-list-url="/Vehicle/JsonList"** *is a* **data-** *attribute containing the metadata* **list-url="/Vehicle/JsonList".**

To select all of the elements that carry the **data-list-url** attribute shown in the previous HTML listing, you could use the following JavaScript code.

```JavaScript
// Example: select the element(s) with a data-list-url attribute
var myVehicleElement = myVehicleList.find('[data-list-url]');
```

The jQuery library also supports **data-** attributes directly through the **data** method, which can get and set multiple values on the attribute. The following example shows how you can get the value of the metadata (the value of the name/value pair) from a referenced element using the **data** method. Note that when using jQuery's **data** method, the "**data-**" part is omitted and just the remainder of the attribute name is used.

```JavaScript
// Example: get the value of a data-list-url attribute
var myUrl = myVehicleElement.data('list-url');
```

Because **data-** attributes are ideal for selecting elements, and for getting or setting data associated with those elements in the DOM, you should use them wherever possible. If your designer changes the layout and style information in the HTML, your JavaScript won't break. In addition, **data-** attributes allow the server to easily provide the client with useful data without the client having to parse UI-specific HTML. Use **data-** attributes wherever it is appropriate to specify metadata in the server-generated HTML or with JavaScript on the client.

Keep in mind that the HTML represents the logical structure of the UI, not the visible layout and style. The use of **data-** attributes provides you with a mechanism for annotating the structure and adding metadata without using style class names or element identifiers.

MODIFYING EXISTING ELEMENTS

After you select your target element or set of elements, you can modify them as required. The following sections provide some examples of scenarios and solutions for modifying existing elements within the HTML structure of the page.

Showing and Hiding Content

When the user first navigates to your application, the server will return the HTML for the page. This HTML includes the locations (URLs) for the resources such as images, scripts, and HTML fragments that the browser will download as secondary requests in order to create the complete page. However, there will be a noticeable delay as the content and scripts are downloaded, the HTML and CSS is parsed, and any startup scripts run. While usually short, this delay can affect the user experience, especially if there are a large number of secondary requests for scripts, images, or other assets, or if the user is on a slow Internet connection.

One solution is to include in the HTML sent from the server a progress indicator that shows that the application is loading. Then, once the rest of the content is available, the application can use JavaScript to change the UI by hiding the progress indicator and replacing it with the desired HTML (which was also part of the server response, but hidden using CSS styles). The code needs only to change the CSS styles applied to the relevant elements. This technique means that the user perceives a reduced waiting time and better responsiveness, even though there is no actual increase in performance.

> **Note:** *Many applications require JavaScript. One approach to communicating this requirement to the user is to include a notice in the initial HTML that the site requires JavaScript. The first action the application script takes is to hide the notice, so that it remains visible only when the client does not support JavaScript. A more common approach is to require that the application run on a recent browser and check that features such as JavaScript are enabled. This is often easier for users, who are immediately aware that the application requires JavaScript or other features, and it simplifies the work of technical support teams who do not encounter errors caused by the use of older browsers.*

Updating Element Attributes

Interactivity in the page can be implemented using JavaScript code that runs in response to user actions, or when events such as completion of page load occur. Typically, the HTML sent from the server will contain all of the structure (the HTML element hierarchy) required to render the page. Unless you actually need to build all or part of the UI dynamically on the client, having the initial structure in place is much faster than creating the same structure in the script each time. However, you may need to modify the HTML elements after the page has loaded in the browser.

For example, the Mileage Stats main page contains a header with links to the dashboard and chart views (The HTML is shown here with some content removed for clarity).

HTML
```html
<!-- Rendered from _Layout.cshtml -->
<div class="nav">
  <span id="welcome">Welcome <span data-display-name>Sample User</span></span>
    [ <a href="/Dashboard" id="dashboard-link">Dashboard</a>
    | <a href="/Chart/List" id="charts-link">Charts</a>
    ...
</div>
```

These hyperlinks must be updated when the page loads to include in the URL any subfolder name (if the application is installed on the server in a subfolder of the default website). If this is not done, the links will not work correctly. When the page load is complete, the following JavaScript runs in the browser to update the **href** attributes of these hyperlink elements to include the correct URL.

JavaScript
```javascript
// Contained in mstats.header.js
_adjustNavigation: function () {
    var state = $.bbq.getState() || { },
        url = this.element.data('url'),
```

```
        newUrlBase = mstats.getRelativeEndpointUrl(url);

    state.layout = 'dashboard';
    this.element.find('#dashboard-link')
        .attr('href', $.param.fragment(newUrlBase, state));

    state.layout = 'charts';
    this.element.find('#charts-link')
        .attr('href', $.param.fragment(newUrlBase, state));
},
```

The first part of this code uses the jQuery Back Button and Query (BBQ) plug-in to create a **state** object and get the actual base URL of the page. This value is discovered on the server and can be obtained from the **getRelativeEndpointUrl** method of the global **mstats** object defined in the JavaScript of the page. Chapter 9, "Navigation," discusses in more detail the BBQ plug-in, the use of a **state** object, and how this section of code works.

After the base URL has been established, the code changes the name/value pair named **layout** within the **state** object instance so that it specifies the correct layout style (**dashboard** or **charts**) for each hyperlink. It then uses the **find** method to select the appropriate hyperlink element based on the value of its **id** attribute, and sets the value of the **href** parameter to the correct URL. This URL is a combination of the base URL of the application and the relevant **layout** property held in the **state** object instance.

Mileage Stats uses **data-** attributes both to locate elements and to store data values in the DOM. As another example, the **_bindNavigation** method of the fill ups widget (part of which is shown below) relies on the presence of a **data-action** attribute to locate navigation buttons. The method also uses the **data-action** and **data-fillup-id** attributes to determine which action to take and which fill up to target.

JavaScript
```
// Contained in mstats.fillups.js
_bindNavigation: function () {
    var that = this;
    this.element.delegate('[data-action]', 'click.' + this.name, function (event) {
        if ($(this).data('action') === 'select-fillup') {
            that._setOption('selectedFillupId', $(this).data('fillup-id'));
            event.preventDefault();
        }
    });
},
```

The above sample uses a specific type of jQuery selector, named the "Has Attribute" selector, which simplifies the selection of elements having a specific attribute. For more information on this type of selector, see "jQuery Selectors" in the "Further Reading" section of this chapter.

Generating and Loading New HTML in a Page

In the previous section, you saw how you can select HTML elements and manipulate them. This obviously requires existing elements to work with. However, you will often need to create new elements and content within the existing HTML structure. There are several ways to generate new HTML and modify the existing HTML structure on the client. Typical techniques, which are discussed in this chapter, are:

- Generating the HTML structure dynamically using JavaScript and jQuery
- Retrieving HTML fragments from the server and injecting them into the page
- Using templates both to retrieve and to generate the HTML structure to insert into the page

GENERATING HTML DYNAMICALLY WITH JAVASCRIPT AND JQUERY

When developing a hybrid or SPI application, you often need to modify the existing page by inserting into it fragments of new HTML. You can, of course, remove elements from the page as well, but it is usually easier to change the CSS styles that control visibility.

Mileage Stats generates and inserts fragments of HTML into its pages in several places. For example, it uses JavaScript to add new elements to the page structure as the user navigates through the application. The following code (it is part of the info pane widget) creates the HTML structure that displays a vehicle's details.

```JavaScript
// Contained in mstats.info-pane.js
_setupDetailsPane: function () {
    var elem = this.element,
        options = this.options;

    if (!elem.find('#details-pane').length) {
        elem.find('div:first')
            .append('<div id="details-pane" class="tab opened section" />');
    }
    this.vehicleDetails = elem.find('#details-pane').vehicleDetails({
        // options for the widget
    });
},
```

This code uses the **find** method to check if the Details pane is already present in the structure. If it does not exist, the code locates the first **div** element within the current context and uses the **append** method to insert a new **div** element with **id="details-pane"** into the page.

Generally, the amount of HTML generated with script should be small. Script that creates large amounts of HTML is difficult to read and can easily create a structure that is invalid because of syntax errors in the code. If you need to generate a large amount of HTML, you should reevaluate the design or consider using one of the other methods described in this section to retrieve or generate the HTML you require.

RETRIEVING HTML FRAGMENTS FROM THE SERVER

In some situations, it may make sense to retrieve an HTML fragment from another source (for example, a URL on the web server) and inject it directly into the page, perhaps after manipulating it, rather than dynamically generating the content on the client. For example, it may make sense to reuse an HTML form generated on the server and dynamically embed it in a web page, rather than generating the entire form and its contents with JavaScript. This approach can simplify the client-side code by moving some of the complexity to the server.

Typically, you will use Ajax methods, including the **load** method of existing elements, to load the new content asynchronously, directly into the target element. An alternative is to retrieve the new content in the background, perhaps in a hidden element or as a string variable, and then insert it into the page at the appropriate location using JavaScript and jQuery. The final version of Mileage Stats does not retrieve HTML fragments from the server. However, this technique was investigated during development.

Content Retrieval Decisions in Mileage Stats

Now that we've arrived at the topic of using HTML fragments and templates, let's take a moment to talk about the design process our team followed while looking for the optimal solution. Since we knew that we wanted to support both a full-page reload and a hybrid experience for most of the features in Mileage Stats, we realized that we needed to generate HTML on the server as well as manipulate the HTML on the client. Our goal was to reuse as much HTML as possible, following the Don't Repeat Yourself (DRY) principle. Unfortunately, this was more difficult than expected. The markup necessary for the full-page reload scenarios was rendered as large chunks of HTML combined with data, while the markup needed for the SPI scenarios was focused and generally independent of the data.

Our strategy was to break the server-side HTML views into small, granular, partial views (small fragments of the UI). The client-side code could request the partial views using an Ajax call, and use the result to replace a small portion of the rendered UI. When we needed to reload a full page, the server could assemble the requested page from the granular partial views and send the complete page to the client. In this way, none of the HTML would be duplicated. We envisioned the final result as a set of composable blocks that could be used to build the UI structure for both scenarios.

Once we began implementing this strategy, we found that the code quickly became very complicated. Both the controller and the view code became intertwined and confusing. Many conditional blocks were required to share the numerous partial views between the server-side and client-side code.

Back on the client side, widgets were given URLs to request the partial views they needed. This had a number of drawbacks. First, it increased the surface area of the server by exposing the additional endpoints the widgets needed to request the necessary HTML fragments. Second, the number of Ajax calls made by the client increased because each widget needed to retrieve both the required data and the partial views. The increase in calls also created additional failure points and made the error handling code for the widgets more complex.

As an alternative, we had considered using a client-side templating engine such as the jQuery Templates plug-in. That would have involved using the server-generated HTML for the full-page reload experience, and creating a second set of client HTML templates for use only on the client. We initially decided against this approach because we thought that we would be duplicating all of the HTML code that was generated on the server.

However, after working through the difficulties of managing the small partial views, we decided that it would actually be easier to maintain the application if we used two methods to generate the HTML—one on the server side and one on the client side—so we chose to rewrite the application using the jQuery Template plug-in. Ensuring that the HTML that was duplicated in both the server and client code remained synchronized was a bit of a challenge. However, we were able to mitigate this issue through developer diligence when changing HTML or HTML templates, through test automation, and through either paired programming or code reviews (a practice we already followed to mitigate other risks). There were also several cases where we intentionally generated different HTML on the client than we generated on the server in order to accommodate the different UIs for the JavaScript-enabled experience and the non-JavaScript experience. These situations were handled on a case-by-case basis and communicated to the entire team.

USING TEMPLATES TO RETRIEVE AND GENERATE HTML

As mentioned in the previous section, another option for generating HTML is to use HTML templates. The idea behind templates is fairly simple: given a set of data and a template with placeholders for the data, you merge the HTML in the template with the data to generate an HTML fragment that can be inserted into the DOM. Templates provide the opportunity for generating HTML dynamically without the need for a lot of JavaScript code. This approach also allows you to generate the HTML using standard design tools, and to insert the placeholders for the data afterwards.

There are a number of HTML templating engines that can be used. As you saw, Mileage Stats uses the jQuery Templates plug-in because it was a natural fit after the team decided to use jQuery and jQuery UI.

Anatomy of a jQuery Template

jQuery templates consist of HTML and placeholders for data. By convention, jQuery templates usually reside in a **script** element that has a unique value for its **id** attribute, and a **type** attribute set to **type="text/x-jquery-tmpl"**. The template **script** element can be located within any HTML element in the structure; it does not have to be located where the result will be displayed.

The **id** attribute allows the jQuery template plug-in to locate the template. The **type** attribute is the Internet media type (also known as the MIME Type or Content Type), and the value shown above is unknown to browsers. When the browser parses the HTML, it will not parse the content of any section with the unknown type, which is the desired result.

The following example shows part of the template used in Mileage Stats to generate the Statistics panel located on the Dashboard screen. The **${...}** expression is a placeholder within the template that the jQuery Template plug-in uses to render a JavaScript value or expression when the data is applied to the template. The generated HTML fragment will contain several values, including the value of the **AverageFuelEfficiency** property of the data applied to the template. Only the section containing the first of these placeholders is shown in this listing.

JavaScript
```
// Contained in _TemplateFleetStatistics.cshtml
<script id="fleet-statistics-template" type="text/x-jquery-tmpl">
  <h1>Summary Statistics</h1>
  <div class="statistic mile-per-gallon">
      ${mstats.makeMPGDisplay(AverageFuelEfficiency)}<span
    class="units">mpg</span></div>
  ...
</script>
```

The template in this example runs other JavaScript code to create a string representing the value that is inserted into the placeholder. It calls the **mstats.makeMPGDisplay** method, which formats the **AverageFuelEfficiency** value of the original data to ensure that it displays correctly.

The example below shows the **_applyTemplate** method, which uses the previous template to generate an HTML fragment, and places this fragment in the element with the id of **statistics-content**.

JavaScript
```
// Contained in mstats.statistics.js
_applyTemplate: function (data) {
    var options = this.options,
        $template = $(options.templateId);
    ...

    this.element.find('#statistics-content')
        .html($template.tmpl(data));
}
```

When the user runs the application, the following HTML is generated:

HTML
```
// Run-time HTML
<div id="statistics-content">
  <h1>Summary Statistics</h1>
  <div class="statistic mile-per-gallon">24<span
    class="units">mpg</span></div>
  ...
</div>
```

For more information on the jQuery Template plug-in and authoring templates, see "jQuery Templates" in the "Further Reading" section.

Server-Side Rendering and jQuery Templates

jQuery Templates are a powerful feature of the jQuery library. Developers can use their chosen server-side rendering engine to dynamically create or inject values into jQuery templates on the server instead of, or in addition to, having the templates combined with data on the client. This dynamic server-side rendering of the template provides many additional options when developing your application.

In one respect, the approach of populating a template on the server instead of on the client resembles the approach described earlier of retrieving HTML fragments that contain the final HTML for display. There is no requirement to merge the data and template on the client. However, there is no reason why you cannot combine both approaches. Your server code could populate some of the dynamic content in the template, but leave other placeholders in the content that will be populated by merging the template with data on the client.

Mileage Stats uses server-side code to generate jQuery templates in several places. For example, templates were used in cases where the URLs for buttons and links in the rendered page depended on where the application was deployed. For example, if the application is deployed in a subfolder instead of in the root of the website on the server, the URL must include the folder name.

Mileage Stats jQuery templates are in the Views\Shared folder of the application and use the "_TemplateNAME.cshtml" naming convention so that they will be processed by the Razor rendering engine. This allows the server-side code to inject values into the template HTML before it is sent to the client. For example, the **@Url.Action** view helper method can render the correct URL of the **add** action of the **vehicle** controller, whether or not the application is deployed in a subfolder on the server, as shown here.

CSHTML
```
<-- Contained in _TemplateVehicleList.cshtml -->
<script id="mstats-add-vehicle-button-template" type="text/x-jquery-tmpl">
  <div class="framed command section">
    <div>
      <a data-action="vehicle-add-selected"
         href="@Url.Action("add", "vehicle")">+ Add Vehicle</a>
    </div>
  </div>
</script>
```

The **_TemplateVehicleList** template shown above is processed by the Razor rendering engine using the **@Html.Partial** view helper method in _Layout.cshtml, as shown below.

CSHTML
```
<!-- Contained in _Layout.cshtml -->
@Html.Partial("_TemplateVehicleList");
```

The HTML fragment shown below is the rendered **_TemplateVehicleList** template when the web application is deployed to the root web site on the server.

HTML

```
<!-- Rendered to the browser at runtime -->
<script id="mstats-add-vehicle-button-template" type="text/x-jquery-tmpl">
  <div class="framed command section">
    <div>
      <a data-action="vehicle-add-selected"
         href="/vehicle/add">+ Add Vehicle</a>
    </div>
  </div>
</script>
```

If, instead, the web application is deployed to the **MileageStats** folder in the root website, the rendered HTML will be the code shown below. You can see the folder name in the value of the **href** attribute.

HTML

```
<!-- Rendered to the browser at runtime -->
<script id="mstats-add-vehicle-button-template" type="text/x-jquery-tmpl">
  <div class="framed command section">
    <div>
      <a data-action="vehicle-add-selected"
         href="/MileageStats/vehicle/add">+ Add Vehicle</a>
    </div>
  </div>
</script>
```

Now the template can be used within the client application, and will provide the correct URLs for the current deployment on the web server.

Summary

There are three key technologies that work together in the browser to enable interactive applications: HTML, CSS, and JavaScript. HTML specifies the structure of the elements available within the UI, CSS controls the styling and positioning of those elements, and JavaScript allows the elements to respond to user gestures and other events such as timers and animations.

Within an application, there is often a requirement to manipulate the HTML that generates the page the user sees, and there are a number of options for selecting the HTML elements whose appearance or behavior you wish to change. Of these, the use of relative position provides the best performance, while using **data-** attributes can significantly help with both the selection of HTML elements and the transmission of metadata to the client code. **Data-** attributes also help to ensure separation between the HTML and the metadata the application requires.

Finally, you saw how you can create new HTML structure within a page by using JavaScript and jQuery, by retrieving fragments of HTML from the server, or by using jQuery Templates on the client to combine data retrieved from the server with HTML included in the templates.

Further Reading

jQuery Home Page: http://jquery.com

jQuery Browser Compatibility: http://docs.jquery.com/Browser_Compatibility

jQuery Selectors: http://api.jquery.com/category/selectors

jQuery Templates: http://api.jquery.com/category/plugins/templates

For more information on how the server can provide the correct initial HTML to the client, see "Providing HTML Structure" in Chapter 11, "Server-Side Implementation."

For more detail on the BBQ plug-in and the use of a **state** object, see Chapter 9, "Navigation."

To access web resources more easily, see the online version of the bibliography on MSDN: http://msdn.microsoft.com/en-us/library/hh404094.aspx.

8   Communication

Introduction

In a client-side application composed of discrete objects, many of those objects need to communicate with one another. You have a few options when deciding how they do this. Generally, your options are direct method invocation, and an indirect communication mechanism such as events. These options give you the ability to control the amount of complexity applied to the object's interface and implementation, and allow you to control the level of coupling the objects have with each other. For example, an object that invokes a method on another object must have a direct reference to that object. If you chose to implement a form of events, the objects may either have a direct dependency or use a broker object to enable them to communicate in a loosely coupled manner. This broker prevents the objects from needing to have direct knowledge of each other.

Comparison between direct and loosely coupled communication

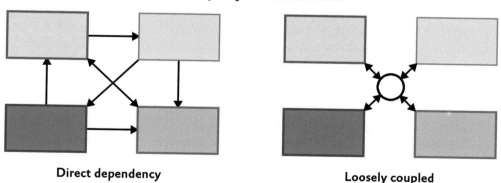

Direct dependency   Loosely coupled

Most applications will use more than one form of communication between their objects because there are advantages and disadvantages to each option. Your responsibility is to apply an appropriate balance based on the application.

In this chapter you will learn:
- How to implement direct method invocation between widgets.
- The advantages and disadvantages of direct method invocation.
- How to implement event triggering and handling between widgets.
- How to control dependencies between the objects triggering events and those handling them.
- When using the Publish/Subscribe (pub/sub) pattern is appropriate.
- How to use pub/sub to manage multiple handlers and reduce coupling.
- How the Mileage Stats Reference Implementation (Mileage Stats) implements these options and how the team chose various communication options.

Direct Method Invocation

When a widget needs to communicate with another widget and no other objects are interested in the communication, the calling widget can use direct method invocation. This option is the easiest to understand, the easiest to implement, and the easiest to follow when tracing code paths. You could use this option for all communication, but if your application has many objects and many calls between those objects, this approach will force the objects to have more methods on their interface than the loosely-coupled options require and it can greatly increase the coupling between those objects.

GETTING A WIDGET REFERENCE

Many of the JavaScript objects in Mileage Stats are implemented as jQuery UI Widgets, which have a specific way to expose public methods. After a widget has exposed a method, the calling widget needs a reference to it before it can invoke the method. One option would be for the calling widget to know how to get a reference to the widget it needs to call. The widget pseudo selector is a good way to do this without having to know the exact elements the widget is attached to. This approach to getting a widget reference requires the calling widget to know that it is invoking the method on a specific widget by name. Another option is to have the references passed in as part of the **options** object. This allows the calling widget to invoke the method without having to know the name of the widget it is calling. For information on how to expose and invoke methods on widgets, see "**Public Methods**" in Chapter 3, "jQuery UI Widgets." For more information on the widget pseudo selector see "Using the Pseudo Selector" in Chapter 3, "jQuery UI Widgets."

METHOD INVOCATION IN MILEAGE STATS

In the following example, an object reference called **charts** is captured when the **charts** widget is created. This reference is then passed as the value to the **charts** option when initializing the **layoutManager** widget.

```
JavaScript
// Contained in mileagestats.js
charts = $('#main-chart').charts({
    sendRequest: mstats.dataManager.sendRequest,
    invalidateData: mstats.dataManager.resetData
});

$('body').layoutManager({
    subscribe: mstats.pubsub.subscribe,
    pinnedSite: mstats.pinnedSite,
    charts: charts,
    header: header,
    infoPane: infoPane,
    summaryPane: summaryPane,
    vehicleList: vehicleList
});
```

The layout manager uses this reference to invoke methods on the **charts** widget. For example, when the layout manager is coordinating the transition to the charts layout, it calls the chart's **moveOnScreenFromRight** method.

```
JavaScript
// Contained in mstats.layout-manager.js
_goToChartsLayout: function() {
    this._summaryPane('moveOffScreen');
    this._vehicleList('moveOffScreen');
    this._infoPane('moveOffScreenToRight');
    this._charts('moveOnScreenFromRight');
},
```

You probably noticed that the method calls in **_goToChartsLayout** are not using the calling convention described in the see "Public Methods" section in Chapter 3, "jQuery UI Widgets."

A Helper for Method Invocation

Rather than using **this.options.widgetName.widgetName('methodName')**, many of the calls in Mileage Stats, and particularly in the previous code example, have been simplified to **this._widgetName('methodName')**. Mileage Stats uses a helper for method invocation to improve readability. This isn't necessary; the long form works fine, but the helper method does take advantage of the dynamic nature of JavaScript and can make the code more readable and less repetitive. The **setupWidgetInvocationMethods** function dynamically creates an underscore-prefixed method on the **host** argument for each widget whose name is passed in the **widgetNames** argument. The **options** argument tells the helper function where to find the implementation of the widget functions.

```javascript
// Contained in mstats.utils.js
function buildFunction(widget, options) {
    var context = options[widget],
        fn;

    if(!context) {
        mstats.log('Attempted to create a helper for ' +
            widget + ' but the widget was not found in the options.');
        return;
    }

    fn = context[widget];
    return function() {
        var result = fn.apply(context, arguments);
        return result;
    };
}

mstats.setupWidgetInvocationMethods = function(host, options, widgetNames) {
    var i,
        widgetName;

    for (i = widgetNames.length - 1; i >= 0; i -= 1) {
        widgetName = widgetNames[i];
        host["_" + widgetName] = buildFunction(widgetName, options);
    }
};
```

The **setupWidgetInvocationMethods** function is called when the layout manager is first created. This function call dynamically creates new methods called **_charts**, **_header**, **_infoPane**, **_summaryPane**, and **_vehicleList** that will make invoking methods on those widgets much easier, as you can see in the **_goToChartsLayout** method above.

```javascript
// Contained in mstats.layout-manager.js
_create: function() {
    ...
    // add on helper methods for invoking public methods on widgets
    mstats.setupWidgetInvocationMethods(this, this.options,
        ['charts', 'header', 'infoPane', 'summaryPane', 'vehicleList']);
    ...
},
```

In addition to the layout manager, the above helper method is also used in the **_create** method of the info pane, summary, and vehicle details widgets.

Direct method invocation is useful when an object must invoke a method on another object. However, depending on the direction of the method call, it may result in incorrect dependencies. For example, in the case of a widget that manages other widgets in a parent/child relationship, the child widgets should not have knowledge of their parent. This is where events can be helpful.

Raising and Handling Events

Events allow an object to communicate with other objects without a direct reference to them. Rather than having to know how to resolve the reference to the receiver or how to invoke a specific method, event handlers only need to know the name of the event and any data sent with it. Therefore, using an event is more appropriate than invoking a method when a child widget needs to communicate with its parent. It's acceptable for a parent in a hierarchy to know about its children, but not the other way around. When a child widget knows too much about its parent, it makes it difficult or impossible to relocate the widget and use it from inside a different parent.

In Mileage Stats, the **registration** widget is created by and contained within the **summary** widget, which means that there is a parent/child relationship. When a user registers with the Mileage Stats application, the **registration** widget raises an event through its **displayNameChanged** event callback. The **summary** widget handles this event by setting the **displayNameChanged** option on the **registration** widget to the handler, which sets an option on the **header** widget.

```JavaScript
// Contained in mstats.summary.js
_setupRegistrationWidget: function () {
    var that = this,
        elem = this.element.find('#registration');

    this.registration = elem.registration({
        dataUrl: elem.data('url'),
        publish: this.options.publish,
        sendRequest: this.options.sendRequest,
        displayNameChanged: function (event, args) {
            that._header('option', 'displayName', args.displayName);
        }
    });
},
```

When the user successfully registers, the **registration** widget raises the **display NameChanged** event using the **_trigger** method. The **_trigger** method is available on the base jQuery UI Widget and accepts three arguments:

- The name of the event to trigger.
- The original event if it originated from a DOM event such as **click**.
- The data to be sent to the event handler.

```javascript
JavaScript
// Contained in mstats.registration.js (in the saveProfile method)
this.options.sendRequest({
    url: this.options.dataUrl,
    data: formData,
    cache: false,
    success: function () {
        that._startHidingWidget();
        that._showSavedMessage();
        // we update the username after successfully the updating the profile
        that._trigger('displayNameChanged', null,
            { displayName: formData.DisplayName } );
    },
    error: function () {
        that._showSavingErrorMessage();
    }
});
```

Using events is a powerful way to reduce coupling without sacrificing communication between widgets. For more details on raising and handling events, see "Events" in Chapter 3, "jQuery UI Widgets."

Using options to expose the callback and wire up the handler reduces the coupling between the sender and receiver, but this requires that some other code, usually the code that creates the widgets, to perform the connections, as you can see in the **_setup RegistrationWidget** method above. An alternative to wiring up event handlers is to use the Publish/Subscribe pattern, which employs a broker to manage these connections.

Publishing and Subscribing

A common strategy for reducing the coupling between objects is for those objects to use an intermediary object, referred to as a broker, rather than communicating directly with each of their dependencies. The Publish/Subscribe pattern (commonly referred to as pub/sub) applies this strategy. The pattern provides a way for objects to communicate without needing a reference to the source or the destination of the messages. Rather, the objects have references to the pub/sub implementation and know how to use it based on their needs.

In its most general form, the Publish/Subscribe pattern identifies *publishers, topics,* and *subscribers.* Publishers and subscribers are software components that need to communicate with each other. *Topics* represent the contract between the sender and receiver and are made up of a name and an optional message. The following figure illustrates the Publish/Subscribe pattern.

The Publish/Subscribe pattern

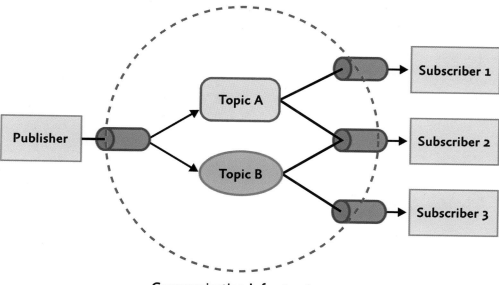

Communication Infrastructure

The pattern has two phases. The first phase is the subscription phase. Objects sign up to be notified when information about particular topics becomes available. For example, in the figure, Subscriber 2 is subscribed to messages about Topic A and Topic B, while Subscriber 1 is subscribed only to Topic A. The second phase is the publication phase, when publishers provide information about topics. For example, in the figure, the Publisher creates messages about Topic A and Topic B.

Each implementation of the Publish/Subscribe pattern provides the communications infrastructure that receives and delivers messages. However, the details of how messages are routed between publishers and subscribers can differ between implementations. For example, it is possible that messages can be delivered synchronously or asynchronously, depending on the situation.

PUB/SUB IN MILEAGE STATS

Mileage Stats uses a pub/sub JavaScript object to broker communication between the objects and widgets that make up the client-side application. Global events are events that are not constrained to an isolated part of the application. These events may cause multiple widgets to update their data and UI, such as when a vehicle is deleted or a reminder is fulfilled. Publishers and subscribers do not communicate directly with each other. Instead, widgets subscribe using callback functions for relevant topics. The widgets managing UI elements publish topics in response to lower-level DOM events caused by user actions.

The pubsub Object

The Mileage Stats' **pubsub** interface provides **publish**, **subscribe**, and **unsubscribe** methods. Each method requires an event name. These events are defined in mstats.events.js as objects that behave like string constants. The following code shows the interface of the **pubsub** object.

```JavaScript
// Contained in mstats.pubsub.js
mstats.pubsub = (function () {
    var queue = [],
        that = {};
    that.publish = function (eventName, data) { ... };
    that.subscribe = function (eventName, callback, context) { ... };
    that.unsubscribe = function (eventName, callback, context) { ... };
    return that;
}();
```

The mechanism for creating the **pubsub** object uses an immediate function which executes as soon as its definition is parsed. As a result, the **pubsub** object is available simply by adding the mstats.pubsub.js file to the page.

The **subscribe** method stores event subscriptions, which are comprised of a callback in the form of a function and a context in the form of an object. More than one subscription is possible for a single event name. Here is the code.

```JavaScript
// Contained in mstats.pubsub.js
/**
 * @param {string} eventName  The name of the event to publish
 *                            Uses a slash notation for consistency
 * @param {function} callback The function to be called when the
 *                            event is published.
 * @param {object} context    The context to execute the callback
 */
that.subscribe = function (eventName, callback, context) {
    if (!queue[eventName]) {
        queue[eventName] = [];
    }
    queue[eventName].push({
        callback: callback,
        context: context
    });
};
```

The **subscribe** method modifies the **queue** variable. It adds a new array element for the name that is passed as the **eventName** argument if that element does not already exist. Then, it adds a new object to that array with the **callback** and **context** fields. These fields store the function to be invoked when the event is published, and the context that function should execute within.

JavaScript allows you to use the context of one object to call an instance method of a different object. This is what happens with the context value that is provided to the **subscribe** method. The callback method will be invoked with the given context.

The **publish** method invokes the registered callback for a given **eventName**. The **publish** method executes all callbacks that are associated with **eventName** by using the context that was provided in the subscription.

JavaScript

```
// Contained in mstats.pubsub.js
/**
 * @param {string} eventName  The name of the event to publish
 *                            Uses a slash notation for consistency
 * @param {object} data       Any data to be passed to the event
 *                            handler. Custom to the event.
 */
that.publish = function (eventName, data) {
    var context, intervalId, idx = 0;
    if (queue[eventName]) {
        intervalId = setInterval(function () {
            if (queue[eventName][idx]) {
                context = queue[eventName][idx].context || this;
                queue[eventName][idx].callback.call(context, data);
                idx += 1;
            } else {
                clearInterval(intervalId);
            }
        }, 0);
    }
};
```

The code successively invokes each function that is stored in the **queue** array. It uses the **setInterval** function with a timeout of 0 milliseconds to execute the callbacks asynchronously. This allows each subscriber callback to be invoked before the previous callback finishes. This also means callbacks can be invoked before other callbacks have finished. A consequence of asynchronicity is that you cannot predict the order in which callbacks are invoked or finish.

In Mileage Stats, only the unit tests take advantage of the **unsubscribe** method. However, other applications may need to allow the dynamic subscription and unsubscription of events.

An Example of Subscribing and Publishing

When a user fulfills a reminder, several areas of the UI need to refresh their own lists of reminders. The application uses the **mstats.events.vehicle.reminders.fulfilled** event name (this is the topic) to communicate the fact that a reminder was fulfilled. This variable is initialized with the value "reminders/fulfilled" in the mstats.events.js file.

The Mileage Stats layout manager widget is a coordinating widget. It subscribes to the **mstats.events.vehicle.reminders.fulfilled** event when it is created. Whenever this event is published, the registered callback refreshes each of the layout manager's child widgets. The following code shows how the subscription is implemented, and what happens during the callback.

JavaScript

```javascript
// Contained in mstats.layout-manager.js
_subscribeToGlobalEvents: function () {
    var state = {},
        that = this;

    ...

    this.options.subscribe(mstats.events.vehicle.reminders.fulfilled,
        function() {
            // we need to refresh the summary reminders, fleet statistics,
            // details pane, reminders pane, charts, and jump list
            that._summaryPane('requeryStatistics');
            that._summaryPane('requeryReminders');
            that._infoPane('requeryVehicleDetails');
            that._infoPane('requeryReminders');
            that._charts('requeryData');
            that.options.pinnedSite.requeryJumpList();
        }, this);
},
```

When the user fulfills a reminder, the **reminders** widget uses the **pubsub** object to publish the event. By passing the **subscribe** method into the layout manager as an option, the layout manager is able to participate in pub/sub without having to know how to resolve the dependency to the **pubsub** object.

JavaScript

```javascript
// Contained in mstats.reminders.js
_fulfillReminder: function (fulfillmentUrl) {
    var that = this;

    this._showFulfillingMessage();

    this.options.sendRequest({
        url: fulfillmentUrl,
        dataType: 'json',
        cache: false,
        success: function () {
            that._showFulfilledMessage();
            that.options.publish(mstats.events.vehicle.reminders.fulfilled, {});
        },
        error: function () {
```

```
            that._showFulfillErrorMessage();
        }
    });
},
```

The **options.publish** method is initialized to be the value of **mstats.pubsub.publish** when the **reminders** widget is created. Even though the **reminders** widget does not have a direct connection to the layout manager, the layout manager receives notification of the **reminders/fulfilled** event because it has subscribed to that event. The **reminders/fulfilled** event does not require a data payload, so the second parameter to the **publish** call is an empty object.

Finding the Right Balance

While building Mileage Stats, the team initially wanted the widgets to be as loosely coupled as possible in hopes of gaining the most flexibility. To this end, pub/sub was used exclusively for communication between widgets. Because each widget had to manage all of its subscriptions and the topics it published, this approach reduced readability by making it difficult to follow code paths. It is reasonable to have some level of coupling between widgets, especially if it improves the readability of the code base. Reducing the number of pub/sub topics also simplified the implementation of the widgets.

After this experience, the team replaced some pub/sub messages with direct method calls and jQuery events. The following guidelines can be used to determine when you might choose one option over the other.

- Use direct method invocation when only two objects are participating in the action, and when readability and simplicity are more important than coupling and flexibility.

- Trigger an event when it is unacceptable for the sender and receiver to know more about each other than the message they are passing.

- Use pub/sub when multiple subscribers are needed for a single message or the same message needs to be sent from multiple publishers to a single subscriber. Pub/sub is also a good choice when subscribers may be added and removed during the lifetime of the page.

Summary

When a client-side web application is composed of multiple, discrete objects, those objects have a number of communication options to choose from. To keep the solution flexible, pub/sub can be used to keep the objects from having to take dependencies on all the other objects they communicate with. Pub/sub implementations, such as the one in Mileage Stats, typically have a way to publish, subscribe, and unsubscribe. If only pub/sub is used, it can complicate the implementation of the objects that have to manage the many subscriptions and handlers. Alternatively, if only direct communication, such as method invocation, is used, it can complicate the interface of the object by requiring more members. Balancing these options allows the application to have flexibility while keeping the interfaces and implementations as simple as possible. Mileage Stats accomplishes this by using pub/sub for global messages that multiple objects must react to and uses method calls and events for everything else. Independent of the approach you take, you should understand the implications and balance them to achieve the simplicity and flexibility appropriate for your application.

Further Reading

For more information about the Publish/Subscribe pattern, see http://msdn.microsoft.com/en-us/library/ms978603.aspx.

For more information on how to use JavaScript to implement the Publish/Subscribe pattern, see "Understanding the Publish/Subscribe Pattern for Greater JavaScript Scalability" at http://msdn.microsoft.com/en-us/scriptjunkie/hh201955.aspx.

For more information about closure, see the Wikipedia entry: http://en.wikipedia.org/wiki/Closure_(computer_science).

For more information on how to expose and invoke methods on widgets, see "Public Methods" in Chapter 3, "jQuery UI Widgets."

For more information on the widget pseudo selector see "Using the Pseudo Selector" in Chapter 3, "jQuery UI Widgets."

For more information on raising and handling events, see "Events" in Chapter 3, "jQuery UI Widgets."

To access web resources more easily, see the online version of the bibliography on MSDN: http://msdn.microsoft.com/en-us/library/hh404094.aspx.

9 Navigation

Introduction

This chapter describes how the Mileage Stats Reference Implementation (Mileage Stats) manages navigation as users interact with the application, and how it uses animated transitions from one state to another to provide an attractive and immersive user experience.

Traditional web applications and websites implement navigation between pages and states by loading separate pages from the server. Hyperlinks and other controls such as buttons typically initiate a request to the server, which sends back the next page or an updated version of the same page. This is the static or server-rendered model.

In some cases the pages may contain client-side code that adds interactivity to the page without initiating a request to the server, or by reloading only a part of the page. This is the hybrid model; it provides islands of interactivity within the site that do not require a full-page reload.

Mileage Stats uses the hybrid model. However, the majority of user interactions occur within a single page, portions of which are updated with data retrieved from the server using background requests. This is the Single-Page Interface (SPI) pattern. When a user performs an action such as selecting a hyperlink or clicking a button, the application modifies the current web page without reloading the entire page, resulting in a more responsive, less jarring experience.

Adherence to the SPI pattern presents a number of navigation challenges. These challenges include managing the browser's history mechanism so that the back button works as expected, providing direct access to a specific layout or state of the page (deep linking), and implementing anchors that allow users to bookmark the application so that it displays in a specific state.

Fortunately, these challenges can be addressed by using some of the features of modern browsers, by using JavaScript, and by taking advantage of some useful libraries to progressively enhance the way that browsers manage navigation. The approach used in Mileage Stats, and described in this chapter, augments the way the browser handles history and hyperlinking.

In a few cases, navigation in Mileage Stats triggers an animation sequence that transitions between screen layouts. Performing these layout changes requires coordination of the necessary transitions, manipulation of the document object model (DOM) elements that make up portions of the screen, and appropriate modularity to manage the complexity of the animation code.

In this chapter you will learn:

- How to keep your users within a single-page interface
- How to manage hyperlinks and respond to user actions
- When to rewrite URLs and when to handle the click event
- How to ensure that deep linking, bookmarking, and the back button work as expected
- How to coordinate and animate screen transitions

Supporting the Single-Page Interface Pattern

To support the SPI pattern, an application must handle user interactions that would, in a traditional web application, cause a request to the server and a full reload of the page to occur. The way that the interaction is handled for both hyperlinks and buttons varies depending on the behavior and requirements of the link. This figure shows the types of links used in Mileage Stats.

Comparison of different kinds of links used in Mileage Stats

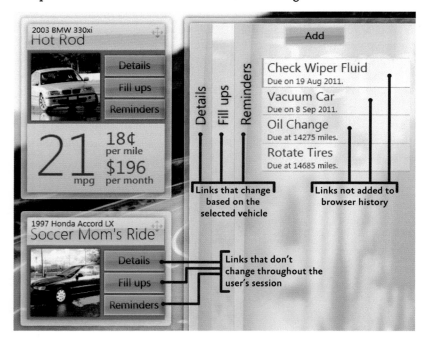

As you can see, there are three different types of links. Links in the vehicle tiles on the left must specify the identifier of the vehicle to which that tile applies, which doesn't change throughout the user's session. Links in the vehicle details panel on the right, which change based on the selected vehicle, must specify both the identifier of the currently selected vehicle and the currently selected view tab (Details, Fill ups, or Reminders) so that deep linking and bookmarks work correctly.

You can also see that the page includes links that are not added to the browser's history list. When links are added to history, users can return to the previous page or any page in the list using the back button or the browser's history explorer. From a user experience perspective, it is not likely users would want to use the back button to return to a previously viewed reminder or fill up on the same view tab.

Applications that partially or fully apply the SPI pattern create page transitions by using JavaScript to override default user navigation actions and control the resulting action. Even though the application is taking over responsibility for the action, it must help the browser understand the important details of the action so the browser will continue to behave as expected.

This partnership between your code and the browser isn't difficult to implement if you have some understanding of how the browser works. Sometimes hyperlinks can be rewritten after the page loads, and other times the user action is better handled dynamically, when the user clicks the link. In either case, you have full control over the response to the user, and can include support for deep linking and bookmarking, as well as for the back button.

Browser History and the Back Button

On a traditional hyperlinked website, the browser can adequately manage the history list and behavior by itself. Each time the browser is instructed by the user or by code to navigate to a unique URL, it registers the URL as a new entry in the browser's history. Clicking the browser's back and forward buttons causes the browser to load the corresponding URL from the history list.

These URLs can contain a *fragment identifier* (often known as a *hash*). This is the part after the # delimiter character in the URL. For example, in the URL **/article.html#intro**, the fragment identifier is **intro**. This may represent a named location on the page (the name of an anchor element in the page) to support deep linking and bookmarking, or a value that corresponds to the state of the page. A fragment identifier may also include a series of name/value pairs. For example, the following URL contains a fragment that includes two name/value pairs, where **layout** equals **details** and **vid** equals **4**.

HTTP URL

```
http://mileagestats.com/Dashboard#layout=details&vid=4
```

Mileage Stats uses the name/value pairs in the fragment identifier to manage state related to the view tab and the vehicle being displayed.

> **Note:** *Do not confuse the fragment identifier with the query segment of a URL. The query segment (or query string) is the part that follows the **?** delimiter. It usually contains name/value pairs that the server uses to generate the appropriate output. For more information about the structure of URLs, see "RFC 3986, Uniform Resource Identifier (URI): Generic Syntax" at* **http://www.ietf.org/rfc/rfc3986.txt**.

Most URLs cause the browser to perform a full-page refresh, which conflicts with the requirements of the SPI pattern. However, if the URL added to the history is identical to the previous URL except for the fragment identifier, the browser will not perform a full-page refresh when the user presses the back button. Therefore, URLs such as the one shown above, which refers to the **Dashboard** resource on the server, and vary only in the content of the fragment identifier, do not result in multiple entries being added to the browser's history list.

When a user selects one of these links, the client-side handler for the **click** event can perform the necessary actions to update the user interface (UI), but the browser does not treat it as a different URL or add it to the history list.

In some cases, however, it is necessary for URLs to be added to the history list even if they vary only in the content of the fragment identifier (and would not, therefore, be added automatically). Mileage Stats uses the Back Button & Query (BBQ) plug-in for jQuery to achieve this, as well as to help make the appropriate modifications to the URL where required.

THE BBQ PLUG-IN

According to the BBQ project page (http://benalman.com/projects/jquery-bbq-plugin/), the BBQ plug-in "... leverages the HTML5 **hashchange** event to allow simple, yet powerful bookmarkable #hash history. In addition, jQuery BBQ provides a full **deparam** method, along with both hash state management, and fragment / query string parse and merge utility methods."

> **Note:** *The HTML5* **hashchange** *event is raised from the* **window** *object each time any values in the fragment identifier of the current URL change;* **hashchange** *is supported in Windows® Internet Explorer® versions 8 and 9. The* **deparam** *method can extract the values of name/value pairs from the fragment identifier and coerce them into the appropriate types. Documentation for the BBQ plug-in is available at* **http://benalman.com/code/projects/jquery-bbq/docs/files/jquery-ba-bbq-js. html.**

Mileage Stats only uses a fraction of BBQ's features. For some navigation scenarios, BBQ is used to parse and merge the fragment identifier values when creating or updating hyperlinks that include the fragment identifier. For hyperlinks that must change based on the state of the application, such as the selected vehicle link, BBQ is used in the **click** event handler to dynamically modify the URL. As you will see in "Responding to User Actions" later in the chapter, BBQ also helps when the browser doesn't support the **hashchange** event.

Modifying Hyperlinks

Mileage Stats uses two different approaches to modify the URLs sent from the server. The approach depends on the lifetime of the hyperlink. If the URL of the hyperlink doesn't change throughout the lifetime of the user's session, such as the hyperlinks in the vehicle tiles (these look like buttons), the URL is modified in the anchor tag's DOM element when the page first loads.

Note: *As you will see in the next section, this approach allows the application to support browsers that do not have JavaScript enabled. This causes the application to send a request for a full-page reload each time the user clicks a link. This is a form of progressive enhancement that provides an improved user experience when JavaScript is enabled.*

If the hyperlink's URL is based on the current state of the application, such as the currently selected vehicle, the **click** event is handled and the URL is applied dynamically, as opposed to using the URL created on the server, which would cause a full-page post back.

The following sections describe the way Mileage Stats implements these different approaches for managing navigation and browser history.

MODIFYING URLs WHEN THE APPLICATION LOADS

Some of the links in Mileage Stats use a URL that does not change throughout the lifetime of the user's session. These URLs include a fragment identifier that contains the identifier of the vehicle to which they apply. For browsers that do not support JavaScript, Mileage Stats supports a traditional static model of navigation, where every user interaction requires the server to create the updated page. To achieve this, each of the hyperlinks sent from the server refers to a specific resource on the server. For example, the URL that the Details view uses to display the details of the vehicle with identifier 4 is sent in the following REST-style format.

HTTP URL
```
http://mileagestats.com/Vehicle/Details/4
```

If the browser has JavaScript enabled, these hyperlinks are modified on the client to use the fragment identifier instead. This ensures the correct behavior of the back button. The link shown above will be converted into the following format so that all of the state information is included in the fragment identifier. "Dashboard" is the location Mileage Stats uses as its SPI.

HTTP URL
```
http://mileagestats.com/Dashboard#layout=details&vid=4
```

This approach means that deep linking, bookmarking, and the back button will continue to work as expected because you are changing the URL in a way the browser understands.

The **Details**, **Fill ups**, and **Reminders** buttons on the individual vehicle tiles are examples of hyperlinks that must be updated only once, when the user starts the application. The code must convert the URL from the REST-style format delivered by the server to the format where the state information is included as name/value pairs in the fragment identifier.

A section of the server-side code that creates the vehicle tiles is shown below. It uses the **Url.Action** method to generate the REST-style URLs for the links.

```
CSHTML
<!-- Contained in _TemplateVehicleList.cshtml -->
<a href="@Url.Action("List", "Reminder")/${VehicleId}"
   data-action="vehicle-reminders-selected"
   alt="Reminders" title="Reminders">
       <div class="hover"></div>
       <div class="active"></div>
       <img alt="Reminders"
           src="@Url.Content("~/Content/command-reminders.png")" />
       <div class="glass"></div>
</a>
```

This creates a URL for the hyperlink in the format **http://mileagestats.com/ reminder/list/4**. Notice that the hyperlink contains a **data-action** attribute, in this case with the "**vehicle-reminders-selected**" value.

> **Note:** *Attributes that begin with the prefix* **data-** *are treated as metadata. The part of the name after the hyphen can be used for querying the value of the attribute using jQuery's* **data** *method.*

The client-side code in Mileage Stats includes the **_adjustNavigation** function, part of which is listed below, to modify the URLs in hyperlinks. The code takes advantage of jQuery's support for HTML5 **data-** attributes to retrieve the value of the **data-action** attribute and store it in a variable named **action**. Next, it obtains the identifier of the vehicle from the widget's **options** collection, then uses the BBQ **getState** method to read the fragment identifier (if one exists) and store it in an object variable named **state**. If there is no fragment identifier (which will be the case when the application starts) it stores an empty object literal instead.

```
JavaScript
// Contained in mstats.vehicle.js
_adjustNavigation: function () {
    var that = this;

    this.element.find('[data-action]').each(function () {
        var $this = $(this),
            action = $this.data('action'),
            vehicleId = that.options.id,
            state = $.bbq.getState() || {},
            newUrlBase = mstats.getBaseUrl();

        state.vid = vehicleId;
        switch (action) {
            case 'vehicle-details-selected':
                state.layout = 'details';
                break;
            case 'vehicle-fillups-selected':
```

```
                    state.layout = 'fillups';
                    break;
            case 'vehicle-reminders-selected':
                    state.layout = 'reminders';
                    break;
            case 'vehicle-add-selected':
                    state.layout = 'addVehicle';
                    state.vid = undefined;
                    break;
        }
        $this.attr('href', $.param.fragment(newUrlBase, state));
    });
},
```

The code then sets the value of a variable named **newUrlBase** by calling the **get BaseUrl** function. This is a helper function defined in mstats.utils.js that retrieves the current base URL without the fragment identifier. The value will usually be **/Dashboard** in Mileage Stats (but may change depending on how the site is deployed).

> **Note:** *The base URL will be different if the site is deployed to a virtual directory versus being deployed to the root of the web server. For example, if the virtual directory is* **mstats***, the base URL (without the domain name) would be* **/mstats/Dashboard***. This is why relying on the server-side* **Url.Action** *function is essential, as it takes into account how the application is hosted.*

Next, the code sets the **vid** property of the state object to the vehicle's ID, and then uses a **switch** statement to set the **layout** property (when adding a vehicle, the **vid** property is set to **undefined**). Finally, the code updates the **href** attribute of the hyperlink to the required URL using the BBQ **fragment** method (which extends **jQuery.param**) to merge the values in the **state** object with **newUrlBase**. The result is a URL that is changed from **http://mileagestats.com/reminder/list/4** to **http://mileagestats.com/dashboard# layout=reminders&vid=4**.

Modifying URLs When the User Activates a Link

The preceding section showed how to use the BBQ plug-in and HTML5 **data-** attributes to modify hyperlinks so they include a fragment identifier that defines the state. This is fine if the links are not likely to change (or will not change very often). However, if the URL can be determined only when the link is activated, it is usually more appropriate to handle the **click** event.

When a user activates one of these links, the client-side handler for the **click** event can perform the necessary actions to update the UI and prevent the default click behavior from sending the request to the server. Alternatively, if required, the code can initiate navigation and page reload by setting the **location** property of the browser's **window** object within the event handler or in code that is executed from the event handler.

The vertical accordion links for Details, Fill ups, and Reminders are examples of links that change each time a different vehicle is selected because they must include the identifier of the selected vehicle. The following listing shows a section of the server-side code that creates the HTML for the hyperlink in the Fill ups view tab.

CSHTML
```
<!-- Contained in _TemplateFillups.cshtml -->
<a class="trigger"
   href="@Url.Action("List", "Fillup")/${VehicleId}"
   data-info-nav="fillups"></a>
```

This creates a URL for the hyperlink in the format **http://mileagestats.com/fillup/list/1**. Notice that the hyperlink contains a **data-info-nav** attribute, in this case with the "**fillups**" value.

The info pane widget that implements this section of the UI is responsible for handling the **click** event of these accordion links and initiating the required transition. The code in the **_bindNavigation** method (shown below) creates a delegate on the **click** event, which uses the widget's name as the namespace, for all elements that include a **data-info-nav** attribute.

> **Note:** *Using the widget's name as the namespace and appending it to the event allows the delegation to automatically be cleaned up when the widget is destroyed.*

Inside the delegate, the code uses the jQuery **data** method to read the value of the **data-info-nav** attribute into a variable named **action**, and then passes this value to another method named **_setHashLayout**. It also prevents the default behavior of the hyperlink from initiating navigation.

JavaScript
```
// Contained in mstats.info-pane.js
_bindNavigation: function () {
    var that = this; // closure for the event handler below

    this.element.delegate('[data-info-nav]', 'click.infoPane', function (event) {
        var action = $(this).data('info-nav');
        that._setHashLayout(action);
        event.preventDefault();
    });
},
```

The **_setHashLayout** method, also defined within the info pane widget, is responsible for setting the layout according to the user's selection. It uses the BBQ **getState** method to retrieve the existing navigation details, which are stored as name/value pairs in the fragment identifier of the current URL, as an object named **state**. After setting the **layout** property for the new layout, it uses the **pushState** method to modify the fragment and update the browser's address bar. The value **2**, passed as the second argument, tells the **pushState** method to completely replace any existing fragment identifier values with the contents of the first argument.

```
JavaScript
// Contained in mstats.info-pane.js
_setHashLayout: function (newLayout) {
    var state = $.bbq.getState() || {};
    state.layout = newLayout;
    $.bbq.pushState(state, 2);
},
```

The result is a URL that is changed from **http://mileagestats.com/fillup/list/1** to **http://mileagestats.com/dashboard#layout=fillups&vid=1**.

Although the server isn't required to do anything special to support these URLs, the client must perform some specific steps to respond to user actions.

Responding to User Actions

At this point, as explained in the preceding sections of this chapter, the URLs in the hyperlinks or in the **click** event handlers have been updated with the required fragment identifier values. Links where the URL does not change during the session have been updated by code that modifies the anchor tag's **href** attributes when the main SPI page loads. Links where the URLs do change have a delegate attached to the **click** event, and this delegate updates the browser's location with the modified URL.

The next stage is to write code that responds when a user clicks on a link. This is done by handling the **hashchange** event, which is raised when the user clicks a link that contains a fragment identifier, or when code programmatically sets the **location** property of the **window** object, which is what BBQ's **pushState** method does, as shown in the previous code example. The **hashchange** event can be used for applications that need to maintain a history of user actions without reloading the complete page.

Mileage Stats uses the BBQ plug-in to manage the browser's history in a uniform manner that works across all browsers. When BBQ detects browser support for the **hashchange** event, it uses the browser's implementation. When it doesn't detect support for the **hashchange** event, it uses its own implementation of the event. Internet Explorer 8 and Internet Explorer 9 support the **hashchange** event.

> **Note:** *In addition to the* **hashchange** *event, HTML5 also defines a mechanism for managing browser session history without using the fragment identifier, which adds* **pushState** *and* **replaceState** *methods to* **window.history***. Internet Explorer 9 supports this mechanism. You should consider using a library such as* Modernizr *to determine if the browser supports the HTML5 history mechanism. The BBQ plug-in and similar libraries can still be used for browsers that do not support it.*

The **hashchange** event handler in Mileage Stats, shown below, is defined in mstats.layout-manager.js. When the **hashchange** event occurs, the handler uses BBQ's **deparam** method to deserialize the name/value pairs in the fragment identifier into a **state** object. The **true** argument instructs the **deparam** method to coerce numbers **true, false, null**, and **undefined** to their actual values rather than the string equivalent. This avoids the need to use the **parseInt** function to convert the **vid** property from a string to a number.

JavaScript

```javascript
// Contained in mstats.layout-manager.js
_subscribeToHashChange: function() {
    var that = this;
    $(window).bind('hashchange.layoutManager', function() {
        var state = $.deparam.fragment(true);
        that._changeLayout(state);
    });
},
```

The handler then updates the page to the required layout by calling the **_change Layout** method, shown next, which is also defined in mstats.layout-manager.js. This method uses the **state** argument that is passed to it to set the widget's **layout** option and to navigate to the appropriate layout.

JavaScript

```javascript
// Contained in mstats.layout-manager.js
_changeLayout: function(state) {
    this._setOption('layout', state.layout || 'dashboard');

    this._setupInfoPaneOptions(state);
    switch (this.options.layout) {
        case 'dashboard':
            this._header('option', 'title', 'Dashboard');
            this._goToDashboardLayout();
            break;
        case 'charts':
            this._header('option', 'title', 'Charts');
            this._goToChartsLayout();
            break;
        case 'details':
            this._setHeaderForSelectedVehicle('Details');
            this._goToDetailsLayout();
            break;
        case 'fillups':
            this._setHeaderForSelectedVehicle('Fill ups');
            this._goToDetailsLayout();
            break;
        case 'reminders':
            this._setHeaderForSelectedVehicle('Reminders');
            this._goToDetailsLayout();
            break;
    }
},
```

The call to the **_setOption** method uses either the layout that is passed in, or it defaults to the Dashboard if no layout is specified. The code then executes the **_setupInfo-PaneOptions** method (not shown here), which sets the **selectedVehicleId** option on the vehicle list and info pane widgets, and sets the **activePane** option on the info pane widget. The code then uses a **switch** statement based on the value of the **layout** option to set the header text option of the widget (in some cases using a private method within the widget) and then it calls another private method to begin animating the transition to the required layout. You will see an example of these animation methods in the next section of this chapter.

Animating Screen Transitions

Mileage Stats uses a widget named **layoutManager** both for managing navigation and for controlling the animation sequences that are triggered by navigation. For example, if you are on the Dashboard and you select **Details** for a specific vehicle, you see an animated sequence that shifts the summary pane off the left side of the screen, moves the info pane onto the screen from the right, and adjusts the vehicle list so that the currently selected vehicle is prominently displayed. This requires coordination of the summary, info pane, and vehicle list widgets.

> **Note:** *For applications that do not use animations, implementing a layout manager is unnecessary. However, animations can help provide a great user experience by making the application appear more responsive and by allowing users to maintain context as they navigate the application.*

THE LAYOUT MANAGER

Early in the development of Mileage Stats, it became clear that something needed to have responsibility for coordinating between the dashboard, details, and charts layouts. Without centralized coordination, each widget that makes up a particular layout would need to know the current layout and when to transition to the next layout. This central coordinator, the layout manager, knows how and when to instruct the appropriate widgets to move to the correct layout, which reduces coupling and simplifies the implementation. By using a layout manager widget, each of the other widgets only needs to know how to perform the transition, not when to do so or what the other widgets must do to complete the transition.

The layout manager is initialized in mileagestats.js with references to all the necessary widgets (such as the summary pane, vehicle list, and info pane) and it knows when to take action based on subscriptions to the following two types of events:

- **Global events**. These are events that are not constrained to an isolated part of the application. They are published to the publish/subscribe object and subscribed to with the layout manager's **_subscribeToGlobalEvents** method. You can learn more about this method in "An Example of Publishing" in Chapter 8, "Communication."

- **hashchange events**. These events are raised through user navigation and handled in the **_subscribeToHashChange** method, as described in the previous section of this chapter.

When these events are raised, the layout manager uses its **_changeLayout** method, described in the previous section of this chapter, to invoke methods directly on the widgets that will take part in the animation, and to update the header widget with the appropriate title based on the layout and selected vehicle. To learn more about how the layout manager invokes these widgets, see "Method Invocation" in Chapter 8, "Communication."

COORDINATING TRANSITIONS

One of the more complex transitions is to and from the dashboard and details layouts. The remainder of this section deals with the specifics of this transition.

Transitioning from dashboard to details

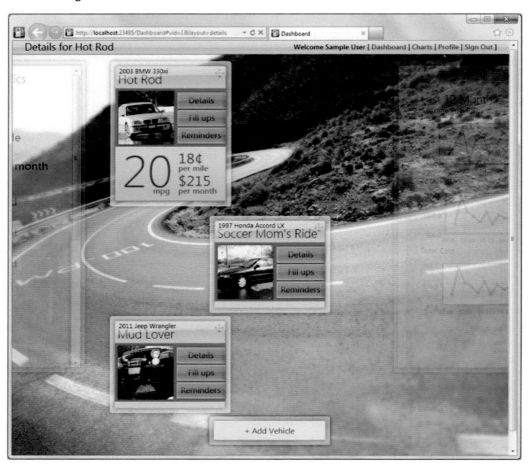

The following code shows one of the methods that the **layoutManager** widget uses to update the layout in response to a navigation event. This example, the **_goTo DetailsLayout** method, is used to navigate to the vehicle details layout.

```
JavaScript
// Contained in mstats.layout-manager.js
_goToDetailsLayout: function() {
    this._charts('moveOffScreenToRight');
    this._summaryPane('moveOffScreen');
    this._infoPane('moveOnScreenFromRight');
    this._vehicleList('moveOnScreen');
    this._vehicleList('goToDetailsLayout');
},
```

The code calls methods in each of the widgets to move them to the appropriate locations on the page. These methods check the widget's current state before doing anything. For example, calling **moveOffScreenToRight** on the charts widget won't do anything if the chart is not currently displayed.

The following figure doesn't show all of the necessary widget interactions to complete the transition to details layout, but it illustrates the roles that the vehicle list, vehicle, and tile widgets play in the transition.

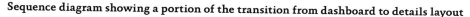

Sequence diagram showing a portion of the transition from dashboard to details layout

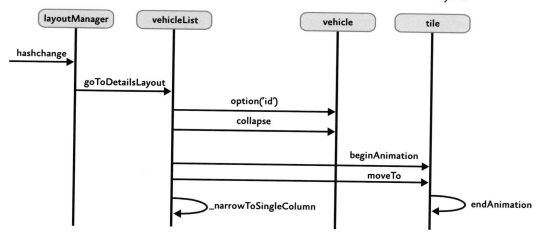

When the **hashchange** event occurs, the **_goToDetailsLayout** method of the layout manager calls the **_goToDetailsLayout** method of the vehicle list widget. The vehicle list widget is responsible for coordinating the animation of the list from a two-column to a one-column layout as it moves to the left side of the screen while, simultaneously, all but the selected vehicle widgets shrink to a compact size. The details of these interactions are addressed in the next section.

ANIMATING VEHICLE TILES

During the transition to the details layout, the vehicle list widget directs the vehicle widget to collapse all unselected vehicles, and the tile widget to animate the tiles left and down.

As you can see in the previous diagram, the **goToDetailsLayout** method of the vehicle list (shown below) starts the process of animating the vehicle tiles. After defining some variables, it calls the private **_checkSelectedVehicleId** method.

```JavaScript
// Contained in mstats.vehicle-list.js
goToDetailsLayout: function () {
    var selectedVehicle,
        vid = 0,
        that = this,
        runningTop = 0,
        animationInfoArray,
        state = $.bbq.getState() || {};
    this._checkSelectedVehicleId();
    selectedVehicle = this.options.selectedVehicleId;
    ...
},
```

The **_checkSelectedVehicleId** method compares the **selectedVehicleId** option with the **vid** property in the URL. If they are different, it calls the **_setOption** method to update the value.

```JavaScript
// Contained in mstats.vehicle-list.js
_checkSelectedVehicleId: function () {
    var vid,
        state = $.bbq.getState() || {};

    if (state.vid) {
        vid = parseInt(state.vid, 10);
        if (vid !== this.options.selectedVehicleId) {
            this._setOption('selectedVehicleId', state.vid);
        }
    }
},
```

When the **selectedVehicleId** option is set, code in the **_setOption** method calls the **_expandVehicle** and **_collapseVehicles** methods.

```JavaScript
// Contained in mstats.vehicle-list.js
_setOption: function (key, value) {
    $.Widget.prototype._setOption.apply(this, arguments);
    if (value <= 0) {
        return;
    }
    switch (key) {
        case 'layout':
```

```
            this._setLayoutOption(value);
            break;
        case 'selectedVehicleId':
            this._expandVehicle(value);
            this._collapseVehicles();
            break;
    }
},
```

The **_expandVehicle** method ensures that the selected vehicle is not collapsed. The **_collapseVehicles** method loops through all vehicles, comparing their **id** option with the **selectedVehicleId** option. When a vehicle's **id** doesn't equal the selected one, the **collapse** method is called on the vehicle widget. This is the vehicle widget interaction shown in the sequence diagram above.

JavaScript
```
// Contained in mstats.vehicle-list.js
_collapseVehicles: function () {
    var selected = this.options.selectedVehicleId;

    this.element.find(':mstats-vehicle').each(function () {
        var $this = $(this);
        if ($this.vehicle('option', 'id') !== selected) {
            $this.vehicle('collapse');
        }
    });
},
```

Going back to the **goToDetailsLayout** method, after **_checkSelectedVehicleId** executes, all vehicle tiles will be collapsed or expanded appropriately. The next step is to animate the tiles into position. The following is a more complete view of the **goTo DetailsLayout** method shown earlier.

JavaScript
```
// Contained in mstats.vehicle-list.js
goToDetailsLayout: function () {
    var selectedVehicle,
        vid = 0,
        runningTop = 0,
        animationInfoArray,
        that = this,
        state = $.bbq.getState() || {};
        this._checkSelectedVehicleId();
        selectedVehicle = this.options.selectedVehicleId;

    if (!this.options.isCollapsed) {
        this.element.find(':mstats-tile').tile('beginAnimation');
```

```
        this.element.find(':mstats-tile').each(function () {
            var $this = $(this);
            vid = $this.find('.vehicle').vehicle('option', 'id');
            animationInfoArray = [{
                position: { top: runningTop },
                duration: animationLength
            }, {
                position: { left: 0 },
                duration: animationLength
            }];

            $this.tile('moveTo', animationInfoArray, function () {
                that.element.find(':mstats-tile').tile('endAnimation');
            });

            // calculate the runningTop for next time around
            if (vid === selectedVehicle) {
                runningTop += 321;
            } else {
                runningTop += 206;
            }
        });

        this._narrowToSingleColumn();
    }

    this._scrollToSelectedVehicle();
    if (state && state.layout) {
        this.options.layout = state.layout;
    }

    this.options.isCollapsed = true;
},
```

Not to be confused with the vehicle widget, the vehicle list widget also has an **is Collapsed** option that indicates if it is currently displayed as a single column (collapsed) or as two columns. If it is not collapsed, it immediately calls the **beginAnimation** method on all tile widgets, as you can see in the sequence diagram above.

> **Note:** *The tile widget was created to reduce the complexity of the tile animations. Initially, the vehicle list and vehicle widgets contained all of the animation logic. Creating the tile widget freed up the vehicle widget to focus only on vehicle concepts. In contrast, the vehicle list widget still contains a significant amount of logic specific to the animations. A future refactoring might employ an additional widget that specializes in animating generic tiles between a one-column and two-column layout (or N-columns to N-columns).*

CALCULATING COORDINATES

Mileage Stats uses relative positioning for many elements, which means that an element's position is based on that of the preceding element (an element's positioning style, such as **relative** or **absolute**, is a CSS property). However, when elements are moving during an animation their position must be **absolute** so that their location values can be controlled. The **beginAnimation** method establishes the **top** and **left** CSS values based on the current top and left values. These values will be used when positioning is switched to **absolute**.

JavaScript

```javascript
// Contained in mstats.tile.js
beginAnimation: function () {
    var $element = this.element;
    $element.css({
        top: $element.position().top + 'px',
        left: $element.position().left + 'px'
    });
},
```

Now that the tiles have been prepared, they can be instructed to move. The **go ToDetailsLayout** method loops through each of the tile widgets and constructs an **animationInfoArray** with properties for **position** and **duration**. The **runningTop** variable is updated within the loop to specify the top of the next tile. This helps with the process of collapsing the two-column list into a single column and ensures that the items in the resulting list do not visually overlap.

The duration, **animationLength**, is defined in the file's closure at the top of the file with the value 600 (milliseconds). To move the tiles, the **moveTo** method is called on all tile widgets with two arguments. These are the **animationInfoArray**, and a callback function that executes when the **moveTo** method completes. The **moveTo** method is shown in the sequence diagram above.

The **moveTo** method calls its **_unlock** method, which sets the position to **absolute**, and then loops over the **animationInfoArray**, calling **_animate** for each item in the array.

JavaScript

```javascript
// Contained in mstats.tile.js
moveTo: function (animationInfoArray, callback) {
    var that = this,
        arrayLength = 0;

    this._unlock();

    // if this is an array, iterate over it
    if (animationInfoArray.length) {
        arrayLength = animationInfoArray.length;
        $.each(animationInfoArray, function (index, info) {
            if (index === arrayLength - 1) {
```

```
            that._animate(info, callback);
        } else {
            that._animate(info);
        }
    });
}
// otherwise just animate one step with the data
else {
    this._animate(animationInfoArray, callback);
}
},
```

Next, the vehicles line up and form a single column. Although these actions seem to be two separate animations, they form a single animation that contains a 400ms delay that separates the two parts (height adjustment and the move left).

When **moveTo** completes, the code calls the **endAnimation** method. This method sets the position attribute back to **relative**, as shown in the following code.

JavaScript
```
// Contained in mstats.tile.js
endAnimation: function () {
    this.element
        .attr('style', '')
        .css({
            top: 0,
            left: 0,
            position: 'relative',
            float: 'left'
        });
}
```

This method also removes all style attributes, sets the **top** and **left** to zero because these values do not matter when using **relative** positioning, and sets **float** to **left**. This completes the animation sequence.

Summary

Even partially applying the SPI pattern to your application means that your client-side JavaScript must take some responsibility for handling navigation actions. Fortunately, with a little help, the browser is capable of performing most of the work. Depending on the nature of your hyperlinks, such as whether they change during a session, or are set only at the start of a session, and whether they should be added to the browser's history, the URLs can either be sent from the server in the correct format or modified on the client once the DOM is ready. If the links are to be modified on the client, they can either be rewritten when the page loads, or modified dynamically when activated.

Animations can be used to ensure that transitions don't confuse or disorient the user by keeping them *in context*. However, animations should not be too slow or annoy the users through extended use of the application. Depending on the complexity of the animation, you should look for opportunities to separate animation logic into modules. This will help with code readability and troubleshooting because the modules can be enabled or disabled easily, and they facilitate reusability.

Further Reading

For more information about the BBQ plug-in, see http://benalman.com/projects/jquery-bbq-plugin/.

For more information about Modernizr, see http://www.modernizr.com/.

For the RFC 3986 Uniform Resource Identifier generic syntax, see http://www.ietf.org/rfc/rfc3986.txt.

To learn more about the layout manager's **_subscribeToGlobalEvents** method and how the layout manager invokes widgets, see Chapter 8, "Communication."

To access web resources more easily, see the online version of the bibliography on MSDN: http://msdn.microsoft.com/en-us/library/hh404094.aspx.

10   Application Notifications

Introduction

All web applications that users consider responsive have one thing in common: they provide appropriate and timely feedback to the user. This feedback can come in many forms, including a save or success message following a completed task, subtle animations in response to a user interface (UI) gesture, a progress message for long-running tasks or input error messages displayed before a page is submitted.

How the application displays notifications to the user is almost as important as the information itself. Intrusive message boxes, modal dialogs, and overlays (floating messages) that require the user to dismiss messages, can interrupt the user's workflow, get in the way, and degrade the overall user experience.

In addition to providing feedback during normal use, the website must also provide quality feedback when a non-recoverable error occurs. Quality feedback means providing understandable information about what has occurred, along with clear instructions on how to proceed.

In this chapter you will learn:

- How to provide unobtrusive user notification messages.
- How to handle multiple simultaneous notification messages raised by the application.
- The benefits of encapsulating the display and management of user notifications in a single JavaScript object.
- How to display a helpful global error page.
- How to set up a global error handler for Ajax requests.
- Alternatives to modal dialogs for prompting users.
- How to enable application notifications on the desktop with the Pinned Sites API.

The technologies discussed in this chapter are jQuery UI Widgets and Pinned Sites in Windows® Internet Explorer® 9.

For a comprehensive look at input validation error messages, see Chapter 11, "Server-Side Implementation."

Notifying the User

Providing a high-quality application notification experience requires careful planning that emphasizes where notifications will be displayed, what events initiate a message, how potential multiple simultaneous messages will be handled, and how to decouple the message originator from the object that displays the message.

During the design phase of the Mileage Stats application, the Project Silk team discussed *where* and *how* notification messages would be displayed. We spent time prototyping several different notification designs.

Where notification messages are displayed is an essential part of the overall application user experience (UX) and UI design. Our initial design called for messages and progress bars to be displayed within the boundaries of each jQuery UI widget. After building several prototypes and performing usability testing, the team determined that this design was unnecessary because the UI loaded quickly, eliminating the need for a loading progress bar. The team decided that displaying user messages in a single location made for a much better experience than having messages displayed within individual widgets.

During the development cycle, the team relied on usability testing to refine their approach to generating user messages. Initially, the team displayed messages each time an Ajax request was invoked. This caused the UI to be too busy; we then used a time delay so that the message would only display if the request took longer than the delay. This too got messy, requiring a good deal of code that added little or no value to the application. In the end, the "less is more" principle triumphed, resulting in a good balance of informative messages.

Interactive and engaging applications such as Mileage Stats can execute multiple asynchronous operations. For example, the Dashboard page loads data for several jQuery UI widgets in addition to the chart widget. Each of these operations loads data for a region of the UI. Any of these operations is a potential point of failure requiring an error message. It's important that the application's notification implementation be able to manage multiple simultaneous or nearly simultaneous messages.

From an architectural design perspective, it's critical that message initiators not be responsible for determining how to coordinate the display of messages in the UI. Decoupling the message initiator from the rendering object allows both of them to evolve independently and to be tested in isolation.

This section gave a glimpse into how the team worked together to maintain the delicate balance of UX, UI, and engineering concerns. It's this type of designer-developer collaboration that enabled the team to deliver a successful notification feature.

WHERE NOTIFICATION MESSAGES ARE DISPLAYED

Mileage Stats is composed of widgets. The decision to create and use a widget for displaying notification messages is a natural architectural choice for this application. Widgets have flexible and powerful UI capabilities, provide for encapsulation of behavior, and can have external dependencies like the publish and subscribe (pub/sub) JavaScript object injected into their **options** object during creation.

Mileage Stats uses a single widget called **status** for displaying messages to the user. The **status** widget subscribes to the Mileage Stats **status** pub/sub message. It also handles the placement and rendering of messages as well as the coordination of multiple simultaneous messages.

Location of the status widget

The **status** widget is rendered within the **header** widget UI, as pictured above. This top, semi-central location was chosen because it's easier for the user to notice the message in this location, as opposed to a message area along the bottom of the browser window. The balance of easily noticed, easy-to-read, yet unobtrusive user notifications took time, patience, and usability testing, but the multiple design iterations were worth the extra investment of effort.

How Notification Messages are Initiated

Mileage Stats notification messages are initiated by widgets and communicated to the **status** widget using the pub/sub JavaScript object. Like other pub/sub messages, the status message has an associated payload object that is passed with the message.

Notification messages passed using Pub/Sub

The code snippet below is from the **vehicleDetails** widget. The **_publishStatus** method is responsible for making the pub/sub call. It's called internally by other widget methods to initiate the display of a message. The **status** argument is the message payload and is forwarded in the **publish** call. The **publish** method was passed in the widget **options** object when the widget was created and points to the **pubsub** JavaScript object. The jQuery **isFunction** method verifies that **publish** is a valid JavaScript function object before it's called.

JavaScript

```
// Contained in mstats.vehicle-details.js
_publishStatus: function (status) {
    this.options.publish(mstats.events.status, status);
},
```

As stated earlier, Mileage Stats does not bother the user with data request messages. However, when initiating an Ajax operation such as a save or delete, it's important to keep the user informed by updating the UI as the request proceeds and concludes.

The following functions show how easy it is to initiate the display of a user message:

- The **_showDeletingMessage** function is called after the user confirms his or her intent to delete the vehicle. This message is intended to inform the user that the vehicle deletion has been submitted to the server.

- The **_showDeletedMessage** function is called after a successful deletion of the vehicle, informing the user that the deletion was successful.

- The **_showDeleteErrorMessage** function is called if an error occurred while deleting the vehicle.

JavaScript

```
// Contained in mstats.vehicle-details.js
_showDeletingMessage: function () {
  this._publishStatus({
    type: 'saving',
    message: 'Deleting the selected vehicle ...',
    duration: 5000
  });
},
_showDeletedMessage: function () {
  this._publishStatus({
    type: 'saved',
    message: 'Vehicle deleted.',
    duration: 5000
  });
},
_showDeleteErrorMessage: function () {
  this._publishStatus({
    type: 'saveError',
    message: 'An error occurred deleting the selected vehicle. Please try again.',
    duration: 10000
  });
}
```

Each function creates an object literal containing a **type**, **message**, and **duration** property. The **type** property is used by the **status** widget to prioritize multiple or overlapping display message requests. The **message** is the text of the message to display and the **duration** is how long the message should display.

For detailed information on the inner workings of the Mileage Stats pub/sub implementation, see Chapter 8, "**Communication**."

HOW INDIVIDUAL OR MULTIPLE NOTIFICATION MESSAGES ARE DISPLAYED

In the following **_create** method, the **status** widget subscribes to the **status** event. When this event is raised, the **_statusSubscription** method is invoked.

The **_statusSubscription** method is responsible for displaying and hiding messages as well as managing multiple simultaneous messages. If a message is being displayed and another message with a higher priority arrives, the higher priority message will be shown.

```JavaScript
// Contained in mstats.status.js
_create: function () {
  // handle global status events
  this.options.subscribe(mstats.events.status, this._statusSubscription, this);
},

...
_statusSubscription: function (status) {
  var that = this,
          current = this.currentStatus;

  status.priority = this._getPriority(status);

  // cancel displaying the current message if its priority is lower than
  // the new message. (the lower the int the higher priority)
  if (current && (status.priority < current.priority)) {
    clearTimeout(current.timer);
  }

  current = status;

  this.element.text(status.message).show();

  // set the message for the duration
  current.timer = setTimeout(function () {
    that.element.fadeOut();
```

```
    that.currentStatus = null;
  }, status.duration || this.options.duration);
},

_getPriority: function (status) {
  return priorities[status.type];
},
```

USER SESSION TIMEOUT NOTIFICATION

Mileage Stats uses forms authentication, with a session time-out threshold of 20 minutes. If the session has timed out, the request (Ajax or non-Ajax) is redirected to the page specified by the forms authentication **loginUrl** in the web.config file.

In traditional websites that perform page reloads between pages, it's common to redirect the user to a sign-in page when their session times out. Applications like Mileage Stats that make heavy use of Ajax calls to retrieve data perform few full-page reloads. Consequently, if a session timeout occurs, it's usually during an Ajax request. Let's examine what happens when an Ajax request is redirected because of an authentication session timeout:

1. Ajax JavaScript Object Notation (JSON) data request initiated.

2. Forms authentication runtime detects an expired session and redirects the request to the sign-in page.

3. A parsing error occurs because the Ajax handler is expecting JSON data and not HTML. The HTML is the content of the sign-in page to which the request was redirected.

4. An Ajax error callback is invoked.

5. A global Ajax error callback is invoked.

Errors that can occur anywhere in the application can often be handled in a centralized location so that individual objects don't need to repeat the same error handling code. Mileage Stats implements the global **ajaxError** method handler shown below to catch errors occurring during an Ajax request. In Mileage Stats, the primary purpose of this method is to identify whether the initiating Ajax request caused a session time-out error and, if so, to redirect the user to the sign-in page.

When looking at the code below, "jqXHR.status === 200" appears out of place or incorrect. Remember, this method is only executed when an Ajax error occurs. If the session times out and the request is redirected to the sign-in page, the response status code will be 200 because the redirect succeeded. In addition to checking for the response status code, this method also verifies that the returned HTML contains the sign-in page's title. If both conditions are met, the browser is redirected to the sign-in page.

```JavaScript
// Contained in mileagestats.js
$(document).ajaxError(function (ev, jqXHR, settings, errorThrown) {
    if (jqXHR.status === 200) {
        if (jqXHR.responseText.indexOf('Mileage Stats Sign In') !== -1) {
        window.location.replace(mstats.getRelativeEndpointUrl('/Auth/SignIn'));
        } else if (jqXHR.responseText.indexOf('Mileage Stats | Accident!') !== -1) {
        window.location.replace(mstats.getRelativeEndpointUrl('/GenericError.htm'));
        }
    }
});
```

Note: *If the originating Ajax calling code also implements an error handler, the originating Ajax caller's error handler will be called first, and then the above global Ajax error handler will be called.*

Website Error Notification

ASP.NET allows you to specify a default error page that the ASP.NET runtime will redirect users to when an unhandled exception occurs. This error page is configured in the web.config file's **customErrors** section.

```C#
// Contained in web.config
<customErrors defaultRedirect="GenericError.htm" mode="RemoteOnly" />
```

The error page should look and feel like it is part of the website, contain a brief explanation of why the user has been redirected to this page, and provide links that allow a user to continue using the site.

Mileage Stats GenericError.htm page

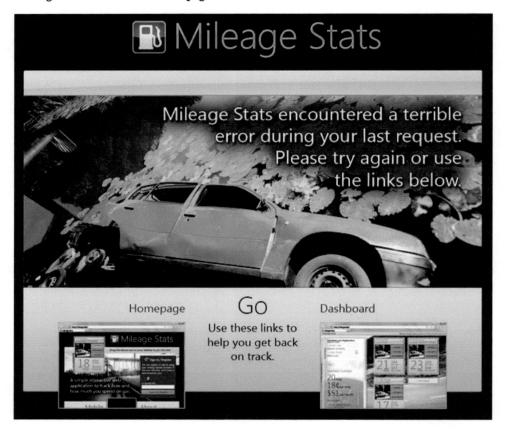

Prompting Users

During the design phase of Project Silk, the team had a goal of not prompting users with modal dialogs. Website UX designers are getting away from modal dialogs that ask the user questions like, "Are you sure?" Instead, designers prefer an undo feature that allows users to undo the previous task. The undo feature also enhances the application by extending undo capabilities to tasks that did not require a confirmation dialog. Because Mileage Stats is only a sample application, it has limited functionality. The team wanted to implement the undo feature, but other features took priority. A production application could include it.

The following code uses the JavaScript **confirm** function to validate the user's request to fulfill a maintenance reminder.

```javascript
JavaScript
// Contained in mstats.reminders.js
fulfillReminder: function (fulfillmentUrl) {
    var shouldfulfill = confirm('Are you sure you want to fulfill this reminder?');
    if (shouldfulfill) {
        this._fulfillReminder(fulfillmentUrl);
    }
},
```

Note: *The jQuery UI dialog provides an alternative to using the JavaScript* **confirm** *dialog. If you are leveraging jQuery UI plug-ins, you should consider using the jQuery UI dialog for consistency in your UI.*

Desktop Notifications

Given that modern web applications can provide excellent user experiences that rival desktop applications, the team wanted to take the next logical step and integrate the Mileage Stats application with the user's desktop to provide dynamic user notifications. This integration was made possible by the Internet Explorer 9 Pinned Site API.

Websites that implement the Pinned Site API can feel more like a native Windows application. They take advantage of the Microsoft® Windows® 7 taskbar capabilities and, when launched, the browser window is customized specifically for the website. The full Pinned Sites experience requires Internet Explorer 9 running on Windows 7. Windows Vista® has a reduced experience that provides: site pinning, customized reduced chrome, and the disabling of browser add-ons.

Mileage Stats uses Pinned Sites to provide Windows 7 taskbar notifications that indicate whether the user has one or more overdue maintenance reminders. In addition, a dynamic jump list provides a direct link to each overdue maintenance reminder.

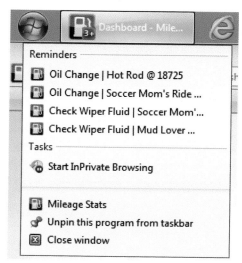

Mileage Stats taskbar integration

Note: *Jump list items will be available whether the site is opened in a browser or not. However, the notification icons are only displayed when the site is opened in the browser.*

The two images below contrast Mileage Stats running in a normal browser window and a customized Pinned Sites browser window. The Pinned Sites image shows the cleaner, pared down browser window with potentially distracting browser features removed, allowing the user to focus on the application features. Applications run in the customized browser window when they are launched from a taskbar or the Start Menu Pinned Sites icon.

Mileage Stats without using Pinned Sites

Mileage Stats using Pinned Sites

In addition to a cleaner browser window, Pinned Sites also allows the developer to customize the color of the browser back and forward buttons, and the browser displays the website favicon to the left of the back button. This favicon is also a link to the website home page.

IMPLEMENTING PINNED SITES

Microsoft provides documentation for implementing Pinned Sites in their web applications on MSDN®. The title of this topic is, "Pinned Sites Developer Documentation," and is located at http://msdn.microsoft.com/en-us/library/gg491731(v=VS.85).aspx.

PINNED SITES IN MILEAGE STATS

The following sections do not attempt to duplicate the MSDN documentation or cover every line of code pertaining to Pinned Sites. Instead, the Mileage Stats implementation will be explained, enabling you to understand the pieces, requirements, capabilities, and value of the Pinned Sites API.

The Pinned Sites implementation in Mileage Stats includes feature detection, site pinning, dynamic jump list updating, and display of notification icons. These features are encapsulated in the **mstats.pinnedSite** JavaScript object that is contained in the mstats.pinnedsite.js file. The **pinnedSite** object is initialized differently depending on whether or not the user is signed in. This initialization will be described below.

Feature Detection

Pinned Sites feature detection is provided by the Internet Explorer 9 **msIsSiteMode** function. Verifying that the page is opened as a pinned site before executing the Pinned Site API methods prevents unnecessary JavaScript errors.

The **msIsSiteMode** function returns **true** if the current page is launched as a pinned site and **false** if it is not. The following **isPinned** function wraps the **msIsSiteMode** call and returns **false** if the page is not launched as a pinned site, or the browser is not Internet Explorer 9.

```JavaScript
// Contained in mstats.pinnedsite.js
isPinned: function () {
    try {
        return window.external.msIsSiteMode();
    }
    catch (e) {
        return false;
    }
}
```

Enabling Website Pinning

Unauthenticated users visiting the site are directed to the landing page, which is shown below. This page allows users to sign in, pin the site, and view the Mileage Stats video (not pictured). The Pinned Sites icon will glow when it is draggable, allowing the user to pin the site to the taskbar or Start Menu. The callout text displays for 5 seconds when the page loads. It will also show and hide the text as users move the mouse over or away from the Pinned Sites icon.

Note: *Developers are not required to implement a draggable site icon as Mileage Stats does to enable site pinning. Providing a draggable icon gives the website more control over the pinning experience. Without a draggable icon, sites can still be pinned by dragging the tab or the favicon to the taskbar.*

Landing page

The Pinned Sites JavaScript object is initialized when the above page loads with the following JavaScript function.

```
CSHTML
// Contained in Index.cshtml
<script>
  $(function () {
    mstats.pinnedSite.intializePinnedSiteImage();
  });
</script>
```

If the browser is Internet Explorer 9 and the website is not currently pinned, the **intializePinnedSiteImage** method will attach appropriate event handlers for hiding and showing the callout text. It also adds the **active** CSS class to the Pinned Sites icon so that the icon appears to glow.

```
JavaScript
// Contained in mstats.pinnedsite.js
initializePinnedSiteImage: function () {

  // Do not enabled site pinning for non-Internet Explorer 9+ browsers
  // Do not show the callout if the site is already pinned
  if (!(!document.documentMode || this.isPinned())) {
    $('#pinnedSiteImage')
                .bind('mousedown mouseout', hideCallout)
                .bind('mouseover', showCallout)
                .addClass('active');
    $('#pinnedSiteCallout').show();
    setTimeout(hideCallout, 5000);
  }
},
```

The following HTML snippet shows the required **msPinSite** class applied to the Pinned Sites icon. This class is used by Internet Explorer 9 to enable the user to drag the Pinned Sites icon to the taskbar or Start Menu and pin the site.

```
CSHTML
// Contained in Index.cshtml
<img id="pinnedSiteImage" class="msPinSite" ... />
```

To call the user's attention to the draggable Pinned Sites icon, the **active** CSS class below adds an attractive outer glow to it.

```
CSS
// Contained in static.css
#pinnedSiteImage.active
{
    cursor: pointer;
    box-shadow: 0px 0px 15px #6Dffff, inset 0px 0px 10px #6Dffff;
    border-radius: 12px;
}
```

The user can pin a website by dragging the Pinned Sites icon, browser tab, or favicon to the taskbar or Start Menu. Internet Explorer 9 integrates with the Windows shell to accomplish the pinning.

Dynamic Jump List Updating and Notification Icons

Mileage Stats uses the jump list and notification icons to notify users of overdue maintenance reminders. When users click on the jump list entry, they will be taken to that reminder. The notification overlay icon displays 1, 2, 3, or 3+ to provide a taskbar indication of outstanding reminders.

Jump list and notification icon

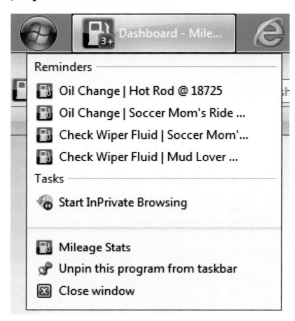

On the initial page load after the user authenticates, the client-side widgets and JavaScript objects are invoked by code in the mileagestats.js file. The **pinnedSite** object is initialized by passing it a delegate to the data manager's **sendRequest** method.

JavaScript
```
// Contained in mileagestats.js
mstats.pinnedSite.intializeData(mstats.dataManager.sendRequest);
```

The **initializeData** function saves the **sendRequestFunc** in the **sendRequest** property for future calls to the data manager by the **requeryJumpList** function.

JavaScript
```
// Contained in mstats.pinnedsite.js
intializeData: function (sendRequestFunc) {
  sendRequest = sendRequestFunc;
  this.requeryJumpList();
},
```

The **requeryJumpList** function, shown below, is called when the **pinnedSite** object is initialized, and also by the layout manager widget when a reminder is fulfilled. It's the layout manager's call that initializes the dynamic updating of the jump list and notification icon.

> **Note:** *Only the essential lines of code that demonstrate the loading of the jump list and updating of the notification icon are listed below.*

All of the following **msSite** functions are provided by Internet Explorer 9. After using feature detection to determine if the site is pinned, the jump list and overlay icon are cleared, and a new jump list is created.

If the Ajax request is successful and the **data.Reminders** array has data, a URL will be constructed for each data item and added to the jump list. Next, the appropriate overlay icon is set. Finally, **msSiteModeShowJumpList** is called to update the jump list.

```JavaScript
// Contained in mstats.pinnedsite.js
requeryJumpList: function () {
  var getRelativeUrl = mstats.getRelativeEndpointUrl;

  try {
    if (this.isPinned()) {

      sendRequest({
        url: '/reminder/overduelist/',
        contentType: 'application/json',
        cache: false,
        success: function (data) {

          try {
            var g_ext = window.external,
              ...

            g_ext.msSiteModeClearJumpList();
            g_ext.msSiteModeCreateJumpList("Reminders");
            g_ext.msSiteModeClearIconOverlay();

            if (data.Reminders) {
              for (i = 0; i < numReminders; i += 1) {
                reminder = data.Reminders[i];
                reminderUrl = getRelativeUrl('/reminder/details/' +
                  reminder.Reminder.ReminderId.toString());
                g_ext.msSiteModeAddJumpListItem(reminder.FullTitle, reminderUrl,
                  faviconUrl, "self");
              }
```

```
            if (numReminders > 0) {
              iconOverlayUrl = '/content/overlay-' + numReminders + '.ico';
              iconOverlayMessage = 'You have ' + numReminders.toString() +
                ' maintenance tasks that are ready to be accomplished.';
              if (numReminders > 3) {
                iconOverlayUrl = '/content/overlay-3plus.ico';
              }
              g_ext.msSiteModeSetIconOverlay(getRelativeUrl(iconOverlayUrl),
                iconOverlayMessage);
            }
          }

        g_ext.msSiteModeShowJumpList();
      }
      ...
```

This code demonstrates that with a small investment, you can deliver dynamic desktop notifications in your websites.

REQUIREMENT FOR JUMP LIST ITEMS TO APPEAR

The Windows 7 taskbar jump list items can be disabled by your users, preventing them from displaying even though the website has been pinned to the taskbar.

If your website implements the jump list feature, you should provide this information to your users and advise them that the **Store and display recently opened items in the Start menu and the taskbar** property setting needs to be checked for the jump list items to appear.

Taskbar and Start menu properties

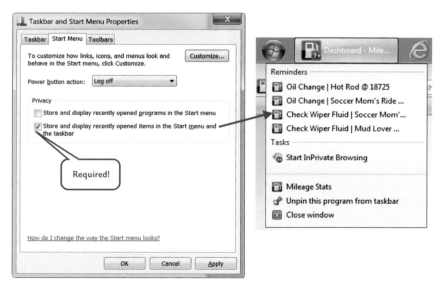

In addition to be being able to disable jump list items, users can customize the number of jump list items displayed on their computers. The default value is 10 and can be changed in the **Customize Start Menu** dialog box below. This dialog box is opened by clicking the **Customize** button in the **Taskbar and Start Menu Properties** dialog box shown above.

Customizing Start menu properties

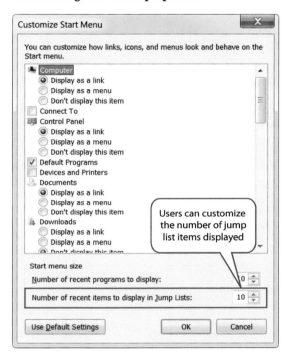

Summary

Providing timely feedback that is uniformly displayed, context sensitive, and understandable to your users without breaking their workflow takes planning by designers and developers alike. Your users will appreciate this extra effort, which results in a polished UX. By encapsulating the display and management of user notifications in a single JavaScript object, your application will be easier to code, maintain, and test. You have also learned about integrating your website with the Windows 7 desktop to provide users with dynamic notifications and jump list items, as well as allowing them to browse your site using a customized browser window.

Further Reading

For a comprehensive look at input validation error messages, see Chapter 11, "Server-Side Implementation."

For detailed information on the inner workings of the Mileage Stats pub/sub implementation, see Chapter 8, "Communication."

For more information about the **isFunction** method, see **jQuery.isFunction()**: http://api.jquery.com/jQuery.isFunction/.

For more information about Pinned Sites, see the Pinned Sites developer documentation: http://msdn.microsoft.com/en-us/library/gg491731(v=VS.85).aspx.

To access web resources more easily, see the online version of the bibliography on MSDN: http://msdn.microsoft.com/en-us/library/hh404094.aspx.

11   Server-Side Implementation

Introduction

Creating a well-architected web server application requires meeting the needs of the web client while properly factoring the Microsoft® .NET Framework code on the web server. A web server application is responsible for more than just returning HTML content. Web server applications also involve data models, data access and storage, security, communication, resource management, and internationalization. This chapter covers ways you can integrate technologies in the Microsoft web platform into a coherent architecture that is reliable, testable, and capable of handling demanding web client applications.

The following diagram shows the architecture of the Mileage Stats Reference Implementation (Mileage Stats). In this chapter, the data access and repository layers are discussed first, and then the Model View Controller (MVC) and business services layers. In the context of these layers, we also discuss the distinctions between data models, domain models, and view models. Lastly, you will learn how to provide asynchronous data and validation to web clients.

Mileage Stats high-level architecture

In this chapter you will learn:
- How to use ADO.NET Entity Framework and the Microsoft SQL Server® Compact Edition to create a data model.
- Techniques to separate concerns among your data model, business logic, and user interface (UI).
- How to support interactive web clients with asynchronous data.
- How to manage data validation at each level of the stack.

The technologies discussed in this chapter are ASP.NET MVC 3, ADO.NET Entity Framework 4, SQL Server Compact Edition 4, and Unity Application Block 2.0.

Creating a Data Access Layer

Data access is a key part of your application. The choice of storage technology and data access patterns can affect the entire application. This section covers an approach that uses rapid modeling techniques and tools while allowing you to migrate to high-scale data storage in the future.

A well-designed data access layer captures the essential structure of the data but omits conditional logic that is specific to the application. When you separate concerns that are specific to data access from those that are specific to the application's logic, the application remains robust and maintainable as you add features over time. The typical concerns of a data access layer include the type of data, the relationships between entities, and constraints.

The data you store is often in a format that is optimized for the storage technology, such as a relational database. Frequently, this format is not convenient for consumption by the application. For example, duration may be stored as a number representing the number of computer clock ticks, but having an instance of a **TimeSpan** would be easier for the application to use. In this case the data access layer should encapsulate the translation between the storage and in-memory formats. Ideally, the data access layer should not contain any UI or application logic and should fully abstract the underlying storage implementation.

In Mileage Stats, the **MileageStats.Model** project contains the data model. The data model is part of the data access layer. The structure and strong typing of the classes in this project express the data types, relationships, and constraints inherent in the data. For example, the **PricePerUnit** property of the **FillupEntry** class is a **double** to allow for dollars and cents, the **Fillups** property of the **Vehicle** class is an **ICollection<FillupEntry>** to express a one-to-many relationship, and the **DueDate** property of the **Reminder** class is a nullable **DateTime** to allow it to be optional.

When your application has significant complexity or conditional interaction with the data, you should consider creating a separate domain model that is distinct from your data model. See the "Composing Application Logic" section for guidance about whether or not to create a separate domain model.

RAPID DATA MODELING USING THE ADO.NET ENTITY FRAMEWORK AND SQL SERVER COMPACT

The ADO.NET Entity Framework provides three ways for you to rapidly create a data model:

- You can use the code-first approach to author standard classes that the ADO.NET Entity Framework uses to generate a database schema.
- You can use the database-first approach, where the ADO.NET Entity Framework generates data model classes from an existing database.
- You can choose to use the model-first approach, where an Entity Data Model (.edmx) can be used to generate the code and database.

The code-first approach is well suited to scenarios like Mileage Stats where developers are defining a new data model that will likely evolve as the application is written and there is no existing database. If you have an existing database, prefer to use stored procedures, or have a data architect on your team, then you may want to use more traditional database modeling techniques that let you generate the data model code from the database.

Using SQL Server Compact with the ADO.NET Entity Framework allows you to use an on-disk database that can easily be recreated whenever your schema changes. It can be seeded with a small dataset for debugging and unit testing. SQL Server Compact has a small footprint and can be migrated to SQL Server Express, SQL Server, or SQL AzureTM when the application is deployed.

> **Note:** *SQL Server Compact provides query and update functionality, but does not support conditional syntax (such as IF EXISTS), nor does it support stored procedures. Consider other SQL Server editions as your starting point if you need database-centric logic.*

Mileage Stats uses the code-first approach with the ADO.NET Entity Framework and SQL Server Compact. This approach allowed the data model to be built quickly and adapt to changes, and it minimized the day-to-day cost of database setup for the development team.

The ADO.NET Entity Framework lets you seed your database with sample data each time the database is rebuilt. This gives you the opportunity to use realistic sample data while you develop the application. We discovered many issues early in the development process of Mileage Stats because the sample data forced the UI and application logic to work with realistic data.

To use the code-first approach, you first create standard CLR object (POCO) classes. The ADO.NET Entity Framework then infers the database schema from your class structure and your property types. In the following example, the **FillupEntry** class defines properties that the ADO.NET Entity Framework can map to a database schema.

```csharp
C#
// Contained in FillupEntry.cs
public class FillupEntry
{
  ...

  public int FillupEntryId { get; set; }
  public int VehicleId { get; set; }
  public DateTime Date { get; set; }
  public int Odometer { get; set; }
  public double PricePerUnit { get; set; }
  public double TotalUnits { get; set; }
  public string Vendor { get; set; }
  public double TransactionFee { get; set; }
  public double TotalCost
  {
    get { return (this.PricePerUnit*this.TotalUnits) + this.TransactionFee; }
  }

  ...
}
```

The ADO.NET Entity Framework maps property types like **double, string,** and **int** to their equivalent SQL data type. Fields that represent unique entity identifiers, such as **FillupEntryId** and **VehicleId,** are automatically populated. Calculated properties, like **TotalCost**, that are not saved to the database can be added.

The ADO.NET Entity Framework has three mechanisms for determining the database schema from the class definition:

- **Class Inspection**. This is inspection of the classes to create a schema. Some of the decisions the ADO.NET Entity Framework makes are based on convention. For example, property names that end in **Id** are considered unique identifiers. They are auto-populated with database-generated values when records are inserted into the database.

- **Attribute Inspection**. This involves inspection of data annotation attributes attached to properties. These attributes are found in the **System.Component Model.DataAnnotations** namespace. For example, the **KeyAttribute** indicates a unique entity identifier. Attributes such as **RequiredAttribute** and **StringLength Attribute** cause the ADO.NET Entity Framework to create column constraints in the database.

- **Explicitly using DbModelBuilder**. This involves calls to the **DbModelBuilder** as part of the database creation. These methods directly determine the data types, entity relationships, and constraints for the database schema.

Note: *Using the data annotation attributes with the ADO.NET Entity Framework affects how the ADO.NET Entity Framework generates the database schema and performs validation of values when the data is saved using* **DbContext.SaveChanges**. *However, using the* **DbModelBuilder** *only changes the database schema. Which approach you choose can change the error messages you see when invalid data is submitted as well as determine whether a database call is made.*

See the "Further Reading" section for the ADO.NET Entity Framework documentation. It contains the detailed API reference and the steps required to apply each of these techniques.

Mileage Stats used the **DbModelBuilder** approach to define the storage schema and did not apply any data annotation attributes to the data model classes. This prevented database-specific concerns from being incorporated into the data model and made it possible to change the database schema, if necessary, for other kinds of database deployments. This approach was part of the decision to create a separate data model and domain model. See the "Creating a Business Services Layer" section for more information on this decision.

The domain model in Mileage Stats uses data annotation attributes extensively. See the "Data Validation" section for details on using attributes for validation.

Using the DbModelBuilder to Create a Data Model

In Mileage Stats, the **MileageStats.Data.SqlCE** project contains the **MileageStats DbContext** class. A data model built using the ADO.NET Entity Framework has at least one class derived from **DbContext**. This class provides the starting point for accessing the data model. It is also used for defining the data model, which results in a database schema.

The **MileageStatsDbContext** class overrides the **OnModelCreating** virtual method and uses the **DbModelBuilder** parameter to provide the ADO.NET Entity Framework with more information about the schema. The task of defining each entity is factored into separate methods that **MileageStatsDbContext.OnModelCreating** invokes. The following example is one of those methods. It builds the model for the **Vehicle** class.

```csharp
// Contained in MileageStatsDbContext.cs
private void SetupVehicleEntity(DbModelBuilder modelBuilder)
{
  modelBuilder.Entity<Vehicle>().HasKey(v => v.VehicleId);
  modelBuilder.Entity<Vehicle>().Property(v => v.VehicleId)
    .HasDatabaseGeneratedOption(
      DatabaseGeneratedOption.Identity);
  modelBuilder.Entity<Vehicle>().Property(v => v.Name)
    .IsRequired();
  modelBuilder.Entity<Vehicle>().Property(v => v.Name)
    .HasMaxLength(100);
  modelBuilder.Entity<Vehicle>().Property(v => v.SortOrder);
```

```
modelBuilder.Entity<Vehicle>().Property(v => v.MakeName)
  .HasMaxLength(50);
modelBuilder.Entity<Vehicle>().Property(v => v.ModelName)
  .HasMaxLength(50);
modelBuilder.Entity<Vehicle>().HasOptional(v => v.Photo);
modelBuilder.Entity<Vehicle>().HasMany(v => v.Fillups);
modelBuilder.Entity<Vehicle>().HasMany(v => v.Reminders);
}
```

DbModelBuilder allows you to chain calls together because each method returns an object that can be used in subsequent calls. The calls in the preceding example use the **Entity<T>** method to locate an entity based on the type of the class. The chained **Property** method locates a property for that entity. Lambda expressions like **v => v.Vehicle EntryId** allow the **Property** method to work without having to provide the name of the property as a string. The last method call defines the data model type, relationship, or constraint.

It is possible for you to use data annotation attributes in conjunction with calls to **DbModelBuilder**. Data annotation attributes allow a decentralized approach where relationships and constraints are attached to individual properties on the class. The **Db ModelBuilder** approach gives you centralized control of the data model and a powerful set of modeling options. You should be careful to keep the constraints in sync when mixing approaches. For this reason, it is recommended that you use either data annotation attributes *or* the **DbModelBuilder**, and avoid mixing approaches.

> **Note:** *There is an order of precedence in the ADO.NET Entity Framework when all three mechanisms are used:* **DbModelBuilder** *calls override data annotation attributes, which override convention by inspection.*

Creating the Database

Once you define the data model in code, you need to create the database. When you use the code-first approach, the ADO.NET Entity Framework doesn't create the database until the first request for data occurs. You should create the database on application startup rather than on the first request so that the first user isn't forced to wait. Initializing during application startup also reduces the chance of a race condition during database creation.

> **Note:** *Many web applications built using the ADO.NET Entity Framework contain the auto-generated* **WebActivatorAttribute** *code. This attribute automatically calls the database creation and initialization code. Mileage Stats forgoes this approach because the Unity dependency injection container controls the lifetime of the* **MileageStats-DbContext** *instance.*

In **Global.asax.cs**, the **Application_Start** method initializes the dependency injection container and then initializes the database. The **InitializeDatabase** method uses the dependency injection container to resolve an instance of the **IRepositoryInitializer** and then calls the **Initialize** method. In the following example, the constructor of the **RepositoryInitializer** configures the database connection and initializer, and the **Initialize** method requests some data to ensure that the database is created before user requests are processed.

```csharp
C#
// Contained in RepositoryInitializer.cs
public RepositoryInitializer(IUnitOfWork unitOfWork)
{
  ...
  Database.DefaultConnectionFactory =
      new SqlCeConnectionFactory("System.Data.SqlServerCe.4.0");

  Database.SetInitializer(
      new DropCreateIfModelChangesSqlCeInitializer<MileageStatsDbContext>());
}

public void Initialize()
{
  this.Context.Set<Country>().ToList().Count();

  ...
}
```

Initializing the Database

The ADO.NET Entity Framework lets you control how your database is created and initialized through the **IDatabaseInitializer<T>** interface and the **Database.SetInitializer** method. You can write the initializer with the logic you need to create and populate your database.

In Mileage Stats, the **MileageStats.Data.SqlCe** project contains three classes that can initialize the database: **CreateIfNotExistsSqlCeInitializer**, **DropCreateAlwaysSqlCeInitializer**, and **DropCreateIfModelChangesSqlCeInitializer**. All three inherit from the **SqlCeInitializer** base class that implements the **IDatabaseInitializer<T>** interface.

> **Note:** *When you use **NuGet** to add the ADO.NET Entity Framework to your project, the package manager will generate some default initializers similar to those found in Mileage Stats. Mileage Stats classes are modified versions of the original generated classes. The modifications allow each initializer to share the database seeding code used to start the application with sample data.*

Each class implements a different strategy for creating the database. Mileage Stats defaults to the **DropCreateIfModelChangesSqlCeInitializer** to drop and create the database anytime the data model changes the schema. This can be very useful during product development when the data model is evolving and the database doesn't contain real data.

Depending on how your database is deployed, you may need to change the default initializer or use another mechanism for initializing the database. If you deploy a new version of the application where the schema needs to be upgraded, you would either need to write an initializer that upgrades the database, or run upgrade scripts before deployment of the newer version. Otherwise, you would lose all the data stored in the database.

Optimized Data Access

Many application data models are hierarchical, with one-to-many and many-to-many relationships between entities. On the other hand, web applications are connectionless and stateless; they take a request and produce a response. You should avoid loading large model hierarchies for requests that only need a subset of the data. Loading more data than is necessary places additional processor, memory, and bandwidth pressure on the server and can limit scalability and performance.

Fortunately, the ADO.NET Entity Framework provides powerful querying support in the **DbSet** class that allows you to return just the data you need. In Mileage Stats, the **VehicleRepository** class uses the **Where** and **Include** methods on the **DbSet** to control the data retrieved, as shown in the following code.

```C#
// Contained in VehicleRepository.cs
public Vehicle GetVehicle(int userId, int vehicleId)
{
        return this.GetDbSet<Vehicle>()
                .Include("Fillups")
                .Include("Reminders")
                .Where(v => v.VehicleId == vehicleId && v.UserId == userId)
                .Single();
}
```

The ADO.NET Entity Framework does not automatically populate **ICollection<T>** properties like **Vehicles**, **Fill-ups**, and **Reminder**, but does lazy load them when accessed. When lazy loading is turned off (as it is in Mileage Stats,) these properties must be included explicitly. Properties marked optional by data annotation attributes or **DbModel Builder** calls, such as the **FillupEntry.Distance** property, must also be included explicitly to be retrieved. The previous code sample is an example of calling **Include** explicitly.

The ADO.NET Entity Framework has features that support lazy-loaded properties and change tracking. When using the code-first approach, lazy loading is done by applying the **virtual** keyword, and change tracking is done through having standard **get** and **set** methods along with using **ICollection<T>** for one-to-many relationships. The ADO.NET Entity Framework also supports these features by implementing the **IEntityWithChange Tracker** or **IEntityWithRelationships** interfaces.

IMPLEMENTING THE REPOSITORY PATTERN

The Repository pattern assists in separating data storage concerns from the application logic. This pattern is especially beneficial when you use the ADO.NET Entity Framework because it allows you to hide ADO.NET Entity Framework-specific classes such as

DbContext and **DbSet**, to optimize the shape of the data returned to the application, to coordinate updates, and to unit test your application without requiring access to physical data storage. See the "Further Reading" section for a formal definition of the repository pattern.

A repository is a set of interfaces and implementations providing methods for data access. The interfaces do not expose any types specific to data storage. You can choose how many repositories to create based on how granularly you want to control data access within your application.

In Mileage Stats, the MileageStats.Data project contains the repository interfaces and the MileageStats.Data.SqlCe project contains the repository implementations. The Mileage Stats repositories map closely to the data entities to match the usage pattern from the business services layer. The following code shows the **IReminderRepository** interface.

```csharp
// Contained in IReminderRepository.cs
public interface IReminderRepository
{
  void Create(int vehicleId, Reminder reminder);
  Reminder GetReminder(int reminderId);
  void Update(Reminder reminder);
  void Delete(int reminderId);

  IEnumerable<Reminder> GetRemindersForVehicle(int vehicleId);
  IEnumerable<Reminder> GetOverdueReminders(int vehicleId,
    DateTime forDate, int forOdometer);

  IEnumerable<Reminder> GetUpcomingReminders(int vehicleId,
    DateTime forStartDate, DateTime forEndDate,
    int odometer, int warningOdometer);
}
```

> **Note:** *The **IReminderRepository** interface returns collections as **IEnumerable<T>**, rather than **IList<T>** or **ICollection<T>**. This was an intentional design choice to prevent the direct addition of entities to the collections. To create a new reminder, the developer must use the **Create** method.*
>
> *In Mileage Stats, the implementation of the **IReminderRepository** calls **ToList** before returning the **IEnumerable<T>**. This is to ensure that the query is executed inside the repository. If **ToList** was not called, then the repository would return an **IQueryable<T>** and the database would not be accessed until something iterated over the **IQueryable<T>** object. The problem with returning an **IQueryable<T>** is that a developer consuming the API is likely to assume that the query has already executed and that you are working with the results. If you iterate over the query more than once, it will result in multiple calls to the database.*
>
> *If you specifically want your repository to return queries instead of results, use the **IQueryable<T>** on the interface in order to make your intention explicit.*

Because web applications and services follow a request/response pattern, incoming data is built from the POST form data. This means that the incoming object class was not retrieved from the **DbContext** and cannot be updated because it is not attached to the context. Using the repository pattern with the ADO.NET Entity Framework creates the proper place to deal with attached and detached entities and set entity state.

In the following example, the **Update** method in the **VehicleRepository** is passed an entity that is not attached to the ADO.NET Entity Framework context. The **Update** method locates the corresponding attached entity, updates the attached entity, and ensures the attached entity state is set correctly.

```C#
// Contained in VehicleRepository.cs
public void Update(Vehicle updatedVehicle)
{
  Vehicle vehicleToUpdate =
    this.GetDbSet<Vehicle>().Where(v => v.VehicleId ==
        updatedVehicle.VehicleId).First();

  vehicleToUpdate.Name = updatedVehicle.Name;
  vehicleToUpdate.Year = updatedVehicle.Year;
  vehicleToUpdate.MakeName = updatedVehicle.MakeName;
  vehicleToUpdate.ModelName = updatedVehicle.ModelName;
  vehicleToUpdate.SortOrder = updatedVehicle.SortOrder;
  vehicleToUpdate.PhotoId = updatedVehicle.PhotoId;

  this.SetEntityState(vehicleToUpdate,
      vehicleToUpdate.VehicleId == 0 ? EntityState.Added : EntityState.Modified);

  this.UnitOfWork.SaveChanges();
}
```

Composing Application Logic

Web client applications built for rich user interactivity are often more complex than those built for clients that post back synchronously on each mouse click and always display static HTML in response. Web applications that provide interactive behavior on a single page (via Ajax method calls, JavaScript templates, and secondary data requests) require careful composition of server application code. This section covers several techniques and considerations to help you create maintainable applications that provide a rich set of services to interactive clients.

FACTORING APPLICATION CODE WITH ASP.NET MVC

Because ASP.NET MVC is a web platform technology built around a design pattern, following the MVC pattern is a key step in properly factoring your application logic. Well-designed MVC applications have controllers and actions that are small and views that are simple. Keeping your application code DRY (Don't Repeat Yourself) as the application is built is far easier than trying to clean it up later.

> **Note:** *The routes you create in global.asax.cs define the URL hierarchy of your application. Defining your URL strategy, routes, and controller topology early in a project can help prevent having to change your client application code later.*

Because the majority of the application logic is contained within the models, MVC applications contain different kinds of models:

- **View models** are built solely for a view to data-bind against. These models are contained within the MVC application and often follow the same composition hierarchy as the views. They are focused on presentation. That is, they are only concerned with presenting data in the UI. Sometimes a special type of view model, called a form model, is also used to represent the data coming into an application from the user.

- **Domain models** are based on the solution domain. They are focused on handling the business logic of the application. They represent the logical behavior of the application independent of the UI and the storage mechanism. They may be annotated or extended to support some application features such as validation or authentication. Because these models need to be shared between the server and client browser, they are sometimes contained within view models. Domain models are sometimes referred to as application models or service models.

- **Data models** are built for data services and storage. These are not exposed by the application and are often encapsulated by a services layer.

Organizing your application into these categories is a way of separating concerns in your code. This separation becomes increasingly important as an application grows in complexity. If you find that changes to your application logic are affecting storage or presentation (or vice versa), you should factor the code into separate models.

In some cases, the models may be very similar to one another. In other cases, the models may radically diverge. If your domain model and your data model are very similar, you can consider aggregating an instance of your data model class into your domain model class. If your domain and data models have a matching hierarchy and compatible interfaces, you can also consider using inheritance to derive your domain model classes from your data model classes.

> **Note:** *Inheritance has the advantage of less coding because you reuse your data model as your domain model, but it is at the cost of tighter coupling. If you can ensure that you will not need to substitute a different data model and that the domain and data models will not diverge, inheritance can be effective.*

As you're writing your controller actions, you should factor complex methods into helper methods or classes in your models and services layer. Use action filter attributes such as **HttpPostAttribute** to avoid writing conditional logic in each action that inspects the **HttpContext**. Also, use action filters for cross-cutting concerns such as authentication (for example, **AuthorizeAttribute**) and error handling (for example, **HandleError Attribute**). Ideally, methods that handle GET should contain only a few method calls and should not contain much conditional logic; methods that handle POST should validate the incoming data, perform the update when the data is valid, and conditionally return a view depending on the success of the update. The following examples from Mileage Stats show two versions of the **FillupController**'s **Add** method (first the GET version, and then the POST version). In these examples, the generic method **Using<T>** is a helper method used to delegate logic to the classes in the services layer.

C#

```csharp
// Contained in FillupController.cs
public ActionResult Add(int vehicleId)
{
        var vehicles = Using<GetVehicleListForUser>()
                .Execute(CurrentUserId);

        var vehicle = vehicles.First(v => v.VehicleId == vehicleId);

        var newFillupEntry = new FillupEntryFormModel
                {
                        Odometer = (vehicle.Odometer.HasValue)
                                        ? vehicle.Odometer.Value : 0
                };

        var fillups = Using<GetFillupsForVehicle>()
                .Execute(vehicleId)
                .OrderByDescending(f => f.Date);

        var viewModel = new FillupAddViewModel
        {
                VehicleList = new VehicleListViewModel(vehicles, vehicleId)
                                {IsCollapsed = true},
                FillupEntry = newFillupEntry,
                Fillups = new SelectedItemList<Model.FillupEntry>(fillups),
        };

        ViewBag.IsFirstFillup = (!fillups.Any());

        return View(viewModel);
}
```

C#

```csharp
// Contained in FillupController.cs
[HttpPost]
[ValidateInput(false)]
```

```csharp
[ValidateAntiForgeryToken]
public ActionResult Add(int vehicleId, FillupEntryFormModel model)
{
        var vehicles = Using<GetVehicleListForUser>()
                .Execute(CurrentUserId );

        if (ModelState.IsValid)
        {
                var errors = Using<CanAddFillup>()
                        .Execute(CurrentUserId, vehicleId, model);

                ModelState.AddModelErrors(errors, "AddFillup");

                if (ModelState.IsValid)
                {
                        Using<AddFillupToVehicle>()
                            .Execute(CurrentUserId, vehicleId, model);

                        TempData["LastActionMessage"] = Resources
                            .VehicleController_AddFillupSuccessMessage;

                        return RedirectToAction("List", "Fillup",
                            new { vehicleId = vehicleId });
                }
        }

        var fillups = Using<GetFillupsForVehicle>()
                .Execute(vehicleId)
                .OrderByDescending(f => f.Date);

        var viewModel = new FillupAddViewModel
        {
                VehicleList = new VehicleListViewModel(vehicles, vehicleId)
                                    { IsCollapsed = true },
                FillupEntry = model,
                Fillups = new SelectedItemList<Model.FillupEntry>(fillups),
        };

        ViewBag.IsFirstFillup = (!fillups.Any());

        return View(viewModel);
}
```

Note: *As you're writing your controllers, injecting dependences through the controller's constructor will benefit unit testing. In Mileage Stats, the controller depends on interfaces and not concrete implementations, so we were able to easily replace the actual dependencies with mock implementations. This allowed us to test just the code for the action and not the entire functional stack. For more information, see Chapter 13, "Unit Testing Web Applications."*

After factoring your models and controller actions, your views will use the models to produce HTML. When building views, you should keep the amount of code to a minimum. Code contained in views is not easily testable. Errors in views are harder to debug because the exception occurs during the view engine's rendering pass. However, some very simple logic in views is acceptable. For example, looping over items to build a repeating section of the UI or conditional logic for toggling the visibility of specific sections is fine. Any HTML that is repeated in multiple views is a candidate for being factored into a partial view. However, if you find that you need something more complicated, try to push that logic into the view model. If the logic is a cross-cutting concern, then consider placing that logic inside an HTML helper extension method. Examples of built-in HTML helper extension methods in MVC include **BeginForm**, **RenderPartial**, and **ActionLink**. Examples of helper methods in Mileage Stats are **AverageFuelEfficiencyText** and **AverageFuel EfficiencyMagnitude**.

Note: *The MVC Razor syntax allows you to write code more compactly as well as easily mix code and markup. Don't let this powerful view engine tempt you into writing a lot of code in your views. Instead, let it help you keep the code you do write clear and maintainable.*

DESIGN CHECKLIST FOR MVC APPLICATIONS

The following checklist is useful when reviewing your MVC web application code.

Check	When reviewing your MVC web application code, ensure that:
☐	Each controller handles a common set of concerns, either for a particular model type or a related set of interactions with the user.
☐	Action methods consist of a sequence of calls to helper methods, helper classes, and/or model classes. They do not contain complex branching conditional logic. They should be easy to unit test and self-documenting.
☐	The same code is not repeated in multiple action methods. Action filter attributes are used to handle cross-cutting concerns.
☐	The majority of the application logic is contained within the model or service layer.
☐	The hierarchy of model classes used by controller actions and views is effective for the application. If required, separate data model classes are contained within another assembly.
☐	Views contain only small conditional statements and calls to HTML helper methods.
☐	The same HTML is not repeated in multiple views. Commonly used HTML is factored into partial views.

See the "Further Reading" section for links to more MVC best practices.

CREATING A BUSINESS SERVICES LAYER

As you factor your application code from your controllers' action methods into helper methods and classes, you may find that there are classes and methods that help to properly retrieve, validate, and update data in your data model. This business logic is distinguished from the controller code because it encapsulates logical operations on the domain model and is *not* specific to any view.

When you have a significant amount of business logic, you may need to create a business services layer. The business services layer is another layer of abstraction, and there is a cost to adding it to the application. However, creating this layer allows you to test the business logic in isolation, and it simplifies the tests for your controllers. Because the business services layer is unaware of the UI, you can also reuse it in the future when exposing additional interfaces such as a web service (using service technologies like Windows® Communication Foundation (WCF)). This allows you to support both desktop and mobile clients from a single business services layer.

When deciding whether or not to create a business services layer, you should also consider whether or not to create a separate domain model. See the section "Factoring Application Code with ASP.NET MVC" for details on the different kinds of models and techniques for separating a domain model from a data model. Creating a separate domain model along with a business services layer is most beneficial when you need to fully encapsulate your data model, your data model does not perform validation, and the domain model functionality will make it easier for you to write your controllers and views. However, having a separate domain model and data model does incur a cost for transforming values between the two models.

The services layer in Mileage Stats consists primarily of handlers and domain models. The handlers are a set of classes that implement the core behavior of the application. They are completely independent from and unaware of the UI. Reading over the names of the handler classes is like reading a list of the features of Mileage Stats. The domain models are a second set of classes in the services layer that differ from both the data models and the view models. The data models in Mileage Stats are primarily concerned with persisting data to the database. The view models are very specific to the needs of the UI. However, the domain models in the services layer are not concerned with either persistence or the UI. The handlers and the domain models in the services layer represent the business logic of the application. Together they provide validation, calculation of statistics, and other services. For more information on data validation, see the "Data Validation" section.

The following illustration shows the high-level design of the services layer and data model.

Mileage Stats service layer and data model

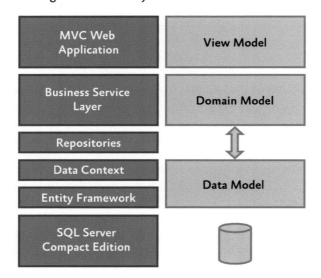

The following example from Mileage Stats shows the **Execute** method from the **AddFillupToVehicle** handler. This handler is represented as a single class with a single public method. We chose the convention of naming the method **Execute**. The general dependencies of the handler are injected into the constructor of the handler. Any specific values that may be needed to invoke the handler are passed as arguments to the **Execute** method. Unity is responsible for managing and injecting the dependencies for the handler's constructor, whereas the **Execute** method will be invoked by some consumer with the necessary arguments. In the case of Mileage Stats, the consumer is a controller action.

Also note that the handler has two private helper methods: **ToEntry** and **Adjust SurroundingFillupEntries**. **ToEntry** is responsible for converting the data to the form needed by the data layer. **CalculateInterFillupStatistics** (which is called within **Adjust SurroundingFillupEntries)** is responsible for calculating the statistics.

```C#
// Contained in AddFillupToVehicle.cs
public virtual void Execute(int userId, int vehicleId,
                            ICreateFillupEntryCommand newFillup)
{
        if (newFillup == null) throw new ArgumentNullException("newFillup");

        try
        {
                var vehicle = _vehicleRepository.GetVehicle(userId, vehicleId);

                if (vehicle != null)
```

```
            {
                newFillup.VehicleId = vehicleId;
                var fillup = newFillup;

                var entity = ToEntry(fillup);
                AdjustSurroundingFillupEntries(entity);

                _fillupRepository.Create(userId, vehicleId, entity);

                // update calculated value
                newFillup.Distance = entity.Distance;
            }
        }
        catch (InvalidOperationException ex)
        {
            throw new BusinessServicesException(Resources
                    .UnableToAddFillupToVehicleExceptionMessage, ex);
        }
    }
}
```

In Mileage Stats, the handlers are responsible for implementing the core business logic of the application. The controllers have the responsibility of accepting the user's input and invoking the handler. Controllers then take the results of invoking handlers and compose any data necessary for rendering views. This data frequently takes the form of classes that we call view models.

Overall, the business services layer provides functionality that makes writing controllers, actions, and views much easier.

Supporting Interactive Web Clients

Interactive web clients communicate asynchronously with the server and manipulate the document object model (DOM). Because multiple interactions can occur simultaneously, managing state and tracking events can be difficult. This section outlines ways the web application server can support web clients by providing services that reduce the complexity of the JavaScript.

PROVIDING HTML STRUCTURE

Traditionally, the server in a web application returns HTML as content that the client's browser renders directly. Because interactive web clients manipulate the HTML structure, you will need to focus less on the appearance of the HTML and more on providing a useful hierarchy for the client. You should think of the HTML structure as part of the contract between the client and the server.

In order to modify the content, web clients first need to locate elements in the DOM. The jQuery library provides a selector syntax that can be used to locate elements in many ways (such as by ID, class, relative position, and so forth). If the web client depends on the hierarchical structure of the HTML you produce, you will likely break the client application when you modify the structure.

To avoid tightly coupling the client JavaScript with the HTML structure, you can use **data-** (pronounced "data dash") attributes in your HTML. The **data-** attributes are attributes whose names are prefixed with "data-" and represent metadata on elements.

Many JavaScript developers use the **id** and **class** attributes to locate elements. The **id** attribute is limited because there can be only one per element and **id** values are generally expected to be unique within a page. The **class** attributes cause confusion because they are also used to apply layout and style to the element through Cascading Style Sheets (CSS).

Because **data-** attributes are independent of the HTML structure, they allow you to restructure the HTML without impacting the client. See Chapter 6, "Client Data Management and Caching" and "Using Data- Attributes" in Chapter 7, "Manipulating Client-Side HTML" for more information on how clients can use **data-** attributes.

Below are two **data-** attribute examples from Mileage Stats. In the first example, the **data-vehicle-id** attribute allows the client to locate the associated element. Notice that we are rendering the value for the **data-** attribute on the server and that it will be consumed by JavaScript on the client.

```
HTML
// Contained in Views\Vehicle\List.cshtml
<a class="list-item @(item.Reminder.IsOverdue ? "overdue" : null)"
  href="@Url.Action("Details", "Reminder", new { id = item.Reminder.ReminderId })"
  data-vehicle-id="@item.Vehicle.VehicleId">
  ...
</a>
```

In the second example, the **data-chart-url** attribute provides the client a URL to use in an Ajax call.

```
HTML
// Contained in Views\Vehicle\List.cshtml
<div id="main-chart" class="article framed"
  data-chart-url="@Url.Action("JsonGetFleetStatisticSeries", "Home")">
```

Ideally, your JavaScript should use only **data-** attributes to locate elements and to discover contextual data from the server. However, there are cases where using a selector to manipulate all elements having a given element name, unique ID, or class is a more practical approach. In both cases, you should write the JavaScript code to allow for the case where the set of selected elements is empty.

> **Note:** *If you have a team of developers writing the web client independently of the web application, we **strongly** recommend you ensure agreement on the expected HTML structure before writing the web client JavaScript.*

USING VIEW MODEL AND VIEW BAG

ASP.NET MVC 3 introduced the **ViewBag**. A **ViewBag** is a dynamic object that wraps the **ViewData** property that was present in previous versions of ASP.NET MVC. A **ViewBag** is a name/value keyed collection that lets you store loosely typed data. This differs from the **Model** property on the **View**, which contains strongly typed data. Having two ways to provide the view data can cause confusion about when to use **View.Model** versus **ViewBag**.

The strongly typed **View.Model** property has several benefits over **ViewBag**. It enables IntelliSense® auto-complete in the view, and it provides type safety when generating the view model from a controller action. In addition, many of the helpers are specifically designed to work with a strongly typed model, and they can extract metadata from the model to help automatically construct a view.

When you use the **View.Model** in a **form** element, you will have an associated controller action (marked with the **HttpPostAttribute**) that accepts the model as a parameter. When the form is submitted, the MVC model binder uses the posted form data to construct and populate an instance of your view-model class.

Often the view model representing the form that is passed into a controller action will be significantly different from the view model returned from the controller action. In those cases you can create a *form model* that contains only the data from the form. An example of this in Mileage Stats is the **Add** action on **VehicleController**. It has a parameter of type **VehicleFormModel** and returns a view model of type **VehicleAddViewModel**. The **VehicleAddViewModel** contains data such as the current user and a list of vehicles, as well as the original form model.

If possible, create a view model for each of your views. This gives you complete control over the data sent to and from the client. It also reduces confusion by making the relationship between views and view models explicit. Likewise, using form models that are specific to views prevents the ASP.NET MVC model binder from setting properties that you didn't expect to receive from the client. In many cases, if you follow this practice you will never need to use **ViewBag**.

However, there can be cases when your view needs additional data that doesn't belong in your view model and you don't want to make a round trip to the client. In these cases, consider placing the data in **ViewBag**.

In Mileage Stats, the **_ProfileForm** partial view uses the **User** class as the **View.Model**. Part of the view is a drop-down list of countries. The following example shows the **ViewBag** used to populate the drop-down list.

```
CSHTML
//Contained in Views\Shared\_ProfileForm.cshtml
@model MileageStats.Domain.Models.User
...
<div class="editor-label">
  @Html.LabelFor(model => model.Country)
</div>
<div class="editor-field">
  @Html.DropDownListFor(model => model.Country, ViewBag.CountryList as SelectList,
```

```
  "-- Select country --", new { @class = "editor-textbox" })
 @Html.ValidationMessageFor(model => model.Country)
</div>
...
<div class="editor-commands">
 <button data-action="profile-save" class="button generic small editor-submit"
type="submit">
   <img src="@Url.Content(
    "~/Content/button-save.png")"
    title="Save Profile" alt="Save" />
 </button>
</div>
<div style="clear: both;">
</div>
@Html.ValidationSummary(true)
```

Mileage Stats could have had a separate view-model class containing the **User** and an **ICollection<Country>** object. However, doing so would make the partial view less reusable because every view model in the hierarchy of views and partial views would have to contain the new view model.

Providing Data Asynchronously

Requesting data asynchronously is at the heart of a responsive, interactive web client. One option for requesting data asynchronously is to use WCF to expose a service API for the client. This is a good choice when the application is not responsible for serving the web UI. ASP.NET MVC web applications are a great endpoint for serving data to web clients when the application must also serve the site's UI. You can use the same routing, controllers, security, and models for returning data that you use for returning HTML structure. This allows the web client to use the relative URLs you provided in the **data-** attributes as well as some knowledge of the site's URL structure to create requests for data.

Choosing a Data Format

Web clients typically request data as HTML, JavaScript Object Notation (JSON), XML, or binary (for example, images and video) from the server. Each of these formats has its unique strengths.

The JSON format is recommended when the web client needs to bind data to existing HTML elements, generate new HTML from the data, transform the data, or make logical decisions based on the data. JSON is a very concise format that has serialization support on the client and in ASP.NET MVC. Because JSON contains no markup, it helps separate UI and data service concerns.

The HTML format is useful when the client makes minimal or no changes to the returned content and simply places the entire HTML result into a pre-determined area of the page. Examples of where HTML works well are advertisements, content aggregators, and content management systems.

The XML format is useful when the client receives data based on a pre-defined schema. XML is also used when working in open-standards formats such as **RSS**, **Atom**, and **oData**. Web clients can use the known schema structure to process the XML into HTML.

Binary formats are generally employed for media. Images are the most common example; the server returns an **img** element with a **src** attribute, the browser makes a secondary request to the server and then renders the binary result as an image.

> **Note:** *Not all browsers send the same data to the server when requesting images and other resources. Some browsers will send authentication headers and cookies while others will not. If you have secondary requests that must be authenticated, you need to verify that those requests work on the browsers you intend to support. In addition, you should perform testing in both the ASP.NET development server and in a Microsoft Internet Information Services (IIS)-deployed web application.*

To support a particular format in ASP.NET MVC, return a **JsonResult**, **ContentResult**, or **FileResult** instead of a **ViewResult** from your action methods.

The following example from Mileage Stats returns a **JsonResult**. The view model is created and then the **Controller.Json** method is called to convert the object into JSON for the response.

C#

```csharp
// Contained in VehicleController.cs
[Authorize]
[HttpPost]
public JsonResult JsonDetails(int id)
{
        VehicleModel vehicle = Using<GetVehicleById>()
                .Execute(CurrentUserId, vehicleId: id);

        // we are limiting this to 3 reminders
        // after we retrieve the full set from the server
        var overdue = Using<GetOverdueRemindersForVehicle>()
            .Execute(id, DateTime.UtcNow, vehicle.Odometer ?? 0)
            .Take(3);

        var vm = ToJsonVehicleViewModel(vehicle, overdue);

        return Json(vm);
}
```

> **Note:** *Controller actions that return a **JsonResult** are easy to unit test because you can inspect the **JsonResult.Data** property directly. However, debugging a serialization issue with a **JsonResult** is harder because it requires you to inspect the returned data from the web service in the web client.*

Factoring Controller Actions for Ajax

The same set of principles used to build controller actions in general still apply when those actions return JSON. If you decide to create a separate set of URLs for returning data (for example, if you create an independent data service API), you can create separate controllers and routes. This approach is beneficial when you expect multiple types of clients (for example, a web client and a Microsoft Silverlight® browser plug-in) to use the data actions, but only the web client to use the view-based actions.

If your data actions are closely related to your view-based actions, you can put data actions in the same controller as the view-based actions. Mileage Stats is an example of this scenario because the data actions focus on the same domain models as the view-based actions.

If your web client needs to use the same URL to request different data formats, you can extend your controller action methods by using the **HttpRequestBase.IsAjax Request** extension method to determine which to determine the format of the request and the data format to return. This is beneficial when you can reuse your view model as your JSON model. If you find that you have large **if-else** blocks in your controller actions, you should factor the view-based and JSON actions into different helper methods. Alternatively, you can write a custom **AjaxAttribute** action filter that uses **IsAjaxRequest**. This action filter would provide overloaded action methods similar to those in **HttpPost Attribute**.

When errors occur, your data actions can throw exceptions just like view-based actions do. The jQuery library supports **beforeSend**, **send**, **success**, **error**, and **complete** handlers to handle server responses and failures. If you don't want the friendly error page HTML content returned when a JSON data action throws an exception, you may need to apply a different **HandleErrorAttribute** value to your data actions.

As you design your data actions, you should consider how many round trips to the server will be required for each interaction with the user. Every Ajax request requires separate threading on the client as well as resources for the connection, server response, data download, and client processing. If you create overly granular data actions, your web client may encounter performance issues because it must manage a large number of requests in order to satisfy a user action. If you create very large data actions, your web client and server may encounter performance issues because of both the creation and processing of large amounts of data.

> **Note:** *You may find it helpful to use web browser debugging and tracing tools such as Windows Internet Explorer® F12 developer tools, Fiddler, and FireBug to see the relative cost of the different parts of each round trip to the server. Depending on the connection speed and distance between your users and your server, creating a connection can be much more costly than downloading the data once a connection is made. Many web applications that are used globally are designed to request larger chunks of data when that data cannot be cached closer to the user.*

Data Validation

Interactive web applications need to let users know when they have provided data that is invalid. Data validation checks need to happen in three places: on the client in the context of what the user is trying to accomplish, on the server to protect from untrustworthy callers, and in the database to ensure data integrity. Having data validation occur at multiple levels in the stack makes creating common and consistent validation logic important to the user experience. This section covers data validation techniques you can use to validate your data on both the server and the client.

DATA ANNOTATION ATTRIBUTES

Applying data annotation attributes to your model allows ASP.NET MVC and the ADO. NET Entity Framework to provide data validation at the server level. As mentioned in the "Creating a Data Model" section, the ADO.NET Entity Framework also inspects the data annotation attributes on your entity classes in order to create the database schema. You can find the standard data annotation attributes in the **System.ComponentModel.Data Annotations** namespace. In this section, data annotation attributes that provide validation are referred to as validation attributes.

The following example shows the validation attributes applied to the **VehicleForm Model** class in the MileageStats.Domain project. The attributes applied to the **Vehicle FormModel.Name** property validate that the name is not null, is not an empty string, is no more than 20 characters, and does not contain script injection characters.

```C#
// Contained in VehicleModel.cs
[StringLength(20,
  ErrorMessageResourceName = "VehicleNameStringLengthValidationError",
  ErrorMessageResourceType = typeof(Resources))]
[TextLineInputValidator]
[Required(AllowEmptyStrings = false,
  ErrorMessageResourceName = "VehicleNameRequired",
  ErrorMessageResourceType = typeof(Resources))]
public string Name
{
    get { return this.Vehicle.Name; }
}
```

Validation attributes also support localization. By using the resource names, the error messages are loaded from a RESX file.

VALIDATING DATA IN MVC

The ASP.NET MVC default model binder uses the **Validator** and **ValidationContext** classes when parsing incoming data into an instance of your model class. These two classes work together to validate the data based on the validation attributes you have applied.

If any of the validation fails, **AddModelError** is called on the **ModelState** class. **ModelState.IsValid** returns false when **ModelState** has one or more errors. Because all of this happens before your action is called, validating data in your controller actions is easy. The following example shows the **FillupController** using **ModelState.IsValid** before making the update.

```C#
// Contained in FillupController.cs
[HttpPost]
[ValidateInput(false)]
[ValidateAntiForgeryToken]
public ActionResult Add(int vehicleId, FillupEntryFormModel model)
{
        var vehicles = Using<GetVehicleListForUser>()
                .Execute(CurrentUserId );

        if (ModelState.IsValid)
        {
                var errors = Using<CanAddFillup>()
                        .Execute(CurrentUserId, vehicleId, model);

                ModelState.AddModelErrors(errors, "AddFillup");

                if (ModelState.IsValid)
                {
                        Using<AddFillupToVehicle>()
                                .Execute(CurrentUserId, vehicleId, model);

                        TempData["LastActionMessage"] = Resources
                                .VehicleController_AddFillupSuccessMessage;
                        return RedirectToAction("List", "Fillup",
                                        new { vehicleId = vehicleId });
                }
        }
        ...
        var viewModel = new FillupAddViewModel
        {
                ...
        };
        return View(viewModel);
}
```

In the previous example, invoking the handler **CanAddFillup** returns a **Validation Result** collection. These validation results are returned from the business services layer. The **AddModelErrors** extension method iterates over the **ValidationResult** collection and calls **ModelState.AddModelError** for each. This level of indirection keeps the business services layer from depending on ASP.NET MVC.

Note: *The previous example turns off the ASP.NET-provided input validation of cookies, form data, and* **querystring** *properties by using the* **[ValidateInput(false)]** *attribute. This was done to allow certain characters that the default input validation does not allow. However, to prevent the user from using these characters to introduce malicious data into the system, the* **TextLineInputValidator** *data validation attribute is applied to the text properties of the* **FillupEntryFormModel** *class.*

It is recommended that you be very careful when disabling the default input validation and ensure that there are mitigations in place to stop malicious input.

CREATING CUSTOM VALIDATION ATTRIBUTES

When the standard validation attributes don't provide what you need, you can write your own. All the standard validation attributes derive from the **ValidationAttribute** class that contains the abstract **IsValid** method.

The following example validates a postal code. The implementation is much simpler than would be used in many applications, but it shows how a model object can validate one field based on the value of a different field.

C#
```
// Contained in PostalCodeValidatorAttribute.cs
protected override ValidationResult IsValid(object value, ValidationContext context)
{
  var userToValidate = context.ObjectInstance as User;
  var memberNames = new List<string>() { context.MemberName };

  if (userToValidate != null)
  {
    if (string.IsNullOrEmpty(userToValidate.Country) &&
      string.IsNullOrEmpty(userToValidate.PostalCode))
    {
      return ValidationResult.Success;
    }
    if (string.IsNullOrEmpty(userToValidate.PostalCode))
    {
      return ValidationResult.Success;
    }
    if (userToValidate.Country == Resources.UnitedStatesDisplayString)
    {
      if (USPostalCodeRegex.IsMatch(userToValidate.PostalCode))
      {
        return ValidationResult.Success;
      }
      return new ValidationResult(Resources.USPostalCodeValidationErrorMessage,
        memberNames);
    }
    else
```

```
  {
    if (InternationalPostalCodeRegex.IsMatch(userToValidate.PostalCode))
    {
      return ValidationResult.Success;
    }
    return new ValidationResult(
      Resources.InternationalPostalCodeValidationErrorMessage, memberNames);
  }
 }
 return ValidationResult.Success;
}
```

HANDLING COMPLEX DATA VALIDATION

You may have noticed in the earlier example that the **FillupController.Add** method calls **ModelState.IsValid** twice. The **CanAddFillup** handler in the following example contains validation logic that uses multiple objects in the domain model and requires additional database access. This validation logic is not suited for a single custom **ValidationAttribute**. It returns a collection of validation results that the controller uses to call **ModelState.AddModelError**. In cases like these you should factor complex validation logic into helper methods or a business services layer.

```C#
// Contained in CanAddFillup.cs
public virtual IEnumerable<ValidationResult> Execute(int userId,
        int vehicleId, ICreateFillupEntryCommand fillup)
{
        var foundVehicle = _vehicleRepository.GetVehicle(userId, vehicleId);

        if (foundVehicle == null)
        {
                yield return new ValidationResult(Resources.VehicleNotFound);
        }
        else
        {
                var fillups = _fillupRepository.GetFillups(vehicleId);

                if (!fillups.Any()) yield break;

                var priorFillup = fillups
                                        .Where(f => f.Date < fillup.Date)
                                        .FirstOrDefault();

                if ((priorFillup != null) &&
                    (priorFillup.Odometer >= fillup.Odometer))
```

```
                    {
                        yield return new ValidationResult(
                            "Odometer",
                            string.Format(CultureInfo.CurrentUICulture,
                                Resources.OdometerNotGreaterThanPrior,
                                priorFillup.Odometer));
                    }
            }
    }
}
```

SUPPORTING VALIDATION ON THE CLIENT

ASP.NET MVC supports client-side validation of data by sharing validation information from the server. This is done by implementing the **IClientValidatable** interface on your custom validation classes. **IClientValidatable** contains only the **GetClientValidation Rules** method that returns a **ModelClientValidationRule** collection.

In the following example, the **PostalCodeValidatorAttribute** implements **GetClient ValidationRules** by returning a single **ModelClientValidationRule**. By setting the **ValidationType** property to **"postalcode"** the client will use the validation routine with the same name that is registered on the client. The validation parameters are added to provide the client-side code with the information it needs to implement the validation rule.

C#

```
// Contained in PostalCodeValidatorAttribute.cs
public IEnumerable<ModelClientValidationRule> GetClientValidationRules(
  ModelMetadata metadata, ControllerContext context)
{
  var rule = new ModelClientValidationRule()
  {
    ErrorMessage = Resources.InvalidInputCharacter,
    ValidationType = "postalcode"
  };

  rule.ValidationParameters.Add("internationalerrormessage",
    Resources.InternationalPostalCodeValidationErrorMessage);
  rule.ValidationParameters.Add("unitedstateserrormessage",
    Resources.USPostalCodeValidationErrorMessage);
  rule.ValidationParameters.Add("internationalpattern",
    Resources.InternationalPostalCodeRegex);
  rule.ValidationParameters.Add("unitedstatespattern",
    Resources.USPostalCodeRegex);

  return new List<ModelClientValidationRule>() { rule };
}
```

Note: *In the previous example, you can see that the validation type and the names of the validation parameters are lowercase. These values are converted into HTML attributes and used by the client-side JavaScript code. Due to the limitations of this transformation, these values must contain only numbers, lowercase letters, and dashes.*

When MVC HTML helper extension methods such as **TextBoxFor** and **EditorFor** are called, MVC inspects the property definition for validation attributes. When a validation attribute implements **IClientValidatable**, MVC uses the client validation rules to include **data-val** attributes. The following HTML fragment shows the **data-val** attributes present on the postal code field in the registration form.

```HTML
<!-- sent from server using Views/Shared/_ProfileForm.cshtml -->
<div class="editor-field">
<input data-val="true"
  data-val-length="Postal code must be less than 10 characters."
  data-val-length-max="10"
  data-val-postalcode="Only alpha-numeric characters and [.,_-&amp;#39;]
                       are allowed."
  data-val-postalcode-internationalerrormessage=
    "Postal codes must be alphanumeric and ten characters or less."
  data-val-postalcode-internationalpattern="^[\d\w]{0,10}$"
  data-val-postalcode-unitedstateserrormessage=
    "United States postal codes must be five digit numbers."
  data-val-postalcode-unitedstatespattern="^[\d]{5}$"
  data-val-textlineinput=
    "Only alpha-numeric characters and [.,_-&amp;#39;] are allowed."
  data-val-textlineinput-pattern="^(?!.*--)[A-Za-z0-9\.,&#39;_ \-]*$"
  id="PostalCode" maxlength="10" name="PostalCode" size="10" type="text" value=""
  />
<span class="field-validation-valid" data-valmsg-for="PostalCode"
  data-valmsg-replace="true">
</span>
</div>
```

The JavaScript that participates in MVC validation on the client side can be found in jquery.validate.js and jquery.validate.unobtrusive.js. These files include standard validation attributes, methods to register validation routines, and unobtrusive validation adapters. The following example shows the registration of the **postalcode** validation routine. Notice how it uses the **params** object to access the **data-val** attributes.

```JavaScript
// Contained in mstats.validation.js
$.validator.addMethod('postalcode', function (value, element, params) {
  if (!value) {
    return true; // not testing 'is required' here!
```

```
  }
  try {
    var country = $('#Country').val(),
        postalCode = $('#PostalCode').val(),
        usMatch = postalCode.match(params.unitedStatesPattern),
        internationalMatch = postalCode.match(params.internationalPattern),
        message = '',
        match;

    if (country.toLowerCase() === 'united states') {
      message = params.unitedStatesErrorMessage;
      match = usMatch;
    } else {
      message = params.internationalErrorMessage;
      match = internationalMatch;
    }

    $.extend($.validator.messages, {
      postalcode: message
    });

    return (match && (match.index === 0) &&
      (match[0].length === postalCode.length));
  } catch (e) {
    return false;
  }
});
```

IClientValidatable helps you to share validation information, but you still have two copies of your validation logic to maintain. You may choose remote validators (that is, by implementing validation actions in your controller) and call them using Ajax from the client. However, the round trip to the server will not be as responsive as validating directly on the client.

> **Note:** *It is important to remember that client-side validation only helps improve the user experience and is not a substitute for proper validation and security on the server. Hackers won't use your web client JavaScript or even the browser when maliciously posting data to the web application on the server, so you **must** ensure that any client-side validation is repeated on the server before any data changes occur.*

UNIT TESTING VALIDATION LOGIC

Because validation occurs at multiple levels of the stack, you may end up with duplicate validation attributes and validation logic to keep in sync. While proper factoring of your application logic, your models, and data validation information can help, you should always unit test each layer in isolation to make sure the validation works as expected.

While you don't need to unit test the standard validation attributes, you should test that the validation attributes are properly applied to your model and validate as expected (just as if you had written code inside the setter of your model property). The following example shows a unit test verifying that the **Title** of the **Reminder** is required.

```csharp
// Contained in ReminderFixture.cs
[Fact]
public void WhenTitleSetToNull_ThenValidationFails()
{
  Reminder target = new Reminder();

  target.Title = null;

  var validationContext = new ValidationContext(target, null, null);
  var validationResults = new List<ValidationResult>();
  bool actual = Validator.TryValidateObject(target, validationContext,
                                    validationResults, true);

  Assert.False(actual);
  Assert.Equal(1, validationResults.Count);
  Assert.Equal(1, validationResults[0].MemberNames.Count());
  Assert.Equal("Title", validationResults[0].MemberNames.First());
}
```

> **Note:** *The **true** parameter at the end of the **TryValidateObject** call is important because it causes the validation of all properties on the target. This means your unit test must ensure all other properties are set to valid values when you verify that one invalid property fails validation.*

Other Considerations

This section describes some other areas of server architecture you may want to consider.

DEPENDENCY INJECTION

Mileage Stats uses Unity for dependency injection. The unity.config file in the web application maps interfaces to concrete classes. It also determines the lifetime for each mapping. For example, Unity ensures that the **VehicleController** constructor receives implementations of the **IUserServices**, **ICountryServices**, **IServiceLocator**, and **IChart DataService** interfaces.

In an effort to manage dependencies and improve testability in the MVC pattern, ASP. NET MVC also provides a dependency resolver. This gives ASP.NET MVC applications a designated place to resolve dependencies for framework-created objects such as controllers and action filters. In the following example, Mileage Stats registers Unity as the MVC dependency resolver as part of initializing the dependency injection container for the application.

```csharp
C#
// Contained in global.asax.cs
private static void InitializeDependencyInjectionContainer()
{
  IUnityContainer container = new UnityContainerFactory()
      .CreateConfiguredContainer();
  var serviceLocator = new UnityServiceLocator(container);
  ServiceLocator.SetLocatorProvider(() => serviceLocator);
  DependencyResolver.SetResolver(new UnityDependencyResolver(container));
}
```

See the "Further Reading" section for more information on dependency injection and Unity.

UNIT TESTING

One of the main reasons ASP.NET MVC follows the MVC pattern is to allow for unit testing of the application logic. The **System.Web.Abstractions** assembly was introduced primarily to allow substitution of mocked instances of classes like **HttpContextBase** during unit testing. You should unit test as much of your application logic as possible; it will not only help ensure the quality of your application but will also help identify design issues early when they are less expensive to fix.

Mileage Stats uses the xUnit.net unit test framework as well as Moq for mocking interfaces. The application is unit tested at the data model, business services, and controller layers. As mentioned in the "Composing Application Logic" section, keeping controller actions simple and factoring application logic into a business services layer makes unit testing much easier. In Mileage Stats, unit testing was much easier because interfaces like **IUserServices** could be mocked.

For more information on unit testing see Chapter 13, "Unit Testing Web Applications."

ERROR MANAGEMENT

Web clients expect proper HTTP status code responses when a web application cannot fulfill a request. This means you should avoid hiding errors like a resource not being found (404), failure to authorize (403), and internal server errors (500+). When an exception is thrown from a controller action, ASP.NET MVC will respond with the correct HTTP status code. There may be cases where you need to catch an exception from a call and throw a different exception type.

Generally, users don't want to see all the developer details for an exception, and showing more than is needed is not recommended from a security standpoint. ASP.NET MVC provides a **HandleErrorAttribute** that provides a friendly error page when an exception occurs. The friendly page displayed is determined in the web.config **customErrors** section. Mileage Stats applies the **HandleErrorAttribute** to all controller actions in the **RegisterGlobalFilters** method in Global.asax.cs.

Although friendly errors are an improvement, the user experience shouldn't be interrupted with an HTTP error if the user enters an invalid value. Use the Post/Redirect/Get pattern (PRG) when handling a POST action. When the user submits invalid data, you should return the same view as the GET action populated with the incoming data. When a POST action succeeds, it can redirect.

In the following example, if a **ReminderFormModel** doesn't pass data validation, the **Add** view result is returned populated with the reminder data that was passed into the action method.

```C#
//Contained in ReminderController.cs
[HttpPost]
public ActionResult Add(int vehicleId, ReminderFormModel reminder)
{
        if ((reminder != null) && ModelState.IsValid)
        {
                var errors = Using<CanAddReminder>()
                                    .Execute(CurrentUserId, reminder);

                ModelState.AddModelErrors(errors, "Add");

                if (ModelState.IsValid)
                {
                        Using<AddReminderToVehicle>()
                                .Execute(CurrentUserId, vehicleId, reminder);
                        return RedirectToAction("Details", "Reminder",
                                new { id = reminder.ReminderId });
                }
        }

        var vehicles = Using<GetVehicleListForUser>()
                .Execute(CurrentUserId);

        var vehicle = vehicles.First(v => v.VehicleId == vehicleId);

        var reminders = Using<GetUnfulfilledRemindersForVehicle>()
                .Execute(CurrentUserId, vehicleId, vehicle.Odometer ?? 0)
                .Select(r => new ReminderSummaryModel(r, r.IsOverdue ?? false));

        var viewModel = new ReminderAddViewModel
        {
                VehicleList = new VehicleListViewModel(vehicles, vehicleId)
                                { IsCollapsed = true },
                Reminder = reminder,
                Reminders = new SelectedItemList<ReminderSummaryModel>(reminders),
        };

        return View(viewModel);
}
```

Concurrency

Because Mileage Stats tracks vehicles per user account, concurrency conflict detection and management was not a scenario for the application. Even though we chose not to implement it, the ADO.NET Entity Framework does support optimistic concurrency by adding time stamps to the data model and taking appropriate action when handling the **DbUpdateConcurrencyException**.

Summary

Hopefully you now have a frame of reference for architecting your server-side web application. There are many choices you will make to structure your site, factor code, and model data. Successful architectures provide the layers of abstraction required to solve the problem at hand while affording a way to accommodate future features and technologies.

The key points made in this chapter are:

- Understand your web client needs and build a contract for the HTML structure, URL structure, and data formats between the client and server early in the process.

- Decide whether or not to create a business services layer and whether or not to create separate domain and data models.

- Create small controllers by placing the majority of your application logic in your domain models, a services layer, or helper classes and methods.

- Keep application logic simple and partitioned.

- Provide a data API that allows web clients to consume data asynchronously in the right format and with the right granularity for the application.

- Structure your validation logic to support validation both on the client and on the server.

Further Reading

Evans, Eric. *Domain-Driven Design: Tackling Complexity in the Heart of Software.* Addison-Wesley Professional, 2003.

Nilsson, Jimmy. *Applying Domain-Driven Design and Patterns: With Examples in C# and .NET.* Addison-Wesley Professional, 2006.

ADO.NET Entity Framework on MSDN®:
http://msdn.microsoft.com/library/bb399572.aspx

The Repository Pattern on MSDN:
http://msdn.microsoft.com/en-us/library/ff649690.aspx

Unit of Work Pattern:
http://www.martinfowler.com/eaaCatalog/unitOfWork.html

Catalog of Patterns of Enterprise Application Architecture:
http://martinfowler.com/eaaCatalog/

Understanding Models, Views, and Controllers on ASP.NET:
http://www.asp.net/mvc/tutorials/understanding-models-views-and-controllers-cs

Best Practices for ASP.NET MVC:
http://blogs.msdn.com/b/aspnetue/archive/2010/09/17/second_2d00_post.aspx

Dependency Injection in *MSDN Magazine*:
http://msdn.microsoft.com/en-us/magazine/cc163739.aspx

Unity Application Block on MSDN:
http://www.msdn.com/unity

Post/Redirect/Get Pattern:
http://en.wikipedia.org/wiki/Post/Redirect/Get

For more information on how clients can consume and use **data-** attributes, see Chapter 6, "Client Data Management and Caching" and "Using Data- Attributes" in Chapter 7, "Manipulating Client-Side HTML."

For more information on unit testing see Chapter 13, "Unit Testing Web Applications."

To access web resources more easily, see the online version of the bibliography on MSDN: http://msdn.microsoft.com/en-us/library/hh404094.aspx.

12   Security

Introduction

This chapter addresses security-related topics for the Mileage Stats Reference Implementation (Mileage Stats) and is divided into three sections. The first section introduces security threats relevant to Mileage Stats. The second section gives a guided tour of Mileage Stats security features that provide countermeasures against those threats. The third section describes possible security modifications to consider if you make changes to the deployment environment and to the security requirements for the application. After reading this chapter, you should understand how relevant security threats are mitigated in Mileage Stats and what some of its extensibility points are.

In this chapter you will learn about:

- Major security threats that you should address in any web application, including unauthorized access, malicious input, content injection, cross-site scripting, eavesdropping, message tampering, message replay, and cross-site request forgery.

- Security features in Mileage Stats that provide countermeasures against the relevant threats, including authentication, input validation, anti-forgery measures, and ways to prevent JavaScript Object Notation (JSON) hijacking.

- Security modifications to accommodate changes in the deployment environment and to the security requirements for the application.

This chapter will also cover some security features of ASP.NET and ASP.NET MVC, and OpenID.

Security Threats

The section describes some security threats that need to be addressed in any web application. If you're already familiar with these security threats and how to mitigate them, skip to the "**Mileage Stats Application Security**" section where the security features for Mileage Stats are described.

UNAUTHORIZED ACCESS

To prevent the wrong people from entering your website and changing its data, you need to limit who can access it. This is typically accomplished by requiring users to authenticate. The most common form of authentication requires a user to provide his or her user name and password as credentials. Once verified, the user has access. If the credentials are not recognized by the website, the user does not have access.

MALICIOUS INPUT – CONTENT INJECTION AND CROSS-SITE SCRIPTING

There are a variety of ways to corrupt content by uploading malicious input to your website. Such attacks can not only corrupt the data but can even make your website unusable. If links can be uploaded to a website, malicious users can potentially execute a cross-site scripting (XSS) attack, enabling them to collect potentially sensitive form data and security information. A common way to prevent the uploading of malicious input to a website is to limit the length and type of input that users are allowed to provide. Removing the ability to submit tags by filtering out tag characters ("<" and ">") goes a long way towards preventing malicious users from submitting scripts or HTML tags. As a rule of thumb, acceptable input to the website should be as limited as possible based on expected length, content, and data type for a particular data field.

EAVESDROPPING, MESSAGE TAMPERING, AND MESSAGE REPLAY

Eavesdropping, message tampering, and message replay are grouped together because they are often detected and mitigated by similar measures. A common and relatively simple way to exploit a web application through eavesdropping is to use a network data capture utility to find and record HTTP requests and responses between a website and a client. Without protection from eavesdropping and tampering, an attacker can alter the contents of a captured HTTP request and re-submit it to the website. This type of attack is commonly referred to as a message replay attack. Even if the website requires authentication, it processes the request as if it came from the client because it contains a legitimate security token. HTTP requests can be altered to cause the website to behave undesirably, to delete data, to change data, or to cause large numbers of transactions to be executed. A common way to mitigate message replay in web applications using HTTP is by requiring communication via Secure Sockets Layer (SSL). When you use SSL in a non-anonymous mode, you prevent the ability to replay messages back to the server. Two additional and very important benefits of using SSL are that it prevents any sensitive content in the HTTP traffic from being disclosed to eavesdroppers and prevents message tampering.

CROSS-SITE REQUEST FORGERY

Cross-site request forgery (CSRF, often pronounced as "sea surf",) occurs when malicious commands are sent to a website from the browser of a trusted user. An attacker constructs a seemingly harmless HTML element on a different website that surreptitiously calls the target website and attempts to do something malicious while posing as a trusted user. CSRF has great potential to damage the website being exploited; an attacker can potentially tamper with or delete data, or execute large numbers of unwanted transactions on the targeted website.

This section is an introductory overview and not a substitute for more comprehensive guidance or a threat model. For more information on ASP.NET security, see the **ASP.NET Web Application Security** reference at the end of this chapter.

Web Platform Security

This section describes some of the out-of-the-box security features that are built into the various components of the web application platform.

MVC VIEW ENCODING

The Razor syntax uses the @ operator in Model-View-Controller (MVC) views to specify Microsoft® .NET Framework code. Any output written to the client in the view from code that uses the @ operator is automatically HTML encoded for you. This traps malicious content by preventing it from being rendered back to the client. Trapping malicious content goes hand-in-hand with input filtering, because you should never assume that any data that comes from users or other applications is safe.

ASP.NET INPUT FILTERING

Starting with version 1.1, ASP.NET has provided input filtering out of the box as a secure default. Any attempt to submit a request containing bracketed tags ("<" or ">") in any of its form data, query string parameters, or cookies results in an error page indicating that malicious input has been detected. The following figure is a screenshot of the default ASP. NET input validation failure page.

Input validation failure

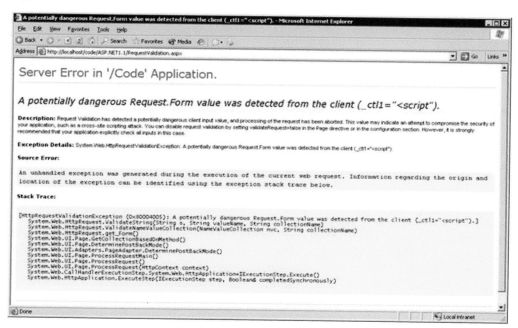

While the default ASP.NET input filtering is good, it is very basic. You should still validate user input in your application.

Protecting Application-Specific Data

Sometimes applications host their own data sources instead of accessing them from a centrally hosted location. Whenever you create an application-specific data source, it should be hosted in the App_Data subdirectory. For example, if you add a SQL membership provider for a specific application, the Microsoft SQL Server® Express .mdf file should be created in the App_Data directory. ASP.NET protects application-specific data in a few ways. Files stored in the App_Data folder cannot be accessed directly by clients because, by default, the folder is protected from browsing.

An additional layer of protection for application-specific data files is configured using HTTP handlers in the machine's web.config file. Requests for certain file types are routed to the ASP.NET **HttpForbiddenHandler** by default. The following code shows the configuration to handle HTTP requests for .mdf and .mdb files that are used by SQL Server Express and Microsoft Access®, respectively, via the **HttpForbiddenHandler** in the machine's web.config file:

```XML
<!-- Contained in machine's default web.config -->
<add path="*.mdf" verb="*" type="System.Web.HttpForbiddenHandler" validate="True" />
<add path="*.ldf" verb="*" type="System.Web.HttpForbiddenHandler" validate="True" />
```

Note that the HTTP handlers defined above are for standard ASP.NET applications. Handlers for an ASP.NET MVC application are defined via route mappings in the application's Global.asax.cs file. All .mdf and .mdb files are normally inaccessible when using ASP.NET MVC unless you explicitly create a route mapping for them; you can also configure ASP.NET MVC to ignore routing for the file types and let ASP.NET handle the file types using the settings described above. Neither approach is recommended for ASP.NET MVC applications because the files should be protected from client browsing by routing all requests to the MVC controllers. For more information on MVC routing best practices, see the reference on "**Best Practices for ASP.NET MVC**" on the ASP.NET and Web Tools Developer Content Team's blog at the end of this chapter.

Mileage Stats Application Security

This section explains security measures implemented in Mileage Stats that mitigate security threats against it.

Authentication

Mileage Stats implements authentication using a third-party authentication provider (OpenID) and ASP.NET forms authentication tickets to prevent unauthorized access. Whenever an unauthenticated user attempts to access the site, he or she is redirected to the login URL via ASP.NET forms authentication. The following diagram depicts the logical flow for user authentication in Mileage Stats.

Third-party user authentication

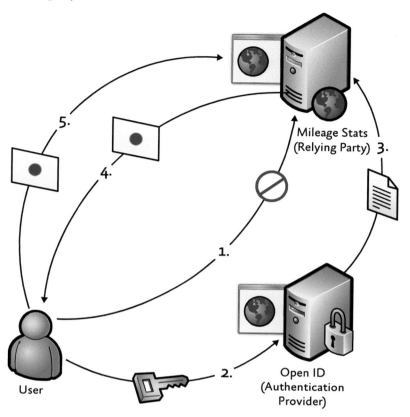

1. The user attempts to access the site without authenticating first and is redirected to the Mileage Stats home page.

2. The user navigates from the Mileage Stats home page to the OpenID sign-in page to authenticate.

3. An authentication result is attached to the response by OpenID and picked up by Mileage Stats for processing.

4. Mileage Stats converts a successful authentication result from OpenID to an encrypted ASP.NET forms authentication ticket and caches it client-side as a session cookie in the web browser.

5. The user accesses the site successfully with a valid forms ticket. Whenever a request is processed with a valid authentication ticket, the expiration time of the ticket is reset to provide a sliding expiration window.

The significance of this authentication model is that a third party (OpenID) is responsible for managing and validating the user's credentials as opposed to more commonly encountered authentication models in which the owner of the website is the same party that maintains and validates the user's credentials.

While out-of-the box ASP.NET forms authentication is not being used, encrypted forms authentication tickets and forms ticket validation are being leveraged programmatically. Forms ticketing is an effective mechanism that you can leverage to work with OpenID authentication instead of creating a security ticketing mechanism from the ground up.

There are several configuration settings and segments of code responsible for implementing authentication end-to-end in Mileage Stats. Let's take a look at how configuration works, and at the major components that make up the authentication mechanism.

Configuration

While the forms tickets are generated manually in Mileage Stats, the code still leverages the configuration settings used for configuring out-of-the-box forms authentication. The following configuration snippet in the Mileage Stats web.config file is responsible for configuring the application for forms authentication and setting the login redirect URL.

```XML
<!-- Contained in web.config -->
<authentication mode="Forms">
  <forms loginUrl="~/Auth/SignIn" timeout="20" />
</authentication>
```

The relying party class validates a user's credentials with an authentication provider, then uses them to create a forms authentication ticket. The relying party implementation is configured in the unity.config file.

```XML
<!-- Contained in unity.config -->
<!-- NOTE: This is a real openId authentication mechanism -->
<type type="MileageStats.Web.Authentication.IOpenIdRelyingParty, MileageStats.Web"
      mapTo="MileageStats.Web.Authentication.DefaultOpenIdRelyingParty,
      MileageStats.Web">
  <lifetime type="perRequest" />
</type>
```

There are two unity.config files available, and the one used by Mileage Stats depends on which solution configuration is selected when you compile the application. The one shown above is used with the Release solution configuration. When Debug is selected, a different unity.config file is used that contains a mock authentication relying party class that can be used to get the application up and running. The mock authenticator will put the user through a mock authentication workflow that does not validate any credentials. To deploy the application, we strongly recommend that you compile the application using the Release solution configuration in order to use the actual relying party class that does validate the user credentials.

Both the mock authenticator and the OpenID relying party class implement the **IOpenIdRelyingParty** interface, which acts as a wrapper around the DotNetOpenAuth interfaces to expose only what is required to interact with the authentication provider and to process the results. Implementing **IOpenIdRelyingParty** enables you to configure a different relying party implementation if your application requirements change.

AuthController

AuthController is an MVC controller in Mileage Stats that is responsible for handling the user redirect for authentication and converting the response from a successful authentication attempt into an ASP.NET forms authentication ticket. The **AuthController** uses the relying party implementation specified in the unity.config file. AuthController's **Sign InWithProvider** method is invoked to redirect the user to the authentication provider's sign-in page. The following code snippet shows the **SignInWithProvider** method.

```csharp
C#
// Contained in AuthController.cs
public ActionResult SignInWithProvider(string providerUrl)
{
  if (string.IsNullOrEmpty(providerUrl))
  {
    return this.RedirectToAction("SignIn");
  }

  var fetch = new FetchRequest();
  var returnUrl = this.Url.Action("SignInResponse", "Auth", null,
      this.Request.Url.Scheme);

  try
  {
    return this.relyingParty.RedirectToProvider(providerUrl, returnUrl, fetch);
  }
  catch (Exception)
  {
    this.TempData["Message"] =
        Resources.AuthController_SignIn_UnableToAuthenticateWithProvider;
    return this.RedirectToAction("SignIn");
  }
}
```

The **AuthController**'s **SignInResponse** method is invoked to process the response from the user's authentication attempt with the authentication provider. **SignInResponse** calls the **GetResponse** method on the relying party class and processes the result. If the result is a successful authentication, **AuthController** creates an ASP.NET forms authentication ticket and attaches it to the response. If anything other than a successful authentication result is returned from the authentication provider, the user is redirected back to the authentication provider's sign-in page.

```csharp
C#
// Contained in AuthController.cs
public ActionResult SignInResponse(string returnUrl)
{
  var response = this.relyingParty.GetResponse();

  switch (response.Status)
  {
    case AuthenticationStatus.Authenticated:
        var user = this.userServices.GetOrCreateUser(response.ClaimedIdentifier);
        this.formsAuthentication.SetAuthCookie(this.HttpContext,
            UserAuthenticationTicketBuilder.CreateAuthenticationTicket(user));

        return this.RedirectToRoute("Dashboard");

    case AuthenticationStatus.Canceled:
        this.TempData["Message"] = "Cancelled Authentication";
        return this.RedirectToAction("SignIn");

    case AuthenticationStatus.Failed:
        this.TempData["Message"] = response.Exception.Message;
        return this.RedirectToAction("SignIn");

    default:
        this.TempData["Message"] =
            Resources.AuthController_SignInResponse_Unable_to_authenticate;
        return this.RedirectToAction("SignIn");
  }
}
```

The following sequence diagram shows the calls made in **AuthController.SignIn Response** to authenticate the user with the relying party and to attach the encrypted forms ticket as a cookie if the authentication attempt was successful.

Authentication sequence diagram

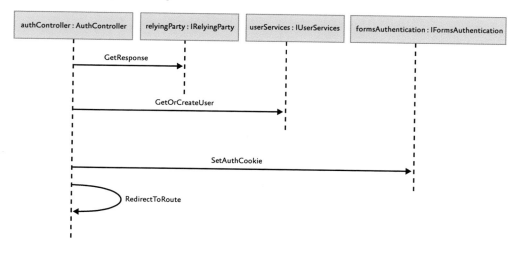

1. **AuthController** calls the **GetResponse** method of its referenced **IOpenId RelyingParty** implementation to get the authentication result from the authentication provider.

2. **AuthController** calls the **GetOrCreateUser** method of its referenced **IUserServices** implementation.

3. **AuthController** calls the **SetAuthCookie** method of its referenced **IFormsAuthentication** implementation.

4. **AuthController** invokes its own **RedirectToRoute** method and sends the user to its landing page after a successful authentication.

Let's take a closer look at the relying party implementation used in Mileage Stats.

DefaultOpenIdRelyingParty

DefaultOpenIdRelyingParty implements **IOpenIdRelyingParty**, which is a façade for the **OpenIdRelyingParty** class provided as part of DotNetOpenAuth that validates the user's credentials with OpenID. The following code snippet shows the **Redirect ToProvider** method on the **DefaultOpenIdRelyingParty** class, which is responsible for redirecting the user to the authentication provider's login page.

```
C#
// Contained in DefaultOpenIdRelyingParty.cs
public ActionResult RedirectToProvider(string providerUrl, string returnUrl,
    FetchRequest fetch)
{
 IAuthenticationRequest authenticationRequest =
   this.relyingParty.CreateRequest(providerUrl, Realm.AutoDetect,
```

```
  new Uri(returnUrl));
authenticationRequest.AddExtension(fetch);

return
  new OutgoingRequestActionResult(authenticationRequest.RedirectingResponse);
}
```

Forms Authentication Sliding Expiration

Sliding expiration of the forms authentication ticket in Mileage Stats is accomplished by resetting the expiration time of the ticket whenever the user makes a new request to the server. Normally, the reset is enabled by setting the **slidingExpiration** attribute to **true** on the forms security configuration in the web.config file; however, because the ticket is being manually created and attached to the response in the **AuthController**, the ticket needs to be refreshed manually. A custom handler for the **HttpApplication.Post AuthenticateRequest** event implements the sliding expiration for the forms ticket.

```csharp
C#
// Contained in Global.asax.cs
private void PostAuthenticateRequestHandler(object sender, EventArgs e)
{
  HttpCookie authCookie =
      this.Context.Request.Cookies[FormsAuthentication.FormsCookieName];
  if (IsValidAuthCookie(authCookie))
  {
    var formsAuthentication =
        ServiceLocator.Current.GetInstance<IFormsAuthentication>();

    var ticket = formsAuthentication.Decrypt(authCookie.Value);
    var mileageStatsIdentity = new MileageStatsIdentity(ticket);
    this.Context.User = new GenericPrincipal(mileageStatsIdentity, null);

    // Reset cookie for a sliding expiration.
    formsAuthentication.SetAuthCookie(this.Context, ticket);
  }
}
```

The advantage of using a forms ticket with a sliding expiration is that it does not force the user to authenticate again if he or she maintains a reasonable level of activity in the application. Otherwise, the user would be redirected to the authentication page after a fixed amount of time had elapsed after the original authentication. While sliding expiration greatly enhances the usability of the application, it is also a potential security risk because the user's authenticated session can be kept alive indefinitely by submitting requests to the server before the sliding expiration time on the forms ticket has passed. This risk can be mitigated by introducing an additional timeout value that does not slide, after which the ticket will expire regardless of user activity. While this approach is effective, it was not implemented in Mileage Stats because it would add complexity to the forms ticket handling that is beyond the scope of the application.

INPUT VALIDATION

One of the primary ways of preventing an application from accepting malicious content is validating any input before it is accepted by the application. While out-of-the-box ASP. NET input validation does a good job of preventing script or HTML injection, it is not always practical to use this mechanism in an ASP.NET MVC application. In Mileage Stats, this mechanism is disabled to handle input validation directly within the MVC model classes. If you don't implement your own input validation and rely on the built-in ASP.NET input validation instead, two things will happen. First, the input will not be validated until *after* the controller has processed it and before the view has rendered. Next, you will get the default "yellow screen of death" input validation page, which is not a pleasant user experience. When the out-of-the box ASP.NET input validation is disabled, you also lose HTML encoding on your input. To account for this, the **@** operator in Razor syntax automatically HTML-encodes output that is rendered in an MVC view.

Although input validation can be done on the client side to reduce round trips to the server, it must also be performed on the server because client-side validation can be bypassed by an attacker. One of the advantages of ASP.NET MVC is that it can be configured to render client-side validation based on server-side validation attributes defined on MVC model properties. This provides a single point in the application to define and maintain data validation rules. For example, in Mileage Stats, the **_ProfileForm** view is configured to use the **MileageStats.ServicesModel.User** class as its MVC model via the **@model** directive. If you look at the **DisplayName** property on the class, you will see attributes that limit the length of the value, that require a value for the property, and that use a custom text input validator that filters input using a regular expression.

```csharp
// Contained in User.cs
[StringLength(15,
    ErrorMessageResourceName = "UserDisplayNameStringLengthValidationError",
    ErrorMessageResourceType = typeof(Resources))]
[TextLineInputValidator]
[Required(AllowEmptyStrings = false,
    ErrorMessageResourceName = "UserDisplayNameRequired",
    ErrorMessageResourceType = typeof(Resources))]
[Display(Name = "UserDisplayNameLabelText", ResourceType = typeof(Resources))]
public string DisplayName { get; set; }
```

Here is the custom input validator class that is behind the **TextLineInputValidator** attribute.

```csharp
//Contained in TextLineValidatorAttribute.cs
public class TextLineInputValidatorAttribute : RegularExpressionAttribute,
                                               IClientValidatable
```

```
{
  public TextLineInputValidatorAttribute()
    : base(Resources.TextLineInputValidatorRegEx)
  {
    this.ErrorMessage = Resources.InvalidInputCharacter;
  }

  public IEnumerable<ModelClientValidationRule>
    GetClientValidationRules(ModelMetadata metadata, ControllerContext context)
  {
    var rule = new ModelClientValidationRule()
    {
      ErrorMessage = Resources.InvalidInputCharacter,
      ValidationType = "textlineinput"
    };

    rule.ValidationParameters.Add("pattern", Resources.TextLineInputValidatorRegEx);
    return new List<ModelClientValidationRule>() { rule };
  }
}
```

The **TextLineInputValidatorAttribute** class uses a set of regular expressions it loads from the resources file. If any of the regular expression patterns are matched in the input, it fails validation. The regular expression pattern used to validate text input is **^(?!.*--) [A-Za-z0-9\.,'_ \-]*$**. This limits the text assigned to the property to alphanumeric characters and allows only a limited range of punctuation characters. Notice that the regular expression pattern is used to validate legitimate characters rather than to exclude invalid characters. By default, anything not explicitly defined in the regular expression is excluded from the application data. The list that limits input by only allowing what is known to be valid is commonly referred to as a *safe list*. The advantage of safe lists is that anything that falls outside of the valid set of characters is not allowed; you don't have to worry about accidentally omitting a character from the regular expression that shouldn't be allowed in the application input.

What's nice about this validation mechanism is that the client-side validation for these properties is generated for you based on the server-side validation defined in the MVC model when the HTML for the MVC view is rendered. The following code shows you what the rendered client-side validation looks like for the user display **name** form field when you view the HTML source for the page.

HTML
```
<!-- Rendered HTML in the client browser -->
<input data-val="true"
  data-val-length="Display name must be less than 15 characters."
  data-val-length-max="15" data-val-required="Display name is required."
  data-val-textlineinput="Only alpha-numeric characters and [.,_-&amp;#39;]
are allowed."
```

```
data-val-textlineinput-pattern="^(?!.*--)[A-Za-z0-9\.,&#39;_ \-]*$"
id="DisplayName"
maxlength="15"
name="DisplayName"
type="text"
value="Sample User" />
```

Note: *If you want to accept HTML tags or other types of input that would normally be rejected by simple input validation, you can leverage the regular expression/input validation mechanism to do it. However, you will need to create more sophisticated patterns to allow the input you want to be accepted while still excluding the input that you don't want submitted to your application.*

ANTI-FORGERY

As previously explained in the "Security Threats" section, CSRF has a high damage potential and should be prevented. ASP.NET MVC has a simple yet effective mechanism for mitigating CSRF attacks. In your MVC view content, add an **@Html.AntiForgeryToken** directive to the view, as shown here.

CSHTML

```
<!-- Contained in _ProfileForm.cshtml -->
@model MileageStats.ServicesModel.User
@Html.AntiForgeryToken()
```

When the view HTML is rendered to the client, MVC places a unique value for the user in a hidden form field and in a session cookie. The form field in the rendered HTML might look like this.

HTML

```
<!-- Rendered HTML in the client browser -->
<input name="__RequestVerificationToken"
  type="hidden"
  value="H4zpQFvPdmEdGCLsFgeByj0xg+BODBjIMvtSl5anoNaOfX4V69Pt1OvnjIbZuYrpgzWxWHIjbn
  zFOLxP5SzVR4cM9XZeV78IPi8K4ewkM3k2oFkplrXL4uoAqy+aoSOg8s1m1qxrE7oeBBtvezEHCAs6nKE
  h2jAwn3w0MwmhkcDQiJfJK7hGvN0jXA4d7S8x7rbLxp4Y8IJZS9wka2eOLg==" />
```

There's another piece to implementing the anti-forgery tokens in ASP.NET MVC. You must also put a **ValidateAntiForgeryToken** attribute on corresponding MVC controller actions that you want to protect. The following code is an example of the attribute decorating the edit action on the **ProfileController** class.

C#

```
// Contained in ProfileController.cs
[HttpPost]
[ValidateInput(false)]
[ValidateAntiForgeryToken]
public ActionResult Edit(User updatedUser)
```

When ASP.NET MVC checks for a request forgery, it verifies that the request verification token form field and cookies are present and that the values match each other. If either the cookie or the form field values are missing, or the values don't match, ASP.NET MVC does not process the action and returns an authorization failure instead.

> **Note:** *MVC anti-forgery tokens do not work using HTTP GET requests because the* **_RequestVerificationToken** *value from the client needs to be sent as a posted value. Therefore, it is important to make sure that you only accept client requests that use HTTP POST when you want to implement anti-forgery tokens. This shouldn't be an issue because you should already be using HTTP POST only for data updates, and using HTTP GET exclusively for read-only operations.*
>
> *If you want to implement more tightly controlled anti-forgery measures so that the tokens will only validate to a particular set of MVC views and actions, you can pass a salt as a parameter to the* **@Html.AntiForgeryToken** *directive in the MVC model. A salt is a value combined with a cryptographic key to make the output of an encryption algorithm more random and less susceptible to attack.*

Make sure that you are using the same salt values in the **@Html.AntiForgeryToken** directive in the MVC model and in the parameter for the **ValidateAntiForgeryToken** attribute on the MVC controller action; otherwise, the anti-forgery token will not validate properly when the MVC action is called. For more information about using a salt with an MVC anti-forgery token, see the reference to "Prevent Cross-Site Request Forgery (CSRF) using ASP.NET MVC's **AntiForgeryToken()** helper" at the end of the chapter.

JSON Hijacking Prevention

In some situations, it may be possible for an attacker to access data via a JSON request by using an attack that closely resembles a CSRF attack. If an attacker can get a user to click on a malicious link that makes a JSON request via HTTP GET and returns a JSON array, it may dump the contents of the array in the response, making it accessible to the attacker. The mitigation for JSON hijacking is fairly straightforward: either you can make sure to never return JSON arrays in a response, or you can restrict JSON requests to respond only to requests that use the HTTP POST action. To configure a JSON action on an MVC controller to respond to requests only via HTTP POST, add the **HttpPost** attribute to it. The following code shows the **HttpPost** attribute on the **ProfileController**'s **JsonEdit** action.

```csharp
// Contained in ProfileController.cs
[HttpPost]
[ValidateInput(false)]
public ActionResult JsonEdit(User updatedUser)
```

This may not be an issue if you don't care whether or not someone can gain unauthorized access to data that is not sensitive; however, as a general practice you should protect your JSON calls against hijacking. For more information, see the reference to JSON Hijacking in the "Further Reading" section at the end of the chapter.

Additional Security Considerations

This section describes other security issues to consider when deploying and configuring Mileage Stats. Securing communication between the client and the server is critical for protecting the data that goes back and forth between them. You may also want to use a different method of authenticating users for the application, whether that means using a different relying party for the existing authentication mechanism or switching to an ASP. NET membership provider. If you expand the functionality of your application, you may want to restrict different levels of functionality to a limited subset of application users. In some cases, you may want to deploy the data tier to SQL Server or SQL Server Express instead of running it on SQL Server Compact Edition.

SECURING COMMUNICATION BETWEEN CLIENT AND SERVER

When properly configured, Secure Sockets Layer (SSL) is an effective way to prevent eavesdropping, session hijacking, message replay and tampering between the client and the server. Mileage Stats does not use SSL out of the box because the use of SSL depends on your infrastructure and not on the application itself. There's already a lot of documentation on how to set up SSL on your server, so the specifics won't be covered here. For more information, see the reference on **"How to Set Up SSL on IIS 7"** in the "Further Reading" section at the end of this chapter. Make sure that when you configure SSL on your server that you do **not** configure anonymous SSL. Otherwise, communication between the client and server will still be susceptible to several different attacks.

> **Warning:** *When communicating with the server via SSL, a client verifies the identity of the server with which it is communicating by checking the host name provided in the SSL certificate against the URL of the server. Sometimes the client does not have a certificate that can be used to identify the server, and sometimes the server is configured to use SSL protocols that do not incorporate identification of the server; these are examples of anonymous SSL. Anonymous SSL can be configured intentionally on some web servers but not on others. It can be "forced" intentionally by breaking the mechanisms inherent to SSL that tie a host to the identity specified in an SSL certificate. While this provides protection against tampering and eavesdropping, it does not protect against message replay or spoofing attacks, where one party can pose as someone else during the communication.*

Once SSL has been set up in your environment, there are two changes to the web. config file that you'll need to make in Mileage Stats. The first change is to require that ASP.NET forms authentication use SSL. To do this, the **requireSSL** attribute needs to be added to the forms element.

```xml
XML
<!-- Contained in web.config -->
<authentication mode="Forms">
  <forms loginUrl="~/Auth/SignIn" timeout="20" requireSSL="true"/>
</authentication>
```

The default timeout for a forms authentication ticket is 20 minutes. However, you can adjust this value to a reasonable time that preserves the usability of the sliding expiration but minimizes the security risk of indefinitely authenticated users.

The second change is for OpenID to require an SSL-encrypted communication with the relying party.

```XML
<!-- Contained in web.config -->
<openid>
  <relyingParty>
    <security requireSsl="true" />
```

The value of **requireSsl** needs to be set to **true**. That way you can ensure that the authentication provider will only attempt to communicate with your application via HTTPS.

Any use of the **UrlHelper.Action** method that specifies a protocol (such as HTTP) in your application for constructing URLs will need to be updated to HTTPS for any URL references that are now secured via SSL. For more information on the **UrlHelper.Action** method, see the reference on the UrlHelper.Action **method** at the end of the chapter.

Protecting Connection Strings

If you change data sources for the application, you will likely end up changing the connection string in the web.config file. As a good practice, you should protect these connection strings from discovery. For more information on protecting connection strings, see the reference on **Protecting Connection Information (ADO.NET)** at the end of the chapter.

Deploying to a Shared Environment

In situations where you are deploying your web application to a server that is being shared by multiple parties, you may want to protect your application from the other applications that are hosted on the server. In addition to protecting sensitive information in the web.config file, ensure that the application pools on the server are configured to run per web application and that the temporary ASP.NET files cached on the server are in a location that is not shared with the other web applications on the server. For more information, see "How To: Secure an ASP.NET Application on a Shared Server" on MSDN®.

Summary

This chapter provided an overview of security threats that impact Mileage Stats. These include: unauthorized access, malicious input (content injection and cross-site scripting), eavesdropping, message tampering, message replay, and cross-site request forgery. The chapter also described how these threats are mitigated through various security features. Finally, a few ideas were suggested for extending or changing security for Mileage Stats to accommodate different deployment environments and security requirements.

Further Reading

"ASP.NET Web Application Security" on MSDN:
http://msdn.microsoft.com/en-us/library/330a99hc.aspx

"How to set up SSL on IIS 7":
http://learn.iis.net/page.aspx/144/how-to-set-up-ssl-on-iis-7/

"UrlHelper.Action Method" on MSDN:
http://msdn.microsoft.com/en-us/library/dd505232.aspx

"Understanding the Forms Authentication Ticket and Cookie" on Microsoft Support:
http://support.microsoft.com/kb/910443

"Authenticating Users with Forms Authentication" on ASP.NET:
http://www.asp.net/mvc/tutorials/authenticating-users-with-forms-authentication-cs

Protecting Connection Information (ADO.NET) on MSDN:
http://msdn.microsoft.com/en-us/library/89211k9b(v=VS.100).aspx

"How To: Secure an ASP.NET Application on a Shared Server" on MSDN:
http://msdn.microsoft.com/en-us/library/ms228096.aspx

"A Guide to Claims–based Identity and Access Control" on MSDN:
http://msdn.microsoft.com/en-us/library/ff423674.aspx

"OWASP Top 10 Project" on OWASP.org:
https://www.owasp.org/index.php/Category:OWASP_Top_Ten_Project

"JSON Hijacking" on Phil Haack's blog:
http://haacked.com/archive/2009/06/25/json-hijacking.aspx

"Best Practices for ASP.NET MVC" on the ASP.NET and Web Tools Developer Content Team's blog: http://blogs.msdn.com/b/aspnetue/archive/2010/09/17/second_2d00_post.aspx

"Prevent Cross-Site Request Forgery (CSRF) using ASP.NET MVC's AntiForgeryToken() helper" on Steve Sanderson's blog:
http://blog.stevensanderson.com/2008/09/01/prevent-cross-site-request-forgery-csrf-using-aspnet-mvcs-antiforgerytoken-helper/

"Hack Proofing Your Microsoft ASP.NET Web Forms and MVC Applications" by Adam Tuliper on Channel 9: http://channel9.msdn.com/Events/TechEd/NorthAmerica/2011/DEV333

To access web resources more easily, see the online version of the bibliography on MSDN: http://msdn.microsoft.com/en-us/library/hh404094.aspx.

13   Unit Testing Web Applications

Introduction

Unit testing, sometimes referred to as developer testing, focuses on testing small pieces of code, such as a class, that a developer is writing. These tests are critical for helping you ensure that the pieces you build work as expected and will operate correctly when combined with other parts of the application. Such testing helps support management of the application over time by ensuring that changes you make don't inadvertently affect other parts of the system.

This chapter shows you how to get started unit testing JavaScript as well as server-side code, but does not cover all aspects of unit testing. References to more detailed discussions about unit testing can be found at the end of this chapter. While the unit tests for the Mileage Stats application were written using Test-First Development (or Test-Driven Development), this chapter will only cover the test-oriented aspects of unit testing, not the design aspects.

This chapter does not cover other important aspects of testing, such as performance, stress, security, automation, deployment, localization, and globalization. Nor does it discuss other important aspects to consider when testing the client side, such as cross-browser compatibility or usability. However, these areas are important for you to consider when testing your web application.

In this chapter you will learn:

- How to get started unit testing your JavaScript and ASP.NET MVC code.

- The arrange-act-assert unit test structure.

- Techniques to isolate your tests and components.

- Things you should consider when testing your jQuery UI widgets.

The technologies discussed in this chapter are QUnit, used to test your JavaScript and jQuery client-side code, and xUnit.net and Moq, for testing your server-side, ASP.NET MVC code.

JavaScript Unit Testing

Unit testing, functional testing, and performance testing of the client-side portion of a web application present different challenges than server-side testing presents. In addition to testing the structural layout of a page and basic application functionality, you may want to verify that animations execute properly, that a page with a large amount of JavaScript has no memory leaks, and that the application maintains its functional and performance expectations across multiple browsers.

As a web application developer, you will use JavaScript for the user interface (UI) logic in your application to dynamically build the structure, to enable or disable portions of your UI, or to load data in the background. Some of this functionality may rely on libraries you adopt, such as jQuery. You'll want to be sure that each piece operates as you expect so that the application as a whole works as planned.

Unit testing allows you to verify that individual pieces work as you expect and provides a way for you to verify that they continue to work as libraries or tools evolve. For example, you may build a jQuery UI widget to manage a piece of your UI. When the next version of jQuery is released, you can quickly and easily verify that your widget is still working by executing the unit tests using the new jQuery libraries.

While unit testing isn't difficult, the learning curve can be somewhat steep for those unfamiliar with it. One common objection to adopting unit testing is the perception that it takes extra time to write unit tests. While it is true that it will take longer to build something with unit tests than without (after all, you need to write the unit tests), what is often not considered is the time you will save later in tracking down bugs or verifying that things still work after changing the code or upgrading to a new version of a library. For the uninitiated, it can also be difficult to determine what should be tested or how to approach testing for a particular behavior. Unit testing can be a complicated topic. This section seeks to provide you with the basics to get started. It will give you an idea of what to test and provide some approaches to solving common challenges in unit testing JavaScript in your application.

GETTING STARTED WITH UNIT TESTING

The Project Silk team decided to use the QUnit unit testing framework to help with unit testing their JavaScript components, which rely heavily on jQuery and the jQuery UI widget framework, which also use QUnit. The QUnit unit testing framework can be found on the jQuery website at **http://docs.jquery.com/QUnit**. The site provides examples, documentation, and links to the download.

To set up QUnit, you will typically create an HTML page containing specific QUnit elements with certain class attributes specified, and add and reference the **qunit.js** and **qunit.css** files. In Mileage Stats, these were added to the tests folder under the Scripts folder.

QUnit files in project

- ▲ 📂 Scripts
  - ▷ 🗀 Debug
  - ▲ 📂 tests
    - 📄 jquery.simulate.js
    - 📄 mstats.charts.tests.js
    - 📄 mstats.data.tests.js
    - ...
    - 📄 mstats.vehicle-list.tests.js
    - 📄 mstats.vehicle.tests.js
    - 📄 qunit.css
    - 📄 qunit.js
    - 📄 test-utilities.js
    - 📄 tests.htm
  - 📄 excanvas.min.js

Once this structure is in place, you will create a test JavaScript file for each set of tests you want to run. A set is typically focused on a specific JavaScript object. For example, in Mileage Stats there is a JavaScript test file for each of the jQuery UI widgets that the application implements.

Each of these JavaScript test files and the JavaScript file of the item being tested are referenced from the test.htm file so the QUnit framework can locate and execute the tests.

HTML
```html
<!-- Contained in test.htm -->
<!-- Code under test -->
<script src="../Debug/mstats.utils.js"></script>
<script src="../Debug/mstats.events.js"></script>
<script src="../Debug/mstats.pubsub.js"></script>
...
<!-- Unit tests -->
<script src="mstats.utils.tests.js"></script>
<script src="mstats.pubsub.tests.js"></script>
<script src="mstats.data.tests.js"></script>
...
```

These unit tests can be run by viewing the test HTML file in a browser. From the Microsoft® Visual Studio® development system, you can right-click the test HTML file and select **View in Browser**. For Mileage Stats, the output would look like this while executing the tests.

QUnit test run output

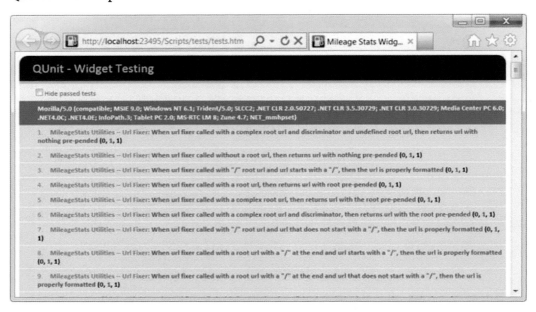

CREATING UNIT TESTS

There are typically multiple unit tests in one file and they are often grouped around a particular topic or type of test. In QUnit, the **module** function is used to denote a group of tests.

JavaScript
```javascript
module('Test Group');
test('Test one', function () {
  // Test logic goes here
});

test('Test two', function () {
  // Test logic goes here
});
```

Let's look at the structure of a typical test. This is a test from mstats.data.test.js to test a data caching component within the solution.

JavaScript
```javascript
// Contained in mstats.data.test.js
test('When data is saved, then it can be retrieved', function () {
  expect(1);
  // Arrange
```

```
    var value = 'some-data';

    // Act

    mstats.dataStore.set(' /some/url', value);

    // Assert
    equal(
      mstats.dataStore.get(' /some/url'),
      value,
      'mstats.datastore saved and returned ' + value);
});
```

The **test**, **expect**, and **equal** methods are specific to QUnit.

Most unit tests follow an arrange-act-assert pattern, a common test pattern employed when unit testing. Its purpose is to make a clear distinction between the set up for the test, the action that is to be tested, and the evaluation of the results. In most unit tests, arrange, act, and assert occur in that order.

In the above code example, the "act" step ensures the value can be set in the store and the "assert" verifies that the value was appropriately set. The QUnit framework provides a number of functions to help with assertions. The **equal** assertion is shown in the example, but **ok** (which performs a Boolean check) is also frequently used.

Notice that we execute a single assertion in this test. In general, keep the number of assertions low (preferably to a single assertion) for smaller, more focused unit tests. Writing unit tests in this manner encourages you to write code that is also small and focused. This tends to lead to code that is more composable because each piece of code has a single responsibility. Each unit test should generally take one action and make one assertion. However, there are cases in which a group of similar assertions will be made, such as when verifying the property values on a deserialized JavaScript Object Notation (JSON) object.

The QUnit framework provides the **expect** function, which verifies that the proper number of expected assertions ran. At the beginning of the test you will see that **expect(1)** was called to let QUnit know how many assertions should be run. If QUnit does not encounter that number of assertions, then it will produce an error in its output.

WHAT TO TEST

Now that you know how to write a unit test, the really important question concerns *what* should be tested. Generally, in a unit test you are trying to verify the functionality of a relatively small component, such as a JavaScript object or a jQuery UI widget. Each test verifies independent pieces such as whether a calculation happened correctly or whether the proper document object model (DOM) modification occurred.

When you are testing UI widgets, you may be uncertain about what should be tested. The basic rule of thumb is to test anything a designer would not change. Logic that drives the UI might be tested to determine, for example, that the proper navigation action was invoked, that an element had the proper class attribute applied (or removed), or that the correct event was raised. But, you would not test that a specific font value was set or a specific background color of an element was used.

ISOLATING YOUR TESTS

Often your object under test will rely on other objects, functions, or libraries. You may have an object that makes Ajax calls to retrieve data. If you attempt to make Ajax calls when running the unit tests you might get unpredictable results because the server responding to the calls may be unavailable when you run your tests. Generally, you want to isolate your component from these types of problems.

When testing, you will also want to isolate your component from other objects you build within your system. In Mileage Stats, many jQuery UI widgets rely on a publish-subscribe object for communication. When you test objects with dependencies, you do not want to invoke the *actual* dependencies. If you did, you would be testing more than one thing at a time. Instead, it is important to test that the component *attempts* to invoke a dependency. The typical strategy for isolating your component under test is to supply an alternative component or function that the component calls instead of the real component. These alternatives may be referred to as fakes, doubles, stubs, or mocks. As it turns out, the ability to isolate your component in this manner also helps the overall design of your application because you will tend to create smaller, more focused components.

With a substitute object employed, you can verify that the correct calls were made with the right values. For example, when testing that the Mileage Stats data cache component makes an Ajax call with the appropriate URL, a mock **ajax** function is supplied for testing in the **jQuery** object (represented as the dollar sign in the example). In this alternate, we verify that the expected URL is invoked by the component.

```javascript
// Contained in mstats.data.tests.js
test('when sendRequest is called, then the url from options is used', function () {
  expect(1);
  // Arrange
  $.ajax = function (options) {
    // Assert
    equal(options.url, '/url', 'Url was properly set');
  };

  // Act
  mstats.dataManager.sendRequest({
    url: '/url'
  });
});
```

Note also that this somewhat changes the typical arrange-act-assert order of the test structure because the assertion is in the supplied Ajax function. It is important to use the **expect** function at the beginning of your tests to help ensure that all the expected assertions are made.

When providing these alternative functions or components, it is also imperative to capture and restore the original values to avoid interfering with any other test that may have relied on these values. In QUnit this can be done when defining the test module where the **setup** and **teardown** functions can be supplied.

JavaScript

```javascript
// Contained in mstats.data.tests.js
module(
        'MileageStats DataManager sendRequest Tests',
        {
          setup: function () {
            this.savedAjax = $.ajax;
            ...
          },
          teardown: function () {
            $.ajax = this.savedAjax;
            ...
          }
        }
    );
```

jQuery UI Widget Testing

When unit testing jQuery UI widgets, there are some additional considerations. Since a widget is attached to a DOM element, you will need to create these elements either in the test or, if they are more complicated, in the setup for a module. In Mileage Stats, because many of the widgets interact with a section of the DOM, some of that structure needs to be created during the test setup. For example, the setup for the header widget test recreates that portion of the DOM structure it manipulates.

JavaScript

```javascript
// Contained in mstats.header.tests.js
module('Header Widget Tests', {
  setup: function () {
    $('#qunit-fixture').append(
        '<div class="header" id="header">' +
          '<div><div><h1>Dashboard</h1>' +
            '<div id="notification"></div>' +
            '<div class="nav">' +
              '<span id="welcome">Welcome <b>Sample User</b></span>' +
```

```
                                '[ <a id="dashboard-link" href="/Dashboard">Dashboard</a>' +
                                '| <a id="charts-link" href="/Chart/List">Charts</a>' +
                                '| <a id="profile-link" href="/Profile/Edit">Profile</a>' +
                                '| <a id="login-link" href="/Auth/SignOut">Sign Out</a> ]' +
                        '</div>' +
                    '</div></div>' +
                '</div>'
                );
        }
});
```

In QUnit, any DOM elements added for your test should be added to the element with the id attribute containing **qunit-fixture**, as shown above. You should only add the minimal amount of structure needed to appropriately simulate your test needs as this will make the structural dependencies of the test clearer.

When testing jQuery UI widgets you will also often need to supply an alternate implementation of dependent functions or objects. Because you don't control the creation of the jQuery UI widgets directly, you will typically do this as part of the **options** object passed into the widget (See Chapter 3, "jQuery UI Widgets" for more details about the use of an **options** object). For example, when testing the Mileage Stats vehicle details widget, an alternative implementation for the event publisher is supplied as part of the options.

JavaScript
```javascript
// Contained in mstats.vehicle-details.tests.js
test('when loading data errors out, then triggers error status', function () {
    expect(2);
    var eventType = 'loadError',
        details = $('#details-pane').vehicleDetails({
            templateId: '#testTemplate',
            sendRequest: function (options) { options.error({}); },
            publish: function (event, status) {
                if (status.type === eventType) {
                    ok(status, 'status object passed to publisher');
                    equal(status.type, eventType, 'status is of type : ' +
                        eventType);
                }
            }
        });

    // force a data refresh
    details.vehicleDetails('option', 'selectedVehicleId', 1);
});
```

Server-Side Unit Testing

Unit testing code on the server typically involves many more interactive pieces than what you encounter when testing client-side JavaScript. In an ASP.NET MVC application, controllers will interact with services or repositories to handle each request. As each piece is built, these interactions can be tested using unit tests to instill confidence that the system continues to work as new features are added or new versions of dependent libraries are supplied.

This section is intended to provide you with enough information to get started unit testing your server-side application. Since each application is different, illustrating all testing scenarios is not possible. To find out more about unit testing your applications, see the "Further Reading" section.

GETTING STARTED WITH UNIT TESTING

There are a number of unit testing frameworks to choose from when unit testing server-side Microsoft .NET Framework components. Most unit testing frameworks are conceptually similar, and any one of them can be a reasonable choice. Microsoft offers two technologies that can be used for writing unit tests: Microsoft Test and xUnit.net. Microsoft Test is supplied with certain versions of Visual Studio, and xUnit.net is a Microsoft developed, open-source unit testing framework available on CodePlex and NuGet.

Regardless of your unit testing framework choice, unit tests are placed in a separate assembly that the unit testing framework can discover and use to execute the tests. A typical Visual Studio solution organization includes all the unit test files under a single solution folder with an appropriate name. For example, the Mileage Stats solution has its test projects in a Unit Tests solution folder.

Unit test location in the MileageStats project

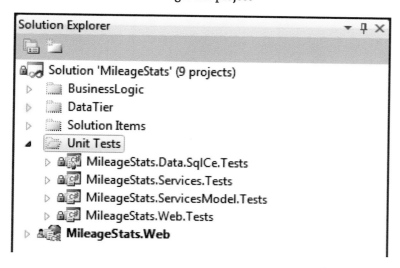

There is a unit test project for the Services, ServicesModel, SqlCe, and Web projects. Some projects don't have a corresponding unit tests project primarily because these projects contain only shared interfaces and data transfer classes that do not have significant logic to test.

The team chose xUnit.net as the unit testing framework for the Mileage Stats project. While you can accomplish unit testing with either Microsoft Test or xUnit.net, the team chose xUnit.net because it was built specifically for developer unit testing. The remainder of this section discusses unit testing using examples in xUnit.net, but you can readily implement the same approaches with Microsoft Test or another unit testing framework, although some of the exact mechanics may be different.

To create a new unit test project, add a C# or Microsoft Visual Basic® Class Library project, and reference the xUnit.net assemblies. In the test project, there will be a class to contain all the related tests for a particular component. For example, the **MileageStats. Web.Tests** project contains a test class for each controller in the Web project. They generally have the same name as the controller name with the term "Fixture" appended.

To write a test, create a method with the **Fact** attribute specified. The xUnit.net framework searches for these attributes and executes these methods. Each test should follow the arrange-act-assert pattern. In this pattern all the setup for the test is done first (arrangement), then the action to be tested is executed (act), and then the validation is done (assert).

```C#
//Contained in ReminderFixture.cs
[Fact]
public void WhenReminderIsNotOverdue_ThenIsOverdueReturnsFalse()
{
  // Arrange
  var reminder = new ReminderFormModel()
                     {
                         Title = "future reminder",
                         DueDate = DateTime.UtcNow.AddDays(2),
                         DueDistance = 10000
                     };

  reminder.UpdateLastVehicleOdometer(10);

  // Act
  bool isOverdue = reminder.IsOverdue;

  // Assert
  Assert.False(isOverdue);
}
```

In addition to **Assert.False**, xUnit.net supplies a number of other built-in asserts available on the **Assert** static class.

After the tests have been built, you can execute them using the xUnit.net test runner to see if they pass. The test runner is located where you unpackaged the xUnit.net contents retrieved from CodePlex. After you add the test assembly into the runner, you can run all the tests to see if they succeed.

Running unit tests

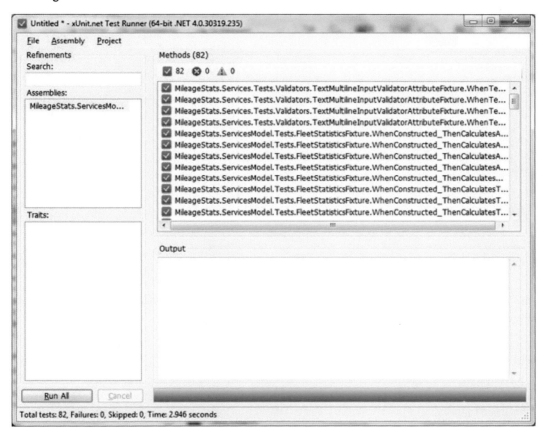

If a test fails, a message appears in the console.

Running unit tests with errors

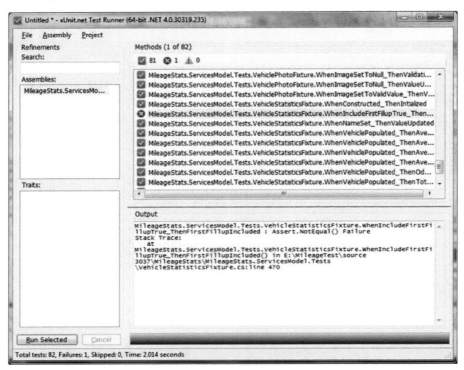

Alternatively, you can run tests by using TestDriven.Net or Resharper, which run the tests from within Visual Studio. For more details on how to do this, see **http://xunit. codeplex.com.**

WHAT TO TEST

On the server side, you should create unit tests for any classes and components that contain logic or must interact with other components. You should not write unit tests for generated code or code you don't own. The team wrote unit tests for classes in each of the major layers.

Repository Layer. The repository layer provides the basic persistence for information throughout the system. In Mileage Stats, this relies heavily on Entity Framework Code-First and Microsoft SQL Server® Compact Edition. Many of the tests written against this layer verify that the persistence and retrieval implementations for the various repositories produce the correct results. These tests, because they are writing to an actual database, cannot strictly be considered unit tests, but are useful in verifying that the persistence mechanism for all the models works as expected. Often, these are referred to as integration tests.

These tests were also useful because the Entity Framework Code-First library was adopted before its final release, so these tests helped demonstrate that the expectations around Entity Framework were maintained between releases.

Business Logic Layer. The business logic layer is invoked by the controllers in the Web Layer in order to execute business rules and store data in the repository. Unit tests for the business logic layer focus on verifying the business rules and their interactions with the repository layer. The tests do not actually store data in the repository, but use a fake repository and verify that the business services layer uses it correctly. The models in the business logic layer often contain validation logic that is also verified in unit tests.

Web Layer. The actual controllers that respond to requests have unit tests to verify that they interact with the services and models appropriately and return correctly built View Models for the Views or jQuery template.

ISOLATING YOUR COMPONENTS

It is common for the classes you are testing to rely on other classes. For example, a class may rely on a repository to persist a model. During testing, you want to isolate the interaction of your class with these other objects to ensure that only the behavior of the class in question is tested. Additionally, it can sometimes be painful to set up these other classes appropriately. For example, if the class calls a web service, it would be unrealistic to expect that the web service be available when you want to run your unit test.

Instead of trying to create the actual context for the class under test, you supply it with alternative implementations of the object it depends on. These alternatives may also be called fakes, doubles, stubs or mocks. Using these alternative implementations has the side effect of also helping separate the responsibilities of your classes.

To provide this separation, instead of creating a class that depends on a specific technology, you can provide an abstraction for the class to depend on. This allows you to provide different implementations of the dependency at different times, such as at unit test time. Often this abstraction could be an interface definition, but it could also be a base or abstract class.

For example, suppose you had a class to test that needed to store values somewhere. Instead of tying the class directly to a specific store implementation, it can depend on an **IStore** abstraction.

```C#
public interface IStore
{
  void Persist(string item);
}


public class ClassToTest
{
  private IStore store;

  public ClassToTest(IStore store)
  {
    this.store = store;
  }

  public void Save(string value)
```

```
{
    ...
    store.Persist(value);
    ...
}
}
```

When you write a test for this class that depends on **IStore**, you can then provide an alternative implementation.

```
C#
[Fact]
public void WhenSaving_ThenSendsValueToStore()
{
  var mockStore = new StoreMock();
  var classToTest = new ClassToTest(mockStore);

  classToTest.Save("Test");

  Assert.Equal(mockStore.ValueSaved, "Test");
}

private class StoreMock : IStore
{
  public string ValueSaved { get; set; }
  public void Persist(string item)
  {
    ValueSaved = item;
  }
}
```

The **StoreMock** object captures the saved item to verify that **ClassToTest** sends the correct value to the store. Instead of making these mocks by hand, as shown above, the team relied on Moq—a mocking framework—when writing Mileage Stats tests. The test shown above would look like this using Moq.

```
C#
[Fact]
public void WhenSaving_ThenSendsValueToStore()
{
  var mockStore = new Mock<IStore>();
  var classToTest = new ClassToTest(mockStore.Object);

  classToTest.Save("Test");

  mockStore.Verify(s => s.Persist("Test"));
}
```

Moq dynamically builds the objects needed for testing, and in the case of the **Verify** method can automatically verify that methods or properties were called with the correct values. For more information about using Moq, see the Moq CodePlex site at http://moq.codeplex.com.

There are times when you don't control the class that you want to mock. For instance, if you use a static class built into the .NET Framework library, such as **FormsAuthentication**, you do not have control over that class. In these cases, you will often create an interface for just the functionality you use and provide a default implementation for run-time use and a mock implementation to use at test time. This was the approach employed with Mileage Stats when using the DotNetOpenAuth library. This is a third-party library used by Mileage Stats to handle various authentication protocols. To isolate the components and make them more testable, the **IOpenIdRelyingParty** interface was created.

```csharp
// IOpenIdRelyingParty.cs
public interface IOpenIdRelyingParty
{
  ActionResult RedirectToProvider(
                  string providerUrl,
                  string returnUrl,
                  FetchRequest fetch);
  IAuthenticationResponse GetResponse();
}
```

Mileage Stats has a default implementation that uses the real **DotNetOpenAuth** library at run time and a mock implementation when testing the **AuthController** MVC controller.

At run time, all these pieces are connected using a technique known as dependency injection. See "**Dependency Injection**" in Chapter 11, "Server-Side Implementation" to better understand how this works.

TESTING YOUR ASP.NET MVC CONTROLLERS

ASP.NET MVC was designed to support the testability of the controllers, filters, and actions that developers typically write when developing a Model-View-Controller (MVC) application. Since each controller is responsible for handling a request, and MVC automatically maps input from the query string or from form data to the data types on your controller's methods, you can easily write tests for your controllers and simply supply them with the necessary inputs. For instance, the **ReminderController**'s **Add** method takes an integer value for the vehicle identifier, and a **Reminder** object.

```csharp
// Contained in ReminderController.cs
public ActionResult Add(int vehicleId, ReminderFormModel reminder)
{
  ...
  return View(viewModel);
}
```

In a unit test, it is very simple to provide these parameter values during testing of the **Add** method. The example below demonstrates how you would supply the reminder and vehicle ID directly in the test.

```csharp
C#
// Contained in ReminderControllerFixture.cs
[Fact]
public void WhenAddReminderWithValidReminder_ThenReturnsToReminderDetailsView()
{

  ...
  var result = (RedirectToRouteResult)controller.Add(vehicle.VehicleId, formModel)
;

  Assert.NotNull(result);
  Assert.Equal("Details", result.RouteValues["action"]);
  Assert.Equal("Reminder", result.RouteValues["controller"]);
}
```

While many unit tests for controllers can use this approach, there are still cases in which the controllers require access to the **HttpContext**. Providing alternate implementations of **HttpContext** is usually very difficult, making certain scenarios very hard to test. But because the MVC base controller class, **Controller,** relies on the abstract **Http ContextBase** class instead of **HttpContext** itself, it can be substituted much more easily. Mileage Stats uses a mock **HttpContextBase** in many of its controller tests to ensure that the **HttpContextBase.User** property is set appropriately.

To do this, Mileage Stats uses an **MvcMockHelpers** class that wraps the building of a Moq object that substitutes **HttpContext** information. This controller context is then set on the controller under test by calling the static **SetFakeControllerContext** extension method in the **MvcMockHelpers** class. The **RemindersControllerFixture** sets this when it builds a testable controller.

```csharp
C#
// Contained in ReminderControllerFixture.cs
private ReminderController GetTestableReminderController()
{
var controller = new ReminderController(_mockUserServices.Object,
                                        _serviceLocator.Object);
controller.SetFakeControllerContext();
controller.SetUserIdentity(new MileageStatsIdentity(_defaultUser.AuthorizationId,
                                        _defaultUser.DisplayName,
                                        _defaultUser.UserId));

return controller;
}
```

The fake context creates a series of Moq objects that the controller will interact with under test. If you want to adjust what they're doing, you can recover the mock and change its behavior. The static **SetUserIdentity** extension method above does this for a controller to set an identity context for the test into the **HttpContext**.

```csharp
// Contained in ControllerMockHelpers.cs
public static void SetUserIdentity(this Controller controller, IIdentity identity)
{
  Mock.Get(controller.HttpContext)
        .Setup(x => x.User)
        .Returns(new GenericPrincipal(identity, null));
}
```

The types of tests you typically write around your controller include:

- **View Models**. You will want to test that the controller provides the correct model data for a specific view.

- **Navigation**. You will want to test that the controller will provide the correct redirection when it is finished processing the request or when there is an error processing the request.

- **Interaction**. You will want to test that the controller makes the appropriate calls to your repository or service layers (which will be mocked in the tests). You will also want to test that your controller appropriately handles the situation when the model data supplied to a controller is in an invalid state.

- **JSON Endpoints**. If you have JSON data endpoints, you want to make sure these return appropriate JSON results for the call.

Summary

You should make a conscious decision about whether or not you are going to unit test your code. Unit testing is not difficult, but it does require an investment of time to learn and apply. However, the time initially spent writing unit tests will save time over the life of your project and deliver better quality code. Frameworks that help you write unit tests are available for most languages and platforms. Visual Studio includes unit test support for C# and Visual Basic, among other languages, and you can readily find them for languages such as JavaScript.

Further Reading

Meszaros, Gerard. *xUnit Test Patterns: Refactoring Test Code*. Addison-Wesley, 2007.

Kaner, Cem, Jack Falk, and Hung Q. Nguyen. *Testing Computer Software*, 2nd Edition. Wiley, 1999.

patterns & practices Acceptance Test Engineering Guidance on CodePlex:
http://testingguidance.codeplex.com/

Performance Testing Guidance for Web Applications on MSDN®:
http://msdn.microsoft.com/en-us/library/bb924375.aspx

Guidance for Build, Deploy and Test Workflows on MSDN:
http://msdn.microsoft.com/en-us/library/ff972305.aspx

QUnit unit testing framework on the jQuery website:
http://docs.jquery.com/QUnit

xUnit.net on CodePlex:
http://xunit.codeplex.com

Moq on CodePlex:
http://moq.codeplex.com

"Testing the User Interface with Automated UI Tests" on MSDN:
http://msdn.microsoft.com/en-us/library/dd286726.aspx

"How to: Create a Coded UI Test" on MSDN:
http://msdn.microsoft.com/en-us/library/dd286681.aspx

Resharper:
http://www.jetbrains.com/resharper/

TestDriven.NET:
http://testdriven.net

For more information on dependency injection in Mileage Stats, see Chapter 11, "Server-Side Implementation."

For more information about testing in Project Silk, see the following:

- "How to: Check UIElement Properties Using Coded UI Test" on MSDN:
  http://msdn.microsoft.com/en-us/library/hh404081.aspx.

- "How to: Create an Automated Negative Test Case Using Coded UI Test" on MSDN:
  http://msdn.microsoft.com/en-us/library/hh404089.aspx.

- "How to: Create a Web Client UI Test Using Coded UI Test" on MSDN:
  http://msdn.microsoft.com/en-us/library/hh404082.aspx.

To access web resources more easily, see the online version of the bibliography on MSDN: http://msdn.microsoft.com/en-us/library/hh404094.aspx.

14

Widget QuickStart

This Widget QuickStart illustrates the way Project Silk uses the jQuery UI Widget Factory to create maintainable widgets that implement client-side behavior.

Business Scenario

Our team has been asked to enable cross-browser keyword lookup capabilities in our web pages by hyperlinking select keywords to popular websites. This feature will need to be added dynamically to all company web pages.

Another team has been tasked with tagging the keywords in the web pages. The words will be tagged dynamically, based on server-side business logic driven by agreements with third parties.

The focus of this QuickStart is to enable the client-side behavior for the tagged keywords. When a user hovers over a keyword, the browser will display a pop-up list of popular links for that keyword from the Delicious.com bookmarking service.

Walkthrough

Project Silk includes the source code for the Widget QuickStart. To run the QuickStart, ensure you have an Internet connection and follow the steps below:

1. If you have not already installed Project Silk, download it from the **Microsoft Download Center** at **http://www.microsoft.com/download/en/details. aspx?id=27290**. To extract the download, run the .exe file. This will extract the source code and documentation into the folder of your choice.

2. Open the **default.htm** file from the {silk}\QuickStarts\DeliciousWidget QuickStart folder using Windows® Internet Explorer® 9. After the file's content is displayed, you'll need to click on the **Allow blocked content** button at the bottom of the browser window to enable scripts to run. Blocking active content by default is a security feature of Internet Explorer 9.

Widget QuickStart (default.htm)

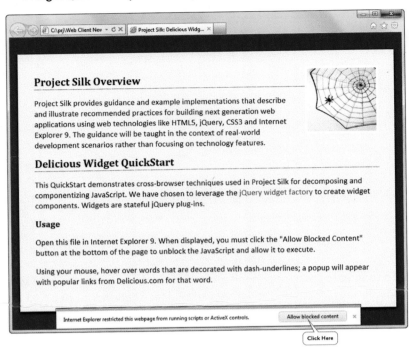

3. After allowing blocked content, you'll notice that the keywords are displayed in a new color and have been underlined with a dashed line, as pictured below.

Widget QuickStart after scripts are unblocked

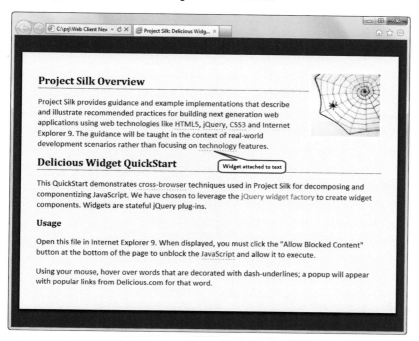

4. Using your mouse, hover over an underlined keyword. A pop-up list with the ten most popular links for that keyword will be displayed. Notice that the keyword has been repeated in the title of the pop-up list.

    1. One second after moving your mouse away from the keyword, the pop-up list will close unless your mouse is within the boundaries of the pop-up list.

    2. If the keyword is on the left side of the page, the pop-up list will open to the right of the cursor. If the keyword is on the right side of the page, the pop-up list will open to the left of the cursor, as in the image below.

Pop-up list for the keyword "jQuery"

Project Silk Overview

Project Silk provides guidance and example implementations that describe
and illustrate recommended practices for building next generation web
applications using web technologies like HTML5, jQuery, CSS3 and Internet
Explorer 9. The guidance will be taught in the context of real-world
development scenarios rather than focusing on technol

Popular Links for jQuery

Diapo | A Pixedelic free jQuery slideshow
15 Useful jQuery Tab-Based Interfaces
FlexSlider - The Best Responsive jQuery Slider
6 Useful & Creative Jquery Plugins For August...
spin.js
Freebie: Responsive jQuery Slider Plugin Flexsl...
Chosen - a JavaScript plugin for jQuery and Pr...
Sticky - An unbelievably simple notification sys...
deck.js » Modern HTML Presentations

Delicious Widget QuickStart

This QuickStart demonstrates cross-browser techniques
componentizing JavaScript. We have chosen to leverage
components. Widgets are stateful jQuery plug-ins.

5. Move your mouse over the pop-up list. You can now click on a link, which will
    open in a new browser window.

Links from Delicious.com in the pop-up list

Project Silk Overview

Project Silk provides guidance and example implementations that describe
and illustrate recommended practices for building next generation web
applications using web technologies like HTML5, jQuery, CSS3 and Internet
Explorer 9. The guidance will be taught in the context of real-world
development scenarios rather than focusing on technolog

Popular Links for jQuery

Diapo | A Pixedelic free jQuery slideshow
15 Useful jQuery Tab-Based Interfaces
FlexSlider - The Best Responsive jQuery Slider
6 Useful & Creative Jquery Plugins For August...
spin.js
Freebie: Responsive jQuery Slider Plugin Flexsl...
Chosen - a JavaScript plugin for jQuery and Pr...
Sticky - An unbelievably simple notification sys...
deck.js » Modern HTML Presentations

Delicious Widget QuickStart

This QuickStart demonstrates cross-browser techniques
componentizing JavaScript. We have chosen to leverage
components. Widgets are stateful jQuery plug-ins.

6. Moving your mouse outside the boundaries of the pop-up list will cause the
    pop-up list to close.

Conceptual View

This section illustrates the relationship of the jQuery UI widgets to the HTML page. A single **infobox** widget is attached to the page's **body** element. After it's attached, it creates a <div> element and dynamically adds it to the page's <body> element. Additionally, a **tagger** widget is attached to each keyword.

Relationship of the jQuery UI widgets to the HTML page

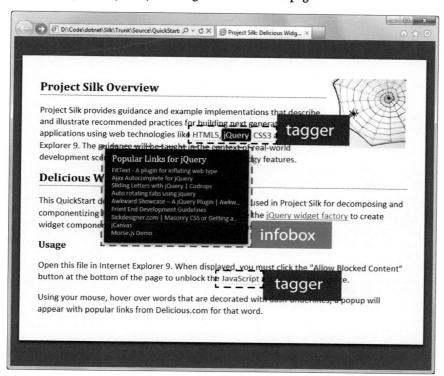

The HTML below reveals a keyword tagging strategy that takes advantage of HTML5 data attributes. Each of the keywords has been wrapped in a **span** tag with the **data-tag** attribute applied. In this scenario, the keyword wrapping was accomplished on the server side.

```
HTML
<!-- Contained in default.htm -->
<!DOCTYPE html>
<html>
<head ...>
<body>
```

```
<div id="container">
  <img src="projectsilk.png" />
  <h1>Project Silk Overview</h1>
  <p>
    Project Silk provides guidance and example implementations
    that describe and illustrate recommended practices for
    building next generation web applications using web
    technologies like <span data-tag>HTML5</span>,
    <span data-tag>jQuery</span>, <span data-tag>CSS3</span>
    and Internet Explorer 9. The guidance will be taught in
    the context of real-world development scenarios rather
    than focusing on <span data-tag>technology</span>
    features.</p>
```

Attaching Widgets

Once created, the widget is attached to an HTML element and its **options** can be set.

```
JavaScript
// Contained in startup.js
(function ($) {
    var infobox = $('body').infobox({
        dataUrl: 'http://feeds.delicious.com/v2/json/popular/'
    });

    $('span[data-tag]').tagger({
        activated: function (event, data) {
            infobox.infobox('displayTagLinks', event, data.name);
        },
        deactivated: function () {
            infobox.infobox('hideTagLinks');
        }
    });
} (jQuery));
```

The code above demonstrates how the **infobox** widget is attached to the **body** element. The **dataUrl option** value will be used when performing popular keyword link lookups.

The jQuery selector **span[data-tag]** returns a jQuery wrapped set that contains all **span** tags with a **data-tag** attribute. A **tagger** widget will be attached to each of the **span** tags in the returned collection. The **tagger** widget has **activated** and **deactivated** options that are used as callbacks. These callbacks are used to handle events raised when the mouse hovers over the tag.

Widget Initialization

When a widget is created (attached), the jQuery UI widget factory will call the private method **_create**. This method provides the developer an opportunity to perform widget setup actions. Examples include building and injecting markup, adding CSS classes, and binding events.

```JavaScript
// Contained in jquery.qs.infobox.js
_create: function () {
    var that = this,
        name = that.name;
    that.infoboxElement = $('<div class="qs-infobox" />');
    that.infoboxElement.appendTo('body')
    .bind('mouseenter.' + name, function () {
        mouseOverBox = true;
    })
    .bind('mouseleave.' + name, function () {
        mouseOverBox = false;
        that.hideTagLinks();
    });
},
```

The code snippet above first creates a variable for **this** called **that** within the closure, so the widget can be referenced within the **mouseenter** and **mouseleave** event handlers.

Recall that the **infobox** widget is attached to the **body** element. The element **div. qs-infobox** will contain the UI for this widget. It is stored in **that.infoboxElement**, attached to the **body** element, and bound to some events. The **name** variable holds the name of the widget and is appended to the name of the event it's binding to. This is a recommended practice when using jQuery; the reasons why will be explained later in the QuickStart.

> **Note:** *Most of the time, widgets are attached to the element that they will control; however, there are times when a widget will need to create additional elements.*
>
> *In the above **_create** function, the **infobox** widget creates a **div** to hold the list of links. The default.htm HTML page could have been modified to include the **div** in the first place, making it unnecessary for the widget to add an additional structure. However, the code was written this way to illustrate a widget adding UI elements to an existing HTML structure.*

Widget Interactions

An interesting challenge in this scenario is giving the user enough time to click the links without showing the pop-up list longer than needed. The implementation requires coordination between the two widgets.

Mouse Entering a Keyword Span

When the mouse enters the keyword span, the **mouseenter** event handler in the **tagger** widget is invoked. The **name** being appended to the event name is the name of the widget and is used as a namespace for the event binding. This is a recommended practice. Any string can be used as the namespace, but using the name of the widget allows you to tap into a feature of the widget factory described later in the QuickStart.

```JavaScript
// Contained in jquery.qs.tagger.js
.bind('mouseenter.' + name, function (event) {
    clearTimeout(timer);
    that._trigger('activated', event, {name: tag});
})
```

The **clearTimeout** call uses the **timer** variable, which is defined outside of the widget prototype and set in the handler for **mouseleave**, discussed in the next section. This means there will be only one timer created and shared among all instances of the **tagger** widget.

The next line raises the **tagactivated** event. It doesn't raise the **taggeractivated** event because the widget sets the **widgetEventPrefix** property, as shown in the next code snippet. It also doesn't raise the **activated** event, as you may have suspected, because the widget factory changes the name of raised events by prepending the name of the widget to the name of the event being triggered.

```JavaScript
// Contained in jquery.qs.tagger.js
$.widget('qs.tagger', {

    widgetEventPrefix: 'tag',

    options: {
```

When the **tagactivated** event is raised, the **displayTagLinks** method is called on the **infobox** widget. As you will notice from having a look at **jquery.qs.infobox.js**, it never binds to this event. Doing so would create a dependency between the widgets. A better option is to follow a recommended pattern that takes advantage of a related jQuery UI feature. It is recommended that a widget provide callback options for all of the events it raises.

```JavaScript
// Contained in jquery.qs.tagger.js
options: {
    activated: null,
    deactivated: null
},
```

The jQuery UI widget factory will automatically call any option with the same name as the event being raised. This feature allows the event handlers to be associated with the event by setting the value of the option. The QuickStart does this in the startup file.

JavaScript

```javascript
// Contained in startup.js
$('span[data-tag]').tagger({
    activated: function (event, data) {
        infobox.infobox('displayTagLinks', event, data.name);
    },
    deactivated: function () {
        infobox.infobox('hideTagLinks');
    }
});
```

This approach is also a nice way to avoid having to know if the event is called **tag activated** or **taggeractivated** or something else. The **displayTagLinks** method accepts a browser event and the name to look up. The first part of the method sets up enclosed variables to be used in the second part of the method.

JavaScript

```javascript
// Contained in jquery.qs.infobox.js
displayTagLinks: function (event, tagName) {
    var i,
        html,
        that = this,
        options = that.options,
        elem = that.infoboxElement,
        top = event.pageY + offsetY,
        left = event.pageX + offsetX,
        url = options.dataUrl + tagName + '?count=' + options.maxItems,
        displayResult = function () {
                elem.html(html);
                elem.css({top: top, left: left});
                elem.show();
            };

    if (event.pageX > window.screenWidth / 2) {
        left = event.pageX + leftSideAdjustment;
    }
```

After the closure is prepared, **left** is adjusted in case the tag is on the right-hand side of the page. The second part of the **displayTagLinks** method is an Ajax call to the **url**, constructed above, for the Delicious bookmarking service.

```
JavaScript
// Contained in jquery.qs.infobox.js
$.ajax({
    url: url,
    dataType: 'jsonp',
    success: function (data) {
        if (data != null) {
            html = '<h1>Popular Links for ' + tagName + '</h1><ul>';
            for (i = 0; i < data.length - 1; i += 1) {
                html += '<li><a href="' +
                        data[i].u +
                        '" target="_blank">' +
                        data[i].d + '</a></li>';
            }
            html += '</ul>';
        } else {
            html = '<h1>Data Error</h1><p>[snipped]</p>';
        }
        displayResult();
    },
    error: function (jqXHR, textStatus, errorThrown) {
        html = '<h1>Ajax Error</h1>' +
               '<p>The Ajax call returned the following error: ' +
               jqXHR.statusText + '.</p>';
        displayResult();
    }
});
```

The local **displayResult** function is scoped only to the **displayTagLinks** method since it was needed for both **success** and **error** conditions and nowhere else. This is the method that applies the result to the element for the user to see.

MOUSE LEAVING A KEYWORD SPAN

When the mouse leaves the tag's **span**, a similar coordination occurs. The **tagger** widget has a namespaced event bound to the span's **mouseleave** event.

```
JavaScript
// Contained in jquery.qs.tagger.js
.bind('mouseleave.' + name, function () {
    timer = setTimeout(function () {
        that._trigger('deactivated');
    }, hideAfter);
});
```

The **timer** is set to raise the **tagdeactivated** event after 1000 milliseconds, which is the value of **hideAfter**.

When the **tagger** widget was applied to the span elements, a function was supplied to the **deactivated** callback, as you also saw earlier in the QuickStart.

JavaScript
```
// Contained in startup.js
$('span[data-tag]').tagger({
    activated: function (event, data) {
        infobox.infobox('displayTagLinks', event, data.name);
    },
    deactivated: function () {
        infobox.infobox('hideTagLinks');
    }
});
```

The function invokes the **hideTagLinks** method on the **infobox** widget.

JavaScript
```
// Contained in jquery.qs.infobox.js
hideTagLinks: function () {
    !mouseOverBox && this.infoboxElement.hide();
},
```

The **infobox** is only hidden if the mouse is not over it. Effectively, the 1000 ms delay provides the user time to move the mouse from the keywords to the links.

Mouse Entering the Pop-up List

Internally, the **infobox** widget uses the **mouseOverBox** variable to maintain state indicating whether or not the mouse is over the pop-up list. This variable is defined in the closure created by the self-executing anonymous function wrapping the file.

JavaScript
```
// Contained in jquery.qs.infobox.js
(function ($) {
    var offsetX = 20,
        offsetY = 20,
        mouseOverBox = false,
        leftSideAdjustment = -270;
    $.widget('qs.infobox', {
```

When the mouse enters the **infobox**, **mouseOverBox** is set to **true**.

JavaScript
```
// Contained in jquery.qs.infobox.js: _create
.bind('mouseenter.' + name, function () {
    mouseOverBox = true;
})
```

Mouse Leaving the Pop-up List

When the mouse leaves the pop-up list, **mouseOverBox** is set to **false** and **hideTagLinks** is invoked.

```JavaScript
// Contained in infobox.js
.bind('mouseleave.' + name, function () {
    mouseOverBox = false;
    that.hideTagLinks();
});

hideTagLinks: function () {
    !mouseOverBox && this.infoboxElement.hide();
},
```

Further Reading

For more information about the jQuery UI widget factory, see the following resources:

- Chapter 3, "jQuery UI Widgets"
- "jQuery UI API Developer Guide" on jQuery UI:
  http://jqueryui.com/docs/Developer_Guide
- "Widget factory" on the jQuery UI wiki:
  http://wiki.jqueryui.com/w/page/12138135/Widget-factory
- "Tips for Developing jQuery UI 1.8 Widgets" on Eric Hynds' blog:
  http://www.erichynds.com/jquery/tips-for-developing-jquery-ui-widgets/
- "Understanding jQuery UI widgets: A tutorial" on bililite.com:
  http://bililite.com/blog/understanding-jquery-ui-widgets-a-tutorial/

To access web resources more easily, see the online version of the bibliography on MSDN: http://msdn.microsoft.com/en-us/library/hh404094.aspx.

Appendix A

Glossary

arrange-act-assert pattern. A common pattern employed when writing unit tests. Its purpose is to make a clear distinction between the setup for the test, the action that is to be tested, and evaluation of the results. In most unit tests the arrange-act-assert occur in the order of arrange, act, and then assert. However, when unit testing JavaScript it is common to define the **assert** in a callback function that may be defined before the **act**.

authentication provider. The party responsible for validating a user's credentials and issuing a token that can be used to access other sites. This is the web site you visit to do the actual authentication.

content injection. In a web application that accepts data input from users, content injection refers to the act of an attacker attempting to insert HTML or client script content that will be processed by a client browser, or SQL commands that the server may process. If successful, content injection of HTML or client scripts will cause the website to behave undesirably for any user that views the injected content because it's being processed by their browser as legitimate HTML or client script. Content injection can result in many undesirable effects, such as causing parts of a web page to disappear, diverting user requests to a malicious location, or allowing an attacker to eavesdrop. SQL injection does not affect the client browser, but if a web application accepts user input and uses it to dynamically create a SQL query without verifying the content, an attacker can inject syntax into the SQL query to manipulate the database and even the database server if it's not locked down properly. This type of attack can lead to deleted data, dropped databases, or even allow operating system commands to run as if you were typing them at the command line.

closures. A JavaScript feature that ensures that an inner function always has access to the variables and parameters of its outer function, even after the outer function has returned. For a good explanation of closures, see "A Graphical Explanation of JavaScript Closures in a jQuery Context" by Ben Nadel at http://www.bennadel.com/blog/1482-A-Graphical-Explanation-Of-Javascript-Closures-In-A-jQuery-Context.htm.

cross-site scripting (XSS). An attack whereby scripts from a malicious source are executed on a client browser as part of a trusted web page. Websites that build pages with data elements originating from other sources, such as user input or shared databases, are vulnerable to XSS attacks.

cross-site request forgery (CSRF). An attack in which a client browser is manipulated into performing malicious actions on a server with which the client has some form of trusted relationship through authentication, HTTPS, or IP filtering. An attacker embeds a link or a script in a piece of untrusted content that does something on the trusted site to which the user is currently authenticated. A simple example is an image element embedded in an HTML email that includes a URL query string, which performs a malicious action. If users click the image, they unknowingly initiate the act on the site where they are authenticated.

data- attributes. HTML5 attributes that provide metadata for HTML elements. They can be used to provide additional information for the JavaScript application, and provide a mechanism for selecting HTML elements via JavaScript without negatively impacting the page's visual design.

Data Model. An object that represents an entity built for data storage services. These are not available for use outside the boundaries of the application and are often encapsulated behind a services layer.

Domain Model. An object that represents an entity in the problem domain, which may also be annotated or extended to support some application features such as validation or authentication. Because these models need to be shared between the server and client browser, they are sometimes contained within view models and used directly for data-binding in HTML forms. Application models and service models are variations of domain models.

eavesdropping. Exploiting a web application using a network data capture utility to find and record HTTP requests and responses between a website and a client. Eavesdropping can lead to disclosure of sensitive information such as passwords, personal, or financial information, and can potentially allow the execution of spoofing, tampering and message replay attacks.

flow diagram. A diagram that defines the pages in the site, actions available on those pages, and navigation between pages. This diagram reflects the user stories identified in the requirements.

Forms authentication. Forms authentication enables user and password validation for web applications that do not require Windows authentication.

Form Model. An entity that represents all of the fields in an HTML form that is specific to a controller action. It contains only the data that is passed into the action. Generally, this corresponds to whatever form is posting back to the server. Form Models (sometimes called Request Models) are a special case of View Models. View Models are more generic in that they may also include additional data needed to render a page. A Form Model might end up being a property on another View Model.

fragment identifier. The portion of a URL identified by the hash (#). With regard to browser navigation, hyperlinks include them to make the hyperlink unique. When used in conjunction with the **hashchange** event, page content is able to change without performing a full-page reload.

full-page reload. When a user operation such as clicking a hyperlink causes the browser to load an entirely new page from the server. This is in contrast to using Ajax to request data from the server so the client-side JavaScript can update only the parts of the page that should change.

functional mockup. Functioning HTML pages that include CSS and possibly JavaScript. These pages are autonomous and don't yet interact with the server and use fake data when needed. They give you the chance to balance browser capabilities with HTML, CSS, images, and JavaScript before integrating the pages with the server-side implementation.

given-when-then template. A helpful template for defining acceptance criteria that include the context of the test (given), the action being tested (when), and the expected outcome (then). This template provides clear and concise documentation that can be understood by team members and can be used to generate both manual and automated test scripts.

hybrid-design web application. Web application with the same characteristics as the server-rendered web application, except that it relies heavily on client-side JavaScript to deliver an engaging experience. This type of application has pages that act as islands of interactivity that do not require full-page reloads as well as pages that do require a full-page reload. Mileage Stats is an example of a hybrid design.

integrator. A role on the team building a web application that is responsible for combining the images, HTML, CSS, and JavaScript with the server-side technologies in a way that closely represents the final implementation. The person responsible for this role may not be a specialist in design or development, but has a solid grasp of all technologies involved.

jQuery selectors. A syntactical aspect of jQuery that allows you to select all DOM elements based on specific criteria (tag name, id, attribute name, value, and more). Once the selection is made, jQuery is used to operate on the selected elements.

jQuery templates. HTML markup with inline JavaScript expressions that are used to populate values in the markup. The jQuery Template plug-in applies data to the template and renders the output into the DOM.

Jump List. List of commonly used tasks and destinations, enabling easy user access to destinations by eliminating the need to launch the browser and then load the relevant content. Also allows users to perform common tasks without launching the web application in advance. This is a feature of Windows® Internet Explorer® 9.

JSON hijack. If an attacker gets a user to click on a malicious link that makes a JavaScript Object Notation (JSON) request via HTTP GET and that request returns a JSON array, the attacking code within the link may gain access to the contents of the array in the response, which may become accessible to the attacker.

malicious input. Bad data that causes your system to behave undesirably and/or corrupts data.

message replay attack. An attack that alters the contents of a captured HTTP request and re-submits it to the website.

message tampering. When an attacker maliciously alters the content of request and/or response messages flowing between two parties across a network. For example, if a customer submits an order for 100 widgets to an online merchant, an attacker might alter the order request to order 10,000 widgets instead. Message tampering can be part of a message replay attack or a man-in-the-middle attack.

mock. The typical strategy for isolating your component under test is to supply an alternative component or function that the component calls instead of supplying the real component. These alternative components may also be referred to as fakes, doubles, or stubs.

mockup. A visual representation that shows what the site will eventually look like. Mockups contain details such as typography, color, gradients, images, and transparency, but no functionality. Mockups should communicate all necessary details of the UI. To do so, multiple mockups for a single page may be required to convey details of the different states of the application.

mood board. A visual collage made up of images and color palettes from a variety of sources that communicate the emotional connection the application aims to have with the users.

persona. A representation of a particular type of user the team can identify with. A persona is a user in context that embodies work style, role, motivation, skills, and goals. If you have a complicated or large application, some features might target multiple personas.

pinned site. A feature of Windows Internet Explorer 9 that integrates your website with the Windows 7 desktop. Pinned sites enable easy access to favorite websites and add shortcut functionality similar to shortcuts in Microsoft® Windows applications. With pinned sites enabled for a website, users can pin the site to the Windows 7 taskbar or add the site to the desktop or Start menu. With this feature, you can add site metadata, create custom jump lists, notification icons, and Thumbnail Preview toolbar controls for the websites you develop.

polyfill. Polyfills and shims consist of JavaScript, HTML, and CSS code that helps to provide the technology and functionality that you expect the browser to provide natively. In simple terms, they provide support for missing features. With polyfills, the code tries to replicate the real, standards-based API, making it easier to port your applications once a standard feature is included in a future version of a browser. This makes it easier to "future-proof" your code since you shouldn't have to change anything for the new feature to work. For more information about polyfills, see "Making HTML4 and CSS3 work with polyfills and shims" by Rey Bango in .net magazine at http://www. netmagazine.com/features/making-html5-and-css3-work-polyfills-and-shims.

Plain Old CLR Object (POCO). Refers to a class in the Microsoft .NET Framework that does not have any dependencies on external libraries such as the Entity Framework. For example, if a class inherits from a base class provided in an external library, it is not a POCO.

progressive enhancement. Adds features to the client-side experience based on browser capabilities.

prototype. A prototype is a JavaScript object from which other objects inherit their members. Every object has a prototype and any object can be used as a prototype for creating new objects. For more information on prototypes, see "Prototypes and Inheritance in JavaScript" by Scott Allen on Script Junkie at http://msdn.microsoft.com/en-us/scriptjunkie/ff852808.

Publish/Subscribe pattern (pub/sub). A messaging pattern that enables loose communication between publishers and subscribers. A pub/sub object manages communication, relieving the publishers and subscribers from having direct knowledge of one another.

relying party. The party trying to validate a user based on a security token that was issued by an authentication provider.

repository. A set of interfaces and implementations providing methods for data access.

Repository pattern. This pattern assists the data model in separating data storage concerns from the application logic. The interfaces do not expose any data storage-specific types and the implementation classes use them. You can choose how many repositories to create based on how granular you want to factor the methods and the expected data access pattern from your application.

rule of thirds. This is a rule of thumb for visual composition that states that an image should be imagined as divided into nine equal parts by two equally-spaced horizontal lines and two equally-spaced vertical lines. Important compositional elements should be placed along these lines or their intersections.

safe list. A list that limits input by only allowing what is known to be valid. The advantage of safe lists is that anything that falls outside of the valid set of characters is not allowed.

salt. A salt is a value combined with a cryptographic key to make the output of an encryption algorithm more random and less susceptible to attack.

sandboxing. Technique that allows components of the application to be tested before the entire application is complete. It also makes testing more robust by preventing software defects in one module from blocking or affecting the testing of other modules.

server rendered web application. Web application where the server dynamically assembles each page from one or more source files and incorporates data and calculated values during the rendering. The client-side script in these applications might perform some data validation or simple hover effects, but few Ajax calls. As each page is navigated to, the browser performs a full-page reload. ASP.NET applications that don't make heavy use of client-side JavaScript are examples of server rendered web applications.

Single-Page Interface (SPI) pattern. A pattern for web applications that reduces the number of full-page reloads during user navigation. When a user performs an action, such as selecting a hyperlink, which traditionally requires the site to load a new web page, the application instead modifies the current web page without reloading it.

single-page interface web application. Web application where the user is only required to perform a full-page load once. From that point on, all page changes and data loading is performed without a full-page reload. Hotmail, Office Live, and Twitter are examples of single-page interface web applications.

shim. Polyfills and shims consist of JavaScript, HTML, and CSS code that helps to provide the technology and functionality that you expect the browser to provide natively. In simple terms, they provide support for missing features. Shims offer features that are not available in the standard implementation and no polyfill is available. For more information about shims, see "Making HTML4 and CSS3 work with polyfills and shims" by Rey Bango in .net magazine at **http://www.netmagazine.com/features/ making-html5-and-css3-work-polyfills-and-shims**.

sliding expiration. A pre-determined amount of time where an authenticated user can use the site. The amount of time is reset whenever the user makes a new request to the server. The advantage of using a sliding expiration is that it does not force the user to authenticate again if he or she maintains a reasonable level of activity in the application. Otherwise, the user would be redirected to the authentication page after a fixed amount of time had elapsed after the initial authentication.

static web application. Web sites consisting of static HTML pages, CSS, and images. As each page is navigated to, the browser performs a full-page reload.

structure. The HTML of the page as it relates to the hierarchy of elements that make up the page, rather than the visual appearance or layout of the UI.

topic. The message between the publisher and subscriber in a pub/sub environment. This message, also often referred to as an event, represents the contract between the sender and receiver, and is made up of a name and an optional message body.

user gestures. A specific action that a user takes in order to interact with an application. Traditionally, gestures include mouse clicks and keys presses. However, many modern applications also employ interactions in which a user acts more directly on an application. For example, they may touch a screen to swipe, pinch, or pull content.

ViewBag. The name/value keyed collection that lets you store any loosely typed data. ASP.NET MVC 3 introduced the **ViewBag** (called **ViewData** in previous versions) in addition to **View.Model**.

View Models. Models contained within the MVC application which are built solely for a view to data-bind against. They often follow the same composition hierarchy as the views and partial views.

widget. An object attached to a page element that supplies services for managing lifetime, state, inheritance, theming, and communication with other widgets or JavaScript objects. A widget is a jQuery plug-in.

widget method. The method that represents the primary interface for applying the widget to elements and using the widget after it's applied. The widget method is named after the name of the widget.

wireframe. A diagram that depicts rough placement of the text, data, and basic controls of a UI. These diagrams are tools used to help organize the page's information. A wireframe does not show details of the page.

wrapped set. A wrapped set is the result of a query that uses a jQuery selector to find elements in the DOM. To call a method on a wrapped set of elements, a selector is used to select elements in the DOM. For example, to add the **listing** CSS class to all **ul** elements directly inside a **div** element, you can use **$('div ul').addClass('listing')**.

Appendix B   Project Silk Road Map

This topic presents a road map that will help you locate the appropriate guidance topics within *Project Silk: Client-Side Web Development for Modern Browsers.*

About the Topic Areas

To help you find relevant content, this document divides the topics into particular areas, and then drills down into each of them. It provides a brief overview of the topic area, followed by considerations and recommendations for each topic area and the location of the relevant guidance content. The high-level topic areas are:

- Immersive Web Applications
- Technology Choices
- Mileage Stats
- Widgets
- UI and UX Design
- Modularity
- Data
- Client-Side HTML
- Communication
- Navigation
- Application Notifications
- Server-Side Implementation
- Security
- Unit Testing
- Automated Acceptance Testing

The following sections describe the content and reference materials for each of these topic areas.

IMMERSIVE WEB APPLICATIONS

There is a spectrum of web applications being built today. While there are many types of modern web applications that address many different needs, they all have some common characteristics.

What are the different kinds of web applications?

- "Spectrum of Web Applications" on page 3 in Chapter 1, "Introduction" and online at http://msdn.microsoft.com/en-us/library/hh404096.aspx.
- "Characteristics of Modern Web Applications" on page 3 in Chapter 1, "Introduction" and online at http://msdn.microsoft.com/en-us/library/hh404096.aspx.

TECHNOLOGY CHOICES

The Project Silk team built the Mileage Stats Reference Implementation (Mileage Stats) using JavaScript, jQuery, jQuery UI, the BBQ plug-in, the jqPlot plug-in, Ajax, Modernizr, QUnit, ASP.NET MVC, xUnit.net, Moq, the Entity Framework, Unity Application Block, HTML5, and CSS3.

What are the technology choices I should consider when building a web application?

- "Technologies" on page 5 in Chapter 1, "Introduction" and online at http://msdn.microsoft.com/en-us/library/hh404096.aspx.
- "Architectural Alternatives" on page 29 in Chapter 2, "Architecture" and online at http://msdn.microsoft.com/en-us/library/hh404097.aspx.

What do jQuery and jQuery UI offer?

- "Introduction" on page 33 in Chapter 3, "jQuery UI Widgets" and online at http://msdn.microsoft.com/en-us/library/hh404085.aspx.

MILEAGE STATS

Mileage Stats is a comprehensive sample application demonstrating a real-world, interactive, cross-browser, consumer-facing, rich web application. This reference implementation is intentionally incomplete, but does illustrate the core concepts, design patterns, coding patterns, security requirements, web technologies, and unit testing necessary to be successful. Below you will find the locations of material that will answer the following questions.

What is Mileage Stats?

- "Exploring the Mileage Stats Reference Implementation" on page 8 in Chapter 1, "Introduction" and online at http://msdn.microsoft.com/en-us/library/hh404096.aspx.

- "Introduction" on page 21 in Chapter 2, "Architecture" and online at http://msdn.microsoft.com/en-us/library/hh404097.aspx.

How do I install Mileage Stats?
- Readme on page XVII and online at http://msdn.microsoft.com/en-us/library/hh404100.aspx.

How did the design of Mileage Stats evolve?
- "Designing the Mileage Stats Reference Implementation" on page 60 in Chapter 4, "Design and Layout" and online at http://msdn.microsoft.com/en-us/library/hh404087.aspx.

How does Mileage Stats implement modularity?
- "JavaScript Module Implementations" on page 89 in Chapter 5, "Modularity" and online at http://msdn.microsoft.com/en-us/library/hh404079.aspx.

How does Mileage Stats manage and centralize application data requests?
- "Data Request" on page 99 in Chapter 6, "Client Data Management and Caching"
- "Providing Data Asynchronously" on page 192 in Chapter 11, "Server-Side Implementation" and online at http://msdn.microsoft.com/en-us/library/hh404093.aspx.

How does Mileage Stats cache data?
- "Data Cache" on page 104 in Chapter 6, "Client Data Management and Caching" and online at http://msdn.microsoft.com/en-us/library/hh404101.aspx.

How does Mileage Stats use **data-** attributes?
- "Using Data- Attributes" on page 112 in Chapter 7, "Manipulating Client-Side HTML" and online at http://msdn.microsoft.com/en-us/library/hh404083.aspx.
- "Providing HTML Structure" on page 189 in Chapter 11, "Server-Side Implementation" and online at http://msdn.microsoft.com/en-us/library/hh404093.aspx.

How does Mileage Stats generate HTML dynamically?
- "Generating HTML Dynamically with JavaScript and jQuery" on page 116 in Chapter 7, "Manipulating Client-Side HTML" and online at http://msdn.microsoft.com/en-us/library/hh404083.aspx.

How does Mileage Stats generate jQuery templates?
- "Server-Side Rendering and jQuery Templates" on page 120 in Chapter 7, "Manipulating Client-Side HTML" and online at http://msdn.microsoft.com/en-us/library/hh404083.aspx.

How does Mileage Stats choose between various communication options?
- "Finding the Right Balance" on page 133 in Chapter 8, "Communication" and online at http://msdn.microsoft.com/en-us/library/hh404091.aspx.

How does Mileage Stats implement direct method invocation between widgets?

- "A Helper for Method Invocation" on page 125 in Chapter 8, "Communication" and online at http://msdn.microsoft.com/en-us/library/hh404091.aspx.
- "Method Invocation in Mileage Stats" on page 124 in Chapter 8, "Communication" and online at http://msdn.microsoft.com/en-us/library/hh404091.aspx.

How does Mileage Stats raise and handle events?

- "Raising and Handling Events" on page 127 in Chapter 8, "Communication" and online at http://msdn.microsoft.com/en-us/library/hh404091.aspx.

How does Mileage Stats implement pub/sub?

- "Pub/Sub in Mileage Stats" on page 129 in Chapter 8, "Communication" and online at http://msdn.microsoft.com/en-us/library/hh404091.aspx.

How does Mileage Stats keep users within a single-page interface?

- "Supporting the Single-Page Interface Pattern" on page 136 in Chapter 9, "Navigation" and online at http://msdn.microsoft.com/en-us/library/hh404077.aspx.

How does Mileage Stats modify the URLs sent from the server?

- "Modifying Hyperlinks" on page 138 in Chapter 9, "Navigation" and online at http://msdn.microsoft.com/en-us/library/hh404077.aspx.

How does Mileage Stats respond to the user clicking on a link?

- "Responding to User Actions" on page 143 in Chapter 9, "Navigation" and online at http://msdn.microsoft.com/en-us/library/hh404077.aspx.

How does Mileage Stats manage the browser's history?

- "Responding to User Actions" on page 143 in Chapter 9, "Navigation" and online at http://msdn.microsoft.com/en-us/library/hh404077.aspx.

How does Mileage Stats coordinate widget transitions between the various layouts?

- "The Layout Manager" on page 145 in Chapter 9, "Navigation" and online at http://msdn.microsoft.com/en-us/library/hh404077.aspx.

How does Mileage Stats animate screen transitions?

- "Animating Screen Transitions" on page 145 in Chapter 9, "Navigation" and online at http://msdn.microsoft.com/en-us/library/hh404077.aspx.

How does Mileage Stats implement Pinned Sites?

- "Pinned Sites in Mileage Stats" on page 165 in Chapter 10, "Application Notifications" and online at http://msdn.microsoft.com/en-us/library/hh404084.aspx.

What does Mileage Stats server-side architecture look like?
- "Introduction" on page 173 in Chapter 11, "Server-Side Implementation" and online at http://msdn.microsoft.com/en-us/library/hh404093.aspx.

How does Mileage Stats implement the Repository Pattern?
- "Implementing the Repository Pattern" on page 180 in Chapter 11, "Server-Side Implementation" and online at http://msdn.microsoft.com/en-us/library/hh404093.aspx.

How are data annotation attributes used in Mileage Stats?
- "Data Annotation Attributes" on page 195 in Chapter 11, "Server-Side Implementation" and online at http://msdn.microsoft.com/en-us/library/hh404093.aspx.

How does Mileage Stats implement authentication?
- "Authentication" on page 210 in Chapter 12, "Security" and online at http://msdn.microsoft.com/en-us/library/hh404095.aspx.

How does Mileage Stats validate input?
- "Input Validation" on page 217 in Chapter 12, "Security" and online at http://msdn.microsoft.com/en-us/library/hh404095.aspx.

What security measures were implemented in Mileage Stats?
- "Mileage Stats Application Security" on page 210 in Chapter 12, "Security" and online at http://msdn.microsoft.com/en-us/library/hh404095.aspx.

What tools were used to facilitate unit testing in Mileage Stats?
- "Introduction" on page 225 in Chapter 13, "Unit Testing Web Applications" and online at http://msdn.microsoft.com/en-us/library/hh404088.aspx.

What is an example of a unit test on the client side in Mileage Stats?
- "Creating Unit Tests" on page 228 in Chapter 13, "Unit Testing Web Applications" and online at http://msdn.microsoft.com/en-us/library/hh404088.aspx.

What is an example of a unit test on the server side in Mileage Stats?
- "Testing Your ASP.NET MVC Controllers" on page 239 in Chapter 13, "Unit Testing Web Applications" and online at http://msdn.microsoft.com/en-us/library/hh404088.aspx.

WIDGETS

When building rich, client-side web applications, some of the visual elements on the page will naturally take on roles, responsibilities, and state. A concept that is central to jQuery UI is the *widget*.

What is a widget?

- "Introduction" on page 33 in Chapter 3, "jQuery UI Widgets" and online at http://msdn.microsoft.com/en-us/library/hh404085.aspx.

What is an example of a widget?

- Chapter 14, "Widget QuickStart" on page 243 and online at http://msdn.microsoft.com/en-us/library/hh404102.aspx.

- "Factors That Influence a Modular Design" on page 80 in Chapter 5, "Modularity" and online at http://msdn.microsoft.com/en-us/library/hh404079.aspx.

- "Using Widgets as Modules" on page 91 in Chapter 5, "Modularity" and online at http://msdn.microsoft.com/en-us/library/hh404079.aspx.

How do I define and apply widgets?

- "Defining a Widget" on page 35 in Chapter 3, "jQuery UI Widgets" and online at http://msdn.microsoft.com/en-us/library/hh404085.aspx.

- "Using a Widget" on page 35 in Chapter 3, "jQuery UI Widgets" and online at http://msdn.microsoft.com/en-us/library/hh404085.aspx.

How do I manage the lifetime of widgets?

- "Managing Lifetime" on page 36 in Chapter 3, "jQuery UI Widgets" and online at http://msdn.microsoft.com/en-us/library/hh404085.aspx.

How do I define default options that permit overrides and change notifications?

- "Defining Options" on page 38 in Chapter 3, "jQuery UI Widgets" and online at http://msdn.microsoft.com/en-us/library/hh404085.aspx.

How do I decouple widget behavior?

- "Functions as Options" on page 40 in Chapter 3, "jQuery UI Widgets" and online at http://msdn.microsoft.com/en-us/library/hh404085.aspx.

How do I define and use public methods, properties, and events?

- "The Widget Method" on page 41 in Chapter 3, "jQuery UI Widgets" and online at http://msdn.microsoft.com/en-us/library/hh404085.aspx.

How do I use private methods to improve the readability of the code?

- "Private Members" on page 43 in Chapter 3, "jQuery UI Widgets" and online at http://msdn.microsoft.com/en-us/library/hh404085.aspx.

How do I define a variable that's available to all instances of the widget, but nowhere else?

- "Static Members" on page 44 in Chapter 3, "jQuery UI Widgets" and online at http://msdn.microsoft.com/en-us/library/hh404085.aspx.

How should widgets communicate with each other?

- "Events" on page 46 in Chapter 3, "jQuery UI Widgets" and online at http://msdn.microsoft.com/en-us/library/hh404085.aspx.

How do I inherit from a base widget?
- "Inheritance" on page 48 in Chapter 3, "jQuery UI Widgets" and online at http://msdn.microsoft.com/en-us/library/hh404085.aspx.

UI AND UX DESIGN

The design process includes the collaboration of stakeholders and team members with different skills and perspectives. If your team invests in a design process, you are more likely to create an application that users enjoy, find useful, and continue to use. Your user experience (UX) design specifies the site's structure, the web pages it uses, what actions users can perform on each page, and the transitions that can occur after a user performs an action. Your user interface (UI) design should be unified and provide a visual signal to your audience that all your elements belong together.

What is the value of design?
- "Design is a Worthwhile Investment" on page 51 in Chapter 4, "Design and Layout" and online at http://msdn.microsoft.com/en-us/library/hh404087.aspx.

What are the designer roles?
- "Web Project Designer Roles" on page 52 in Chapter 4, "Design and Layout" and online at http://msdn.microsoft.com/en-us/library/hh404087.aspx.

What are UX and UI design artifacts?
- "Design Prototyping" on page 53 in Chapter 4, "Design and Layout" and online at http://msdn.microsoft.com/en-us/library/hh404087.aspx.

What are UX considerations?
- "User Experience Design Considerations" on page 54 in Chapter 4, "Design and Layout" and online at http://msdn.microsoft.com/en-us/library/hh404087.aspx.

What are UI considerations?
- "User Interface Design Considerations" on page 57 in Chapter 4, "Design and Layout" and online at http://msdn.microsoft.com/en-us/library/hh404087.aspx.

What are some guidelines for assigning IDs to elements and naming CSS classes?
- "CSS Organization" on page 70 in Chapter 4, "Design and Layout" and online at http://msdn.microsoft.com/en-us/library/hh404087.aspx.

What are vendor-prefixed attributes?
- "Vendor-Prefixed Attributes" on page 71 in Chapter 4, "Design and Layout" and online at http://msdn.microsoft.com/en-us/library/hh404087.aspx.

How do I debug CSS styles?
- "Debugging" on page 72 in Chapter 4, "Design and Layout" and online at http://msdn.microsoft.com/en-us/library/hh404087.aspx.

MODULARITY

A modular design can make it easier for you to develop, test, deploy, and extend your application. Modular designs also have well-understood benefits that help you unit test your applications and make them easier to maintain over time. However, achieving a modular design in a complex JavaScript application requires specific techniques that may not be immediately obvious.

What are the benefits of modularity when building hybrid-designed web applications?
- "Modularity" on page 24 in Chapter 2, "Architecture" and online at http://msdn.microsoft.com/en-us/library/hh404097.aspx.
- "Benefits of Modularity for Hybrid-Design Web Applications" on page 78 in Chapter 5, "Modularity" and online at http://msdn.microsoft.com/en-us/library/hh404079.aspx.

What are the factors that influence a module's boundaries?
- "Factors that Influence a Modular Design" on page 80 in Chapter 5, "Modularity" and online at http://msdn.microsoft.com/en-us/library/hh404079.aspx.

What are the types of modules to consider in your application?
- "Functional Roles and Categories for Modules" on page 88 in Chapter 5, "Modularity" and online at http://msdn.microsoft.com/en-us/library/hh404079.aspx.

When should I use a JavaScript object, a jQuery plugin, or a jQuery UI Widget?
- "JavaScript Module Implementations" on page 89 in Chapter 5, "Modularity" and online at http://msdn.microsoft.com/en-us/library/hh404079.aspx.

DATA

In rich, interactive, client-centric applications, users expect the application to respond quickly to mouse gestures, page transitions, and the saving of form data. Delays caused by data retrieval or saving data can negatively impact the user's experience and enjoyment of the site. Therefore, carefully managed data retrieval and caching is critical to today's web applications.

How can a loosely coupled data layer simplify caching for client-side data requests?
- "Data" on page 28 in Chapter 2, "Architecture" and online at http://msdn.microsoft.com/en-us/library/hh404097.aspx.
- Chapter 6, "Client Data Management and Caching" on page 97 and online at http://msdn.microsoft.com/en-us/library/hh404101.aspx.

Why do I need a client-side data management strategy?
- "Introduction" on page 97 in Chapter 6, "Client Data Management and Caching" and online at http://msdn.microsoft.com/en-us/library/hh404101.aspx.

What are the benefits of a client-side data manager and the abstraction of data requests?

- "Benefits of the Data Manager Abstraction" on page 99 in Chapter 6, "Client Data Management and Caching" and online at http://msdn.microsoft.com/en-us/library/hh404101.aspx.

How do I improve application performance by caching and prefetching data?

- "Client-Side Data Design" on page 98 in Chapter 6, "Client Data Management and Caching" and online at http://msdn.microsoft.com/en-us/library/hh404101.aspx.

CLIENT-SIDE HTML

Both hybrid and single-page interface web applications that do not perform full-page post backs in order to change the rendered UI must use client-side techniques for manipulating the document object model (DOM). The three client-side technologies you can use when implementing these techniques are HTML, cascading style sheets (CSS) and JavaScript.

What are options and strategies for getting the right HTML to the client?

- "Structure" on page 23 in Chapter 2, "Architecture" and online at http://msdn.microsoft.com/en-us/library/hh404097.aspx.
- Chapter 7, "Manipulating Client-Side HTML" on page 107 and online at http://msdn.microsoft.com/en-us/library/hh404083.aspx.

What are the roles and responsibilities of HTML, CSS, and JavaScript within a client application?

- "The Roles and Responsibilities of Client-Side Languages" on page 107 in Chapter 7, "Manipulating Client-Side HTML" and online at http://msdn.microsoft.com/en-us/library/hh404083.aspx.

How do I use jQuery to select and manipulate HTML elements?

- "Selecting and Manipulating Existing HTML Elements" on page 110 in Chapter 7, "Manipulating Client-Side HTML" and online at http://msdn.microsoft.com/en-us/library/hh404083.aspx.

How do I use jQuery to generate new HTML within the client?

- "Generating and Loading New HTML in a Page" on page 116 in Chapter 7, "Manipulating Client-Side HTML" and online at http://msdn.microsoft.com/en-us/library/hh404083.aspx.

How do I use jQuery Templates to generate new HTML within the client?

- "Using Templates to Retrieve and Generate HTML" on page 118 in Chapter 7, "Manipulating Client-Side HTML" and online at http://msdn.microsoft.com/en-us/library/hh404083.aspx.

How do I choose the most appropriate option when manipulating HTML?

- "Structure, Appearance, and Behavior" on page 108 in Chapter 7, "Manipulating Client-Side HTML" and online at http://msdn.microsoft.com/en-us/library/hh404083.aspx.

COMMUNICATION

In a client-side application composed of discrete objects, many of those objects need to communicate with one another. You have a few options when choosing how they do this. Generally, your options are direct method invocation, and an indirect communication mechanism such as events.

What are the options for communicating between objects?

- "Communication" on page 26 in Chapter 2, "Architecture" and online at http://msdn.microsoft.com/en-us/library/hh404097.aspx.

- Chapter 8, "Communication" on page 123 and online at http://msdn.microsoft.com/en-us/library/hh404091.aspx.

How can the Publish/Subscribe (pub/sub) pattern be used for loosely coupled communication?

- "Loose Communication" on page 27 in Chapter 2, "Architecture" and online at http://msdn.microsoft.com/en-us/library/hh404097.aspx.

- "Publishing and Subscribing" on page 128 in Chapter 8, "Communication" and online at http://msdn.microsoft.com/en-us/library/hh404091.aspx.

How do I implement direct method invocation between widgets?

- "Direct Method Invocation" on page 124 in Chapter 8, "Communication" and online at http://msdn.microsoft.com/en-us/library/hh404091.aspx.

What are the advantages and disadvantages of direct method invocation?

- "Direct Method Invocation" on page 124 in Chapter 8, "Communication" and online at http://msdn.microsoft.com/en-us/library/hh404091.aspx.

How do I implement event triggering and handling between widgets?

- "Raising and Handling Events" on page 127 in Chapter 8, "Communication" and online at http://msdn.microsoft.com/en-us/library/hh404091.aspx.

How do I control dependencies between the objects triggering events and those handling them?

- "Publishing and Subscribing" on page 128 in Chapter 8, "Communication" and online at http://msdn.microsoft.com/en-us/library/hh404091.aspx.

When should I use the Publish/Subscribe (pub/sub) pattern?

- "Finding the Right Balance" on page 128 in Chapter 8, "Communication" and online at http://msdn.microsoft.com/en-us/library/hh404091.aspx.

How do I use pub/sub to manage multiple handlers and reduce coupling?

- "Publishing and Subscribing" on page 128 in Chapter 8, "Communication" and online at http://msdn.microsoft.com/en-us/library/hh404091.aspx.

NAVIGATION

When a user performs an action such as selecting a hyperlink or clicking a button, the application modifies the current web page without reloading the entire page, resulting in a more responsive, less jarring experience. Adherence to the Single-Page Interface pattern presents a number of navigation challenges. These challenges include managing the browser's history mechanism so that the back button works as expected, providing direct access to a specific layout or state of the page (deep linking), and implementing anchors that allow users to bookmark the application so that it displays in a specific state.

How do I solve browser history and back-button problems when the site doesn't perform full-page reloads?

- "Navigation" on page 27 in Chapter 2, "Architecture" and online at http://msdn.microsoft.com/en-us/library/hh404097.aspx.

- Chapter 9, "Navigation" on page 135 and online at http://msdn.microsoft.com/en-us/library/hh404077.aspx.

How do I keep users within a single-page interface?

- "Supporting the Single-Page Interface Pattern" on page 136 in Chapter 9, "Navigation" and online at http://msdn.microsoft.com/en-us/library/hh404077.aspx.

How do I manage hyperlinks and respond to user actions?

- "Modifying Hyperlinks" on page 138 in Chapter 9, "Navigation" and online at http://msdn.microsoft.com/en-us/library/hh404077.aspx.

- "Responding to User Actions" on page 143 in Chapter 9, "Navigation" and online at http://msdn.microsoft.com/en-us/library/hh404077.aspx.

When do I rewrite URLs and when should I handle the click event?

- "Modifying Hyperlinks" on page 138 in Chapter 9, "Navigation" and online at http://msdn.microsoft.com/en-us/library/hh404077.aspx.

How do I ensure that deep linking, bookmarking, and the back button work as expected?

- "Browser History and the Back Button" on page 137 in Chapter 9, "Navigation" and online at http://msdn.microsoft.com/en-us/library/hh404077.aspx.

How do I coordinate and animate screen transitions?

- "Animating Screen Transitions" on page 145 in Chapter 9, "Navigation" and online at http://msdn.microsoft.com/en-us/library/hh404077.aspx.

APPLICATION NOTIFICATIONS

Web applications that users consider responsive have one thing in common: they provide appropriate and timely feedback to the user. How the application displays the notifications to the user is almost as important as the information itself.

How do I provide unobtrusive user notification messages?

- "Where Notification Messages are Displayed" on page 156 in Chapter 10, "Application Notifications" and online at http://msdn.microsoft.com/en-us/library/hh404084.aspx.

How do I handle multiple simultaneous notification messages raised by the application?

- "How In dividual or Multiple Notification Messages are Displayed" on page 159 in Chapter 10, "Application Notifications"

What are the benefits of encapsulating the display and management of user notification in a single JavaScript object?

- "Where Notification Messages are Displayed" on page 156 in Chapter 10, "Application Notifications" and online at http://msdn.microsoft.com/en-us/library/hh404084.aspx.

How do I display a helpful global error page?

- "Website Error Notification" on page 161 in Chapter 10, "Application Notifications" and online at http://msdn.microsoft.com/en-us/library/hh404084.aspx.

How do I set up a global error handler for Ajax requests?

- "User Session Timeout Notification" on page 160 in Chapter 10, "Application Notifications" and online at http://msdn.microsoft.com/en-us/library/hh404084.aspx.

What are alternatives to modal dialogs for prompting users?

- "Prompting Users" on page 161 in Chapter 10, "Application Notifications" and online at http://msdn.microsoft.com/en-us/library/hh404084.aspx.

How do I enable application notifications on the desktop with the Pinned Sites API?

- "Desktop Notifications" on page 163 in Chapter 10, "Application Notifications" and online at http://msdn.microsoft.com/en-us/library/hh404084.aspx.

SERVER-SIDE IMPLEMENTATION

Crafting a well-architected web server application requires meeting the needs of the web client while properly factoring the Microsoft® .NET Framework code on the web server. A web server application is responsible for more than just returning HTML content. Web server applications also involve data models, data access and storage, security, communication, and resource management.

How do I use ADO.NET Entity Framework and the Microsoft® SQL Server® Compact Edition to create a data model?

- "Rapid Data Modeling Using the ADO.NET Entity Framework and SQL Server Compact" on page 175 in Chapter 11, "Server-Side Implementation" and online at http://msdn.microsoft.com/en-us/library/hh404093.aspx.

How do I store loosely typed data?

- "Using View Model and View Bag" on page 191 in Chapter 11, "Server-Side Implementation" and online at http://msdn.microsoft.com/en-us/library/hh404093.aspx.

How do I separate concerns between my data model, business logic, and user interface?

- "Composing Application Logic" on page 182 in Chapter 11, "Server-Side Implementation" and online at http://msdn.microsoft.com/en-us/library/hh404093.aspx.

What are the different kinds of models in an MVC application?

- "Factoring Application Code with ASP.NET MVC" on page 182 in Chapter 11, "Server-Side Implementation" and online at http://msdn.microsoft.com/en-us/library/hh404093.aspx.

What are the things I should think about when designing my MVC application?

- "Design Checklist for MVC Applications" on page 186 in Chapter 11, "Server-Side Implementation" and online at http://msdn.microsoft.com/en-us/library/hh404093.aspx.

Should I create a business services layer?

- "Creating a Business Services Layer" on page 187 in Chapter 11, "Server-Side Implementation" and online at http://msdn.microsoft.com/en-us/library/hh404093.aspx.

How do I support interactive web clients with asynchronous data?

- "Providing Data Asynchronously" on page 192 in Chapter 11, "Server-Side Implementation" and online at http://msdn.microsoft.com/en-us/library/hh404093.aspx.

What are the different types of data that web clients request from the server and what are the differences between these types?

- "Choosing a Data Format" on page 192 in Chapter 11, "Server-Side Implementation" and online at http://msdn.microsoft.com/en-us/library/hh404093.aspx.

How do I manage data validation at each level of the stack?
  • "Data Validation" on page 195 in Chapter 11,
    "Server-Side Implementation" and online at
    http://msdn.microsoft.com/en-us/library/hh404093.aspx.

How do I create custom validation attributes?
  • "Creating Custom Validation Attributes" on page 197 in Chapter 11,
    "Server-Side Implementation" and online at
    http://msdn.microsoft.com/en-us/library/hh404093.aspx.

What other things should I consider when designing my server-side architecture?
  • "Other Considerations" on page 202 in Chapter 11,
    "Server-Side Implementation" and online at
    http://msdn.microsoft.com/en-us/library/hh404093.aspx.

SECURITY

You should think about security threats that need to be addressed in any web application and what you should do to mitigate these threats.

What are key security threats that I should address in my web application?
  • "Security Threats" on page 207 in Chapter 12, "Security" and online at
    http://msdn.microsoft.com/en-us/library/hh404095.aspx.

What security features are built into ASP.NET MVC?
  • "Web Platform Security" on page 209 in Chapter 12, "Security" and
    online at http://msdn.microsoft.com/en-us/library/hh404095.aspx.

How do I protect my application from Cross-Site Request Forgery (CSRF)?
  • "Anti-Forgery" on page 219 in Chapter 12, "Security" and online at
    http://msdn.microsoft.com/en-us/library/hh404095.aspx.

How do I protect my application against JSON hijacking?
  • "JSON Hijacking Prevention" on page 220 in Chapter 12, "Security"
    and online at http://msdn.microsoft.com/en-us/library/hh404095.aspx.

How do I secure communication between the client and server?
  • "Securing Communication between Client and Server" on page 221
    in Chapter 12, "Security" and online at
    http://msdn.microsoft.com/en-us/library/hh404095.aspx.

What are security modifications I should think about to adjust for changes in the deployment environment and security requirements for the application?
  • "Additional Security Considerations" on page 221
    in Chapter 12, "Security" and online at
    http://msdn.microsoft.com/en-us/library/hh404095.aspx.

Unit Testing

Unit testing, sometimes referred to as developer testing, focuses on testing small pieces of code, such as a class, that a developer is writing. These tests are critical for helping you ensure that the pieces you build work as expected and will operate correctly when combined with other parts of the application. Such testing helps support management of the application over time by ensuring that changes you make don't inadvertently affect other parts of the system.

How do I get started unit testing my JavaScript code?
- "JavaScript Unit Testing" on page 226 in Chapter 13, "Unit Testing Web Applications" and online at http://msdn.microsoft.com/en-us/library/hh404088.aspx.

How do I get started unit testing my ASP.NET MVC code?
- "Server-Side Unit Testing" on page 233 in Chapter 13, "Unit Testing Web Applications" and online at http://msdn.microsoft.com/en-us/library/hh404088.aspx.

What is the arrange-act-assert unit test structure?
- "Creating Unit Tests" on page 228 in Chapter 13, "Unit Testing Web Applications" and online at http://msdn.microsoft.com/en-us/library/hh404088.aspx.

What are techniques to isolate my tests and components?
- "Isolating Your Tests" on page 230 in Chapter 13, "Unit Testing Web Applications" and online at http://msdn.microsoft.com/en-us/library/hh404088.aspx.

- "Isolating Your Components" on page 237 in Chapter 13, "Unit Testing Web Applications" and online at http://msdn.microsoft.com/en-us/library/hh404088.aspx.

What are things I should consider when testing my jQuery UI Widgets?
- "jQuery UI Widget Testing" on page 231 in Chapter 13, "Unit Testing Web Applications" and online at http://msdn.microsoft.com/en-us/library/hh404088.aspx.

What are things I should consider when testing my ASP.NET MVC controllers?
- "Testing Your ASP.NET MVC Controllers" on page 239 in Chapter 13, "Unit Testing Web Applications" and online at http://msdn.microsoft.com/en-us/library/hh404088.aspx.

AUTOMATED ACCEPTANCE TESTING

Automated acceptance tests are tests that use code to implement a manual test. Automated acceptance tests are usually written at the user interface level and can validate a high-level of functionality.

How do I ensure that the **UIElement** properties are displayed with the correct values?

- How to: Check UIElement Properties Using Coded UI Test online at http://msdn.microsoft.com/en-us/library/hh404081.aspx.

How do I test the error handling capability of the application at the user level?

- **How to: Create an Automated Negative Test Case Using Coded UI Test** online at http://msdn.microsoft.com/en-us/library/hh404089.aspx.

How do I create an automated test for my web application using Coded UI Test in Microsoft Visual Studio® 2010 Premium or Ultimate edition?

- How to: Create Web Client UI Test Using Coded UI Test online at http://msdn.microsoft.com/en-us/library/hh404082.aspx.

Index

Printed in Great Britain
by Amazon.co.uk, Ltd.,
Marston Gate.